1994

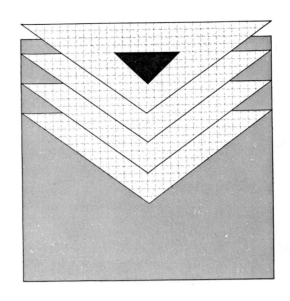

Fourth Edition

STRATEGIES OF Community Organization

Macro Practice

Editors

FRED M. COX, University of Wisconsin—Milwaukee

JOHN L. ERLICH, California State University, Sacramento

JACK ROTHMAN, University of California, Los Angeles

JOHN E. TROPMAN, University of Michigan

 F. E. PEACOCK PUBLISHERS, INC. ITASCA, ILLINOIS

Contents

Preface to the Fourth Edition   **vii**

GENERAL INTRODUCTION

1. Models of Community Organization and Macro Practice Perspectives: Their Mixing and Phasing, *Jack Rothman with John E. Tropman*   **3**
2. A History of Community Organizing Since the Civil War With Special Reference to Oppressed Communities, *Charles D. Garvin and Fred M. Cox*   **26**

PART ONE. COMMON ELEMENTS OF PRACTICE

Introduction, *John E. Tropman*   **67**
3. Need Identification and Program Planning in the Community Context, *Larry M. Siegel, C. Clifford Attkisson and Linda G. Carson*   **71**
4. The Knowledge Base of Planned Change in Organizations and Communities, *Joseph Katan and Shimon E. Spiro*   **98**
5. How To Be An Advocate in Bad Times, *Nancy Amidei*   **106**
6. Working With Task Groups, The Middle Phase, *Ronald W. Toseland and Robert F. Rivas*   **114**
7. Interpersonal Transactions in Community Practice, *Herbert Bisno*   **143**
8. Community Problem Solving: A Guide to Practice With Comments, *Fred M. Cox*   **150**
9. Program Evaluation and Administrative Control, *Steven Maynard-Moody*   **168**

PART TWO. ARENAS

Introduction, *Fred M. Cox*   187

10. Society: American Values as a Context for Community Organization and Macro Practice, Part I, *John E. Tropman;* Part II, *Fred M. Cox*   213
11. Communities: Alternative Conceptions of Community: Implications for Community Organization Practice, *Fred M. Cox*   232
12. Organizations: Organizations as Polities: An Analysis of Community Organization Agencies, *Mayer N. Zald*   243

PART THREE. STRATEGIES

Introduction, *John E. Tropman and John L. Erlich*   257
I. SOCIAL POLICY
Introduction   270
13. Social Planning, Social Policy and Political Change, *Eugen Pusic*   273
14. Theories of Choice and Making Decisions, *James G. March*   279
15. Homelessness as a Public Concern: How to Develop a Community Approach to Solving the Problem, *Milan J. Dluhy*   297
II. SOCIAL PLANNING
Introduction   308
16. Social Planners and Social Planning in the U.S., *Armand Lauffer*   311
17. Political Strategy for Social Planning, *Barry Checkoway*   326
18. Citizen Input and Professional Responsibility, *Carl V. Patton*   343
III. LOCALITY DEVELOPMENT
Introduction   351
19. Community Development: Potentials and Limitations, *S. K. Khinduka*   353
20. Needs Assessment and Community Development: An Ideological Perspective, *Sylvia Martí-Costa and Irma Serrano-García*   362
21. Community Involvement in Desegregation: The Milwaukee Experience, *Ian Harris*   373
IV. SOCIAL ACTION
Introduction   384
22. Community Organizing in Historical Perspective: A Typology, *Robert Fisher*   387
23. Can't Ya Hear Me Knocking?: An Organizing Model, *Lee Staples*   398
24. The Tactics of Organization Building, *Warren Haggstrom*   405
V. ADMINISTRATION AND MANAGEMENT
Introduction   423
25. Organization Theory for Social Administration, *Burton Gummer*   427
26. Program Development, *Yeheskel Hasenfeld*   450
27. The Circuit Riding Administrator: A Network Based, Macro Generalist Approach to Capacity Building in Small Communities, *Lynne Clemmons Morris*   473

STUDENT STUDY GUIDE, *Fred M. Cox*   487

BIBLIOGRAPHY   525

INDEXES   536

Preface to the Fourth Edition

At times, it seems as if everything important in the field of community organization has changed since the Third Edition was published in 1979. At other times, it feels as if almost everything of importance has remained the same. Perhaps, in a way, both perspectives are accurate reflections of what has been happening in the field. In that sense, this Fourth Edition has undergone a major revision which attempts to take into account the many new trends, developments, and program approaches and also illuminates continuing issues, dilemmas, and activities.

The most significant change is that the central conceptual design around which the earlier editions were organized, the three models of community organization practice (locality development, social planning, and social action), has been broadened to include two additional practice perspectives: social policy, and administration and management. We believe that this design gives the book a coherence often lacking in anthologies about the practice of community organization and social change. It has emerged from our collective experience as colleagues at the University of Michigan and, more recently, at Michigan State University; California State University, Sacramento; University of Wisconsin-Milwaukee; and University of California, Los Angeles. Indeed, the models continue to be reshaped in the crucible of our work with students, practitioners, community organizations, and colleagues. It is not neat, or complete, or finished.

The three macro practice perspectives—social policy, community organization, and administration and management—and the three models of community organization are delineated and explored in the first chapter of the General Introduction. Most recent trends in the field are also considered as part of this overview. The second article in the section addresses the history of community organization practice from the period following the Civil War.

Part One, the common elements section new to the Third Edition, has, with the exception of one article, been completely revised. The focus is on those things that can facilitate or constrain the day-to-day work of the practitioner. These include such areas as need identification, advocacy in times of adversity, program evaluation, and a systematic guide to community problem solving. In a sense what this section does is give form to some of the most pressing questions that we believe will confront policymakers, administrators, planners, and organizers alike in the latter half of the 1980's.

Part Two addresses three arenas which impact social change—the society, the community, and formal organizations. We are especially concerned about the linkages among these arenas as well as the community context in which they are often played out. Thus the community may be either a context, a target, or both in this scheme. Although the urban community receives the greatest emphasis, attention is also paid to the important and rapidly changing suburban and rural environments. While the community is experienced as a complex and fluid social configuration, we find it useful for analysis and practice to give special attention to certain variables that are functionally important, accessible, and manipulable. Primary groups and formal organizations (and their interrelationships) are viewed as central for the practitioner—whether he or she is trying to develop, sustain, or sever existing linkage patterns or create new ones. Each possibility invokes different strategic and programmatic options.

The heart of the book, Part Three, deals with action strategies as they relate to the three perspectives noted earlier: social policy, community organization, and administration and management. In addition, three models of community practice—social planning, locality development, and social action—are explored using a framework that will be familiar to those who have used earlier editions of this work.

As with past editions, it continues to be our aim to distinguish this volume from other works on the subject by an emphasis on strategic and tactical considerations in planned community change. We have in mind a practitioner based in an organizational structure (be it a social agency, interorganizational planning body, community-based action group or the like) that determines policy and offers intervention opportunities and resources, while at the same time carrying with it limitations and constraints. One major resource the practitioner brings to his or her task is an ability to use analytical skills in a thoughtful and committed fashion, no matter how conflict-ridden the community setting. We attempt to offer individuals and groups performing this role a set of guides for strategic planning and the tools to implement those plans.

We have tried, as in the past, to take into account shifting patterns of funding and community support for social change efforts. It is scarcely a time of unbridled optimism. Often it feels like maintaining programs at their current levels takes all of our creative energy. From the grassroots to the councils of national government we are called upon to defend and justify planned social change efforts. We must operate in an era of distrust and skepticism. But there are trends that bode well for the future—like a resurgence of interest in the family (in its many and emerging forms), concern about the elderly, advances in health care (including such areas as spouse and child abuse), and awareness of the special needs of newer minority communities (like those from Southeast Asia and Central America). The quality of community life is, again, becoming a more important part of the national agenda.

A very special debt is owed to a number of people who have contributed to the succeeding editions of this book. Louis Ferman, then our colleague, first pointed to the need for such a collection from his experiences as consultant to several federal agencies. Former deans of the University of Michigan's School of Social Work: Fedele Fauri, Robert Vinter, Phillip Fellin; and the current Dean, Harold Johnson; Jesse McClure, former Dean of the School of Social Work at California State University, Sacramento; and the current Director of the now Division of Social Work, Priscilla Alexander; and Leonard Schneiderman, Dean of the School of Social Work at the University of California, Los Angeles, provided invaluable assistance, making time and other resources available to us that considerably eased the task of completing each edition. Mitchell Lazarus, who worked with us on the first edition of the book until he returned to professional practice, made his wise counsel available throughout the initial stages of the undertaking. Ted Peacock and Tom LaMarre, our publisher and editor, were most encouraging in the early stages of the project. Ted's steadfast support during the tribulations of producing this fourth edition has been especially appreciated, as were the efforts of Joyce Usher, managing editor. Many people have helped with the consuming tasks of typing portions of the manuscript, obtaining permissions from authors and publishers, and a welter of clerical details. To all of them we are most grateful. Our wives—Gay Cox, Judy Rothman, Lizabeth Russell-Erlich, and Penny Tropman—have, with understanding supportiveness, suffered the disruptions of family life that made this fourth edition possible. The support and assistance of the staff of the Alabama Public Library Service in Montgomery (and Megan who slept on the floor of the Alabamiana Room while her father worked) are deeply appreciated. Gay Cox must be singled out for her unstinting efforts in securing permissions, proofreading, and overall coordination of the evolving revised manuscript.

The major part of what is good about this book we owe to the authors of the included works. However, we must bear full responsibility for the selections chosen, and the organization and preparation of introductory materials, together with whatever faults may be found.

FRED M. COX
JACK ROTHMAN
JOHN L. ERLICH
JOHN E. TROPMAN

GENERAL
INTRODUCTION

1.

Jack Rothman with John E. Tropman

MODELS OF COMMUNITY ORGANIZATION AND MACRO PRACTICE PERSPECTIVES: THEIR MIXING AND PHASING

INTRODUCTION

This article is an expanded version of an earlier one entitled "Three Models of Community Organization Practice, Their Mixing and Phasing."* The body of this discussion will remain essentially the same. What we will do in this instance is place community organization in the broader context of macro social work practice. This involves consideration of policy and administrative perspectives among the constellation of methods of macro intervention.

Macro intervention involves methods of professional changing that target systems above the level of the individual, group, and family, i.e., organizations, communities, and regional and national entities. Macro practice deals with aspects of human service activity that are nonclinical in nature, but rather focus on broader social approaches to human betterment, emphasizing such things as developing enlightened social policy, organizing the effective delivery of services, strengthening community life, and preventing social ills. Macro prac-

tice, thus, includes the areas of community organization, social policy, and administration. It is useful to view these methods both together and in relationship to one another, as the boundaries between them are often unclear, and many schools of social work teach them collectively in generic courses rather than as separate specializations. We will refer to the three areas of policy, community organization, and administration as perspectives within macro practice. The community organization area will be differentiated further in terms of distinct models within that practice. In keeping with previous editions of this text, community organization will receive primary and extended treatment. Hence, we will begin this discussion with consideration of community organization as a perspective on social intervention, including the variant models within that practice. This will be followed by a broader, but brief, discussion of the three perspectives and their relationship to one another. That discussion will constitute a first preliminary step toward a comparative analysis of macro perspectives.

As we are using the term here, a perspective represents a broad approach or strategy direction. A model, in contradistinction, is more specific, detailed, and coherently patterned internally.

Source: This article was written expressly for this volume.

*An expanded version of Jack Rothman, "Three Models of Community Organization Practice," from National Conference on Social Welfare, *Social Work Practice 1968* (New York: Columbia University Press, 1968). Copyright ©1968, National Conference on Social Welfare. Revised, 1978.

The contrast is between a somewhat loosely defined general orientation and a more tightly organized ideal-type. In discussing macro practice, we will use an interperspective analysis which compares the community organization approach with policy and administrative practice. In examining community organization more comprehensively, we will employ an intraperspective analysis which focuses on patterned variations within this approach to intervention.

THE COMMUNITY ORGANIZATION PERSPECTIVE AND ITS SUBMODELS

A welter of differing, contrasting, and sometimes clashing formulations of community organization practice exists, and this condition has been a source of immense perplexity and discomfort to the struggling practitioner and to the teacher of community organization. Taylor and Roberts describe the fluid nature of community organization theory, stating that "eclecticism, pragmatism and practice wisdom of professionals foster a turbulence and diversity that makes categorization and model building especially difficult tasks."[1] Kramer and Specht indicate that "there are some wide gaps in the theory used by community organizers and social planners."[2] Another scholar has been led to characterize "macro so-cial work," including community organization, as "a practice in search of some theory."[3]

Inadequate conceptual development prevails in professional areas which have community organization and planning aspects. In fields such as social work, education (adult education), and psychology (community psychology), the community organization dimension is somewhat peripheral and outside the main thrust of the profession. Until recent years, the social planning aspect of city planning has similarly been neglected. These areas have accordingly suffered from inadequate conceptualization and research efforts.

With the foregoing as backdrop, we shall endeavor to achieve some greater measure of clarity in conceptualizing community organization practice. One of the difficulties has been that writers on the subject originally attempted to set forth a single model or conception of community organization which was presumed to embrace all forms of this professional practice. Often these models were actually disparate, touched on different aspects of practice, or made discrepant assumptions about goals, methods, or values. The position advanced here holds that in empirical reality there are different forms of community intervention and that at this stage in the development of practice theory it would be better to capture and describe these rather than attempt to establish a grand, all-embracing theory or conception. The implication is that we should speak of community organization *methods* rather than *the* commu-

---

[1]Samuel H. Taylor and Robert W. Roberts (Eds.), *Theory and Practice of Community Social Work* (New York: Columbia University Press, 1985), pp. 24-25.

[2]Ralph M. Kramer and Harry Specht (Eds.), *Readings in Community Organization Practice,* Third Edition (Englewood Cliffs, NJ: Prentice Hall, 1983), p. 17.

[3]Edward E. Schwartz, "Macro Social Work: A Practice in Search of Some Theory," *Social Service Review,* 51, No. 2 (1977), pp. 201-227.

nity organization method. At the same time the actual and theoretical blending of alternative approaches should be acknowledged. Indeed, a basic intent of this analysis is to encourage purposeful and skilled mixing of different strategies and the presentation will culminate in just such a discussion.

Three important orientations to deliberate or purposive community change have been manifested over the past two decades in contemporary American communities, both urban and rural, and overseas. We will refer to them as approaches or models A, B, and C, although they can be given the appellations respectively of *locality development, social planning,* and *social action.* We will use these terms in a particular way, as will become clear in the passages which follow. These modes of action are not seen as exhaustive of all actual or potential possibilities. Because of their contemporary significance they have been selected for analysis; for reasons of economy in a single presentation others have been excluded.

It should also be noted that we are referring to activity which is of a somewhat continuing nature and which includes staff (professionally trained or not) who are responsible for sustained action processes. Thus the category of events which includes sporadic, ad hoc, voluntary civic action to obtain a new traffic light or displace an arrogant public official is not included.

Model A, locality development, presupposes that community change may be pursued optimally through broad participation of a wide spectrum of people at the local community level in goal determination and action. Its prototypic form will be found in the literature of a segment of the field com-

monly termed "community development." As stated by a major U.N. publication: "Community Development can be tentatively defined as a process designed to create conditions of economic and social progress for the whole community with its active participation and the fullest possible reliance on the community's initiative."[4] According to Dunham, some themes emphasized in locality development include democratic procedures, voluntary cooperation, self-help, development of indigenous leadership, and educational objectives.[5]

Some examples of locality development as conceived here include neighborhood work programs conducted by settlement houses and other community based agencies: Volunteers in Service to America; village-level work in some overseas community development programs, including the Peace Corps; community work in the adult education field; and self-help and informal helping network activities of various kinds. Writings that express and elaborate the community organization method according to Model A are those by the Biddles,[6] Henderson and Thomas,[7] Mayer,[8]

---

[4]United Nations, *Social Progress through Community Development* (New York: United Nations, 1955), p. 6.

[5]Arthur Dunham, "Some Principles of Community Development," *International Review of Community Development,* No. 11 (1963), pp. 141-151.

[6]William W. and Loureide J. Biddle, *The Community Development Process: The Rediscovery of Local Initiative* (New York: Holt, Rinehart & Winston, 1965).

[7]Paul Henderson and David N. Thomas, *Skills in Neighborhood Work* (Winchester, MA: Allen & Unwin, 1980).

[8]N. Mayer, *Neighborhood Organization and Community Development* (Washington, D.C : Urban Institute, 1984).

Blakely,[9] Bedics and Doelker,[10] and Lappin.[11] We will draw on the Blakely and Biddle volumes in particular for illustrative purposes.

Model B, the social planning approach, emphasizes a technical process of problem-solving with regard to substantive social problems, such as delinquency, housing, and mental health. Rational, deliberately planned, and controlled change has a central place in this model. Community participation may vary from much to little, depending on how the problem presents itself and what organizational variables are present. The approach presupposes that change in a complex industrial environment requires expert planners who, through the exercise of technical abilities, including the ability to manipulate large bureaucratic organizations, can skillfully guide complex change processes. The design of social plans and policies is of central importance, as is their implementation in effective and cost efficient ways. By and large, the concern here is with establishing, arranging, and delivering goods and services to people who need them. Building community capacity or fostering radical or fundamental social change does not play a major part.

Within the field of social work, programs emphasizing substantive decision making typify this approach. It also finds expression in university departments of public administration, urban affairs, city planning, and so forth. It is practiced in numerous federal bureaus and departments, in social planning divisions of housing authorities, in some United Ways and community welfare councils, and in various facets of community mental health planning. Some writings which reflect Model B include Lauffer,[12] Rein,[13] Morris and Binstock,[14] and Rothman and Zald.[15] The Morris and Binstock volume will be referred to liberally in this discussion.

Model C, the social action approach, presupposes a disadvantaged segment of the population that needs to be organized, perhaps in alliance with others, in order to make adequate demands on the larger community for increased resources or treatment more in accordance with social justice or democracy. It sometimes aims at making basic changes in major institutions or community practices. Social action often seeks redistribution of power, resources, or decision making in the community and/or changing basic policies of formal organizations. Examples of the social action approach have included consumer and environmental

[9]Edward J. Blakely, "Toward a Science of Community Development," in Edward J. Blakely (Ed.), *Community Development Research: Concepts, Issues and Strategies* (New York: Human Sciences Press, 1979), pp. 15-23.

[10]B.C. Bedics and R. Doelker, "Mobilizing Informal Resources in Rural Communities." *Human Services in the Rural Environment,* 8(1): 18-23, 1983.

[11]Ben Lappin, "Community Development: Beginnings in Social Work Enabling," in Samuel H. Taylor and Robert W. Roberts (Eds.), *Theory and Practice of Community Social Work* (New York: Columbia University Press, 1985), pp. 59-94.

[12]A. Lauffer, "The Practice of Social Planning," in Neil Gilbert and Harry Specht (Eds.), *Handbook of the Social Services* (Englewood Cliffs, NJ: Prentice Hall, 1981), pp. 588-97.

[13]M. Rein, *Social Policy: Issues of Choice and Change* (White Plains, NY: M.E. Sharpe, 1983).

[14]Robert Morris and Robert H. Binstock, *Feasible Planning for Social Change* (New York: Columbia University Press, 1966).

[15]Jack Rothman and Mayer N. Zald, "Planning Theory in Social Work Community Practice," in Samuel H. Taylor and Robert W. Roberts (Eds.), *Theory and Practice of Community Social Work* (New York: Columbia University Press, 1985, pp. 125-153).

protection organizations, feminist action groups, gay and lesbian organizations, civil rights and black power groups, La Raza, Alinsky's Industrial Areas Foundation projects, labor unions, and radical political action groups. Alinsky's *Reveille for Radicals* and *Rules for Radicals*[16] have typified the orientation of the social action model. Other more recent writings also reflect this orientation.[17] Social action does not enjoy the currency it once had. Its practice is more sporadic and contained. Nevertheless, opportunities and fashions in use of community organization rise and fall over time as changes occur in ideology, political climate, and economic circumstances. Social action methods remain tools of sophisticated community·organization practitioners, to be drawn upon selectively as situations allow in the current context, or to be used more extensively as historical forces transform the social landscape.

Several schools of social work have in the past developed specialized programs for training according to these three models. Thus a community development program that was situated at the University of Missouri has epitomized Model A; the doctoral program in planning at Brandeis University, Model B; and the social action program which was based at Syracuse University, Model C.

Morris and Binstock suggest a similar threefold division in the field of community planning and action:

[A] ... to alter human attitudes and behavioral patterns through education, exhortation and a number of other methods for stimulating self-development and fulfillment. [B] ... to alter social conditions by changing the policies of formal organizations. It is undertaken to modify the amount, the quality, the accessibility, and the range of goods, services, and facilities provided for people. [C] ... to effect reforms in major legal and functional systems of a society. It relies upon political agitation ... and a host of other instruments for coping with powerful trends and developments.[18]

Having set off each of these models or ideal-types, it would be well to indicate that we are speaking of tendencies or emphasis and that in actual practice these orientations are overlapping rather than discrete. Practice in any of these orientations may require techniques and approaches that are salient in another orientation. For example, neighborhood social actionists may be required to draw up a social plan in order to obtain funding for desired projects from HUD or DHHS (Models C and B). Or social planners may decide that the most effective way of solving the

[16]Saul D. Alinsky, *Reveille for Radicals* (Chicago: University of Chicago Press, 1946), and *Rules for Radicals* (New York: Random House, 1972).

[17]Douglas Glasgow, "Black Power through Community Control," *Social Work,* XVII, No. 3 (1972), 59-65; Jeffry H. Galper, *The Politics of Social Services* (Englewood Cliffs, NJ: Prentice Hall, 1975); Roy Bailey and Mike Brake, *Radical Social Work* (New York: Pantheon Books, 1975); S. Burghardt, *Organizing for Community Action* (Beverly Hills: Sage Publications, 1982); R. Browning, *Protest Is Not Enough* (Berkeley: University of California Press, 1984); S. Burghardt, *The Other Side of Organizing* (Cambridge, MA: Schenkman, 1982); Richard Cloward and Frances Piven, *Poor People's Movements* (New York: Pantheon, 1977); R.E. Roberts and R.M. Kloss, *Social Movements: Between the Balcony and the Barricade* (St. Louis: C.V. Mosby Co., 1974); S. Weisner, "Fighting Back: A Critical Analysis of Coalition Building in the Human Services," *Social Service Review,* 57 (2) (1983), 291-306; S. Kahn, *Organizing* (New York: McGraw-Hill Book Co., 1982).

[18]Morris and Binstock, op. cit., p. 14.

problem of resistant attitudes toward family planning is through wide discussion and participation in developing a community program (Models B and A). This issue will be discussed at greater length in the concluding section of this presentation.

At this point we will not attempt to deal with variants or mixed forms which may constitute unique separate models. Instead, for analytical purposes, we will view the three approaches as "pure" forms. The virtue in this is suggested by Morris and Binstock when they refer to their own classification system:

The categories are somewhat arbitrary, for it is sometimes difficult to say that a particular planning experience fits one category but not another. For these reasons it is particularly important to achieve as narrow a focus as possible in analyzing planning: otherwise a systematic treatment is virtually impossible.[19]

To proceed with the analysis, we will attempt to specify a set of practice variables which will help describe and compare each of the approaches when they are identified in the ideal-type form. Each of the orientations makes assumptions about the nature of the community situation, the definitions of one's client population or constituency, goal categories of action, concepts of the general welfare, appropriate strategies of action, and so on. A set of such variables will be treated in the passages that follow. (The reader may find it useful to scan Table 1.1, p. 10 at this point.)

1. Goal Categories. Two main goals which have been discussed recurrently in the community organization and macro practice literature are referred to

frequently as "task" and "process." Task goals entail the completion of a concrete task or the solution of a delimited problem pertaining to the functioning of a community social system—delivery of services, establishment of new services, passing of specific social legislation. Process goals are more oriented to system maintenance and enhancement, with aims such as establishing cooperative working relationships among groups in the community, creating self-maintaining community problem-solving structures, stimulating wide interest and participation in community affairs, fostering collaborative attitudes and practices, and increasing indigenous leadership. Murray Ross characterizes this set of goals as "community integration" and "community capacity." Process goals are concerned with a generalized or gross capacity of the community system to function over time; task goals, with the solution of delimited functional problems of the system.[20]

In locality development, process goals receive heavy emphasis. The community's capacity to become functionally integrated, to engage in cooperative problem solving on a self-help basis, and to utilize democratic processes is of central importance. This point of view is expressed by Blakely as follows:

The community ... must be totally involved in all of the frustrations as well as the successes in arriving at the objective. It is in this process that growth in 'community' (relationships among people) occurs, and it is

[19]Morris and Binstock, op. cit., p. 15.

[20]Neil Gilbert and Harry Specht, "Process Versus Task in Social Planning," *Social Work,* XXII, No. 3 (1977), 178-83; also Jack Rothman, "An Analysis of Goals and Roles in Community Organization Practice," *Social Work,* IX, No. 2 (1964), 24-31.

this process and not its outcome that stimulates and advances the science of community development.[21]

In the social planning approach, stress is placed on task goals, oriented toward the solution of substantive social problems. Social planning organizations often are mandated specifically to deal with concrete social problems, and their official names signify this—mental health departments, city planning and housing authorities, commissions on physical rehabilitation or alcoholism, and so on.

The social action approach may lean in the direction of either task goals or process goals. Some social action organizations, such as civil rights groups and cause-oriented organizations, emphasize obtaining specific legislative outcomes (higher welfare allotments) or changing specific social practices (preferential hiring). Usually these objectives entail the modification of policies of formal organizations. Other social action groups lean more in the direction of process goals—building a constituency with the ability to acquire and exercise power—as exemplified by Saul Alinsky and the Industrial Areas Foundation, ACORN, or the early black power movement. This objective of building local-based power and decision-making centers transcends the solution of any given problem situation. Goals are often viewed in terms of changing power relationships rather than tinkering with small-scale or short-range problem situations. These small-scale activities are often pursued, however, because they are feasible and they help to build an organization. Creating power may also be associated with building personal self-esteem. This

dual perspective has been put by Kahn as follows:

Organizing has both short- and long-range benefits. In the short run it's an effective tool for getting things done: for improving schools, for lowering taxes, for establishing rights on the job, for improving transportation and health care, for protecting and defending neighborhoods and communities .... But it is also an end in itself. As we organize, we clarify ourselves as individuals because we learn to speak for ourselves in ways that make us heard.[22]

2. Assumptions Concerning Problem Conditions. In Model A (locality development) the local community is frequently seen as overshadowed by the larger society, lacking in fruitful human relationships and problem-solving skills and peopled by isolated individuals suffering from anomie, alienation, disillusionment, and often mental illness. As Ross develops this theme, technological change has pressed society toward greater industrialization and urbanization with little consideration of the effects on social relations:

The processes of urbanization have almost destroyed "man's feeling of belonging to" a community ... The problem of developing and maintaining common or shared values (the basic ingredient for cohesion) is made vastly more difficult by industrialization and urbanization .... This tendency for large subgroups to develop cohesion as separate entities in the community produces social tension, potentially dangerous in any community ... Democracy will weaken, if not perish, unless supporting institutions are supported and new institutions (to meet new ways of living) are developed .... The barriers that prevent active participation in the direction of social change inhibit personal development.[23]

---

[21]Blakely, op. cit., p. 19.

[22]Kahn, op. cit., pp. 7-8.
[23]Murray G. Ross, *Comunity Organization: Theory and Principles* (New York: Harper and Brothers, 1955), pp. 80-83.

TABLE 1.1
Three Models of Community Organization Practice
According to Selected Practice Variables

	Model A (Locality Development)	Model B (Social Planning)	Model C (Social Action)
1. Goal categories of community action	Self-help; community capacity and integration (process goals)	Problem solving with regard to substantive community problems (task goals)	Shifting of power relationships and resources; basic institutional change (task or process goals)
2. Assumptions concerning community structure and problem conditions	Community eclipsed, anomie; lack of relationships and democratic problem-solving capacities; static traditional community	Substantive social problems; mental and physical health, housing, recreation	Disadvantaged populations, social injustice, deprivation, inequity
3. Basic change strategy	Broad cross section of people involved in determining and solving their own problems	Fact gathering about problems and decisions on the most rational course of action	Crystallization of issues and organization of people to take action against enemy targets
4. Characteristic change tactics and techniques	Consensus: communication among community groups and interests; group discussion	Consensus or conflict	Conflict or contest: confrontation, direct action, negotiation
5. Salient practitioner roles	Enabler-catalyst, coordinator; teacher of problem-solving skills and ethical values	Fact gatherer and analyst, program implementer, facilitator	Activist advocate: agitator, broker, negotiator, partisan
6. Medium of change	Manipulation of small task-oriented groups	Manipulation of formal organizations and of data	Manipulation of mass organizations and political processes
7. Orientation toward power structure(s)	Members of power structure as collaborators in a common venture	Power structure as employers and sponsors	Power structure as external target of action: oppressors to be coerced or overturned
8. Boundary definition of the community client system or constituency	Total geographic community	Total community or community segment (including "functional" community)	Community segment
9. Assumptions regarding interests of community subparts	Common interests or reconcilable differences	Interests reconcilable or in conflict	Conflicting interests which are not easily reconcilable: scarce resources
10. Conception of the client population or constituency	Citizens	Consumers	Victims
11. Conception of client role	Participants in an interactional problem-solving process	Consumers or recipients	Employers, constituents, members

Ross sums up his basic assumptions regarding the contemporary community situation:

This is the problem of man's loss of his essential human dignity. For surely man is being overwhelmed by forces of which he is only dimly aware, which subjugate him to a role of decreasing importance and present him with problems with which he has no means to cope. Aspects of this central problem are the difficulty of full expression of a democratic philosophy and the threats to the mental health of individual members of societies.[24]

Alternatively, the community may be seen as tradition-bound, ruled by a small group of conventional leaders, and composed of an illiterate population who lack both skills in problem solving and an understanding of the democratic process.

The planner represented in Model B comes to his situation with quite a different viewpoint. He/she is likely to see the community as comprised of a number of substantive social problem conditions, or a particular substantive problem which is of special interest, such as housing, employment, or recreation. Warren, while taking account of the outlook set down by Ross, expresses also a perspective that is more congruent with that of the social planners:

It is apparent that certain types of 'problems' are broadly characteristic of contemporary American communities. While most noticeable in the metropolitan areas, most of them are apparent in smaller communities as well. They appear in such forms as the increasing indebtedness of central cities, the spread of urban blight and slums, the lack of adequate housing which people can afford, the economic dependence of large numbers of people in the population, poorly financed and staffed schools, high delinquency and crime rates, inadequate provisions for the mentally ill, the problem of the aged, the need for industrial development, the conflict of local and national agencies for the free donor's dollar, the problem of affording rapid transit for commuters at a reasonable price and at a reasonable profit, and the problem of downtown traffic congestion. This list is almost endless, and each of the problems mentioned could be subdivided into numerous problematic aspects.[25]

The social action practitioners in Model C have still a different mind-set. They would more likely view the community as comprised of a hierarchy of privilege and power. There exist islands of oppressed, deprived, ignored, or powerless populations suffering social injustice or exploitation at the hands of oppressors such as the "power structure," big government, corporations, the establishment, or the society at large. (Oppression can imply material deprivation or psychological harassment.) Kahn states the point:

In the United States today power is concentrated in the hands of a small number of well-organized individuals and corporations. These corporations and the individuals involved in them have extraordinary power to make decisions that affect all our lives ... regardless of the suffering that it has caused people ... [26]

Again, we caution that the above describes dominant motifs rather than discrete categories. Many social actionists are greatly concerned about apathy and substantive problems, even as some social planners are concerned about both the quality of social relations and specific problems. We are

---

[24]Ibid., p. 84.

[25]Roland L. Warren, *The Community in America* (Chicago: Rand McNally & Company, 1963; rev. 1972), p. 14.

[26]Kahn, op. cit., p. 3.

defining dominant tendencies rather than mutually exclusive properties.

3. *Basic Change Strategy.* In locality development the change strategy may be characterized as, "Let's all get together and talk this over"—an effort to get a wide range of community people involved in determining their "felt" needs and solving their own problems.

In planning, the basic change strategy is one of "Let's get the facts and take the logical next steps." In other words, let us gather pertinent facts about the problem, and then decide on a rational and feasible course of action. The practitioner plays a central part in gathering and analyzing facts and determining appropriate services, programs, and actions. This may or may not be done with the participation of others, depending upon the planner's sense of the utility of participation in the given situation and the organizational context within which he/she functions.

In social action the change strategy may be articulated as, "Let's organize to overpower our oppressor," that is, crystallizing issues so that people know who their legitimate enemy is and organizing mass action to bring pressure on selected targets. Such targets may include an organization, such as the welfare department; a person, such as the mayor; or an aggregate of persons, such as slum landlords.

4. *Characteristic Change Tactics and Techniques.* In locality development, tactics of consensus are stressed—discussion and communication among a wide range of different individuals, groups, and factions.

Blakely underlines the importance of cooperative, deliberative techniques for the practice we are designating as locality development:

Development specialists attempt within the conflict situation to place the stress on problem solving as opposed to win-lose strategies and attitudes. The community developer's role is to provide avenues for the problem to be confronted objectively and dealt with intelligently.[27]

In social planning, fact-finding and analytical skills are important. Tactics of conflict or consensus may be employed, depending upon the practitioner's analysis of the situation. For example, a recent writing on managerial planning emphasized the cooperative participation aspect.[28]

In social action, conflict tactics are emphasized, including methods such as confrontation and direct action. Ability to mobilize relatively large numbers of people is necessary to carry out rallies, marches, boycotts, and picketing. Kahn has stated the issue as follows:

Most of the rights and benefits we have now weren't given to us. People organized to get them. Many of the things we now take for granted had to be fought for.[29]

Alinsky adds:

Issues which are noncontroversial usually mean that people are not particularly concerned about them; in fact, by not being controversial they cease to be issues. Issues involve differences and controversy. History fails to record a single issue of importance which was not controversial. Controversy has always been the seed of creation.[30]

Warren, in his discussion of types of purposive social change, suggests a var-

---

[27]Blakely, op. cit., p. 21.
[28]T.J. Peters and R.H. Waterman, *In Search of Excellence* (New York: Harper & Row, 1982).
[29]Kahn, op. cit., p. 6.
[30]Saul D. Alinsky, "Citizen Participation and Community Organization in Planning and Urban Renewal" (Chicago: Industrial Areas Foundation, 1962; mimeographed), p. 7.

iation among conflict tactics: campaign strategies when there are differences among parties but issue consensus can eventually be reached; and contest strategies when the external group refuses to recognize the issue or opposes the change agent's proposal so that issue dissensus is quite pervasive and inherent.[31] Specht analyzes a variety of disruptive tactics.[32]

5 and 6. Practitioner Roles and Medium of Change. In locality development the practitioner's characteristic role is that of an "enabler" or, as suggested by Biddle, "encourager." According to Ross, the enabler role is one of facilitating a process of problem solving and includes such actions as helping people express their discontents, encouraging organization building, nourishing good interpersonal relationships, and emphasizing common objectives.[33] The role has been described in this way:

Community developers study group behavior in community settings in an attempt to identify new avenues for catalyzing citizen awareness and community action.[34]

The practitioner employs as a major medium of change the creation and manipulation of small task-oriented groups, requiring skill in guiding processes of collaborative problem finding and problem solving.

In social planning, more technical or "expert" roles are emphasized, such as fact finding, implementation of programs, relationships with various bureaucracies and with professionals of

various disciplines and so on. Referring again to Ross, the expert role is suggested as containing these components: community diagnosis, research skill, information about other communities, advice on methods of organization and procedure, technical information, and evaluation. In Model B the practitioner employs as a salient medium of change the manipulation of formal organizations (including interorganizational relationships) as well as data collection and analysis.

The social action model is likely to incorporate what Grosser has called the "advocate" and "activist" roles. According to Grosser, the advocate is "a partisan in social conflict, and his expertise is available exclusively to serve client interests."[35] The roles in Model C entail the organization of client groups to act on behalf of their interests in a pluralist community arena. The practitioner seeks to create and manipulate mass organizations and movements and to influence political processes as an important medium of change. Mass organization is necessary because the constituency has few resources or sources of power outside its sheer numerical strength. This is stated as follows:

The power of a lot of people working together is enough to make changes where one person can do very little.[36]

7. Orientation Toward Power Structure(s). In locality development the power structure is included within an all-embracing conception of community. All segments of the community are thought of as part of the client system. Hence, members of the power structure

---
[31]Warren, op. cit.

[32]Harry Specht, "Disruptive Tactics," *Social Work,* XIV, No. 2 (1969), pp. 5-15.

[33]Ross, op. cit.

[34]Blakely, op. cit., p. 20.

---
[35]Grosser, op. cit., p. 18.

[36]Kahn, op. cit., p. 2.

are considered to be collaborators in a common venture. One consequence of this might well be that in Model A only goals upon which there can be mutual agreement become legitimate or relevant; the goals which involve incompatible interests are ignored or discarded as inappropriate. Values and constraints narrow the goals to those upon which all factions can agree. Hence, goals involving fundamental shifts in configurations of power and resource control are likely to be excluded.

In social planning, the power structure is usually present as sponsor or employer of the practitioner. Sponsors may include a voluntary board of directors or an arm of city government. Morris and Binstock state the case this way: "Realistically, it is difficult to distinguish planners from their employing organizations. In some measure, their interests, motivations, and means are those of their employers."[37] Planners are usually highly trained professional specialists whose services require a considerable financial outlay in salary as well as support in the form of supplies, equipment, facilities, and auxiliary technical and clerical personnel. Frequently, planners can only be supported in their work by those in a power position in the society, especially with regard to the possession of wealth, control of the machinery of government, or a monopoly of prestige. As Rein suggests, much planning is by "consensus of elites" who are employers and policymakers in planning organizations.[38] Usually this consensus is clothed in strong factual data.

In social action the power structure is seen as an external target of action; that is to say, the power structure lies outside the client system or constituency itself, as an oppositional or oppressive force vis-à-vis the client group.

The fact that you're right usually has very little to do with whether or not you win. People with power or privilege rarely give it away because it would be 'right' to do so. The question is, are you powerful? If you have power, then you can get something done.[39]

The power structure, then, usually represents a force antithetical to the client or constituent group whose well-being the practitioner is committed to uphold. Those holding power, accordingly, must be coerced or overturned in order that the interests of the client population may find satisfaction.

8. Boundary Definition of the Client System or Constituency. In locality development the total community, usually a geographic entity, such as a city, neighborhood, or village, is the client system. According to Dunham, "Community Development is concerned with the participation of *all* groups in the community—with both sexes, all age groups, all racial, nationality, religious, economic, social and cultural groups."[40] Blakely states that

The development of projects or programs in community development requires considerable preplanning or diagnostic work to insure that the total system is being considered adequately.[41]

In social planning the client system might be either a total geographic com-

[37]Morris and Binstock, op. cit., p. 16.
[38]Martin Rein, "Strategies of Planned Change," American Orthopsychiatric Association, 1965.

[39]Kahn, op. cit., p. 2.
[40]Dunham, op. cit.
[41]Blakely, op. cit., p. 22.

munity or some area or functional subpart thereof. Community welfare councils and city planning commissions usually conceive of their client groups as comprising the widest cross section of community interests. On the other hand, sometimes the client populations of social planners are more segmented aggregates—a given neighborhood, the mentally ill, the aged, youth, juvenile delinquents, or the Jewish community.

In social action the client is usually conceived of as some community subpart or segment which suffers at the hands of the broader community and thus needs the special support of the practitioner. According to Kahn:

When people in government, such as community planners and developers, talk about community development, they often mean the development of an entire city. This idea is misleading. You can't develop an entire city. What's good for some people is not good for others. If something is good for one group, another group loses out. There are conflicts within groups. The poverty of one group may be caused by the profits of another.[42]

In social action, practitioners are more likely to think in terms of constituents or fellow partisans[43] rather than in terms of the "client" concept, which may be patronizing or overly detached and clinical.

9. Assumptions Regarding Interests or Subsystems. In locality development the interests of various groups and factions in the community are seen as basically reconcilable and responsive to the influences of rational persuasion, communication, and mutual good will. Hence:

Community developers accept the notion that people, regardless of race, sex, ethnicity or place of birth, can find ways to solve their problems through group efforts. The community development movement is humanistic in orientation . . . . Interpersonal competencies are the skills required to deal with others in face-to-face relationships. This implies a genuineness or authenticity in relationships that permits open, honest communication and feedback.[44]

In social planning there is no pervasive assumption about the degree of intractability of conflicting interests; the approach appears to be pragmatic, oriented toward the particular problem and the actors enmeshed in it. Morris and Binstock set down the social planning orientation as follows:

A planner cannot be expected to be attuned to the factional situation within each complex organization from which he is seeking a policy change; nor can he always be aware of the overriding interests of dominant factions. Considerable study and analysis of factions and interests dominant in various types of organizations will be needed before planners will have sufficient guidance for making reliable predictions as to resistance likely in a variety of situations.[45]

The social action model assumes that interests among community subparts are at variance and not reconcilable, and that often coercive influences must be applied (legislation, boycotts, political and social upheavals) before meaningful adjustments can be made. Those who hold power or privilege and profit from the disadvantage of others do not easily give up their advantage; the force

[42]Kahn, op. cit., p. 80.
[43]William Gamson, *Power and Discontent* (Homewood, IL: Dorsey Press, 1968).

[44]Blakely, op. cit., pp. 18, 21.
[45]Morris and Binstock, op. cit., p. 112.

of self-interest would make it foolish to expect them to do so. Saul Alinsky states:

All major controlling interests make a virtue of acceptance—acceptance of the ruling group's policies and decisions. Any movement or organization arising in disagreement, or seeking independent changes and defined by the predominating powers as a threat, is promptly subjected to castigation, public and private smears, and attacks on its very existence.[46]

10. Conception of the Client Population or Constituency.

In locality development, clients are likely to be viewed as average citizens who possess considerable strengths which are not fully developed and who need the services of a practitioner to help them release and focus these inherent capabilities. The Biddles express this viewpoint as follows:

1. Each person is valuable, and capable of growth toward greater social sensitivity and responsibility.
    a. Each person has underdeveloped abilities in initiative, originality, and leadership. These qualities can be cultivated and strengthened.[47]

In social planning, clients are more likely to be thought of as consumers of services, those who will receive and utilize those programs and services which are the fruits of the social planning process—mental health, public housing, recreation, welfare benefits, and so forth. Morris and Binstock specifically refer to "consumers" rather than "clients" in their social planning analytical framework.

In social action, clients or constituents are likely to be considered as victims of "the system," most broadly, or of portions thereof, such as slum landlords, the educational system, city government. Those on behalf of whom action is initiated are often characterized in "underdog" terms.[48]

11. Conception of Client or Constituent Role.

In locality development, clients are viewed as active participants in an interactional process with one another and with the practitioner. Considerable stress is placed on groups in the community as the media through which learning and growth take place. Clients engage in an intensive group process of expressing their "felt needs," determining desired goals, and taking appropriate conjoint action.

In planning, clients are recipients of services. They are active in consuming services, not in the determination of policy or goals, a function reserved for the planner or some policymaking instrumentality, such as a board of directors or a commission. According to Morris and Binstock:

Opportunities for members and consumers to determine policy are severely limited because they are not usually organized for this purpose. If they are organized, and if the central issue which brings them together is sufficiently strong, they are likely to withdraw to form a separate organization. If the issue is weak the opportunity to control policy is short-lived because the coalition will fall apart, lacking sufficient incentive to bind together the otherwise diverse constituent elements.[49]

---

[46]Alinsky, "Citizen Participation and Community Organization in Planning and Urban Renewal," op. cit., p. 6.

[47]Biddle and Biddle, op. cit., p. 60.

[48]These categories are similar, respectively, to those of: (1) clients or patients; (2) customers; and (3) victims as described by Martin Rein, "The Social Service Crisis," *Trans-Action,* 1, No. 4 (1964), pp. 3-6.

[49]Morris and Binstock, op. cit., pp. 109-110.

Decisions, then, are made through the planner in collaboration with some community group, usually composed of elites, who are presumed to represent either the community-at-large or the best interests of the client group.

In social action the benefiting group is likely to be composed of employers of the practitioner or constituents. In unions the membership ideally runs the organization. Alinsky's Industrial Areas Foundation will ideally not enter a target area until the people there have gained a controlling and independent voice in the funding of the organization. The concept of the organizer as an employee and servant of the people is stressed. Kahn holds that the "staff director of the organization, if there is one, should be directly accountable to the board and should be held accountable by the board."[50] The client group, whether employers or constituents, is in the position of determining broad goals and policies. Those not in continual or central participatory roles may participate more sporadically in mass action and pressure group activities, such as marches or boycotts.

THE COMMUNITY ORGANIZATION MODELS VIEWED VERTICALLY

We have examined the three models horizontally; that is, we have looked at them comparatively in a way that has cut across the practice variables. We may also view the models from a vertical standpoint, by describing each separately in terms of all the listed practice variables. Doing this illustratively in two instances—locality develop-

ment and social action—yields a product described here.

Locality Development

In Model A, locality development, goals of action include self-help and increased community capacity and integration. The community, especially in urban contexts, is seen as eclipsed, fragmented, suffering from anomie, and with a lack of good human relationships and democratic problem-solving skills. The basic change strategy involves getting a broad cross section of people involved in studying and taking action on their problems. Consensus strategies are employed, involving small-group discussion and fostering communication among community subparts (class, ethnic, and so forth). The practitioner functions as an enabler and catalyst as well as a teacher of problem-solving skills and ethical values. He/she is especially skilled in manipulating and guiding small-group interaction. Members of power structures are collaborators in a common effort since the definition of the community client system includes the total geographic community. The practitioner conceives of the community as composed of common interests or reconcilable differences. Clients are conceived of as citizens engaged in a common community venture, and their role accordingly is one of participating in an interactional problem-solving process.

Social Action

In the social action model, goals include the shifting of power, resources, and decision-making loci in the society as well as, on the short-range basis,

[50]Kahn, op. cit., p. 70.

changing the policies of formal organizations. System change is viewed as critical. The community is conceived of as being composed of a hierarchy of privilege and power, with the existence of clusters of deprived populations suffering from disadvantage or social injustice. The basic change strategy involves crystallizing issues and organizing indigenous populations to take action on their own behalf against enemy targets. Change tactics often include conflict techniques, such as confrontation, and direct action as in rallies, marches, boycotts, or "hard-nosed" bargaining. The practitioner functions in the role of activist, agitator, broker, "hard-nosed" negotiator, and partisan. He/she is skilled in the manipulation of mass organizations and political processes. Power structures are viewed as an external target of action—oppressors or exploiters who need to be limited or removed. The client group or constituency is a disadvantaged community segment (blacks, the poor, women, gays, workers). It is assumed that interests among related parties are at conflict or not easily reconcilable since those who possess power, resources, and prestige are reluctant to relinquish or share them. Clients are viewed as victims of various forces and interests in the society, and their role is that of employer or constituent with regard to the practitioner, as well as participants in mass action and pressure group activities.

A COMPARISON OF MACRO PERSPECTIVES

Having set off and dissected the community organization practice perspective, we are ready to place it in context with policy and administration practice perspectives. This discussion is an initial entry to the subject and suggestive of its analytic utility. Considerations of length and complexity of this presentation dictate a brief and heuristic treatment. For ease of discussion we will treat each of these perspectives in general terms, that is, along lines of the dominant mode of conceptualizing these practices. We will deal with community organization now on a more abstract level that encompasses the three models. There are losses as well as gains in this approach. Administration could be subdivided into at least two models, hierarchical and participatory. Likewise, there are rationalistic and political conceptualizations of the policy process. For ease of analysis, we will emphasize the former concept in each case in our discussion.

We will start this phase of the discussion with social policy formation and enactment, the broadest or most encompassing of macro perspectives. Social policy frequently sets the framework within which all other areas of social work function. It often becomes necessary to adopt new policy or change existing policy in order to structure conditions under which other macro methods may function optimally. Also, social policy often operates at the societal or state level, offering the broadest scope of coverage and effect.

Community is on the next level down, and has already been treated. Finally, we will conclude with consideration of the administrative perspective, which focuses on the agency or organization through which programs and services flow. The organizational unit is the smallest or most bounded of the macro systems we will be discussing.

Policy Practice

There are several phases to the policy process, including generation of initial ideas, selecting some goals for further consideration, the management of the ratification process itself, and the link, after ratification, to more detailed planning and design, programming and evaluation. Typically policy includes the setting of goals and the establishing of rules for implementation. Most writers on policy methods have a set of stages similar to these five steps.[51]

Policy practice ordinarily entails the development and improvement of written and formally approved guidelines for action.[52] While it often may be thought that policy is what governments, and especially the federal or national governments do, in fact policy can be made at each of the levels of social intervention: individual, family/group, organizational, community as well as state/national arenas. Personal goal statements, wills, marriage contracts, directives passed by the board of an agency, city ordinances, as well as national laws, fall into the policy category. This expanded view of policy realms has been developed recently in works by Pierce, Jansson, and Tropman.[53]

The idea of policy management is a more proactive or practice-related concept than has characterized policy definitions in the past. Such definitions have often focused upon learning what policies exist and which affect social welfare concerns. Another step, policy analysis, was sometimes taken, in which the policies were analyzed in terms of sources, implications and effects, using a variety of analytic techniques.[54] Both of these efforts tend to focus upon policy documents. Recent conceptualizations have added several elements to policy practice, including a focus on the policy process just mentioned, the policy context (those structures and beliefs which advance certain policies and retard others), policy implementation (what happens after a policy is passed), and policy management (the orchestration of the policy process through the series of requisite steps, and attention to increasing the supply of new policy ideas). The policy manager, thus, becomes, like the community organizer and administrator, an individual actively seeking to improve the process of policy making much as the case manager seeks to improve the situation for a particular client. We are speaking here of policy as a professional practice method, not merely an analytical tool for understanding cognitively social welfare programs and services.

Certainly these efforts were implicit in the early treatment by Baumheier and Schorr[55] in their discussion of four policy practice roles (enacting laws and regulations, advising, researching social problems, and advocating) but policy practice has now expanded the realms and specified the ways in which

[51]John E. Tropman. "Methods and Techniques for Social Policy Analysis: The Practice of Policy Management," *The Encyclopedia of Social Work* (New York: NASW, Forthcoming).

[52]John E. Tropman, *Policy Management in the Human Services* (New York: Columbia University Press, 1984).

[53]Dean Pierce, *Policy for Social Work Practice* (New York: Longman, 1984); Bruce Jansson, *Theory and Practice of Social Welfare Policy* (Belmont, CA: Wadsworth Publishing, 1984); and Tropman, ibid.

[54]Tropman, 1984, op. cit.

[55]Edward C. Baumheier and Alvin L. Schorr, *Social Policy, The Encyclopedia of Social Work* (New York: NASW, 1977), pp. 1453-1462.

these activities are carried out. In a sense, policy practice involves the mobilization and guidance of ideas through the decision process. This process was often approached casually, as suggested in the "Garbage Can Model of Decision Making."[56] However, policy management can act to improve the process of decision making by explicit attention to the essential elements (information, people) and their configurations, the use of skills and techniques to improve the process (mediating, negotiating, brokering, decision structuring techniques) and the use of assigned roles in the decision process (researcher, documentor, facilitator).

Some of the more limited perspectives on policy came, perhaps, because of the focus in social work on one kind of policy—social policy. However, there remains even today considerable confusion about what social policy is, and what is included, and excluded, from its purview.[57] But whatever it was, social policy was thought of in public policy terms, that is, to be largely done by government. Hence there was a tendency to think of policy activity as governmental and especially concerned, perhaps, with the disadvantaged. While we reaffirm social work's historic concern with the disadvantaged group, it became increasingly difficult to separate policy for that group from policy for other groups, to distinguish "welfare" policy for the "poor" from "welfare" policy for the

"rich" (tax support, etc.). Our perspective is that decisions which concern people and their lives are the appropriate target for policy practice, and as noted, those decisions may occur at all levels of the social order. Pension protection through Social Security, for example, needs to be considered along with that same protection provided (or not provided) by one's place of employment. Social policy pertains to the range of processes and pronouncements that deal with human services.

Administrative Practice

The administration perspective recognizes that community organization, as well as other methods of social work, is practiced within organizations.[58] The functioning of those organizations is crucial as a necessary, but not sufficient, condition to effective and efficient intervention by the community organization practitioner and the policy practitioner. Administration has, after some uncertainty, come to be recognized as a legitimate method of social work intervention in and of itself. The journal, *Administration in Social Work,* provides a range of relevant articles for the administrative practitioner. Often, community organizers and administrators are one and the same person, and it is the role, not the person, which shifts. Increasingly, schools of social work offer specialties in administration, and some schools of social work are developing joint ventures with schools of

---

[56]M. Cohen, J. G. March and J. Olsen, "A Garbage Can Model of Organizational Choice," *Administrative Science Quarterly,* 17 (1) 1972, 1-25.

[57]For an explicit treatment of this issue, see Tropman, 1984 (op. cit.), Chapter 13, "Social Policy: Old Concerns, New Perspectives."

[58]See for example, Armand Lauffer, *Strategies of Marketing* (New York: Basic Books, 1984); Robert D. Vinter and Rhea Kish, *Budgeting for Non-Profit Organizations* (New York: Free Press, 1984); Yeheskel Hasenfeld, *Human Service Organizations* (Englewood Cliffs, NJ: Prentice-Hall, 1983).

business for these purposes. In addition, some schools of management, such as at Yale and UCLA, are looking toward the "nonprofit" sector as a source of jobs. While the nonprofit sector is not exclusively made up of social work agencies, it includes "human service agencies," the traditional context of social work practice.

Organizational structures provide the *vehicles* through which services and programs are formulated and implemented. The organization provides resources, legitimation, personnel, know-how, "good will" and other instrumentalities through which action is articulated.

Organizations are often the *targets* of professional activity. Frequently the practitioner's goal is the modification of policies or practices of some external organization or institution in the community. Service agencies seek clients and information from other organizations and use them for referral purposes. Planning agencies attempt to coordinate programs among agencies. Locality development agencies bring community agencies into deliberation processes with citizens groups in order to assess community needs and collaborate in developing ameliorative actions. Social action organizations often pressure organizations and agencies to drop certain policies and programs or to adopt new ones.

Organizations also serve in many instances as the *context* within which practice takes place. Existing patterns of good cooperation and communication among organizations may lead a change organization into one mode of action; a climate of distrust and conflict will suggest a different *modus operandi*. Likewise, if agencies generally exhibit high levels of professionalism or have

an ample resource base, the form of action by a change agency will be different than when agencies have a low level of expertise or are poor in resources available for programmatic purposes.

If organization is the framework within which action takes place, administration is the practice of organizational development and manipulation. Administration is the means through which organizations are shaped and directed to pursue particular goals and carry out particular strategies and programs. While administration is viewed as a delineated method in social work practice, it also cuts across all other methods of practice. Administration provides a basis for steering the organizational process of direct service organizations. It does the same for all three models of community organization, whether social planning, locality development, or social action. In a similar vein, policy development and enactment take place within an organizational framework that ought to be shaped in such a way as to allow the policy process to unfold optimally.

Particular elements of administration can be singled out to identify facets of the practice. First of all, there is the matter of choosing the goals that an organization should pursue and determining the strategies and programs that are consistent with attaining those goals. This draws upon the skills of the administrator in executive leadership, including the ability to assess community needs, design programs, maintain community relationships, and facilitate consensus among organizational constituencies. Next there is the capacity to execute strategies and services in an effective way. These technical tasks of implementation require the ability to mobilize people, information and resources so as to make an impact on the needs or problems being addressed. Additionally, there is the task of managing organizational operations. This may be stated in simplest terms as keeping an organization going. Such maintenance activities involve things as basic as having a supply of paper clips available, getting the right staff people to the right place at the right time, acquiring and keeping in good condition equipment and facilities necessary for program implementation, etc. Parsons[59] has identified these respectively as institutional, technical, and managerial levels of administrative function.

Having described the three macro perspectives, it is possible to examine them cross-sectionally, using the same set of practice variables applied to the analysis of alternative models within community organization practice. We will do this type of analysis suggestively, selecting out a few practice variables to illustrate the utility of the approach. A fuller explication will require treatment in a separate analysis.

Looking first at *characteristic change tactics and techniques, policy practice* may use either consensus or conflict orientations. Political power and its deployment is a central consideration. The particular issue and the array of interests and forces surrounding an issue may lead to one or the other tactical approach. In *community organization practice* different models lean in the direction of either consensus or conflict. Locality development relies heavily on the former and social action on the latter. *Administrative practice* often involves use of formal authority as a

mode of influence and generally favors stability, good will, economy, and efficiency of operation. However, this is a preferred rather than an "ordained" tactic and administrators will employ conflict as well when organizational objectives are viewed as enhanced through such initiatives.

Examining *practitioner roles* provides interesting insights. In *policy practice,* there are two basic roles: the policy analyst who studies policy formulation looking for weakness and defects, and the policy manager who guides the policy generation and development process. The policy practitioner is often attached to policy committees, requiring him or her to assist the committee in a staffing capacity. *Community organization practitioners* function in the role of enabler, fact-gatherer, and activist, depending on the given model of action. *Administrative practitioners* tend to rely on their position of an authority figure in a core role, such as executive, associate executive manager, or supervisor.

The *medium of change* in each perspective is quite distinctive. For *policy practitioners,* two media are central; one is the decision group. This group can be a board, an executive committee, a legislature, or other group which has formal ratification power. A second medium is that which the group *acts* upon—the policy draft or document, in other words, the actual law itself. Changes in the text of laws and regulations are an important medium of change. *Community organization practitioners* work with other kinds of groups—neighborhood groups, associations of all kinds as well as with formal organizations. Planners also deal with data. For *administrative practitioners* the key medium is the human service

[59]Talcott Parsons, *Structure and Process in Modern Societies* (New York: Free Press, 1960).

agency itself. Changes in the structure and programs within the agency are the media through which change occurs.

In each perspective there is a somewhat different *orientation toward the structure. Policy practitioners* work with the power structures in most instances, but at arm's length. While they are usually not members of it, they do participate in it. In a sense, they have a marginal or arm's length relationship, as they know the "out-group" perspectives as well. *Community organization practitioners* have variable relationships to the power structure, from employees and allies to militant adversaries, depending on the model of action. From an *administrative practice* point of view, the chief executive often *is* the power structure as the implementer of programs and services. It is interesting that sometimes practitioners who become administrators find themselves the targets of the very techniques they had used against their predecessors.

The *conception of the client role* varies within each perspective. *Policy practitioners* see elite participants as highly involved and active, but view nonelites as tending to review and approve or disapprove of policy direction. In *community organization practice,* client roles are varied, from active to passive, depending on the model of practice. *Administrative practitioners,* particularly in service-providing agencies, tend to view clients in the same way as planners, that is, as consumers of the agency's product. In this sense, they are subordinate participants in the organizational system. In administration, then, the client role is passive, entailing consumer or recipient forms of participation. The consumer may be active in seeking and obtaining services, but is typically not active in determining the form and availability of services.

This same type of analysis could be applied to all the practice variables as a way of gaining greater conceptual grasp of the perspectives. A larger question has to do with the value of constructing such typologies.

IMPLICATIONS OF MULTIPLE APPROACHES

There are a variety of implications of constructing typologies of practice. In the first place, it is important for a practitioner immersed in the organizational and methodological vortex of one of these perspectives or models to be aware of his or her grounding. What are the basic assumptions, orientation toward clients, preferred methods of action, etc., of the situation? In this way, the practitioner may perform appropriately, consistent with the expectations of other relevant actors.

Going beyond conformance to what exists, the practitioner may be in a position to create a form of action to deal with specific problems. Some rough rule-of-thumb guidelines can be sketched out. In community organization, when populations are homogeneous or when consensus exists among various community subparts and interests, it would be useful to employ locality development. When subgroups are hostile and interests are not reconcilable through usual discussional methods, it may be functional to use social action. When problems are fairly routinized and lend themselves to solution through the application of factual information, social planning would appear to be the preferred mode of action. When the problems seem to be located

suggests that values are certainly plural and conflicting, and may well come in pairs of semiopposed commitments. Adequacy *"vs."* equity, a pair just mentioned, is one example. There are others.[64] Mixing may occur when more than one value is being pursued at a given time.

However, it is clear that these options, despite divergent value emphases, can be applied in such a way as to foster and support social change and human betterment. The position taken here accepts the validity of each of these value orientations and encourages the simultaneous and interrelated development of varying macro practice intervention modes which stem therefrom. In the absence of research or experience which confirms the overarching superiority of only one, change agent competency can only be enriched and society benefited by such multiple development of macro practice technologies. Appropriate mixtures and phasing can be attended to within such a development.

[64]John E. Tropman, "Value Conflict in Decision Making," in F. M. Cox, et al., *Tactics and Techniques of Community Practice, Second Edition* (Itasca, IL: F. E. Peacock, 1984).

2.

Charles D. Garvin and Fred M. Cox*

A HISTORY OF COMMUNITY ORGANIZING SINCE THE CIVIL WAR WITH SPECIAL REFERENCE TO OPPRESSED COMMUNITIES

This paper traces the development of community organization within American communities since 1865. It is concerned both with community activities in which professionals were engaged and also with indigenous community efforts. Sometimes these two activities are seen as separate. Fisher, for example, identifies three dominant approaches to organizing: social work, political activism, and neighborhood maintenance.[1] He characterizes the social work approach as one that is reformist with a professional at the core; activism as one oriented to a government; and maintenance as a middle-class oriented approach to neighborhood improvement.

In this article, in contrast, we see these three approaches as affecting one another in ways that are determined by historical and contemporary forces. We

Source: This article was written expressly for this volume.
*The authors are grateful to John Tropman, Barry Checkoway, and Howard Brabson for contributing their views on the most recent developments in community organizations.

[1]Robert Fisher, "Neighborhood Organizing: Lessons from the Past," *Social Policy* (Summer, 1984), pp. 9-10.

shall, therefore, present our analysis of interactions among various kinds of organizing activities in the United States, yet pay special attention to indigenous efforts within oppressed groups. This is because of our conviction, somewhat yet not entirely contrary to Fisher's characterization of social workers as organizers, that the most effective kind of organizing is that which complements and supports such indigenous efforts. We seek to describe, therefore, from a historical view (1) how relevant professional social work efforts were to indigenous ones and (2) how responsive both were to the issues embedded in the larger society.

In order to organize this analysis, we shall emphasize the many important community efforts in which ethnic communities have been engaged. Such organizing has occurred in virtually all ethnic communities. For example, there are many organizations devoted to improved conditions within Jewish, Italian, and Polish enclaves. In this article, however, we focus upon the history of organizing in ethnic communities which are now economically and socially oppressed. These include black, Chicano, Native American, and Asian American ones.

Other ethnic groups also have organized to secure their rights. The same has been true of the elderly, gay persons, and the handicapped. Space limitations, however, make it impossible for us to explore each. We have, however, included the women's movement because of our conviction regarding its broad scope and impact.

For purposes of this analysis, we divide American history since the Civil War into five stages. For each stage we outline the social forces and ideologies which affected community organizing;

the specific community organization activities; and the institutions that sponsored the organizing efforts. We also describe the types of organizing occurring in oppressed communities. Finally the effects of these social forces, activities, and institutions upon the education of community organization practitioners are described.

1865 TO 1914

During the period between the end of the Civil War and the beginning of World War I, a number of social issues emerged in the United States that had strong impact upon welfare practices. Ideologies developed in response to these social conditions, and solutions were proposed for those defined as problematic. These social issues were the rapid industrialization of the country, the urbanization of its population, problems growing out of immigration, and changes in oppressed populations after the Civil War. These are described and their relevance for the emergence of community organization practice highlighted.

Social Conditions

Industrialization. The growth of technology and the centralization of industry brought with them a wide range of social problems. These included problems of working hours and conditions, safety, and child labor.[2]

Urbanization. A direct consequence of industrialization was the movement of large parts of the population from the

---

[2]For a social worker's perception of these conditions, see Jane Addams, *Twenty Years at Hull House* (New York: The Macmillan Co., 1910), pp. 99, 109ff.

country to the city.[3] The many unskilled workers who moved into the city from rural areas, particularly from the South and from Europe, were often forced to take up residence within the oldest and most crowded sections. These districts were inadequate in sanitation, building conditions, and city services. As Jane Addams wrote:

The streets are inexpressibly dirty, the number of schools inadequate, sanitary legislation unenforced, the street lighting bad, the paving miserable, and altogether lacking in the alleys and smaller streets, and the stables foul beyond description. Hundreds of houses are unconnected with the street sewer.[4]

Immigration. In the early part of the nineteenth century, many immigrants came from northwestern Europe and spread out across the country. By 1890 the frontiers were gone. A large number then came from southern and eastern Europe until the tide of immigration was stemmed by legislation passed shortly after World War I. Asian and Mexican people went to the West and Southwest; small numbers of Puerto Ricans settled in the East.

These people brought with them not only their own social and religious institutions, but a variety of problems. Many came from peasant origins and sought a rural environment. However, most of those who came in the later waves were unable to escape the cities where they landed. Impoverished and often sick from the crossing, they were forced to take whatever work they could find. They clung to their former

ways. This later brought them into conflict with their children who took on American habits and manners.[5]

Minorities After the Civil War

Blacks. During reconstruction there were many organizations that sought to support and sustain newly won civil rights. After the period of reconstruction there were many efforts on the part of black people to organize themselves "to the point where they could demand those rights which had slipped away since reconstruction."[6] The Supreme Court decision which declared the Civil Rights Act of 1875 unconstitutional was a major source of frustration for it placed the responsibility for protecting the rights of black people largely on the states.

During this period, the Populist Movement in the South was a major political force which attempted to secure black support. Fishel and Quarles quoted the white president of a Populist convention in Texas as saying that the black "is a citizen as much as we are." However, these authors noted that "the elections of 1892 saw their [Populists'] defeat in the South and the end of any political effort to work with the Negro on an equitable basis."[7]

A major concern of the black community was to solve the problem of educational deficits, particularly in vocational and higher education. In this context, an important event was the founding of Tuskegee Institute in 1881. Also, in the fifteen years before 1900

---

[3]For details, see Allan Nevins and Henry Steele Commager, *The Pocket History of the United States* (New York: Pocket Books, 1942), pp. 326-357.

[4]Addams, op. cit., pp. 97-100.

[5]See Oscar Handlin, *The Uprooted* (New York: Grosset and Dunlap, 1951).

[6]Leslie H. Fishel, Jr., and Benjamin Quarles, *The Negro American: A Documentary History* (Glenview, IL: Scott, Foresman & Co., 1967), p. 308.

[7]Ibid., p. 309.

over fifteen hundred black people were lynched, and between 1900 and 1910 another nine hundred black people perished in the same way. "The sickening brutality of the act of lynching was matched only by its lawlessness and, in too many cases, the innocence of its victims."[8] Black support of other oppressed minorities during this period is illustrated by black poet Alberry Whitman's *The Rape of Florida,* an exposition of white degradation of the Seminoles (published in 1884).

Toward the end of this period many industries in the North encouraged black people to migrate from the South. Workers were needed because of the termination of the large European immigrations and the expansion of war industry. As a consequence their urban living conditions were deplorable.

Chicanos.[9] Although we describe community organizing primarily since the Civil War, we must recognize that the history of protest among Chicanos began with the Treaty of Guadalupe Hidalgo, signed on February 2, 1848, which brought a formal end to the Mexican-American War. Under this treaty, Mexico lost 45 percent of its territory including the wealth of the oil fields of Texas and the gold of California. More than a hundred thousand persons who had previously been citizens of Mexico were added to the United States. From this beginning, the rights of these "conquered" people were heavily infringed upon with little legal redress available. Protest took the form of guerrilla activity by so-called bandits and armed rebellions that were vigorously repressed by the government. According to one authority, "Organized hunts, murders, robberies, and lynchings of Mexicans were everyday happenings, and cattle rustling and assaults on Mexican merchants were carried out with brutality and savagery."[10]

Native Americans. In the period just before the Civil War, the status of Native Americans was largely determined by the Removal Act of 1830. This act gave the president the right to remove any Indians who lived east of the Mississippi.[11] The Seminoles of Florida and the Sac and Fox of Illinois fought, but most were moved peacefully. A particularly shameful action was that taken against the Cherokees, who were forcibly removed in 1838 from Georgia to what was to become Oklahoma, with a great loss of lives on the way despite their enormous effort to adapt to the new culture forced upon them.

After the Civil War, the removal to reservations continued until the passage of the Dawes Act of 1887 which authorized the president to distribute 160 acres to each Indian adult and 80 acres to each child. This followed a series of major fights with tribes such as the Sioux in 1876, Nez Percé in 1877, Cheyenne in 1878, and Apache a few years later.

---

[8]Ibid., p. 358.

[9]Although the term *Chicano* has not been used throughout all of the historical periods described in this chapter, we use it whenever we refer to those United States residents and citizens who are descended from Mexicans. For details of the evolution of the Chicano movement, see Gilberto Lopez y Rivas, *The Chicanos: Life and Struggles of the Mexican Minority in the United States* (New York and London: Monthly Review Press, 1973), pp. 57-74.

[10]Ibid., p. 33.

[11]John R. Howard, ed., *Awakening Minorities: American Indians, Mexican Americans, Puerto Ricans* (New Brunswick, NJ: Transaction Books, 1970), p. 17.

them to reap the benefits bestowed by government.

Community Organization Institutions

As we have stated, community organization activities during the period between the Civil War and World War I can be divided into two categories: the first are those which were carried on by individuals or institutions related to present-day social welfare activities. The charity organization societies, settlement houses, and urban leagues are important examples.

A second category of activities are those that were conducted by those with no direct connection to contemporary community organization programs but which have become areas of interest for community practitioners. Examples include the organization of political, racial, and other action groups.

The Charity Organization Society. A number of factors noted above contributed to the emergence of charity organization societies in England in 1869 and, by 1873, in the United States.[22] These societies initially came into existence to coordinate the work of the private agencies which provided for the needs of the poor. Soon, however, these societies began to offer direct relief and other services, as well as to coordinate the work of other agencies.[23] Murphy summarized their program as follows:

They established social service indexes or exchanges listing individuals or "cases" known to cooperating agencies. They evolved the "case conference," in which workers from different agencies interested in the same "case" or the same family— workers from the settlement house, the relief-giving agencies, the child-placing agencies, the agencies established to protect children from cruelty, the visiting nurse association, and others—would meet to plan a constructive course of action in behalf of the "case." In some instances, too, the charity organization societies made broad studies of social and economic problems and recommended specific remedial measures.[24]

These social forces contributed to this development in several ways. The movement of large populations into the cities, as well as the waves of immigration which met the manpower needs of growing industries, led to many social problems associated with poverty, inadequate housing, illness, and exploitation. Both humanitarian impulses and fear of what these people might do in desperation produced agencies directed to ameliorating conditions. In a sense, this was an effort to counter the more radical ideologies.

Separate efforts also were made by groups associated with different neighborhoods and ethnic and religious groups, and those with different problems. Difficulties which arose repeatedly were: (1) The same people were approached over and over again to provide resources for such agencies, and they began to look for ways to make charitable solicitations more efficient and less demanding on the few. (2) Duplication of aid was apparent, and those who offered it sought ways to avoid this

---

[22]Charles Loch Mowat, *The Charity Organization Society, 1869-1913* (London: Methuen and Co., 1961), pp. 16-21 and 94.

[23]The direct services which had significance for the emergence of social casework will not be pursued in this paper. Only the community organization antecedents will be noted.

[24]Campbell G. Murphy, *Community Organization Practice* (Boston: Houghton Mifflin Co., 1954), p. 35.

and prevent the pauperization of the recipients which they believed was the inevitable result of indiscriminate relief. (3) Paid functionaries arose who sought to rationalize these activities, drawing their inspiration from the same wellsprings that fed a developing pragmatic philosophy. (4) The resources of some charitable societies were insufficient for the maintenance of required services, prompting an incessant search for new sources of funds.

During this period, leaders of charity organization societies harbored serious reservations about the wisdom of public activity on behalf of the poor. In general, they doubted government's ability to administer aid so that it would be rehabilitative. Darwinian ideology and a hedonistic theory of motivation strongly influenced their views on the matter. The Social Darwinians regarded relief as interference with the operation of natural law, and the hedonists held that the only assurance of hard work among the poorer classes was the fear of hunger and exposure. This was tempered somewhat by humanitarian impulses. The charity organization societies distinguished between the "worthy" and the "unworthy" poor and chose to aid the former who, for reasons beyond their control, were unable to support themselves and who, through the moral example of the societies' "friendly visitors," could be rescued from pauperization. The rest were relegated to the not-too-tender mercies of the public poor law authorities, never to be supported at a level equal to the lowest wages in the community so that they would constantly be goaded toward self-support.

The functions of the charity organization societies were cooperative planning among charitable institutions for the amelioration or elimination of various social problems and the creation of new social agencies and the reform of old ones. Charity organization leaders were actively engaged in securing reforms in tenement housing codes, developing antituberculosis associations, obtaining legislation in support of juvenile court and probation work, establishing agencies and programs for the care of dependent children, cooperating with the police in programs for dealing with beggars and vagrants, and supporting legislation requiring absent fathers to support their children.[25]

Some of the most significant contributions of the charity organization societies to community organization were the development of community welfare planning organizations and of social survey techniques. One of the earliest and most important examples was that of the Pittsburgh organization. Writing in 1922, Frank Watson discussed the significance of the Pittsburgh survey:

Few of the offspring of the charity organization movement have had more far-reaching consequences or given greater promise of the future than the Pittsburgh Survey, the pioneer social survey in this country. Interpretation of hours, wages, housing, court procedure and all the rest, in terms of standards of living and the recognition that the basis for judging of social conditions is the measure of life they allow to those affected by them, constitute the very essence of the developments that have since taken place in social work.[26]

Out of the Pittsburgh survey came a council of social agencies which took

[25]For details on these activities see Frank D. Watson, *The Charity Organization Movement in the United States* (New York: The Macmillan Co., 1922), pp. 288-323.
[26]Ibid., pp. 305-306.

Municipal reform was viewed, in part, as a process of helping communities gain the capacity to deal with their problems more effectively.

The settlement idea spread rapidly. In 1891 there were six settlements in the United States; by 1910 the number had jumped to over four hundred. Most of them were located in the large industrial cities of the East and Midwest; there were very few in the South or West.

The Organization of Ethnic Minorities and Women. A variety of forms of organization among black Americans was tested during this period as black people coped with their shifting status in American life. One of the earliest of these forms was developed by a group of prominent black people in 1865 and led by Frederick Douglass and George T. Downing who were "charged" with the duty to look after the best interests of the recently emancipated.[31] Almost twenty-five years later, in 1883, a very different kind of step was taken by the Louisville Convention of Colored Men which "concentrated on large issues of political, as distinct from partisan, rights, education, civil rights and economic problems."[32] Five years later, the Colored Farmers Alliance and Co-operative Union came into existence. In 1890, the Afro-American League organized in another direction, emphasizing legal redress rather than politics.[33] In 1890, blacks from twenty-one states and the District of Columbia organized the Afro-American League of the United States. Issues which concerned this group included school

funds, and legal and voting rights. In 1896, the National Association of Colored Women was formed.

Crosscurrents, similar to those which affect the organizations of black people today, were operative between the Civil War and World War I. On the one hand, many efforts were under the influence of Booker T. Washington, who sought an accommodation with white interests in order to maintain their support. In contrast, W. E. B. DuBois epitomized an opposition to this approach in 1905 when he called for "a conference 'to oppose firmly the present methods of strangling honest criticism.'"[34] The Niagara movement grew out of this meeting and by 1909 resulted in the formation of the National Association for the Advancement of Colored People. Such social workers as Jane Addams, Florence Kelly, and Lillian Wald assisted in these organizing efforts.

The Committee on Urban Conditions among Negroes in New York City, later to become the National Urban League, was another organization in which social workers were involved during this period. Its first executive, George Edmund Haynes, "was on the faculty of Fisk University and particularly interested in training black social workers."[35]

As noted earlier, Mexican-Americans, as well as Native Americans, were confronted with efforts that took away their lands. One response to this trend was the development of small groups for protection and support. Some, for survival, became bandits. Organized protest, however, for Mexican-Americans began in agriculture or, as Howard states, "The

---

[31]Fishel and Quarles, op. cit., pp. 259-260.
[32]Ibid., p. 308.
[33]Ibid., p. 312.

[34]Ibid., p. 357.
[35]Ibid., p. 361.

roots of the Chicano movement lie in the fields."[36]

In 1903, for example, Mexican- and Japanese-American sugar beet workers struck in Ventura, California.[37] In addition, throughout this period, but particularly from the 1880s on, many organizations came into existence whose function was, according to Alvarez, to preserve a Mexican-American way of life through "celebrations, social events, provision of facilities, information and communication networks."[38] The function of such organizations was to preserve a bicultural and bilingual existence. Some examples include the Penitente Order in New Mexico in the 1880s and Mano Negra, also in New Mexico, in the 1890s.[39]

The Native Americans during this period continued to have well-developed forms of tribal organization, partly as a heritage of their early struggles for survival against white encroachment. However, the tribes were separated from one another geographically and structurally, thus often rendering them easy prey for governmental manipulation. Nevertheless, the militancy of the period in actual warfare, as well as persistent legal action, represents an impressive, though unsuccessful, effort to secure a greater measure of justice from American society.

The early Chinese immigrants were organized into family or benevolent associations, tongs, or business interests.[40] For the Japanese, the Japanese Association for Issei (first-generation Japanese in the United States) had some similar functions.

Thus, for these Asian groups, a major function of community organizations during this period was mutual benefit and cultural participation. For example,

people from the same *ken,* or Japanese state, often cooperated in various ways, and this was noticeable in particular trades. For example, Miyamoto writes that the first Japanese barber in Seattle was from Yamaguchi-ken. After he became established, he helped his friends from the same ken with training and money, so that, eventually, most of the Japanese barbers in Seattle were from Yamaguchi-ken.[41]

During this era, when associations existed or were created in many ethnic groups, organizations for the benefit of women also emerged. In 1868, Susan B. Anthony was a leading organizer of a working women's association to fight economic discrimination against women. In addition, during the next decade unions of women working in a number of industries such as laundries and shoe factories were organized. By 1886, there were 113 women's assemblies in the Knights of Labor.[42] Other organizations also were concerned

---

[36]Howard, op. cit., p. 95.

[37]Ibid.

[38]Salvador Alvarez, "Mexican-American Community Organizations," in *Voices: Readings from El Grito, A Journal of Contemporary Mexican American Thought, 1967-1973,* ed. Octavio Ignacio Romano-V (Berkeley: Quinto Sol Publications, 1971), pp. 205-214.

[39]Ibid., p. 209.

[40]For a discussion of evolving forms of Chinese-American community organizations, see Melford S. Weiss, "Division and Unity: Social Process in a Chinese-American Community," in *Asian Americans: Psychological Perspectives,* ed. Stanley Sue and Nathaniel N. Wagner (Palo Alto: Science & Behavior Books, 1973), pp. 264-273.

[41]Kitano, *Japanese Americans,* op. cit., p. 19.

[42]For details of these and other endeavors, see "A Century of Struggle: American Women, 1820-1920," in Barbara Deckard, *The Women's Movement: Political, Socioeconomic, and Psychological Issues* (New York: Harper & Row, Publishers, 1975), pp. 243-284. This section draws heavily on that chapter.

about the poor working conditions of women. For example, in 1894, the New York Consumer's League presented information on these conditions. By 1896, this organization had branches in twenty states. In 1900, the International Ladies' Garment Workers' Union was organized and throughout the pre-World I period it continued to organize despite many obstacles.[43]

While working women were organizing themselves in their workplaces, more affluent women organized to secure the vote. The women's suffrage movement and the movement for the abolition of slavery had originally been one. The split came partially because northern business interests stood to gain from the black vote but could see no value in women having the same right.[44] This was symbolized when the American Equal Rights Association, working for black and women's rights, split in May 1869. Later that year moderate women organized the American Woman Suffrage Association while radical women formed the National Women Suffrage Association. These organizations remained separate until 1890 when they merged to form the National American Woman Suffrage Association. Unfortunately, the class bias of these organizations was evident in attacks on blacks as less fit to vote than women and in other statements made to ensure the acceptability of the women suffrage movement in the South.

The women's suffrage movement was able to see to it that the Nineteenth Amendment was proposed every year from 1886 to 1896, although it was defeated each time. The lack of strength to pass the amendment, according to one authority, was due to "their own conservative tactics and racist, elitist positions, which alienated their potential allies."[45] With the emergence of militant supporters, however, such as radical farmers, the Progressive Party, and the socialists and a shift to more militant leadership, many states did come to adopt woman suffrage. By 1916, both major parties supported suffrage. In 1917, the Women's party turned to more militant tactics and picketed the White House. Partly, also, because of women's activities in the war and the public support of President Wilson, the House of Representatives finally passed the Nineteenth Amendment in January 1918. It took, however, another eighteen months for Senate approval.

Development of the Profession and Professional Education

For this period it is impossible to discuss community organization as a specialization in social work, which had itself not yet emerged as a separate entity. There were individuals concerned with coordinating charity, organizing neighborhood settlements, or mobilizing protest in racial matters, but these people had little common professional identity. Some training activities began to emerge in 1898 when the New York Charity Organization Society started a summer training course. This was expanded to a one-year program a few years later, and by the end of World War I seventeen schools of social work had come into existence in the United States and Canada. The Association of Training Schools for Professional Social Work was formed at that time also.

---

[43]Ibid., p. 270.
[44]Ibid., p. 262.

[45]Ibid., p. 269.

The emphasis, however, was more on what became casework than on methods of community organization.

While the ethnic organizing of the period as well as that among women may have secured the support of social workers as *individuals,* this did not represent activities of the profession or of a social work method called community organization. Nevertheless, many precedents were being created for and lessons learned by those who sought to create a more humane society and this included social workers.

1915 TO 1929

Social Conditions

After World War I, several new conditions emerged that had a significant impact on community organization practice: urbanization increased markedly, industrial potential escalated, and racial conflicts intensified. By 1920 more than half of the population of the United States lived in cities, and industrial innovations were accelerated by the heavy demands on production created by World War I.

The twenties, nevertheless, was a decade of confidence in the economic system. As Lerner stated, "Big business of the 1920's, certain that it had found the secret of perpetual prosperity, claimed the right to the policymaking decisions not only in the economy but in the government."[46]

Ironically, this period also brought some major crises in civil liberties. "After World War I there was a wave of raids and deportations; it arose from the uneasy feeling that the Russian Revolution had caused a shift in the

world balance of power and spawned a fanatic faith threatening American survival."[47] The period also witnessed the intensification of activities of groups such as the Ku Klux Klan with antagonism directed against blacks, Jews, and the foreign born.

The Condition of Minorities

Blacks. This was a period during which black Americans made strong attempts to improve their lives and were simultaneously subjected to major efforts at repression. Seventy-six black people were lynched in 1919,[48] and "the white national secretary of the NAACP was badly beaten on the streets of Texas."[49] Chicago experienced a severe "race riot" in 1919 which resulted in the death of 15 white and 23 black persons as well as injury to an additional 537.[50]

However, progress occurred in many spheres of American life. The term *the New Negro* became prevalent in the 1920s, and this was supported by the increased self-respect of many black war veterans. During this period, distinguished people such as Langston Hughes, Countee Cullen, and Paul Robeson began their careers. Black school attendance jumped from 45 to 60 percent of the eligible school population between 1910 and 1930.[51] In fact, in many ways the current emphasis on black power and black identity has ideological antecedents in this period.

Chicanos. These years saw a large immigration of persons from Mexico into what had become the United

[46]Lerner, op. cit., p. 279.

[47]Ibid., p. 455.
[48]Fishel and Quarles, op. cit., 403.
[49]Ibid.
[50]Ibid., p. 405.
[51]Ibid.

States. Between 1910 and 1919, almost two hundred and twenty-five thousand persons came, and in the next decade the number was almost double.[52] According to one writer, "that striking increase is directly related to the miserable economic conditions in Mexico after ten years of armed struggle."[53] Specifically, the Mexican economy was in a poor state after the Mexican Revolution while the southwestern United States was experiencing considerable economic growth.

There was an expansion and development of nonagricultural worker organizations during this period. As Moore notes:

In 1920 Mexican workers struck the Los Angeles urban railway. In later years the strikes in the fields and mines of the Border States were both more numerous and more sophisticated. The earlier ones were significant, however, because Mexicans were generally denied normal channels of political expression in any of the Border States except New Mexico.[54]

Native Americans. During this period, the conditions of Native Americans continued to deteriorate as the government persisted in its policy of implementing the Dawes Act of 1887 which distributed land to individuals. The attempt to undermine the widely practiced custom of holding land in common for the good of all was continued. The act not only created severe economic problems but eroded traditional tribal government.[55] In fact, "the Indi-

an Agent and his staff were 'the government' for most tribes from the cessation of treaty making to the 1930s."[56]

In addition to the effects of the Dawes Act, two other actions also diminished tribal ties. From 1917 to 1921, the trust on land allotments of Indians of less than one-half Indian blood was terminated. Many Indian agents were also eliminated and their wards placed under school superintendents and farmers reporting directly to the Commissioner of Indian Affairs.[57] This focused activities on individuals, not tribes, and presumably moved Indians as individuals into non-Indian education and agriculture.

Asian Americans. The Immigration Act of 1924 epitomized the attitudes of the American government, if not of the society, to the foreign born. No immigration was to be permitted for Asians; low quotas were set for southern Europeans, and high ones for northern Europeans. This made it impossible, particularly for the Chinese who had not come as families, to form or reunite families. In Japanese communities, these years marked the birth and early development of many *Nisei,* or second-generation Japanese-Americans. With great determination, many Nisei moved into middle-class occupations.

Ideological Currents

The ideologies that were prevalent in the earlier period continued to exert a strong influence. The sense of complacency and optimism stemming from economic growth and affluence did find

---

[52]Lopez y Rivas, op. cit., p. 85.

[53]Ibid., p. 39.

[54]Joan Moore, *Mexican-Americans* (Englewood Cliffs, NJ: Prentice-Hall, 1970), p. 24.

[55]Theodore W. Taylor, *The States and Their Indian Citizens* (Washington, DC: United States Department of the Interior, Bureau of Indian Affairs, 1972), p. 17.

---

[56]Ibid.

[57]Ibid., pp. 17-18.

perceptive social critics, however. In addition, the following are ideas which developed during this period and which also molded social work practice.

Psychoanalysis. Some may find it strange to regard psychoanalysis as an ideology; nevertheless, the conditions of the period were conducive to the introduction of psychoanalysis as a major intellectual force in social work. This was a period of affluence, and many believed that the social environment offered so many opportunities and was otherwise so benign that any problems must be the result of individual failure. Psychoanalytic practice was clearly oriented toward changing the individual and not the system. Social workers, as Jesse Taft observed, became preoccupied with the person and all but forgot the situation: "The most daring experimental caseworkers have all but lost connection with social obligation and are quite buried in their scientific interest in the individual as he has evolved through his own unique growth process."[58] The social worker disassociated herself from charity to be reborn a psychotherapist.[59]

Anti-Intellectualism. Despite the increasing popularity of Freud's ideas, this was not a period of intellectual activity in the United States. Vice-President Coolidge attacked the colleges and universities as "hot beds of sedition."[60] Many intellectuals, along with T. S. Eliot, fled to Europe, finding

America a "wasteland."[61] American writers such as Sinclair Lewis castigated the American middle class, as F. Scott Fitzgerald did the upper class. It should also be remembered that the Scopes trial, testing the legal right to teach evolution in the schools, took place in 1925. According to one authority "only one event in the 1920s succeeded in arousing intellectuals of every kind of political loyalty: the arrest, trial, and execution of two Italian anarchists, Nicola Sacco and Bartolomeo Vanzetti."[62]

Development of Community Organization Institutions

The Community Chest and United Fund. This period saw a continued increase in the number of welfare institutions. This proliferation of agencies generated insistent demands for coordination. The increase in such institutions was prompted primarily by accelerating urbanization. The war increased the pace as "some three hundred American communities organized war chests to cope with the mounting flood of appeals from national and local agencies."[63] The agencies' increasing needs for financing, despite the affluence of the period, prompted demands from both the philanthropists and the professionals for better fund-raising methods. The interests of these two groups were not identical, and this led to the development of two separate yet interrelated institutions—the community chest or united fund, on the one

---

[58]Roy Lubove, *The Professional Altruist: The Emergence of Social Work As a Cause, 1880-1930* (Cambridge, MA: Harvard University Press, 1965), p. 89.

[59]Ibid.

[60]Samuel Eliot Morison, *The Oxford History of the American People* (New York: Oxford University Press, 1965), p. 909.

[61]Ibid., p. 910.

[62]For a brief summary of the case and its effects on opinion, see Frederick J. Hoffman, *The Twenties: American Writing in the Post War Decade* (New York: The Viking Press, 1955), pp. 357-364.

[63]Lubove, op. cit., p. 189.

hand, and the community welfare council on the other. The separation of interests between the suppliers of philanthropic dollars and the dispensers of them had effects which can be seen to this day in community welfare institutions.

Lubove reflected this situation accurately when he declared:

Financial federation captured the imagination of businessmen by promising efficient coordination and organization of the community welfare machinery, immunity from multiple solicitation, economical collection and distribution of funds, and the development of a broad base of support which would relieve the pressure on the small circle of large givers. The corporation, increasingly regarded as a source of gifts, appreciated the conveniences of federated finance.[64]

There was also opposition to this development. National organizations resented the competition for local funds. Of particular importance to the contemporary scene in community organization is resistance to the erosion of "democracy" implicit in the development of a fund-raising bureaucracy. Lubove cited one chest executive who stated, "We are facing here the age-long and inevitable conflict which exists in any society between the urge for individual independence and initiative on the one hand, and the need for social control on the other."[65]

Philanthropists wanted their funds spent efficiently and desired relief from the constant appeals of charitable solicitors. United appeals for financial support were created to serve these objectives, originating with the United Jewish Appeal in Boston in 1895.[66]

Community chests evolved in several ways. First, welfare agencies joined to solicit funds, hoping to raise more money than each could obtain separately. In 1887, the Charity Organization Society in Denver initiated joint fund-raising among fifteen of its twenty-three cooperating agencies, an effort which proved financially successful in its first year of operation.[67] Community chests were also organized by councils of social agencies. In 1915, two years after its organization, Cincinnati's Council of Agencies brought twelve agencies together in a united appeal for funds. Before 1927, councils in St. Louis, Minneapolis, Columbus, New Haven, and Detroit had followed suit.[68]

For the most part, however, community chests were initiated by large contributors. Often their first step was a charity endorsement bureau which later reorganized as a community chest. Businessmen and industrialists believed that welfare services, like public utilities, should be held accountable to the public. Because contributors rarely had time to investigate agencies that asked for support, local chambers of commerce organized bureaus to (1) establish standards for welfare agencies; (2) investigate individual agencies and measure their operations against their standards; (3) recommend those agencies that met the test; and (4) encourage members and the public to

---

[64]Ibid., p. 183.

[65]Ibid., p. 196. Lubove, here, was quoting Raymond Clapp, "Who Shall Decide Personnel Policies?" *Survey* 65 (1930), p. 103.

[66]Lyman S. Ford, "Federated Financing," in Harry L. Lurie (ed.), *Encyclopedia of Social Work* (New York: National Association of Social Workers, 1965), p. 331.

[67]William J. Norton, *The Cooperative Movement in Social Work* (New York: The Macmillan Co., 1927), pp. 50-54.

[68]Ibid., pp. 93-99.

support organizations that received endorsement.[69]

The endorsement bureau had its critics. Because it mainly represented the large business and industrial contributors, agencies viewed the bureaus as potentially autocratic and a threat to their autonomy. Furthermore, agencies believed that the organization might dampen contributors' interest and enthusiasm.[70] The demands upon a small number of contributors also became very great. The first major effort to remedy these conditions was taken by the Cleveland Chamber of Commerce. After initiating a study of the problem in 1907, the chamber launched the Federation for Charity and Philanthropy in 1913. Cleveland's federation is generally considered to be a major landmark in the history of community chests,[71] a name which was first used in Rochester, New York, in 1919.[72]

Community chests were dominated by three kinds of people: contributors, particularly those who gave large sums; solicitors, the small businessmen, service club members and middle management types who helped to raise the chests' funds; and volunteers representative of the health, welfare, and recreation agencies that were supported by the chests. The membership delegated much of the decision making to a board of directors, which hired an executive. In the beginning, much of the work was done by volunteers. Volunteers still continue to play an important part in community chests.

World War I gave a great impetus to the development of chests. Overseas relief and other war-created welfare needs stimulated the development of nearly four hundred "War Chests." During the 1920s the number of communities with community chests increased from 39 to 353.[73]

The Council of Social Agencies and Community Welfare Council. The first decades of the twentieth century saw the development of an increasing professionalism among those who helped the poor. The friendly visitor was replaced by the paid agent. The charity organization societies founded schools of philanthropy which, beginning around the turn of the century, became graduate schools of social work. The development of the social survey—a disciplined effort to obtain facts necessary for planning—was another manifestation of the growing professionalism. In short, the growing cadre of welfare professionals, with the support of many volunteers who served as board members of charitable societies, was interested in organizing a rational, systematic approach to the welfare needs of communities. Their interest included providing for the gaps in service, detecting problems, and looking to future needs. This combination of professionals and volunteers formed councils. The first councils were organized in Milwaukee and Pittsburgh in 1909. By 1926 there were councils in Chicago, Boston, St. Louis, Los Angeles, Detroit, Cincinnati, Columbus, and New York.[74]

Because of the potential conflicts noted earlier, one of the problems ex-

---

[69]Ibid., pp. 24-29.
[70]Ibid., pp. 29-30.
[71]Ibid., pp. 68-71.
[72]Guy Thompson, "Community Chests and United Funds," *Social Work Year Book, 1957,* ed. Russell H. Kurtz (New York: National Association of Social Workers, 1957), p. 176.

---

[73]Ford, op. cit., pp. 327-328.
[74]Ibid., p. 37.

their patronizing nature was unsupportive of indigenous institutions.

One author, in an attempt to characterize efforts to organize women after the adoption of the Nineteenth Amendment, titles her chapter "Forty Years in the Desert: American Women, 1920-1960."[88] In the first place, there was no indication of a women's bloc vote, which some had feared. This was not to deny the fact, however, that in specific elections in those states that had adopted women's suffrage, the proportions of women voting differently than men made a difference in the outcome. An example was the defeat of antisuffrage senator John Weeks in 1918.[89]

The National Women's Party, however, continued to operate. It maintained a platform committed to full equality and supported the first introduction of the Equal Rights Amendment into Congress in 1923. However, it was quite small and in 1923 had only eight thousand members as compared to fifty thousand three years before.[90]

The League of Women Voters was founded in 1920. This group was much less militant than the National Women's Party and it declared in 1931 that "nearly all discriminations have been removed."[91] The League was less concerned about women's issues than child labor laws, pacifism, and other general reforms.

The general conservatism of the 1920s took its toll on the women's movement. The prohibition against child labor, which women's groups favored, was attacked as a subversive plot.[92] It was even charged that all liberal women's groups were part of a communist plot.[93] Despite this, women continued to found organizations including the National Federation of Business and Professional Women's Clubs (1919) and the American Association of University Women (1921).

Development of the Profession

Most of those who trained for social work in the first two decades of the twentieth century were studying to become caseworkers. However, by 1920 Joseph K. Hart had written a text entitled *Community Organization,* and between then and 1930 at least five books were written on the subject.[94] It is easy to see why the casework emphasis existed in view of the prevalent ideologies and issues of the period, emphasizing individual conformity to the "system." In fact, community organization practice during this period was aimed largely at enhancing agencies oriented toward personal adjustment. Except, perhaps, for the workers in settlement houses, the "social unit plan," and the organizations developing in the black community, little thought was given to changing social institutions to meet the needs of individuals. Even in the case of settlements, the workers there often thought of themselves as educators, recreation leaders, or group workers. In the black community, organizers rarely identified with social work.

Nevertheless, some different ideas were beginning to emerge. Mary Follett foresaw the advantages to democracy of the organization of primary groups

[88]Deckard, op. cit., p. 285.
[89]Ibid., p. 286.
[90]Ibid., p. 287.
[91]Ibid.
[92]Ibid., pp. 288-289.

[93]Ibid.
[94]Meyer Schwartz, "Community Organization," *Encyclopedia of Social Work,* op. cit., 1965, p. 177.

in the local communities.[95] Eduard Lindeman, who taught for many years at the New York School of Social Work, also spoke of the value of "an attempt on the part of the people who live in a small, compact local group to assume their own responsibilities and to guide their own destinies."[96]

The emphasis of this period, however, was aptly summed up by Lubove when he wrote the following:

Federation employed the rhetoric of the early community organization movement, but its intensive concern with the machinery and financing of social welfare diverted attention from cooperative democracy and the creative group life of the ordinary citizen to problems of agency administration and service. It substituted the bureaucratic goal of efficiency through expert leadership for what had been a quest for democratic self-determination through joint efforts of citizen and specialist. Community organization had barely emerged as a cause before it had become a function absorbed into the administrative structure of social work.[97]

1929 TO 1954

Social work, as well as other institutions in the United States, was deeply affected by the two major cataclysms of this period: the depression and World War II. To regard these years as a single period in American history may seem odd to some readers, but they cover a coherent period in the development of ideas and issues in community organization practice. A departure from this

pattern took place in the fifties, marked by the desegregation decision of the Supreme Court and the end of McCarthyism, that period of ideological repression which received its name, as well as much encouragement, from the late Senator Joseph McCarthy of Wisconsin.

Social Conditions

To set the stage for the discussion of the history of community organization during the period, one should call attention to several social forces.

Depression Issues. The most apparent of the social forces at play was the vast increase in unemployment. The bank and stock market failures also removed whatever reserves people might otherwise have utilized in such a crisis. Mortgage foreclosures deprived many of their homes, farms, and small businesses.

The Growth of Government. The expansion of government programs was a direct result of the depression. Government expenditures, programs, and controls grew in unprecedented ways. The government became an employer, a producer of goods and services, and a vast resource to restore the industrial processes. The federal government also became the most significant planner and promoter of welfare programs through the enactment, in the mid-thirties, of such legislation as social security and the minimum wage.

The Growth of Unionism. The depression also stimulated a major upsurge of trade unionism. The founding of the CIO showed that the labor movement was at last free from the limits of a craft basis for organization. The passage of the National Labor Relations

---

[95]See for example, her book, *The New State: Group Organization, the Solution of Popular Government* (New York: Longmans, Green and Co., 1918), p. 217.

[96]Eduard C. Lindeman, *The Community: An Introduction to the Study of Community Leadership and Organization* (New York: Association Press, 1921), p. 58.

[97]Lubove, op. cit., p. 180.

Act in 1935 marked the beginning of an era in which government facilitated the development of unions and thereby became less the biased protector of business interests. The development of strong unions in the auto, steel, electrical, meat-packing, and other industries had a major impact upon the industrial scene. The organization of the Brotherhood of Sleeping Car Porters gave the black community an important labor spokesman, A. Phillip Randolph.

The International Scene. During this period, it became evident that the Communist party was firmly entrenched in the USSR. In Spain, Italy, and Germany, fascist governments seized power. American counterparts of these movements were apparent in the developments within the United States.

On the international level, these developments had consequences of the most serious nature for the United States. Just at the time in the thirties that many programs to solve the social problems of the country were being tested, the need to prepare for and then wage World War II increasingly absorbed the attention and resources of the American people. In fact, only with the war did the country clearly come out of the depression.

The Condition of Minorities

Blacks. The creation of many New Deal agencies "added credence to the emergent fact that for the first time the federal government had engaged and was grappling with some of the fundamental barriers to race progress."[98] On the other hand, there were many times when Roosevelt, who was highly re-

garded by many black leaders, failed to deliver on expectations because of political considerations. Where local control was strong, the effect of some of those programs was to continue the exclusion of black people from necessary benefits.

It is undeniable, however, that important strides were made during this period. There was a considerable expansion of opportunities for black people in important governmental positions. Civil service brought many black people into white-collar positions in government. World War II increased this momentum. The Committee on Fair Employment Practice, established by Roosevelt in 1941 to improve employment opportunities in defense industries, was a significant development. In 1948, Truman created the civil rights section of the Justice Department and established the President's Committee on Equality of Treatment and Opportunity in the Armed Services. The courts struck down restrictive housing covenants and outlawed segregation on buses in interstate travel.

Chicanos. During this period, Chicanos began to move beyond the Southwest into many parts of the United States. This was due in part to the processes of acculturation but also to the fact that new Mexican immigrants were willing to work for lower wages than second-generation persons, who then tended to move to new areas. Particularly in the North, jobs were more available and wages better. A pattern of migrant farm labor was also established emanating from the Southwest and spreading to other parts of the country, as Chicanos followed the crops.

Much of the immigration during this period was illegal but responsive to em-

---

[98]Fishel and Quarles, op. cit., p. 447.

ployers seeking cheap labor. Employers aided the smuggling in of such persons.[99] The need for labor was heightened as Asian immigration ended.

In summarizing the period prior to 1940, however, one authority states:

The lot of the Mexican-Americans, except as they were affected by the immigration, changed little during this period prior to 1940. In a real sense, they were forgotten Americans; there was little assimilation to the majority society. They remained a Spanish speaking, largely rural, and generally poor minority. The decline of the small farmer and sheepherder forced many off the land altogether. But even as wage earners, they received no proper return in comparison to their contribution to the building of the economy of the Southwest.[100]

Native Americans. Early in the period being described here, a new approach was adopted to Native Americans: the Indian Reorganization Act of 1934. The intent of this act was to reverse the land policy of the Allotment Act of 1887 and the intent of trying to "stamp out everything that was Indian."[101] The 1934 act specifically provided authorization for the purchase of new land, the initiation of tribal organization, the creation of loan funds for individuals *and tribes,* and extended the trust of Indian lands "until otherwise directed by Congress."[102]

This new policy of a more humane concern for Indians was a part of FDR's New Deal. The Commissioner of Indian Affairs from 1933 to 1944, John Collier, was an anthropologist with a long career of interest in Indian affairs, and this may also have made a difference. Collier was critical of many American values and was identified with the aspirations of many Indian groups, as well as having his own ideas about the potential of Indian society.[103]

Tribal governments, established under this act, were helped to develop constitutions and carry on many operations required of modern governments, economic as well as political. In contradiction to this, however, was the policy of promoting assimilation by urging states to provide the same services for individual Indians as for other citizens.

Asian Americans. This period saw the gradual improvement of the economic status of Chinese-Americans although not necessarily of their social status. As Kitano states:

In the late 1930's and during World War II the Chinese became our friends and allies, although the general tone of the friendship was condescending . . . . Their peace loving nature was emphasized; they had fought valiantly against the "sly, tricky Jap;" they were different from their more aggressive neighbor . . . . In many ways, this praise deflected from the everyday humiliation, harassment, and deprivation faced by many Chinese, even with the relatively favorable attitude toward all Orientals (except the Japanese) at this time.[104]

The most devastating event affecting the Japanese-American community was the wartime evacuation of all persons with as little as one-eighth Japanese blood from the West Coast. By March 1942, one hundred and ten thousand such persons, most citizens of the United States, were in virtual concentration camps in such states as

---

[99]Wayne Moquin with Charles Van Doren, *A Documentary History of the Mexican Americans* (New York: Praeger Publishers, 1971), p. 252.

[100]Ibid., p. 253.

[101]Taylor, op. cit., p. 20-26.

[102]Ibid.

---

[103]Ibid., p. 22.

[104]Kitano, *Race Relations,* op. cit., p. 200.

Colorado, Utah, and Arkansas. There was widespread compliance by most Japanese-Americans, even though they had to abandon their homes and possessions. This terrible injustice continued until 1944 when the Supreme Court revoked the policy. Most families who survived the experience had to begin all over again. Little remained of their property or belongings.

Ideological Currents

The most important ideological issues of the period were those stimulated by the conditions of the depression. The emphasis of the twenties upon the individual's responsibility for his or her own destiny could not hold up under the circumstances of the thirties. The literature of this period emphasized the effects of the social order on people and the need to modify that order to solve the spiritual as well as the economic problems which plagued Americans.[105] Many came to regard government, rather than business, as the preferred means for developing a better society. However, except for small minorities, people wanted their government to operate through much the same political processes as it always had, and the economy to remain capitalist, though under strong government controls.

These ideas were not basically shaken by the war. Fascism as an international enemy was further proof that there are forces which transcend the individual and must be controlled by collective action. Although congressional investigations of "un-American activities" received support, the external enemy and wartime prosperity took many people's attention away from problems within the United States. Moreover, Americans' faith in their own political and economic system may have been reinforced by wartime victory. However, the specter of an external enemy acting in concert with internal agents returned with a vengeance with the cold war and the Korean War, dampening criticism of the "American way of life" and making it difficult to gain support for proposals to confront the country's social problems.

Development of Community Organization Institutions

Community organization agencies, like others in social welfare, found themselves unable to cope with the massive needs of the country during the depression. This period marked a shift of emphasis in operations from local and private to regional or national and public. The federal government through its agencies became the main impetus for social planning. At first through the Federal Emergency Relief Administration and later through the Federal Security Agency, standards for welfare activity were set, coordination was promoted, fact finding was conducted, and plans for public education were launched.

World War II advanced the trend toward community planning under national auspices, both public and private. The need for welfare services grew as new and expanding communities of defense workers and soldiers sprang up. The Office of Community War Services in the Federal Security Agency was created to handle some of the planning for

---

[105]It was noted earlier that the ideological antecedents of some Negro militancy were in the twenties. Current white militancy had similar antecedents in the thirties.

recreation and public health needs in affected areas.

Organization of Ethnic Minorities and Women. Organization in the black community remained primarily on a national level, and some authorities have noted a degree of apathy regarding anything beyond that.[106] The NAACP continued to wage campaigns in the courts, the Congress, and the press for the rights of blacks. The Urban League expanded its programs of employment, family welfare, health, and education. The thirties and forties did not foster any prominent new organizational efforts. In addition to the external threats noted earlier, this may have been due to the development of governmental programs, trade union activity, and local activity, which black people believed would provide long-hoped-for access to the "American Dream."

During the 1930s, the organizing activities of the *Confederacion de Uniones Obreras Mexicanas* continued. Efforts to build union organizations also included those of the National Farm Workers' Union. Other organizations emerged, and some examples of these are the League of United Latin American Citizens (Texas, 1929), the *Associacion de Jornaleros* (Texas, 1933), the *Sociedad Mutualista Mexicana* (Ohio, 1936), the Pan American Student Forum of Texas (1943), and the Community Service Organization (California, 1947).[107] The vitality of Chicano life is apparent in the organizations that were created during these years. These developments may well have provided support for the new programs which emerged in the 1960s.

These years also saw movements within Native American tribes. Through new government policies, many tribal governments were established or strengthened. Tribes assumed authority to:

employ legal counsel; prevent sale or encumbrance of tribal land or other assets without the consent of the tribe; negotiate with Federal, State, and local governments; determine tribal membership; assign tribal land to individuals; manage economic affairs; appropriate money for salaries or other public purposes; levy taxes, license fees, or community labor in lieu thereof; control conduct of members of the reservation by enactment of ordinances. . .[108]

As was true of Mexican-Americans, it seems likely that the organizational development of the depression, war, and postwar years was a precursor to militant organizing in the next decade.

A somewhat different type of organizational experience characterizes Chinese-American life. Chinese-Americans had been living within their own communities, but a trend toward some dispersion began at this time. The control exerted by the traditional associations weakened in many Chinese-American communities. Some who had gained status in the broader community did not have it in the ethnic community because of age and cultural difference, including language. Thus, new institutions began to emerge to meet their needs.[109] In many ways, the situation was similar for Japanese-Americans, although recovery from the "relocation" of the war years was a long and hard process.

---

[106]Fishel and Quarles, op. cit., p. 450.
[107]Alvarez, op. cit., pp. 209-210.

[108]Taylor, op. cit., pp. 23-24.
[109]For a discussion of this development, see Weiss, op. cit., pp. 264-273.

The period between the depression and the 1950s was not a good one for the women's movement. During the war years many women were employed, and this may have diminished demands for equal employment opportunities for women. However, such issues as adequate child care were central. The conservative swing after the war discouraged militancy among women. Even the League of Women Voters, hardly a radical organization, showed a decline in membership during this time.

Development of the Profession and Professional Education

This, while not a period of innovation in community organization beyond the shift from a local to a national emphasis, was a time of intensive efforts to conceptualize the nature of community organization practice. Writers had three overriding concerns.

The *first* bore upon the relation between community organization and social work. Some contended that community organization was not really a legitimate form of social work practice, and others took pains to establish community organization's affinity to the basic values and concerns of social work.

The *second* was an interest in the objectives of community organization. On the one hand, practitioners regarded the Industrial Revolution as destructive of personal, face-to-face relations between people and believed that community organization practice should strengthen community cohesion. At the same time, they were disturbed about a number of social problems and thought that community organization practice should prevent or at least ameliorate them.

Third, they struggled with the appropriate role for the practitioner. Neighborhoods and communities needed the help of practitioners if localities were to achieve their objectives. And yet practitioners must not impose their views on those served. One must somehow strike a balance between giving help and fostering self-determination.[110]

1955 TO 1968

The beginning of this period coincides with the end of the McCarthy era and the Supreme Court decision on school desegregation. Whether or not causally related, these events appear to have anticipated a number of other phenomena.

Social Conditions

The Growth of the Civil Rights Movement. Marked by the 1954 Supreme Court decision ending legal school segregation, the rising dissatisfaction of black Americans gave birth or renewed vitality to a number of organizations which have sought to end the inequality of opportunity afforded black people. The Montgomery, Alabama, bus boycott, which began in December of 1955, brought Martin Luther King, Jr., and the Southern Christian Leadership Conference forward as leaders in the civil rights struggle.[111] The Congress of Racial Equality (founded in 1943) sponsored nonviolent resistance in the form of sit-ins, freedom rides, and demonstrations.[112] The Student Non-Violent Coordinating Committee, the Mississippi

---

[110]For further details, see Schwartz, op. cit., pp. 177-190.

[111]Martin Luther King, Jr., *Stride toward Freedom* (New York: Ballantine Books, 1958).

[112]James Peck, *Freedom Ride* (New York: Simon & Schuster, 1962).

Freedom Democratic party, the Black Panther party, the Black Muslims, the Republic of New Africa and other black nationalist groups, and the NAACP were among the organizations affected by the rising tide of civil rights activities. The quest for black power grew out of the experiences of the Student Non-Violent Coordinating Committee and other active groups who came to despair of achieving genuine integration. As they began to fight for black pride and capability, they demanded autonomy in black affairs, including neighborhood control of schools and economic institutions.[113]

Subsequently other minority groups asserted themselves, claiming their rights and developing pride in their special identity. The Chicanos of the Southwest made substantial progress in organizing. Stimulated by Cesar Chavez and his success in organizing California farm workers, Chicanos organized groups such as *La Raza Unida* in such places as south Texas, New Mexico, and even where migrant farm workers traveled in search of employment, such as Michigan, where many Chicano farm workers settled down and sought education and regular jobs. American Indians, whose living conditions are generally worse than those of any other minority in this country, likewise demonstrated solidarity in such ways as occupying Alcatraz Island in San Francisco Bay and obtaining legislative support for expanded fishing rights in Michigan.

As the period continued, one trend was clear: a growing effort to create ethnic minority institutions. Examples include neighborhood control of schools, black-owned business, black professional societies, black-led Model Cities programs, powerful interest groups such as the National Welfare Rights Organization, and black labor unions. Nevertheless, conflicts were evident among the leaders of these groups, often traceable to ideological differences. For example, some black leaders sought parallel black economic organizations, i.e., black capitalism, while others worked for changes in the power bases of all American institutions to include major input from black people and other minorities.

Late in this period, other groups asserted themselves, feeling deprived in comparison with their fellow citizens and encouraged by the achievements of blacks and other minorities. Gay men and lesbians demanded social and economic rights and fought discrimination in jobs and housing. The elderly, sometimes with the support of Grey Panther groups, demanded greater attention to their needs, especially for health care. The handicapped also drew attention to the discrimination they suffer in education, employment, and public facilities. Women, oppressed by the requirements of their traditional roles, demanded liberation and equality. A not fully successful achievement was congressional approval of the Equal Rights Amendment to the federal Constitution and its ratification by many state legislatures. "Middle America" became a potent political force. Disgruntled citizens such as Irene McCabe mobilized large numbers of people who opposed the busing of school children to achieve racial integration. Political candidates (George Wallace, for example) captured the support of large numbers of disenchanted voters who felt strongly about school busing and high taxes and were distrustful of government. An anti-gay move-

---

[113]Stokely Carmichael and Charles V. Hamilton, *Black Power: The Politics of Liberation in America* (New York: Vintage Books, 1967).

also were perpetuated. An alternative "dropout" culture grew as a spin-off of this process. Some community organizers, for example, developed and lived within a growing network of communes.

Alongside interests in added government responsibility and participation of the people has been a strong tide of disengagement from society on the one hand and of violent opposition to those who control society on the other. These currents were reflected in social work, with some students planning government jobs, others looking forward to participation in anti-establishment grassroots organizations, and still others asking if social work and "revolution" are compatible orientations. Moderation and social planning formed the dominant orientation of community organization students, while social work as a whole experienced a marked increase of interest in professionalization, psychotherapy, self-realization and "making a good living."

Development of the Profession and Professional Education

Training for community organization practitioners in social work grew markedly at first. Both the number of programs and the number of students rose sharply. By 1969 the number of schools of social work providing training programs for community organizers increased to forty-eight, from thirty-six in 1965.[114] Community organization was taught in some form in virtually all schools.

Parallel with the increase in numbers were efforts to clarify the nature of community organization, identify what community organizers need to know to be effective, and give recognition to the development of community organization as a specialized form of practice within social work. In the late 1950s, the Council on Social Work Education embarked upon a wide-ranging study of the curriculum in schools of social work which included separate attention to community organization.[115] The National Association of Social Workers created a Committee on Community Organization which prepared working papers and bibliographies designed to codify practice knowledge and establish the position of the community organization specialty within social work.[116] In 1962 the Council on Social Work Education gave formal recognition to community organization as a method of social work comparable with casework and group work.[117]

An ambitious effort to develop curriculum for training community organizers was initiated in 1963. It, too, was sponsored by the Council on Social Work Education and received financial support from HEW's Office of Juvenile Delinquency and Youth Development.[118] This study culminated in the publication of five book-length reports and numerous journal articles and con-

---

[114]Arnold Gurin, *Community Organization Curriculum in Graduate Social Work Education: Report and Recommendations* (New York: Council on Social Work Education, 1970), p. 10.

[115]Harry L. Lurie, ed., *The Community Organization Method in Social Work Education,* Vol. IV, Project Report of the Social Work Curriculum Study (New York: Council on Social Work Education, 1959).

[116]See especially National Association of Social Workers, *Defining Community Practice* (New York: NASW, 1962).

[117]Council on Social Work Education, *Curriculum Policy Statement* (New York: CSWE, 1962).

[118]Gurin, op. cit., pp. vii-viii.

ference reports.[119] Earlier efforts pointed up the similarities of community organization practice and other forms of social work practice. Perhaps the most significant theme of this latest curriculum study was the recognition that community organization practitioners required professional training that is, in many ways, differentiated from training for other social work specializations.

1969 AND AFTER

We have chosen 1969 as the beginning of the current phase of community organization history because of the political events that began that year and the many social changes related to these events. That year was the first one in which Richard Nixon held office as president of the United States. In his, as well as succeeding administrations, many of the programs initiated by Kennedy and Johnson were terminated, particularly those that were associated with the Office of Economic Opportunity and the Department of Health and Human Services (formerly the Department of Health, Education, and Welfare). Nixon's administration did, however, present some alternatives that were intended to link community and social planning more fully to the traditional political structures through such devices as revenue sharing and a community development block grant program.

This trend abated somewhat in the one term administration of Carter but continued in an even more extensive manner as President Reagan sought to implement his philosophy of reducing

the role of government, particularly the national government, in offering programs to solve social problems. This view was closely related to other ideas regarding how to cope with the economic crises brought on by severe unemployment and inflation, namely to reduce government spending while increasing purchasing power through reduction in taxation.

Social Conditions

John Naisbitt in his treatment of trends in society does an excellent job of highlighting the social conditions as well as ideological currents of this period and we draw heavily upon his work in the discussion that follows.[120] We have chosen to emphasize these kinds of trends at this point rather than specific events or programs because of the impact we believe they are having on social work practice at community and societal levels.

The Emergence of an Information Society. This development is associated with a shift in the occupational structure of the United States along with technologies that make this possible. By the 1980s, more than 60 percent of those employed work with information "...as programmers, teachers, clerks, secretaries, accountants, stock brokers, managers, insurance people, bureaucrats, lawyers, bankers, and technicians... Most Americans spend their time creating, processing, or distributing information."[121]

This trend has had major effects upon people who were already employed but

---

[119]For a summary and reference to the various publications of this project, see Gurin, op. cit.

[120]John Naisbitt, *Megatrends: Ten New Directions Transforming Our Lives* (New York: Warner Books, 1982).

[121]Ibid., p. 14.

lacked some of the skills now required, upon those seeking employment, and upon the skills people must obtain in order to be employable. This last point has obvious implications for an assessment of the adequacy of educational institutions as well as the educational preparation of the population.

Important technological developments associated with this shift to an information society are those of "high technology." In almost every sphere of life, technological developments have changed the ways we live. Some examples of this are the utilization of computers for virtually every information processing task; the creation of many devices for monitoring and improving our health; the use of video associated mechanisms for entertainment, education, and marketing; and the employment in the factory of countless new ways of mechanizing production. These changes, in addition to the ways they have altered our lives, have also produced counterforces, according to Naisbitt, in that people have also sought new ways to be together doing simple things with each other.[122]

Growth of a World Economy. The changes that have taken place in the economic status of the United States are that it no longer plays the dominant role in the world economy, its economic growth has stalled, and its domestic market is dominated by foreign products in many sectors. The role of Japan, for example, is well known as a producer of many of the technological products used in the United States. What may not be as well known is the growth of South Korea in steel, of Brazil and Spain in ship building, and of China in textiles.

This is leading to vast shifts in investment patterns, interorganizational relationships on a global scale, and the effects that economic developments within the United States have on those in others.

Decentralization. Despite the seeming concentration of power implied by a world economy, the actual trend is toward decentralization. According to Naisbitt, "the decline of American industry and the rise of the new information economy neutralized the pressure to centralize and we began to decentralize."[123] Some of the examples he cites of this are the proliferation of cable TV stations and lower-powered broadcast TV stations; the increased role that state as opposed to national government is playing in our lives; a vast increase (that we shall discuss later) in neighborhood organizations; the interest in local magazines; and the shift of population to rural areas and small towns.

Ideological Currents

Perhaps the ideological development with the most impact on the current phase of community organizing is the belief in the value of self-help activities—although this might, in a classic social work sense, be thought of as *mutual aid*. In a limited way, this development has been seen by some as an outgrowth of President Reagan's emphasis on reducing people's reliance on government, but we join Naisbitt in seeing this as a culmination of a long historical process in which people reacted to their alienation from their

---

[122]Ibid., pp. 39-53.

[123]Ibid., pp. 98-99.

government, their welfare institutions, and their occupations.

Some of the spheres in which we can see the development of self-help are in the ways people are seeking to improve their health through running, eating natural foods, monitoring their weight, and acting to prevent illness. They are also providing each other with mutual support in a manner that often imitates the highly successful program of Alcoholics Anonymous, such as Gamblers Anonymous, Parents Anonymous, Tough Love, Compassionate Friends (for those whose children have died), and groups for those who have had cancer, a mastectomy, a colostomy, Acquired Immune Deficiency Syndrome (AIDS), or who lost a close friend or relative because of suicide. These are only a few of the hundreds of organizations that have arisen for mutual aid in the last few years and that continue to be created on almost a daily basis somewhere in this country.

As we mentioned earlier in this article the federal programs of the sixties required "maximum feasible participation" of their consumers. While this requirement has abated, in most societal spheres the move toward participation has grown. Naisbitt illustrates this in the creation and development of new political parties, the increase in splits among legislators of the same political party, the rise in the use of initiatives and referenda, and the tax "revolts." He also points to what he refers to as the "participatory corporation" which offers "workers, shareholders, consumers, and community leaders a larger say in determining how corporations will be run."[124] He sees this as occurring through consumerism, the appoint-

ment of more outside board members, shareholder activism, and worker participation.

Another trend noted by Naisbitt is toward "networking" in which people seek ways of locating others who can help them achieve desired ends. This has been facilitated by computer utilization in which computer files are maintained that can locate others of similar interests and needs. Examples cited by Naisbitt are the Denver Open Network, the National Women's Health Network in Washington, D.C., and the Newton, Massachusetts WARM LINES.[125]

Finally, we are becoming a society of even more diversity in all of life's spheres. A major example is that of the family in which the traditional notion of a household composed of two adults of different sexes who are married to each other (each for the first time) and who have children is the exception rather than the rule. Blended families, one-parent families, gay male and lesbian couples, and "living together" families are increasingly likely to be found in every community. The options available to women to work in every occupation and to play any and all family roles are accepted and, if not, are fought for. And people living each of these life styles, and many others that exist or are emerging, are developing networks, literature about their aspirations, and unique ways of coping.

Development of Community Organization Institutions

The major shift in community organization practice after 1969 was the withdrawal of federal funding from

---

[124]Ibid., p. 175.

[125]Ibid., p. 193.

Students and others learning to practice at these macro levels are likely to be taught this range of skills while being afforded opportunities to practice roles that are defined as management within an organization, organizing within a community, or policy creation and/or implementation within regional and societal institutions.

The tools available to these practitioners have grown over this period and include utilization of computer and other technological resources for communication and data manipulation purposes as well as knowledge regarding organizational, community, and societal phenomena drawn from major advances in the social sciences, particularly sociology, social psychology, anthropology, political science, and economics. Whether this "new world" leads to more successful efforts at social change than those engaged in by previous generations of organizers remains to be seen.

A unity of thinking among all social workers regarding micro and macro practices of change is, at least, encouraged by the spread of systems-oriented and ecologically-based thinking throughout the profession. Presumably all social workers are coming to see the necessity for systems changes and the participation of the consumer of social services in these changes. The negative side of the picture is some tendency for social work students and practitioners to be highly concerned about career advancement and to emphasize *therapy* rather than social change in their career goals.

SUMMARY AND CONCLUSIONS

Community organization practice has been examined in its social and ideological context during four periods of its history, separated by events with particular significance for that practice: the First World War and the end of the Progressive Era (1914); the stock market crash (1929) and the Supreme Court decision ending legal racial segregation in the public schools (1954).

It is impossible to understand community organization as an isolated phenomenon or merely as a technique of social engineering, for it is so closely related to what is most important in the lives of those it touches. Industrialization, urbanization, immigration, and minority emancipation created great opportunities and problems. The perspectives of Social Darwinism, socialism, pragmatism, and liberalism through which social conditions were perceived set the stage for many institutional developments important for community organization practice. Among these were charity organization societies designed to coordinate unplanned efforts to rescue the poor, and social settlements intended to help the urban poor get themselves together, unite rich and poor in a common enterprise, and reform the oppressive conditions of life that victimized the poor. Minorities organized, in some cases, to accommodate themselves to the system and, in others, to fight it.

Following World War I, the American people expressed a strong desire to return to "normalcy" and the principles of free enterprise, and they developed a sense of profound optimism toward capitalism. The newly emerging profession of social work withdrew from its prior efforts to change pernicious social conditions. In its place, the profession cultivated a preoccupation with the individual psyche. In this context, efficiency-oriented community chests were organized by businessmen to spread the cost and reduce the annoy-

government, their welfare institutions, and their occupations.

Some of the spheres in which we can see the development of self-help are in the ways people are seeking to improve their health through running, eating natural foods, monitoring their weight, and acting to prevent illness. They are also providing each other with mutual support in a manner that often imitates the highly successful program of Alcoholics Anonymous, such as Gamblers Anonymous, Parents Anonymous, Tough Love, Compassionate Friends (for those whose children have died), and groups for those who have had cancer, a mastectomy, a colostomy, Acquired Immune Deficiency Syndrome (AIDS), or who lost a close friend or relative because of suicide. These are only a few of the hundreds of organizations that have arisen for mutual aid in the last few years and that continue to be created on almost a daily basis somewhere in this country.

As we mentioned earlier in this article the federal programs of the sixties required "maximum feasible participation" of their consumers. While this requirement has abated, in most societal spheres the move toward participation has grown. Naisbitt illustrates this in the creation and development of new political parties, the increase in splits among legislators of the same political party, the rise in the use of initiatives and referenda, and the tax "revolts." He also points to what he refers to as the "participatory corporation" which offers "workers, shareholders, consumers, and community leaders a larger say in determining how corporations will be run."[124] He sees this as occurring through consumerism, the appoint-

ment of more outside board members, shareholder activism, and worker participation.

Another trend noted by Naisbitt is toward "networking" in which people seek ways of locating others who can help them achieve desired ends. This has been facilitated by computer utilization in which computer files are maintained that can locate others of similar interests and needs. Examples cited by Naisbitt are the Denver Open Network, the National Women's Health Network in Washington, D.C., and the Newton, Massachusetts WARM LINES.[125]

Finally, we are becoming a society of even more diversity in all of life's spheres. A major example is that of the family in which the traditional notion of a household composed of two adults of different sexes who are married to each other (each for the first time) and who have children is the exception rather than the rule. Blended families, one-parent families, gay male and lesbian couples, and "living together" families are increasingly likely to be found in every community. The options available to women to work in every occupation and to play any and all family roles are accepted and, if not, are fought for. And people living each of these life styles, and many others that exist or are emerging, are developing networks, literature about their aspirations, and unique ways of coping.

Development of Community Organization Institutions

The major shift in community organization practice after 1969 was the withdrawal of federal funding from

---

[124]Ibid., p. 175.

[125]Ibid., p. 193.

many community organizations and the termination of many community-oriented federal programs. This trend became most pronounced during the Reagan administration. The casual observer might conclude *incorrectly,* therefore, that there was a decrease in the quantity of community organizations. Nothing could be farther from the truth!

As Perlman states:

The contemporary grassroots movement is new, growing, diverse, and effective. Although its lineage can be traced back to the social movements of the 1960s, the early Alinsky organizations of the 1950s, and the union struggles of the 1930s and 1940s, in its present form it is not yet a decade old. Most of the groups we shall be describing started in the early 1970s, and many are five years old or less. They are growing in numbers and expanding in size so rapidly that any estimates of their size and numbers are outdated as quickly as they are calculated.[126]

Although, as Perlman states, the number of grassroots organizations is expanding, efforts have frequently been made to assess their quantity. She quotes a figure cited by the National Commission on Neighborhoods of 8,000 groups and the Department of Housing and Urban Development (HUD) has begun a clearinghouse with 4,000 groups. In addition, the Alliance for Volunteerism estimated there were six million voluntary associations in the United States in 1975. Perlman adds that there are some 10,000 block clubs in New York City alone.[127]

Many local groups are affiliated with regional or national organizations.

Among these are Association of Community Organizations for Reform Now (ACORN); National People's Action, and Massachusetts Fair Share. Some organizations also were created to provide support and technical assistance to grassroots groups such as the Center for Community Change, the National Center for Urban Ethnic Affairs, National People's Action, and the National Association of Neighborhoods.[128]

The important difference, however, between this and earlier periods is that these organizations cannot rely on federal financing but, instead, have generated many alternative forms of support. This often comes from state and local governments but also from voluntary donations, fund-raising efforts, and support from various constituencies such as labor organizations, churches, and businesses.

The focus of many of these organizations is on specific issues such as housing, the creation of cooperatives, obtaining adequate health care in the community, and a host of consumer related topics. They exist in all ethnic communities and among all socioeconomic groups.

Organization of Ethnic Minorities and Women

The growth of neighborhood organization that we have just described also characterizes some of the major developments within oppressed ethnic communities. A few examples demonstrate the geographical spread as well as breadth of

---

[126]Janice E. Perlman, "Grassroots Participation from Neighborhood to Nation," in Stuart Langton, *Citizen Participation in America,* (Lexington, MA: D.C. Heath, 1978), p. 65.

[127]Ibid., p. 67.

[128]More information on these organizations may be found in Robert A. Rosenbloom, "The Politics of the Neighborhood Movement," *South Atlantic Urban Studies,* Vol. 4 (1979), pp. 103-119.

purpose of this. Native American organizations include the Seminole Employment and Economic Development Corporation (Florida); the Menominee Restoration Committee (Wisconsin); and the Zuni Craftsman Cooperative Association and the All Indian Development Association (New Mexico). Hispanic ones include the Mexican American Unity Council (Texas); *Chicanos Por La Causa* (Arizona); and the Council for the Spanish Speaking (California). Asian-American examples are the East Bay Asian Local Development Corporation and the Asian Neighborhood Association (California).

Within the black community, as well as the others we have named, these organizations have been highly issue oriented. The issues in that community have included reducing poverty through neighborhood job creation and training, reversing the trend toward the dismantling of services for children, and reducing illiteracy. Many black organizations have also sought to identify ideologically with peoples of the third world.

An example of these developments is PUSH in Chicago and the activities of its leader Jesse Jackson. That organization has heavily focussed on creating economic opportunities through such campaigns as encouraging black people to spend their money within the black community. Many black churches in keeping with this approach have created credit unions within their communities.

Many developments are continuing to occur within the women's movement and women's organizations. As progress was made in securing women's rights in the workplace, in academic institutions, and in government, this has provided impetus to even stronger commitments of women and women's organizations to refuse to settle for anything less than full opportunity. A recognition that, despite this progress, the "feminization of poverty" continues to be an issue for the entire society has contributed to the specific agendas of women's organizations. The candidacy of Geraldine Ferraro for vice-president has reinforced the conviction that women can and should seek every role available within the political and economic structure of society, and is likely to have effects that have not yet been predicted.

Development of the Profession and Professional Education

We shall not explore this topic at any length here as it is expressed throughout all of the chapters in this book. We believe that an important shift took place during this period, however, that we should draw attention to in this historically oriented analysis. This was the shift to thinking of community organization activities as part of "macro" practice that also includes interventions at organizational and societal levels.

This shift is important because it recognizes that social change takes place through a set of activities that sometimes focuses on a single organization, sometimes on a community, and sometimes on a society as a whole. The skills the practitioner uses when engaged in these activities are sometimes unique to the level (i.e., organization, community, society) but more often are appropriate to several levels. Such skills include needs assessment, group leadership, budgeting, and class advocacy—to name a few. The current edition of this book attests to this evolution.

Students and others learning to practice at these macro levels are likely to be taught this range of skills while being afforded opportunities to practice roles that are defined as management within an organization, organizing within a community, or policy creation and/or implementation within regional and societal institutions.

The tools available to these practitioners have grown over this period and include utilization of computer and other technological resources for communication and data manipulation purposes as well as knowledge regarding organizational, community, and societal phenomena drawn from major advances in the social sciences, particularly sociology, social psychology, anthropology, political science, and economics. Whether this "new world" leads to more successful efforts at social change than those engaged in by previous generations of organizers remains to be seen.

A unity of thinking among all social workers regarding micro and macro practices of change is, at least, encouraged by the spread of systems-oriented and ecologically-based thinking throughout the profession. Presumably all social workers are coming to see the necessity for systems changes and the participation of the consumer of social services in these changes. The negative side of the picture is some tendency for social work students and practitioners to be highly concerned about career advancement and to emphasize *therapy* rather than social change in their career goals.

SUMMARY AND CONCLUSIONS

Community organization practice has been examined in its social and ideological context during four periods of its history, separated by events with particular significance for that practice: the First World War and the end of the Progressive Era (1914); the stock market crash (1929) and the Supreme Court decision ending legal racial segregation in the public schools (1954).

It is impossible to understand community organization as an isolated phenomenon or merely as a technique of social engineering, for it is so closely related to what is most important in the lives of those it touches. Industrialization, urbanization, immigration, and minority emancipation created great opportunities and problems. The perspectives of Social Darwinism, socialism, pragmatism, and liberalism through which social conditions were perceived set the stage for many institutional developments important for community organization practice. Among these were charity organization societies designed to coordinate unplanned efforts to rescue the poor, and social settlements intended to help the urban poor get themselves together, unite rich and poor in a common enterprise, and reform the oppressive conditions of life that victimized the poor. Minorities organized, in some cases, to accommodate themselves to the system and, in others, to fight it.

Following World War I, the American people expressed a strong desire to return to "normalcy" and the principles of free enterprise, and they developed a sense of profound optimism toward capitalism. The newly emerging profession of social work withdrew from its prior efforts to change pernicious social conditions. In its place, the profession cultivated a preoccupation with the individual psyche. In this context, efficiency-oriented community chests were organized by businessmen to spread the cost and reduce the annoyance of charitable solicitations. A growing cadre of welfare professionals promoted councils of agencies to rationalize their efforts, fill the gaps in services, and promote disinterested and effective services supported by dependable and expanding resources. The social unit plan, oriented toward grassroots participation, found little sympathy in the climate of the times.

The depression brought the federal government into welfare planning and strengthened grass-roots activities, particularly through the labor movement. World War II and the government's response to the demands of blacks and others for equality were the beginning of important developments in community organization. Small programs for training community organization practitioners to work with community chests and welfare councils were organized, and their teachers produced the beginnings of a professional literature.

Recent periods are characterized first by the civil rights movements and those of oppressed minorities and by student activism and discontent with the war in Vietnam, generating strong professional interest in grass-roots organizing and planning with local citizens, plus a pervasive sense of anger and alienation.

This was followed by major reverses in the government's commitment to community organizing. Shifts in social attitudes, particularly among young people, were not conducive to organizing. Nevertheless, particularly within ethnic groups and among women, these commitments were kept alive and are now intensifying through the growth of neighborhood organizations.

Where does all this lead? Several major questions dangle precariously overhead like the sword of Damocles: How will impatient underclasses, and particularly the large ethnic minorities, respond to current social conditions? Will the necessary wisdom and determination be forthcoming to put our resources to work on the social problems that threaten to divide the nation? What are the most effective ways to accomplish our objectives consistent with our values? The first is a question that only those who are oppressed can answer, and the most persuasive answers are likely to be deeds rather than words. The second is a question for the whole nation, especially the president and Congress, the governors, the state legislatures, the city councils, and the neighborhood groups themselves. The last is a particular responsibility of macro practitioners, including community organizers.

PART ONE:

COMMON ELEMENTS
OF PRACTICE

Introduction

Among practitioners and teachers of community organization there is little consensus about which practice aspects bear most heavily upon the success or failure of any range of interventive efforts. Perspectives are as diverse as the field itself. In part, this lack of agreement has been a function of the continuing struggle to define and describe what ought to be included under the concepts of practice. Also, the widely varying perspectives among organizers, planners, administrators, community developers, and policy-makers have contributed to the difficulty of sorting out which aspects are central and which should be peripheral to the community organization enterprise.

At the same time, the historical development of community organization has made the task of seeking out and identifying common elements of practice more difficult. Because of the dominance of "interpersonal" modes of practice, a major task of community organization in the past had been to develop its unique and distinctive features. Thus, while specification of a set of distinguishing community organization characteristics was occurring, along with a vigorous attempt to separate "CO" from the "interpersonal" fields of practice, one consequence was the tendency to ignore some very useful ideas developed in casework and group work. A second problem occurred because as the traditional "third" method in social work practice (i.e., casework, group work, and community organization), community organization tended to include in a fairly undifferentiated way most or all methods that we now call macro practice. Hence, CO skills ran from advocacy to policy analysis, from needs assessment to evaluation, from task to process. It is only within recent years that more systematic attempts to define community organization skills have been developed which facilitated the ability to link community organization skills with other elements of macro practice.

While this section cannot remedy oversights of the past thirty years, it seeks to address some of those issues, and continues to develop the perspective in the third edition of this book of emphasizing some of the common elements of practice. We certainly do not claim to have touched on *all* the aspects of practice that are vital in day-to-day work in the community area. But we do believe that areas considered in Part One constitute an important part of what must be taken into account if interventive approaches are to have any reasonable level of success. The broader focus of this edition means that our selection was informed not only by elements common to CO practice; certainly those are present, as they were in the last edition, but also elements which are common to all macro practice. Since the actual work of the community practitioner tends to include administration and policy matters, she or he needs to have a broadened awareness of common elements. These continue to include need identification and program planning; the social scientific knowledge base upon which planned change efforts build; and the ways in which one can be an advocate of social programs especially given social work values and the difficult economic conditions of the 1980s. In addition, we include a focus upon task groups and their use in the accomplishment of social purpose; an analysis of interpersonal transactions within the community organization context; and, finally, aspects of program evaluation and administrative control.

Community organization and macro practice are ultimately based upon theories of social organization and social disorganization. But the successful practitioner needs to be more than a documenter of social structure and a describer of social breakdown. She or he observes the structures and problems in structure and develops a sense of what kinds of interventions are needed and in what order, and is able to structure intervention so that practice goals have some likelihood of being accomplished. The Siegel, *et al.* piece, "Need Identification and Program Planning in the Community Context," tries to assist in this regard. For the harried practitioner, "theory" is often an annoyance and a distraction. Frequently the practitioner is right in this perspective, for much social science knowledge has not been formulated with the idea of application in mind. The ability to identify client system needs and to devise a program of intervention to meet those needs is certainly an element of practice which is common to all levels of social work effort. The potential complexity of such assessments at the macro level make it exceptionally difficult. Siegel and his colleagues provide help in this area.

While the practitioner should not become a theorist, and indeed does not need to become a theorist, he or she must be aware of the knowledge base of practice to apply tactics and techniques. The lack of understanding of theory and the scientific basis of practice mechanizes the practitioner. No longer is she or he the thoughtful applier of skills and competencies but rather the "Pavlovian practitioner" who automatically responds with a certain practice technique when an apparent problematic stimulus is manifest. Katan and Spiro help us understand these knowledge bases and help provide bridges from the islands of theory to the mainland of practice.

The history of social work has resembled a roller coaster in recent years. We saw a negative period in the 1950s followed by increasing popularity of our field during the 1960s and, to some extent, into the 70s; that period followed by, once again, lack of esteem for social programs and the individuals those programs help. In this rising negative climate the importance of the role of advocacy is central to all social workers. Because community practitioners and other macro practitioners are likely to be in contact with decisionmakers as part of their daily job the advocate role and knowledge about it takes on a special significance. Amidei's piece on "How To Be An Advocate In Bad Times" reflects and distills the knowledge of importance to social advocates.

Perhaps one of the more ignored areas in the macro practice field has been the skills necessary to work with decision-making groups. These might include not only boards of directors, executive committees, advisory councils, and others, but also might involve staff groups and other kinds of task groups formed within the agency to accomplish particular purposes. Toseland's piece on "Working With Task Groups" is an outstanding example of new work in this area.[1] Toseland provides not only an analytic framework but a variety of specific skills which are applicable across the whole range of community organization and macro practice. Since so much of what macro practitioners must do involves the use of tasks groups, it is imperative to have a more central focus upon them and a more thoroughgoing understanding of the skills needed to work with them than has often been presented in many CO courses.

The lack of attention to groups was perhaps one casualty of the attempt to develop a "unique" set of skills for CO. We failed to borrow where appropriate. A second failure of this same sort lies in the unfortunate de-emphasis of interpersonal skills. Perhaps as an overreaction to the period in our history when every remark was interpreted and assumed to mean something else we tended to eschew appropriate borrowing from casework in other interpersonal practice arenas.[2] Bisno seeks to remedy this deficiency by providing us with a perspective on interpersonal transactions within the community organization context. Across all social work, the disciplined use of self in "the relationship" is central to our interventive success. Bisno reminds us of this truth and provides some helping guidelines. However, unlike the interpersonal practitioner in social work, he focuses on bargaining and negotiation rather than "helping."

Another feature which certainly encompasses all of macro practice is the process of problem solving. In discussing the importance of need identification and plan formulation, it was assumed that these "somehow" occurred.

---

[1]See also John E. Tropman, *Meetings: How to Make Them Work for You* (New York: Van Nostrand Reinhold, 1984).

[2]A simple humorous story illustrates the parallels of that period. As two mental health practitioners were passing in the hallway of their agency, one said to the other, "Good morning." The recipient of this salutation looked puzzled and said to himself, "Hummmmmm, I wonder what he meant by that?"

There is very little "somehow" about it. There is a set of steps practitioners historically have found useful in going through the problem-solving process. In the several editions of *Strategies,* we have always included the Cox piece on this topic. Not only is a set of steps presented, but a discussion of the steps is presented, so that the student will be able to have a fuller and richer idea of the process of problem solving itself and the ways that one may move from one step to the other.

Finally, a common element of community organization and macro practice is evaluation. This area is one in which we have not, perhaps, been as vigorous as would have been appropriate. Many community organizers or macro practitioners are so delighted to even get a program off the ground that the idea of evaluating it seems unnecessary, if not ludicrous. Yet in these more stringent times, evaluation and the attendant processes of adjustment and control of agency practices is essential. But it is not only financial stringency which is encouraging us in evaluative directions; clients are demanding it. It is unfortunate but not surprising that attempts at evaluation and appropriate program refurbishment and improvement are less vigorously undertaken when our clients are among the poorer segments of society. Programs serving the poor do not have a lot of money for evaluation but it may also be that society does not care a great deal about whether those programs work or not. Certainly as the client base of social work has broadened to encompass the full range of social standings in America the press for evaluation and improvement has increased as well. The Maynard-Moody piece provides some suggested ways in which evaluation can proceed.

It is important to reiterate that these selections in no way represent the totality of common elements. They do touch upon ones the editors felt to be of central importance. As community organizers and other practitioners of macro practice become more comfortable with their identity we are able to pay more attention to the links and commonalities. It is possible and desirable for methods in the field of social work to have both differences as well as similarities and this volume seeks to attend to both.

JOHN E. TROPMAN

3.

Larry M. Siegel, C. Clifford Attkisson, and Linda G. Carson

NEED IDENTIFICATION AND PROGRAM
PLANNING IN THE COMMUNITY CONTEXT

Assessment of service needs is a neglected and misunderstood aspect of human service program planning. Optimally, legislative blueprints for national social and health programs should emerge from systematic, scientific need assessment efforts that are designed to identify the extent and degree of need for specific services in the general population. In practice, however, national programs emerge from a political context of confrontation between special and general interests, social service ideologies, demands for service, and the competition for access to resources. As a result, our communities are peppered with uncoordinated and loosely integrated programs that overlap and compete for sparse resources. Without adequate assessment of human service needs, this poorly monitored and uncoordinated situation will persist and worsen.

This article describes the central issues of need identification and assessment. Following the initial discussion, several basic need assessment methodologies are described and illustrated. The basic assumptions on which the article is based are that identification and assessment of service needs (a) must be undertaken at the local community and

regional level in a fashion that stimulates coordination and integration of human services at the community level; (b) must be a rationalizing force in the regional health and human service planning process; and (c) must carefully blend citizen and consumer participation with professional personnel in a planning process designed to stimulate program relevance to human service needs.

A DEFINITION OF NEED
IDENTIFICATION AND
ASSESSMENT

Need identification describes health and social service requirements in a geographic or social area, whereas *need assessment* is aimed at estimating the relative importance of these needs. The process of need identification and assessment involves two distinct steps: (a) the application of a measuring tool or an assortment of tools to a defined social area; and, following this attempt at measurement, (b) the application of judgment to assess the significance of the information gathered in order to determine priorities for program planning and service development (Blum, 1974). Assessment is a research and planning activity that is focused on a specific social area. Within social areas, need assessment strategies are designed to provide data that will enable planners to determine the extent and kinds

Source: From Larry M. Siegel, C. Clifford Attkisson and Linda G. Carson, "Need Identification and Program Planning in the Community Context," *Evaluation of Human Service Programs,* Academic Press, Inc., 1984. Reprinted with permission of Academic Press, Inc.

of needs there are in a community; to evaluate existing service resources systematically; and to provide information for planning new service programs in the light of the community's needs and human service patterns.

Basically, the various known assessment techniques produce information that describes or defines social conditions or situations. These conditions are not necessarily predetermined to be positive or negative. The interpretation of social situations depends on the values and expectations of those individuals doing the interpreting. As Blum (1974) states, "The identical situation may be seen as good by those whose value expectations are met, and as bad by those whose values are not; those whose values are unrelated, or who do not connect the condition to values, may not perceive the condition at all, or view it as a natural state of affairs [pp. 219–220]."

The same rationale may be applied when considering the term "need" in situations where assessment activities are characterized as "need identification." Need in this context might usefully be defined as the gap between what is viewed as a necessary level or condition by those responsible for this determination and what actually exists. Need is at best a relative concept and the definition of need depends primarily upon those who undertake the identification and assessment effort.

JUSTIFICATION AND GOALS FOR NEED STUDIES

The concepts of need identification and assessment are such that there is no set of generally agreed upon steps which, when carefully followed, lead one to a comprehensive assessment of needs. The reality is that planners and program administrators must decide what information will generate the most comprehensive identification and assessment of needs in a specific geographic service area, and what proportion of program resources should reasonably be allocated for this effort. Some of the relevant variables that merit careful consideration when planning an assessment of human service needs include:

1. Information

What assessment data are most relevant for the local program? How easily can the desired data be obtained? What is the potential accuracy and usefulness of the data?

2. Resources Available

What staff and fiscal resources are available to the assessment effort? What is the cost estimate of collecting (purchasing) these data? Will the expected benefits from the data outweigh their cost? Are these resources sufficient to obtain the desired information?

3. State of Program Development

Is the service system new or in early program planning stages? How wide is the range of services currently available? Is there a service system organizational network?

4. Community Attitudes

What is the community tolerance for surveys, community forums, and other approaches to assessment?

Planning human service programs for the future will require an approach to need identification that has clear sanctions and sufficient resources. Collaborative networks must be formed to act as regional information-gathering systems. These regional systems, probably organized at the multicounty level, should perform intensive field surveys and serve as a conduit through which appropriate information will be channeled to the community level.

CONVERGENT ANALYSIS

In a comprehensive need assessment effort *convergent analysis* may be conceptualized as the second of the two operational stages, the first one being need *identification.*

Convergent analysis is a methodological framework in which information relative to human service needs may be identified, defined, evaluated, and given priority in a progressive manner. The tasks to be completed in this final analytical stage are synthesis and integration of all collected information from a variety of data collection methods.

Convergent analysis usually begins with data internal to the service system, such as legal and fundor mandates, historical trends relevant to service delivery, and client utilization information. Other forces feeding into the initial phase of convergent analysis are the orientation, training and interests of administrators and providers, and the perspectives of advisory and policy board members. The process then integrates information assembled about a specified social area or target community via a network of techniques designed to capture a wide range of perceptions about conditions in the community.

Convergent analysis is used here in the sense that the information gathered from a range of need assessment methods, deployed both systematically and sequentially, will yield a reasonably accurate identification of community needs and an assessment of the relative priorities among the needs identified. "Convergent" in this context has several meanings. First, there is a convergence of different information coming from divergent sources (e.g., citizens, consumers, service providers, and political leaders). Second, there is a convergence of different assessment strategies, each with some overlapping, yet unique, bits of information. Third, convergent also describes the cumulative nature of an ideal assessment procedure viewed across time. Information obtained at different (though sequential) points in time (information from a wide range of data collection methods and perspectives) are convergent to the extent that they can be pooled in an ongoing fashion to yield an accurate depiction of human service needs of a particular social area. All three of the above concepts of convergence analysis imply that, with each stepwise increment of information, one more clearly approximates a valid description of the social area under study. In other words, convergent analysis provides a dynamic process for reaching a convergent and discriminant validation of the needs in a social area (Campbell & Fiske, 1959). Finally, the last meaning of convergence in our formulation is to be found in the range of organizational levels through which assessment information must be channeled. Information from both state and national perspectives "converges" on service program networks at the community level. When integrated with regionally and locally generated "need" data, this information allows for more systematic program planning and development.

BASIC PURPOSES OF NEED IDENTIFICATION AND ASSESSMENT

Assessment provides one important informational input to a much broader *planning process* that leads to (*a*) the selection of and priority setting among problems and target populations to be addressed; (*b*) the selection and operationalization of specific community program activities; and (*c*) the evaluation of these program activities. Assessment information helps to assure that there will be additional inputs to prevent sole reliance on professional formulations of service needs and/or to prevent overriding influence by the most vocal or powerful community groups in program planning.

Assessment also has an important role in established community programs. In such agencies, assessment can provide a continuing examination of the relevance of existing service activities to changing human service needs and priorities.

Assessment strategies are varied, and selection of a particular strategy is dependent upon the type of information sought. Assessment efforts may study the distribution of social problems in a population and the factors that influence the distribution. In the mental health field, for example, some assessment studies attempt to relate certain social or health characteristics of a population to various rates of mental disorder; or, studies may focus upon the relation between ecological characteristics of a social area and the rates of

mental disorder (Bloom, 1975). Other studies employ field survey strategies in order to identify mental health problems and service needs more specifically (Warheit, Bell, & Schwab, 1974).

Most field survey efforts are designed to assess the prevalence and incidence of those who already suffer from particular disorders and to identify those subpopulations having the highest risk of experiencing specific mental health problems within a social area. When it is possible to identify populations at risk, such findings are very important in planning for services, especially preventive ones. In addition to collecting information about the range of social and health problems in a community and specification of populations at risk, program planners must also identify cultural and linguistic barriers or other features of the service system that impede effective delivery of services—such as awareness, acceptability, accessibility, and availability of services.

Beyond describing needs, assessment is also useful in identifying those factors within the human service network which aid or impede attempts to meet those needs. First, assessment may be used to specify current and/or potential resources that can be channeled or reallocated to respond to unmet needs. Second, an assessment effort is useful in gaining an understanding of the political and social value system underlying a particular social area. These values often determine what needs are identified and also tend to determine which needs receive priority in the program planning process. Finally, analysis of assessment data may suggest new interventions and may ultimately be helpful in uncovering the etiology of certain conditions. Knowledge about social, environmental, and biologic etiology will eventually lead to more effective preventive programs (Blum, 1974; Broskowski & Baker, 1974).

ASSESSMENT CONTRASTED WITH PROGRAM EVALUATION

Care must be taken not to confuse community need assessment with evaluation. Both program evaluation and need assessment are parts of a larger program planning-implementation-development cycle, but need assessment is an environmental monitoring system. As an environmental monitoring system, it is a conceptually separate and operationally different process when compared to and contrasted with program evaluation.

WHEN TO DO A NEED IDENTIFICATION

Considerable attention must be given by human service programs to clarification and specification of the purposes and potential uses of a proposed assessment effort. Since the process requires a substantial expenditure of resources, it should primarily be considered when there is both an opportunity and a commitment either for planning new services or for restructuring existing ones on the basis of needs that may be identified. If there is no commitment to planning or restructuring programs in accordance with those needs identified, no useful purpose is served by an assessment effort. At best, failure to use need assessment information in planning represents a waste of resources and, at worst, certain assessment procedures (such as the "community forum") may serve to heighten community expectations that needs identified will be

addressed in actual service or preventive operations.

AN OVERVIEW OF NEED IDENTIFICATION AND ASSESSMENT METHODOLOGIES

A comprehensive, convergent analysis of human service needs requires utilization of information resources that exist in (or can be obtained from) national, regional, state, and community depositories. At the local level each human service agency has unique informational needs that logically can be identified through local effort. Beyond this, however, there is a large body of information held in common by, and/or is mutually relevant to, a number of agencies comprising the human services network within a given social area. Where informational requirements overlap, a cost-efficient and effective need assessment effort can only be undertaken and/or coordinated at the regional planning level.

The various approaches to need assessment presented in this article may be undertaken at any planning level: community, regional, state, and more rarely, national. The auspices for any particular need assessment will vary accordingly. Nevertheless, mounting effective need assessment programs will require each planning body to develop a master strategy which will coordinate assessment and dissemination of assessment information throughout an area.

A need assessment program that is organized at the regional planning level affords a number of advantages. First, a single regional assessment effort instead of numerous community efforts could guarantee a substantial conservation of financial and human resources. Tremendous duplication of effort and greatly exaggerated cost could ensue if each social agency in a given area were to undertake a unilateral assessment of community needs. Second, an ongoing regional assessment effort could also share successful models that are practical to employ on a smaller scale and that would be more appropriately undertaken at the community agency level. Third, the regional assessment activity could provide readily available, decision-relevant data to community-based programs on a regular, planned basis. And fourth, need assessment conducted under regional auspices would be less influenced by local political pressure, and in that way, could serve as a vehicle for more "objective" data than that which could be obtained at the agency level.

Without the integrative capacity, production capacity, and economic advantages of this regional approach to need assessment, it is doubtful that individual community-based programs will be able to conduct assessment programs that can adequately provide the necessary information. This state of affairs would not only be a serious blow to the development of flexible, responsive human service networks but also would seriously affect the relevance of specific agencies and services.

Several constraints limit the depth and scope of need assessment efforts undertaken by community-based agencies. First, the financial base for program planning and development may be too sparse to support an extensive assessment effort. Second, the time-frame in which an assessment activity is performed may limit the scope of its findings. Many, if not most, need assessments undertaken by community-based agencies are carried out in a relatively short period of time to meet, for example, governmental grant deadlines. These efforts tend to monopolize agency assessment lines. Third, internal pressure from highly vocal consumer groups often requires that immediate action be taken on a human service problem. In such circumstances, a comprehensive, time-consuming assessment effort is neither feasible nor appropriate. In these instances, where accessibility to time and/or money is limited, need assessment plans at the agency level may still be implemented to provide useful information. Excellent examples of such an effort are provided by Beigel, Hunter, Tamerin, Chapin, and Lowery (1974) and Beigel, McCabe, Tamerin, Lowery, Chapin, and Hunter (1974).

Regardless of the level at which need assessment is undertaken (local, regional, or state) there are eight need identification and assessment approaches that can provide the basis for a convergent analysis of human service needs. Each approach can be described as serving one or more information gathering functions: (a) *compilation* of information which is available but not yet disseminated within the boundaries of the social system, (b) *development* of new information, and (c) *integration* of all relevant information that is developed from within the system or gathered from outside the system's boundaries. One of the eight approaches performs all three informational functions, three serve two functions, and four represent only one function. The various approaches to need assessment, where the information may be obtained, how the data are formulated, and where "need" information is best utilized in the planning and development process, are summarized in Table 3.1. Table 3.1 is developed from the

TABLE 3.1
Need Identification and Assessment Methods

Methods and method families		Characteristics and technical considerations regarding the use of each method					
		Perspective being represented	Optimal sponsor	Source of information	Information processing function	Measurement expertise needed	Time and resources needed
Indicator approaches	1. Social and health indicator analyses	Government and private agencies	Local, state, regional or federal planners	Public archives, planning agencies	Compilation of existing data	Moderate to high	Moderate to extensive
	2. Demands for services	Service agencies and consumers	Community agencies along with above	Information systems	Compilation	Moderate	Moderate
Social area survey approaches	3. Analysis of service providers and resources	Planners	Local and regional planners	Local records and surveys	Compilation and development of new data	Low	Moderate
	4. Citizen surveys	Private citizens	Regional, state or federal planners	Face-to-face, telephone, or mailed surveys	Development of new data	High	Extensive
	5. Community forums	Private citizens and consumers	Community agencies	Public meetings	Integration of existing and new data	Low	Moderate
	6. Nominal group techniques	Planners, service providers, citizens	All levels	Specific projects	Development of new data	Moderate	Minimal
Community group approaches	7. Delphi technique	Planners, service providers, experts	All levels	Specific projects	Development and integration	Moderate	Moderate
	8. Community impressions	Citizens, key informants, consumers, providers	Community agencies, regional planners	Specific projects	Development, compilation, and integration	Moderate	Minimal

perspective of the community-based human service program, and assumes that regional planning bodies will soon join the local community agency in the need assessment data collection, analysis, and dissemination process.

A need assessment approach that collects information from already existing sources and subsequently organizes it in some coherent fashion illustrates a data *compilation* function. Frequently the required information exists outside the boundaries of the community-based program, for example, the National Clearinghouses of Drug Abuse Information, Mental Health Information, and Alcohol Information. Assessment approaches may also *develop* or collect new information. Here, original information bearing on the needs of a particular community is generated. Finally, a technique is classified as an *integrator* of information when data from two or more sources are organized to effect a more valid description of human service needs than is possible when information is drawn from a single source. It is in the combination of all three informational functions (compilation, development, and integration) that a convergent analysis of human service needs is achieved.

There are several important methods that can be employed to obtain information about human service needs. This section provides an outline of the various approaches including (*a*) a brief definition for each strategy, (*b*) the time at which utilization of a particular technique is appropriate, and (*c*) the source(s) from which data can be obtained. Each method provides a different perspective on needs. A more lengthy discussion of each technique follows in the final major sections of this article.

Social and Health Indicator Analysis

The Social and Health Indicator approach to need identification consists of compiling and making inferences of need from descriptive statistics found in public records and reports. It is based on the assumption that particular descriptors such as proximity to the urban core and socioeconomic status, are viable indicators of human service needs (Bloom, 1975; Siegel, Attkisson, & Cohn, 1977). The viability of particular indicators depends upon three factors: (*a*) the validity and reliability of the descriptive information, (*b*) the logical and statistical appropriateness of procedures used to derive the social and health indicators for the community (Schulberg & Wechsler, 1967), and (*c*) the subjective sense or feel for the given community which is developed through these sources of information about the community.

The Social and Health Indicator approach is invaluable as an initial descriptive approach to understanding a given social area (Sheldon & Parke, 1975). Social indicator approaches range from the very simplistic designs using one or two indicators, such as census data on income, housing or a population density index, to very complex designs that consist of many variables requiring the use of complex statistical procedures such as cluster or factor analysis (Bloom, 1975).

Social Area Surveys

1. Demands for services. This approach to need identification includes compilation of existing information and integration of those sources of information. Here the aim is to review the various human service providers' (both individual and agency) past and current services-rendered patterns and requests for service by citizens in an attempt to understand the number and types of human services demanded in a particular community. These data may be secured through structured interviews with appropriate staff and board members, extrapolations from past and current clinical records and management information systems, or analysis of agency charters, licenses, funding applications, contracts, and grants. Analysis can also identify current commitments, mandates, policies, and goal statements within the human service system. Appropriate target groups include agency management, agency staff and board members, funding organizations, and citizen advocacy groups.

2. *Analysis of service resources.* This need assessment device involves a descriptive enumeration of the human service agencies and individual providers within a community. It can best be classified as a compilation and integration of information that exists at the agency level. This integration may take the form of a human services directory for a particular community. Important to the process of identifying existing service resources is the assessment of whether current efforts are efficiently and effectively focused on known needs.

3. *Citizen surveys.* Here the assessment effort is concerned with eliciting differing perspectives on the nature and magnitude of human service needs from community residents. The main function of this technique is the development of new information through stratified random sampling of the community residents. This technique is most appropriately used to supplement generalized and indirect assessments,

such as social and health indicator analyses, with the more personal perspective of community residents.

Ascertaining Community Views Through Community Group Approaches

1. *Community forum.* This approach consists of an open meeting to which all members of a community are invited and at which all participants are urged to present their views regarding the human service needs of a particular social area. Although this information is often used to validate previously existing data, the technique itself is concerned with generating new information only; that is, obtaining community residents' input on a particular issue or issues.

2. *Nominal group approach.* The nominal group approach is principally a noninteractive workshop designed to maximize creativity and productivity and to minimize the argumentative style of problem-solving and competitive discussion. Within this format, a *selected group of community residents* is invited to share group subject views regarding community needs or to identify barriers to relevant, effective human service delivery in a social area. The nominal group approach is most appropriately used as a method for obtaining citizen and consumer input into the need assessment and program planning process.

3. *Delphi approach.* This approach to need identification includes the development of a questionnaire, which is distributed to a panel of resource persons and/or a select group of community residents whose opinions on a particular issue or issues are highly valued. From their responses, a perspective can be derived regarding human service needs. This technique is quite useful and most appropriate when respondents have a minimal amount of time available for an identification effort. The Delphi process of obtaining individual opinions on a particular issue is best classified as development of new information.

4. Community impressions approach. There are three steps to this assessment procedure. First, a small but representative group of individuals is interviewed about their views of human service needs. Second, this information is then integrated with existing data taken from public records and other assessment efforts to yield a richer understanding of the community needs. Third, the resulting community portrait is then validated and/or revised according to information gained from various groups in the community through the community forum process.

This approach serves as an information integrator and validator. It employs data from three different assessment efforts, and at the same time provides new information in the form of community impressions. The community impressions approach is an economical and necessary step on the path to a creative convergence of need assessment information gained from the various other need assessment approaches.

SOCIAL AND HEALTH INDICATOR ANALYSIS

This approach consumes preexisting, publicly available information (census data, public health data, and criminal justice data, for example) and inte-

grates this information in an attempt to gain a clear and parsimonious description of a social area. It does not produce new information. Rather, it analyzes, integrates, and disseminates already existing information. Although the task sounds simple, most social and health indicator analyses are complex, expensive and time-consuming.

Social and health indicator analysis cannot be treated in a detailed and systematic manner here. For more details, see Attkisson, *et al.,* chapters 9 and 10.

SOCIAL AREA SURVEY APPROACHES TO NEED IDENTIFICATION

One of the first steps in a convergent analysis of human service needs is to survey existing community service resources. Surveys of social and health agencies provide information about major problems existing in a community, about help-seeking behaviors in a community, about service resources and gaps in these resources, and about existing outreach and preventive efforts in a community.

There are three main types of information that a survey of practitioners and agencies can provide. They are (*a*) the analysis of *demands* for service placed upon agencies and private practitioners; (*b*) the specification, by type, of the various human services resources in a designated social area and their corresponding capacity to respond to human service problems; and (*c*) a description of the pattern and the extent of interrelationships among human service resources in the community.

In analyzing demands for service, the objective is to understand the magnitude and types of requests for human services. When assessing human service resources, however, planners are concerned with comprehending the capacity of the service systems to respond to those requests and with the quality of such responses. In delineating the interagency relationships in a particular community, we hope to clarify the extent and kind of collaborative efforts that characterize the human service network.

Need Identification Through Analysis of Demands for Service

This approach requires a survey of the entire human services network within a community. The typical survey seeks information not only from the primary health service agencies, for example, or institutions within a community but also from other community agencies which interface with and provide a range of supporting and interlocking services to the primary health care network. Many agencies can potentially be included: mental health clinics and centers, hospitals (including psychiatric and general hospitals), drug and alcohol treatment and related service programs, private practitioners, family service programs, public health departments, churches, probation and family courts, and other social and health organizations or service providers.

Although analysis of demand for services is an important element of a broader assessment strategy, there are a few caveats related to using this approach exclusively in assessing service needs (Feldstein, 1973; Schaefer, 1975). Even though a service is well utilized, it does not necessarily follow that this service is addressing a high-priority need in the community. A high utilization rate may possibly be due to any of the following: (*a*) the service is well publicized; (*b*) it is inexpensive; (*c*) it is one of the only services available in the community; (*d*) the various professionals in the community are unaware of alternative services; and/or (*e*) more pejoratively, high utilization may reflect professional preferences for particular service modalities. Reciprocally, services addressing high-priority problems may be underutilized because they are unpublicized, because client referral procedures are too cumbersome, or because they have marginal relevance to professional investments. In addition, high service utilization rates may signal the need for the development of preventive programs in a particular service area. And, finally, there are likely to be important differences between those who seek or receive care and those who do not. Many "needers" are not utilizers and some utilizers are, relatively speaking, "non-needers." These caveats should be carefully considered as indicators of the hazards involved in extrapolating from populations receiving services to the population at large.

In analyzing demands for services it may be possible to secure satisfactory response from a fairly brief, well-designed, mailed questionnaire. A followup letter or phone call to nonrespondents is usually necessary to increase the response rate. A method for substantially increasing the number of returns from mailed questionnaires has been described by Robin (1965). It involves a minimum of two and a maximum of five contacts with the potential respondent. The first contact is a prequestionnaire letter which, if possible, should be written on letterhead and cosigned by someone who represents broadly recognized authority and who is able to validate the importance of the survey and the appropriateness of the respondent's participation. Optimally, the letter must (*a*) request individual participation; (*b*) explain the assessment methodology, its importance, and possible applications; (*c*) inform the respondent that he or she will soon receive an assessment questionnaire; and finally (*d*) describe procedures for safeguarding confidentiality in handling all information. The second contact consists of a cover letter and the questionnaire. Contacts three to five consist of a series of followup strategies, should these be necessary. The reader is referred to Robin's article for further explanation of this survey strategy (Robin, 1965).

When possible, utilization surveys should be conducted in a systematic site visit format. Personal interviews with through-the-mail followups almost always produce greater reliability and validity of survey results.

Analysis of Existing Service Resources

Beyond assessing demands for human services it is also important for every community to identify and assess its human service resources. A count of resources by type and capacity allows human service program planners to identify gaps and duplications among existing services. This knowledge of existing resources may then be contrasted with information derived from other assessment strategies relative to estimates of met and unmet needs. Usually a single survey can produce information about both (*a*) demands for services in the community, and (*b*) existing service resources.

The specific content and format of social and health agency surveys must vary from community to community to the extent that agencies in a given social area differ in structure and service objectives. Nevertheless there are a number of general interest areas that are applicable to most agencies when conducting this type of survey:

1. Range of human services provided
2. Client entry policies, conditions of eligibility for service, including age, sex, financial criteria, geographic restrictions, and particular focal or target population groups
3. Personnel characteristics and personnel development efforts
   a. Service providers by training and credentials
   b. Provider training and continuing education opportunities
   c. Treatment modalities provided
   d. Number of individuals providing various services
   e. Average client load per staff member
4. Financial characteristics
   a. Charge for services—fee schedule, eligibility for third party reimbursement, sliding scale provisions
   b. Agency support—public or private, fees and other sources of funding categorized as percentage of total support budget
5. Accessibility, availability, and awareness of services
   a. Location of facility—proximity to target populations and proximity to public transportation
   b. Intake procedure—amount of information required, publicity for the available ser-

vices, hours when services are provided, comfort and acceptability of the facility to clients, and availability of child-care when necessary

6. Referrals (demand)
   a. Number within a standardized time frame
   b. Source categorized by service type or status of referring agent
   c. Reasons (symptoms, problem areas)
   d. Other characteristics such as geographic locale of referring agents, geographic origin of clients who are referred, and temporal patterns of referrals

7. Accepted for service
   a. Number over a specified time period
   b. Diagnosis or other nomenclature for designated problems
   c. Sociodemographic characteristics of clients—age, race, sex, census tract, socioeconomic status
   d. Those refused service and reasons for refusal

8. Waiting list
   a. Number of persons on waiting list
   b. Reasons for waiting list
   c. Symptoms or problem areas of individuals placed on waiting lists
   d. Other characteristics, such as average time on waiting list and proportion of those placed on waiting list who do not eventually receive service

9. Services provided
   a. Human service problem areas thought to be of highest priority as well as services that are in increasing demand
   b. Range of actual services provided categorized by units of service
   c. List of referral resources that interface the agency

10. Referrals initiated
    a. Frequency of referrals made (listed across the range of agencies within the social area)
    b. Problems in making referrals—including such factors as transportation, financial, language, and cultural barriers.

Identification of Need Through Analysis of Interagency Relationships— Some Further Thoughts

An analysis of the interagency relationships including the extent of collaboration among human service resources in a community is thought to be important in a comprehensive approach to need assessment. Such exploration will *(a)* uncover underutilized resources; *(b)* give an indication of how these resources are perceived and utilized by peer agencies; *(c)* determine the extent to which continuity exists, the degree of service duplication, and the extent to which there is inadequate integration within the human service network; and *(d)* identify those agencies or providers who maintain collaborative ties and who might work well in a collective effort. Suggestions for restructuring or in other ways improving services may result. This type of inquiry is probably best accomplished by site visits conducted by skilled interviewers with appropriate credentials.

The main advantages of assessing need through analysis of interagency relationships are the relatively low cost of collecting and analyzing the information and the ready availability of such information. In addition, this type of survey, which tends to increase communication between human service agencies and providers, often leads to a greater sensitivity to the needs of community residents and as a result to a more adequate integration of human services. This strategy also allows for a general inventory of community resources—information that is useful when integrating need assessment information into program planning. One particularly useful subsidiary benefit of human services resource identification is the publication and distribution of a human services information directory complete with referral procedures applicable to the network of human service providers.

The two main disadvantages to this type of need identification involve, first, the difficulty in obtaining reliable data and second, drawing conclusions about a population solely on the basis of service utilization. One must proceed with caution when attempting to estimate the needs of an entire community on the basis of information obtained from an analysis of information about a sample of persons receiving services from the community's public and private care providers. In the mental health field, for example, there is a great deal of research which suggests that there is a wide gulf between the mental health needs of a community as determined by field prevalence surveys and the number of persons receiving mental health care in the same community. Other research has shown that many residents of a community may not require new or additional mental health services, because they are receiving services from agencies or providers outside of the community. A systematic need identification and assessment program must always include data concerning (a) the extent to which identified needs are being met by resources within or outside the social area being studied, and (b) the appropriateness of reliance on external resources to meet social area needs.

Citizen Surveys: Community Residents' Perspectives on Human Service Needs

In this section, we describe three survey techniques that allow broader citizen and community participation in the identification of needs and the establishment of service priorities than those discussed to this point. Such surveys provide citizen perspectives on the nature and magnitude of service needs in the community. Either anonymous, through-the-mail, stratified random sampling or direct interview-based methods can be employed to assemble this type of information.

Through-the-mail surveys should include a random sample of people living within a geographically defined service area. The sample may be stratified by such variables as census tract, age, race, or economic status. Almost always, respondents in such surveys are anonymous.

The following types of information that were viewed as particularly relevant to mental health planning were included by Meier (1973) in a survey of residents in Contra Costa County, California: (a) community problems in order of perceived importance; (b) sources of help perceived as available for particular problems; (c) mental health problems thought most important; (d) attitudes toward utilization of a public mental health program; (e) mental health services thought most important; (f) mental health problems experienced in their own families; (g) help received for these problems; (h) satisfaction obtained from mental health services received; and (i) nomination of providers from whom one would seek help for problems of drug abuse in children and adolescents.

In some social areas face-to-face interviews with citizens have produced a better response rate and more useful information than anonymous mailed surveys. Since most surveys of this type are not particularly complex, it may be possible, without undue difficulty, to train community volunteers as interviewers (Warheit, et al., 1974). This use of community interviewers may have several secondary benefits, which include (a) involving a cadre of community people in the actual planning phase of a program; (b) educating both the interviewers and interviewees about existing or potential services; and (c) conducting the survey in an atmosphere of familiarity, which decreases interviewee's reluctance to provide survey information. Since any survey of community residents requires considerable energy and a significant amount of financial resources, a human service program should carefully contrast the advantages and disadvantages of community surveys with those of community forums as described in this article. An approach that combines some survey features with the methodology of a community forum will be described in a later section of this article.

Still another option worth consideration when planning a resident survey is the telephone approach, which yields a much higher rate of response than a mailed questionnaire. This may be a more viable technique for programs serving middle-income areas where more people have telephones than in low-income areas, although the bias of an increasing number of unlisted telephone numbers should not be overlooked. One study comparing advantages and disadvantages of mailing or telephoning a followup questionnaire on discharged hospital patients showed that approximately 85% of the patients and relatives completed the telephone interviews as compared with a 35% return of the mailed questionnaires. It was found that certain questions provoked markedly different responses when the type of interview was by mail rather than phone (Schwartz, 1973). We would expect that the differences in response to questions would not be as great when contrasting telephone with personal interviews as they would be when comparing telephone and mail techniques. Nevertheless, design characteristics of any type of survey determine to a great extent the response rate achieved with a survey strategy. Meier (1973), for example, employed a mailed questionnaire survey format that was unusually successful—both in terms of response rate and results.

There are three primary advantages in using the survey approach to need identification. According to Warheit et al. (1974), carefully designed and conducted surveys provide the most scientifically valid and reliable information obtainable regarding citizen views of their service needs and utilization patterns. It is also the most direct method of obtaining data about the needs of persons in a community. Finally it is very flexible and can be designed in an extremely wide variety of ways to answer questions related to human service needs. The value of selective use of surveys to assess in depth the specific needs of known high-risk populations cannot be overemphasized.

Disadvantages of the survey method of need identification include the following: In comparison to other methods, it tends to be more expensive. Some respondents are reluctant to offer information about themselves or other family members. Finally, the data obtained are based on self-report and are not independently verified in the typical case. A more thorough description of community survey methodology is presented in Attkisson et al., Chapter 10 [not reprinted here].

ASCERTAINING COMMUNITY VIEWS THROUGH GROUP APPROACHES

In addition to surveys, there are many different ways in which citizen and consumer views of human service needs can be ascertained. In this section, we describe four methods that are useful in undertaking a relatively quick and inexpensive assessment from the perspective of the community: (*a*) community forums, (*b*) workshops using the nominal group technique, (*c*) the Delphi technique, and (*d*) the community impressions approach.

When a human services network must conduct a community assessment rapidly, any one of the community group methods may be used independently; however, they are most usefully employed in conjunction with approaches described in previous sections of this article. Once surveys have been undertaken and social and health indicator analyses have been conducted,

community group methods can be used to gain an additional perspective on the reliability or the interpretation of the previously collected information. The more formal data collection procedures do not capture all relevant information and the data that are collected by formal data collection approaches may not provide an up-to-date portrait of the human service system in a community.

The community group methods can also be invaluable in determining which need areas among those detected during the formal data gathering have highest priority in the community. Because of disparate values and perspectives, different interest groups in a community will view certain conditions as more important than others; they will also hold varying notions as to the distribution of needs and the most appropriate approaches to interventions.

Linking survey with community group approaches is the only reliable mechanism for achieving a convergent analysis of needs and priorities—an analysis on which planning decisions can be based.

Community Forums as a Means of Needs Assessment

Any person living or working in a community is potentially an information resource on the sociological and psychological aspects of that community. Community residents either directly, through personal experience, or indirectly, through observation or study, form impressions about the human service needs in a social area. The perspectives of residents concerning the accessibility, availability, acceptability, and organization of services comprise indispensable clues about the human service needs of the community as a whole. It is unlikely that any one person has a comprehensive view of human service needs or that two people have the same view. Yet, each person's view portrays some potentially important aspect of the existing reality. In the process of integrating these various viewpoints, a useful, although impressionistic, picture of the human service needs in a community begins to emerge. The community forum represents a quick and effective method of eliciting this desired information.

A community forum is an open meeting for all members of a designated community. Its purpose is to provide a setting for members of a community to express their opinions about a particular issue—in this case the human service needs of the community. Forums resemble an old fashioned "town meeting," but can be more open and flexible. Any person attending is considered an important information resource and is encouraged to express his or her views. In general, forums last 3–4 hours and may include a wide range of activities: information exchange, communication of details about new programs or projects, introduction of various community members, and more general social interaction. The major function of the forum, however, is to elicit views from as many people as possible on a single issue. Although it is possible, the forum itself rarely involves decision making on the basis of views presented. At heart it is a means of problem identification and of obtaining citizen reaction to service efforts.

For further details on planning and carrying out community forums, see Attkisson, et al. (1978), pp. 240–241 and Cox, et al. (1984).

There are four advantages in using the community forum approach. First, community forums are, without question, quite economical in relation to other methods of need assessment. Planning for the meeting, including publicity, can be accomplished in a matter of weeks, and the forum itself may only last a few hours. The costs include the publicity, the time of any paid personnel in planning and implementing the forum and in analyzing the forum results, the time of a recording secretary, the provision of necessary transportation and child-care services to facilitate attendance of certain community members, and perhaps the rental of a meeting place. Many of these tasks may be accomplished by community volunteers.

Second, forums allow a wide range of individuals from the community to express their opinions about human service needs. Since the forum is open to all members of the community, a presentation of all important views can potentially be heard. Of particular importance is the fact that the views of those individuals who fall into the underserved or nonserved category in the community can be heard.

Third, the forum may serve as a catalyst for the initiation of plans and actions about the human service needs in the community. During the forum, those who have not previously considered the question of service needs may be stimulated to do so. As a result of interest generated by the forum, one could well expect the initiation of certain activities related to meeting human service needs.

Fourth, the forum provides those responsible for the need assessment with an opportunity not only to hear from many different elements of the community about unmet needs, but also to identify those participants and agencies most interested in doing something about them. These individuals can be invaluable in the convergent analysis phase of assessment and in developing plans to meet the needs identified.

There are also four main disadvantages to community forums. First, given a sizable forum attendance, it is unlikely that everyone who wishes to speak will have a chance to do so. Thus, certain information that could be quite relevant to the assessment of needs may never be presented.

Second, not all members of the community can or will attend a forum. Certain viewpoints about unmet human service needs may not be represented at the forum. The results of the forum provide an impressionistic and probably incomplete picture of needs.

Third, although the forum does provide an opportunity for expressing many valuable perspectives, particularly concerning need identification, it is usually the case that the discussion does not go beyond this point.

Fourth, the forum may mobilize certain elements of the community, or at least heighten the awareness of existing human service needs in the community. As a result, the expectations of community members may be raised in ways that cannot or will not be met. Organizers of the forum have a responsibility to inform attendees of realistic outcomes that may be expected from the forum and to advise participants that the process of problem identification is only the first phase of a problem-solving process.

From the advantages and disadvantages of the community forum ap-proach, it can be concluded that forums are most appropriate if there is interest in (*a*) uncovering citizen feelings and impressions about human service needs—particularly citizens who represent those groups that are underrepresented in census data and utilization rates; and (*b*) identifying directly in a public arena the concerns of citizens as well as enlisting stimulating support for planning efforts directed at those needs.

The Nominal Group Technique

A second community group approach to need identification in human services is the nominal group technique (Delbecq & Van de Ven, 1971) that is used extensively in industrial, governmental, educational, and health organizations. The nominal group technique was developed through a series of experiments over a period of 10 years by Delbecq and his colleagues, and is a model approach to problem identification and program planning (Delbecq, Van de Ven, & Gustafson, 1975). This group process method was designed for the identification of organizational problems and formulation of appropriate and innovative tactics to solve them. Following an initial problem identification and ranking process, the nominal group is a methodology for involving critical reference groups in successive phases of program planning and development: (*a*) clients (consumers) and first-line staff, in the problem exploration stage; (*b*) external resource people and internal specialists, in solution and resource exploration; (*c*) key administrators and resource controllers, in priority development; (*d*) organizational staff, in program proposal inception and development; and

(e) all constituencies, in final approval and designs for evaluation.

The usefulness of the nominal group technique is based on Delbecq and Van de Ven's research, which indicated that a nominal group—one in which individuals work in the presence of one another but initially do not interact—allows production of a greater number of problem dimensions, more high-quality suggestions, and a larger number of more highly differentiated kinds of solutions than groups in which members are encouraged or allowed to interact during the generation of critical problem variables (Delbecq & Van de Ven, 1971).

The nominal group process initially involves silent, individual effort in a group setting, with working groups limited to eight to ten individuals. Basically, the process includes posing a question or a series of questions to a group and inviting each group member to list brief responses or answers to the question during a silent period of 10–15 minutes. These questions may seek possible solutions to a particular problem or may merely seek opinions about a particular human service problem in a community. When used in human service need assessment, participants may be asked to identify their own human service needs, to list the needs they perceive for other groups in the community, or to identify important factors or issues to be considered in a community program planning process. This initial silent time spent in idea generation is followed by an interval in which all ideas generated by individuals are shared with the total group. The group leader, in round-robin fashion, asks each participant to offer one idea from his or her list. Each idea is then recorded on large sheets of paper, which are then displayed for continued review by the total group. Every effort is made to record the ideas exactly as they are offered from the participants. The leader continues the round-robin until all ideas on each participant's list are exhausted. This procedure may take from 1 to 2 hours, depending upon the type of questions posed and the number of ideas generated. During this phase, participants are asked to refrain from making comments or discussing any of the ideas, as the round-robin is for enumeration of ideas only.

Once the round-robin is completed, a discussion period follows in which participants are free to clarify, elaborate, or defend any of the ideas presented. During this discussion, participants may add new ideas to the list; they may eliminate certain ideas; they may combine ideas that seem to overlap substantially; or they may condense ideas that appear similar. One means of facilitating this process is for the leader to read one idea at a time from the list generated, to ask for discussion, comments, or questions in reference to that idea, and then to move on to the next. Participants are not required to defend or otherwise substantiate an idea.

Once the leader feels that sufficient clarification has been achieved, each participant is then asked to select those ideas (from the total list) that are considered most important. Each person selects five or more (as desired) ideas judged personally to be most important, and ranks them accordingly. These "votes" are then tallied, and the result is the group's rank ordering of those ideas generated in order of importance. In a human services need assessment, for example, individuals may be asked to rank those identified needs which are the most critical for program planning and intervention. All selection and ranking is done individually and anonymously.

The nominal group technique allows for group decision making or idea sharing without the typical competitive problems of the interacting group. Also, each participant privately expresses his or her perception of the relative importance of the many different problem areas or need areas generated by the group as a whole. The silent period in the nominal group process is critical to the production of ideas. It allows each member time for reflection and thought. It encourages the generation of minority ideas; it avoids hidden agendas; it imposes a burden on all present to work and contribute and to have a sense of responsibility for the group's success; it facilitates creativity; it allows for the airing of personal concerns; and it is especially useful in a heterogeneous group as it does not allow any one person or point of view to dominate.

By following the silent period with round-robin sharing, all ideas are shared with the group before they are discussed and each member has assurance that all of his or her ideas will be heard. In the discussion that follows, the feedback and information-sharing benefits of the interacting group are gained. The group has a chance to question and to clarify each idea presented. Other advantages accruing to the nominal group technique include social modeling of disclosure by more secure group members, which facilitates disclosure on the part of less secure members; a setting in which the pooling of resources from a heterogeneous, potentially noncollaborative group may occur; and finally, the potential for new perspectives on or cognitive remapping of "old" or existing problems.

The main disadvantage of the nominal group technique is that it lacks precision. Votes or rankings are made without thorough or careful sorting out of all of the ideas generated into appropriate categories. Another disadvantage, and quite an important one in our experience, is that although most participants enjoy the process and feel satisfied with the results, some participants may feel manipulated because they are not used to participating in a highly structured process. These disadvantages are minor and can be handled by careful planning, preparation of participants, and followup feedback to participants.

The Delphi Technique

An additional community groups approach to human service need identification is the Delphi technique (Dalkey, 1967; Dalkey & Helmer, 1963). The Delphi is a procedure for the systematic solicitation and collation of informed judgments on a particular topic (Delbecq et al., 1975). The Delphi is usually composed of a set of carefully designed sequential questionnaires. With each subsequent questionnaire, summarized information and opinion feedback derived from earlier questionnaires are provided. This summarized information is carefully organized to provide a common reference point against which the Delphi judges base their responses. The sequential questionnaires take the form of a structured dialogue between persons who do not meet, but whose opinions are valuable to the issue at hand.

This method for systematically eliciting and refining group judgments has three defining characteristics (Dalkey,

1969; Delbecq et al., 1975): (*a*) anonymous response to question or questions, (*b*) iteration or controlled feedback of various stages of the information collection process, and (*c*) statistical analysis and formulation of group responses.

First, anonymity may be ensured by the use of questionnaires or, where resources permit, on-line computer communication. Second, the Delphi exercise is conducted in a series of rounds between which a summary of the results of the previous round is distributed to each participant. Third, the form in which this controlled feedback is given is statistical, and usually consists of the group medium (Dalkey, 1967, 1969; Delbecq et al., 1975), although other less directive forms of iteration are being considered (e.g., the quantity of the individual's score).

The Delphi technique consists of five basic steps:

1. A questionnaire is developed relative to a key issue or set of issues
2. Questionnaires are distributed to a panel of experts or key individuals. Since it is not necessary and often not desirable to have these experts meet, the questionnaire can be mailed to the participants serving on the panel
3. When the questionnaires are returned, the results are tallied to determine areas of agreement and disagreement
4. When disagreement occurs, a second questionnaire containing the various reasons given by the experts for their initial judgments is distributed to the panel
5. The above steps are repeated, hopefully until an agreement can be reached

The Delphi has typically gained widest use in areas of broad- or long-range policy formulation in, for example, the U.S. Air Force and in industry for technological forecasting and evaluation of corporate planning (Helmer, 1967). Various public agencies are beginning to use the Delphi for planning exercises related to education, health, and urban growth. Although the original experiments relating to the Delphi centered around questions having definitive factual answers, the originators believe this method is appropriate in areas of "value judgment" where preset "answers" are not available.

This method of assessment has a number of possible human service applications: to determine or develop a typology of human service needs; to explore or expose underlying assumptions or information leading to different judgments as to human service needs; to correlate informed judgments on a topic spanning a wide range of social roles and/or disciplines; and to educate the respondent group as to the diverse and interrelated aspects of human service needs (Turoff, 1971).

The Delphi involves at least two separate groups of individuals. First, the user body is composed of the individual or individuals expecting some product from the exercise which is useful to their purposes. Next there is a design and monitor team, which constructs the initial questionnaire, summarizes the returns, and designs the followup questionnaires. The final group of individuals involved in a Delphi effort are the respondents. It is important to note that this latter group of persons who are chosen to respond to the questionnaires may in some cases also be the user body.

There are four advantages to the Delphi technique. First, because participation can be anonymous, the inhibiting influences of dominant and more verbal participants are minimized. Second, due to the fact that feedback is controlled in a systematic manner, the negative influences of individual vested interests are reduced to a minimum. Third, because responses are anonymous, group pressure to conform is significantly decreased. Fourth, the Delphi is an efficient user of the respondents' time. Efficiency in the use of time allows the involvement of individuals who cannot otherwise become involved in other more time-consuming procedures.

The main disadvantage of the Delphi technique is the lack of certainty in guidelines on its use or design. For example, there are a number of important questions for which general agreement does not exist among practitioners, users, and critics: (*a*) Is the respondent group completely anonymous among its own members, to the design team, or to the user body? (*b*) Should the Delphi be used in conjunction with a committee or ongoing study effort? (*c*) Should the iterations (controlled feedback) be cycled to the same respondent group, or is there a series of separate respondent groups interacting independently or parallel with one another? (*d*) How many iterations are needed? and (*e*) What form should the feedback take? A further disadvantage is that extreme positions may be dropped in order to obtain agreement and consequently many divergent, yet creative ideas may be lost. This latter disadvantage is also shared by the nominal group and other similar approaches.

A use of the Delphi at the national planning level illustrates this technique (National Institute of Drug Abuse, 1975). The Prevention Branch of the National Institute of Drug Abuse employed the Delphi process as a part of an attempt to develop "a National Strategy for Primary Drug Abuse Prevention." The project involved 420 prevention planners, administrators, and programmers from community programs, state agencies, and federal departments. The main objective was to promote the evolution of a national strategy for primary prevention that would be conceptually sound and capable of implementation. Furthermore, the effort was designed (*a*) to involve in the strategy development those federal, state and community-based practitioners who would be directly affected by it, and (*b*) to facilitate collaboration and resource sharing among the scattered advocates of primary prevention.

In order to attain these objectives, the following three tasks were proposed:

1. Development of a sound, supportable definition of primary drug abuse prevention
2. Clarification of what is being done now in prevention, as well as recommendations on the kinds of new strategies that should be implemented
3. Descriptions of the training and technical assistance resources needed at state and local levels.

The project was divided into two phases. In Phase I, a total of 70 participants were convened at three sites to address the objectives. The information generated at these sessions was then refined by 30 of the participants before and during a fourth meeting.

In Phase II, the Phase I recommendations were presented to an additional 340 prevention workers at five regional conferences. The results of the entire process were then tabulated and incorporated into a final report that included:

1. A working definition of primary drug abuse prevention
2. An exhaustive list of those activities that are now being done or should be done by preventors
3. A section devoted to training and technical assistance. This latter section describes the information and program support needs that were identified at all nine conferences.

The Community Impressions Approach

The community impressions approach was developed by Cohn and her colleagues at the School of Public Health at the University of California, Berkeley (1972). It allows for direct focus on those groups in the population that have been identified as having the greatest human service needs and is a procedure for involving those groups in subsequent planning and evaluation activities directed at establishing programs to reduce their needs. A comprehensive view of needs combines hard data with impressions and feelings about need. In this process it is very important to identify and involve those groups with the greatest human service needs in both the assessment and subsequent planning and program development activities.

The community impressions approach integrates existing data about human service needs with community impressions about such needs. First, community impressions are obtained from key individuals living or working in the community. Then, on the basis of all available sources of data (social indicator, survey and community group data) groups identified as having the greatest human service needs are approached in order to verify findings and/or to explore human service needs further. The approach has three major steps:

1. Key informant interviews. In this approach, interviews are conducted with 10 or 15 individuals who have extensive first-hand knowledge of the community and who either live or work in the community. Interviewees are selected on the basis of the longevity of their involvement in the community and/or the nature of their involvement with the community. These informants are asked to provide their perspectives on the human service needs of different groups in the community. Thus, a public health nurse, members of any community action agencies, long-time residents, a policeman or fireman, the local health officer, and others are interviewed in order to elicit their impressions. The interviews are conducted from a list of questions about the existing human services in the community and about certain demographic characteristics of the population with the aid of a map of the community under study. Answers to questions such as "Where do the elderly live?" and "What public transportation exists between different parts of the community and the local community mental health center?" are recorded on the map. Slowly, a picture of the community, from service and demographic viewpoints, begins to emerge. Typically, the interview will result in some fairly concrete statements of need. Once 10 to 15 key community members have been interviewed, their impressions are collapsed onto one map. It is highly probable that there will be some discrepancies in both information and impressions. In analyzing the discrepancies in impressions about need, the need assessor should settle the discrepancies by erring "in favor" of identifying groups as having unmet needs (i.e., if one interviewee identified a group as having many human service problems, and another interviewee identified that same group as having few, the group should be recorded at this time as having many—this will be verified with the group under question at a later date).

2. Integration of existing information. Existing data from the widest possible range of needs assessment methods are then integrated with the community impressions. Emphasis here should be on balancing efforts to integrate as much available, existing data as possible in order to move toward a convergent analysis of needs. Once enough information has been collected to satisfy the assessor's need for factual information about the community, this "hard data" should be added to the map of impressions from interviewees, thus yielding a richer understanding of the needs of the community. This combined picture should not be taken as complete, however. It should ideally be validated with relevant groups in the community.

3. The community forum. A community forum is planned and held for each group or section of the community identified as having significant unmet human service needs (see the section on community forums). One purpose of the forum is to allow those groups identified as having unmet needs to validate or invalidate those needs. In addition to validation, however, the forum serves as an opportunity to explore in greater depth the nature and perceived etiology of these needs. Moreover, the forum serves as an opportunity to involve those persons with the greatest need in the process of defining and placing priorities on those needs. In this manner, the forum helps to complete the need assessment process while initiating the process of responding to the needs identified.

The community impressions approach has a number of advantages and disadvantages. First, it can be carried out with minimal expenditure of time and resources.

Second, it allows for consideration and convergence of a variety of informational sources, both those that represent what might be regarded as "factual clues" about human service needs and those that might be regarded as "impressionistic clues" about human service needs.

Third, it relies on more than information generated by "outsiders." Those identified as having unmet human service needs have an opportunity to determine whether or not they think and feel that they do in fact have unmet needs. Additionally, these groups have an opportunity to voice opinions about better procedures for meeting their needs and to become involved in activities that may lead to reduction of those needs.

Fourth, through the discussion and interaction that characterizes this approach, channels of communication among different human service agencies in the community may be strengthened or in some cases established. As a result, a more effective, broad-based, community approach to need assessment, to the establishment of priorities, and the allocation of resources may take place.

As fruitful as the community impressions approach may be, the results insofar as possible must be subjected to the same tests of reliability and validity that are applied to the results from the various types of need assessment surveys. Typically it is found that reasonable standards of reliability and validity cannot be confirmed, and the results must be generally considered as impressionistic. Due to this problem, there is no way to ensure that every group with human service needs will be identified or that all of the needs of those identified will have been recorded. Community impressions must be considered as one perspective about needs among many others, and divergencies in perspectives must be resolved in the subsequent program planning process.

The community impressions approach is most useful when one is interested in undertaking quickly and at little cost an assessment of the unmet human service needs in different groups within the community. The approach takes into consideration the content of data from other approaches *and* also the thoughts and feelings of various community members. The approach is particularly useful if one is committed to involving those with greatest needs in processes which will help reduce their needs.

SUMMARY

Need identification and assessment are integral aspects of human service planning and development. *Need identification* is the process of describing the health and social service needs of a geographic area. In the *need assessment* process, planners set priorities on identified needs with reference to relative importance, available resources, and available service technology.

The area of need assessment-identification is in its nascence, and no universally accepted methodology exists that will yield a comprehensive assessment of need. Moreover, the evaluation and interpretation of human service need is influenced by (*a*) the vested interests and values of those formulating program goals; (*b*) the diffuse and interrelated nature of social and health needs; (*c*) the rapidly changing character of human service needs; and (*d*) the capabilities and interests of staff as well as the availability of appropriate service technology and adequate financing.

Within the limits of current assessment methodologies, information about needs is useful in (*a*) describing demands for services; (*b*) assessing service resources; (*c*) developing detailed community descriptions; (*d*) delineating groups likely "to be at risk"; (*e*) examining the relevance of existing services; (*f*) clarifying those factors that influence the occurrence of social and health problems; and (*g*) enumerating factors that aid or impede effective service delivery.

The most comprehensive picture of human service need can be obtained through a convergent analysis of need. Convergent analysis assumes that useful information about need emerges out of a process that receives input (*a*) at different, although sequential points in time; (*b*) from a number of different organizational levels; (*c*) from a variety of informational sources (community members, public records, service agency data, professional staff); and (*d*) through a family of assessment strategies. Further assumptions basic to a convergent analysis are that no single stakeholder, no one informational source, no single organizational level, no specific technique, and no single point in time will provide a comprehensive human service need assessment. It is only through the systematic, progressive convergence of multiple perspectives filtered through multiple assessment methods that the most useful information for planning is obtained. A convergent analysis identifies the widest range of need information that is relevant for program planning and service development by assessing need at all community and organizational levels.

The variety of assessment strategies used in a convergent analysis provides three different informational functions: (a) *compiling* existing information; (b) *developing* new information; and (c) *integrating* existing and newly developed information. There are advantages and disadvantages of each need assessment strategy when viewed in isolation. However, when seen as part of a total convergence of information, deployment of a range of methods provides the basis for an integrated perspective on need.

There are three basic orientations to assessing human service need: (a) the social and health indicators approach; (b) social area surveys; and (c) the community groups approaches. The *social and health indicator approach* to need assessment compiles publicly available information, and, on the basis of these data, needs are inferred. *Social area surveys* compile and integrate information about demands for service; provide information about resources that are currently available to meet the needs of the community; and provide

citizens' views about needs and need priorities. In addition, new information can be generated on a personal self-report level from community members through direct interview surveys. Finally, the *community group approaches* to assessment are quick and inexpensive methods to use in conjunction with other assessment techniques. The group methods provide perspectives from community members by developing new information, compiling already existing information, and integrating existing information with the perspectives of persons living in the community.

REFERENCES

Attkisson, C. C., Hargreaves, W. A., Horowitz, M. J., & Sorenson, J. E. (Eds.). *Evaluation of human service programs.* New York: Academic Press, Inc., 1978.

Beigel, A., Hunter, E. J., Tamerin, J. S., Chapin, E. H., & Lowery, M. J. Planning for the development of comprehensive community alcoholism services: I. The prevalence survey. *American Journal of Psychiatry,* 1974, *131,* 1112–1115.

Beigel, A., McCabe, T. R., Tamerin, J. S., Lowery, M. J., Chapin, E. H., & Hunter, E. J. Planning for the development of comprehensive community alcoholism services: II. Assessing community awareness and attitudes. *American Journal of Psychiatry,* 1974, *131,* 1116–1120.

Bloom, B. L. *Changing patterns of psychiatric care.* New York: Human Sciences Press, 1975.

Blum, H. L. *Planning for health.* New York: Human Sciences Press, 1974.

Broskowski, A., & Baker, F. Professional, organizational, and social barriers to primary prevention. *American Journal of Orthopsychiatry,* 1974, *44,* 707–719.

Campbell, D. T., & Fiske, D. W. Convergent and discriminant validation by the multitrait-multimethod matrix. *Psychological Bulletin,* 1959, *56,* 81–105.

Cohn, A. H. *Solutions to unique problems encountered in identifying the medically underserved and involving them in the planning process.* Unpublished manuscript, School of Public Health, University of California, Berkeley, California, 1972.

Cox, F. M., Erlich, J. L., Rothman, J., & Tropman, J. E. (Eds.). *Tactics and techniques of community practice,* 2nd ed. Itasca, Illinois: F. E. Peacock Publishers, Inc., 1984.

Dalkey, N. C. *Delphi.* Santa Monica, California: Rand Corporation, 1967.

Dalkey, N. C. *The Delphi method: An experimental study of group opinion.* Santa Monica, California: Rand Corporation, 1969.

Dalkey, N. C., & Helmer, O. An experimental application of the Delphi method to the use of experts. *Management Science,* 1963, *9,* 458–467.

Delbecq, A. L., & Van de Ven, A. H. A group process model for problem identification and program planning. *Journal of Applied Behavioral Science,* 1971, *7,* 466–492.

Delbecq, A. L., Van de Ven, A. H., & Gustafson, D. H. *Group techniques for program planning: A guide to nominal group and Delphi processes.* Glenview, Illinois: Scott, Foresman & Company, 1975.

Demone, H. W., & Harshbarger, D. (Eds.). *A handbook of human service organizations.* New York: Behavioral Publications, 1974.

Feldstein, P. J. Research on the demand for health services. In J. B. McKinlay (Ed.), *Economic aspects of health care.* New York: Prodist, Milbank Memorial Fund, 1973.

Goldsmith, H. F., Unger, E. L., Rosen, B. M., Shambaugh, J. P., & Windle, C. D. *A typological approach to doing social area analysis.* (DHEW Publication No. ADM 76-262.) Washington, D. C.: U.S. Government Printing Office, 1975.

Helmer, O. *Analysis of the future: The Delphi method.* Santa Monica, California: Rand Corporation, 1967.

Meier, R. *Contra Costa mental health needs.* Unpublished manuscript, Contra Costa County Mental Health Services, Martinez, California, 1973.

National Institute of Drug Abuse, Prevention Branch, Division of Resource Development. *Pyramid,* 1975, *1,* 1–2. (Available from: NIDA, 1526 18th Street, N.W., Washington, D.C. 20036.)

Robin, S. A procedure for securing returns to mail questionnaires. *Sociology and Social Research,* 1965, *50,* 24–35.

Schaefer, M. E. Demand versus need for medical services in a general cost-benefit setting. *American Journal of Public Health,* 1975, *65,* 293–295.

Schulberg, H. C., & Wechsler, H. The uses and misuses of data in assessing mental health needs. *Community Mental Health Journal,* 1967, *3,* 389–395.

Schwartz, R. Follow-up by phone or by mail. *Evaluation,* 1973, *1*(2), 25–26.

Sheldon, E. B., & Parke, R. Social indicators. *Science,* 1975, *188,* 693–699.

Siegel, L. M., Attkisson, C. C., & Cohn, A. H. Mental health needs assessment: Strategies and techniques. In W. A. Hargreaves, C. C. Attkisson, & J. E. Sorensen (Eds.), *Resource materials for community mental health program evaluation* (2nd ed.). (DHEW Publication No. ADM 77-328.) Washington, D.C.: U.S. Government Printing Office, 1977.

Turoff, M. Delphi and its potential impact on information systems. *AFIPS Conference Proceedings,* 1971, *39,* 317–326.

Warheit, G. J., Bell, R. A., & Schwab, J. J. *Planning for change: Needs assessment approaches.* Rockville, Maryland: National Institute of Mental Health, 1974.

4.

Joseph Katan and Shimon E. Spiro

THE KNOWLEDGE BASE OF PLANNED CHANGE IN ORGANIZATIONS AND COMMUNITIES

INTRODUCTION

The profession of social work has occasionally been described as being long on values and commitment and short on scientific knowledge. This may explain the somewhat precarious status of social work among the professions, its occasional treatment as a "semi-profession" (Toren, 1969), and the tendency of social workers to be preoccupied with the status and the knowledge base of their profession.

It is our purpose to explore, in this paper, the knowledge base of one specific area of social work practice, i.e., the initiation of planned change in communities and organizations. Planned change will be defined broadly, as any initiative designed to alter the structure of positions and roles, or patterns of activity, within a community or an organization. This may include the initiation of new program activities, the formation of new groups, facilitating the flow of communication, or any activity affecting the distribution of knowledge, resources, power, and authority among individuals and groups.

Commitment to change is one of the main tenets of the social work profession. The literature provides ample evidence of the involvement of social workers in projects designed to change organizations and communities. Community workers are engaged in the development of new welfare services, in efforts to change attitudes of residents toward their neighborhood, in the establishment of interorganizational linkage among welfare agencies, etc. Social workers employed as executives or administrators in human service organizations (HSO's) are engaged in tasks such as: adopting new treatment technologies, changing workers' attitudes toward clients, modifying organizational procedures and rules, developing new services or abolishing existing ones. Not only executives, but front-line and middle level workers as well, are involved in the initiation, adoption, development and implementation of change programs.

In practice, the outcomes of professional efforts are not always consistent with an ideology of change. Wittingly or unwittingly social workers are often found to contribute to the maintenance of the status quo in organizations and communities. Their change efforts are occasionally half-hearted, and often frustrated. But the planned change of organizations and communities is still an accepted goal of professional practice. Hence the importance of examining the knowledge on which it is founded, and from which it derives guidelines for practice.

Source: This article was written expressly for this volume, reproduced by permission of the authors.

SOURCES OF KNOWLEDGE

All social and behavioral sciences share an interest in change. *Psychologists,* for instance, have studied the personality traits characterizing creative and nonconformist individuals capable of initiating or adopting changes, even if these changes are incongruent with the social norms and patterns predominant in their social circles. Among other issues concerning change, *social psychologists* have dealt extensively with the effects of group norms on the attitudes and behavior of their members and examined the conditions under which groups may initiate new ideas and contribute to their adoption and implementation, or, contrarily, resist changes and prevent their adoption. Especially, *community psychologists* have devoted their attention to factors affecting the participation of individuals in organizations, networks and political action. *Sociological and anthropological* studies have embraced a wide range of subjects relating to changes in communities and organizations. To name a few of them: the contextual and structural attributes of the change-producing and the change-resisting organization, the effect of environmental contingencies on organizational changes, social and demographic attributes of workers and their effect on attitudes toward change, the generation and adoption of changes in communities and their linkage to various community characteristics, and the role of social networks as channels for the diffusion of changes. *Political scientists* and *sociologists* have examined the power and decision-making structures of communities and their impact on capability for generating or adopting changes and implementing them. Economic models of organizational and community change offered by *economists* and *sociologists* have focused the attention on market conditions, availability of resources and organizational slack as possible predictors of change. Various rational and systematic techniques of developing, planning and implementing change programs have been proposed in the *management* literature. The vital function played by the court system in spurring and even obliging HSO's to change their policies and patterns of activity has drawn attention to the discipline of *law* as another source of knowledge and information that may be used by practitioners engaged in planned change.

The foregoing discussion might leave the impression that *social work* knowledge relevant to issues of planned change in organizations and communities is derived entirely from other disciplines. This is definitely not the case. Recent decades have seen the emergence of a body of knowledge which in some respects is specific to social workers operating in the fields of community organization, administration, and policy. This body of knowledge is still relatively underdeveloped and uncrystallized. Much of it goes under different headings such as "planned change" (Mayer, 1972), "community organization" (Perlman & Gurin, 1972), "community development" (Goetschius, 1971, Kramer, 1970), "community organizing" (Brager & Specht, 1973), "changing human service organizations" (Brager and Holloway, 1978), and "neighborhood work" (Henderson and Thomas, 1980). Still, there seems to emerge some coherence in terms of questions asked relative to planned intervention in social organization, which are:

1. The goals and underlying values of planned change.
2. Assumptions about the nature of social organizations which guide planned intervention.
3. The roles of change agents.
4. The strategies and tactics of planned intervention and their outcomes.

However, like other applied disciplines such as engineering and medicine, social work has to draw on the basic social sciences for an understanding of the phenomena with which it deals and the settings in which it operates. These sources provide knowledge and information on the various units or systems relevant to planned change: individuals, small groups, social networks, informal and formal organizations, local communities, social groupings, networks of organizations, etc. All of these figure in practice as actors, targets of change, or contexts of action.

TYPES OF CONTRIBUTION

What are the contributions of these various disciplines to the understanding of the relevant systems involved in the process of planned change and to the specification of possible interventions and their expected outcomes? Elaborating on Thomas (1967) we see the social and behavioral sciences providing practitioners operating as change agents with concepts, hypotheses, theories (or models), bits of information, methodological approaches, a general scientific stance, and specific guidelines for practice.

Concepts

Many of the concepts used by practitioners have been elaborated and clari-

fied (or, occasionally, obscured) through the work of social and behavioral scientists. These include the distinction between the various stages of planned change (the initiation and generation of change, the development of a change program, its diffusion, adoption, implementation, and institutionalization), as well as concepts such as: resistance to change, creative organizations, resources mobilization, diffusion of innovation, cooptation, etc. These concepts compose a common terminology shared by social scientists and human service practitioners.

Hypotheses

The literature in a variety of fields is abundant with studies that have examined specific hypotheses dealing with the association between change and a wide range of variables. Many of these hypotheses can be of relevance to practice even when not imbedded in more complex theories or models.

Following are some of the variables that have been tested as correlates of the ability of organizations to initiate, plan, implement, or adopt change. First, internal organizational characteristics such as size, age, formalization, differentiation, specialization, goals, ideology, internal power structure, centralization, worker participation, availability of resources, and type of technology (Mansfield, 1963; Hage and Aiken, 1967; Mohr, 1969; Delbecq and Pierce, 1978; Hasenfeld, 1980, 1983; Zaltman, Duncan & Holbek, 1973; Meyer, 1982, Bullock and Stewart, 1984). Second, environmental characteristics such as market condition, the composition of the organizational set, and the stability of the environment (Mohr, 1969; Hasenfeld, 1971, 1980, 1983). Third, characteristics of individuals such as attitudes toward change, and personal, social and demographic attributes (Hage and Dewar, 1973, Pierce and Delbecq, 1977). Fourth, attributes of the change program itself such as its radicalness, i.e., the degree to which it is costly and requires significant organizational changes (Hasenfeld, 1983), its congruence with the organization's main goals, ideology, structure, and procedures, and its degree of contribution to organizational survival and maintenance (Kemp, 1981, Bullock and Stewart 1984).

Various studies have tested hypotheses relating to conditions effecting changes in communities. In this context we will mention three of them: Turk's study (1970) on the association between a community's local and extralocal integration and its capability of adopting new programs; and Aiken and Alford's (1970) and Smith's (1979) studies on the association between the characteristics of a community's structure and its capacity to deal with new issues, and to develop programs and implement them. Not less important are studies of the variables affecting participation in neighborhood groups and community affairs (Wandersman, 1981).

Theories or Models

Occasionally, practice is guided or at least informed by theories or models purporting to explain conditions in organizations and communities effecting changes and to predict the outcomes of these changes. Field theory (Lewin, 1951) as well as system and contingency theories (Katz and Kahn, 1966, Lawrence and Lorsch, 1967), symbolic interaction theory (Blumer, 1969), conflict theories (Dahrendorf, 1959; Rex, 1961), the political economy perspective (Zald, 1970), the distinction between organic and mechanistic organizations (Burns and Stalker, 1961), and the social movements approach (Zald and McCarthy, 1977) may be used as examples of these theories.

Possibly one of the best known concrete examples of a theory that has guided planned change programs in a community context was Cloward and Ohlin's theory of delinquency which for better or worse served as the theoretical underpinning for "Mobilization for Youth" (Moynihan, 1969). This may be an example of a not-too-common situation where a complex theory is directly applied to an ambitious program designed to affect a major social problem.

Information

In addition to tested hypotheses, the social and behavioral sciences provide practitioners with information which may or may not be related to theories or hypotheses. Such "mere facts" may, however, shape the working hypotheses guiding professional practice. One example of this kind of information is the amount and degree of change occurring in organizations facing turbulent environments (Goldberg, 1976, cited in Brager and Holloway, 1978).

Methods and Tools

Some of the most important contributions of the social and behavioral sciences to practice are methodological. As part of their work, practitioners involved in one way or another in the development and implementation of planned change in communities and organizations have to gain entry into organizations, groups and subcultures, to get to know their structure, to evaluate the relative costs and benefits of proposed changes, and to engage in a variety of other activities for which social and behavioral scientists from different disciplines have developed specific methods and tools. Recently, there is also a strong emphasis on the utilization of research techniques used by social and behavioral scientists as parts of the intervention process itself (Mutschler, 1984). No less important for practitioners is the acquisition of a generalized scientific stance, namely, the willingness and ability to question pat answers and easy explanations, and to search for hard evidence and attempt to evaluate it objectively.

Strategies and Guidelines for Practice

The social and behavioral sciences have dealt extensively with different facets of the issue of change in organizations and communities and, as we have shown, provided concepts, theories, hypotheses, information, and methods. For these to be useful, their practice implications need to be made explicit. As we shall argue below, this is to a large extent dependent on a variety of mechanisms which link the knowledge base to practice. However, the social and behavioral sciences themselves provide some orientations to strategies of change, as for example, when Johnson, Frazier, and Riddick (1983) suggest four types of strategies of planned change: (1) problem solving, (2) social interaction, (3) power coercion, and (4) research, development, and diffusion.

At a still lower level of abstraction social scientists provide practitioners with specific and sometimes very detailed "action guidelines" and instructions concerning practical issues such as how to assess community needs and plan programs designed to meet them, or how to convince organizations and communities to adopt and implement innovations. Some of these techniques and action guidelines are directly derived from empirical studies, such as the propositions for practice included in the works of Rogers and Shoemaker (1971) on the diffusion and communication of innovations; Bennis, Benne, Chin, and Corey (1976) and Havelock (1969) on the planning of change; Rothman (1974) and Rothman and his associates (1976, 1977, 1978) on planning and organizing for social change in communities and organizations; and Brager and Holloway (1978) on changing human service organizations. Other implications for practice which relate mainly to decision making and planning methods and procedures in organizations and communities are mainly based on the management literature, and include specific techniques such as O.D., P.E.R.T, the Gantt system, Adelphi, etc. (Golombiewski and Eddy 1978, Lauffer, 1978).

THE PROBLEM OF LINKAGES

In our discussion so far we have pointed to types of knowledge relevant to practice, and to the possible sources of such knowledge in the social and behavioral sciences. The link between the two is, however, problematic. Thomas (1967) has suggested a number of criteria to be used in selecting knowledge for application. These include considerations of validity and predictive potency, as well as the identifiability, accessibility, and manipulability of empirical referents.

Since much of social science knowledge is not produced with usefulness to practice as a main motive (Gouldner, 1957), issues of potency, referent, accessibility, and manipulability have not been the central concern of most scientists. Furthermore, these dimensions are mostly not self-evident, and require specific judgment by potential users. On top of all this, there is the problem of accessibility: how is a practitioner engaged in planned change to know of possibly relevant and usable knowledge scattered through numerous journals and books?

One could suggest a number of different answers to the problem of the practitioner's access to relevant knowledge. Professional education for the human service professions always includes a significant input from the social and behavioral sciences. Thus, practitioners trained in schools of social work get, as part of their training, basic or specific courses in sociology, psychology, political science, and other disciplines (Gurin, 1970). The main problem with transmission of social science knowledge to practitioners as part of their basic professional education is its being a one-shot affair. At best the knowledge thus transmitted reflects the "state of art" in the relevant disciplines at a given point in time. It does not provide the practitioner with continuing access to developments in the social science disciplines. Continuous linkage could theoretically be achieved through appropriate continuing education programs, but, at this stage of development, in most countries, these provide only a partial solution to our problem. This, in itself, does not detract from the importance for practitioners of a basic training in the social and behavioral sciences. On the contrary, only through internalization of basic ideas and key concepts, and the acquisition of the "scientific stance" and some basic methodology, can practitioners understand, evaluate and possibly utilize more specific contributions.

Professional supervision or guidance may also play an important role in creating linkages between knowledge and practice. However, often supervisors have completed their professional education long ago, and many of them may have been less exposed to new developments in the behavioral and social sciences than their supervisees.

Another possible channel for ongoing transmission of knowledge from the social sciences to the practitioners could be through current professional literature. However, a recent study reports that practitioners rarely read professional literature which reports research findings (Gordon, 1984). A possible reason for this may be the workers' inability to perceive the specific uses of research for their practice. One way to overcome this situation is to equip students, during their professional training, and later in continuing education programs, with skills that will enable and help them to derive practice applications from research reports relevant to their area of practice. Thus, the capability of drawing practice application from social and behavioral sciences research can be seen as a learnable skill (ibid.). Not less important is the involvement of social and behavioral scientists in efforts to translate knowledge into practice. Of special relevance are recent developments in the methodology of meta-analysis (Glass, et al. 1981), which give practitioners access to syntheses of numerous studies with other conflicting findings. Even more directly relevant are efforts, akin to R & D (research and development) in engineering, to collect, evaluate, and abstract contributions from the social sciences and draw out their major implications for practice. Thus Rothman, et al. (1975, 1976, 1977, 1978) reviewed close to a thousand studies from the relevant disciplines, drew from them hundreds of key propositions and their corollaries, tried to evaluate the power of the knowledge thus acquired, and pointed to the implications of the propositions for practice. In an advanced stage of their work, they trained a group of senior community workers employed in various human service organizations (HSO's), community mental health centers, family service agencies, schools, courts, planning councils, etc. to apply propositions relating to the introduction of changes into organizations. They followed the implementation process and, based on the field experience composed a working manual with action guidelines for the use of practitioners. The value of an undertaking of this sort is not only in the knowledge retrieved and made available to practitioners, but in the systematic examination and evaluation of that knowledge, leading to the identification of gaps, inconsistencies, and difficulties in operationalization and application.

So far, attempts to collect, codify, and digest knowledge from the social and behavioral sciences and present their consequences for practice have been costly and cumbersome and, consequently, sporadic. The introduction of more flexible mechanisms for the retrieval and codification of social science knowledge relevant to practice remains a task for the future. This again may serve to underline the importance of a broad education in the basic concepts and ideas of the relevant disciplines.

THE DYNAMICS OF
THE KNOWLEDGE BASE

Finally, we should like to draw attention to the dynamics of the knowledge base. Social work practice dealing with organizations and communities is constantly in flux. There is little similarity between community organization for social welfare as practiced in the 1950s, the community action movements of the 1960s (Grosser 1976) and the emphasis on neighborhood coalitions in the 1970s and early 1980s (Warren and Warren, 1977). Administration and policy as relatively young areas of practice in social work are undergoing a continuous process of development. Our arguments, however, are presented here at a level of generality which make them equally valid (or invalid) for different times and places. Thus we have to remind ourselves that the knowledge base of any profession has to be relevant to practice as it is at any given point in time. This may be more a matter of shifting emphasis than of changing boundaries. One would expect conceptions of professional roles, settings of practice, and ideological orientation to affect the selection of concepts, hypotheses, and methodological approaches. On the other hand, knowledge available for practice is, at any given time, affected by the current "state of the art" in the relevant disciplines. The knowledge base of practice is determined through the interplay between these various factors. An ongoing, free and open interaction between the field, social work academia, and the relevant social science disciplines may enhance mutual adaptation between the knowledge base, current practice, and changing social condition and needs.

REFERENCES

Aiken, M., and R. Alford. "Community Structure and Innovation." *American Sociological Review,* 35(1970):650–665.
Bennis, W. G., K. D. Benne, R. Chin, and K. Corey, eds. *Planning of Change.* 3rd ed.

New York: Holt, Rinehart & Winston, 1976.

Blumer, H. *Symbolic Interaction: Perspective and Method.* Englewood Cliffs, NJ: Prentice-Hall, 1969.

Brager, G., and S. Holloway. *Changing Human Service Organizations: Politics and Practice.* New York: Free Press, 1978.

Bullock, C. S., and J. Stewart. "New Programs in Old Agencies." *Administration and Society,* 15(1984):387–412.

Burns, T., and G. M. Stalker. *The Management of Innovation.* London: Tavistock, 1961.

Dahrendorf, R. *Class and Class Conflict in Industrial Society.* Stanford, CA: Stanford University Press, 1959.

Delbecq, A. L., and J. L. Pierce. "Innovation in Professional Organizations." *Administration in Social Work,* 2(1978): 411–424.

Glass, G. V., P. McGow, and M. L. Smith. *Meta-Analysis in Social Research.* Beverly Hills: Sage Publications, 1981.

Goetschuis, E. *Working with Community Groups.* London: Routledge and Kegan Paul, 1971.

Golombewski, R. T., and W. B. Eddy. *Organization Development in Public Administration.* New York: Marcel Dekker, 1978.

Gordon, J. E. "Creating Research-Based Practice Principles: A Model." *Social Work Research & Abstracts,* 20(1984): 3–6.

Gouldner, A. W. "Theoretical Requirements of the Applied Social Sciences." *American Sociological Review,* 22(1957): 92–103.

Grosser, C. F. *New Directions in Community Organization.* New York: Praeger, 1976.

Gurin, A. *Community Organization Curriculum in Graduate Social Work Education.* New York: Council on Social Work Education, 1970.

Hage, J., and M. Aiken. "Program Change and Organizational Properties." *American Journal of Sociology,* 72(1967):503–519.

Hage, J., and M. Aiken. *Social Change in Complex Organizations.* New York: Random House, 1970.

Hage, J., and R. Dewar. "Elite Values versus Organizational Structure in Predicting Innovation." *Administrative Science Quarterly,* 18(1973):279–290.

Hasenfeld, Y. "Organizational Dilemmas in Innovating Social Services: The Case of Community Action Centers." *Journal of Health and Social Behavior,* 12(1971): 208–216.

Hasenfeld, Y. "Implementation of Change in Human Services Organization: A Political Economy Perspective." *Social Service Review,* 54(1980):508–520.

Hasenfeld, Y. *Human Service Organizations.* Englewood Cliffs, NJ: Prentice-Hall, 1983.

Havelock, R. G. *Planning for Innovation through Dissemination of Knowledge.* Ann Arbor: University of Michigan, Institute for Social Research, 1969.

Henderson, R., and D. Thomas. *Skills in Neighborhood Work.* London: George Allen and Unwin, 1980.

Katz, D., and R. Kahn. *The Social Psychology of Organizations.* New York: Wiley, 1966.

Kemp, K. A. "Innovations in Human Services Organizations." *The Journal of Applied Social Science,* 5(1981): 100–112.

Kramer, R. *Participation of the Poor.* Englewood Cliffs, NJ: Prentice-Hall, 1969.

Kramer, R. *Community Development in Israel and the Netherlands.* Berkeley: Institute of International Studies, University of California, 1970.

Johnson, K. W., W. D. Frazier, and M. F. Riddick. "A Change Strategy for Linking the Worlds of Academia and Practice." *The Journal of Applied Behavioral Sciences,* 19(1983):439–451.

Lauffer, A. *Social Planning at the Community Level.* Englewood Cliffs, NJ: Prentice-Hall, 1978.

Lawrence, P. R., and J. W. Lorsch. *Organization and Environment.* Cambridge: Harvard Graduate School of Business Administration, 1967.

Lewin, K. *Field Theory in Social Science.* London: Tavistock, 1951.

Mayer, R. R. *Social Planning and Social Change.* Englewood Cliffs, NJ: Prentice-Hall, 1982.

Meyer, A. D. "How Ideologies Supplant Formal Structures and Shape Responses to Environments." *Journal of Management Studies,* 19(1982):45–61.

Mohr, L. "Determinants of Innovations in Organizations." *American Political Science Review,* 63(1969):111–126.

Moynihan, D. P. *Maximum Feasible Misunderstanding*. New York: Free Press, 1969.

Mutschler, E. "Evaluating Practice: A Study of Research Utilization by Practitioners." *Social Work,* 29(1984): 332–337.

Perlman, R., and A. Gurin. *Community Organization and Social Planning*. New York: Wiley, 1972.

Pierce, J. L., and A. L. Delbecq. "Organizational Structure, Individual Attitudes and Innovation." *Academy of Management Review,* 2(1972):27–37.

Rex, J. *Key Problems in Sociological Theory.* London: Routledge and Kegan Paul, 1961.

Rogers, E. E., and F. Shoemaker. *Communications of Innovations: A Cross Cultural Approach*. 2nd ed. New York: Free Press, 1971.

Rothman, J. *Planning and Organizing for Social Change*. New York: Columbia University Press, 1974.

Rothman, J. *Social R & D: Research and Development in the Human Services*. Englewood Cliffs, NJ: Prentice-Hall, 1980.

Rothman, J., J. L. Erlich, and J. G. Teresa. *Promoting Innovation and Change in Organizations and Communities*. New York: Wiley, 1976.

Smith, R. "Decision Making and Nondecision Making in Cities: Some Implications for Community Structural Re-

search." *American Sociological Review,* 44(1979):141–161.

Thomas, E. *Behavioral Science for Social Workers*. New York: Free Press, 1967, pp. 3–13.

Toren, N. "Semi-Professionalism and Social Work." In Amitai Etzioni, ed., *The Semi-Professions and Their Organization*. New York: Free Press, 1969, pp. 141–195.

Turk, H. "Interorganizational Networks in Urban Society." *American Sociological Review,* 35(1970):1–19.

Wandersman, A. "A Framework for Participation in Community Organizations." *Journal of Applied Behavioral Science,* 17(1)(1981):25–58.

Warren, R., and D. I. Warren. *The Neighborhood Organizers Handbook*. Notre Dame, IN: University of Notre Dame Press, 1977.

Zald, M. N. "Political Economy: A Framework for Comparative Analyses." In M. N. Zald, ed., *Power in Organizations*. Nashville, TN: Vanderbilt University Press, 1970.

Zald, M., and J. D. McCarthy, eds., *The Dynamics of Social Movements: Resources, Mobilization, Social Control and Justice*. Cambridge, MA: Winthrop Publishers, 1979.

Zaltman, G., R. Duncan, and J. Holbek. *Innovations and Organizations*. New York: Wiley, 1973.

5.

Nancy Amidei

HOW TO BE AN ADVOCATE IN BAD TIMES

It may seem arrogant to nominate something as "worst consequence" of the disastrous budget and policy decisions of 1981, but I have a candidate: it is paralysis. The changes adopted in just

Source: Reprinted with permission from *Public Welfare,* Vol. 40, No. 3. Copyright 1982 by the American Public Welfare Association.

one year by the Congress were so complex and so sweeping that many people who are normally active in working to influence public policy simply gave up. Concerned people all across the country saw programs they had spent their entire professional lives working on disappear in a matter of weeks; fights they had won twenty years ago were suddenly having to be fought again. They talked of being "overwhelmed," of being so depressed they could not decide where to start, of feeling that what was happening was too big for any individual to tackle. The speed, complexity, and enormity of what happened had paralyzed them. That was understandable—but a year of paralysis is enough.

This article is addressed to those who are concerned about what has happened and is still happening. All of us in this category have been going through culture shock since we woke up and found ourselves in a country where no one seemed to share our values. But it is time to learn how to act in our new surroundings.

In order to help get ourselves back in gear, I have developed an action plan. The plan has evolved as I have worked with various groups throughout the country. As people respond to it and make suggestions, the plan changes. So it is a very dynamic thing, adaptable to many kinds of situations. The plan certainly is not intended as a strict prescription, but rather as a set of strategies that can—and should—be adapted to local circumstances. Taken together, each step builds on the one before.

Before getting into particulars, it helps to recognize that political change always occurs within some kind of context, never in a vacuum. Congress follows the public. That is worth remembering as we think about the many vital programs now under attack. "We" did not somehow "put one over" on the Congress and the public in getting them enacted. There are Medicaid, Medicare, environmental standards, food stamps, and civil rights laws because within the last thirty years a consensus was developed—often after years of protest and hard work—and the Congress followed.

Moreover, broad issues of social responsibility—like hunger, access for the handicapped, nursing home standards, food and drug safety, protection of the environment, employment policy, mental health—all cut across class lines even though they affect the poor most directly (just because poor people have no other recourse when public services are no longer available). Social security, for example, is our premier weapon in the fight to prevent poverty among the elderly, but it benefits people of all classes and draws much of its political support from that fact. The national climate that produced existing social legislation was one in which elected officials saw a broad base of support for their actions.

Now we find ourselves in a different situation. In the new political environment, many people in public life believe that endorsement of tax-supported social programs is a one-way street to defeat. Members of Congress fear they will lose their seats if they support these programs and the budgets they require. But the reverse is not true: they do not expect to win or hold a seat because they *do* support them. Supporting social programs strikes many people in political life today as all risk and little or no gain—a fact that makes all the more impressive the many individual votes cast in *favor* of social programs in 1981 and 1982.

If we mean to get a different result from this or any other Congress on issues that we care about, we have to convince enough members of Congress that votes *against* issues that matter to us could cost them their seats, and that votes *for* these issues will put or keep them in office—just as surely as votes on tax relief or foreign policy. This action plan offers one approach that could lead to different results in the budget debates and elections yet to come.

FORM "TRUTH SQUADS"

The biggest obstacle to better social policies is the pervasive public misunderstanding of benefits, services, and the people who depend on them. We are constantly on the defensive, fighting battles against myths about "welfare queens" and public hostility toward what are regarded as giveaways. The president has complained in public about parents with "incomes in six figures" whose children get food stamps just because they are in college. It does not seem to trouble him, or anyone else who makes the same complaint, that students were virtually eliminated from the food stamp program by amendments adopted in 1977. In 1982 students are just two-tenths of one percent of all food stamp users, but the myths—and the hostility—persist.

Wild charges appear in newspapers, small and large, and are repeated by ill-informed people on radio talk shows. These charges get the stamp of truth when television news programs and newspapers present information inaccurately or in ways that reflect public prejudices. The background graphic for a recent network news item on aid to families with dependent children (AFDC), for example, showed a line of able-bodied young men, though women and children are virtually the only recipients of AFDC.

We can do something to solve this problem, but it means setting out deliberately to change public attitudes toward public programs and the people who ben-

efit from them. That will require a conscious effort to set the record straight whenever misinformation about social programs or those who depend on them appears; it means joining with others to form "truth squads" of people who view winning a better understanding of social programs as part of their civic or professional responsibility.

First, concerned people, armed with good information, need to divide up the media in their states and communities, and use information at their command to present a more accurate picture of public benefits and those who use them.

After identifying the newspapers, television news shows, and radio call-in shows (including those disc jockeys who encourage listeners to call in) in the area, the group should decide who will monitor which media. It would work like this: If you are usually driving home from work between 5:30 and 6:00 p.m. and there is a radio call-in show during that time, that can be your assignment. If you hear a caller denounce a social program or base a comment on misinformation, it is your job to call that show as soon as you get home (you can put your car keys down, but nothing else) and set the record straight. If you are not the right expert but think the caller was mistaken, it is your task to quickly alert another member of the truth squad who can respond knowledgeably.

The same thing applies to newspapers. If you have agreed to monitor a local newspaper's coverage of public programs and something misleading or incorrect appears, then you are responsible for writing a letter to the editor or an "op ed" piece, calling the editor, or finding another member of the truth squad who will. You will not always get into print, but a point will be made with the editors all the same. Think what an impact it makes whenever statistics used by the president are shown to be incorrect. Then consider the impact if, each time someone in public office "misspoke," newspapers and local television or radio news shows all across the country had access to information called in by local people demonstrating how the official was wrong. Television news shows will not allow you to air your views on the show, but producers tend to be sensitive to carefully documented charges of inaccuracy. If they get the sense that their shows are viewed as inaccurate or prejudiced, they will take note; and the responsible shows will improve the quality of their coverage.

Doing nothing is more damaging than most people realize. Misinformation that goes unchallenged becomes accepted; it often accounts for why elected officials vote as they do. We need to create a climate that reflects the realities rather than misperceptions. Truth squads will help create the climate necessary for responsible social policy.

UNDERSTAND HOW POLITICAL POWER WORKS AND USE IT

If you want to wield power in the political arena (federal, state, or local), there are six ways you can do it:

- contribute money to political campaigns;
- mobilize voters;
- gain access to the media;
- have public sympathy on your side;
- cultivate a link with a credible "establishment;" and
- develop the ability to embarrass.

Using this as a kind of check list, it is easy to determine the political leverage you can muster for your particular issues, whether it is mental health centers, welfare benefits, protective services, runaway shelters, or food stamps. Issues with several of these factors working for them tend to get favorable attention. Compare how the oil industry and food stamp users fare on the check list, and you will see the point. The oil industry can count on four or more of these factors working in their favor at any given time: money for campaigns; voters; almost unlimited access to the media—including full-page ads to tell the public how poor they are; association with powerful business interests; and the ability to embarrass elected officials who do not vote as they wish.

Food stamp recipients are a very different story: they have no money for campaigns; they have a reputation as nonvoters; there is no public sympathy; media attention is mostly negative; and few "establishment" groups are associated with their issue. The only tool readily available to food stamp users is the ability to embarrass. The same could be said of many social issues: Medicaid, subsidized housing, welfare, and mental health, for example. The elderly, on the other hand, are powerful because they vote, can get good media coverage, and usually have public sympathy working for them even though they generally do not have money for campaigns.

If all you have going for your issue is the ability to embarrass, you should use it. This tactic should not be misunderstood. "Embarrassment" is simply a way of holding politicians accountable. Just bear in mind that people in political positions never want to appear foolish, uninformed, or on the "wrong side" of an issue. Politicians tend to be better informed on issues that are continually raised in public and on which they are forced to take a public position.

Consider the antiabortion movement. Leave aside how you stand on the issue and think just about the way abortion became a public issue. Ten years ago, abortion was considered so controversial that few public figures had a public position on the subject. Then people opposed to abortion went to work. Even without money or substantial numbers, they made their point by appearing at public gatherings and raising questions about a candidate's or official's stand on abortion. Today, every public figure has a position on abortion. In the process, a lot of people in public life have learned a great deal about the fine points of the abortion debate; and the media got an education as well.

The same can be done for other issues. All that is required is a willingness to speak up in public every time an elected official or candidate is present, and ask questions about their position on issues you care about. You only need the ability to put up your hand in a public meeting and press that person for answers to questions that make clear where you stand.

For example, you can ask Representative X to justify voting for changes in Medicaid that leave elderly, disabled, and other vulnerable people unable to pay for health care, but *not* voting to end inappropriate contracting and waste by the Pentagon at a cost of billions of federal tax dollars every year. It helps to have media people on hand. Politicians do not like to appear uninformed in front of reporters. Once political figures know that every time they appear in public they will be confronted with angry questions about bad votes on Medicaid, two things will happen: they will learn more about Medicaid and the facts surrounding it, and they will come to understand that voters in their district care about the issue. The same is true of housing, food stamps, Title XX, child welfare, or any other issue.

REGISTER VOTERS AROUND BUDGET ISSUES

If you can not check off mobilized voters as a source of political power on the list above, there is still hope. You can organize voters around your particular issue. The first step is getting people registered to vote. Politicians begin to pay attention to people they see as voters. It was no accident that 70 percent of the 1981 budget cuts came from programs that poor people depend on—even though poor people constitute only about 15 percent of the population. More relevant than their numbers is the fact that the people who depend on public services and benefits are generally not seen as voters. It is also worth remembering that the present administration and Congress were put in office by just 27 percent of all eligible voters.

But many people who care deeply about social justice and the availability of services and benefits that make society more humane do not think to get involved in voter registration. That has to change. Many of the political races in 1980 were decided by margins of from 5 to 10 percent of those voting. The task becomes clear when you consider the number of potential voters directly affected by the budget issues: everyone, rich or poor, with someone in their family who is elderly or disabled; everyone whose state and local taxes have gone up to replace lost federal funds; everyone who is spending more now to get to work; everyone whose health insurance costs more; everyone concerned about health, housing, roads, the environment, the safety of our food, water, and air; everyone worried about the nuclear issue and the military build-up; everyone who thinks we should not give $20,000 in new tax benefits to families with incomes over $200,000 while the deficit stands well above $100 billion. If we can deliver from 5 to 10 percent of the voters in a close race—people who are prepared to vote based on where the candidates stand on the budget issues—then we can influence not only the decisions made by politicians this year but also the outcome of future state and federal election campaigns. So many people are being affected that the numbers, for once, are clearly on our side.

There have been some dramatic successes in registering voters among people waiting to be served at social agencies. In one state, volunteers registered 11,500 low-income people in just eight days. Newly registered voters received a follow-up letter and telephone call plus a reminder call on election day, and 66 percent of them turned out to vote. Poor people are like everyone else: they do not vote if they think their votes do not matter. When they come to see that their votes do count, they vote.

In many states, voter registration is relatively simple. Postcard registration is increasingly common; and registration can go on at grocery stores, outside churches, and at social functions. Each of us can be registering our friends, neighbors, clients, and relatives. We can register people at exercise classes, poker games, professional meetings,

and on the bus going home from work. And making follow-up telephone calls to talk about issues plus reminder calls on voting day does not cost any money.

Door-to-door get-out-the-vote efforts are thought to be most effective, but lacking the people power for door-to-door work is no excuse for doing nothing. One group in upstate New York is talking about an event that features autographs from popular athletes at a free concert. The price of admission will be four accurately completed voter registration cards. Teenagers who want to get the athletes' autographs and hear the music will have to persuade their relatives and neighbors to fill out their cards. Telephone calls and visits to the newly registered will follow.

It is important to bear in mind that this is not a partisan activity. The issue at hand is whether there will be enough people in Congress willing to vote responsibly on the budget. Programs and issues we all care about will continue to need Republican *and* Democratic supporters in both the House and Senate. Men and women of either party who will say "no" to throwing money at the Pentagon and "no" to consistently higher tax breaks for people who are already wealthy should be elected; they deserve support. Those of you who cannot work for a political party *can* do voter education and registration work that is nonpartisan.

Another likely outcome of this process could be counted as a plus. In the past, many people chose not to vote simply because they saw so little difference between the candidates on issues that were important to them. By organizing voter registration campaigns that focus on the budget, you can be sure voters will have a personal stake in the outcome. Then those who are elected will owe their victories to voters whose priority is a socially responsible federal budget.

FORM COALITIONS

Coalition building is so basic that is sometimes goes unmentioned, but it is worth discussing in this context both because it is so important and because the coalition building required for this kind of action plan is something new.

The three strategies I have just described clearly cannot be undertaken by a handful of people working alone. The information demands alone are beyond the resources of most small, specialized groups. Part of the job is knowing who has information and how to make it available—quickly and in usable form. No one person or group is going to be able to respond to misinformation on ten different issues, or be able to cover every public appearance of every candidate once the campaigns get underway. But coalitions that represent everyone who is affected can do this.

One possibility is already shaping up in many cities and states. A broad range of groups around the country have been getting together as part of an effort called Fair Budget Action Campaign. The campaign's national endorsers run the gamut from the National Council of Churches and the National Farmers' Union, through Congress Watch, the Coalition for a New Foreign and Military Policy, Friends of the Earth, and a number of labor unions. The success of the campaign can be attributed to the fact that it has consolidated the concerns of people with a wide range of interests: civil rights, religious, antimilitary build-up, tax reform, labor, elderly, children, health, housing, employment, and the environment. The power

of the effort is being felt at the state and local levels where, last spring, fair budget committees held "accountability sessions" with their members of Congress *before* the first major votes were taken on the budget. More of these will increase the impact of the movement in the future, and plans call for intense efforts during the upcoming fall campaigns.

The expertise of special-focus groups remains critical, but is not enough in a world in which everything is being cut. We could afford to concentrate on food stamps or subsidized housing or welfare when there was broad support for moving forward on more than one front. Today, however, winning additional funds for food stamps may mean losing Medicaid coverage for the same people. Working in coalition makes it possible to track several issues at the same time, while still maintaining specialized expertise.

The fair budget campaign recognizes that programs for poor people constitute less than 10 percent of the federal budget, while the big money continues to flow into the defense department or, by means of tax benefits, remains in the pockets of the well-to-do. People who care about cuts in social programs have to relate them to each other and to such budget items as nuclear weapons and tax expenditures. Fair budget committees can combine the expertise of specialists in all those areas, and fit their work into the broader budget context.

Broad based coalitions allow groups of disparate interests to consolidate their resources for greater impact. In many places, environmental issues have attracted solid, middle-class support. Most poor people's issues have not. By linking environmentalists with groups concerned about the poor, it may be possible to broaden the base of support for both. In Appalachia, for example, the strip mine forces often move with greater impunity against the lands where poor people's houses stand. However, strip mine foes do not automatically link up with people organizing around food stamps or welfare, although the two may prove to be valuable allies. In Ohio and Michigan, where the auto industry slump has sent entire state economies into a tailspin, or in Oregon and Washington states, which are so badly affected by the slump in construction industries, a broad range of special-issue groups now have common interests simply because everything is threatened.

DON'T GIVE UP

We are all being told that we have to be pragmatic and recognize that this is not a "good" time for social issues, especially if they cost money. That implies that there may yet *be* a better time for social issues, if only we have patience. But no Congress has ever come to Washington vowing to make things right for the poor, the vulnerable, for workers, or for the environment. In that sense, this time is different only in degree.

If you detect a note of unfounded optimism in that comment, it may be helpful to consider briefly the history of the antihunger movement.

In 1981, 23 million people got food stamps, 27 million children got a lunch at school (half of them free or at a reduced price) 8 million children got breakfast, 2.2 million pregnant women and young infants got specially nutritious foods through the WIC program, and both congregate and home-delivered meals were available to about

three million elderly. That was not always the case.

In 1967, when the current antihunger movement began, federal food assistance scarcely existed. Some help was administered by the states and localities—as the president would have us do again—in ways that left millions of Americans malnourished. We got from almost nothing then to where we are today though everyone would have agreed that 1967 was not a "good" year for a new social cause.

In 1967 President Johnson was fighting a costly war in Vietnam, and the last thing he wanted was an expensive new social issue on his hands. Those were also years of social unrest, with demands being made for government assistance for minorities, the cities, the poor. Johnson's view was shared by the Congress. Neither wanted to go into the 1968 elections having voted for higher taxes, and it was all they could do to finance the war.

Had they asked, the people who brought national attention to the plight of hungry children would have been told that 1967 was not the right year to launch a campaign to wipe out hunger. Feeding people costs money, and money to feed poor people cannot at the same time be used to buy fighter planes or to rebuild cities.

But those who were concerned chose to act, based not on the practical politics of the day, but on the fact that having children starve in a country as rich as ours is intolerable. Thanks to the efforts of all the people who chose to get and stay involved over the years, they prevailed. As a result, food assistance was made available.

The cynics are right; this is not a good time. But anxiety levels in poor neighborhoods are high and rising. The suffering of millions is growing daily. The needs are real and compelling; the issues deserve better treatment from the Congress than they are getting; and the president's plans to divert massive amounts of federal spending to the wealthiest individuals, corporations, and the Pentagon by taking food, housing, medical care, income, and jobs away from vulnerable people could not be more wrong.

Given the stark clarity of the issues, this may be the best possible time to get ourselves together, plan, and act deliberately to put the country back on track with respect to social issues.

It is not a question of whether we should try to do something in a politically bad year. The question is: How can we not try? In times like these, doing nothing is a political act. The action plan for advocates is one way to stop talking about how terrible things are— and begin to act now to make them better.

6.

Ronald W. Toseland and Robert F. Rivas

WORKING WITH TASK GROUPS: THE MIDDLE PHASE

It has been said that Americans are involved in committees and other task groups more than any other people (Tropman, Johnson, and Tropman, 1979). Participation in the decisions that affect our lives is characteristic of our democratic society. Every day millions of meetings take place throughout the United States. Social service agencies could not function without meetings of committees, treatment conferences, teams, boards, and other work groups.

Social workers and other helping professionals are often called upon to chair committees, teams, and other task groups. For example, the social worker is frequently designated as the team leader in interdisciplinary health care settings, because social work functions include coordination, case management, and concern for the biopsychosocial functioning of the whole person (Kane, 1975, 1976; Wise, 1974; Siporin, 1980a). Workers also are asked to "staff" task groups (Tropman, Johnson, and Tropman, 1979). In general, the staff person plays a supportive role, helping the group to clarify its goals and to carry out its work. Acting under the direction of the task group's leader, the staff person reports directly to the group. The duties and roles of staff persons are quite varied, and they include serving as a resource person, consultant, enabler, analyst, implementer, tactician, catalyst, technical catalyst, and technical advisor (Tropman, Johnson, and Tropman, 1979).

Source: Edited with permission of Macmillan Publishing Company from *An Introduction to Group Work Practice* by Ronald W. Toseland and Robert F. Rivas. Copyright © 1984 by Macmillan Publishing Company.

Despite the importance and the widespread use of task groups in social service agencies, relatively little has been written about how to lead or staff them. Brill (1976) and Trecker (1946) point out that teams and other task groups have great potential for helping clients receive effective services. Yet, with a few notable exceptions (see, for example, Brill, 1976; Bradford, 1976; Delbecq, Van de Ven, and Gustafson, 1975; Napier and Gershenfeld, 1981), the human services have paid little attention to how task groups work.

Although task groups can be useful, they can be a source of frustration for their participants when they function ineffectively. For example, Napier and Gershenfeld (1981, pp. 310–349) describe the "incredible meeting trap" in which little is accomplished and members leave feeling frustrated by the group process. In one of the few articles published in a social work journal about leading task group meetings, Edson (1977) suggests unorthodox methods that can be used to guard against the irrational and manipulative strategies used by "narrowminded, pigheaded, sly, opinionated, bigoted manipulators" who often dominate committee meetings (Edson, 1977, p. 224).

Edson's (1977) comments are strongly stated, but they make the important point that many workers are dissatisfied with task group meetings and indifferent or suspicious about their outcomes. Meetings that are not well run are boring and dissatisfying to members. They suffer from a lack of participation and corrective feedback from members, who lose interest.

Although task group meetings are often seen as a chore to be endured by members for the good of the organization, meetings that are well run can be a positive experience. They help draw people together, creating effective teamwork in which ideas are shared, feelings are expressed, and support is developed for group members, as well as for the decisions made by the group. There are few experiences in the workplace that equal the feelings of cohesion, commitment, and satisfaction that members feel when their ideas have been heard, appreciated, and used in resolving a difficult issue and arriving at a mutually agreed upon decision.[1]

This article focuses on the skills, procedures, and methods that workers will find useful when staffing or leading task group meetings. First the authors describe some generic skills in conducting task group meetings during the middle phase, then discuss some of the most common functions of task groups and the generic practice principles that are helpful in carrying out each function. Because effective problem solving is basic to many task group efforts, the authors describe a six-step model for effective problem solving in groups. The model includes a discussion of the practice skills workers use during each step.

CONDUCTING MEETINGS

The middle stages of task groups are characterized by repetition and by diversity. Repetition occurs because meetings generally follow a similar pattern: an opening portion for warming up, a middle portion for working, and a

---

[1]See the film *Meeting in Progress,* Round Table Films, 113 North San Vincente Blvd., Beverly Hills, California 90211, for a vivid example of task group members who are ready to end a meeting as soon as a decision is reached.

closing portion for summarizing and ending. At the same time, there can be great diversity among task groups during the middle stage of their development. Diversity is fostered by the wide range of functions and the great variety of procedures that can be used to help task groups conduct their business.

During the middle stage, work is accomplished between meetings as well as during the beginning, middle, and end of each meeting. The following sections include a brief discussion of the ways that workers can help groups to accomplish their tasks during each of these periods.

Between Meetings

Between meetings, the worker has two major tasks: seeing that decisions and tasks decided upon at the previous meetings are carried out, and preparing for the next group meeting. The worker can prepare for the first task by reading the minutes of the meeting. Properly kept minutes should include a summary of the actions taken, tasks that were assigned, and the time frame for reporting back to the group. It is also helpful for the worker to make brief notes during a meeting or soon after the meeting ends about decisions made by the group, which need to be followed up prior to the next meeting.

In seeing that the decisions decided upon by the group are carried out between meetings, Tropman (1980) suggests that a worker should become "a bit of a nag." The worker ensures that members work on and complete reports and other assignments that are necessary for the next group meeting. This does not mean that the worker takes over these tasks. The worker's function is to encourage and to facilitate the

progress of those whose responsibility is to carry out a task.

The second major task of the worker between meetings is to prepare for the next group meeting. When there is a written agenda for each meeting, the worker or the member designated as the group's secretary should send a memo to each group member soon after a meeting to receive agenda items well ahead of the next meeting. This allows enough time for agenda items and background or position papers to be completed and sent to group members so they can be read before the next meeting. Meeting agendas should be established to facilitate discussion. One effective framework is to:

1. Examine and approve (with any corrections) brief, relevant minutes from the last meeting.
2. Make informational announcements.
3. Vote to include special agenda items.
4. Work on less controversial, easier items.
5. Work on difficult items.
6. Break.
7. Work on "for discussion only" items.
8. Consider any special agenda items if there is sufficient time.
9. Summarize.
10. Adjourn.

In preparing for the next meeting, the worker should also organize opening remarks and administrative summaries that he or she will present during the meeting. Special care should be taken in preparing for meetings that do not have a written agenda. In such instances, the worker should be clear about how to direct the meeting, what tasks the group will work on, and what goals are to be achieved.

During Meetings

Beginning. At the beginning of a meeting, the worker is responsible for several tasks. The worker begins by introducing new members and distributing additional handouts not included with the material distributed before the meeting. Before working on agenda items, the worker should make a brief opening statement about the purpose of the meeting. In this statement, the worker may want to call members' attention to previous meetings and to the mandate of the group as a way to indicate that the meeting will undertake a necessary and important function. Making members aware of the salience of the particular agenda items they will consider is important for maintaining the members' interest and willingness to work during the group meeting.

The worker should seek members' approval of written minutes that were distributed before the meeting and request that members raise any questions, changes or amendments they would like to enter into the minutes. After the minutes are approved, the worker makes announcements and calls upon group members to make designated reports. Reports should be kept brief and to the point. Members should verbally summarize written reports that have been circulated with the agenda rather than reading them verbatim. Reading lengthy reports can be boring and can result in the loss of interest and attention of other members.

Middle. During the middle portion of meetings, the worker's task is to help the group follow its planned agenda. Whatever the particular purpose of a specific meeting, the middle portion is the time when the group accomplishes much of its most difficult work. To avoid getting stuck on one item of business in meetings that have extensive agendas, details of a particular item should be worked out prior to the meeting. If this is not possible, Tropman (1980) points out, the group can agree "in principle" on overall objectives and goals about a particular task and a subcommittee or an individual group member can be charged with working out the details and bringing these back to the group at a later date.

The worker should model the behavior that is expected of all members. A worker who shows respect, interest, integrity, and responsibility will convey these feelings to members. By encouraging equitable participation, the expression of minority group opinions, and an appreciation of all sincere contributions to the group's work, the worker sets a positive example for group members to follow.

Ending. The worker should ensure that the pace of the meeting leaves enough time at the end to accomplish the items specified in the agenda. Task groups can make serious mistakes when they rush through important decisions because they are pressed for time at the end of a meeting. Members also become frustrated when they are expected to present or to discuss ideas but have no time to do so, because the group has spent too much time discussing earlier items on the agenda. Part of the responsibility of an effective worker in preparing for a meeting is making sure that the number of agenda items is manageable and can be accomplished in the available time. Items sometimes take longer to discuss than anticipated, so it is a good practice to plan some extra time into an agenda. When too many agenda items are submitted for a meeting, items should be prioritized by the worker. Items that are assigned a low priority should be postponed to a later meeting.

Before adjourning, the worker should summarize the meeting's accomplishments, identify issues and agenda items that need further attention, and mention major topics for the next group meeting. When the group is working on a large task, the worker should also mention where the meeting has placed the group in terms of its overall schedule. At this time, the worker should also summarize as clearly as possible the tasks that members agreed to accomplish before the next meeting. This avoids confusion, clarifies responsibilities, and reduces the possibility that members might forget assignments that were agreed to during earlier portions of the group's discussion.

FUNCTIONS OF TASK GROUPS

Whereas the main focus of treatment groups is on the functioning and the socioemotional needs of individual group members, task groups are focused on the projects and results that the group as a whole produces. Task groups, of course, are also concerned with individual members. Attention to members' satisfaction, comfort, motivation, and skills are essential if the group as a whole is to accomplish its tasks. However, unlike treatment groups, the primary concern of task groups is not to change members. Task groups are created to accomplish work that will meet evaluative criteria set both from within and from outside of the group.

Many important functions of task groups are similar to those of treatment groups. Despite this overlap, the differing foci of task and treatment groups are evident in their respective functions. Task groups, for example, are more concerned with creating new ideas, developing plans and programs, solving problems that are external to the group, and making decisions about the organizational environment than are treatment groups.

Although problem solving and decision making are important functions, several others have been identified in the literature (see, for example, Scheidel and Crowell, 1979; Napier and Gershenfeld, 1981; Bradford, 1976). Functions that govern the work of task groups during their middle phase include

1. Sharing information, thoughts, and feelings about common concerns and issues that workers encounter as they function in their assigned roles within an agency.
2. Helping members feel involved and committed to the group and the agency in which they work.
3. Developing facts and information about particular issues, concerns, and problems facing the group.
4. Making effective decisions.
5. Monitoring and evaluating decisions and program components for which the task group is responsible.
6. Problem solving.

Sometimes, task groups perform only one of the functions described. Usually, however, task groups attempt to perform several functions simultaneously. Task groups often develop primary and secondary functions. For example, in a community agency serving homebound older persons, paraprofessional outreach workers meet together with their supervisor on a weekly basis to discuss common problems which they confront in obtaining psychological, social and medical services for their clients. Because they spend so much time out of the office, a secondary function of the group is to help workers identify with the organization for which they work. In the following pages, task group functions are described separately to illustrate particular work skills, but in practice they are frequently combined so that several purposes can be accomplished simultaneously.

Sharing Information

Perhaps the most common function of task groups is to help members share information, thoughts, and feelings with one another. Teams, committees, delegate councils, and boards use group meetings as a means for members to share their concerns, their experiences, their perspectives, and their expertise with one another. This is an important function because, as a result of highly differentiated work roles, there is infrequent contact among workers in many agencies. Job assignments such as individual treatment sessions and home visits limit opportunities for communication among workers.

Social issues and problems often have an interagency impact, and task groups serve as the vehicle for bringing workers from different agencies together. A group meeting is a convenient way for workers from different agencies to share unique viewpoints and differing perspectives on issues, problems, or concerns they face in their own agen-

cies. By providing a forum for sharing knowledge and resources, interagency task groups encourage cooperative and coordinated problem solving.

Open communication and unimpeded sharing of information are prerequisites for other functions of task groups. Brill (1976), for example, suggests that the communication network that is established in a group is the key to effective work in teams and other task groups. Empirical findings regarding group productivity and group process confirm that the way information is communicated and used in a group has an important effect on the quality and the quantity of a group's productivity (Hackman and Morris, 1975; Steiner, 1972).

What steps can be taken to aid effective communication and open sharing of information in task groups? The first step is to ensure that all members have a clear understanding of the topic being discussed and the task facing the group. In order to stimulate all members' participation in the discussion, the topic must be relevant. If members have little interest in the topic and no stake in the outcome, there is little reason for them to participate. In many groups, members become bored, uninterested, and dissatisfied because they do not understand the importance of a particular topic. It is important for the task group's leader to help each member see the relevance and importance of issues as they are brought before the group. When it is clear that a discussion topic is relevant to only a subset of members of a task group, the worker should consider forming a subgroup to meet separately from the larger group. The subgroup can provide a brief report of its deliberations and recommendations at a later meeting of the entire group.

In order to focus interest, promote task-relevant discussions, and reduce confusion among members, Zander (1977), Huber (1980), and Steiner (1972) suggest developing clear procedural steps that can be followed during the discussion. Maier (1963, p. 41) refers to discussions that follow clear procedural steps as "developmental discussions." Later in this article, a six-step problem-solving model for conducting task group discussions is presented.

Workers also can use their leadership skills during the group meeting by summarizing frequently and by helping the group to remain task-focused. Summarizing can be used to check understanding, to review previously discussed subjects, to go back to items that were not fully discussed, to help separate a problem or issue into several parts, and to bring members' attention to a particularly important aspect of the discussion. Focusing can be accomplished by suggesting that the group discuss one issue at a time, by pointing out that the group has digressed from the discussion topic, and by making task-relevant statements.

Another method of establishing open communication channels and promoting information sharing among all group members is to ensure equitable participation in the group. Domination by a few members who have high status or who are very expressive leads to less felt freedom to participate among all members and to a reduction in the quality of group decisions (Torrance, 1957; Chung and Ferris, 1971; Delbecq, Van de Ven, and Gustafson, 1975). Workers should help task groups develop mechanisms that ensure equitable participation.

The worker should help the group develop a standard of fairness in partici-

pation (Huber, 1980). This can be done by helping the group develop rules for participation. Members may agree to keep their comments brief, to be attentive to the communication of others when they are speaking, and to encourage silent members to participate. In addition to modeling appropriate behavior, the worker can help members follow the rules that are established. For example, the worker can interrupt long speeches, ask members to summarize their comments briefly, or suggest that members give others a chance to reply. When a member presents an idea, the worker can invite participation by asking other members for feedback about the proposal. In some cases, it is helpful to structure the discussion by using a round robin procedure or the rules of parliamentary procedure.

In a round robin procedure, each member is asked to present one idea or one piece of information. Going around the group, members take turns at presenting one piece of data. This procedure is continued and each member takes as many turns as needed. Members who do not have any additional ideas or information simply pass during their turn. The cycle is completed when all ideas have been shared by all members.

The round robin procedure has several advantages over unstructured, interacting communication procedures. It does not force members to participate equally although all members have an equal opportunity to participate. Because only one idea is presented at a time, the procedure avoids the boredom that often results when one member enumerates several ideas at the same time. By continuing to go around the group until all ideas are heard and by asking members to pass if they do not have any new information to present, a norm is established for sharing as many ideas as possible.

In large task groups, round robin procedures are often too time-consuming. Unless the group is divided into subgroups, the procedure is not useful. In order to facilitate equitable participation in large groups, the worker should consider using parliamentary procedures (Gully, 1968; Maier, 1963; Scheidel and Crowell, 1979) following *Robert's Rules of Order* (Robert, 1970) which provide for orderly and structured participation in large group meetings.

Getting Members Involved

A second function of task groups is to help members feel that they are a vital part of the agency for which they work. Because much of any organization's work is done by individuals, there is a danger that staff can become isolated and alienated from an organization. Task groups provide support for their members and a sense of belongingness that reduces alienation. For example, an individual worker in an agency for disabled children spends much of her time helping new parents with the trauma associated with giving birth to physically and mentally handicapped children. Weekly team meetings with other professionals who work with the infants in a pre-school program provide support and recognition for the worker who is faced with the difficult, often emotionally charged, task of helping parents become adjusted to having handicapped children.

What can be done to help task group members feel that their input is vital to the agency's sound functioning? First, workers should make sure that members understand the importance of the group's work, its relationship to the agency's purpose, and how the group fits into the agency's administrative structure. This can be accomplished by making a clear statement of the group's purpose, by using flow charts to explain how the group fits into the entire agency's administrative and decision-making structure, and by clarifying the duties, responsibilities, authority and power that results from membership in the group. At first, this explanation might mean little to members. However, as work is accomplished within the group and recommendations and reports are prepared for the larger agency, members gather a more personal, first-hand experience of the governance structure of their agency.

Assigning members specific roles can also help them become actively involved in their agency. Roles that encourage members to become dependent on one another for task accomplishment and roles that place them in the position of representing the group to a larger constituency increase the attractiveness and cohesion of the group, and help members feel that they are part of a collective effort that is of vital importance for effective agency functioning (Deutsch, 1973).

A third, and extremely important, step in getting members involved in and committed to a task group and their agency is to invite their input into the agenda and the decision-making processes of the group. This can be done by encouraging members to develop and submit agenda items for future group meetings. Circulating the agenda and any background papers prior to a meeting can help members prepare their thoughts and concerns before a meeting and increase the chances that they will participate by sharing them during the meeting. It has been shown that the greater a member's effort and sacrifice in preparing for and working on a task, the more likely the member is to stay involved and committed to the group (Kiesler, 1978). Therefore, asking members to prepare for a meeting by reading background papers, collecting information, and submitting agenda items will tend to increase involvement and commitment to the group and the larger organization.

A fourth method of helping members become involved is to encourage them to participate in the decision-making process to the extent possible (Scheidel and Crowell, 1979). Shared decision making has been found to increase motivation (Kiesler, 1978), increase acceptance and understanding of decisions (Bradford, 1976), increase the information available for decision making (Huber, 1980), and help in processing complex information (Carnes, 1980). Although some writers suggest that decision making should always be shared among members (Bradford, 1976), there are potential disadvantages to giving members decision-making authority. According to Huber (1980), these include (1) the great amount of personnel time spent in group decision making, (2) the tendency for groups to produce decisions that are not acceptable to management, (3) expectations that future decisions will also be make through group participation, (4) the tendency for groups to take longer than individuals to reach decisions, and (5) the possibility that group decision making could cause conflict between group members who may have to work together on a daily basis. Thus, the decision to delegate decision making to groups should be made only after carefully

considering both the advantages and disadvantages of shared decision making in the particular situation. When the advantages of group decision making are questionable, it is often possible to have the group make several recommendations but to reserve the final decision-making authority to one person.

Developing Information

A third function of task groups is to generate information and develop creative alternatives for responding to difficult issues and problems facing the group. Although task groups are often used for this function, the available evidence suggests that ordinary interacting group discussions inhibit rather than increase the disclosure of information, ideas, and creative solutions. (See, for example, Van de Ven, 1974; Miner, 1979; Van de Ven and Delbecq, 1971; Delbecq, 1967.)

Reasons that group processes may inhibit information sharing and the development of creative ideas include:

1. Status-conscious group members feel intimidated by those with higher status (Torrance, 1957). Lower-status members will tend to share less information and will avoid making suggestions that will offend higher-status members.
2. Norms and social pressures for conformity tend to limit the expression of new and creative ideas (Van de Ven, 1974; Vroom, Grant and Cotton, 1969).
3. Groups have the advantage of the wide variety of opinions and knowledge offered by the members, but group members may censor controversial opinions.

4. Covert judgments are often made but not expressed openly in groups (Collaros and Anderson, 1969). Members, therefore, become concerned about the effects that their self-disclosures will have on future interactions with group members.
5. Interacting groups tend to reach premature solutions without considering all the available evidence (Maier and Hoffman, 1960; Van de Ven, 1974).

In order to reduce or eliminate the difficulties associated with generating information and developing creative solutions in interacting groups, several methods, such as brainstorming, the nominal group technique, and social judgment analysis, have been suggested as alternative procedures. However, because interacting group discussions are commonly used in task groups, workers should be aware of procedures that can help to overcome the limitations often associated with them.

The worker can help in several ways to improve group members' opportunities to present new ideas, combine information, and generate creative solutions in interacting groups. First, the worker must clearly indicate to all members that their input is welcome. This means that the worker must be able to address the members' concerns about sanctions that may result from expressing sensitive or controversial ideas in the group. When the worker cannot guarantee freedom from sanctions, he or she should try to be as clear as possible about the boundaries of the discussion. For example, it might be possible for committee members to discuss new policies regarding service delivery, but it might not be acceptable for them to criticize existing supervisory staff who have to follow current policy guidelines. When sanctions are possible from individuals outside the group, the worker can encourage the group to consider making their discussions confidential. If lower-status members fear reprisals from higher-status members, the worker can discuss the use of sanctions with higher-status members prior to the group meeting and gain their cooperation in refraining from applying them. The worker can suggest that higher- and lower-status members discuss this issue in the group.

Feedback can have a beneficial or a detrimental effect in helping the group to develop information and form creative solutions. It is commonly thought that all feedback is useful because it helps group members to detect and correct errors in information processing. (See, for example, Argyris, 1977; Bowers and Franklin, 1976; and Nadler, 1977.) This is not true in all circumstances. In the early phase of developing information and forming creative solutions, evaluative feedback can have the effect of suppressing further suggestions (Van de Ven, 1974, Nadler, 1979). Members fear that their ideas may be evaluated negatively and that this will reflect on their competence and their status in the agency. Under these circumstances, few members will risk making suggestions, giving opinions, or volunteering information that will not be readily accepted. To encourage free discussion, creative ideas, and new insights about a problem or issue, the worker should ask members to refrain from evaluating ideas early in the group's discussion.

Several other steps can also be taken to help the group develop information and creative ideas to solve a problem. The worker can encourage the group to develop norms that promote free discussion of ideas. As the meeting progresses, it is often helpful to point out group pressures that inhibit members' free discussion. By presenting creative, controversial, and thought-provoking ideas, the worker can act as a model for the group. Workers can also encourage members to continue to share unique ideas by praising those who present innovative suggestions. Since it is more difficult for lower status members to present their ideas after higher status members have expressed their opinions, lower status members should be encouraged to share their ideas as early as possible in the group's discussion. To avoid premature solutions during group discussions, the worker should help the group separate information and idea-generating steps from decision-making steps. When these suggestions are implemented, interacting groups can develop more creative solutions than they would under ordinary conditions.

Making Effective Decisions

A fourth function of task groups is to make effective decisions. Although groups are often used to make decisions, the evidence as to their effectiveness is mixed. Groups are better than individuals in influencing opinions and obtaining commitments from members (Kelley and Thibaut, 1969; Lewin, 1948). Napier (1967) found that groups are better at integrating complex perceptual and intellectual tasks, because members can rely on one another for assistance. However, for other types of problems, groups may not be any more effective than individuals working

alone (Campbell, 1968; Rotter and Portugal, 1969). In summarizing the literature that has compared the problem-solving activities of task groups with that of individuals, Hare (1976) has drawn the following conclusions:

1. Groups are superior to individuals in solving manual problems such as puzzles. This is particularly true when the problem can be subdivided so that each person can use his or her own expertise to work on a problem component. The superiority of groups has been less consistently documented when the task to be accomplished is of a more intellectual nature, such as a logic problem.
2. While groups are better than the average individual, they are not better than the best individual. Therefore, a group of novices may perform worse than one expert.
3. Groups have the advantage of the wide variety of opinions and knowledge offered by the members, but group members may censor controversial opinions.
4. A part of the superiority of group problem solving is due to the pooling of individual judgments to converge on a group norm. For some problems, similar accuracy may be achieved by averaging the decisions of non-interacting individuals.
5. When groups solve intellectual tasks, members' rational information-processing orientation may be impeded by socioemotional concerns.
6. Because task groups require the time of a number of members who deliberate until they reach a decision, task groups may be more

costly than work done by one or more individuals working alone.

In order to improve group decision making, workers should help members to avoid the phenomenon known as "groupthink" (Janis, 1972). "Groupthink" occurs when group contagion takes over and members fail to express their own thoughts and feelings. Instead, they go along with the predominant sentiment of the group.

Before 1960, it was generally thought that problem-solving groups make more conservative decisions than individuals. Experiments by Ziller (1957) and Stoner (1961), however, indicated that groups made riskier decisions than individuals. Stoner (1961) called this phenomenon the "risky shift." As evidence began to accumulate, it became clear that this shift may either be toward greater or lesser risk. Riskier decisions are made in groups whose members approve of risk taking (Teger and Pruitt, 1967; Wallach and Wing, 1968), when persuasive information is presented (Ebbesen and Bowers, 1974), when the responsibility for the decision is shared among group members (Myers and Arenson, 1972; Zajonc, Wolosin, and Wolosin, 1972), or when the leader approves of a risky decision (Myers and Arenson, 1972). On the other hand, in some groups risk taking is discouraged, and members are rewarded for developing solutions that result in conservative group decisions (Stoner, 1968).

Several steps can be taken to help groups avoid "groupthink" and "risky shifts." Norms and a group climate that encourages free and open discussion of ideas tend to discourage conformity and to decrease "groupthink." Procedures that clarify how a group will use information and arrive at a decision also tend to reduce conformity. Early in the decision-making process, the group should decide how to use the information it possesses in making a decision. For example, in a family service agency, a personnel committee deciding between many qualified applicants for a clinical position develops decision criteria. They are the rules and the standards that govern rational choices between alternative candidates. Criteria for making decisions should include all the factors that group members consider to be essential in making a good judgment. The personnel committee arrived at decision criteria that included the clinical competency of the applicant, the needs of the agency for a worker who could speak Spanish, a worker with skill and experience in supervision, and a worker who was familiar with the use of psychotropic medications in outpatient mental health settings.

To avoid disagreements later in the decision-making process, the worker should allow the group to discuss the rationale behind each decision criteria. To avoid confusion, it is often helpful to ask members about their understanding of each criteria and to use examples to illustrate how each criteria would be applied in rating alternative solutions. After developing and clarifying the criteria, the group should rate their relative importance so that the group can decide between alternative solutions. In the previous example, group members decided that clinical competency and supervisory experience were twice as important as the other criteria for this particular position. They then used the criteria to review each job applicant's folder in order to select the best candidate.

During the decision-making process, conflict may occur between members.

It is important for workers to realize that conflicts occur even in effective task groups (Scheidel and Crowell, 1979; Napier and Gershenfeld, 1981). Conflicts often occur over control of resources, values, beliefs, preferences, and the nature of the relationship between members (Deutsch, 1973). Maier (1963) and Filley (1974) suggest that disagreement between members can either lead to increased conflict and failure to accomplish a task or to the development of creative solutions. The outcome of a disagreement depends on how the worker and the group members handle it (Lowe and Herranen, 1978).

In their analyses of hundreds of decision-making groups, Guetzkow and Gyr (1954) distinguished between two types of conflict, substantive conflict and affective conflict. Affective conflict is based on the emotional and interpersonal relationships among members within and outside of the group. Substantive conflict is based on members' differing opinions about ideas, information, and facts presented during the task group's work. In general, affective conflict is more difficult to resolve than substantive conflict because it is resistant to persuasive reasoning. When conflict is avoided and remains unresolved, the group may (1) decide not to decide, (2) delegate its decision-making responsibilities to others, or (3) decide on a solution that is not substantiated by accurate information (Kiesler, 1978).

Guetzkow and Gyr (1954) and Burke (1970) suggest that substantive and affective conflicts can be reduced by the following procedures:

1. Help members to recognize the conflict.

2. Help members to express the reasoning behind conflicting opinions and alternatives.
3. Develop facts and expert judgments to help resolve the conflict.
4. Emphasize those factors in the group discussion that promote consensus.
5. Follow orderly, pre-planned steps for considering alternatives and deciding on a solution.
6. Use decision criteria that are mutually agreed upon by group members.
7. Clarify and summarize the discussion frequently so that all members have a similar understanding of what is being discussed and the decision criteria that will be used.
8. Be sensitive to members' personal concerns and needs in developing solutions and arriving at a decision.
9. Remain neutral in the conflict, asking questions that seek clarification whenever possible.

To arrive at a final group decision, a procedure for choosing among alternatives is needed. Most groups make their final decisions using one of the following procedures: consensus, compromise, or majority rule (Gulley, 1968). In certain situations, each of these procedures can result in quite different decisions. To avoid the suspicion that a particular decision-making procedure is being chosen to influence a decision about a particular issue, a method of choosing among alternatives should be agreed upon as early as possible in a task group's deliberations.

Consensus is often considered the ideal way to select among alternatives because all group members commit themselves to the decision. When reviewing conditions for effective work with groups, Whitaker (1975) suggests that helping a group to achieve consensus reduces conflict within the group and helps to make the group more effective. Consensus does not, however, necessarily imply agreement on the part of all group members. As Napier and Gershenfeld (1981, p. 402) point out, consensus "simply requires that individuals must be willing to go along with the group's predominant view and carry out the implications of the decision in good faith."

Consensus is sometimes difficult to achieve in groups. Reaching consensus can be time-consuming and tension-provoking because each alternative must be discussed thoroughly along with dissenting viewpoints. Also, there is the danger that members will acquiesce and decision quality will be sacrificed in order to arrive at a solution that is acceptable to all group members (Napier and Gershenfeld, 1981). Although other decision-making procedures are quicker, reaching consensus often brings considerable support for a decision because members are more likely to cooperate in implementing decisions that they have thoroughly discussed and agreed upon.

When issues are controversial and there is much dissenting opinion, it is often possible to reach a decision by modifying original proposals. In order to develop amendments to proposals that are acceptable to all group members, the discussion of each alternative should focus on the reasoning behind members' objections to the alternative.

This process helps all group members identify the acceptable and unacceptable parts of each alternative. After a discussion of all the alternatives, the acceptable parts of several alternatives can often be combined into one solution that is acceptable to most, if not all, members.

Majority rule is a frequently used procedure to decide between alternatives in task groups. It is less time-consuming than consensus or compromise procedures, and when the vote is done by secret ballot it protects the confidentiality of members. Majority rule is an excellent procedure to use when deciding about routine and relatively minor issues. However, because there can be a significant minority who may not agree with the final outcome, majority rule is a less appealing procedure when the issue is important and when the support and cooperation of the entire group is needed for successful implementation. For important decisions, a two-thirds majority vote is an alternative to simple majority rule. A two-thirds majority vote ensures substantial, if not total, support for a decision made by the group.

In recent years, simple mathematical procedures have also been recommended to achieve majority rule (Huber, 1980; Delbecq, Van de Ven, and Gustafson, 1975). For example, each member of a task group can be asked to rate alternative solutions on a five-point scale from 5 = best alternative to 1 = worst alternative. The group's chairperson or staff person tabulates the vote on each alternative solution. Because this procedure is easily done without identifying members' individual ratings, it also preserves their anonymity during the decision-making process. Another mathematical procedure is to have all members rank order alternative solutions. Ranks are tallied, and the mean of the ranks is calculated for each alternative.

Monitoring and Evaluating

Monitoring and evaluating are also important functions of task groups. Task groups may monitor and evaluate their own functioning or be called upon to monitor and evaluate the functioning of other systems. For example, the board of a social service agency is responsible for monitoring and evaluating the functioning of the agency. Because boards are ultimately responsible and legally liable for the proper conduct of social service agencies, monitoring and evaluating functions are a critical component of an effective board's work (Swanson, 1978; Houle, 1960). In another case, an alcoholism treatment team monitors and evaluates its own performance by reviewing recidivism data on all former clients at three-month "progress review" meetings.

For effective monitoring and evaluation during the middle phase, task groups must be clear about their mandate from the agency and their ethical, moral, and legal obligations, as expressed by regulatory agencies, professional societies, legislative bodies, and the larger society. At times these are clear, but it is often part of the responsibilities of the task group to develop a set of standards, rules, or guidelines that can be used to monitor and evaluate performance. For example, a large, private social service agency decided to encourage evaluations of several of its service programs. In order to ensure that the research would serve a useful purpose, protect the rights and the con-

fidentiality of their clients, and meet state and federal rules and regulations, an institutional research review board was formed. The first meeting of this task group focused on reviewing the procedures of similar review boards at other agencies and examining state and federal regulations. The group then prepared guidelines governing its own operation and guidelines for researchers to use when preparing proposals to be reviewed by the board.

To fulfill their monitoring and evaluating function adequately, task groups develop feedback mechanisms to help them obtain information about the results of a decision and take corrective actions when necessary (Nadler, 1979). The type of feedback that is useful to a task group depends to a great extent on the group's mandate and the monitoring and evaluating that is required in the particular situation. A board, for example, may require periodic reports from the agency director, the director of clinical services, the agency executive, and the coordinator of volunteer services. In addition, the board may review program statistics, quarterly financial statements from a certified accountant and reports from funding sources about the performance of the agency. In other cases, a task group may use formal data gathering procedures to perform its monitoring and evaluation functions.

Problem Solving

Problem solving has been given more consideration in the group work literature than any of the other functions of task groups. Task groups spend a great deal of time performing other functions, but problem solving is often seen as a task group's major function. Although problem solving is a separate function from sharing information, involving others, or making decisions, it incorporates many of the other functions of task groups. Problem solving is really a complex set of functions that vary with the type of problem facing the group. The next section describes a generic, six-step problem-solving model that can be used effectively in a variety of task groups.

A MODEL FOR EFFECTIVE PROBLEM SOLVING

Problem solving can take as little as five or ten minutes or as long as several months. The length of any problem-solving process depends on a variety of factors, including the nature of the problem, the structure and function of the group, and the capabilities and willingness of the group members and group leader to solve the problem. The effectiveness of any problem-solving effort depends on the extent to which an optimal solution is developed and implemented. It also depends on how satisfied the members of the group are with the problem-solving process and the extent to which they support the decision made by the group. It is important for task group leaders to become thoroughly familiar with the problem-solving model presented here so they can apply it in a manner that will satisfy group members and gain necessary cooperation and support. There are six steps in problem solving, including:

1. Identifying a problem.
2. Developing goals.
3. Collecting data.
4. Developing plans.
5. Selecting the best plan.
6. Implementing the plan.

These steps are not discrete. In practice they often tend to overlap. For example, preliminary goals are often discussed during problem identification. Goals are modified and refined as data collection continues. Similarly, data collection often continues as the group begins to develop plans for problem resolution.

Problem-solving processes are often described as if they occur once. This may be true in groups convened to solve a single problem, but problem-solving processes are generally used repeatedly by groups as they conduct their business. A task group may have to use two or more cycles of a problem-solving process to accomplish a single task. An adult protective service team, for example, spends three meetings developing a plan for emergency evening coverage for all clients on team members' caseloads. The plan is implemented for a two-month trial period. After the trial period, the team reconsiders aspects of the plan. Using the problem-solving process for a second time, the team decides on a modified version of the plan that proves effective in assuring adequate emergency evening coverage. Thus, over the course of several months the team is involved with two problem-solving attempts to accomplish its task.

Identifying a Problem

How a problem is identified and defined is crucial to effective problem solving. It affects what data will be collected, what range of alternatives will be considered, and who will be called upon to work on the problem, what alternatives will be considered, and who will be affected by the problem's resolution. When they are first identified, problems are often unclear and muddled. They appear to be an unsolvable, complicated maze of tangled or disjointed components. Even when problems appear to be fairly well delineated, there is often a need for further clarification. For example, the staff of a social service agency perceives that it has a problem in serving a large group of Mexican-Americans who live in the area served by the agency. Although at first glance this appears to be a fairly clear problem, it could be defined in a number of different ways, including (1) not having Spanish-speaking workers, (2) not conducting any outreach efforts to this population, (3) having a poor public image with Mexican-Americans in the community, (4) not having the financial resources to develop programs for Mexican-Americans, or (5) providing the wrong services to meet the needs of Mexican-Americans.

Several things can be done to help a group define a problem so as to promote rather than hinder problem solving, including

1. Clarifying the boundaries of the problem.
2. Seeking out members' perceptions of the problem and their expectations about how it will be solved.
3. Developing a problem-solving orientation.
4. Defining a solvable problem.
5. Specifying the problem as clearly as possible.

Because identifying and defining a problem adequately are critical to the effectiveness of the entire problem-solving process, each of these will be described in more detail.

Clarifying Boundaries. The first issue that confronts workers and mem-

bers as they define the boundaries of a problem is how to handle large problems that may have several interrelated components. Groups are often confronted with large problems that seem to be unmanageable and unsolvable. In other cases, a vague concern or problem expressed by a group member may emerge as a large problem as members begin to discuss the issues that the member raises. One method of handling large problems is to partialize them. Several manageable, solvable problems should be developed from problems that are first presented as unsolvable, unmanageable issues.

When the group partializes a problem, it must decide on which aspect of the large problem to work on first. Some guidelines for selecting problems to work on first include:

1. Select a problem that is clearly under the group's legitimate authority.
2. Select a pressing problem.
3. Select a problem that is potentially under the group's control.
4. Select a problem that when resolved will have far-reaching, beneficial effects.
5. Select a meaningful problem whose solution is important to group members and other systems outside of the group.
6. Select a problem that the group has a good chance of resolving successfully.

Boundaries refer to the extent and the scope of a problem or issue facing the group. Defining clear boundaries helps problem solvers to focus and clarify their thoughts and suggestions about a problem, leading to more effective solutions (D'Zurilla and Goldfried, 1971). When setting boundaries the worker is in a delicate position. On the one hand, an effective worker does not want to hamper the group's creative problem-solving ability. The worker would like to encourage the group to consider all the relevant options for problem resolution. On the other hand, the worker is often in a better position than any other group member to recognize what is politically, economically, and organizationally feasible. For example, in a group working on ways to increase services for Mexican-Americans, it would be helpful to inform members that solutions to the problem should not commit the agency to new services that require additional funding because no new funds are available during the current fiscal year. The worker could explain that although the solution should not require new funds, the group might consider making recommendations to the agency's administrative staff about seeking additional funding during the next fiscal year.

Whenever possible, the boundaries of the problem-solving process should be broad and flexible so as not to stifle creative problem solutions. The worker should point out members' freedom within the boundaries and the importance of accomplishing the task within specified limits. The group should be given a convincing rationale for limiting the scope of a problem and the scope of the efforts used to resolve it. Without guidelines, the group may arrive at a solution that is unacceptable to those who have responsibility for its implementation. Members who spend their time and energy developing a solution that is not feasible will feel frustrated and disappointed when they realize their recommended solution is not implemented.

An example of the delicate balance the worker should strike in suggesting boundaries for problem solving occurs in the following statement by the leader of the task group addressing the needs of Mexican-Americans:

The needs assessment we have just completed confirms our suspicions—we are not doing enough to serve Mexican-Americans in our catchment area. As we discuss the problem and decide about what to do we should keep in mind that we have just entered a new fiscal year and the agency's budget does not allow for new programming that requires additional funding. The executive director has informed me that within this constraint she will actively pursue any solutions that you suggest for improving service to this population. She is ultimately responsible for presenting solutions we suggest to the board and getting the solutions implemented in the entire agency. In discussing the problem, we should consider ways that existing services could be redirected or applied differently to the clients we serve. Eligibility requirements and other issues related to access must also be explored. We may also want to consider using regularly scheduled in-service trainings and supervision to increase our awareness of the problem and to enhance our skills in dealing with this population. What are your thoughts about tackling this problem?

This example illustrates that the worker has set some broad guidelines for problem solving and has made some tentative suggestions to the group about what aspects of the problem might be worth exploring. The worker has given the group some indication of what is feasible within the budget constraints of the agency and has clarified who is responsible for implementing potential solutions. By asking for members' thoughts about the problem the worker is inviting them to define the boundaries of the problem within these broad guidelines.

Members' Perceptions and Experiences. Members' perceptions of problematic situations and their expectations about how they should be resolved determine the way they will approach a problem. If the members of a group are to be satisfied with the group's problem-solving process and committed to the solution that is decided upon by the group, the members' views about problems facing the group must be respected. There is no better way to show respect than to solicit members' views and to ensure that they are given a fair hearing by all members. Failure to clarify members' expectations and perceptions about a problem often leads to difficulties later in the group's problem-solving process. For example, hidden agendas develop, in part, because unclarified expectations are acted on by members.

Clarifying boundaries and helping members to express their perceptions and expectations of the problem-solving situation can be helpful techniques in arriving at a common understanding of the problem. An open discussion usually causes a modification of all group members' perceptions and expectations. Common perceptions and expectations form the basis for mutually agreed upon goals.

Careful considerations of the views of individual group members does not mean that every opinion or bit of information should be treated as equally correct or important. Although there is a tendency to equate equality of ideas with equal treatment of group members, these concepts should not be confused (Kiesler, 1978). Members should be treated equitably in the group process, but the importance of their contribution changes as the work of the group changes.

Sometimes, one or more members may hold tenaciously to initial perceptions of a problem or to initial expectations about the ways a problem should be resolved. Group members should be invited to discuss the logic of their assessments as a means of arriving at a shared view of the problem.

When the majority of the group's members agree with the leader's assessment and ideological differences separate one or two members from the rest of the group, workers can acknowledge the conflict and help members to express minority opinions while continuing to carry out decisions made by the majority.

Problem-solving Orientation. During the process of identifying a problem it is important for the worker to help members develop a problem-solving orientation (D'Zurilla and Goldfried, 1971). A problem-solving orientation includes:

1. Minimizing irrational beliefs about problematic situations.
2. Recognizing and being willing to work on problems as they occur.
3. Inhibiting tendencies to either respond prematurely on the first impulse or to do nothing.

Irrational beliefs about "how the world should be" can inhibit members from recognizing problematic situations and can also interfere with members' ability to act on problems that need to be resolved (Ellis, 1962). Irrational beliefs can lead to primitive solutions that can have detrimental consequences for the group as a whole. It is important for the worker to encourage all members to challenge irrational beliefs and to encourage rational approaches to problem solving. Members should be helped to use evidence, logic, and sound reasoning as they identify and define a problematic situation (see, for example, Gouran, 1982; Barker, 1979; Harnack and Fest, 1964; Sattler and Miller, 1968).

An effective problem-solving orientation includes recognizing problems that need attention and being willing to work on them. It is sometimes difficult for task groups to confront and work on problems facing them. For example, a team in a psychiatric hospital avoids discussing problems in its own functioning for fear that the discussion will be viewed as an attack on individual members. In this case, the team leader can help by facilitating the development of a group climate that encourages problems to be discussed as shared concerns whose resolution will benefit all team members.

In developing a problem-solving orientation within the group, it is important to help members reduce their tendency to make immediate and automatic responses (Toseland, 1977). Frequently, members will suggest solutions without carefully considering the problem. It has been found that less effective problem solvers are impulsive, impatient, and quick to give up (Bloom and Broder, 1950). Therefore the workers should help members to stop and think about the problem and to collect data and analyze alternative solutions before deciding on what to do (Dollard and Miller, 1950).

There should be sufficient time during a meeting agenda to grapple with difficult problems. According to Tropman (1980), difficult items should be placed in the middle third of the agenda. This is when members are at the peak of their (1) psychological focus, (2) physiological awareness, (3) attention, and (4) attendance (Tropman, 1980). Easier items should

be placed earlier in the agenda. Items for discussion only can be placed at the end of the agenda because they require less energy at a time when members have little energy for problem solving.

Defining a Solvable Problem. Groups are sometimes blocked in their problem-solving ability because they fail to locate the problem correctly (Maier, 1963). Group members may fail to identify the correct actors, the correct systems, or the correct obstacles that comprise the problem situation. In the early stages of problem solving, the group should be tentative and flexible about its problem definition so that it is possible to modify it when new data are collected about the situation.

How problems are stated can have an effect on the entire problem-solving process. The worker can use several techniques to improve the group's ability to define a solvable problem. Maier (1963) suggests that whenever possible, problems should be stated in situational rather than personal terms. For example, a definition that attributes the problem of lack of services to Mexican-Americans to an inept director of clinical services will tend to alienate the director of clinical services, making the problem more difficult to solve. However, stating the problem as a lack of service hours for the Mexican-Americans opens possibilities for modifying service delivery patterns. Similarly, defining the problem as a lack of knowledge and expertise about Mexican-American clients suggests that the committee should consider assessing members' willingness to learn more about Mexican-Americans.

To help the group obtain a new perspective on a problem, the worker can use the reframing technique, an exercise that can help members to reframe a problem by asking them to imagine themselves experiencing it as another might experience it. For example, members of a program committee who have some reservations about making efforts to improve services for Mexican-Americans are asked to imagine themselves going to an agency where no one speaks English and where most clients and all workers have a different cultural and ethnic background from their own. The exercise helps members to reconsider whether something should be done to improve services for Mexican-Americans.

Reframing may also be done by focusing on the positive aspects of a problem. For example, a problem that is experienced as anxiety-provoking may be reframed as one that motivates the group to improve a situation. In these ways, members' motivation to solve problems can be increased.

Specifying the Problem. Having a clearly defined and mutually understood problem is essential if members are to work effectively together. When problems are first expressed in a meeting, they are often stated as partially formulated concerns. For example, a committee member might say "I get a sense that some of our staff may be having difficulty with the new record keeping system." Many of the terms in this statement are vaguely defined. Terms such as "get a sense," "some of our staff" and "difficulty" can have different meanings for each member of the group.

As concerns are raised by members, the worker should help them to clarify vague or ambiguous terms. The state-ment mentioned previously, for example, could be clarified to indicate that three members of the community team and one member of the day treatment team expressed concerns that the new record keeping system took too long to fill out. The group should be encouraged to continue to clarify terms such as "took too long to fill out" so that it becomes clear what it is the group is being asked to consider. For example "took too long to fill out" might mean "can not complete the case record in the 15 minutes allocated for that purpose" or might mean "being asked to collect data which is not needed to work with clients." Sometimes members of the task group may find that they can't specify the problem further without collecting additional information.

After the group has clarified the problem, the worker should summarize it in a clear, brief statement. Ideally, the problem should be defined in objective terms that have similar meanings for all members. Objective terms with clear, observable referents help members to arrive at a common understanding of the situation. When summarizing, the worker should restate the boundaries of the problem and the group's authority and responsibility so that members will have a clear idea of their role in resolving it.

Developing Goals

The second step in the problem-solving process is goal setting. Goal setting does not occur at only one time in the problem-solving process. Tentative goals are formulated soon after the problem has been identified. These tentative goals aid in data collection because they help to shape the scope of the information that is to be collected. Goals are often modified and specified during data collection as additional information is accumulated. Initial goals may sometimes be abandoned altogether and new goals may be developed on the basis of the data accumulated.

The procedures for developing goals for specific problems are quite similar to goal-setting procedures described in beginning a group. Through a process of exploration and negotiation, the worker and the members share their perspectives about what goals the group should achieve in relating to a particular problem. The emphasis should be on formulating goals that are mutually acceptable. Like problem statements, goal statements should be as clear and specific as possible. Desired changes in problem situations should be stated as objective tasks. For example, goals to increase services to Mexican Americans might include (1) providing eight hours of training for each outreach worker during the next six months, (2) increasing the number of Mexican Americans served by the agency from an average of three a month to fifteen a month by the next fiscal year, (3) translating program brochures into Spanish within three months, and (4) printing four hundred bilingual Spanish-English brochures at the beginning of the next fiscal year. Each of these goals specify tasks that can be readily understood by all members.

Workers can utilize several other principles for developing effective goals, including:

1. Goals should be directed at the mutual concerns of all members.
2. Goals should be consistent with the group's mandate, its overall objectives, and the values which have been agreed upon by the group as a whole.
3. Goals should be attractive enough to gain the commitment, cooperation, and the investment of all group members.
4. Goals should be realistic and attainable through the resources available to the group and its members.
5. Goals should be time-limited.
6. The goal-setting process should set a supportive, encouraging climate for goal attainment.

At the end of the goal-setting process, members should be clear about the tasks they must perform in order to achieve the goals decided on by the group. It is important for the worker to summarize the goals that have been decided upon by the group and to review each member's role in goal achievement. This avoids misunderstandings about who is responsible for what during a specified time period. Members should be clear about the time frame for accomplishing goals and about the mechanisms for reporting their achievements to the group.

It is often helpful to partialize large goals into a series of smaller ones that can be more readily accomplished by the group in a short time period. This is particularly true in recently organized groups, whose members may be overwhelmed by the enormity of a task and unsure about the group's ability to accomplish it. Partializing goals gives members a sense of accomplishment as they reach subgoals. This sense of accomplishment increases the attractiveness of the group, helping to ensure highly motivated members for future problem-solving efforts.

Collecting Data

Data collection, the third step in the problem-solving process, begins as soon as a problem is identified by a group and continues as broad goals are defined and refined and as plans are being developed. As a process, data collection is concerned with idea generation. It should be kept separate from analyzing facts and generating solutions. Data collection relies on creative, imaginative thinking, whereas data analysis relies on evaluative thinking. Groups sometimes arrive at hasty, ill-conceived solutions because they rush to implement initial ideas without carefully exploring the situation, the obstacles to problem resolution, and the ramifications of a proposed solution.

Areas of information that are important for the group to obtain when attempting to solve any problem include (1) the history of the problem; (2) previous attempts at resolving the problem; (3) objective facts about the situation, such as who is involved in the situation, where, how, and when the problem occurred; (4) characteristics of the problem, such as its duration, intensity, scope, and importance; (5) the psychosocial context of the problem; and (6) organizational and societal rules and regulations that impinge on the problem. It is important for the group to have as much information as possible about the problem as it analyzes data and prepares alternative solutions.

Knowing the history of the problem helps the group to develop a longitudinal perspective on its development and its course. Comparing the state of affairs before and after a problem has occurred can often point to potential causes and possible solutions. While gathering data about the history of the problem, the group should become familiar with previous attempts to solve the problem. This can help the group avoid repeating past failures.

The worker should help members to pinpoint as many objective facts about the situation as possible. To help members separate facts from opinions and feelings, the worker should encourage members to describe the situation as if they were uninvolved observers who took a photograph of the situation. After the objective facts of the situation are described, members should be encouraged to share their unique perspectives about the problem. Scheidel and Crowell (1979) list five facilitative conditions that help to create a group climate which encourages members to share their unique perspectives. These include (1) maintaining the group's openness to speculation, (2) encouraging an open search for all pertinent data, (3) encouraging all group members to present their ideas, (4) demonstrating genuine appreciation of differences, and (5) refraining from evaluation (Scheidel and Crowell, 1979).

A supportive group climate reduces the need for members to defend their positions. Gibb (1961) points out that communications should be expressed (1) nonjudgmentally, (2) genuinely, (3) without the intent of controlling others, (4) with tentativeness rather than certainty, and (5) as an equal rather than as a superior. Facilitating this type of communication in a group increases problem exploration and contributes to high-quality solutions.

Members should be helped to become "unstuck" in the ways in which they explore and review the problem (Napier and Gershenfeld, 1981). Members should be encouraged to (1) view problem situations flexibly rather than rigidly, (2) expand rather than restrict the way information is collected and combined, (3) recognize and fill gaps in available information, (4) generate new ideas by viewing situations from alternative perspectives, and (5) use lateral as well as vertical thinking processes.

Vertical thinking processes are often associated with rational problem-solving strategies. Vertical thinking relies on inductive and deductive reasoning. Evidence and reason are used in a logical fashion until a solution is reached. Solutions are grounded in facts that are built one upon another in an orderly, systematic, and linear fashion.

Lateral thinking processes are particularly useful in problematic situations when vertical thinking processes have not yielded a creative solution. Lateral thinking helps to free ideas that have been blocked by stale, routine ways of conceptualizing a problem and its potential solutions. Instead of relying on an orderly, linear combination of facts, lateral thinking is characterized by the use of analogies, metaphors, similarities, contrasts, and paradoxes. Seemingly disparate facts, thoughts, and ideas are put together in new and creative ways. Analogies, for example, help to bring out similarities between objects or situations that were previously considered to be different. Solutions that were found to be helpful in analogous situations might, for example, be tried in the current situation. For further information about lateral

thinking process, see DeBono (1968, 1971, 1972).

Developing Plans

Whereas data collection encourages divergent thinking processes, preparing plans for problem resolution encourages convergent thinking processes (Scheidel and Crowell, 1979). The worker calls on members to organize, analyze, and synthesize facts, ideas, and perspectives generated during problem exploration.

The first step in analyzing the information generated during data collection is to display it so that all members can see it. It is difficult for members to keep a great deal of information in mind as they are attempting to develop alternative solutions. Displaying information on newsprint or a blackboard helps to ensure that all members are aware of the full range of information shared during a discussion.

The next step is to order and clarify the information generated by the group. Techniques that are useful for this purpose include (1) separating relevant from irrelevant facts, (2) combining similar facts, (3) identifying discrepancies, (4) looking for patterns across different facts, and (5) ordering facts from most important to least important. During the process of organizing data into a coherent whole, members should be encouraged to discuss the logic behind their reasoning rather than to discuss their particular ordering of information. Members should be encouraged to give each other a chance to explain why they see things the way they do, rather than to defend their choices. Defending choices often entrenches group members' opinions, whereas a discussion of how members think information should be used often brings out commonalities and similarities in members' views of the situation.

After the information is ordered, it is helpful to redefine the problem, specifying, refining, and, if necessary, reframing it, in view of the facts, ideas, and perspectives that have been discussed. It is also helpful to reexamine the group's goals by comparing the problem situation to the outcomes the group would like to achieve by resolving the problem. Once a common definition of the problem is reached and a valued end state is specified, the group should have little trouble developing a plan to solve the problem.

Before making a decision, members should be encouraged to develop as many alternative solutions as possible. Because critical and evaluative comments tend to inhibit the production of creative ideas, workers should caution members not to criticize each other's solutions as they are presented. When members generate alternative solutions, they should also keep in mind that their strategies and plans for problem resolution must begin to specify the action system and the tasks, as well as the time, energy, and resources necessary for implementing the solution.

Selecting the Best Plan

After all members have presented their alternatives, the group should review each one. This review has several purposes. It helps to ensure that all members understand each alternative. Misunderstandings at this point can cause conflict and reduce the chances for achieving closure in the problem-solving process. Reviews can be used to clarify the objectives and goals de-

scribed in each alternative plan. Objectives should clearly indicate who will be involved in problem resolution efforts and what they will be doing. Objectives should be developed in a way that allows them to be evaluated. When reviewing each alternative, members can discuss how they would overcome obstacles and challenges likely to be encountered if the alternative were implemented. For large or costly decisions, task groups sometimes recommend that one or more alternatives be tested in a pilot program before full-scale implementation.

Once this is done, members are ready to choose between alternative plans. When selecting among alternatives, members should be encouraged to consider the overall likelihood that a plan will resolve the problem in a manner that is valued by all group members (Edwards, 1961). For this purpose, it is helpful for members to develop criteria that can be used to judge each plan. Rational decision-making methods based on utility theory have been developed to help members develop judgment criteria. Although much has been written about these methods (see, for example, Becker and McClintock, 1967; Shelly and Bryan, 1964; Edwards, Lindman, and Phillips, 1965), until recently they have not been widely applied in the human services (Huber, 1980; Rohrbaugh, 1979, 1981; Toseland, Rivas and Chapman, 1984).

To select among alternatives, groups sometimes rely on decision criteria developed by experts. For example, a task group at HEW was charged with distributing funds for health maintenance organizations in "medically underserved" areas. By using panels of experts, the committee developed four criteria for deciding among programs that applied for funds in "medically underserved" areas. These included (1) the number of physicians per 1,000 population, (2) the percentage of families in the area served with less than $5000 annual income, (3) the infant mortality rate in the area served, and (4) the percentage of the area's population over age 65 (Health Services Research Group, 1975).

At other times, groups rely on the expertise of their own members to develop decision criteria. This is frequently done by having members rate the advantages and the disadvantages of each alternative. Alternatives may be combined or modified to maximize advantages and minimize disadvantages. As members decide between alternatives they should keep in mind the group's mandate, its goals, and the ideal situation they would like to see result if the problem was resolved successfully. Members may also want to consider other factors, such as the benefits and costs of implementing alternative solutions, the comfort and ease with which particular solutions are likely to be implemented, and the political ramifications of alternative solutions. The most effective solution to a problem may not be the most desirable solution if it is costly or if it is likely to offend, inconvenience, or otherwise upset those who will be asked to implement it.

Implementing the Plan

Excellent decisions can be worthless when task groups do little to ensure that they are implemented properly. Effective problem solving requires that a group take an active part in overseeing a plan's implementation.

Input from those who will be influential in implementing the plan should be solicited as early as possible in the problem-solving process. Once a solution is decided upon, members should begin to gain support for the decision from constituencies outside the group. Members should seek the support of those with authority to implement the decision and those who will be held accountable for the decision. For example, the committee that decided to improve outreach efforts to Mexican-Americans by training staff and publicizing agency programs in the Mexican-American community sought the cooperation of the board of directors, the agency's executive director, the directors of programs who are responsible for implementing staff training and publicity campaigns, all direct service staff who were going to be involved in the program, and leaders of the Mexican-American community.

When seeking the support of others, members may have to educate people to the value of a new approach to a problem. Motivating people to cooperate with the implementation of a decision is not an easy task. However, motivation is important because passivity during the implementation phase of problem solving can often mean the demise of a promising solution. In gaining cooperation, individual members or the group as a whole may also have to use some leverage to gain the support of others (Cox, Erlich, Rothman, and Tropman, 1974). This leverage may include persuasion by those with prestige and power or lobbying by those who will benefit by the solution.

Once the receptivity of those responsible for implementing the decision is ensured, the group can begin to organize and supervise the plan's implementation. When a group is responsible for the implementation of a large plan, a division of labor is often helpful. Each member may be assigned specific responsibilities in overseeing the plan's implementation. There may also be a need for training to educate those who will implement the plan.

It is often helpful to delineate steps in the implementation sequence. Objectives can be specified for each step, allowing the group to obtain periodic feedback about the plan's implementation. A time line can be attached to the implementation sequence. This helps to clarify how much time is available for each step during the implementation phase. During this process, members often experience surprise and even shock at how long a plan will take to become fully operational.

Implementing the proposed solution also includes identifying, contacting, and utilizing available resources. A heterogeneous group can be advantageous in the process because of the diversity of resources that members have available. Members can also help the group to prepare for opposition. Obstacles might include inertia, passive resistance, and perceived or actual conflicts of interest that can lead to attempts to block implementation of a plan.

Feedback is essential in the problem-solving process. When planning for the implementation of a decision, group members should establish feedback channels. Access to feedback can keep the group apprised of a solution's utility in terms of its expected outcome. Feedback can be used to overcome obstacles, to stabilize change, and to meet the challenges of a continually changing environment.

BIBLIOGRAPHY

Argyris, C. Organizational learning and management information systems. *Accounting, Organizations and Society,* 1977, *2,* 113–123.

Barker, L. *Groups in process: An introduction to small group communication.* Englewood Cliffs, NJ: Prentice-Hall, Inc., 1979.

Becker, G., and McClintock, G. Value: Behavioral decision theory. *Annual Review of Psychology,* 1967, *18,* 239–286.

Bloom, B., and Broder, L. *Problem-solving processes of college students.* Chicago: University of Chicago Press, 1950.

Bowers, D., and Franklin, J. *Survey-guided development: Data-based organizational change.* Ann Arbor, MI: Institute for Social Research, 1976.

Bradford, L. *Making meetings work: A guide for leaders and group members.* La Jolla, CA: University Associates, 1976.

Brill, N. *Team-work: Working together in the human services.* Philadelphia: J. B. Lippincott Co., 1976.

Burke, R. Methods of resolving superior-subordinate conflict: The constructive use of subordinate differences and disagreements. *Organizational Behavior and Human Performance,* 1970, *5,* 393–411.

Campbell, J. Individual versus group problem-solving in an industrial sample. *Journal of Applied Psychology,* 1968, *52,* 205–210.

Carnes, W. *Effective meetings for busy people.* New York: McGraw-Hill Book Co., 1980.

Chung, K., and Ferris, M. An inquiry of the nominal group process. *Academy of Management Journal,* 1971, *14,* 520–524.

Collaros, R., and Anderson, L. Effects of perceived expertness upon creativity of members of brainstorming groups. *Journal of Applied Psychology,* 1969, *53*(2), part 1, 159–164.

Cox, F., Erlich, J., Rothman, J., and Tropman, J. (eds.). *Strategies of community organization.* Itasca, IL: F. E. Peacock Publishers, Inc., 1974.

DeBono, E. *New think: The use of lateral thinking in the generation of new ideas.* New York: Basic Books, Inc., Publishers, 1968.

DeBono, E. *Lateral thinking for management.* New York: American Management Associations, Inc., 1971.

DeBono, E. *Lateral thinking: Productivity step by step.* New York: Harper & Row Publishers, 1972.

Delbecq, A. The management of decision making within the firm: Three strategies for three types of decision making. *Academy of Management Journal,* 1967, *10,* 329–339.

Delbecq, A., Van de Ven, A., and Gustafson, D. *Group techniques for program planning: A guide to nominal group and Delphi processes.* Glenview, IL: Scott, Foresman & Company, 1975.

Deutsch, M. *The resolution of conflict.* New Haven, CT: Yale University Press, 1973.

Dollard, J., and Miller, N. *Personality and psychotherapy.* New York: McGraw-Hill Book Company, 1950.

D'Zurilla, T., and Goldfried, M. Problem solving and behavior modification. *Journal of Abnormal Psychology,* 1971, *78,* 107–126.

Ebbesen, E., and Bowers, R. Proportion of risky to conservative arguments in a group discussion and choice shift. *Journal of Personality and Social Psychology,* 1974, *29,* 316–327.

Edson, J. How to survive on a committee. *Social Work,* 1977, *22,* 224–226.

Edwards, W. Behavioral decision theory. *Annual Review of Psychology,* 1961, *1,* 473–498.

Edwards, W., Lindman, H., and Phillips, L. Emerging technologies for decision making. In T. Newcomb (Ed.). *New directions in psychology.* New York: Holt, Rinehart & Winston, 1965.

Ellis, A. *Reason and emotion in psychotherapy.* Secaucus, NJ: Lyle Stuart Publishers, 1962.

Filley, A. *Interpersonal conflict resolution.* Glenview, IL: Scott, Foresman & Company, 1974.

Gibb, J. Defensive communication. *The Journal of Communication,* 1961, *11,* 141–148.

Gouran, D. *Making decisions in groups: Consequences & choices.* Glenview, IL: Scott, Foresman & Company, 1982.

Guetzkow, H., and Gyr, J. An analysis of conflict in decision-making groups. *Human Relations,* 1954, *7,* 368–381.

Gulley, H. *Discussion, conference and group process* (2nd ed.). New York: Holt, Rinehart & Winston, 1968.

Hackman, J., and Morris, C. Group tasks, group interaction process and group performance effectiveness: A review and proposed integration. In L. Berkowitz (Ed.). *Advances in experimental and social psychology* (Vol. 8). New York: Academic Press, Inc., 1975.

Hare, A. *Handbook of small group research* (2nd ed.). New York: Free Press, 1976.

Harnack, R., and Fest, T. *Group discussion: Theory and technique.* New York: Appleton-Century-Crofts, 1964.

Health Services Research Group. Development of an index of medical underservedness. *Health Service Research,* 1975, *10,* 168–180.

Houle, C. *The effective board.* New York: Association Press, 1960.

Howard, J. *Please touch.* New York: McGraw-Hill Book Company, 1970.

Huber, G. *Managerial decision making.* Glenview, IL: Scott, Foresman & Company, 1980.

Janis, I. *Victims of group think.* Boston: Houghton Mifflin Company, 1972.

Kane, R. The interprofessional team as a small group. *Social Work in Health Care,* 1975, *1*(1), 19–32.

Kane, R. Teams: Thoughts from the bleachers. *Health and Social Work,* 1976, *18,* 52–59.

Kelley, H., and Thibaut, J. Group problem solving. In G. Lindzey and E. Aronim (Eds.). *Handbook of social psychology* (2nd ed., Vol. 10). Reading, MA: Addison Wesley Publishing Co., Inc., 1969.

Kiesler, S. *Interpersonal processes in groups and organizations.* Arlington Heights, IL: AHM Publishing Co., 1978.

Lewin, K. *Resolving social conflict.* New York: Harper & Row Publishers, 1948.

Lowe, J., and Herranen, M. Conflict in teamwork: Understanding roles and relationships. *Social Work in Health Care,* 1978, *3,* 323–330.

Maier, N. *Problem-solving discussions and conferences: Leadership methods and skills.* New York: McGraw-Hill Book Company, 1963.

Maier, N., and Hoffman, L. Quality of first and second solutions in group problem solving. *Journal of Applied Psychology,* 1960, *44,* 278–283.

Miner, F. A comparative analysis of three diverse group decision making approaches. *Academy of Management Journal,* 1979, *22,* 81–93.

Myers, D., and Arenson, S. Enhancement of the dominant risk in group discussion. *Psychological Reports,* 1972, *30,* 615–623.

Nadler, D. *Feedback and organizational development: Using data base methods.* Reading, MA: Addison-Wesley Publishing Co., Inc., 1977.

Nadler, D. The effects of feedback on task group behavior: A review of the experimental research. *Organizational Behavior and Human Performance,* 1979, *23,* 309–338.

Napier, H. Individual versus group learning: Note on task variable. *Psychological Reports,* 1967, *23,* 757–758.

Napier, R., and Gershenfeld, M. *Groups: theory and experience* (2nd ed.). Boston: Houghton Mifflin Company, 1981.

Robert, H. *Robert's rules of order.* Glenview, IL: Scott, Foresman & Company, 1970.

Rohrbaugh, J. Improving the quality of group judgment: Social judgment analysis and the Delphi technique. *Organizational Behavior and Human Performance,* 1979, *24,* 73–92.

Rohrbaugh, J. Improving the quality of group judgment: Social judgment analysis and the nominal group technique. *Organizational Behavior and Human Performance,* 1981, *26,* 272–288.

Rotter, G., and Portugal, S. Group and individual effects in problem solving. *Journal of Applied Psychology,* 1969, *53,* 338–341.

Sattler, W., and Miller, N. *Discussion and conference* (2nd ed.). Englewood Cliffs, NJ: Prentice-Hall, Inc., 1968.

Scheidel, T., and Crowell, L. *Discussing and deciding: A deskbook for group leaders and members.* New York: Macmillan Publishing Co., Inc., 1979.

Shelly, M., and Bryan, G. (Eds.). *Human judgment and optimality.* New York: John Wiley & Sons, Inc., 1964.

Siporin, M. Ecological system theory in social work. *Journal of Sociology and Social Work,* 1980(a), *7,* 507–532.

Steiner, I. *Group process and productivity.* New York: Academic Press, Inc., 1972.

Stoner, J. *A comparison of individual and group decision including risk.* Masters Thesis, School of Industrial Management, MIT, Cambridge, MA, 1961.

Stoner, J. Risky and cautious shifts in group decisions: The influence of widely held values. *Journal of Experimental Social Psychology,* 1968, *4,* 442–459.

Swanson, A. *The determinative team: A handbook for board members of voluntary organizations.* New York: Exposition Press, 1978.

Teger, A., and Pruitt, D. Components of group risk-taking. *Journal of Experimental Psychology,* 1967, *3,* 189–205.

Torrance, E. Group decision making and disagreement. *Social Forces,* 1957, *35,* 314–318.

Toseland, R. A problem-solving workshop for older persons. *Social Work,* 1977, *22*(4), 325–327.

Toseland, R., Rivas, R., and Chapman, D. An evaluation of decision making in task groups. *Social Work,* 1984, *29,* 339–346.

Trecker, H. *Group process in administration.* New York: Women's Press, 1946.

Tropman, J. *Effective meetings: Improving group decision-making.* Beverly Hills, CA: Sage Publishing Company, 1980.

Tropman, J., Johnson, H., and Tropman, E. *The essentials of committee management.* Chicago, IL: Nelson-Hall, 1979.

Van De Ven, A. *Group decision making and effectiveness: An experimental study.* Ohio: Kent State University Press, 1974.

Van De Ven, A., and Delbecq, A. Nominal versus interacting group processes for committee decision-making effectiveness. *Academy of Management Journal,* 1971, *9,* 203–212.

Vroom, V. Grant, L., and Cotton, T. The consequence of social interaction in group problem solving. *Journal of Organizational Behavior and Human Performance,* 1969, *4,* 79–95.

Wallach, M., and Wing, C. Is risk a value? *Journal of Personality and Social Psychology,* 1968, *9,* 101–106.

Whitaker, D. Some conditions for effective work with groups. *British Journal of Social Work,* 1975, *5,* 423–439.

Wise, H. *Making health teams work.* Cambridge, MA: Ballinger Pub. Co., 1974.

Zajonc, R., Wolosin, R., and Wolosin, W. Group risk-taking under various group decision schema. *Journal of Experimental and Social Psychology,* 1972, *8,* 16–30.

Zander, A. *Groups at work.* San Francisco: Jossey-Bass, 1977.

Ziller, R. Four techniques of group decision making under uncertainty. *Journal of Applied Psychology,* 1957, *41,* 384–388.

7.

Herbert Bisno

INTERPERSONAL TRANSACTIONS IN COMMUNITY PRACTICE

INTRODUCTION

When interpersonal relationships and skills are mentioned in a social work context one tends to think of counseling or related types of activity. A corollary of this is the tendency to minimize the importance of person-to-person, or person-to-group interactions, in such macro aspects of social work practice as policy formulation and implementation, planning, locality development, and social action. Although more attention is given to the place of interpersonal relationships in administration, even here there is less systematic regard for these transactions than might be expected. This general downgrading in emphasis and training of the interpersonal component in macro social work should surely be a matter of concern since, in reality, face-to-face transactions are a critical, and often major element, in community organization and related aspects of social work practice. The following examples are illustrative of the broad range of "non-counseling" types of interpersonal activities which you, as a social worker, might engage in:

Example 1 — You are to meet with representatives of the planning commission in your community to discuss the establishment of a refuge for battered women.

Source: This article was written especially for this volume. Printed by permission of the author.

Example 2 — You have arranged an appointment with the member of congress from your district on behalf of a welfare rights organization, to lobby for an increase in benefits for single parents.

Example 3 — As a member of the policy and social action committee of the local chapter of NASW, you are to attend a meeting with representatives from other concerned organizations for the purpose of formulating a strategy for improving and coordinating services for the "frail aged."

Example 4 — You have been asked by the director of your agency to meet with a representative of a "competing" organization to discuss ways of rationalizing the division of services and functions between your two agencies.

Example 5 — You, and several other workers from your agency, are going to meet the Director and Chairman of the Board to discuss better conditions of employment.

Example 6 — You are planning to do a "needs" and "wants" survey (by interview) of people in your community.

Example 7 — You are coordinating the volunteers working on a community development project.

Example 8 — You are to chair a meeting of workers with different disciplinary backgrounds, in an attempt to improve case planning and reduce interprofessional competition.

Example 9 — You have organized a meeting with local landlords in order to try to reduce harassment of your clients (renters) who are in conflict with them.

Obviously these examples merely "scratch the surface" of the interpersonal transactions involved in macro social work practice. In view of the importance of such activities why is such minimal attention granted to them in the professional literature and in the education of social workers? It would appear that two of the primary reasons for the relative neglect of the interpersonal process in macro social work are: (1) the belief that face-to-face interactions and skills are the same whether in a "helping" (e.g., casework-group work) situation or as part of a community organizing (or similar) activity; and (2) the assumption that the general skills learned in preparing oneself for "helping" activities suffice for all types of interpersonal transactions. A third possible explanation is that the interpersonal skills in macro social work are considered to be "intuitive" or, at least, not susceptible to being systematically taught/learned.

This article is based on the premise that all three of these reasons are invalid. In other words, we believe that although all interpersonal interactions have certain characteristics in common, those which are typically part of macro social work differ in many significant respects from the interpersonal transactions which make up the bulk of traditional "helping-type" practice. In turn, it appears that while some of the same *skills* and qualities are called for in both categories of face-to-face rela-tionships there are many very important competencies which are relatively "unique" to each. Furthermore, there is every reason to believe that those skills required for effective macro social work interpersonal interaction can be learned and taught just as readily as "therapeutic" type competencies, and that neither is more intuitively grasped nor naturally possessed than the other.

Throughout this article we shall refer to those types of interpersonal interactions characteristic of macro social work as *instrumental* activities. More specifically, we are using the term instrumental to refer to those "task-oriented" aspects of social work practice which are not, basically, of a helper-helped character. In so doing we are differentiating the instrumental from the "helping" type of interactions which we shall refer to as *subventionary.* The term subventionary, then, is used to designate those types of transactions commonly associated with the "helping" role of social workers (e.g., counseling, provision of material aid, and certain types of group work) in which the provision of assistance is sought by the recipient (rather than being imposed). The proviso that subventionary refers to desired help means that certain types of *involuntary* social work-client relationships may be more instrumental than subventionary. However, our present concern is with those instrumental activities characteristic of macro social work, such as community organization in the broadest sense.

Of course, all professional interpersonal interactions have some things in common and require certain of the same competencies. For example, basic communication skills, sensitivity to the reactions of others, disciplined use of the self, the ability to secure an appropriate form of rapport, and a fundamental psychosocial understanding of human beings are required of all social workers, regardless of their arena of practice. Nevertheless, the differences between the instrumental and subventionary modes of practice are of particular importance and the remainder of this article will focus on the shaping characteristics of those types of instrumental interpersonal transactions most commonly employed in macro social work.

INSTRUMENTAL ACTIVITIES AND RELATIONSHIPS: CHARACTERISTICS AND PROCEDURES

1. Goals and Interests

In the classic voluntary helping situation the goals/interests of the worker and client are normally shared, or at least similar. However, in instrumental relationships the objectives of the social worker may or may not be the same as those of the persons with whom he is interacting. When the goals are not shared this is often due to conflicting or competing interest. For example, let's consider the situation in which a social worker is meeting with representatives of the landlords' association in order to try to convince them to provide a better level of building maintenance for the welfare clients who live in their apartments. In this instance the social worker may be going counter to the landlords' goal which is to resist any change that will reduce profits from the buildings. Thus, the interest of the social worker in representing the desire of people on welfare to have a decent place in which to live may be in conflict with the land-lords' interest in ensuring a given level of return from their investments. One may argue, of course, that it would be in the "real interests" of the owners of the building to spend more money on maintenance. Regardless of whether this argument is valid or not the fact in the given situation is that at least the perceived interests of the parties in the transaction are in opposition.

Another illustrative situation would be one in which a social worker is trying to convince an "anti-abortion" legislator that there should be a liberalization of the abortion laws. In this circumstance the social worker may be arguing on behalf of the "right" of women to have a choice while the legislator may insist on priority being given to the "right-to-life" of the unborn child.

Of course, the social worker's goals and interests are not always on behalf of "clients," individually or collectively, or some amorphous reference groups. The confrontation may be over the direct interests of the social worker as opposed to the interests of the other party (or groups being represented by that person) with whom she is interacting. For example, a social worker may negotiate, on behalf of her own interests and that of other social workers in the organization, with the director of the agency for higher salaries and better working conditions for all the social work staff, herself included. The director, on the other hand, may claim that greater expenditure on the staff would result in fewer benefits for clients. In turn, the social worker might maintain that an improvement in the conditions of employment is likely to result in a higher quality service being provided to clients. However, the director may respond that as long as there is a fixed sum of money available to the agency it is a matter of the direct interests of the users of service being opposed to the interests of the help providers, and that a gain for the workers will be at the expense of clients. In this situation, multiple interests are involved, or at least invoked, one of which is that of the social workers themselves. There is, of course, nothing inherently wrong or unethical in this type of self-interest being pursued by social workers. It is well to remember that "self-interest" and "selfishness" are not one and the same. One might pursue one's self-interest in the process of giving assistance to another person. On the other hand, the pursuit of self-interest may, in given instances, be "selfish" in the sense of exploiting others for one's own advantage.

The examples, thus far, have been of goals and interests in conflict, or apparent conflict. However, the transactions of the social worker in instrumental relationships may involve differing interests but shared goals. For instance, a social worker, in a conference with a landlord, may agree to support a request by the landlord for higher welfare rent payments in return for a promise that a higher level of service will be provided to the renters. In this situation the transaction involved different interests, but a "superordinate" goal emerged which accommodated both sets of interests. Or, a slightly different version of the same type of situation would be evident in the following example: A social worker representing the professional association, and an environmentalist acting on behalf of his organization may agree to collaborate in formulating a policy statement supporting improved public transportation in the inner city. The social worker's primary interest in doing this

is to secure better transportation facilities for poor people while the environmentalist's main concern is a reduction in the pollution levels.

Finally, there may be an identity of purposes and interests in instrumental transactions. Two social workers, representing different agencies, may support an educational campaign to increase the community's awareness of the social and personal costs of racism and other forms of discrimination and oppression.

2. Obligations and Accountability

The primary obligation of the social worker in interpersonal transactions in the macro arena will vary with the situation. It may be to the community, profession, colleagues, social movement, reference group, user-of-service, or to oneself. The examples in the previous section illustrate this diversity in the primacy of responsibility and ethical obligations of the social worker engaged in instrumental interactions. Once again, a contrast may be drawn with the conventional voluntary social worker-client relationship in which the primary responsibility and ethical obligation of the social worker is usually to the user-of-service, although other accountabilities may also be involved.

The following example highlights the fact that in instrumental interpersonal transactions the social worker's primary concern is not necessarily with the well-being of the interactant (the person with whom the worker is engaged in the transaction): A social worker negotiates with the representative of a civil service (public service) board over the issue of "declassifying" various positions and eliminating the requirement of a social work qualification for them. The social worker argues against the declassification while the civil service representative is an advocate of it. In this case the social worker's primary responsibility is not the satisfaction or perceived self-interest of the public service representative, rather, it is a concern with the well-being of the profession and, indirectly, with an alleged "public interest." Of course, the civil service chap may also contend he is acting on behalf of a group or category of people "out there."

Or take the case of a social worker who is trying to get a retailer to change his "high pressure" credit sales tactics. In this situation the social worker may even "threaten" the economic well-being of the retailer with whom he is disputing the matter. Here again, the social worker's primary responsibility is not to the person occupying the other side of the interactional process (the retailer). Now it might be argued that the social worker is really representing the interest of clients (potential or actual) in this process by his stand but, in reality, this is another instance of an indirect "public interest" being involved, rather than a "client" or "client group" per se. Hence, it is very different from the face-to-face relationship with a client in a helping situation in which the social worker's primary (but not necessarily exclusive) commitment and ethical obligation is normally to the well-being of the person "across the table" from him.

3. Authority and Exchange

In the traditional helper-helped relationship there tends to be a built-in imbalance in terms of authority (expertise), psychological control, and dependency. In other words the "exchange" is not reciprocal, at least in the usual sense of the word. Now this is not necessarily because of the social worker's uncontrolled striving for power and dominance. In a fundamental sense, the very process of asking for assistance from another person tends to create an "imbalance" in that relationship since it usually acknowledges the greater resources or expertise of the potential helper. The situation may be quite different, though, in instrumental interpersonal relationships. In pursuing a matter with a colleague, a "significant other," or some other member of the community, there can be no automatic assumption that the social worker's involvement will be welcomed, nor that her greater resources and expertise will be acknowledged (or exist). Certainly, no inherent imbalance in favor of the social worker, with a resulting "dependence" on the part of the other person, can be assumed to be a characteristic of an instrumental relationship. This fact alone implies that an instrumental interpersonal relationship often will differ fundamentally from that in a helper-helped transaction.

4. Motivation

In a "voluntary" helping relationship the user-of-service is usually motivated to enter into the interactional process by a desire for assistance/provision of some resource (material or nonmaterial). However, the circumstances of an instrumental relationship may be quite different. In the macro arena interpersonal transactions may be entered into in order to secure an advantage (e.g., material gain, policy, professional, power, status); to expedite a task; or even because of legal necessity. Hence, unlike the more focussed motivational characteristic of helping relationships, instrumental transactions may be entered into for virtually any voluntary motive, or because of coercion.

Illustrative of the *range* of reasons for entering into an instrumental relationship are the following examples: (1) two social workers participate in a cooperative, voluntary relationship for the purpose of planning a joint social action campaign on behalf of a program to reduce youth unemployment; and, (2) a social worker is interrogated by a police officer (an instrumental relationship) in respect to his activities during a demonstration against the resurgence of anti-Semitism and racism in the local community. Of course, even a social worker doing counseling may be involved in an instrumental relationship with a client, a case in point being the interaction between a probation officer and his involuntary, antagonistic client.

5. Focus

In instrumental relationships, particularly those that occur in the macro arena, the emphasis tends to be on a task-orientation, with "emotional maintenance" activities relegated to a subordinate position. This is quite different from many types of helping relationships in which there is much attention to "feeling states," as well as to overt behavior. An amusing, though significant, consequence of the emphasis on "feelings" in the traditional view of social work relationships is that social workers frequently get in the habit of saying "I feel," when they mean "I think" or "I believe."

6. Illustrative Roles

The examples already discussed in this article suggest that social workers engaged in macro type instrumental activities occupy a variety of statuses (positions) and fill many different roles. Without trying to be inclusive the following roles can be readily identified: advocate, mediator, colleague, co-worker and co-participant, co-ordinator, administrator, policy-formulator and implementor, planner, representative, organizer, researcher, and ombudsman. Some of these are, of course, much more position-specific than others, but, together, they suggest the versatility required of the social worker engaged in macro type social work activities.

7. Illustrative Procedures
   (methods/techniques)

It should be evident, from the prior discussion, that a wide variety of procedures—methods and techniques—are associated with the instrumental types of transactions that characterize community organization and related activities. Among the most prominent of these are the *Adversative, Developmental, Role-Making,* and *Rule-Implementing.* These may be described as follows:

Adversative. This method is appropriate in situations involving potential or actual conflicts of interest or beliefs. In such conflictual (or competitive) circumstances oppositional and/or conciliatory types of techniques frequently come into play. Among the techniques that might be invoked are bargaining and negotiation, the exercise of power resources, conflict generation through the articulation and advocacy of competing interests, the development of a "superordinate" solution, clarification of positions and interpretations, and the maximizing of similarities and minimizing of differences. Adversative interactions normally are of an instrumental character.

Developmental. This method is suitable in those situations in which the basic concern revolves around a lack of resources, or of the need to mobilize and maximize those that exist, in fact or potentially. The techniques which might be utilized include coordination, use of influence mechanisms, information giving, assistance in problem definition, support, consciousness raising and the enhancement of personal, group, organizational and interorganizational capacities and skills. All of these techniques are expressed in instrumental transactions.

Rule-Making. This method is invoked when it seems desirable, for purposes of attaining an objective or coping with a problem situation, to formulate a new rule or policy/procedure, or to press for the passage of a law (or repeal of a law). Among the techniques which might be employed are lobbying, the preparation of policy briefs, debates, conducting meetings and norm enactment. Many of these techniques involve instrumental interactions.

Rule-Implementing. This method is called for when the situation requires the implementation of laws, policies, programs, and procedures. The techniques, all of which may involve instrumental interactions, include those of administration, policy interpretation, diffusion of information and the translation of policy into programs and procedures.

8. Skills and Knowledge

The preceding discussion of procedures suggests that the effectiveness in instrumental interactions requires a rather imposing repertoire of skills. For example, conflict management, which is one of the most important types of instrumental activities, necessitates skills such as: bargaining; the preparation of public relations materials; the ability to diagnose types of conflicts; the effective use of "third parties" (negotiators); expertise in conducting meetings; the ability to turn "ecological" factors (e.g., seating arrangements in a room) to one's benefit; the assessment of evidence; leadership; and political "manipulation." And this is just a sampling!

Underlying the skill repertoire must be a grounding in an appropriate knowledge base. This knowledge should include not only the "traditional" content found in the professional literature, but also "new" material (e.g., from industrial relations, social-psychology and public speaking) which can then also be incorporated into a social work framework.

Conclusion. In this article we have attempted to demonstrate that instrumental type interpersonal transactions are a vital part of effective community organization and related macro social work activities. Some of the main features of such *instrumental* interactions have been identified and described. Although the material in the article has, of necessity, been covered in a cursory fashion we hope that we have conveyed to you our belief in the importance of the subject matter, and that you will be stimulated to acquire, in the future, the requisite competencies.

8.

Fred M. Cox

COMMUNITY PROBLEM SOLVING: A GUIDE TO PRACTICE WITH COMMENTS

This problem-solving guide was developed by the editors and their students. Community practitioners will find that the guide directs their attention to a number of factors central to assessing community problems and developing a course of action for attacking them.

There have been a number of efforts to provide a model to guide community organization practice. Murray G. Ross developed a set of principles to guide community organization and a discussion of the roles of the organizer. (16, pp. 155-228; 17, pp. 157-231) Ronald Lippitt and his collaborators studied a wide range of planned change efforts, which include efforts at the community level. From this study, they formulated a discussion of the phases of planned change, the role of the change agent, an approach to diagnosis in planned change, and an analysis of the forces operating for and against change. (9) Roland Warren provides a five-stage model of the "development and change of community action systems." (25, p. 315 and pp. 303-39) Robert Perlman and Arnold Gurin offer a "problem solving model" in their study of community organization, prepared under the auspices of the Council of Social Work Education. (12, pp. 61-75) This list is by no means comprehensive (19, pp. 504ff.), but it includes those that have been most influential in shaping the present effort.

The guide is ordered sequentially as the factors considered are likely to be encountered in practice. The guide should be used flexibly. The experienced practitioner may not need to explore each point as carefully as one new to a situation. Few will have the opportunity to employ it systematically in every practice context. Nevertheless, we believe the practitioner will find it useful as a reminder of issues that may otherwise be overlooked or questions that provoke thought that may have an important bearing on practice decisions and outcomes. Some practitioners will be confronted with more "givens" and fewer choices than others. A clear understanding of the "givens" as well as the options is crucial for effective practice.

Like most general models, this one may fail to call attention to certain questions of importance in specific situations. Many practitioners will want to refine and elaborate the guide to suit the particulars of the practice situation in which they are involved. In general, however, we believe that the guide can contribute to a more logical and coherent approach to confronting problems in the multiple pressures and confusions of community practice.

THE GUIDE

I. Preliminary Considerations
    A. *Summary of Assignment.* Brief

description of the worker's assignment and developments leading to it, designed to introduce and make intelligible what follows

B. *Agency* (organization employing the practitioner)

  1. Type

    a. Based on primary beneficiary (2, pp. 45-57), mutual benefit, commonweal, service, and business

    b. Based on locus of control at the top or base (13), corporate or federated

    c. Representative, collegial, bureaucratic, or anomic (23)

  2. Constitution and goal orientation (formal statement and informal "understandings" of purposes, *modus operandi*)

    a. Domain and extent of community consensus on domain (8)

    b. Narrowly defined and specific or broad and general (13)

    c. Change or service orientation (Reading #12)

    d. Member or nonmember targets (Reading #12)

    e. Institutional or individual targets (Reading #12)

  3. Constituency (those who control the agency) and resource base (funds, clients, and personnel and their sources) (Reading #12)

    a. Homogeneous or heterogeneous on various dimensions—social class, ethnic characteristics, sex, interests, etc.

    b. Organizations or individuals

    c. Extent of agency dependence on constituency and resource base

  4. Internal structure (Intro., Part Two)

    a. Authority—hierarchical or collegial

    b. Division of labor—specialist or generalist

    c. Rules—predetermined and imposed on functionaries, based on internalization of goals by functionaries, ad hoc, etc.

    d. Interpersonal relations—impersonal or personal

    e. Personnel assigned on basis of merit or on criteria irrelevant to organization's goals

  5. Programs and functions of agency and their relation to worker's assignment

C. *Practitioner* (person employed by agency who is working on given problem)

  1. Motivation, capacity, and opportunity to perform assigned tasks (14)

  2. Role ambiguity, conflict, discontinuity, and strain in the situation and their management (22)

II. Problems (15)

A. *Problem Analysis* (as perceived by the practitioner)

  1. Nature: What specific kind of problem are you concerned about?

  2. Location: Where is the problem? (geographically, socially, psychologically, institutionally)

  3. Scope: Who (kinds of people, groups) are affected?

  4. Degree: How much are they affected?

B. *Past Change Efforts*

  1. By whom?

  2. How effective?

  3. Reasons for successes or failures

C. *Perceptions of the Problem by Significant Others* (individuals, groups and organizations) (15)

  1. Who perceives the problem as the practitioner does?

2. Who perceives it differently—as nonexistent or insignificant, or as qualitatively different?

III. Social Context of the Problem

A. *Origins of the Problem* (where relevant) (4)

B. *Theory of the Problem*

1. Why this rather than some alternative explanation?

2. Empirical and ideological justification

C. *Structural-Functional Analysis of the Problem*

1. Social structures that maintain, increase, or reduce the problem

a. Societal, regional, state, local, neighborhood

b. Formal organizations, voluntary associations, primary groups

c. Power alignments, social/demographic factors, ecological/economic relations, cultural/technological factors

2. Consequences of the problem for significant elements of the social structure—who gains, who loses. In what ways is the problem situation functional or dysfunctional for the maintenance of the groups having a stake in the problem?

IV. The Client (the population segments or groups that are the primary beneficiary of the practitioner's efforts) (2, pp. 45-57)

A. *Physical Location,* boundaries, size

B. *Social, Economic, Political, and Demographic Characteristics*

C. *Formal Organization of the Client*

D. *Divisions and Cleavages* within the client

E. *Significant Relations* with other parts of the social structure

F. *Significant Changes* in the above, over time

V. Goals (11; 18)

A. *Goals in Their Approximate Order of Priority* for dealing with the problem as identified by:

1. Agency

2. Client

3. Significant others

B. *Practitioner's Preferred Goals and Priorities,* in the light of the above, including:

1. Task goals (goals related to task attainment regarding a substantive community problem)

2. Process goals (system maintenance and enhancement goals—social relationships, problem-solving structures, and processes)

VI. Strategy. In the light of preferred goals and priorities, consider two or three feasible strategies, in the following terms: (9, pp. 71-89)

A. *Minimum Tasks Required for Success*

B. *The Action System.* Identify the resources and supporting groups from within the agency, the client and significant others required to carry out strategy under consideration

C. *Resistance* (opposition) *and Interference* (inertia, distraction) *Forces*

1. Review functional analysis (III.C. 2., above)

2. Identify opposing groups, their probable actions and impersonal difficulties which might be encountered

3. Indicate how the strategy under consideration would cope with these

D. *Evaluation of Practitioner's Ability To Utilize Strategy*

1. Can minimum tasks be carried

out and sustained?

2. Can needed resources and supporting groups be mobilized, and their cohesion and goal-directed behavior maintained?

3. Can resistance and interference forces be managed?

E. *Preferred Strategy.* Of the strategies considered, select one and give the rationale for this choice

VII. Tactics (9)

A. *Gaining Initial Support*

1. Entry—where does one start and with whom?

2. Leverage—what initial actions give one the best chance for sustaining one's strategy?

B. *Involving and Organizing* (or Reorganizing) *the Action System*

1. Clarification of the problem, including gathering and interpretation of relevant data

2. Clarification of goals and preferred strategy

3. Clarification of role expectations of change agent, agency, and various parts of the action system

4. Establishing a "contract" (or basic agreement between the practitioner and those making up the action system)

C. *Implementation of Action*

1. Training and offering organizational and psychological support to the action system

2. Scheduling actions over time

3. Utilizing available resources

4. Utilizing "Action-Reaction-Action" patterns (designing a sequence of actions to take advantage of anticipated responses) (1)

5. Dealing with opposition, as necessary (confrontation, neutralization, questioning legitimacy,

bargaining, etc.)

VIII. Evaluation (Reading #9)

A. *Success of Strategy in Problem Solution*

B. *Effectiveness of Tactics*

IX. Modification, Termination or Transfer of Action

A. *Designing New Goals, Strategy, or Tactics*

B. *Facilitating Termination or Modification of Practitioner's Activity*

1. Disengaging practitioners from action system

2. Transferring relations to new practitioner

3. Maintaining or institutionalizing change effort

4. Moving action system toward terminal goal(s)

COMMENTS[1]

As part of the effort to increase the professional character of community organization practice, we need to develop guidelines for decision making that are grounded upon tested generalities. As our knowledge base expands, it should be possible to rely more heavily on insights drawn from the social and behavioral sciences. The problem in basing decisions on tested knowledge is to find a way to join the hodgepodge which is the reality of community practice and the generalizations derived from research, which necessarily oversimplify, and select a few factors believed to be of overriding importance.

[1]The author acknowledges the contributions made by his colleagues John L. Erlich and Jack Rothman, whose critical comments and suggestions were used extensively in preparing this supplement to the preceding guide.

This problem is a difficult one for at least two reasons. First, our knowledge of what factors are most influential and their effects upon matters of importance to the practitioner, together with the various conditions that affect such cause and effect relationships, is very limited. Typically, we must be content with a combination of practice wisdom and partially tested theory validated under conditions quite different than those faced by each practitioner. For example, conclusions about group behavior are often based on laboratory data rather than field studies.

Second, even when knowledge is very full and based on rigorous study, there are serious problems in applying it. Scientific knowledge is the knowledge of probabilities, of the chances that certain actions or events are likely to be followed by particular consequences. But even a high probability of B being followed by A leaves room for the possibility, in some minority of instances, that A will not produce B. And there are always newly emerging contingencies, the effects of which are unknown, and relatively unique configurations of events and conditions that were not anticipated in the research studies. Thus, even under the best conditions, we must guard against expecting too much from scientific knowledge in guiding practice decisions.

What does the problem-solving guide contribute to this process? First, it suggests the major types of information that must be obtained by the practitioner if he or she is to reach informed decisions. Second, it offers the outline of an interconnected set of frameworks within which to collect this information. It does not, however, provide propositions or generalizations to which decisions must be referred; these comments will suggest some additional sources we have found useful for this purpose. The comments are organized in the same order and under the same headings as the guide above. Wherever possible we relate these comments to the three models of community organization around which this book is organized.

I. PRELIMINARY CONSIDERATIONS

A. Summary of Assignment

The practitioner provides a brief orientation to the nature of the assignment. If the guide is used for training purposes, the instructor may find this summary particularly useful.

B. Agency

The organization that sponsors the practitioner's work is the agency referred to. Its primary significance is in the possibilities it opens and the constraints it places upon practice.

Social action is typically sponsored by groups of like-minded people who feel generally oppressed by the wider society, are offended by particular governmental decisions or social norms, or share common interests they believe can be achieved more effectively through collective action. The group is held together by some common identity (ethnic or racial characteristics, ideological or cultural similarities, goals, a piece of turf, a shared sense of being oppressed by the larger society). While the sponsor is likely to be homogeneous in some respects, necessary funds may be generated by the group itself or may come from outside sources which may not fully identify with the sponsor, its goals, or, particularly, its methods. This constitutes a problem for some social action groups because, as they engage in controversial activities, they may jeopardize their financial support. On the other hand, to the extent they are homogeneous they are able to pursue their objectives single-mindedly, without undue debate over ends and means.

Locality development may be sponsored by a national government, as in the case of many community development programs in developing countries or in industrialized countries with groups of people isolated from modernization. In such cases there may be conflict between the aims and values of the national government and the people toward whom locality development is directed. Governmental sponsorship, however, may bring otherwise unavailable resources to bear upon problems of under-development. In other cases, locality development is sponsored by groups who seek self-development, often at the initiative and with the continued assistance of some outside group (American Friends Service Committee, a community development program in a land-grant college). Under these conditions, considerable emphasis is placed upon representing various segments of local people and upon their voluntary choice of aims and activities. Given the diversity of people within a locality, problems often arise in finding consensus and in sustaining motivation to work on common problems, but, because these are necessary, the programs chosen represent what local people really want and may be more permanent than those imposed from outside.

Social planning may be sponsored by government at various levels or by private organizations. Backed by constituted authorities or the socially or politically elite, these agencies tend to view their mandate as deriving from the established political process or from democratic procedures in which all citizens are at least nominally free to participate. They typically focus on bringing technical skills to bear upon social problems and are dependent upon the sources of legitimacy, so that they often overlook the views of those who are the presumed beneficiaries or targets of their planning efforts. Insistent demands for wider participation may create operating problems for social planning agencies. If the agencies can secure substantial support, both financial and political, and highly qualified specialists, however, they may be able to resolve social problems to a greater degree than if support from those affected by the plans were required or fewer resources were available.

The extent to which organizations are bureaucratized has a major impact upon the kinds of tasks they can undertake and the strategies and tactics available to the practitioner. (Intro., Part Two) Organizations vary not only in internal structure but in relations with the social environment. They emerge out of the needs of particular constituents, with whom they have a variety of understandings about goals and methods. As noted in the text above, social action agencies are oriented toward their members, while social planning agencies are created by elites to control social problems experienced by nonelites. Zald discusses this with special reference to factors affecting the autonomy of the strategies available to the community organization agency. (Reading #12) Rein and Morris discuss the effects of the planning organization's goals and structure upon the strategies it employs. (13, pp. 127-45)

Parenthetically, it should be noted that formal organizations may be important to the practitioner not only as sponsors of action but as allies in a joint effort or as targets of strategy.

The work of the authors mentioned in parentheses in the guide is discussed more fully in the Introduction to "ARENAS" and in the selections included in "STRATEGIES."

C. Practitioner

The practitioner's activities can be analyzed from two perspectives. The first, which examines the practitioner's motivation, capacity, and opportunity, was developed by faculty members at the University of Chicago's School of Social Service Administration. (14) This perspective raises three general questions: (1) To what extent do the personal and professional goals of the practitioner coincide, reinforce, compete, or conflict with the goals of those he is trying to help and with those of the sponsoring agency? (2) Does the practitioner have the basic qualities of intelligence, ability to empathize with others, a sense of personal identity, and the special skills and knowledge necessary to operate effectively in a particular community organization assignment? (3) Does the practitioner have the support of the agency, the human and financial resources that are necessary for him to do the job with a reasonable expectation of effective performance? If there are impediments in the situation, what, if anything, can be done to correct them? Ronald Lippitt and his collaborators give attention to some of these questions. (9, pp. 92-99)

The motivation, capacity, and opportunity required will vary with the type of practice and the nature of the sponsoring agency. For example, the practitioner's ideological predilections and world view will affect the motivation to work for various types of agencies and the willingness to use different strategies and tactics. Skills in working with different kinds of people (poor people, local elite) and in using various techniques (making population projections, teaching people how to handle unfamiliar situations) affect the capacity to work in different settings. The types and amounts of resources needed for effective practice vary for agencies with various scopes, goals, and strategies.

Role theory provides perhaps an even more useful perspective for analyzing the practitioner's work. The ambiguity and conflict in role definitions by various persons with whom the practitioner interacts, the discontinuity between the various roles one plays currently and between past and present roles, and the personal strain involved in learning a new role and coping with the problems inherent in role ambiguity, conflict, and discontinuity must be taken into account in understanding the practitioner's behavior and decisions. (22, pp. 17-50; 9, pp. 91-126)

II. PROBLEMS

This section of the guide directs the community organization practitioner's attention to an analysis of the difficulties he or she is trying to remedy. The problems of concern are usually social rather than personal, affecting a substantial portion of the people served and out of harmony with their preferences. They may be substantive in character, i.e., problems such as mental illness, insufficient housing or delinquency, or they may involve process, affecting the way the society, the community, and its institutions are organized, formally or informally, for dealing with social problems. Often the two are closely connected as, for example, when it is assumed that the negative reaction to the mentally ill stems from the lack of community-based institutions for dealing with them—well-organized family care homes, recreation programs, emergency services for coping with personal life crises, etc. Community practitioners are typically concerned with problems of both substance and process.

At this point the guide calls for careful observation and description. Explaining the problem is reserved for the next section. The practitioner describes the kind of problem dealt with as clearly as possible, where it is located, how widely it is distributed among different kinds of people, and the degree to which one group is affected in comparison to another. The practitioner looks at past efforts to improve conditions, who made them, the extent of their successes or failures, and the probable reasons for these outcomes. He or she gives particular attention to differences in perceptions of the problem among the affected groups.

The varying ways in which the problem is perceived will be of particular importance. The agency, various subgroups of the client, and the practitioner may all see the problem a little differently and thus favor different solutions.

In the context of social action, the problem will be viewed as one of social injustice—an oppressed minority not receiving its fair share of political, economic, and educational resources, a group that has been deprived of some benefit or has had some social cost inflicted upon it, or a group seeking some benefit for itself at the expense of others for reasons it considers justified. Of increasing importance recently, many negatively regarded groups seek improved status and respect.

In a locality development context, the problem will often be defined as a failure to modernize, to develop the necessary capital and skills to facilitate industrialization at an appropriate rate or to build the necessary services ("infrastructure") needed to support an urbanizing population. The problem may be regarded as opposition to change (strong traditional or new but counterproductive forms of social organization), anomie (languishing social organization), or loss of local autonomy (an organized community losing control to national business, philanthropic, and governmental institutions). A normative view held by some community developers is that the problem stems from the failure of local democracy, the lack of concern about and a sense of responsibility for local problems.

Social planning agencies tend to define the problem as one or more fairly discrete social problems (mental illness, crime and delinquency, poverty, poorly organized services) for which they seek various technical solutions. The problems with which social planners deal are seen as forms of deviant behavior or social disorganization. Deviant behavior, such as mental illness, delinquency, or child abuse, is at variance with prescriptions for particular social roles. Merton makes a useful distinction between two types of deviant behavior, nonconformist and aberrant, which is particularly appropriate in the light of unrest among women minority groups, gays and students. (10, pp. 808-11) The nonconformist announces his or her deviant behavior, challenges the legitimacy of rejected social norms, tries to change norms regarded as illegitimate, and calls upon higher social values as justification for actions. Conventional members of society recognize that the nonconformist is dissenting for disinterested reasons. In contrast, the aberrant individual hides his or her acts from public view, does not challenge the legitimacy of broken norms, tries to escape detection and punishment, and serves personal interests through aberrant behavior.

Social action groups of oppressed people may define their behavior as nonconformist and seek responses from the rest of society that first confirm this definition and ultimately redefine the behavior, prompting the nonconformity as acceptable rather than deviant. For example, those seeking abortion law reform, acceptance of homosexual preferences or equality in job opportunities may use nonconformist means to secure redefinitions of abortion, homosexual behavior, and equal employment opportunities as nondeviant. Social planners may assist them through legitimate ("conformist") means that are possible within the context of their work—drafting legislation, taking matters to court, enlisting the support of community leaders, and so forth. Social planners may also participate in efforts to redefine the behavior of some deviants who, by this definition, are aberrant but whose crimes are trivial and are not regarded as morally reprehensible, or as victimless. The smoking of marijuana in moderation may increasingly be regarded as a trivial offense at best or a victimless crime at worse. Those who engage in drug abuse, prostitution, gambling, and homosexuality are often hurting no one but themselves. Even where behavior cannot be redefined as acceptable, social planners may assist in relieving exacerbating responses, through plans for bail reform and community care for the mentally ill, for example. Finally, planning services to modify the behavior of deviants, using new techniques such as behavioral modification, will continue to be useful for a number of forms of deviant behavior.

Other social problems are regarded as symptoms of social disorganization, not necessarily involving deviations from prescribed norms but rather reflecting incompatibilities between various parts of a social system, such as different rates of change (for example, technology changes more rapidly than social values). Poverty, housing shortages, water pollution, unemployment, and racial discrimination are often regarded as examples of social disorganization that constitute social problems social planners seek to solve.

Locality development practitioners typically view social problems from this standpoint, focussing on those that retard the maintenance or enhancement of a society or community (sharply increasing birth rates, general apathy, lack of entrepreneurial skills, or a failure of leadership). They are also concerned with the inability of a locality to obtain resources or achieve results from self-help efforts.

Another way of looking at social problems is offered by Arnold Rose, (15, pp. 189-99) who defines two perspectives. One, which we will call "disjunctive theory," regards social problems as arising from different meanings being attached to objects that form the context of social interaction or from different values being assigned to the behaviors displayed in relation to those objects. Marijuana (an object) is regarded by some as a potentially dangerous mind-altering drug and by others as a means to a pleasant "high." The smoking of marijuana (behavior in relation to the object) is disvalued by some and enjoyed by others. Poverty in the United States today (a set of objects or conditions) is regarded by some as an unfortunate but inevitable by-product of the free enterprise system and by others as a needless hardship inflicted upon substantial (though decreasing) numbers of people by the economic system. Living in poverty (behavior in relation to that condition) is regarded as avoidable and remediable by individual effort or as essentially irremediable "tough luck" by some and as unnecessary deprivation remediable by collective effort by others. In each case, the problem is regarded as arising from lack of agreement on meanings, values, or both.

The disjunctive theory is often held, at least implicitly, by those practicing locality development and leads to emphasis upon the socialization process, education, and communication. If meanings attached to the same objects differ, efforts can be made to give people "the facts" so that increasingly meanings can be shared. If values associated with particular behaviors conflict, communication between those who disagree may ultimately lead to a greater degree of consensus.

The other perspective Rose calls "conflict theory." From this point of view, social problems are the product of competition for scarce resources (wealth, prestige, power) which results in painful struggles over their distribution, with some being dissatisfied at the outcome.

Conflict theory assumes that values are held in common, that is, most people want the same things and will fight over their distribution, while disjunctive theory assumes that social problems arise from wanting different things or defining the same things in different ways. Those engaged in social action tend to regard social problems from the perspective of conflict theory. Although these practitioners may agree that some secondary grounds for conflict may arise from different meanings being attached to the same events (for example, the lack of a common understanding about the "facts" of poverty), they argue that the basic problem is one of maldistribution (of jobs or income). Social action practitioners try to solve social problems by mobilizing power to induce a redistribution of the valued objects in favor of their clients.

III. SOCIAL CONTEXT OF THE PROBLEM

A. Origins

The practitioner must take care to interpret the origins of a problem. He or she may understand how a problem came to be by examining its origins, but cannot thereby explain its persistence. Conditions that brought about a problem originally often fade, so that present conditions can only be explained by reference to factors currently operating. The practitioner must search for contemporary conditions that are causally connected with the problem and try to change them.

An effort should be made to understand the historical roots of the problem, particularly if there is a long or significant history affecting the present state of affairs. Coleman discusses what he calls residues of organization and sentiment that build up as people interact in community life and may take the form of collaborative patterns, expressed in latent or manifest forms of social organization or in organized cleavages such as those between rival political parties or ethnic groups. They may also be expressed in sentiments of liking and respect or of hostility. (4, pp. 670-95)

B. Theory of the Problem

It is at this point in the analysis that attention is directed toward a search for controlling factors. Assuming that most problems are sustained by a wide variety of factors and that some are more influential than others, the practitioner's task is two-fold: First, one must locate factors that have a major effect on the problem to be corrected. Second, one must choose problems one can reasonably expect to influence, given the time, money, personnel and other resources at one's disposal.

In many social action contexts, the problem will be understood as some form of conflict between "haves" and "have-nots." But greater specificity is required. Which particular interests are pitted against one another? What are the dynamics of the conflict? Are there any aspects of the problem or any facts that do not seem to fit into a conflict perspective? What are the implications for intervention? In many cases of locality development, the problem will be regarded as arising from barriers to communication or different rates of change, i.e., some form of disjunction or social disorganization. But it is important which specific theory or set of theories is selected, for this will exercise an important influence on strategies and tactics chosen. Most practitioners engaged in social planning will consider alternative theories explaining various social problems they are charged with ameliorating. But, again, the specific theory chosen is of great importance in shaping the action taken. If, for example, lower-class male delinquency is conceived of as arising from a lack of legitimate opportunities for success in American society, efforts will be made to expand those opportunities. If, on the other hand, delinquency is thought to arise from psychological problems or parental rejection, efforts will be directed toward various forms of counseling or the strengthening or substitution of parental relations. Or, if the labeling of youngsters as delinquent and the consequent processing through the criminal justice system are thought to be responsible for the perpetuation of delinquent behavior, efforts will be made to decriminalize certain behavior and handle young people who transgress social norms outside the criminal justice system.

Unfortunately, the explanation of the problem chosen by (or more typically implicit in the behavior of) the practitioner is usually limited by the ideology and values of the employing organization or the practitioner. The practitioner should explore his or her own preconceptions and those of the employer to determine what limits such preconceptions place on the choice of an explanation for the problem. However the theory of the problem arises, whether it is implicit in various predisposing values or is more rationally developed, it will have a major influence on the goals and strategies chosen for dealing with the problem.

C. Structural-Functional Analysis of the Problem

The practitioner begins with an assessment of available "theories of the problem." He selects the most reliable theories, and within them the factors that are both potent and potentially controllable. The next step is careful observation of the particular social problem in its context, collecting information within the framework of the theories and hypotheses selected earlier. The outline suggests that both the impact of various factors on the social problem in question and the effect of the problem on these factors be assessed. For example, we might identify particular social structures (schools, employers) that systematically deny opportunities to persons of lower socioeconomic or ethnic minority status, thus creating discontent, delinquent behavior, and so forth. We might then show the impact of such behavior on schools, ethnic minorities, and so forth, emphasizing the differential effects on various groups. This, of course, has implications for which groups, individuals, or organizations may be recruited into organized efforts to alleviate the problems.

Two terms used in this section of the outline are functional and dysfunctional: The functional consequences of action strengthen and unify social systems; dysfunctional consequences produce conflict or threaten disruption of existing social patterns. However, these terms should not be confused with "good" and "bad." Functional consequences can perpetuate what is, from the practitioner's perspective, an unde-

sirable system, such as patterns of racial discrimination in housing and employment. Likewise, dysfunctional consequences may be exactly what the practitioner desires. For example, the early sit-ins, in addition to disrupting preexisting patterns of race relations, tended to enhance the self-esteem of black people and provide experience in contentious organized action.

IV. THE CLIENT

The client is defined as the primary beneficiary of the practitioner's activities. It may be a group of people, a formal organization, or a population category. The client can be analyzed in terms similar to other forms of social organization. Some of the factors that may be most important are outlined in the guide. The major implication of this section is that the client must be identified and understood both in its context, i.e., its relations to other social phenomena, and in its internal structure. We must also be sensitive to changes that have taken place in the client and the reasons for them.

The definition of the client forces the practitioner to be clear about whom he or she is trying to help and to differentiate them from others who are regarded in more instrumental terms. There was a time when it was conventional for the community organizer to say that the client is the community. This rhetoric tends to hide the fact that particular actions may benefit some, harm others, and have little effect on still others. The suggested definition makes the practitioner consider whose interests will be sacrificed last if decisions must be made requiring that someone pay a price. It also demands that the practitioner consider how much to expect others to "pay" for the sake of the clients and decide whether the price is justifiable.

If the clientele is a group of individuals with strongly held common interests that can be rather precisely defined, the practitioner will have little difficulty in knowing what benefits to work for on their behalf. On the other hand, one is likely to have difficulty in gaining allies and support for the group. If the clientele is a heterogeneous group with common interests that can be defined only at the most general level, the practitioner probably will have trouble in defining precisely what to aim for. The chances of alienating some faction of the clientele are increased, but the group is likely to be much more inclusive, and thus the practitioner will have less difficulty in gaining needed outside support.

As Rothman notes (Reading #1), the client is viewed differently in the several contexts of practice. In locality development, clients are citizens and participants in local problem solving. In social planning, they are consumers and recipients of services. In social action they are victims of oppression and employers or constituents of the practitioner.

The kind of client one is able to serve is limited, in important ways, by the type of organization that employs one. That is, it is most difficult for a practitioner to give primacy to the interests of a group that is not the primary beneficiary of his or her employer. Blau and Scott have developed a typology of organizations based on the identity of the groups that are the primary beneficiaries of organizations. (2, pp. 42-57) The main implication for practice is that the practitioner experiences grave difficulties in making clients out of groups other than those that are naturally the primary beneficiaries of the type of organization employing him. For example, the primary beneficiary of a mutual benefit association is its members. If the practitioner employed by, say, a labor union defines some nonmembers as the client—perhaps the people living in an impoverished neighborhood—he is likely to run into difficulties with members who resent the diversion of their dues for purposes not directly related to their welfare. Community practitioners employed by such agencies as public assistance bureaus sometimes experience difficulties when they select client-serving goals with which the public is out of sympathy. Part of the reason for these difficulties is a failure to recognize the true character of such social service agencies as commonweal organizations whose prime beneficiary is the general citizen instead of, as commonly believed, service organizations whose primary beneficiary is the clientele.

V. GOALS

At some point in his or her work, the practitioner must define as clearly as possible the particular goals to be achieved with the client. Lack of clarity may lead to goal displacement, i.e., the unintended replacement of goals by new, often unrecognized objectives. Under some conditions—when the situation is very unstable, when there is little experience to guide action, or when knowledge of aims would help those opposed to them—it may be necessary to be vague in public statements or to move toward goal definition through a process of successive approximation. Many other factors also lead to goal displacement—insufficient resources to pursue multiple goals, factional differences in interests, procedures which come to be valued by those who benefit from them, and so forth. Precise goal definition is one defense against goal displacement, however, and provides some criteria against which results can be measured. Resistance to goal displacement should not be used as an excuse to avoid adopting new goals when old ones have been achieved or are no longer appropriate, or new resources make it possible to add goals.

The practitioner must take into account not only his or her personal objective but also the views of the sponsoring organization, the clientele, and other groups whose support is needed or whose resistance or objections must be anticipated. It is not necessary to accommodate the interests of the opposition or of those who are largely indifferent to or unaffected by the action, but one must do so for those whose cooperation, whether as active collaboration or passive awareness and the absence of hindering responses, one must have. Those whose interests must be taken into account if the practitioner is to achieve his or her objectives are called the "action system." (This term is used in the guide under the heading "Strategy.")

As suggested above, various groups have different *goals,* attach varying *importance* to particular goals, and have contrasting sets of *priorities.* Factions within groups may also differ in these ways. In taking these differences into account, the practitioner may decide on a strategy of "something for everyone," or may begin with one easily achieved goal of fairly high importance to all elements in order to build confidence in the organization's capability.

One may develop some other rationale for selecting goals, but information about the relative priorities and salience of the goals of different factions is essential to a reasoned decision. (11, pp. 25-31)

Social problems may reside in a group's relations with its environment (inadequate police protection or unresponsive public officials) or among its members (uncoordinated activities, low morale, lack of commitment). Goals are of two parallel kinds. For example, a welfare council may appeal for additional public funds for a child care center or try to develop support for a human relations commission. These are commonly referred to in the literature as "task goals." Other goals affect the maintenance and enhancement of the organization (resolving destructive factional rivalry or transforming member apathy into involvement and commitment). These are called "process goals." In general, both types of goals must be served, but at particular times one type may be more important than another. At one time it was generally believed that the community practitioner should pursue only process goals, that is, be concerned exclusively with facilitating or "enabling" clients to achieve self-defined goals. Rothman argues persuasively that the practitioner need not be limited in this manner. (18, pp. 24-31)

VI. STRATEGY

Perfect rationality (or anything approaching it) is unattainable in most practice situations. Computer technology may enable some to come a bit closer. But most of us must, as Herbert Simon puts it, "satisfice" rather than "maximize" the efficiency and effectiveness of our decisions. (20, p. xxv)

However, some practitioners approach questions of strategy with predetermined formulas, agency traditions, and little imagination. While it is not feasible to consider every possibility and identify the single best way to achieve objectives, it does not follow that one strategy is as good as the next. The practitioner is asked to consider at least two good possibilities and exercise judgment in choosing the best one.

Perhaps more than any other activity, strategy development offers the practitioner an opportunity for creativity. In applying the guide, he or she sketches each strategy, outlining the minimum tasks required to achieve success; the necessary elements of the action system; the resistance (opposition), interdependence (entanglements), and interference (competition and indifference) forces that may be encountered; and the plans to handle them. (9, pp. 71-89) Finally, the practitioner evaluates his or her ability to carry them out and develops a rationale for choosing between the various strategies being considered. As a general approach to decision making this applies to all types of practice. However, the relative emphasis given to various tactics (research, client participation, confrontation with organizations and their leaders) will vary with the model of practice used.

To the extent that success depends upon a correct theory of the problem and an effective strategy, success may be limited by the choices permitted by the elites or the political process. Because social planning strategies normally depend upon the effective manipulation of large-scale bureaucracies, success may also depend heavily on whether the strategy chosen can be effectively administered. And finally, because those whose actions are required for success—the functionaries and the targets—are not ciphers but people with interests and values that guide what they will respond to and what they will do, strategies that assume values about which there is little consensus or which assume a nonexistent community of interests are likely to enjoy limited success.

Some recent analyses suggest that strategies that operate as much as possible in a way analogous to a competitive market situation are most likely to succeed. They maximize individual choices and allow for individual differences. They require a minimum of bureaucratic complexity, especially detailed rules and numerous functionaries to enforce or monitor compliance. It has been suggested that this is the reason for the failure of such programs as the War on Poverty, the success of Social Security, and the promise of income maintenance programs based on negative income tax principles. (7)

VII. TACTICS

Strategy shades imperceptibly into tactics. The inspiration for much of this part of the guide comes from Lippitt and his colleagues. (9) Among the questions the practitioner is asked to consider are: Where is it possible to gain a foothold in the targets? At what point are efforts likely to be most effective? For example, the practitioner may have access to other practitioners working in low- or middle-echelon positions in a target organization. His or her analysis, however, may lead to the conclusion that, to achieve the objective, the practitioner must gain access to the top executive. One may, therefore, bypass colleagues in the target organization and approach a member of one's board with the necessary social and political contacts to gain the ear of the target agency executive.

In order to avoid misunderstandings, it is important for the practitioner to communicate with key people in the action system (those whose cooperation is needed to carry out the strategy) so that they may develop common ideas about such things as definition of the problem, objectives, approaches, roles each participant will perform, and amount of time each participant will commit to the endeavor. The resulting set of agreements is referred to as the contract. Although the concept is borrowed from the law, it does not imply legal or even written form. The expectations must be as clear and unambiguous as possible, and all necessary participants must understand and commit themselves to the terms of the contract.

In carrying the plan into action, it may be necessary to train and support participants who feel more or less uncertain about what they are doing. This is particularly relevant for those who are inexperienced in the sort of activities required by the contract. The timing of various actions must be carefully planned. Resources of several kinds may require difficult coordination—it may be necessary to induce competing professionals to work together or to provide the press with newsworthy events involving large numbers of people so that politicians will take the action system's demands seriously.

The idea of an "action-reaction-action pattern" is borrowed from Alinsky. (1) We refer to these patterns

when one group makes a move which is intended to elicit a response from an adversary that makes possible further action to achieve objectives that could not have been otherwise undertaken. For example, a group might leak information to an adversary that it plans a massive disruption of the adversary's business. The expected response is an offer to negotiate which, in turn, makes it possible to obtain concessions favorable to the group that would not have been secured by an initial request for negotiations. Such tactics depend on credibility; if the adversary does not believe that there is a genuine threat, it is not likely to negotiate.

The practitioner should anticipate that some form of opposition to the program undertaken by the action system may emerge and make plans to handle it. Under some circumstances, no such opposition will develop—organizing a council on aging or applying for funds from the federal government to mount programs for the aging should arouse no controversy or opposition. If insurmountable opposition can be expected, however, plans should be changed unless the practitioner is deliberately trying to heighten awareness of impotence and stimulate anger as a prelude to other, perhaps stronger forms of action. If opposition is inevitable, a variety of approaches is available to cope with it in ways that may further the action system's objectives.

VIII. EVALUATION (3, 5, 6, 21, 24, READING #9)

Evaluation should be an ongoing process. Plans must be worked out for the collection of information from participants in the action system regarding effectiveness with respect to both task and process goals. This may be quite informal (setting aside a portion of a meeting to discuss "how we're doing") or much more rigorous (standardized data collection, written reports) depending upon the size, complexity, and other requirements of the effort in which the practitioner is engaged. The important thing is that assessment not be overlooked, for the process allows the practitioner and the organization to revise their program if activities are found to be less than satisfactory.

Practitioners often find annual or semi-annual meetings good opportunities for taking stock. The results may be set forth in a periodic report. There is a tendency at such meetings to "put the best foot forward" and overlook difficulties in order to maintain or enhance morale, build financial resources, and avoid offending those who have been active in the organization. Ordinarily it is best to find ways to say what may be the unpleasant truth in a manner that minimizes problems. For example, it is possible to express gratitude for individual contributions while calling attention to persistent difficulties that exist "in spite of the best efforts of everyone involved."

IX. MODIFICATION, TERMINATION OR TRANSFER OF ACTION

Evaluation of program and organizational effectiveness may lead to any one of several conclusions. First, the practitioner may conclude that the program is operating much as expected, is achieving its intended purposes, and should be continued. Second, he or she may find that some aspects are faulty, because of an erroneous analysis of the situation, a poor strategy, or particular actions that were inappropriate or poorly carried out. This conclusion should lead to necessary revisions. Third, the practitioner and those he or she is working with may conclude that the program has served its purpose or, alternatively, is hopelessly inept. In either case, the conclusion should be to discontinue operations and the practitioner must plan carefully for this. Finally, for a variety of reasons the practitioner may be leaving the job. Under these conditions, it is necessary to arrange either the transfer of professional responsibilities to another practitioner or the termination of the program.

CONCLUSION

These comments suggest how the guide may be used and offer some additional references which are intended to give it a broader scope and greater utility. We hope that practitioners will use the guide to remind themselves of some of the more important factors they need to take into account in planning their work.

Obviously the busy community practitioner will be unable to utilize fully the analysis suggested here in daily work. However, many of the steps in the problem-solving process will become part of the professional "equipment" he or she may apply, perhaps less formally and less rigorously but nonetheless effectively, in making day-to-day practice decisions. This is the hope we have had in preparing the guide and using it in teaching community organization practice.

BIBLIOGRAPHY

1. Alinsky, Saul D. *Reveille for Radicals.* Chicago: University of Chicago Press, 1946; and *Rules for Radicals.* New York: Random House, 1971.
2. Blau, Peter, M., and Scott, W. Richard. *Formal Organizations.* San Francisco: Chandler Publishing Co., 1962.
3. Campbell, Donald T. "Reforms as Experiments." *American Psychologist* 24 (April 1969): 409-29.
4. Coleman, James S. "Community Disorganization," in Merton and Nisbet, op. cit., pp. 670-95.
5. Herzog, Elizabeth. *Some Guidelines for Evaluative Research.* Children's Bureau Publication No. 375. Washington, DC: U.S. Dept. of Health, Education, and Welfare, 1959.
6. Hyman, Herbert H., and Wright, Charles R. "Evaluating Social Action Programs," in *The Uses of Sociology,* edited by Paul F. Lazarfeld, William H. Sewell, and Harold Wilensky. New York: Basic Books, 1967. pp. 741-82.
7. Levine, Robert A. *Public Planning: Failure and Redirection.* New York: Basic Books, 1972.
8. Levine, Sol; White, Paul E.; and Paul, Benjamin D. "Community Interorganizational Problems in Providing Medical Care and Social Services," *American Journal of Public Health* 53 (August 1963): 1183-95.
9. Lippitt, Ronald; Watson, Jeanne; and Westley, Bruce. *The Dynamics of Planned Change: A Comparative Study of Principles and Techniques.* New York: Harcourt, Brace and World, 1958.
10. Merton, Robert K. "Epilogue: Social Problems and Sociological Theory," in *Contemporary Social Problems,* 2d ed., edited by Robert K. Merton and Robert A. Nisbet. New York: Harcourt, Brace and World, 1966.
11. Morris, Robert, and Binstock, Robert H. *Feasible Planning for Social Change.* New York: Columbia University Press, 1966.
12. Perlman, Robert, and Gurin, Arnold. *Community Organization and Social Planning.* New York: John Wiley and Council on Social Work Education, 1972.
13. Rein, Martin, and Morris, Robert. "Goals, Structures and Strategies for Community Change." *In Social Work Practice 1962.* New York: Columbia University Press, 1962.
14. Ripple, Lillian. "Motivation, Capacity and Opportunity as Related to the Use of Casework Services: Theoretical Base and Plan of Study," *Social Service Review* 29 (June 1955): 172-93.
15. Rose, Arnold. "Theory for the Study of Social Problems," *Social Problems* 4 (January 1957): 189-99.
16. Ross, Murray G. *Community Organization: Theory, Principles and Practice.* New York: Harper & Bros., 1955.
17. Ross, Murray G., with Lappin, B.W. *Community Organization: Theory, Principles and Practice.* 2d ed. New York: Harper & Row, 1967.
18. Rothman, Jack. "An Analysis of Goals and Roles in Community Organization Practice," *Social Work* 9 (April 1964): 24-31.
19. Sanders, Irwin T. *The Community: An Introduction to a Social System.* 2d ed. New York: The Roland Press, 1966.
20. Simon, Herbert A. *Administrative Behavior,* 2d ed. New York: The Macmillan Co., 1957.
21. Suchman, Edward A. *Evaluative Research: Principles and Practice in Public Service and Social Action Programs.* New York: Russell Sage Foundation, 1967.
22. Thomas, Edwin J., and Feldman, Ronald A. with Kamm, Jane. "Concepts of Role Theory," in *Behavioral Science for Social Workers,* edited by Edwin J. Thomas. New York: The Free Press, 1967,
23. Thompson, James D., and Tuden, Arthur. "Strategies, Structures and Processes of Organizational Decision," *Comparative Studies in Administration,* edited by J. D. Thompson et al., pp. 195-216. Pittsburgh: Pittsburgh University Press, 1959.
24. Tripodi, Tony; Fellin, Phillip; and Epstein, Irwin. *Social Program Evaluation: Guidelines for Health, Education and Welfare Administrators.* Itasca, Ill.: F. E. Peacock Publishers, 1971.
25. Warren, Roland L. *The Community in America.* Chicago: Rand McNally, 1963.

9.

Steven Maynard-Moody

PROGRAM EVALUATION AND ADMINISTRATIVE CONTROL

The history of social science records a long-standing tradition of interdependence between social problems and social research, and program evaluation research is a recent extension of this tradition. Although debates comparing the effectiveness of different responses to social problems were common during earlier periods of social reform (Hofstadter, 1960; Rothman, 1971; Cronbach et al., 1980) and in the 1930s there was some interest in applying social research methods to the assessment of New Deal social action programs (Stephan, 1935; Lynd, 1939), program evaluation research is a product of the 1960s (Freeman, 1977). During the 1960s, government support for applied social science shifted from a small number of grants initiated by researchers to extensive support for research solicited by government agencies to address specific policy questions. Increasingly the policy questions were over the impact of social action programs, and federal funding for program evaluation grew from almost nothing in 1960 to 63.6 million dollars in 1977 (Cronbach et al., 1980, p. 41).[1]

These changes are not isolated events. As Coleman (1980) observed, the recent emphasis in social science on policy problems is evidence of broader social changes. The rapid emergence of the field of program evaluation research over the past twenty years results from two current problems in making and implementing social policy, and each will be discussed below. Program evaluation grew in response to the needs of decision makers in all levels of government to control and justify social action programs.

THE NEED TO CONTROL

Social legislation of the Kennedy and Johnson administrations changed the scope and extent of federal involvement in social welfare. Until the Social Security Act of 1935, the federal government had virtually no role in social policy. In 1854, President Franklin Pierce vetoed as unconstitutional a modest bill authorizing federal land grants for insane asylums and thereby delegated social welfare to charitable societies and state and local governments. The New Deal ended the constitutional constraints, and the War on Poverty brought a dramatic proliferation of social welfare legislation and programs.[2]

Source: Steven Maynard-Moody, "Program Evaluation and Administrative Control," in *Policy Studies Review*, Vol. 2, No. 3 (February, 1983), pp. 371-390. Reprinted with permission of the publisher and the author.

[1]Funding has, however, recently been marginally declining in constant dollars.

[2]The War on Poverty legislation included: in 1962, the Manpower Development and Training Act; in 1963 the Mental Retardation Facilities and Community Mental Health Construction Acts; in 1964 the Economic and the Elementary and Secondary Education Act; and in 1967, the Work Incentives Program, to name only the most prominent initiatives.

But, as Coleman (1980, p. 343) observed, "As the nation assumed public responsibility in matters where responsibility had been local and private, it was ill-equipped to discharge this responsibility." Federal agencies could allocate funds and distribute regulations, but they could not assure that policies would be properly carried out. Although Lowi (1969) charged that implementation problems were the inevitable result of the vagueness of the War on Poverty legislation—he described these initiatives as "policy without law" (p. 233)—the scope of the problems and the scope of the attempted solutions overwhelmed the federal government's ability to control implementation. The vagueness of the laws was the result of reform-mindedness overreaching understanding.

Effective federal control could overcome its structural distance from local programs only by determining if social programs were implemented in the manner intended, how local administrators adapted programs to local needs and constraints, and how programs could be modified. To address these questions, decisionmakers first in the federal government and then in state and local governments turned to social scientists for help. The field of program evaluation research grew in response to their need to assert control over policy implementation. Although the Reagan administration is pressing hard to return much of the responsibility for social services to state and local governments, the scope of social welfare programs is unlikely to greatly diminish, and the extent Reagan can devolve responsibility to state and local governments remains uncertain. Moreover, the problems administrators have in controlling the implementation of social programs may diminish but will not disappear through decentralization.

A RATIONAL IDEOLOGY

Acknowledging the problems government agencies have in controlling the implementation of social policy does not, however, fully answer the question, "Why turn to social scientists for help in evaluating the effects of social programs?" Others—lawyers and accountants, perhaps—could monitor the implementation of social policy without the expense of careful research. Part of the answer was suggested above; federal decisionmakers turned to social scientists to expand their limited understanding of the causes and solutions of social problems. But they also turned to social scientists to legitimate their decisions.[3] The growth of the field of program evaluation is part of a larger trend of reliance on scientific experts in all areas of governance. Interest in program evaluation research grew out of the trend away from justifying social policy decisions on the belief in "doing good" or, as is often the case, "doing good for my district" and towards basing decisions on evidence of the effectiveness of the program in solving the identified social problems (Patton, 1978, chap. 1).

The use of social scientific evidence in making policy does not, however, announce the "end of ideology." Rather, it announces the ascendency of the scientific and technical belief in rational analysis. Patti (1975, p. 170) described rational analysis or scientific manage-

---

[3]For a detailed discussion see Maynard-Moody (1981, p. 8-12).

ment in human services as an ideology that "is not distinguished as much by its technology as it is by a particular socio-political world view, characterized by certain (albeit often implicit) assumptions about how best to understand, control, and change organizational behavior."

Nor is this trend politically neutral. The application of social scientific research techniques to decision making changes who participates in policy discussions. Experts are given an increased role, leading Nelkin (1978, p. 14) to conclude that, "Deference to technical knowledge enables those with specialized competence to exert a powerful influence on public agencies" (see also Ellul, 1964; Benveniste, 1972). As factual information eclipses beliefs, the gatherers and organizers of facts become the eyes of government and management, and how evaluators define their problems and view social programs is a political as well as a conceptual question. This is the general issue that this paper examines.

In sum, program evaluation is much more than an applied research methodology. It is a political innovation that reflects current trends in social policy making and implementing. To examine the implications of this trend, this paper reports on the findings of two closely related studies that examined a series of questions derived from the literature on organizational effectiveness about the current practice of program evaluation research. The specific research questions will be discussed in the following section. Each focuses the discussion on a different aspect of the general research problem of describing how social scientists view the social programs they evaluate.

THREE THEMES IN THE EFFECTIVENESS LITERATURE

Uncertainty and the Assessment of Effectiveness

There are three main themes in the organizational effectiveness literature. The first is the impact of uncertainty on the assessment of effectiveness. Thompson (1967) argued that variation in an organization's certainty about outcome standards and causal knowledge should determine the way effectiveness is measured. Outcome standards refer to criteria, such as goals, for assigning value to effects and causal knowledge as a construct for assigning responsibility for effects. In an earlier paper (Maynard-Moody & McClintock, 1981), three general evaluation strategies that were based on Thompson's model were described. These are briefly discussed below.

In social programs where both causal knowledge and outcome standards are clear, efficiency strategies, which assess whether a given effect was produced for the least cost, are appropriate and powerful (Thompson, 1967, p. 84). In such cases, evaluators can reasonably assume that efforts produced the desired results and the relative costs of equivalent products adequately measures effectiveness. Cost-benefit, cost-effectiveness, and cost-utility procedures are examples of efficiency strategies (Rothenberg, 1975, p. 57; Rossi et al., 1979, chap. 8).

In other organizations in which goals are clear but important causal relations uncertain, the assumptions of efficiency strategies cannot be met (Thompson, 1967, p. 84; Scott, 1977, p. 76). Here strategies that assess the ways in which actions are instrumental in achieving results are appropriate. In such cases the primary evaluative question is "Do the efforts contribute to the results?" Experimental and correlational designs that rigorously rule out alternative explanations are the fundamental instrumental strategies.

Where both outcome standards and causal knowledge are ambiguous, revelatory strategies, to borrow Perrow's (1977, p. 101) term, are appropriate.[4] These strategies follow Weick's (1979, p. 243) advice that where ambiguity dominates organizations the first step in analysis is to accurately register the disorder. A revelatory approach examines a program's history and its staff's choices and actions, lists the actual as well as the intended results, and explores the functions of seemingly counterproductive organizational features, such as persistent staff conflict. Evaluators using revelatory strategies must suspend judgment and remain open-minded.

Thompson's contingency model of basing the assessment strategy on the level and type of organizational uncertainties raises the question: "Do program evaluators use assessment strategies that correspond to the level of uncertainty in the organization about outcome standards and causal knowledge?" Although Thompson argued that assessment strategies should be based on the extent of organizational uncertainty, he stressed the importance of the "norm of rationality." As Scott and Hart (1979, p. 44) concluded, the

belief in purposive action applies "to every manager in every organization in modern society." It is expected, therefore, that this normative pressure of rational decision-making procedures encourages an unjustified reliance on procedures that presume greater certainty of outcome standards and causal knowledge than exists in the program.

Effectiveness for Whom?

The second theme in the organizational effectiveness literature is captured in Perrow's (1977, p. 101) question: "Effectiveness for whom?" Effectiveness criteria always represent someone's values (Cameron, 1978, p. 606), and any complex organization contains points of view that differ systematically in how they define effectiveness. Much organizational behavior is driven by the power struggles, bargaining, and coalition formation over whose definition of effectiveness will dominate the organization (Cyert & March, 1963; Kahn, 1977). Indeed, Scott (1977) takes the extreme position that judging effectiveness is nothing more than an exercise in self-interest.

Yet conflicts over effectiveness criteria are often restrained to the point of inaudibility. Observing established organizations reveals few clashes over goals or evaluation criteria. The main restraint on conflict is the endurance of stable dominant coalitions who because of their formal authority retain control over effectiveness criteria (Pfeffer, 1978).

The second research question is: "Who influences the design and interpretation of the evaluation studies?" It is expected that a coalition of the sponsors of the programs and top adminis-

---

[4]Thompson (1967) suggested that evaluating effectiveness in conditions of great uncertainty shifts from "empirical to social referents" (p. 87). Revelatory strategies differ from his discussion in that they involve the empirical recording and examination of different perspectives.

trators of the programs would retain control over the evaluation.

Effectiveness Is a Heterogeneous Concept

Turning to the third theme, organizational effectiveness is increasingly seen as a heterogeneous concept. Although most of the definitions of effectiveness in the research literature depend on univariate, organization-wide measures (Steers, 1975), effectiveness is a heterogeneous concept because organizations are complex with many outcomes serving diverse constituencies (Katz & Kahn, 1978, p. 224). As Kirchoff (1977, p. 437) observed, "Trying to view organizational effectiveness as a single dimension is much like trying to visualize a cube without depth perception—the result is distortion." The general features of organizational effectiveness can, however, be clustered into three models: the goal, systems-resource, and human relations models.

Foremost among the three is the goal model. This approach is built on Weber's studies of bureaucracy and assumes that organizations are designed to achieve specific ends and that decisionmakers purposively act in accordance with these goals (Simon, 1976, p. 257; Campbell, 1977; Maynard-Moody & McClintock, 1982). Goals are the organizing principle around which procedures, staff responsibilities, and structures are built and the basis of much of current management practice. Management by objectives is but one example.

The usefulness of this view of organizational effectiveness has been persistently challenged, however. Etzioni (1960) argued that goal statements are idealized norms about what organizations should be or do and "are not meant to be realized" (p. 260). Perrow (1961) documented the wide gap between official and operative goals, and Cummings (1977) observed that individuals pursue their own goals that, especially as you move down the organizational chart, compete with organizational goals. Indeed, Perrow (1978) recently asserted that goals are largely irrelevant to what goes on inside organizations.

Because of the problems with the goal model, several theorists have suggested abandoning it in favor of the systems-resource view. This approach is based on the definition of organizations as open systems that must balance production goals with maintenance needs and engage in exchange and competitive relationships with other organizations (Katz & Kahn, 1978, chap. 8). In this view, effectiveness is the "ability of the organization, in either relative or absolute terms, to exploit its environment in the acquisition of scarce and valued resources" (Yuchtman & Seashore, 1967, p. 898). In this view, flexibility and adaptability, not adherence to goals, are considered the essential characteristics of effectiveness.

As with the goal model, there are problems with this view. Focusing on adaptability over-emphasized the openness of most organizations to environmental changes. Through a variety of tactics—such as sheer size, monopoly, lobbying, and secrecy—organizations can successfully "seal themselves off" from environmental influences (Thompson, 1967, p. 19; Weick, 1979, p. 239). A more important problem is that neither the goal nor the systems-resource model tells us much about what goes on inside organizations that contribute to either goal achievement or resource acquisition.

In examining the processes that contribute to or restrict organizational effectiveness, much attention has been paid to how human relations alter performance. Early studies focused on shaping individual behavior in "organizationally useful directions" (Kahn, 1958, p. 74) and on how to elicit commitment and enthusiasm for management goals (Bowers & Seashore, 1966). In this view, an effective organization gets its employees to work (that is, reduces absenteeism); to work diligently, creatively, and with others; and to contribute to the overall functioning of the organization. Procedures for eliciting conformity, commitment, and effort are the cornerstones of contemporary, behavioral management theory (Scott & Hart, 1979), but the relationship between these characteristics of individual performance and overall organizational effectiveness remains tenuous. As Argyris (1968) conceded, utility for the organization is not necessarily related to utility for the individual.

The current trend in research on effectiveness is to accept these various dimensions of effectiveness as complementary and to measure effectiveness on a variety of dimensions (e.g., Cameron, 1978; Cameron & Whetten, 1981).[5] This leads to the third research question: "Do the questions evaluators ask reflect the scope of the concepts relevant to understanding organizational effectiveness?" Although the trend in basic research on organizational effectiveness has moved away from a singular reliance on the goal model, it is

expected that the measurement of goal achievement still dominates evaluation studies. The goal model has so dominated the methodological literature in evaluation research that Rossi (1978) concluded that evaluations are not possible unless an organization's goals are clearly specified. Deutscher (1977) labeled this premise the "goal trap" and concluded that most evaluators are willingly ensnared.

METHODS

These questions were addressed in two closely related studies. The first study examines the relationship between the types of uncertainty and the methods of assessment, and the second study questions what definitions of effectiveness shaped the evaluators' view of the organizations and what groups influenced the design of the evaluations.

Study One

The logic and methods of the first study are discussed elsewhere (Maynard-Moody & McClintock, 1981) and will be described here in brief. The 18 evaluation reports that were reprinted in the first volume of the *Evaluation Studies Review Annual* (Glass, 1976) were selected for study. Although the sample is not representative of the program evaluations since they were chosen for the *Review Annual* for their excellence, they included a wide range of organizational types and are a representative of what the editors consider good evaluation research. They were chosen as "state of the art" studies.

These 18 evaluation reports were examined to code the descriptions of the organizations' certainty of outcome

---

[5]Hall (1982, chap. 13) takes the more extreme position and argues these models of effectiveness are contradictory.

standards and causal knowledge and the assessment strategy used to evaluate those organizations. To examine the relationship between uncertainty and assessment strategy, this information was then coded into two nominal variables, the predicted and observed strategies.

Predicted Strategies. The coding categories for the predicted strategies are displayed in Table 9.1. The evaluators' descriptions of organizational uncertainty were first coded on two variables: (1) the clarity of causal knowledge relating to the programs' efforts and outcomes—causal knowledge can be clear or unclear—and (2) the clarity of outcome standards— outcome standards can be clear or unclear. The evaluations were then classified into one of the three strategies as indicated on Table 9.1. Efficiency strategies were predicted if both features were clear, instrumental strategies if goals were clear but causal knowledge unclear, and revelatory strategies if both were unclear.

Observed Strategies. The observed strategies were derived from the evaluators' descriptions of the evaluation design and methods. Five aspects of the descriptions were coded and the coding categories are summarized in Table 9.2. Based on the pattern across

all five characteristics, the evaluation methods were again coded into the three strategies. In contrast to the predicted strategies, this characterization refers to the actual research design. Although the categories for the two variables are identical, each was derived from coding differing information in the evaluation report. They are therefore independent.

Coding reliability was checked by having a second coder, who did not know the purpose or the expectations of the study, code a randomly selected 30 percent of the reports. Using a Pearson Product Moment Correlation, reliability between coders was .67.

Study Two

The second study is closely related to the first but is broader in scope. The sample was expanded to include evaluations reprinted in the first three volumes of the *Evaluation Studies Review Annuals* (Glass, 1976; Guttentag & Saar, 1977; Cook et al., 1978) and those identified in the Federal Program Evaluations sourcebook (General Accounting Office, 1978). The second source was added to include average, as well as excellent, studies.

In addition to examining the reports, data were collected by mail questionnaire from the evaluators and by

TABLE 9.1
Predicted Strategies by Type of Uncertainty, Study One

	Type of Uncertainty	
Predicted Strategies	Uncertainty About Causal Knowledge	Uncertainty About Outcome Standards
Efficiency Strategies	Low	Low
Instrumental Strategies	High	Low
Revelatory Strategies	High	High

TABLE 9.2
Observed Strategies and Evaluation Design Characteristics, Study One

Evaluation Design Features	Efficiency Strategies	Instrumental Strategies	Revelatory Strategies
Purpose and Application	Compare costs and benefits	Clarify causal relations	Program descriptions, register uncertainty, sense-making
Research Design	Econometric	Experimental, correlational, longitudinal	Case studies, group processes
Causality	Assumes causal relations	Examines expected causal relations	Explores causal assumptions
Measurement Process	Quantitative	Quantitative/ qualitative	Qualitative
Focus of Measurement	Inputs & outcomes	Inputs, process, & outcomes	Process

telephone interviews with recipients of the reports. This triangulation approach expanded the scope and augmented the strength of the measures but made sampling more difficult.[6] As a population, evaluators proved hard to locate; they are often migrant workers moving from grant to grant. When located some were reluctant to discuss their studies and most were reluctant to identify recipients of their reports. After studies were culled from each source if they did not evaluate an identifiable organization, name the authors of the report, or the reports were not publicly available, 40 percent of the evaluators returned usable questionnaires. This low response rate left a small sample size of 22 cases. Nine individuals who were identified as users of these reports were interviewed over the telephone. These open-ended interviews provided a qualitative backdrop to the analysis.

Observed Strategies. As in the first study, the evaluation methods were coded into one of the three evaluation strategies: the efficiency, instrumental, and revelatory strategies. In this study, the evaluators were asked which of 24 possible procedures were used in their research and these responses were then coded into the three strategies. This procedure replicates but does not duplicate the procedure used in the first study.

Effectiveness for Whom? The evaluators were also asked which of seven groups influenced their study. They included: local, state, and federal agencies; other community programs; clients as individuals or in groups; professional associations; program management; and service delivery or frontline staff. Influence was measured on three levels. The lowest was receiving a copy of the report. Although this is not a source of direct influence, receiving reports represents potential influence. The second level was affecting the design of the study and the third the interpretation of the results.

---

[6]For details about sampling procedures see Maynard-Moody (1981, p. 79-90).

Effectiveness Dimensions. The evaluators were then asked two questions about five dimensions of organizational effectiveness that correspond to the three models discussed above. The dimensions were achieving stated goals, providing benefits equal to or greater than costs, adapting to environmental changes, acquiring adequate resources for survival and growth, and maintaining a motivated and satisfied staff. The evaluators were first asked whether these concepts influenced the design of their studies and second if they were relevant to evaluating social programs in general. In addition, statements in the evaluation reports that described the effectiveness questions asked were coded into these five categories.

Use by Recipients of the Reports. The evaluators were also asked to rate on an eight-point scale the extent of actual use of their studies by recipients of the report. Characterizing use is important to measure the extent these evaluations were applied in decision making. These characterizations were qualitatively validated by the descriptions of the recipients of the reports, but because of the small number of recipients interviewed, their observations were not used as a basis of analysis.

Uncertainty. And finally, the certainty of goals and causal knowledge were measured in the evaluator questionnaires. An index of goal uncertainty was created from independent measures of goal agreement, clarity, conflict, and similarity. The certainty of causal knowledge was measured more directly by asking the evaluators to rate the certainty that the programs' efforts could be related to their results.

FINDINGS

Study One

When predicted and observed strategies for conducting evaluative studies were compared, there was no statistically significant correspondence between the two measures. However, the "norm of rationality" would predict that evaluators would (1) use only efficiency strategies in studies where causal knowledge and outcome standards are clear, (2) use efficiency and instrumental strategies when causal knowledge is clear and outcome standards unclear, and (3) use efficiency, instrumental and relevatory strategies where neither causal knowledge nor outcome standards are clear. This is, indeed, what the data reveal. In other words, these evaluators tended to disregard the uncertainties characterizing the organizations they evaluated.

Study Two

The Three Strategies and Use. The results indicate a significant relationship between the type of assessment strategy and the use of evaluations by recipients of the reports. Clearly the recipients of these evaluations preferred efficiency and instrumental strategies.

It is possible, although not expected, that the recipients of the evaluations preferred the efficiency and instrumental strategies based on the extent of certainty about goals and causal knowledge. The analysis of the data shows that the recipients preferred efficiency and instrumental strategies independent of the extent of organizational certainty. Combining these two findings, the evaluators in the first study and the recipients of the reports in the second preferred assessment strategies that presumed greater certainty about goals and causal knowledge than was realistic. Both conformed to the norm of rationality.

Effectiveness for Whom? In addition to the relationship of uncertainty and assessment strategy, the second study examined how the sampled evaluators resolved two other effectiveness questions. First, what interest groups influenced these evaluations? There was little difference between the groups in receiving reports, but as the level of direct influence increased, patterns emerge. State and local officials, service staff, other community agencies, and clients had the least influence. Federal agencies and top administration in the programs had the strongest influence on the design and interpretation of the studies. They form the dominant coalition. This finding explains, in part, the selection of assessment strategies without regard for organizational uncertainties. The primary interests of this dominant coalition are accountability and control, and they would likely use their influence over the criterion setting and evaluation process to stress these issues.

Effectiveness Dimensions. The second study also examined the question "Did the questions the evaluators asked reflect the scope of concepts currently discussed in the organizational effectiveness literature?" The extent that each of five dimensions of organizational effectiveness was used in the evaluation is displayed in Figure 9.1. The solid line represents the frequency the evaluators mentioned a dimension of effectiveness as actually used in their

study, and the broken line the frequency they were mentioned as relevant to evaluations in general. The dotted line represents the frequency that the different effectiveness dimensions were discussed in the evaluation reports. In all three frequencies the evaluators could mention and the reports could include one or all of the dimensions; they are not mutually exclusive categories.

The two dimensions of the goal model, goal achievement and efficiency, clearly dominated the evaluations. According to the evaluators, all of the studies applied the goal achievement criteria to their evaluations. The efficiency dimension, while part of the design in 65 percent of the cases, was considered relevant by all of the evaluators. Adaptability and resource acquisition were next in importance and were reported as influencing 70 and 45 percent of studies. Maintaining staff motivation and satisfaction were the least influential, affecting 35 percent of the studies. These findings contrast sharply with Steers' (1975, p. 549) findings in his review of the theoretical literature. Of the 14 evaluation criteria mentioned, he found that adaptability and flexibility were the most prominent. Productivity, an aspect of the goal model, was second and worker satisfaction third.

Although the evaluators considered four of the five dimensions as relevant more often than they were used, the pattern of the broken line is similar to the other two. This suggests that the evaluations conformed to the evaluators' beliefs about organizational effectiveness. Therefore, if the dominant coalition shaped the design of these studies they did so in a way that conformed to the evaluators' point of

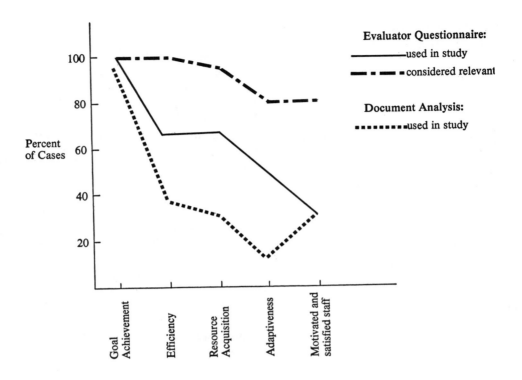

FIGURE 9.1
Percent of Evaluators Using and Considering Different
Effectiveness Dimensions, Study Two

view. The federal agencies, program administrators, and evaluators are of "one mind" regarding organizational effectiveness.

DISCUSSION

Evaluation Strategies and the Norm of Rationality

Finding that the evaluation studies were not designed to correspond to the uncertainties in social programs and that decision makers prefer certain research designs even if they disregard program uncertainty, underscores a

paradox of organizational decision making. Thompson (1967, chap. 7) argued that meaningful evaluations of organizational outcomes require the use of assessment strategies that correspond to the extent of uncertainty about organizational goals and causal knowledge. But Thompson (1967, p. 10) also acknowledged that decisions "are subject to the criteria of rationality and hence needing determinateness and certainty." Rationality norms encourage decision makers to interpret actions in relation to intentions and results, to seek technical solutions to problems, and to value arguments based on evidence. Even though there is mounting evidence that many organizations, especially public sector organizations, suffer from pervasive ambiguity of intentions, understanding, process, history, and structure (Cohen et al., 1972; March & Olsen, 1976; Weick, 1976), the norm of rationality encourages decision makers to overlook these characteristics.

Evaluation research, as a decision tool, is caught in this dilemma (see also Palumbo & Wright, 1981). On one hand, descriptive accuracy requires evaluators to reflect the level of uncertainty about goals and causal knowledge, yet the norm of rationality encourages evaluators to disregard uncertainty on the other. But conforming to the norm of rationality may create more problems than it solves for decision makers. As McGowan (1976) argued, ignoring uncertainties, inconsistencies, and unsurfaced conflicts to employ rigorous research designs gives an unrealistic picture of social programs and creates, in the end, greater uncertainty.

A Dominant Coalition with Interest in Control

In addition, these studies found that, of the many interest groups with a stake in program evaluation, only federal agencies and top program management significantly influenced the design and interpretation of the evaluations. This finding supports the argument that evaluating program effectiveness is an aspect of the formal authority relationships in and surrounding social programs.

Although no evidence was collected on how these dominant groups define effectiveness, the structural concerns of

federal agencies and top program management are with accountability and control. The primary role of top management is to ensure that "the organization serves its mission in an effective way, and also that it serves the needs of those people who control or otherwise have power over the organization. . ." (Mintzberg, 1979, p. 24). Managers are responsible for insuring that the organization meets its official goals and this responsibility clearly converges with that of federal agencies who are responsible for overseeing the implementation of laws and regulations. Both groups look to program evaluation as a means of holding services accountable to their mandates.

In addition, finding that program evaluation augments the formal authority of certain groups corresponds to the findings of Dornbusch and Scott (1975). They found a close relationship between formal authority within organizations and influence over the evaluation of individual performance. They concluded that this relationship was based on two rights: the "criterion setting right" and "appraising right" (pp. 214-226). Extrapolating to the present studies, program evaluation is analogous to personnel evaluation in that the right to evaluate is retained by those with formal authority over the organization. Such groups would likely use their rights and authority to pursue their interest in accountability.

Overstressing the Goal Model

The third finding was the clear dominance in evaluation studies of the goal model of organizational effectiveness. The goal model dominated the effectiveness questions asked, the design of the specific evaluation studies, and how the evaluators defined organizational effectiveness in general.

This emphasis on goals should not surprise anyone familiar with the program evaluation literature. Early contributions in the field—Suchman (1967) and Weiss (1972), for example—were based on the goal model, and the mainstream view currently asserts that only programs with "delimitable, measurable, and not inherently contradictory goals can be evaluated" (Rossi, 1978, p. 586). To paraphrase one respondent, "Goals are the new state religion."

The narrow range of effectiveness questions asked by evaluators has implications for the future of social services, however. To a substantial extent, selecting criteria determines judgments, and consistently emphasizing single criteria, such as goal achievement, not only presents an inadequate picture of the complexity of social programs, it will alter the programs.

Evaluations are not organizationally neutral; they define a set of expectations and encourage conformity to those expectations (Pfeffer, 1978, p. 79). This pressure to conform can be resisted by corrupting the data (Campbell, 1979, p. 85), by thwarting all efforts to evaluate performance (Patton, 1978, chap. 6), and by ignoring pressure to change (Lipsky, 1980, p. 23). Or, as is often the case, the pressure is accommodated by narrowing the organization's attention to those activities stressed in the evaluation. This narrowing of human services has been described as a shift from value to purposive rationality (Maynard-Moody, 1982) and will involve changes in the way human services are justified, administered, and judged. Although such changes are likely to have both positive and negative results, the point

to emphasize here is that evaluation research is an intervention in the twin processes of justifying and managing social programs. It is not passive measurement.

Patterns Across Findings

These findings are disturbingly consistent. As illustrated in Figure 9.2, the influence over the evaluation process of a dominant coalition whose primary interest is in accountability would encourage attention to goal achievement. Evaluating goal achievement does not present a complete picture of the effectiveness of programs, but it does provide a measure of how well programs complied with mandates. This stress on goals would, in turn, increase the reliance on assessment criteria that disregard organizational uncertainties, since examining goals directs the attention of evaluators away from organizational processes. Disregarding uncertainties would, completing the loop, reinforce the stress on accountability by deemphasizing the constraints on the provision of human services. Each individual finding underscores the stress on accountability and the set of findings is mutually self-reinforcing. They form a closed loop.

This pattern of findings is both descriptive and diagnostic. It documents the current emphasis in the field of program evaluation on accountability and identifies potential problems in both program evaluation and social policy implementation. Weick (1979, p. 72) argued that much organizational behavior is determined by how decision makers think about problems and that closed-loop thinking, if unchecked, leads decision makers into an increasingly narrow understanding of prob-

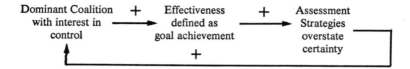

FIGURE 9.2
The Enactment of Effectiveness, A Summary of Findings

lems by progressively precluding alternative points of view.[7] Closed-loops are similar to committees of like-minded individuals; alternative points of view are not just ignored, they are never recognized.

Argyris (1980) argued that closed-loop thinking will, over time, either escalate errors or focus attention on the assumptions behind errors and thereby lead to new ideas about old problems. He acknowledged, however, that re-examining assumptions is rare because the assumptions themselves discourage people from seeing their errors. One solution Argyris advocates is the increased use of scientific evidence and procedures in decision making. Scientific research is, after all, a set of rules for testing assumptions against evidence and for surfacing errors in problem definition.

But the closed-loop pattern across the findings of these two studies is the result of the application of social science research procedures to decision making. These findings indicate that evaluation research by emphasizing accountability may be failing to provide the check on narrow-mindedness that may, in the end, prove to be social science's most important contribution to policy making.

---

[7] For a case study of the negative results of closed-loop thinking see Hall (1976).

REFERENCES

Argyris, C. Some unintended consequences of rigorous research. *Psychological Bulletin*, 1968, 70, 185-197.

Argyris, C. Making the undiscussable and its undiscussability discussable. *Public Administration Review*, 1980, 40, 205-213.

Benveniste, G. *The Politics of Expertise.* San Francisco: Boyd, Fraser, and Glendessary, 1972.

Bowers, D. & Seashore, S. Predicting organizational effectiveness with a four-factor theory of leadership. *Administrative Science Quarterly*, 1966, 11, 238-263.

Cameron, K. Measuring organizational effectiveness in institutions of higher education, *Administrative Science Quarterly*, 1978, 23, 604-632.

Cameron, K. & Whetten, D. Perceptions of organizational effectiveness over organizational life cycles. *Administrative Science Quarterly*, 1981, 26(4), 525-544.

Campbell, D. Assessing the impact of planned social change. *Evaluation and Program Planning*, 1979, 2, 67-90.

Campbell, J. On the nature of organizational effectiveness. In P. Goodman and J. Pennings (Eds.), *New Perspectives on Organizational Effectiveness.* San Francisco: Jossey-Bass, 1977.

Cohen, M., March, J. & Olsen, J. A garbage can model of organizational choice. *Administrative Science Quarterly*, 1972, 17, 1-25.

Coleman, J. The structure of society and the nature of social research. *Knowledge*, 1980, 1, 333-350.

Cook, T., DelRosario, M., Hennigan, K., Mark, M., & Trochim, W. (Eds.). *Evaluation Studies Review Annual* (Vol. III). Beverly Hills, CA: Sage, 1978.

Cronbach, L., Ambron, S.R., Dornbusch, S.M., Hess, R.D., Hornik, R., Phillips, D., Walker, D. & Weiner, S. *Toward Reform of Program Evaluation.* San Francisco: Jossey-Bass, 1980.

Cummings, L. Emergence of the instrumental organization. In P. Goodman and J. Pennings (Eds.), *New Perspectives on Organizational Effectiveness.* San Francisco: Jossey-Bass, 1977.

Cyert, R. & March, J. A *Behavioral Theory of the Firm.* Englewood Cliffs, NJ: Prentice-Hall, 1963.

Deutscher, I. Toward avoiding the goal-trap in evaluation. In F. Caro (Ed.), *The Evaluation of Social Programs.* New York: Russell Sage, 1977.

Dornbusch, S. & Scott, W.R. *Evaluation and the Exercise of Authority.* San Francisco: Jossey-Bass, 1975.

Ellul, J. *The Technological Society.* Translated by J. Wilkerson. New York: Knopf, 1964.

Etzioni, A. Two approaches to organizational analysis: A critique and a suggestion. *Administrative Science Quarterly,* 1960, *5,* 257-278.

Freeman, H. The present status of evaluation research. In M. Guttentag and S. Saar (Eds.), *Evaluation Studies Review Annual* (Vol. II). Beverly Hills: Sage, 1977.

Glass, E. (Ed.). *Evaluation Studies Review Annual* (Vol. I). Beverly Hills: Sage, 1976.

General Accounting Office. *Federal Program Evaluations* (Vol. 1). Washington, DC: U.S. Government Printing Office, 1978.

Guttentag, M. & Saar, S. (Eds.) *Evaluation Studies Review Annual* (Vol. II). Beverly Hills, CA: Sage, 1977.

Hall, R.H. *Organizations: Structure Process.* Englewood Cliffs, NJ: Prentice-Hall, 1982.

Hall, R.I. A system pathology of an organization: The rise and fall of the old *Saturday Evening Post. Administrative Science Quarterly,* 1976, *21,* 185-211.

Hofstadter, R. *The Age of Reform.* New York: Vintage, 1960.

Kahn, R. Human relations on the shop floor. In E. Hugh-Jones (Ed.), *Human Relations and Modern Management.* Amsterdam, Holland: North Holland Publishing, 1958.

Kahn, R. Organizational effectiveness: An overview. In P. Goodman and J. Pennings (Eds.), *New Perspectives on Organizational Effectiveness.* San Francisco: Jossey-Bass, 1977.

Katz, D. & Kahn, R. *The Social Psychology of Organization* (2nd ed.). New York: Wiley and Sons, 1978.

Kirchoff, B. Organizational effectiveness measurement and policy research. *Academy of Management Review,* 1977, *2,* 347-355.

Lipsky, M. *Street-Level Bureaucracy.* New York: Russell Sage Foundation, 1980.

Lowi, T. *The End of Liberalism.* New York: W.W. Norton, 1969.

Lynd, R. *Knowledge for What?* Princeton, N.J.: Princeton University Press, 1939.

McGowan, E. Rational fantasies. *Policy Sciences,* 1976, *7,* 439-454.

March, J. & Olsen, J. *Ambiguity and Choice in Organization.* Bergen, Norway: Universitetsforlaget, 1976.

Maynard-Moody, S. *Strategies for Assessing Organizational Effectiveness in the Public Sector: The Uses and Misuses of Program Evaluation.* Doctoral Dissertation, Cornell University, Ithaca, NY, 1981.

Maynard-Moody, S. Reconsidering charity: Some possible negative effects of program evaluation. *Administration and Society,* 1982, *13*(4), 379-404.

Maynard-Moody, S. & McClintock, C.C. Square pegs in round holes: Program evaluation and organizational uncertainty. *Policy Studies Journal,* 1981, *9,* 644-666.

Maynard-Moody, S. & McClintock, C.C. Organizational goals: A conceptual problem that will not go away. Paper presented at the Albany Conference on Organization Theory and Public Policy, April 1 & 2, 1982.

Mintzberg, H. *The Structuring of Organizations.* Englewood Cliffs, NJ: Prentice-Hall, 1979.

Nelkin, D. (Ed.). *Controversy: The Politics of Technical Decision.* Beverly Hills: Sage Publications, 1978.

Palumbo, D. & Wright, P. Decision making and evaluation research. In D. Palumbo, S. Fawcett, & P. Wright (Eds.), *Evaluating and Optimizing Public Policy.* Lexington, Mass.: Lexington Books, 1981.

Patti, R. The new scientific management. *Public Welfare, 1975, 33,* 23-31.

Patton, M. *Utilization Focused Evaluation.* Beverly Hills: Sage Publications, 1978.

Perrow, C. The analysis of goals in complex organizations. *American Sociological Review,* 1961, *26,* 856-866.

Perrow, C. Three types of effectiveness studies. In P. Goodman and J. Pennings (Eds.), *New Perspectives on Organizational Effectiveness.* San Francisco: Jossey-Bass, 1977.

Perrow, C. Demystifying organizations. In R. Saari and Y. Hasenfeld (Eds.), *The Management of Human Services.* New York: Columbia University, 1978.

Pfeffer, J. *Organizational Design.* Arlington Heights, Ill.: Harlan Davidson, Inc., 1978.

Reynolds, H. *Analysis of Nominal Data.* Beverly Hills: Sage Publications, 1977.

Rossi, P. Issues in the evaluation of human services delivery. *Evaluation Quarterly,* 1978, *2,* 573-599.

Rossi, P., Freeman, H., & Wright, S. *Evaluation: A Systematic Approach.* Beverly Hills: Sage Publications, 1979.

Rothenberg, J. Cost benefit analysis: A methodological exposition. In E. Struening and M. Guttentag (Eds.), *Handbook of Evaluation Research.* Beverly Hills: Sage Publications, 1975.

Rothman, D. *The Discovery of the Asylum: Social Order and Disorder in the New Republic.* Boston: Little, Brown & Co., 1971.

Scott, W. & Hart, P. *Organizational America.* Boston: Houghton-Mifflin, 1979.

Scott, W.R. Effectiveness of organizational effectiveness studies. In P. Goodman and J. Pennings (Eds.), *New Perspectives on Organizational Effectiveness.* San Francisco: Jossey-Bass, 1977.

Simon, H. *Administrative Behavior* (3rd ed.). New York: Free Press, 1976.

Steers, R. Problems in the measurement of organizational effectiveness. *Administrative Science Quarterly,* 1975, *20,* 546-558.

Stephan, A.S. Prospects and possibilities: The New Deal and the new social research. *Social Forces,* 1935, *13,* 515-521.

Suchman, E. *Evaluative Research.* New York: Russell Sage, 1967.

Thompson, J. *Organizations in Action.* New York: McGraw-Hill, 1967.

Weick, K. Educational organizations as loosely coupled systems. *Administrative Science Quarterly,* 1976, *21,* 1-19.

Weick, K. *The Social Psychology of Organizing* (2nd ed.). Reading, Mass.: Addison-Wesley, 1979.

Weiss, C. *Evaluation Research.* Englewood Cliffs, NJ: Prentice-Hall, 1972.

Yuchtman, E. & Seashore, S. A system resource approach to organizational effectiveness. *American Sociological Review,* 1967, *32,* 891-903.

PART TWO:
ARENAS

Introduction

In the past few years, the social sciences have added a great deal to our understanding of the realities which confront community organizers. These contributions have been both conceptual and empirical. We have been greatly assisted by some of the ways they have conceived of the "booming, buzzing confusion" which confronts us as we go into action. We have found a social systems perspective on communities, organizations, and the relations among them to be particularly helpful. In addition, we are beginning to get some glimmerings of the regularities in social phenomena that enable us to make a few tenuous predictions and thus exercise some control over our field of action.

Arenas of Community Practice

One major contribution of the social sciences to the practice of community organization has been in understanding the context in which we work, what we call the arenas of community practice. These arenas include interpersonal relations, small groups, formal organizations, neighborhoods, communities, and societies. We have chosen three of these arenas—society, community and formal organization—for special attention in this volume. We believe they are particularly salient for community organization practice.[1]

---

[1]Other works are available for those who wish to examine the other arenas more closely. On interpersonal relations see: Bruce J. Biddle and Edwin J. Thomas (eds.), *Role Theory: Concepts and Research* (New York: John Wiley & Sons, Inc., 1966); Arthur W. Staats and Carolyn K. Staats, *Complex Human Behavior: A Systematic Extension of Learning Principles* (New York: Holt, Rinehart & Winston, Inc., 1963); on small group: Dorwin Cartwright and Alvin Zander (eds.), *Group Dynamics: Research and Theory* (2d ed.; Evanston, Ill.: Row, Peterson, 1960); Barry E. Collins and Harold Guetzkow, *A Social Psychology of Group Processes for Decision Making* (New York: John Wiley & Sons, Inc., 1964).

To view societies, communities and formal organizations as arenas, instead of as means or ends as others have done, lends a special perspective. As arenas, they are viewed as the context within which action occurs, conditions of the practitioner's work to be understood and, largely, taken as given in doing community work. The reaction of some will be that this is altogether too passive, too accepting of the status quo and quite reactionary from a political point of view. But most of the conditions one finds as one begins to work must be accepted as they are even though a few may be changed. Time and resources—people, influence, etc.—are limited. What is selected for change must be chosen very carefully, calibrated not only to the hopes and aspirations of the clientele and those who serve them but also to available resources. To argue for regarding communities and formal organizations as arenas, then, is to argue for understanding, analysis, and the assessment of objectives and possibilities, not to counsel despair or the inevitability of existing conditions. Only then can one choose wisely what is to be changed. That may well be some aspect of community, some organizations, or some set of relations among them. The decision will be the product of observation and analysis rather than the a priori end of all community organization practice. Murray G. Ross, the author of a widely used text in community organization, assumes that the sense of community has been weakened, if not destroyed, by industrialization and urbanization, and that the major objective of our practice is to build or strengthen community integration.[2] This might well be the outcome of observation and analysis in particular instances. But to take community integration as the goal of all community organization practice, without regard to the circumstances of particular situations, as Ross does, seems inappropriate.

Others will object to viewing community as the context of practice on the grounds that it fails to take hold of possibilities, the dynamics of local life that provide the leverage and power needed to bring about change. But understanding must precede action if success is to be more than accidental. To know what opportunities there are for change is not given in advance or in some formula. The rush to act may prove fruitless unless observation, diagnosis, and understanding come first. Thus, careful observation and analysis of a particular community may lead to the selection of appropriate means to change what needs changing. In contrast, Saul Alinsky, perhaps the best-known practitioner in the field of community organization, regarded the development of powerful local "people's organizations" as the basic means for achieving his clients' objectives, and disparaged other approaches to change.[3] Under certain conditions—intensely felt grievances for which specified persons or organizations may be held responsible, relative powerlessness in the local community, willingness to engage in conflict strategies, resources to ensure persistence through disappointments, requisite

---

[2]Murray G. Ross, *Community Organization: Theory and Principles* (New York: Harper & Bros., 1955), pp. 52, 78-81.

[3]Saul D. Alinsky, *Reveille for Radicals* (Chicago: University of Chicago Press, 1946).

skill and leadership, etc.—Alinsky's strategy may prove best. But one cannot know all this in advance without a careful study of the situation at hand.

Defining the Arenas of Community Practice

Individuals may be understood as persons occupying a variety of social positions. A person, for example, may be a family member, an employee, and a member of a political party. Within each position, a person is expected to play one or more roles. As a member of a political party, a person may be asked to campaign for certain candidates, study and report on political issues, and vote in the party's primary elections. An individual may be subjected to ambiguous or conflicting expectations, arising from the different positions he occupies or the different roles he performs in a given position. He searches for ways of extricating himself from those uncertainties and conflicts.[4]

George C. Homans defines a group as follows:

> We mean by a group, a number of persons who communicate with one another often over a span of time, and who are few enough so that each person is able to communicate with all the others, not at secondhand, through other people, but face to face.[5]

Groups are composed of individuals, and formal organizations contain groups but are not merely "groups writ large."

Formal organizations are patterns of social interaction and shared perspectives "that have been deliberately established for certain purposes."[6] The fact that formal organizations are planned for the achievement of explicit objectives should not be taken to imply that all of its activities occur according to plan. As Peter M. Blau and W. Richard Scott put it:

> It is impossible to understand the nature of a formal organization without investigating the networks of informal relations and the unofficial norms as well as the formal hierarchy of authority and the official body of rules, since the formally instituted and the informally emerging patterns are inextricably intertwined.[7]

Groups are among the most important informal relations found in formal organizations, but such relations also include friendships, common interests such as politics and religion outside the formal organization, etc.

Roland L. Warren defines a community as:

---

[4]Robert K. Merton, *Social Theory and Social Structure* (rev. and enlarged ed.; Glencoe, Ill.: The Free Press, 1957), pp. 368-84; Edwin J. Thomas and Ronald A. Feldman, "Concepts of Role Theory," in E. J. Thomas, *Behavioral Science for Social Workers* (New York: Free Press, 1967), pp. 15-50.

[5]George C. Homans, *The Human Group* (New York: Harcourt, Brace & Co., 1950), p. 1.

[6]Peter M. Blau and W. Richard Scott, *Formal Organizations* (San Francisco: Chandler Publishing Co., 1962), p. 5.

[7]Ibid., p. 6.

... that combination of social units and systems which perform the major social functions having locality relevance. This is another way of saying that by "community" we mean the organization of social activities to afford people daily local access to those broad areas of activity which are necessary in day-to-day living.[8]

Each of these functions, e.g., production, distribution and consumption of goods and services, social control, education of the young, etc., is carried out by congeries of groups and formal organizations, partly dependent on one another but in no way centrally controlled.

This is what Edward O. Moe implies when he suggests that a community may be thought of as a "system of systems." In the same vein, Norton E. Long described the local community as an "ecology of games." Unlike the formal organization, a community is not planned but implicit or emergent. It is not centrally directed, like parts of a formal organization. Rather its parts run themselves and articulate with one another, conflicting, competing, and exchanging resources in unplanned ways.[9]

"A society," says Aberle et al. "is a group of human beings sharing a self-sufficient system of action which is capable of existing longer than the life-span of an individual, the group being recruited at least in part by the sexual reproduction of the members."[10]

Mayhew puts it this way: A society is "a complex of overlapping process systems.... We may abstract from the concrete interaction of concrete social persons a number of types of interaction systems. Economic, religious, political, educational, and other types of activity come to cohere into partially independent systems with units, boundaries and mechanisms of their own. These systems overlap, and when a relatively broad range of such systems cohere around a common population, we may speak of a society."[11] By population, Mayhew means a group at least partially maintained by sexual reproduction. His definition is consistent with that of Aberle et al. except that he casts it in system terms. The links between the systems that form a society include "emotional attraction, orientations of actors to each other, shared cognitive and evaluative perspectives, mutual influence or coercion, economic or functional interdependence, and common participation in an environment."[12]

How may a society be distinguished from a community? By (1) the relatively greater dependence of a society on sustenance through sexual reproduction, in contrast with immigration; (2) relatively permanent residence, whereas movement between communities is more common; and (3) including systems which are not necessarily "locality relevant" or do not necessarily afford local access to activities of daily living.

---

[8]Roland L. Warren, *The Community in America* (Chicago: Rand McNally & Co., 1963), p. 9.

[9]Edward O. Moe, "Consulting with a Community System: A Case Study," *Journal of Social Issues,* Vol. 15, No. 2 (1959), p. 29; Norton E. Long, "The Local Community as an Ecology of Games," *American Journal of Sociology,* Vol. 64 (November, 1958), pp. 251-61.

[10]David F. Aberle, et al., "The Functional Prerequisites of a Society." *Ethics.* Vol. 60 (1950), p. 101.

[11]Leon H. Mayhew, "Society" in *International Encyclopedia of the Social Sciences,* David L. Sills, ed. (N. Y.: The Macmillan Co. and the Free Press, 1968), Volume 14, p. 583.

[12]Ibid., p. 584.

From the perspective of these arenas, community organization practice may be defined as the deliberate effort of a practitioner to influence the ties that bind individuals into small groups, relate two or more groups, connect two or more formal organizations, relate groups to organizations. His or her purpose may be to improve the relations between individuals, groups and organizations, to assist them in collaborating to achieve some tangible goal, or both. Influence may be directed within the community in an effort to change local attitudes, administrative practices, etc. or toward the larger society in attempts to effect national opinion, legislation, etc. The practitioner may do this directly by working with the individuals in groups and organizations, and indirectly by influencing the characteristics of the groups and organizations themselves such as size, representativeness, operating procedures, etc., as well as by intervening in the relations between individuals, groups and organizations, i.e., bringing them into closer communication or cooperation, increasing their autonomy, facilitating confrontation and contention, etc. More detail is given in Part Three. Here we must be content merely with indicating the relation between the arenas and the strategies of community organization practice, and focusing attention on the arenas selected for detailed analysis and some of their important features.

Salient Characteristics of Groups and Organizations

Groups and organizations differ in a number of important respects. Although it is traditional to define primary groups and bureaucracies as "ideal types" representing polar extremes of organizational characteristics, it is more useful to identify continua along which groups and organizations may be placed. Certain features are universal characteristics of organizations, and we discuss these first.

Functions

All social systems must satisfy certain requirements to maintain themselves. Talcott Parsons offers one useful classification of the functions of social systems which we paraphrase as follows: (1) *adaptation to the social environment,* particularly obtaining resources necessary for operation such as money, personnel, and material; (2) *goal attainment,* securing the gratifications desired by the units of the system, such as profit or better housing, usually in response to external units on which the system depends; (3) *integration* or organization of the units of the system and their functioning; and (4) *tension management and pattern maintenance,* developing positive sentiments, including mechanisms for resolving disputes, training of new recruits, etc.[13] Adaptation and goal attainment are called *task* functions. These activities take place across the boundaries of social systems. Integra-

---

[13]Talcott Parsons, "General Theory in Sociology," in Robert K. Merton, Leonard Broom, and Leonard S. Cottrell, Jr. (eds.), *Sociology Today* (New York: Basic Books, 1959), pp. 4-7.

tion and tension management are called *maintenance* functions and occur within systems.

Parsons also pointed out that adaptive and tension management functions are *instrumental,* the *means* for attaining the system's objectives. Obviously obtaining resources (adaptation) is a necessary means for securing the system's objectives; perhaps less obviously, maintaining respect for authority, resolving internal disagreements, and training new recruits (tension management and pattern maintenance) are also means for keeping the organization together and moving forward to achieve its objectives.

Goal attainment and integration are consummatory, the ends or objectives of the system's activity. Again, goal attainment is obviously connected with achieving a system's objectives; less obviously, dividing and sequencing a system's work, assigning various roles to be performed, communicating between various elements of the system (integration) are necessary for achieving the system's ends and are, in effect, among the system's intermediate ends, necessary for goal attainment. The ends may be achieved by interaction among the members of the system, such as those engaged in some joint recreational pursuit, or through exchange with those outside, as when a business earns profits through transactions with its customers or a community organization practitioner helps his clients obtain a piece of legislation.

These ideas may be summarized in a diagram, adapted from Parsons[14] as follows:

	INSTRUMENTAL FUNCTIONS (Means)	CONSUMMATORY FUNCTIONS (Ends)
EXTERNALLY ORIENTED TASK FUNCTIONS	Adaptation	Goal Attainment
INTERNALLY ORIENTED MAINTENANCE FUNCTIONS	Pattern Maintenance Tension Management	Integration

As suggested above, these functions are universals. They are activities in which all social systems must engage. But organizations may differ on which of these functions are their primary *raison d'être.* For example, the community chest is engaged in collecting funds for private welfare agencies, that is, it serves an adaptive function. Welfare agencies help people resolve interpersonal difficulties, overcome physical handicaps, adapt to the demands of social institutions, etc., that is, they help manage tensions that arise in the course of social relations. Councils of social agencies, in the past, brought together representatives of welfare agencies so that they might work together effectively, serving mainly an integration function.

Some groups are largely consummatory in nature, providing direct gratifications for their members. Families, friends, churches, and recreation groups are primarily of this sort. Others are mostly instrumental tools for

[14]Ibid., p. 7.

achieving other purposes. Most social welfare agencies, schools, block clubs, and neighborhood associations are aimed at achieving some external goals rather than providing intrinsic satisfactions for their members.

An organization's primary function may differ for its various units. For example, a local property owners' association may be regarded by some members as instrumental to the protection of property values and the exclusion of "undesirable elements," while it offers other members a sense of participation and belonging. Organizations typically function in several ways for their members. A women's rights group may serve a consummatory function by providing an acceptable outlet for personal frustrations at the same time that it is instrumental in improving women's access to jobs, etc.

The functions served by an organization for its members will often differ from the roles it plays for organizations outside its boundaries. For example, a family may find its interrelations inherently gratifying, while the state regards the family as instrumental to its population policy. A civil rights organization may achieve more equal opportunities for its members (a task function) and serve the community by reducing racial tensions (a maintenance function).

Variables

There are a number of organizational variables which are important in understanding the special capabilities of organizations with which community practitioners must deal. (See Reading #12) These include (1) authority structure which may be hierarchical or collegial, (2) division of labor which may be on the basis of specialized or generalized role definitions, (3) performance guides which may be in the form of predetermined rules, the internalization of the organization's goals by the work force, or unplanned *laissez faire* determination of duties, (4) goal and policy setting which may be done by a separate cadre of policy makers or by those who administer programs, and (5) assignment of personnel on the basis of merit or such ascribed characteristics as race, sex or family status which are essentially irrelevant or detrimental to the achievement of organizational goals.

In addition, there are a number of other significant organizational variables which include the following:

Breadth of Function. Some groups and organizations are very *narrow* in the spectrum of participant interests they encompass, others are very *broad.* A community council may concern itself simultaneously or serially with any of the various interests people who live in a contiguous area may share, while a voluntary association with the same geographic base may confine its interests to the eradication or treatment of a particular disease, the resolution of interpersonal problems in families, or the removal of discriminatory practices based on race.

Characteristics of Participants. Some groups and organizations include persons whose social characteristics are quite similar. Others bring together

people of a widely varied sort. Significant characteristics on which participants may vary include socioeconomic status, age, sex, race, political
sympathies, perspective on organizational goals and methods or work, membership in other groups and organizations, etc. The significant factors will
vary. Thus, members of the National Association of Social Workers are quite
similar with respect to professional training, skills and socioeconomic status,
while they vary as to age, sex, race and perhaps political affiliation. A voluntary association with which a community organization practitioner works
may be quite homogeneous in many respects, or may be deliberately composed to include a sampling of the variety of social characteristics and
opinions to be found in the community.

We have sketched some of the important structural features which differentiate organizations. It remains to show how these are related to distinct
organizational abilities. First we indicate the variables associated with two
"ideal types": bureaucracies and primary groups. Quickly abandoning these
types, we proceed to summarize conclusions drawn from some of the literature which relates these structural variables to particular organizational
capabilities.

Organizational Structure and Capabilities

The traditional view of bureaucracy[15] is that it consists of the following
pattern of characteristics: a hierarchical authority structure, a division of
labor among technically competent specialists, strictly delimited functions,
impersonal relations, and laws or rules as the basis for decisions. Primary
groups fall, in several respects, at the other extreme: personal, face-to-face relations; lack of specialized training and competence; largely consummatory
rather than instrumental in function; and serving broad, ill-defined function.

Eugene Litwak and Henry J. Meyer[16] point out two very important facts:
First, some formal organizations and parts of many are much closer to primary groups in their characteristics than they are to bureaucracies. These
primary group-like organizations called "human relations" organizations
are more capable of dealing with highly complex and idiosyncratic situations
than traditional bureaucracies.

Second, bureaucracies and primary groups are not merely antithetical in
their characteristics. Rather than viewing them as alternative modes for
achieving social objectives, these authors find that, in many respects, they
are complementary.

[15]H. H. Gerth and C. Wright Mills (trans. and eds.), from *Max Weber: Essays in Sociology*
(New York: Oxford University Press, Inc., 1947), pp. 196 ff.; A. M. Henderson and Talcott Par-
sons (trans. and eds.), *Max Weber: The Theory of Social and Economic Organization* (New
York: Oxford University Press, Inc., 1947), pp. 324 ff.

[16]Eugene Litwak and Henry J. Meyer, "A Balance Theory of Coordination Between Bureaucratic Organizations and Community Primary Groups." *Administrative Science Quarterly*,
2:1:31-58 (June 1966).

James D. Thompson and Arthur Tuden[17] found that organizational structure affects the kinds of problems an organization can tackle effectively. They pose four types of problems, based on differences in two variables. One variable is the extent of agreement on the causes of a problem, that is, whether or not knowledge is available or thought to be available for dealing effectively with it. The second is the extent of agreement on objectives for dealing with a problem.

A bureaucratic structure is most effective in dealing with problems where there is agreement on both objectives and causation. A *collegial body*—a group of peers with similar training in whom authority resides—is best for handling problems where there is an agreement on objectives, but knowledge of causes or effective means of intervention is uncertain or a matter of judgment. A collegium is charged with the responsibility for what must be done in the face of uncertainty not about the desired outcome but about what action will be most effective. A *representative body,* bringing together various interests, is best in reaching a compromise on preferred outcomes or in settling differences on the order of priorities when knowledge is available for achieving any of the outcomes under consideration. Finally, an *anomic collectivity,* operating without rules and encouraging inspiration, creativity, and "experimentation," is indicated when there is neither agreement on goals nor the means for their attainment.

In several respects, the conclusions reached by Thompson and Tuden and by Litwak and Meyer converge and complement one another. Litwak and Meyer conclude that uniform events, that is, ones of moderate complexity, which can be mastered through disciplined study and occur with some regularity, can best be managed by a bureaucracy. Thompson and Tuden find that matters on which there is agreement on ends and knowledge of appropriate means are handled most efficiently by a bureaucracy.

These conclusions appear to be related, for uniformity in a phenomenon is required if knowledge of suitable means for mastery is to be developed. Litwak and Meyer fail to take into account the extent of agreement on goals and values. Their analysis assumes agreement on basic objectives. Thompson and Tuden, in effect, specify that nonuniform events of high complexity require a representative structure when agreement on major issues is lacking, but can be resolved by a collegial body if there is agreement on ends. Nonuniform events which are both highly complex and of infrequent occurrence, Thompson and Tuden might have said, can best be handled by an anomic collectivity that can search for and try out various ends and means. On the other hand, Litwak and Meyer suggest that nonuniform events that require only simple, widely distributed skills can best be handled by primary groups, a contingency ignored by Thompson and Tuden.

---

[17]James D. Thompson and Arthur Tuden, "Strategies, Structures and Processes of Organizational Decision," in J. D. Thompson et al. (eds.), *Comparative Studies in Administration* (Pittsburgh: Pittsburgh University Press, 1959), pp. 195-216.

Martin Rein and Robert Morris have suggested that there is a close connection between the goals and structures of organizations engaged in community organization practice.[18]

Community organization practitioners may work with organizations engaged in promoting the interests of some faction or segment of the community, such as the poor, Puerto Ricans, or the mentally ill, or some particular set of objectives, such as birth control or civil rights. In contrast, they may work with organizations which try to harmonize, reconcile, or compromise various goals and interests in the community. In the first instance, the organization's goal orientation may be referred to as the pursuit of *factional interests*,[19] while in the second *community integration* is the goal orientation.

Corporate organizations consist of a small, relatively homogeneous leadership cadre which is in basic agreement on the goals and means of the organization. In such an organization, others may be invited to join in order to assist in the achievement of this preestablished program. In contrast, *federated* organizations are collections of the diversity in the community. They endeavor to be representative of a wide range of groups, interests, or types of people. Others may be invited to join not because they agree with the specific program of the organization but because they represent otherwise unrepresented groups.

Rein and Morris' basic hypothesis is that a corporate structure is most appropriate in pursuing factional interests, while a federated structure is best adapted to the search for community integration. In the long run, achievement of factional interests may relieve strains in the social fabric and contribute to community integration. Likewise, the promotion of community integration, particularly in the reinforcement of norms which set wide limits on the pursuit of special interests, aids factions in achieving their interests. Nevertheless, an organization should select a structure appropriate to its particular goal orientation and allow the long-range effects to work themselves out. If an organization is saddled with a particular structure it should select an appropriate goal orientation. Otherwise, it is likely to fail.

A representative structure and what Rein and Morris call a federated structure appear similar in the diversity of interests which they bring together. Rein and Morris conclude that a federated structure is best adapted to achieving community integration, while Thompson and Tuden believe that a representative structure is useful for achieving compromise in the event of conflicting preferences. These assertions seem quite similar.

Blau and Scott, from their review of the empirical literature, reached related conclusions. Their focus is on situations that require "efficient coordination" in comparison to those that need "a single correct or best an-

---

[18]Martin Rein and Robert Morris, "Goals, Structures and Strategies for Community Change," *Social Work Practice 1962* (New York: Columbia University Press, 1962), pp. 127-45.

[19]Rein and Morris prefer to call this goal "change." But this is so ambiguous a term that we have adopted "pursuit of factional interests" in its place. For example, change can and does occur as practitioners pursue community integration, bringing social values into a better adjustment with one another or, more frequently, bringing action into a closer approximation of the values we espouse.

swer." Where there is agreement on both outcomes and causes, the main problem is to coordinate the necessary means to achieve the desired results. When there is disagreement on either objectives or appropriate methods, the problem is one of deciding which of various possible objectives or methods ought to be sought or employed. While Thompson and Tuden's conclusions are somewhat more refined than Blau and Scott's the latter support the former:

> In sum, groups are superior to individuals, and groups in which there is a free flow of communication are superior to groups in which differentiation impedes communication in solving problems which call for a single correct or best answer; but individuals are superior to groups, and hierarchically differentiated groups are superior to undifferentiated groups, in performing tasks that primarily depend on efficient coordination.[20]

Seldom does an organization deal with but one type of problem or face but one kind of circumstance. In short, organizations must develop a variety of capabilities, and one way they can do this is by incorporating various types of substructures appropriate for dealing with the problems they most typically confront. Thus, a large-scale bureaucracy which must deal with some nonuniform events may create special departments structured along collegial or "human relations" lines to deal with those events. A second way groups, particularly small ones, can deal with this problem is by changing structure over time as the kind of problems confronted shifts. Thus, a community council (representative structure) may meet as a committee of the whole to decide on a program and establish priorities. Once this has been agreed upon, the council may divide into "working committees" and subdivide the job further among subcommittees and individual members, all of whom are responsible to the chairman (bureaucratic structure).

Connor, in a recent comprehensive review of the literature on organizational design, reaches a number of conclusions bearing on the relation between organizational structure and capabilities.[21] For Connor, organization structure is one of several "design variables." From our perspective, Connor discusses organizational capabilities in a number of different contexts. For our purposes, we will refer to organizational capabilities as the ability to: (1) pursue various types of goals, (2) cope with differing environmental conditions, (3) apply varying kinds of technology, (4) make use of different kinds of people, (5) design work in various ways, (6) exercise control over the organization in different ways, (7) make varying types of decisions, (8) develop various sorts of organizational climate, and (9) achieve various kinds of organizational effectiveness.

Connor defines organizational structure as "the organization's official arrangement of roles, authority relationships, and communication patterns."[22]

---

[20]Blau and Scott, op. cit., pp. 125-26.
[21]Patrick E. Connor, *Organizations: Theory and Design.* (Chicago: Science Research Associates, Inc., 1980.)
[22]Ibid., p. 347.

Space does not permit a detailed review of Connor's summary of the literature. At the risk of oversimplification, the following review is quite selective.

Connor identifies four basic dimensions of organizational structure: (1) Complexity, which includes (a) horizontal differentiation, i.e., the degree to which those involved in producing the organization's output is divided, usually measured by the number of departments within an organization. (Labor may be divided either by giving trained specialists a wide range of activities to perform or by minutely subdividing tasks so that non-specialists can perform them. The first is typical of the professional, the second of the unskilled worker.); (b) vertical differentiation, i.e., the number of management levels in the organizational hierarchy; and (c) span of control, i.e., the number of subordinates under each manager's direct supervision, with the clear implication that the larger the number, the greater the complexity.

(2) Specialization, consisting of two types, i.e., (a) task specialization, the degree to which a particular task is divided and assigned to different individuals, and (b) personal specialization, the extent to which an organization employs persons with different types of training. This permits one to distinguish between organizations that divide tasks among unskilled workers (high task specialization, low personal specialization) from organizations that divide tasks among professional workers with different training (low or moderate task specialization and high personal specialization). A combined measure, referred to by Tyler as "role variety . . . the number of completely dissimilar occupational categories in the organization" takes account of both task and personal specialization.[23]

(3) Formalization and Standardization, i.e., (a) "the degree to which rules and regulations governing people's behavior exist; and (b) the degree to which they are enforced."[24] In some organizations, managers depend upon professional training and organizational socialization to guide the work of employees and decisions are reached through consensus in formal discussions or workers respond informally to cues within the work group; in others, general or detailed orders are issued *ad hoc* in the absence of rules; in still others, the organization and rhythm of the assembly line serve this purpose. Thus, formalization and standardization are but one way in which decisions are made in organizations.

(4) Centralization, i.e., "the degree to which members participate in decision making." Connor identifies two factors in centralization: (a) "the location of the actual decision-making function at particular points in the authority structure," and (b) "the promulgation of rules for decisions, which limit the discretion of subordinates."[25]

Connor's discussion bears a strong resemblance to the traditional view of bureaucracy, based on the work of Max Weber, and summarized earlier.

[23]William B. Tyler, "Measuring Organizational Specialization: The Concept of Role Variety." *Administrative Science Quarterly,* 18:385 (1973).

[24]Connor, op. cit., p. 352.

[25]Ibid., p. 352.

However, Connor's approach is to view each factor as a variable rather than a constant, and is clearly more consistent with recent research.

Next, we review selected aspects of Connor's analysis which bear on what we have called organizational capabilities. Space permits consideration only of (1) goals, (2) environment, (3) climate, and (4) effectiveness.

Connor, after reviewing a number of analyses of *organizational goals,* uses the work of Gross as the basis for his synthesis.[26] Gross identifies five major types of organizational goals from his research:

1. Output goals are products or services.
2. Support goals are of four types:
   a. Adaptation or coming to terms with various elements of the organization's environment.
   b. Management or decisions on who should run the organization, handling conflict and determining priorities.
   c. Motivation or efforts to build satisfaction and loyalty among members.
   d. Position or domain, the organization's place in relation to other organizations.[27]

In our terms, when organizational structure is low in vertical complexity, high in horizontal complexity, large in span of control, high in task specialization, low in personal specialization, high in formalization and in centralization, it is most capable of pursuing output goals, and when the opposite structural features are present, it is most capable of pursuing support goals. Of course an organization's freedom to pursue one type of goal or the other will depend upon a variety of other conditions such as environmental constraints, the types of technology and people employed to carry out the work.

Connor uses the dimension of "dynamic" and "static" as the basic, if over-simplified, analysis of variations in *organizational environment.* This includes at least four important subdimensions:

1. Complexity or the number of units in the environment with which the organization must cope.
2. Diversity or the variety of such units.
3. Change or the degree such units vary over time.
4. Uncertainty or the degree to which change in such units is unpredictable.[28]

Another important dimension is the level of dependence on various environmental elements.[29]

---

[26]Edward Gross, "The Definition of Organizational Goals," *British Journal of Sociology.* 20:277-294 (September 1969).

[27]Connor, op. cit., p. 95.

[28]Ibid., pp. 126-127.

[29]Ibid., p. 127.

In our terms, organizations that are not too formalized or centralized, moderate in task specialization and high in personal specialization, moderate or high in vertical complexity but low in horizontal complexity and small in span of control are best able to handle high levels of environmental complexity, diversity, change and uncertainty, while organizations with the opposite structural features are best adapted to dealing with a stable environment.

In discussing *organizational climate,* Connor focuses on the character of an organization as "a psycho-social-emotional environment" as "the public, customers, politicians, employees and prospective employees see it."[30] The dimensions of organizational climate he uses are as follows:

"1. Individual autonomy: the freedom of the individual to be his or her own boss, having considerable decision-making power, and not being continually accountable to higher management.
2. Position structure: the degree to which the objective of, and methods for, the job are established and communicated to the individual by higher management.
3. Reward orientation: the degree of reward/profit/achievement orientation fostered and reflected by managerial and nonmanagerial personnel.
4. Consideration-warmth-support: the degree to which psycho-social-emotional needs are met and nourished by other organizational members, managers and nonmanagers alike."[31]

In our terms, organizations with a structure that is simple, low in specialization, and high in formalization and centralization will support an organizational climate which is low in individual autonomy, reward orientation and consideration, and high in position structure. In contrast, organizations with a structure that is complex, high in specialization, and low in formalization and centralization will support an organizational climate which is high in individual autonomy, reward orientation and consideration, and low in position structure.

Connor analyzes the dimensions of *organizational effectiveness* in the following terms: (1) Efficiency, (2) Quality of Output, (3) Quality of Work Environment (essentially what he referred to elsewhere as organizational climate), and (4) Responsiveness, consisting of (a) adaptability to external and internal change and (b) flexibility in dealing with crisis situations.[32]

In our terms, organizations with structures that are low in horizontal complexity, formalization, and centralization and high in personal specialization will be relatively less capable of efficient operation, but more capable of producing high quality output and creating a high quality work environment, and will be more capable of responding to change. In contrast,

---

[30]Ibid., p. 395, 398.
[31]Ibid., p. 406.
[32]Ibid., pp. 447-448.

organizations with structures that are high in horizontal complexity, formalization, and centralization and low in personal specialization will be relatively more capable of efficient operation, but less capable of producing high quality output and creating a high quality work environment, and will be less capable of responding to change.

Another approach to the analysis of organizational structure is provided by Galbraith and his colleagues.[33] Every organization of any size and complexity must differentiate its activities and coordinate them so that the outcome is the production of some product or service in a timely fashion within budgetary limitations and of a nature that is consistent with the wishes of management (or, more accurately, with the various constituencies that management must satisfy). It is assumed that each differentiated unit must have an authority structure to assign work, allocate resources, monitor performance, and resolve differences.

One principle of differentiation is the organization of units around the production of some product or service. A community development agency might have departments dealing with new subdivisions, zoning, downtown redevelopment, and neighborhood redevelopment. Another such principle is functional organization. A community development agency might have departments dealing with planning, drafting, accounting, and legal matters. The service structure would be effective in providing the service but not very efficient if each of the separately organized services needed, say, legal advice but none were large enough to require the full time services of a lawyer. The functional structure would make it possible to hire one or two lawyers to assist each of the services. The services, however, would not have control over legal services, and would have to confer with the legal department, develop plans and schedules, creating delays and inefficiencies in the operations of each of the services.

These problems can be handled informally, through committees, etc., where new environmental demands occur infrequently and the pace of change is slow and where technical innovations (e.g., changes in the law) are infrequent. But where changes in environment or technology are rapid and cannot be ignored, particularly in very large and complex organizations, functional structure can cause intolerable delays in delivering services. These problems can be mitigated through a number of processes, including the creation of rules and procedures, planning processes, referral of disagreements up the hierarchy, direct contact among line or supervisory personnel from various functional departments, and the creation of liaison departments. But in large, complex organizations experiencing a high volume of demands from their environment which cannot be responded to in a routine manner or a high rate of change in relevant technology, some organizations (Galbraith's examples are from the aerospace industry) find it most effective

---

[33]Jay R. Galbraith, "Matrix Organization Designs: How to Combine Functional and Project Forms," *Business Horizons,* 14:1:29-40 (February 1971) and Jay R. Galbraith and Daniel A. Nathanson, *Strategy Implementation: The Role of Structure and Process.* (St. Paul, MN: West Publishing Co., 1978).

and efficient to develop a matrix organization. This is an organization with both service and functional units linked together by middle level personnel that are responsible to two supervisors, one representing the particular function (e.g., the legal dept.) and the other representing the service provided (e.g., neighborhood redevelopment).

In our terms, the service organization structure is most capable of coping with a stable task environment, particularly when the resources it requires (personnel, equipment, knowledge, clients) are not shared by other service units. The functional organization structure is most capable of coping with a stable task environment, particularly when it must share its resources in the delivery of a variety of services. But the matrix structure is most likely to be of optimum effectiveness and efficiency when the task environment is changing, particularly where the technology is not routine, i.e., it must be specially adapted to each particular service or project, and the organization is large.[34]

The discussion of organizational structure and the relation between various forms of structure and organizational capabilities is premised upon the view that certain capabilities are desirable under specified conditions and their outcomes are measurable. It may be possible to measure the output of certain mass-produced processes, and specify the structural and other design features required to produce them most efficiently at an acceptable level of quality. But this becomes particularly difficult when one must resort to the measurement of behavior, rather than output, and that behavior is highly interdependent, as in the case of sports teams; or when the knowledge of what it takes to produce certain outputs is very imperfect and our ability to measure the outputs is low. This is certainly the case with most human services.

Connor argues that in such cases, dependence on market factors (competition and pricing) or bureaucratic rules (with training and monitoring) for control may be inappropriate, and one may need to rely on what he calls clan control. This is typical of most professional organizations, which depend heavily on lengthy periods of training to develop both technical skills and values of the profession. The extent to which the needs of a particular organization will be met by employing persons of a given profession will vary, of course, with consensus or conflict predominating in particular cases. Low rates of employee turnover and heterogeneity are necessary for clan control to operate, and it is possible to compensate partially for high levels of employee heterogeneity through training and indoctrination, both of a technical nature and in organizational beliefs and values.[35]

In short, the relationships identified between organizational structure and capabilities may serve to provide some general guidance to those working with human service or professional organizations, but aspirations to anything approaching perfect rationality in designing such organizations to achieve explicit and measurable objectives seem out of reach.

---

[34]Ibid., pp. 381-383.
[35]Connor, op. cit., pp. 290-307.

Factors Influencing Linkages between Arenas

Community organization practice, as suggested above, involves bringing influence to bear on the relations among groups and organizations. As the practitioner comes to understand what affects these linkages, he is in a better position to exercise control over them—or to know when to avoid wasting resources on attempting to change what he can do little about.

Groups, organizations, and communities are bound together by two major sets of ties: *cultural* and *social. Cultural ties* consist of shared tools and technology; common sentiments, that is, beliefs about the nature of reality, attitudes toward various institutions and roles within and outside the system, ideas about right and wrong, good and bad, etc. *Social ties* are interactions between people, their nature, pattern, and frequency. Some interactions are direct, face to face; others are mediated by third parties or by various forms of communication, including the mass media. Litwak and Meyer[36] offer us an analysis of the relations between external primary groups such as families and formal organizations like schools or neighborhoods. Basically, they suggest that there is a balance in the social distance between these antithetical structures that maximizes the achievement of social goals, for example, education of the young. The community organization practitioner serves as the link between the two types of structures and employs four principles in deciding how to bring them closer, move them farther apart, or maintain the existing social distance between them. Drawing conclusions from studies of mass communication, Litwak and Meyer point out four barriers to communications or linkages between formal organizations and external primary groups: (1) selective listening to those messages with which one agrees; (2) selective interpretation, perceiving messages that are heard in ways that are consistent with personal attitudes or group characteristics; (3) complexity of messages, varying from simple to complicated; and (4) scope or numbers of people the message must reach.

These authors offer some general guidelines for the practitioner in choosing appropriate methods for overcoming the barriers noted above: (1) In overcoming selective listening, i.e., a predilection not to listen to messages, the practitioner can choose a method which permits a high degree of organizational initiative. Thus, instead of inserting a notice in a local newspaper or distributing handbills, the practitioner may knock on doors or stop people on a busy street corner and engage them in conversation so that the message gets through. (2) In dealing with selective interpretation, i.e., message distortion, one can choose communicators who have the trust of the persons receiving the message or persons who have the time and training to develop positive relationships with message recipients. (3) In coping with complexity, one may use experts or specially trained persons to get the message across, using face-to-face communication to allow message recipients to ask questions and seek clarification. (4) To assure maximum scope, one may use

---

[36]Litwak and Meyer, op. cit.

various forms of mass communications designed to reach the targeted audiences.

The practitioner's first task is to determine the nature of the communication problems with which he or she is faced, and then select one or a set of interrelated methods that are likely to be most effective in dealing with the problems or barriers, diagnosed at the least cost. Obviously, if the practitioner is dealing with people who are ready to listen (e.g., other middle-class people with goals and motives similar to those of the practitioner, or groups of people who must cope with a common disaster) selective listening will not be a problem and a high degree of organizational initiative will not be required. Similarly, if the senders and receivers of messages are much alike in status, age, sex, attitudes and opinions, or are in regular and sympathetic interaction, there will be little problem with selective interpretation. Simple messages can be carried by ordinary people without special expertise, and a few people can be reached without use of the mass media. But if the targets are not predisposed to listen, some degree of organizational initiative will be necessary; if messages are likely to be interpreted selectively, some form of intensive relations between practitioners and targets will be required; if messages are complex, experts must be relied upon and available to answer questions; and if many people must be reached, some form of mass media must be chosen.

Clearly, methods that resolve one problem are not necessarily suitable for handling others, especially as the practitioner must take account of costs. Thus it is difficult to maximize both scope and organizational initiative or intensity of relations. The practitioner's task is to diagnose the problem accurately and then select a set of approaches and activities, often phased over time and otherwise interrelated, that will solve the problem at the least possible cost.

As James D. Thompson and William J. McEwen[37] have suggested, organizations vary in the extent to which they are dependent upon their environments, ranging from something approaching complete control over the environment (e.g., giant cartels and trusts) to total dependence upon the environment (e.g., many service enterprises). Thus they may relate to their environment in a number of different ways, depending upon their strength and independence of the environment.

In descending order of power, organizations relate to their surroundings by (1) absorption of competitors and suppliers; (2) competition; (3) cooperation in the form of *(a)* bargaining and exchange, *(b)* co-optation, *(c)* coalition, alliance, and merger; and (4) conflict in the form of harassment.

Giant corporations often buy up smaller competitors rather than forcing them out of business through competition because their managerial know-how and markets add to the parent corporation's strength, although antitrust

---

[37]James D. Thompson and William J. McEwen, "Organizational Goals and Environment: Goal-Setting as an Interaction Process," *American Sociology Review,* Vol. 23 (February, 1958), pp. 23-31.

legislation puts some brakes on such activity in this country. In the welfare field, the large and well-endowed hospital may buy up nursing homes.

When two or more organizations vie for the resources of third parties, they are engaged in competition. The business example is clear enough. In the health field, the independent health agencies—heart, cancer, etc.—compete for the contributor's dollar. One may find a rehabilitation agency with a wealthy constituency constructing a fine facility in a prime location which reduces the demand for existing services. However, given the paucity of treatment resources, two rehabilitation programs may be able to coexist if trained personnel and income are available in sufficient quantity. Contributions to one organization do not necessarily detract from those received by another; the total amount contributed may be larger.[38]

When two organizations are approximately equal in power and produce goods and services needed by each other, they may negotiate or bargain with one another to settle the terms of their cooperation. Sol Levine, Paul E. White, and Benjamin D. Paul have made an important contribution to our understanding of the conditions affecting exchanges between health and welfare organizations.[39] Based on their research, these authors show that exchanges between organizations depend upon (1) the functions they perform, which, in turn, determine their needs, (2) their access to needed resources from outside the system of health and welfare agencies or, conversely, their dependence on such agencies, and (3) the extent to which there is consensus among health and welfare agencies about their respective domains.

Robert Morris has also studied the conditions affecting cooperation between agencies concerned with chronic illness under Jewish auspices in seven cities in the United States. He found six factors of importance in fostering cooperative relations, in descending order of importance: (1) a simultaneous crisis in the organizations that ultimately engaged in cooperative activities, (2) informal interaction among trustees, (3) availability of a planning organization perceived as objective, neutral, and nonthreatening, (4) leaders possessing qualities of statesmanship, that is, trusted by all parties, skilled in negotiation techniques, and capable of creating formulas for cooperation that alter organizational autonomy without destroying it, (5) expert studies which confirm and legitimate conclusions reached by local leaders, rather than providing blueprints for action, and (6) a discriminating use of incentives.[40] One cannot help but wonder what conclusions Morris would have reached if he had examined relations between agencies that have differing capacities to sustain themselves in their environments.

---

[38]John R. Seeley, et al., *Community Chest* (Toronto: University of Toronto Press, 1957), pp. 365-66, 408-11.

[39]Sol Levine, Paul E. White and Benjamin D. Paul, "Community Interorganizational Problems in Providing Medical Care and Social Services," *American Journal of Public Health,* Vol. 53, No. 8 (August, 1963), pp. 1183-95.

[40]Robert Morris, "New Concepts in Community Organization," in *The Social Welfare Forum* (New York: Columbia University Press, 1961), pp. 128-45.

One organization may absorb or co-opt into its decision-making structures representatives of another to head off potential threats to its stability or integrity. At the same time, it may pay the price of adapting its program in the interests of those so absorbed. Philip Selznick found two types of co-optation in the organization he studied. The first he called informal co-optation. In this type, the co-opted party is not actually found on the boards or committees of the organization, but its interests are considered or informal consultations are held with its leaders before major decisions are reached. Those co-opted exercise real influence in the organization, although they are not formally a part of it. The second type he called formal co-optation. Groups are formally co-opted by bringing representatives into the decision-making bodies of the organization. But real influence on basic decisions is not shared because it doesn't need to be. When formal co-optation takes place, it is not because the co-opted parties represent a potential threat to the organization but because bringing them in provides assistance in administering programs or adds to the legitimacy of the organization in its social context.[41] Co-optation is often the substance of various moves toward "democratic administration," such as those engaged in by local community action agencies under the Economic Opportunity Act of 1964. There is little evidence that formal co-optation of the poor by the War on Poverty was parlayed into control or substantial influence by the poor over funds, programs, content, job opportunities, etc.[42]

When an organization is so powerless in relation to its environment that it is unable to carry out an effective program, it may seek other organizations with which to form coalitions. Coalitions are often short-term agreements to achieve specific purposes but may begin or develop into relatively permanent alliances. For example, coalitions may form to elect a candidate or pass a school bond issue. Most community chests began as alliances of local businessmen and wealthy philanthropists who, working separately, were unable to evaluate the character of the numerous requests for charitable contributions they received. Neither were they able to increase the efficiency of fund-raising efforts. The community chest enabled them to pursue both objectives. When organizations agree to cooperate but give up their separate identity, one speaks of merger.

Eugene Litwak and Lydia F. Hylton found that alliances in the form of coordinating agencies arise when organizations are interdependent, perceive their interdependence, and can define their transactions in standardized units. They concluded that very high levels of interdependence lead to merger, and low levels may be handled by *ad hoc* coordination (for example, a telephone call). Only moderate levels give rise to coordinating agencies such

---

[41]Philip Selznick, *TVA and the Grass Roots* (Berkeley and Los Angeles: University of California Press, 1949), pp. 13-16.

[42]Lillian Rubin, "Maximum Feasible Participation: The Origins, Implications and Present Status," *Poverty and Human Resources Abstracts*, Vol. 2, No. 6 (November-December, 1967), pp. 5-18.

as a council of social agencies. Highly standardized units of action are handled by rules or laws (such as those governing eligibility for public assistance) while low levels of standardization result in *ad hoc* coordination (such as case conferences between agencies making and receiving referrals). Only moderate amounts result in coordinating agencies. Finally, they found that a small number of organizations requiring coordination does not warrant a coordinating agency, but can be handled on an *ad hoc* basis, while a very large number of organizations can only be coordinated through laws, directories of organizations, a competitive market system, etc.[43] The implications for practice are clear. With some knowledge of the presence and magnitude of the factors identified by Litwak and Hylton, the practitioner can select and promote a suitable approach to coordination, ranging from merger to *ad hoc* communications.

Halpert, in an effort to summarize the literature on the antecedents of interorganizational coordination, concludes that the following factors support or hinder such coordination. He begins with a discussion of interpretive factors (attitudes, beliefs, meanings) on the parts of administrators and other organizational members, and then moves to a discussion of contextual factors.[44]

Interpretive Factors that Support Coordination. Agreement among administrators and staff at all levels of the organization on a wide range of matters encourages coordination. These include:

1. Identification of organizations amenable to coordination.
2. Common definition of problems and appropriate methods for their solution.
3. Perception of similar interests among the organizations to be involved.
4. Perception of the need for a joint endeavor.
5. Perception of partial interdependence among the organizations to be involved.
6. Perception of equal status of organizations and their administrators.
7. Agreement to the exclusive rights of each organization to its domain.
8. Perception that the benefits of coordination (e.g., improved service, greater efficiency) exceed the costs.
9. A cosmopolitan world view and ideology supportive of coordination.
10. Perceived ability to maintain each organization's valued ways of operating in the context of coordination.
11. Positive employee orientation toward group approaches to problem solving and goal attainment.

[43]Eugene Litwak and Lydia F. Hylton, "Interorganizational Analysis," *Administrative Science Quarterly,* Vol. 6, No. 4 (March, 1962), pp. 395-420.

[44]Burton P. Halpert, "Antecedents", Chapter 4 in David L. Rogers, et al., *Interorganizational Coordination.* (Ames, Iowa: Iowa State University Press, 1982), pp. 54-72.

Contextual Factors that Support Coordination.
1. Loss of clientele or other necessary resources.
2. A large number and variety of services provided.
3. Environmental uncertainty and turbulence.
4. Innovation is an organizational or community norm.
5. Standardized procedures, including referral procedures.
6. Physical proximity leading to informal interaction, membership in the same community voluntary associations.
7. A reward system that supports coordination.
8. Leadership qualities which include (a) a service ethic, (b) technical competence, (c) forcefulness, and (d) active involvement in providing leadership.
9. Professionalized organizations.
10. Organizations with a high diversity of occupational specialties.
11. A broad conception of the organization's target and a broad range of services.
12. A high level of decentralization of authority.
13. Similarity in organizational structure among participating organizations.
14. Similarity in services, capabilities and resource needs.

Interpretive Factors that Inhibit Coordination.
1. Perceptions of potential coordination partners as threats, that coordination would lead to:
   a. Loss or fragmentation of administrative authority.
   b. Loss of program identity or of separate organizational identity.
   c. Loss of organizational prestige or strategic position. (E.g., potential partners perceived as of lower status or legitimacy, incompetent in dealing with clientele, etc.)
   d. Loss of service effectiveness, client alienation, inability to serve new clients, etc.
   e. Criticism from other network organizations crucial to an organization's current mode of operations if coordination is pursued with a non-network agency.
2. Differences in interests or ideology (e.g., punishment vs. rehabilitation orientation among correctional agencies.).
3. Disparity in training and leadership among organizations or in professional socialization when different professions are employed, leading to the lack of a common language.
4. Institutionalization of norms that question the legitimacy of interorganizational coordination.

Contextual Factors that Inhibit Coordination.
1. Limited amount and quality of interorganizational communication arising from:
   a. Bureaucracy, i.e., long chains of command and rules requiring communication only through prescribed channels.

    b. Professionalization, i.e., causing different ideology, language and communication barriers.
2. Centralization of authority, causing:
    a. Distance of top administrators from the areas to be coordinated.
    b. Barriers to innovation.
3. Structural differences between the organizations to be coordinated.
    a. Smaller, less complex organizations lack resources to implement coordination.
    b. Smaller organizations experience threats to their integrity and autonomy in relation to larger, better financed ones.
    c. The costs of coordination may exceed the benefits.
d. Smaller organizations may be unable to exchange items of equivalent value to maintain the basis for coordination.

The research summarized above is in relation to voluntary coordination. When coordination is mandated, additional barriers have been found where:

1. The environment of coordination is highly fragmented.
    a. Differences in the geographic jurisdiction of the units and sub-units of federal, state, local government and private community organizations.
    b. Similar differences exist within jurisdictions.
    c. Mandates and regulations vary within and between levels of government and units to be coordinated.
    d. Duplications and gaps exist in administration, services and funding sources.
    e. Ambiguity exists in the roles of federal and state agencies with respect to mission or accountability.
    f. Program support and directives change frequently.
2. Conflict exists over the locus of decisionmaking between and within various levels of government.
3. There is frequent turnover in policy personnel and lack of continuity in leadership.
4. There is inadequate training of personnel.
5. Competition exists between single-purpose federally funded agencies and multi-purpose state coordinating agencies.
6. There are threats to authority, autonomy, and survival including disruption of routines, changes of status, increased regulation, reduced funding, and outside evaluation of performance.

A very weak group that is grossly dissatisfied with its social environment, perhaps convinced that it is the victim of great injustice, may relate to other organizations by attack and harassment. Contenders having a major power advantage (for example, an illegal syndicate, state and local governments) may engage in overpowering conflict when it is required. But those at the opposite end of the power hierarchy may be able to create considerable inconvenience, disruption, embarrassment, annoyance, etc., without being able to overpower. By so doing, they put themselves in a position closer to parity with their adversary so that they can bargain effectively for their interests in exchange for ceasing their harassment. Some of the tactics of the civil rights movement may be understood in these terms. The lunch-counter sit-ins, the bus boycotts, and the Poor People's Campaign of the summer of 1968 reflect this type of conflict relations. Saul Alinsky has created and applied such tactics with great skill.

James Coleman has made a major contribution to understanding the way individuals, groups, and organizations relate to one another. He notes that *activities which are independent of one another,* such as the meeting of a welfare agency's board of directors and a family's evening meal, have no effects on the relations between the two groups involved. The directors develop an interest in the social agency, and the family in its dining activity and conversation, and the actions taken are independent of one another. The cultural and social residues created thereby are an attitude of indifference between the meal-takers and the meeting-attenders, and a pattern of noninteraction or mass.

If, on the other hand, people are engaged in *similar activities dependent on the same events,* such as traveling to work on the same set of roads or sending their children to the same schools, then their activities intersect in such a way that all benefit or suffer together. If the roads are bad or the schools poor, all are harmed. In this way, they develop common interests in improving their roads and schools and are likely to take collective action to that end. The residues that are produced include sentiments of identification with one another and patterns of interaction that take the form of communitywide organization.

A more complicated set of results occurs when people engage in *dissimilar but interdependent activities.* For example, one set of families sends their children to the public schools, and another group of people teaches them. In one respect, all benefit from these activities. These families and others pay school taxes, for which they receive, in exchange, educated children. Others contribute their working hours to the education of those children, for which they receive their livelihood. The results are the same as when people engage in similar activities dependent on the same events, discussed above.

But the same situation may produce benefits for some and costs for others which do not balance out. Some parents may prefer to send their children to private schools and resent paying school taxes. Some must pay school taxes even though they have no children in school. Teachers may not be paid adequately for their work and demand higher salaries which the taxpayers find it difficult to meet. Thus, interests are opposed, resulting in *conflict, unilateral action,* or *inaction.* The residues produced include sentiments of hostility and organized cleavages.[45]

---

[45]James S. Coleman, "Community Disorganization," in Robert K. Merton and Robert A. Nisbet (eds.), *Contemporary Social Problems* (2d ed., New York: Harcourt, Brace & World, Inc., 1966), pp. 670-95.

What determines whether activities which hurt some and benefit others will result in conflict, unilateral action, or inaction? At this point, several additional concepts must be introduced. *Density* refers to the number of organizations per unit of population or the proportion of the population who are members of organizations. *Distribution* refers to the proportion of organizations in different sectors of society. For example, in our society, there are proportionately more organizations among middle-class people than lower class people. *Interlocking* refers to the extent to which the same individuals belong to two or more organizations. *Cross pressures* are felt by individuals when they belong to several organizations which hold conflicting expectations for their behavior.

High density is likely to draw many people into controversies. Organizations are the vehicles for the articulation of interests. The more interests that find organized expression, the greater the chances for the emergence of opposed interests. As high density means large numbers of people in organizations, the higher the density, the more people are likely to be involved in controversy.

The greater the degree of interlocking membership, the more likely that controversies, when they do arise, will be compromised or stalemated. The greater the degree of interlocking, the more likely it is that people will be subjected to cross pressures. If they cannot win others over to their point of view or work out the basis for a compromise, they are likely to withdraw from the organizations with which they disagree or urge their organizations to take no action.

If there is a narrow distribution of organization in the community, involving, for example, the middle but not the lower classes, and there is a fair degree of common interests among those who are organized, by virtue of their similar class position, then unilateral action may be expected. For example, the dental and medical societies and the public health department may urge the city council to fluoridate the water supply and, with little discussion, the necessary ordinances are passed. But if the lower classes are mobilized, conflict of an extreme variety is likely to occur, such as the spreading of initial disagreement on one issue to many issues, and from a disagreement on policies to attacks upon individuals. Organizers have frequently entered communities that have instituted fluoridation to mobilize the opposition and appeal to normally apathetic lower class voters through various scare tactics.

In general, a high degree of density plus a low amount of interlocking is conducive to conflict. When Martin Luther King organized the Montgomery bus boycott, he deprived the organized white community of the opportunity for unilateral action and created the conditions necessary for conflict—a Negro organization relatively free from interlocking membership in white organizations. (He also overcame the reluctance to act springing from dependence on the white community.) In contrast, as organized labor has developed increasing ties with management through profit-sharing plans, informal interaction of union leaders with management, upward mobility of working men into management positions, etc., conflict between labor and management has been limited to "bread and butter" issues, and virulent labor-management conflict has all but disappeared.[46]

FRED M. COX

---

[46]James S. Coleman, *Community Conflict* (Glencoe, Ill.: The Free Press, 1957), pp. 20-23.

10.

John E. Tropman and Fred M. Cox*

SOCIETY: AMERICAN VALUES AS A CONTEXT FOR COMMUNITY ORGANIZATION AND MACRO PRACTICE

PART I. A GRAMMAR OF VALUES

Introduction

Other than a global or international context, such as bilateral, multinational or United Nations programs of social assistance, society is the broadest arena in which community organization and social administration are practiced. Society consists of both social organization and culture. By social organization we mean governmental, economic, and social institutions and by culture we mean the technology, values, attitudes, and beliefs of a given society. We have chosen values in general and American values in particular as the focus of our discussion because of their significance as an important factor in shaping what choices in social policy and programs will be made in a society. Increasingly, values are being recognized as an important target of change, especially with respect to social policy.[1]

The relationship between society's values and its social policies has long been a subject of debate.[2] A central question in this debate is this: Does society, gauged by its social policies, behave consistently with its purported values? Often it does not.[3] But even if values cannot be linked consistently with policies they do comprise a key component of the climate in which policies are developed. In order to study relations between values and social policy, it is essential to recognize that policy generally expresses values in operational or behavioral terms. This connection has been made explicitly by Lasswell and Kaplan, who state that "policy is a projected program of goal values and practices: the policy process is the formulation, promulgation, and application of identifications, demands, and expectations."[4]

Because values embody our fundamental assumptions about goals and the meaning of existence, they undergird our behavior and our opinions about appropriate policy. A value can be described as a standard that discriminates the aims or actions we believe are important to pursue. This working definition is close to that of Bengston and

---

*Note: John E. Tropman is the author of Part I., A Grammar of Values. Fred M. Cox is the author of Part II., American Values.

[1] See John E. Tropman, "Societal Values and Social Policy" in J. Tropman, et al., *Strategic Perspectives on Social Policy.* (Elmsford, N.Y.: Pergamon, 1976.)

[2] Ibid.

[3] Perhaps the contrast between early American rhetoric of equality and the institution of slavery provides the sharpest example.

[4] Quoted by Wilfred Harrison, "Policy," in J. Gould and W. L. Kolb, eds., *A Dictionary of the Social Sciences* (Glencoe, Ill.: The Free Press, 1964), p. 509.

Lovejoy, who define values as ". . . conceptions of the desirable which orient toward action. . ."[5] The supposition that values influence behavior helps us understand how people's values relate to their choices and positions within society. Bengston and Lovejoy add that values ". . . represent an important link between social structure and personality. . ."[6] Further, values represent important links among social and cultural structure and social policy. Social structure includes the range of characteristics that distinguish people and groups from one another—their occupation, education, race, sex, etc. Cultural structure is the conceptual, affective, perceptual, imaginative, thinking part of our world. It includes, as Rokeach suggests, values, attitudes, and beliefs.[7] The social system is composed of cultural and social structures, both of which affect what people do individually and what society does collectively, often in the form of social policy.[8]

[5]Vern L. Bengston and Mary C. Lovejoy, "Values, Personality and Social Structure: An Intergenerational Analysis," *American Behavioral Scientist,* 16:6:880 (July/August, 1973).

[6]Ibid.

[7]Milton Rokeach, *Beliefs, Attitudes and Values.* (San Francisco: Jossey-Bass, 1972). Beliefs and attitudes are often thought of interchangeably with values. While beliefs and attitudes are related to values, they are more subject to change. Beliefs are assertions of what is or ought to be true factually. Attitudes reflect the orientation one has toward an experience or belief.

[8]This is as true of private firms (for example, through pension plans) as it is of governments. As we see it, any collectively-derived policies, whether public or private, aimed at assisting people are a kind of social policy. Social policy is a collective expression rather than an individual one; it is addressed to collective needs. Although there are various orientations toward determining what is in the interest of the group the target of social policy is some form of long-run group enhancement through some collective means, either public or private. See John E. Tropman, "New Horizons of Social Policy," paper presented at the Society for the Study of Social Problems, San Francisco, August 1982.

Complicating Factors. There are a number of complications to be considered in an examination of values and their relationship with social policy. These factors fall into four categories: (1) political factors, (2) value conflict, (3) close effects, and (4) theory versus practice.

Political Factors. Values provide only a part of the context in which policies are developed. It is true that most policies address a societal problem and employ value-laden strategies. But political necessity and compromise generally intrude, often obscuring the values originally embodied in the policy. By the time a proposal becomes law it has been subjected to debate and compromise among policymakers, resulting in policies acceptable to the majority but not necessarily totally reflective of their values. Schiltz expresses this concern:

What legislators and commentators often forget is that the public is under no constraint—nor does it possess a mechanism—to arrive at a practical compromise acceptable to the majority. In the practical order, this means that a proposal attracting a relatively small proportion of the electorate—perhaps less than 25 percent—during the discussion stage, may well enjoy a majority or even massive public support for enactment, not because it is everyone's preference, but because it is acceptable to most people.[9]

Value Conflict. Schiltz's comment stresses conflict between interests but overlooks the fact that a given individual or group may have interests which are inconsistent with one another. Our view, which is detailed below, is that we are all ambivalent about the values

[9]Michael Schiltz, *Public Attitudes Toward Social Security 1935-1965* (Washington, DC: U.S. Dept. of Health, Education and Welfare, Social Security Administration, Office of Research and Statistics, Research Report #33, 1970), p. 182.

we seek in any policy, and that there are multiple and contradictory values which people try to satisfy not only between interest groups but also within each person and group. For example, society generally wants to help older people have an adequate income. Yet we also want to encourage independence and self-sufficiency. This is one reason that we attach a contributory requirement to our social security programs for the aged. Providing medical care for the old and needy is another commonly held value. Yet questions are raised concerning whether such care should be provided to those who consciously expose themselves to risks such as smoking, overeating, etc.[10] This perspective both complicates and sheds light on the problems Schiltz raises. It complicates the problem because it recognizes an added complexity in reaching social policy decisions; it sheds light because it gives us a more accurate map of the value system and its relationship to policy.

Close Effects. In understanding factors affecting social policy, other complications arise. People's values tend to vary depending on how closely a policy issue affects them. This is a matter of intensity of preference. Generally we feel more strongly about policies that affect us or our loved ones directly than policies that touch us only indirectly. Older people, as a case in point, may be less interested in property tax increases to support public schools (unless they are property owners or have close relations with grandchildren enrolled in the schools) than they are in increases in Medicare premiums.

Theory vs. Practice. A final complication arises from the relationship between people's general attitude toward a policy and their personal experience with it. As Katz and his colleagues suggest, there is a lack of consistency between the general attitudes people have toward an issue and their personal experience with it.[11] Some younger married people, for example, may be opposed generally to the government taking over what they consider to be a family's responsibilities for children or aging parents. Yet when they are faced with the birth of a severely retarded child, a mentally ill son or daughter or frail elderly parents requiring nursing care, they may want the government to help them. This lack of congruence between theory and practice (or between general attitudes and the pressures of particular circumstances) confounds the relationship between the public's values and its support for specific social policies. Further, as Katz, et al. suggest, the public may more readily view policy stereotypically than they see it accurately.[12] As the public is rarely involved in the day-to-day implementation of policy, it may focus on only the most obvious and emotionally exciting issues, ignoring the unintended consequences of administration which often detract from the achievement of the overall goals of the policy.

In summary, while values clearly provide an important part of the con-

---

[10]Lawrence Brown, "The Scope and Limits of Equality as a Normative Guide to Federal Health Care Policy," *Public Policy.* 26:4 (Fall 1978)

[11]Daniel Katz, et al., *Bureaucratic Encounters: A Pilot Study in the Evaluation of Government Services* (Ann Arbor: Institute of Social Research, 1975). Webster and Driskell point out that Berger's work on status generalization focuses upon how people develop performance expectations of others—*viz.*, specific expectations based upon general characteristics. M. Webster and J. Driskell, "Status Generalization: A Review and Some Data," *American Sociological Review,* 43 (April 1978).
[12]Katz, et al., op. cit

text in which policies are formulated, we must be very cautious in making generalizations about Americans' values based on analyses of social policy. Let us turn next to a general discussion of some salient aspects of values, their structure and meaning.

The Complex Phenomena of Values

To contemplate values is an exercise in thinking about a complex phenomena, about social refractions in which the picture one sees, in the first instance, may not be one that is really there. Much like those old photos which at first blush look like one thing but on further examination reveal something quite different, the study of values is often a study in paradox.[13] Values vary in meaning and in function. They conflict in time and in space. They provide the structure around which social life is understood and infused with meaning. Much like a prism, values provide refractions of interpretation on the "rays" of social activity surrounding us.[14]

In the policy realm of community organization practice, paradox is often the most strikingly persistent quality, for it is possible to describe a set of values which significantly informs policy but which fails to resolve the underlying conflicts and dilemmas of choice; rather, it actually highlights those dilemmas and conflicts by revealing what they are. Therefore, a full understanding of values as a context for practice

must reflect values in all their complexity.

For our purposes, we are not as interested in looking at the effects of values upon policy directly as we are in using values as a prism to illuminate the many aspects of the practice context and especially the contradictions with which community practitioners must deal. An understanding of values and, as important, the system of values provide a conceptual framework that sheds light on the complexities and contradictions faced by practitioners. Policy embodies the solution, for a moment in time, of the multiple and conflicting values that make up our value system. To understand policy for the aged, or for children, or for any group, one not only needs to understand the push of one value, but the pulls of contradictory values as well.

The Hidden Aspects of Values

As Robin Williams, Jr., has indicated, the term value may refer to the actual ratings or grades we assign to objects. Or it may refer to the criteria we employ to make reflective evaluation:

In one meaning we refer to the specific *evaluation* of any object, as in "industrialized countries place a high value on formal education" or "governmental regulation is worthless." Here we are told how an object is rated or otherwise but not what standards are used to make the judgments. The second meaning of value refers to the *criteria*, or standards in terms of which evaluations are made, as in "education is good because it increases economic efficiency." Values-as-criterion is usually the more important usage for purposes of social scientific analysis.[15] (Emphasis in original)

---

[13]One common old photo, for example, shows at a distance, what appears to be a woman sitting at a dressing table fixing her hair. Upon closer examination of this photograph, however, its parts change into a skull! Its title is "Vanity."

[14]To the extent that values illuminate such social activity, "prism" is a good concept; to the extent they limit and constrain possible interpretations, the "prison of values" is a good concept also.

[15]Robin M. Williams, Jr., "The Concept of Values," in David L. Sills, ed., *The Encyclopedia of the Social Sciences* (New York: Macmillan/Free Press), Vol. 16, p. 283.

Values as criteria for evaluation, as exemplified in our discussion of American values, below, often operate in a structure that is not always apparent. Because values operate at different levels of consciousness, an expression of values may in fact be related to some deeper, even conflictual pattern.

An Example from University Life. Social work students have been particularly strong supporters of progressive taxation to provide resources for aiding the disadvantaged. They have been very critical of what they perceive as the unwillingness of most Americans to support these programs. Suspecting that the values of the students did not differ greatly from those they were attacking, the author devised a method of exploring this assumption. A classroom exercise was developed in which the instructor proposed to "tax" the grades of students, so that those who received A and A+ would get lower grades and the surplus would be applied to those who had failed.[16] Immediately students reacted negatively. They argued that grades were their personal property, they had worked hard to earn them, and if someone failed that was the concern of that person, not themselves, especially if it involved subtracting anything from their own grades! But what about their argument, in a past week, that grades are nothing but a product of an instructor's whim? Here, too, contradictory values were expressed. In general, they argued, better grades reflect personal achievement while poor grades do not. However, additional probing revealed a deeper meaning. The key to the matter lay in the assessment of oneself and one's own grades,

versus others. Students tended to believe that their own grade, and grades below them, were due to merit: grades above them were due to luck and professorial whim.[17] Grades *up to one's own grade* reflected merit. At that point assessment changed. Bad grades *down to one's own grade* reflected instructor whim, not personal demerit.

Several points are illustrated by this example. First, the students reacted like the most conservative people with respect to money when their own "coin" (grades) was involved. Second, very quickly they made the link between grades and personal worth, abandoning it only when confronted with a competing argument which they themselves had made. When they thought they would benefit by getting good grades they argued for what Aristotle called proportionate equality, or rewards in relationship to contributions.[18] When they thought they would lose, through lower grades, they switched to what he called numerical equality. Their compromise position was proportionate equality when it benefited them, numerical equality when it did not.[19]

The Social Security Act is a prime example of a program that combines the

[16]John E. Tropman, "The Grade Tax," *Policy Analysis,* 5:3: (Summer 1979).

[17]An experimental situation produced similar results. Students were asked to set performance criteria for themselves on a test, and then take the test. Those who were successful in meeting their criteria attributed the results to high ability. Those who failed to meet the expected level of performance, however, did not attribute low ability to themselves. Rather, they said the test did not work. Grace Kovenklioglu and Jeffrey H. Greenhaus, "Causal Attributions, Expectations and Task Performance," *Journal of Applied Social Psychology,* 63:6 (1978).
[18]Aristotle, *Nicomachean Ethics,* Tr. by R. McKeon (New York: Modern Library, 1947). Book V., Chapter 5.
[19]For an extensive discussion of numerical and proportionate equality, as well as its applications, see E. Walster, G. W. Walster and E. Berschied, *Equity* (Boston: Allyn and Bacon, 1978).

principles of proportionate and numerical equality. In this case the principle of proportionate equality is generally termed equity and the principle of numerical equality is called adequacy. Title II of the program, the retirement portion of the law, employs a very complicated formula in an effort to provide an adequate income floor for older persons with low earnings during their working lives while at the same time requiring people to contribute a proportionate (or equitable) share of their earnings toward their own retirement income. Title XVI of the law, Supplemental Security Income (SSI) attempts to provide an adequate income for needy aged, blind, and disabled persons without requiring a contribution. Programs such as SSI are necessary because a policy based on equity may not always be an adequate one. Providing benefits proportionate to contributions results in an inadequate level of support for those with the lowest incomes, if contributions are proportionate to ability to pay. The grade tax example illustrates this point well. Applying considerations of equity, some students, on the basis of their intellectual investment and effort, may not warrant a passing grade. In thinking about this situation, students felt that in such cases, a failing grade was in order. And the idea of providing supplemental points to raise all grades to an adequate level was soundly rejected.

However, there were several important exceptions which had to do with the consequences of the failing grade in the specific case. Whether or not the failing student had other good grades seemed to be the central concern. If the student's other grades were "ok," then one failing grade was acceptable. However—and here is the crucial

point—when it appeared that the consequences of an inadequate grade were too severe, then students felt that "something should be done" to mitigate the effect. If, for example, a student was marginal, and the grade would result in dismissal from school, then the situation was evaluated quite differently. It would be appropriate, they argued, to permit the student to do some "extra" work so that the grade could meet minimum standards. This should be permitted, students argued, even though the same consideration should not be extended to other students, even other students with poor grades but not in danger of dismissal because the consequences were less severe for them.

The criterion seemed to be the impact of applying the rule in a given case. The students argued that, when the application of the rule has disastrous consequences, then its application (or the results of its application) should be tempered, even though they recognized that the individual "fully deserved" the grade. That is, they were not making the argument that the instructor had been unfair, or that there was need to adjust the standards: *they wanted an exception to the standards,* and an exception such that the rule itself was not imperiled.[20] This might be called the principle of mitigating disastrous results of applying the rule of equity.

Another type of exception was mentioned by the students. This one might be called the principle of mitigating circumstances. This one focused upon reasons why the student could not do

---

[20]While they did not mention it then, students later asked about grading during the Vietnam War, when lower grades for men had ominous implications, as they would be subjected to military service if their grades fell below a certain level.

well. Illness, responsibilities for child care, and "discrimination" were mentioned. If such circumstances existed, then adjustments should be made for the individual in question. Both sets of reasons, mitigating disastrous results and mitigating circumstances, are ones people use for making exceptions to the rule of equity, while retaining the rule itself.

Policy, within the Social Security system, reflects these principles. The older adult whose Social Security benefits are equitable but inadequate qualifies for SSI which "bridges the gap" between adequate and equitable levels of support. The reasoning behind this is much like that of the students—even though people may not "deserve" it, they should not be permitted to become too badly off if the consequences are too severe.[21]

The Conflict of Values

We rely on values to give purpose, meaning, and integrity to life. They span time and space, connecting us to those who have gone before and those who will come after. Insofar as we are

aware of them and can reflect on them, values make life comprehensible.

Everyone needs self-esteem as well as the respect of others. Yet the ways one achieves this represent a "policy conflict" for the individual. Is it best achieved through work or leisure? Machlowitz, for example, points out that "workaholics" seem confident and competent, yet suffer from low self-esteem.[22] One might ask if personal growth is to take priority over work or family? Retirement used to be a time for "leisure." With increasing pressure to work, older people may have to forego some leisure and stay on the job longer. Society is in conflict about what to do, as much as the person is who wonders about the proper balance.

There is also conflict between "independence" and "interdependence." On the one hand, Americans are supposed to be self-reliant. America as a "land of opportunity" means that everyone has a chance to get ahead.[23] On the other hand, Americans need to depend upon others for help in achieving social goals. Not only do we value the help others provide, we have a sense of obligation to them. Thus, Dahrendorf juxtaposes "life chances" and "ligatures"—connections with and obligations to others. If the Lone Ranger is valued, so are Tonto and Silver, two friends who help him out time and again. If the solitary farmer is esteemed, so is the communal barn raising. The values of independence and interdependence exist side by side.

As is perhaps evident by now, the conflict of values means something rather special to us. It represents a particular perspective on the grammar of

---

[21]In this case, discrimination would play a big role. Work opportunities and compensation are heavily influenced by gender and race. One would expect that minorities and women would have lower Social Security benefits than majority group males. Because contributions are proportionate to wages, up to a point, and because benefits are proportionate to contributions (above the minimum benefit to which all covered by the system are entitled), and because women and minorities receive lower wages than majority group males, it follows that disproportionate numbers of women and minorities receive the minimum social security benefit and are eligible in disproportionate numbers for means-tested SSI benefits. Thus, more frequently than with majority group males, the principle of mitigating disastrous results or mitigating circumstances apply to women and minorities.

[22]Marilyn Machlowitz, *Workaholics* (New York: Mentor Books, 1980).
[23]Ralf Dahrendorf, *Life Chances* (Chicago: The University of Chicago Press, 1980).

values. The idea that values are multiple is important, but not new. The idea that values have a hidden structure has been advanced at the psychological level by the concept of the "unconscious" (although that itself is not a "values" concept).[24] Pareto's idea of "residues," though never quite clear, is akin to a latent structure of values which is present at the social level.[25] Jung writes of a "collective unconscious," which is evident in archetypal symbols seen at many times and in many cultures.[26] And Merton has advanced the idea of latent functions which also emphasizes the hidden aspect of social purpose.[27]

The notion advanced here is that a system of values tends to be comprised of juxtaposed pairs of values. Interdependence and independence, adequacy and equity, public and private, are examples of this kind of juxtaposition. Thinking about one of the pair tends to bring the other to mind. The conflict, though never absolute, means that the expression of one requires the diminution of the other.

Change and Stability

Because the value system is patterned, one might expect that constancy would characterize it. Yet one also hears about "the good old days" in which traditional values held sway.

Has there been, then, a significant change in values?[28]

One also hears of generational conflict. Do the values of older and younger people differ, especially as they relate to policy matters? Are old people "conservative" and younger people "liberal?" Thinking about values requires us to look at what people believe. Because values are multiple, and in conflict, we would expect to find both change and constancy. People hold contradictory beliefs. Therefore, a movement from one belief to another is more a shift in emphasis within a system of commitments than a change in that system.

However, even knowing what people value, or at least what they say they value, may not be enough. Acock and Bengston, for example, point out that generational conflict between parents and children is as much influenced by what parents are thought to believe as by what they actually believe.[29] This process of attribution of belief is an important point to keep in mind as value-laden policy-relevant questions are examined.

Conclusion

The value system is that collection of values, attitudes, and beliefs which people use to give life meaning and direction. It is more than a list of cherished commitments; it is a structure

---

[24]C. de Monchaux, "Unconscious," in J. Gould and W. Kolb, eds., *A Dictionary of the Social Sciences* (Glencoe: The Free Press, 1964), p. 732.

[25]Talcott Parsons, *The Structure of Social Action* (Glencoe: The Free Press, 1949), pp. 704-705.

[26]de Monchaux, op. cit.

[27]Robert Merton, *Social Structure and Process*, Rev. Ed. (Glencoe: The Free Press, 1958).

[28]See, for example, D. Garth Taylor, "American Politics, Public Opinion, and Social Security Financing," in F. Skidmore, Ed., *Social Security Financing* (Cambridge: MIT Press, 1981).

[29]A. Acock and V. Bengston, "Socialization and the Attribution Process: Actual Versus Perceived Similarity Among Parents and Youth," *Journal of Marriage and the Family* (August 1980).

and a pattern, containing many specific individual values, often joined in conflict with each other. Older and younger people may differ in their orientation within the system, but almost certainly are part of the same system.

This perspective is a useful one in considering the relationship of values to community organization, administration and policy because it takes complexity as a point of departure. We see macro-practice as an approach to solving some of the problems posed by multiple and conflicting values, providing a tentative and perhaps temporary map through the changing territory of commitments and beliefs.

PART II. AMERICAN VALUES

These are times of unprecedented change, changes that have shaken many Americans from the secure moorings they enjoyed in previous generations. Patriotism, for example, a sincere commitment to the nation and its objectives, especially in time of peril, was relatively uncomplicated during the 1940s. We were fighting a proven menace, the fascists. The war resisters were there but their voice was small. All that has changed, beginning perhaps with the Korean War and certainly during the Vietnam conflict. The pace of such changes has quickened and we are uncertain about what we value. At the same time the values have become even more important as we search for guides to action.

The sources of change are many, among them technological innovation and expansion of education and communications accompanied by rising expectations which remain unfulfilled.

Whatever the source, American values are under assault. Yet we often turn to the traditional verities when decisions are required. Not that our values somehow determine our decisions. Various prudential and expedient considerations enter in. But what we ought to do is often referred to—or rationalized by—values to which Americans subscribe. This is particularly true of public decisions which are of primary importance for social welfare.

Americans are moralists. Many are not content with justifying actions on the basis of legality or tradition. They seek the moral principles behind law and habit. For example, civil disobedience is justified not by reference to law but by higher moral principles. Those on the right, while condemning civil disobedience and declaring their reverence for the law, turn to moral principles in justifying their positions. Various forms of public enterprise, graduated income taxes and court-ordered desegregation of the public schools, for example, are condemned on the grounds that they infringe on the essential liberties of the individual. The point is that we Americans, in addition to acting expediently and sometimes avariciously, refer decisions to basic values. Sometimes these are but rationalizations of our hopes and fears.

However, values need not be misused. They can provide moorings, a sense of direction as the tide of change sweeps over us. But they can work mischief. "There is nothing so dangerous," an old saying goes, "as a principled man." And there is an important truth here. People who come to believe that their principles provide an unerring and detailed guide to action are at the brink of fanaticism. Abstract principles may be carried to absurdities. "Thou shall not kill" seems straightforward and irrefutable at first glance. But when we apply the principle to a specific decision, we may still face problems. Even those who oppose abortion on this basis are faced with an unresolved choice when the decision not to abort a fetus means the sure death of the mother in childbirth. At their best, values sensitize us to important considerations to be taken into account in reaching decisions. They do not prescribe action in detail.

Our own approach may be called humanistic pragmatism. We regard human existence as all of one piece, not divided into mind and body, moral principles and expedient guides to action, values and facts. We believe that decisions should flow from the evaluation of specific consequences. People may differ in abstract principles but agree on the consequences they desire from a particular social welfare program. We do not evaluate policy in terms of abstract principles but consider their impact on flesh and blood human beings living at particular times and places and under specific conditions.

There are many different American values and ways of expressing them. We have approached the subject from a study of American history and philosophy. Our approach is a fairly traditional one. The statement is not very precise, but the concepts are not either. What we hope to do is to give the reader a general sense or feel for American values. We have selected those values which are basic and most relevant to social welfare, values which deal with (1) the individual, (2) the economy, (3) liberty and freedom, (4) equality, (5) democracy, (6) the family, and (7) humanitari-

anism and human rights. We will point up ambiguities and differences in the way American values are interpreted, particularly in the social welfare arena.[30]

The Individual

Society is regarded as existing to serve the interests of each individual. The activities of business, government, voluntary associations, etc., are evaluated in terms of their effects upon individual participants. In other words, the individual is not regarded as subservient to the "higher" purposes of the nation or any other human institution.

Expectations of the Individual. What is expected of the individual? He is expected to (a) be self-reliant, to work with others but not depend upon them in the sense of allowing them to do his share of the work, unless he is sick, disabled, too young or too old. Even then, he is expected to do as much as possible for himself. (b) It is expected he will work hard and strive for success, largely in economic terms. Success is generally measured in terms of income, wealth, possessions, power, occupational prestige plus the style of life that goes with these achievements. He is supposed to be dissatisfied with present achievements, have hopes and plans for the future, constantly improve himself and work for upward mobility. (c) He is expected to work with others to achieve

---

[30]We rely heavily on the work of Robin M. Williams, Jr. *American Society.* (New York: A. Knopf, 1958) and Ralph B. Perry, *Characteristically American.* (New York: A. Knopf, 1949) in this description and analysis of American values. Also, the personal pronoun "he" is used in the general sense, to refer to both men and women.

his objectives. The American does not pursue success alone; he organizes. He does not subordinate his interests to the organization, but pursues his own objectives through it. When the group no longer serves him, the individual abandons it. In other words, he changes jobs frequently in pursuit of career success. If he is "other directed" it is because he believes it will advance him. (d) And lastly, it is expected he will play fair, according to the rules of the game. Although he is often tempted, the American believes he should not achieve his purposes through force, fraud or "pull."

Responses to the Behavior of the Individual. How are we expected to respond to the individual? He is honored for his achievements, not for his station at birth. Americans reject the aristocracy of birth but embrace the aristocracy of the successful, of merit, and achievement. Age, sex, race, ethnic group, etc., are regarded as irrelevant measures of worth. Rewards are supposed to be unequal and in rough proportion to natural ability and character (hard work, self-denial, etc.). Although there has been a growing awareness that race and sex and age have made an important difference in the way people are treated, apart from their achievements, Americans do not accept this state of affairs as right or inevitable.

Those who fail in the competitive struggle for success are regarded as of two types: (1) The "unlucky" and basically respectable, the "worthy poor." These are people who, through no fault of their own, have had circumstances befall them that have prevented them from achieving a measure of success. These are widows, the disabled and el-

derly. (2) The "bums," the able-bodied poor whose character is regarded as defective, the "lazy," and the "vicious." These include the panhandlers who would rather beg than work, the alcoholics and drug addicts who are caught in a vicious habit, and the petty criminals who hope to get something for nothing. Increasingly, these people have come to be regarded as influenced by social conditions and not altogether responsible for their condition. But there remains a strong thread of feeling that to some extent these people are responsible for their own condition and are, therefore, morally reprehensible.

The "worthy poor" are regarded as suitable objects of charity and compassion. Some would say that society has a duty to assure their support, and increasingly Social Security and the adult categories of public assistance have reflected this. The "unworthy poor" are regarded with scorn or exaggerated pity. Although our humanitarian principles do not allow their deliberate slaughter, many people believe they deserve only the barest subsistence given in the meanest, most demeaning fashion. Programs of general relief often reflect this view, as do conditions in many jails and prisons. Increasingly, Americans are coming to believe that these "unfortunates" should be rehabilitated, i.e., efforts should be made to change their behavior so that it will be at least minimally acceptable to the rest of society.

Americans distinguish between the lazy and the inefficient and the vicious. The former are doomed to fail, but the latter may succeed through fraud or deceit. They may fail to live up to contracts, embezzle funds, etc., and be quite successful economically. Americans generally believe that such people should be punished when they don't play fair. However, there is a double standard. The man who cheats on his income tax statement or falsely declares his availability for work to qualify for unemployment insurance benefits is not regarded as reprehensibly as the poor person who lies to qualify for public assistance. Perhaps this is due to his doubly invidious position: he is regarded both as a failure and a cheat. Americans call for justice, retributive justice, punishment that fits the crime, but tend to be more lenient with middle-class criminals.

Individual Motivation. What do Americans believe moves people? The traditional view is that the individual seeks pleasure and avoids pain. This view of human motivation, together with the value placed on self-reliance and hard work, leads to social welfare programs that make the receipt of subsistence, shelter, etc., somewhat hard and disagreeable as well as meager, especially for those who are regarded as potentially employable. In general, efforts are made to build work incentives into social welfare programs. A growing recognition that opportunities are not always available to be self-supporting has led to programs of rehabilitation, work training, and job creation.

Americans have been a hopeful people with faith in the future. This is reflected in the view that hard work and self-discipline will be rewarded by success. It is also reflected in social welfare programs that refuse to accept character defects and disagreeable patterns of behavior as inevitable. We have spent increasing sums on the treatment of the mentally ill and the rehabilitation of the delinquent.

The Economy

The view of man sketched above is essentially that of economic man. To make self-reliance, hard work, and striving for success pay off, certain conditions of the economy are valued. The economy must be free, not only from state interference that deprives the individual of the fruits of his labor but of monopoly control by large corporations. Each man must have a fair and equal chance to compete successfully. With recognition of the difficulties in achieving success, individuals have formed corporations, trade associations, monopolies, labor organizations, etc., all intended to increase their power and control over the difficult situations they face. As such groups have increased their power, the government has increasingly been called upon to mediate disputes and assure each interest as fair an opportunity to compete as possible. Examples are antitrust, labor relations and minimum wage laws. The government, originally regarded as a threat to freedom, has been called upon to assure a measure of freedom and fair competition.

The economy must grow, for growth provides the opportunity for individual success. A stagnant or declining economy deprives individuals of opportunity. Recognition that growth may be thwarted by economic conditions (e.g., depressions, mineral depletion, etc.) has led to government job creation, (e.g., WPA, Emergency Employment Act) together with efforts to stimulate government spending and the supply of credit. Recently serious questions have been raised about perpetual growth of the economy, and alternatives have been sought.

The individual must deny himself the gratification of consuming all he produces, saving so that the economy may grow through the investment of his accumulated capital and so that the individual may protect himself against unexpected illness, unemployment, etc. Recognition that this is not always possible has led to social insurance programs.

The economy must be stable in the sense that wild fluctuations in the rate of unemployment and monetary inflation are to be avoided. In order for the individual to know that hard work will pay off in some measure of success, he must know that he has a reasonable expectation of regular work and that the value of his wages will not shrink with inflation. In order for him to be willing to save and invest his accumulated capital, he must know that it will not be eroded by deflation in the value of the dollar.

Such fluctuations were originally thought to be inevitable concomitants of a free economy, but with advances in economic theory and ability of government to control the economy through adjusting the rate of taxes and government expenditures, and the supply of money, extreme fluctuations are no longer regarded as inevitable. Unfortunately, as steps are taken to increase employment, inflation tends to increase, eroding the value of savings and fixed dollar incomes. Those who are retired and living on fixed incomes suffer greatly from inflation.

Equality

The individual is regarded as equal to others, not in personal attributes or possessions but in rights and opportunities. The value placed on equality is reflected in the stress on fair play, discussed above.

Many forms of discrimination, based on ascribed characteristics rather than personal achievement, i.e., racial, ethnic, religious, sexual, age, etc., are regarded as illegitimate. Although honored very imperfectly, demands for equal access to public accommodations, employment, housing, education, the vote, etc., have been heard in the last three decades. This is reflected in legislative action and court decisions at many levels of government. Discrimination based on characteristics believed to be under the control of the individual is regarded as justified. Where the line is to be drawn, between characteristics under the individual's control and those beyond control, is hotly debated. For example, should a landlord be permitted to discriminate against persons whose lifestyle he finds objectionable? Social welfare programs likewise have been under pressure to eliminate illegitimate discrimination from their policies and practices.

Americans generally prefer government benefits that are universal, i.e., available to all more or less equally as a matter of right rather than at the discretion of bureaucrats. As an example, Social Security is preferred to public assistance in the recipient's eyes. In part this is due to the invidious labeling of the recipient of public assistance. He usually feels he has not earned, and is therefore not entitled to, public assistance. The fact that he needs it is a sign of failure. But it is also due in part to the fact that he feels no assurance of equal treatment, i.e., impartial, impersonal determination of eligibility, and the amount of benefits. At the same time, the individual as a taxpayer is concerned that his taxes not go to support those who he feels either ought to support themselves or do not need support. These kinds of moral judgments can only be made by a functionary operating under some measure of discretion. Furthermore, the taxpayer generally wants to keep his taxes low, a condition best achieved by selective, means-tested programs involving the exercise of judgment and discretion. Thus, Americans are mixed in their evaluation of universal benefits, depending upon whether they are recipients or taxpayers.

Americans endorse equal treatment for equal achievements, contributions, or personal merit. Social Security is for the worthy; public assistance for the questionable or unworthy. Higher Social Security benefits are awarded to those who have contributed more to the system. Veterans, who presumably have sacrificed much for their country, are singled out for special benefits. Disabled veterans get more on easier terms than those who completed their service unscathed. All of these discriminations which Americans, by and large, endorse are justified on the basis of behavior over which the individual is believe to have some control, or which is to his credit or discredit.

Liberty and Freedom

Not only do we value equality of opportunity and treatment for those of equal merit. We also value freedom to exercise choice among alternative opportunities. This applies not only in the economic sector but in a wide range of choices—religious beliefs, marriage partners, political opinions, etc. If an individual has no choices, if his behav-

ior is externally predetermined, he cannot be held responsible for his behavior. But Americans insist upon holding each other responsible for what they do, and therefore freedom of choice is an essential value.

Freedom may be regarded as the personal dimension of choice. The ability to choose is limited by personal characteristics, habits, frame of mind. The authoritarian personality is likely to avoid choice and look toward others for direction. Personal habits such as addiction to drugs may severely limit choice. Knowledge also affects choice. One of the functions of some welfare programs is to help remove personal restraints to choice through psychotherapy, counseling, education, etc. One danger is that instead of freeing the individual to choose, help will be used to control behavior.

Liberty may be regarded as the social dimension of choice. Personal characteristics arise, in part, from institutional factors. The desire to succeed constrains choice, albeit in what is generally regarded as acceptable ways. Originally as a nation we were concerned about the constraints upon freedom imposed by the English crown, later by our own government, and still later by giant corporations and labor unions. One of the justifications for social welfare programs, as well as many other governmental activities, is the protection of the individual's choices and the enhancement of his opportunities for, and abilities to, make choices. For instance, the creation of public service employment or government contracts with private industry increases opportunities and choices open to the individual. Rehabilitation of the disabled and work training enhances the ability of the disabled to make choices, to the extent that market conditions permit.

Should social welfare programs be administered to enhance choice or constrain behavior? Few would argue that the adjudicated delinquent should be treated by the state so as to maximize his choice between acceptable behavior and repeated offenses. It might be argued, however, that he be allowed some choice in the form of rehabilitative services he receives and the range of acceptable behavior permitted him. Is it right that public assistance only be given to mothers of young children if they agree to work, or train for work, while others care for their children? This was seriously proposed by the Nixon administration in its Family Assistance Plan.

Democracy

The individual should be free to choose. But we have noted that American individualism involves collective action, i.e., organization, and working with others to achieve the individual's purposes. The question arises, How should decisions be made when the individual's choice is constrained by others with whom he is associated? The answer is democratically—"the idea of a social group organized and directed by all of its members for the benefit of all of its members."[31]

Democracy rests on the belief in the common man as a relatively wise, skillful person of good judgment, involved in and taking responsibility for common decisions. Widespread apathy, alienation, and susceptibility to demagoguery, together with Michel's observation that organizations—no matter how democratic they may be initially—

end up under the control of a few leaders, raises questions about democracy as a way of reaching collective decisions. This places great importance upon education, by now a traditional social welfare function. It also highlights the importance of programs that reduce alienation and increase the sense of community and regard for others. To this end social welfare makes a contribution through such programs as Model Cities and such policies as citizen participation.

Consensus is the idealized basis for decisions. But size and heterogeneity of the polity of many organizations and most governments make this impossible. Majority rule is, thus, widely accepted. The effectiveness of this rule rests on the assumption that the minority will acquiesce in the decisions of the majority which, in turn, depends upon a belief in the process and rules by which decisions are made. The minority will acquiesce only if they believe the process to be fair and that they have a genuine opportunity to persuade others to accept their point of view so that they may become the majority.

Willingness of the minority to acquiesce is also based partly on the restraint exercised by the majority. Some matters must not be legislated; the minority must be free to make choices. In the voluntary association in which the individual has either little at stake or an alternative means to achieve his goal, he may simply leave the organization and join another. The same does not apply to government or to organizations such as labor unions to whom the individual is bound by long-range commitments. A legal commitment to prescribed constraints by the majority is the essential meaning of our Bill of Rights.

---

[31]Perry, op. cit., p. 127.

This problem arises for social welfare personnel working in a variety of settings. For example, though concerned with the protection of children against abusive or neglectful parents, we find the courts and legislative bodies extremely reluctant to interfere with the rights of parents to handle their children as they see fit except in the most extreme circumstances. What is the correct balance between the society's right to protect its children and the minority's right to raise their children as they please?

"Democratic" and "republican" are concepts representing two ends of a continuum between direct control by the people and indirect control through representatives elected by the people. Out of fear, concern over rule by an alienated and unthinking mob, or the prospect of demagogues seizing power through irrational appeals, some people prefer a republican form of government. They presume that elected representatives will be drawn from those with education and good judgment and therefore better be able to withstand unreasoned pressures from constituents. Others are concerned over the possibility that an elite will maintain control, delivering the people into the hands of big business or other well organized interests. They prefer more direct forms of democracy such as meetings of the whole membership in small organizations or the liberal use of the initiative, referendum, and the recall of elected officials in government. There continues to be a debate over the proper role of the representative, inevitable in all but the smallest organizations. Is he to be guided by his own analysis of the situation and vote his conscience? Or should he merely reflect the opinions of his constituents? Did the people elect him because they thought he would exercise good judgment in complex situations or because they thought he would be guided by them and vote the expressed interests of the public?

Which level of government makes the best decisions? Are the wisest decisions made by the national government which is able to cancel out conflicting parochial interests and get the clearest picture of the public interest? Or is local government, which is closest to the people, more flexible and responsive to the popular will and therefore to be preferred?

As noted in the definition of democracy, there are two components: control and benefits. The concept of political democracy points up the control aspects of democracy. Problems of democratic control are found in the operation of social welfare programs. The clearest examples are the War on Poverty's Community Action Programs which call for "maximum feasible participation" of the poor, and the Model Cities Program which contains similar requirements. However, the question is also salient in public assistance and Social Security, and in private as well as public welfare programs. To the question: Who should control the program, the answer is given "the people." But precisely which people? How broad or narrow should the constituency be? How should that control be exercised, and what is the role of political leadership? These are matters of controversy.

Social democracy raises the question: Who should benefit from government and its social welfare programs? Because paying taxes is the reverse of receiving benefits, there is also the question of who should pay how much in taxes. Again, the answer to both questions is "the people." But the hard questions are how much should various people receive in benefits and pay in taxes, and how to distinguish between people and circumstances in making these decisions. The concepts of justice and equity are used in talking about these matters.

The productive element of society should get the most. In general, we believe that those who work hard and produce the most of the things people want should receive the greatest rewards. Government subsidy programs, justified as providing incentives for production, generally are highest for the wealthiest or most productive. Tax deductions or credits, other forms of subsidy, are generally allowed on the same basis.

The productive element should pay the most in taxes. At the federal level and overall, it is clear that those who have the highest incomes pay taxes at the highest rates. This is based on the view that those who benefit the most from society should pay the most for government which helps to assure them of conditions that permit them to continue to work productively and profitably. However, the extent to which this actually takes places is in doubt. The current debate over tax reform reflects in part a desire for greater equity in taxation.

Those who work hard and save should get more than those who don't work so hard and don't save. Those who, through no fault of their own, are unable to work, should get something. Just what that something should be is the subject of considerable debate. Those who are unable to work but who are held, in some way, responsible for that fact should get even less. Again, how

much they should receive is debatable. And what kind of circumstances the individual should be held responsible for is unsettled. In general, these questions fall under the heading of distributive justice, i.e., differential rewards for various amounts and types of meritorious behavior.

The Family

The family is regarded as the basic social unit. The rights of the family, particularly its adult members, to do as they please within the home, free from the interference of the state, is well recognized in the law. As an example, the state may not search and seize property without a warrant issued by a court; the court is not supposed to issue a warrant without probable cause that a crime has been committed. Apart from the law, the aphorism that a "man's home is his castle" reflects the view that the male head of the household, and increasingly his spouse, are free to do as they please in their home, within wide limits.

Parental rights to children, while not absolute, are strong. The child is the ward of his parents, not of the state except in extreme cases—abandonment, abuse, delinquency, etc. Court proceedings are required to deprive parents of their rights to their children, and legal presumptions favor the parents. Thus, parents are free to educate and discipline their children within broad limits.

The nuclear family is the norm. The extended family, which includes uncles, aunts, cousins, grandparents, etc., is on the decline as a living unit. Houses are small. Families are mobile. Thus, maiden aunts and elderly parents are often lonely and isolated. Some social welfare programs are intended to step in to fill this void.

The nuclear family, while losing functions to other institutions—economic activity to business and industry, education to the schools, care of the sick to hospitals and nursing homes, etc.—is still valued for its role in the early socialization of the child and as a context for intimate interpersonal relations.

The nuclear family is under considerable pressure. Industrialization creates pressures for social and geographic mobility, employment of women outside the home, and consequent role strain for both husbands and wives. It also creates peer group pressures that separate children from their parents, advertising which produces over-spending, and family economic problems. Consequently, Americans experience high rates of divorce and separation. When families experience difficulties, social welfare institutions are called upon to help in counseling around marital, parent-child, and economic problems, and to provide such services as substitute care and counseling for the children. The objective is generally to maintain and improve family functioning and, when that is not possible, to provide substitute care for the children. The preferred form of substitute care is another family. Congregate care in institutional settings is generally regarded unfavorably, especially for young children.

Alternative lifestyles, such as "communes," "swinging" single life, etc., have emerged in recent years. Families, in which both parents work outside the home, and single parent families are increasingly frequent. Nevertheless, the nuclear family appears to be a persistent and valued social institution, not likely to go out of existence in the near future as some have predicted.

Humanitarianism and Human Rights

Humanitarianism is the call to treat the stranger as one would treat a member of the family, particularly when he has been unsuccessful, his family is falling apart, he is plagued with disease or handicapped by disability, or he has behaved badly.

Humanitarian values serve to blunt the consequences of the doctrine of individualism which has been described above. We are asked to take pity on, and lend a helping hand to, those in need. It is not merely enlightened self-interest; we are asked for some measure of altruism, for genuine sympathy, concern, and help for those less fortunate.

The source of humanitarianism in America is its Judeo-Christian tradition. Although religion in the theological sense has lost its grip on many Americans, its moral imperatives still hold sway in the American conscience. It is not difficult to cite biblical sources for our humanitarianism. As the eminent American philosopher, Ralph Barton Perry, has said:

The general Hebraic-Christian-Biblical tradition embraces ideas so familiar that, like the air, they are inhaled without effort or attention. The most fundamental of these is the idea of one personal God, the Creator of nature and the ruler of mankind, flanking human life on all sides... This God is invested with the parental attributes: like a father he both loves and chastens his human children; who, having erred, are restored to favor and perfected in their innate attributes by a way of salvation exemplified, if not mediated, by Jesus of Nazareth...

The personal and social implications of this broad creed are apparent. It raises mankind to the dignity of possessing a family likeness to the maker of the universe. It makes of each human being an object of compassion and solicitude, such as the parent feels for the child regardless of his talents or merit; so that it is love rather than strict justice that speaks the last word. It thus enlivens the pacifist and humanitarian sentiments, and supports social legislation designed to mitigate cruelty and misery. . ..[32]

The concept of human rights joins American humanitarianism with political judgments and decisions. Human rights are not merely desires. "We speak of a right to subsistence, not of a right to luxury. The notion of rights, in other words, springs from the idea that society is a cooperative enterprise, in which all participate, and from which all shall receive certain minimum benefits."[33]

Human rights are not merely legal enactments. They transcend the law. They are the principles which guide the enactment of law, and to which appeals are made for changes in the law, including appeals for social welfare legislation.

Humanitarianism, expressed through the idea of human rights—specific, concrete rights—"is the fundamental force in American reform, in the remorse which is felt for racial or class discrimination, and in the steadily mounting concern for the health, housing and living conditions, and the economic opportunity, of those who are getting the worst of the bargain. Americans are morally 'shocked,' not because they have failed merely, but because they feel that they have been unfaithful to their own idea of what ought to be."[34] Clearly, social welfare institutions have an important role in carrying out if not shaping these reforms.

The assertion of basic human rights often results in conflict and competition between groups in a large and complex society characteristic of America. A basic right of Americans is to come together, concert interests, and give expression to their several competing and conflicting interests. Social welfare institutions have taken responsibility, within their own institutional sector, for encouraging the expression of such differences and, where necessary, helping others give expression to those differences.

The resolution of conflicting and competing assertions of interests and rights is generally desired by Americans. Americans prefer to avoid violence which represents a failure in the democratic process. Social welfare institutions also have a role to play in the resolution of conflicts. Sometimes they have done so through amelioration and diversionary methods which have left basic grievances untouched. We hope that those who provide leadership for American social welfare institutions will be dissatisfied with such approaches except as temporary expedients, and will continue to provide channels for the advocacy of the rights and interests of those with legitimate complaints and will use their influence with those in power to rectify those complaints.

---

[32]Ibid., pp. 94-95.
[33]Ibid., pp. 153-154.

[34]Ibid., pp. 155-156.

11.

Fred M. Cox

COMMUNITIES: ALTERNATIVE CONCEPTIONS OF COMMUNITY: IMPLICATIONS FOR COMMUNITY ORGANIZATION PRACTICE

INTRODUCTION

Students of communities, urban and rural, large and small, have approached their subject from very different perspectives. Following Warren[1] this paper explores these various conceptions, extending Warren's analysis by drawing out their several implications for community organization practice. For the practitioner, as Kramer and Specht have noted,[2] community is context, the arena within which the practitioner operates; target, the source of problems or harmful conditions the practitioner tries to change; and vehicle, or the means by which change is effected. In this discussion I explore community from all of these perspectives with emphasis on community as context and vehicle.

Warren defines community as "that combination of social units and systems which perform the major social functions having locality relevance." He goes on to explain that "this is another way of saying that by 'community' we mean the organization of social activities to afford people daily local access to those broad areas of activity which are necessary in day-to-day living."[3] He identifies five such functions: (1) production-distribution-consumption, (2) socialization—"a process by which society ... transmits prevailing knowledge, social values, and behavior patterns to its individual members";[4] (3) social control—"The process through which a group influences the behavior of its members toward conformity with its norms";[5] (4) social participation; and (5) mutual support—which may take "the form of care in time of sickness, the exchange of labor, or the helping out of a local family in economic distress."[6]

In the following discussion I have divided Warren's categories of approaches to the study of community into three major subgroups: context, vehicle, and problem. The division is based on judgments about the central utility of each approach for the community practitioner.

Source: This article was written for this volume. The author wishes to express appreciation to John L. Erlich for a careful reading and suggestions for improving this article.

[1]Roland L. Warren, *The Community in America,* 2d ed. (Chicago: Rand McNally Co., 1972), pp. 21-51.
[2]Ralph M. Kramer and Harry Specht, eds., *Readings in Community Organization Practice,* 2d ed. (Englewood Cliffs, NJ: Prentice-Hall, 1975), p. 17.
[3]Warren, op. cit., p. 9.
[4]Ibid., p. 10.
[5]Ibid., p. 11.
[6]Ibid., p. 11.

COMMUNITY AS CONTEXT

The Community as the Locus of Daily Activity (Site or Place)

Max Weber defined the city as a settlement with a market.[7] The early rural sociologists were interested in identifying the boundaries within which people traded. By extension, the community may be conceived of as a place where a group of people live and conduct various activities of daily living: earn a living, buy the goods and services they are unable to produce for themselves, school their children, transact their civic and governmental affairs, etc. The early human ecologists of the Chicago school took an interest in identifying urban zones (central business district, transitional zones, workingmen's homes, etc.) and smaller natural areas (apartment house districts, slums, transient areas, etc.) and in examining the processes that established and changed such zones and areas (cooperation, competition, and conflict; concentration and dispersion of people; centralization and decentralization of functions; segregation, invasion, and succession of activities and people; etc.).

The community practitioner will find a number of uses for this concept of community. As one asks, Who shall be organized? the question of community boundaries arises. Is the significant area one that shares a common public school or set of schools? Is it the people who use a particular neighborhood shopping area or the downtown shop-

ping area? Or is it the political boundaries of the city or county that are significant for a particular set of interests around which organization is to occur?[8] In modern urban communities these questions become very complex indeed. How does one measure frequency and intensity of interaction that may serve to establish a community boundary? Assuming that a detailed survey is not feasible, what surrogate measures may be applied? May it be assumed that major roads, highways or freeways bound a neighborhood or community? Or, given the ubiquity of the automobile or public transportation, do such barriers really limit interaction or identification with place? Perhaps there is very little identification with the locality. Has it been replaced by union, occupation, profession, ethnic group, political party, or some other intense interest? Or is there, in fact, very little in the way of any identification with anything that might be called "community?" In recent years the idea of community has been related to a presumably basic human need for "affiliation" or "belonging."

Put somewhat differently, this perspective raises the following questions of importance to the practitioner: (1) Who interacts and shares a common identity with whom? These people might well provide a base for collective action. (2) Who has little interaction with whom? These people may be relatively indifferent to one another. While the parties seem apathetic to one another, they may interact intensely in other

---

[7]Roland L. Warren, ed., *Perspectives on the American Community: A Book of Readings,* 2d ed. (Chicago: Rand McNally College Publishing Co., 1973), p. 2.

[8]It is not uncommon to find that the place itself is irrelevant to organizing unless it also identifies people who share a particular social class or racial, ethnic or religious identity, i.e., institutions and values, discussed below.

arenas (e.g., occupational) or may interact only in secondary relations, characteristic of a mass society. (3) Who competes with whom for the business or resources of third parties? Competitors have an interest in gaining an advantage over one another and may organize internally for this purpose (as when a group of social agencies forms an alliance to increase their chances for obtaining a grant); at the same time, they will come together if there is a threat to their resources (as when trade associations including professions and groups of social agencies organize to resist unfavorable legislation). (4) Who is in conflict with whom over fundamental values (as with racial segregationists and integrationists or with radical and liberal politicians)? Opponents are interested in overwhelming or subduing one another or in protecting vested interests or obtaining a "just" distribution of scarce resources, and each side will organize to these ends.

The dynamic processes identified by the Chicago school of human ecologists are useful in understanding such phenomena as racial "block busting," attempts at residential racial integration, the reactions to returning large numbers of mentally ill persons to the communities from the relative isolation of mental hospitals (and similar programs for juvenile delinquents, adult offenders and the mentally retarded), drives to "get rid" of red-light or skid row districts, and urban renewal that involves major displacement of low-income people. Although it is not possible to give detailed analyses of these phenomena here, the perspectives of the Chicago school lead to asking questions of the following sort: (1) What social, economic and political factors lead to shifts in population groups? (2) What happens to those dis-

placed? To those moving into a new area? (3) Why are efforts to mix people of differing social identification (class, life-style, ethnic group) so often ineffective? Under what conditions can integration (or dispersion) succeed? (4) Which community functions (activities, businesses, etc.) are spatially compatible with one another? Which are incompatible, and why?

The Community as Described by the Demographic Characteristics of Its People

The census provides data on the composition of the population broken down by age, sex, income, occupation, education, race and ethnic identity, etc., some of the data being available for areas as small as a city block, others aggregated by census tracts, cities, counties, and states. Other surveys of the population provide information about birth, death, marriage, divorce, illness, disability, delinquency, and crime. These data are very useful to the community organization practitioner in a number of different ways.

First, by looking for clusters of characteristics and their distribution geographically, it is possible, following Shevky and Bell,[9] to identify the various social areas of cities and use these analyses to plan patterns of services appropriate to the several types of social areas identified. For example, it is clear that areas that include large numbers of young families with school-age children will require a different pattern of services than areas that house mostly older people whose children are grown and out of the family. Depending upon the cluster of characteristics used, social ar-

[9]Eshref Shevky and Wendell Bell, *Social Area Analysis* (Stanford, CA: Stanford University Press, 1955).

eas may be defined for a variety of social planning purposes. Data on health conditions may be used to plan the location of public health programs of various types, mental health programs, etc. Data on the frequency of delinquency and crime will suggest areas in which efforts should be concentrated.

Second, many sets of demographic data are available in time series, showing trends and developments. Using various forms of projection, plans may be created for developing services to meet anticipated needs in growing or declining areas, areas of increasing health problems, or whatever.

The Community as Shared Institutions (Values, Norms, Traditions)

Differences in the ecological relations between communities and neighborhoods, urban zones and natural areas, and differences in the population characteristics found in urban social areas do not explain all of the differences between communities of significance to the community practitioner. Studies cited by Warren[10] demonstrate that communities that are very like one another in these respects may, nevertheless, respond to problems in very different ways that can only be understood as differences in values and the importance attached to and the quality of their institutions. For example, the importance of the public schools and, therefore, the willingness of people to increase school taxes or endorse school bonds will depend, in part, on the proportion of people who send their children to parochial and other private schools and, by implication, value various forms of private education more than the public schools. Reactions to pro-

posals for the fluoridation of the water supply or to campaigns to provide physical examinations for all school age children will depend in part on the value attached to health, trust in public officials and the medical profession vs. dependence on home remedies and folk medicine.

The study of a community's values and institutions will be particularly important when the social identity of the practitioner and the community served are quite different. Ignorance of indigenous values may even exist among those with a surface resemblance to those served. For example, Spanish-speaking South Americans may have little appreciation for the folkways and values of Mexican-American farm workers or Puerto Ricans living in New York City. Likewise, black social workers raised in middle-class families may have been shielded by their parents from learning the street language and mores of the black inner city ghetto.

Plans and proposals for community action or social services may be formulated with little understanding of the values of the population served and the failure of such efforts may be misinterpreted. For example, Gans's study of the working-class Italian population of North Boston suggests that the residents would have been a very poor vehicle for united community action to protect their interests against encroaching urban renewal, in part because of their very strong extended family and friendship ties and their distrust of outsiders, even including other Italian-Americans faced with the same threat of destruction to their community.[11]

Beginning organizing efforts or planning services that are grounded in the

---

[10]*The Community in America,* pp. 32-36.

[11]Herbert J. Gans, *The Urban Villagers* (New York: Free Press, 1962).

basic values and institutions of the people to be served provides a point of entry that may, as trust develops between practitioner and community, lead to possibilities for action not as central to or even at some variance with local traditions. "Beginning where the client is" applies to community work as well as casework. Alinsky insisted his organizers do so, i.e., (1) identify concerns and interests widely held in the community as a basis for mobilization and organizing people and (2) build an organization consisting of an alliance of preexisting indigenous organizations, which means appealing to their interests and values.[12] His work illustrates very well how a "people's organization" can move from issue to issue and transcend parochial interests as the members begin working together.

The Community as a Social System

For the community practitioner, the analysis of communities as social systems serves two primary functions. First, it permits a comparison of communities with other social systems to arrive at what is unique about community in contrast to other social systems. For example, like other social systems, as Moe points out,[13] particularly large ones, the community is a system of systems, with many different organizations, institutions, and groups as components. Unlike a formal organization, e.g., a city welfare department, the community is not centralized. That is, there is no planned hierarchy of authority and command in a community as there is,

say, in city government, but rather a collection of parts that are often relatively autonomous in relation to other subsystems in the community. Finally, Moe points out that the community is implicit in nature rather than explicit in comparison with the formal organization. Put somewhat differently, the community is emergent rather than contrived.

The second value of the social system perspective on the community for the community practitioner is that it permits systematic analysis, using concepts that have been developed and applied to other social systems. It helps the practitioner avoid overlooking some aspect of the community that might otherwise be forgotten. There are a large number of social systems concepts that may be used for this purpose. Three examples: (1) If a community is to be understood as, in some sense, a separate entity, it must have some boundaries, geographic or conceptual. Social systems analysis forces one to identify those boundaries and ask how they are maintained and changed. (2) All systems have vertical and horizontal interactions, that is, relations among various subunits (i.e., Red Cross and Travelers Aid) and between subunits within and units outside the system (i.e., local and national Red Cross and Travelers Aid). One may examine the nature and functions of such interactions (e.g., between families and the public schools or social services, and between local social services and their counterparts in other communities). Warren has concluded that a pervasive feature of American communities is the weakening of horizontal patterns and the strengthening of vertical ones,[14]

[12]Saul D. Alinsky, *Reveille for Radicals* (Chicago: University of Chicago Press, 1946).

[13]Edward O. Moe, "Consulting with a Community System: A Case Study," *Journal of Social Issues,* 15:2:29 (1959).

[14]*The Community in America,* pp. 161 ff.

with the result that the autonomy of American communities is diminishing. (3) Finally, there are various schemes for analyzing the functions of social systems. Parsons' scheme, described in the Introduction to Arenas,[15] is illustrative. This scheme leads one to ask the following questions: With respect to each of the community's subsystems, what functions do they serve for the community? How do they attain their goals and adapt to the environment? How are the various subsystems integrated or coordinated? How do they manage the tensions that arise within and between them?

THE COMMUNITY AS VEHICLE

The Community as Exchanges among People and Institutions (Interaction)

The sociologists who have studied communities from this perspective have concentrated on the action that takes place within them. Some of them, notably Harold F. Kaufman,[16] have carefully distinguished between community action and action involving other social institutions and organizations that takes place within the community. For example, much of the action that occurs in families takes place within localities, but that is not to be mistaken for community action. Rather it is action at the subcommunity level. Certain fund-raising efforts of national health organizations likewise take place within communities but are directed and controlled at the state or

national level and may best be thought of as extra-community action.

The special contribution of this perspective to community organization practice is the attention given to the natural process of interaction, the stages through which community action or community development efforts move, and the implications for practice. If various types of community action or development can be identified, and if stages of interaction can be described through which a given type of community action passes, we are on our way to understanding the relation between action and result and therefore to prescribing what the practitioner must do to achieve desired results through planned intervention. Beyond types of action and stages, it is important to understand how one action leads to another, the reactions that occur, and therefore the possibilities for failure and reversal as well as success.

At this point, we are very far from a prescriptive science of community action, development, and planning. But it is possible to use existing studies suggestively to guide practice. There are, for example, a substantial number of such studies of urban renewal and community action to block the destruction of local communities through the urban renewal process. If one were embarking upon social planning in an urban renewal or related context, one would do well to review a number of these studies.

It should also be pointed out that this is one way in which the community practitioner can make a contribution to the development of practice knowledge. Keeping detailed records of community actions engaged in, particularly if they are related to studies that have similar categories of information col-

---

[15]See the Introduction to Arenas (Part 2, this volume).

[16]Harold J. Kaufmann, "Toward an Interactional Conception of Community," *Social Forces*, 38:1:9-17 (October 1959).

lected and reported, can contribute to inductively developed theories of various types of planned community action.[17]

The Community as a Distribution of Power

This perspective has been so central to the interests of community practitioners that it has been given a special place in the literature of community organization practice. Arising out of the frustration with traditional community organization (we would call it community or locality development) practice principles, these studies, perhaps most notably those by Floyd Hunter and his colleagues, gave the community practitioner new insights and direction. Instead of counseling participation by those affected by community decisions and urging plans based on the felt needs of grassroots people, this literature directed the practitioner to locate those who exercised major influence in the community and bring pressure to bear upon them if one desires to achieve professional objectives. Participation is regarded as secondary to gaining the support of local power figures. Because this point of view is so important to community organization practitioners—because it treats community as vehicle and target, and not merely context—we include an extended excerpt from Warren[18] that summarizes the literature very briefly.

The Community as a Distribution of Power

Few developments in the field of community studies in recent years have made such a vast impact on community theory, research, and practice as the growth of *community power-structure* analysis. This has been a means of coming to grips with the observable fact that certain individuals in the community exercise much more influence on what goes on than do others. Recent study has been concerned with ascertaining the extent to which this is true, just how much influence is wielded, by whom, how, on what issues, and with what results.

The concept of differential ability to influence social behavior is not itself a new one. Thrasymachus, in Plato's *Republic,* gives a vivid description of how members of a ruling group are able to utilize the state and political institutions for their purposes, and a "ruling class" theory has developed through such classic works as those of Machiavelli, Marx, Mosca, and Pareto. The concept of social power is related to this special degree in which some people influence the actions of others. A classical definition of such power was given by Max Weber, who wrote, "In general, we understand by 'power' the chance of a man or of a number of men to realize their own will in a communal action even against the resistance of others who are participating in the action."[19]

In the second Middletown study the Lynds devoted an entire chapter to "The X Family: A Pattern of Business-Class Control" and pointed out the inordinate influence that members of this leading industrial family exerted in various aspects of the institutional life of that city and the channels through which this influence was exercised.[20] Likewise, in the Yankee City study Warner and his associates described the manner in which concentrated power was

---

[17]See also: Ronald Lippitt et al., *The Dynamics of Planned Change* (New York: Harcourt, Brace and World, 1958); and Warren's *Community in America,* pp. 303-39.

[18]Roland L. Warren: *The Community in America,* Third Edition © 1978 by Houghton Mifflin Company. Adapted by permission of the publisher and the author.

[19]From *Max Weber: Essays in Sociology,* trans. and ed. H. H. Gerth and C. Wright Mills (New York: Oxford University Press, 1946), p. 180.

[20]Robert S. Lynd and Helen Merrell Lynd, *Middletown in Transition: A Study in Cultural Conflicts* (New York: Harcourt Brace, 1937), chap. 3.

wielded by the upper classes in that community, and Hollingshead, in his social class analysis of the youth of a small midwestern city, showed specifically how the school system was controlled by a small number of upper-class people and made to function for their own interests.[21]

The more recent interest and activity in the field of the exercise of social power at the community level was largely set in motion by a study of community power structure by Floyd Hunter. Defining power as "a word that will be used to describe the acts of men going about the business of moving other men to act in relation to themselves or in relation to organic or inorganic things," he studied community power in a southeastern city that is a regional center of finance, commerce, and industry.[22] The book focused its attention on the 40 persons who were found to be the top power leaders in the community.

Through carefully planned interviews with these leading power figures and through other community-study methods, Hunter was able to gain a picture of the influence that these individuals wielded, the channels through which they wielded it, the relation of these power figures to each other, and the patterns through which community action in Regional City took place.

Hunter found that these power leaders generally not only knew each other personally but were in frequent interaction with each other, much more so than chance would allow. Their frequent interaction often involved joint efforts in community affairs. This group of leaders was at the top of the power pyramid, and its influence was found to be exerted through organizational positions and through formal and informal connections with a whole group of subordinate leaders who usually did not participate in making major community policy decisions but were active in implementing such decisions. Thus, though major power was exercised by this group of leaders, they were not all necessarily involved in any single action at the same time.

Hunter emphasized two important characteristics of the power system in Regional City. The first was that economic interests tended to dominate it. The second was that the formal leaders of community organizations and institutions were not necessarily the top people. "The organizations are not a sure route to sustained community prominence. Membership in the top brackets of one of the stable economic bureaucracies is the surest road to power, and this road is entered by only a few. Organizational leaders are prone to get the publicity; the upper echelon economic leaders, the power.[23]"

Hunter found that the understructure of leadership through which top power leaders operate is not a rigid bureaucracy but a flexible system, including people described by top power leaders as first-, second-, third-, and fourth-rate. The first-raters are industrial, commercial, and financial owners and top executives of large enterprises. Second-raters include bank vice-presidents, people in public relation, owners of small business, top-ranking public officials, and so on. Third-raters are civic organization personnel, petty public officials, selected organizational executives, and so on, while fourth-raters are ministers, teachers, social workers, small-business managers, and the like.[24]

On community decisions of major importance, actions are considered and developed by top leaders and their immediate followers, or "crowds," and then spread out to a wider group of top leaders and crowds for further support and basic decision-making. Only much later, at the carrying-out stage, are the usual civic organization leaders, the press, and interested citizens' groups brought into the picture.

One of the reasons Hunter's book received so much attention was that it challenged much current thinking in the field of community organization and development, which tended to follow such procedures as "encouraging participation in

[21]W. Lloyd Warner and Paul S. Lunt, *The Social Life of a Modern Community* (New Haven, CT: Yale University Press, 1941); August B. Hollingshead, *Elmtown's Youth: The Impact of Social Classes on Adolescents* (New York: John Wiley & Sons, 1949).

[22]Floyd Hunter, *Community Power Structure: A Study of Decision Makers* (Chapel Hill: University of North Carolina Press, 1953), pp. 2-3.

[23]Ibid., pp. 86-87.
[24]Ibid., p. 109.

policy-making by the people who will be affected by the policy," "letting plans arise
from the felt needs of community people,"
"basing programs on grass-roots decision,"
and so on. If basic community decisions are
not made primarily at city hall or at the
community welfare council but at the country club and even more exclusive clubs as
well as in informal conferences among a
small group of top leaders, then important
community actions must be supported and
approved by these top groups. Community
planning agencies and professional leaders
in such fields as public welfare and public
health recognize this situation.

One question that can be raised with regard to the concept of community power
structure as developed by Hunter is, If the
power structure is so important, how does it
happen that it so often loses in the contest to
determine a public issue? Does the power
configuration surrounding any particular
community issue invariably take the form
that Hunter describes, with top policy being
determined by members of essentially the
same small power group? Or is it not possible that on some community issues, decisive power is exercised by organizations and
minor officials as prime movers, rather than
merely as the henchmen of a small power
group?

Turning to the first, a number of studies
have been made bearing more or less directly on the question of one versus a number of
power structures.[25] With few exceptions,
these studies indicate that the picture is
much more complex than the one Hunter

described, and they indicate a multiplicity
of power structures with the power pyra-
mids being much less a tightly knit group of
leaders in close interaction than was found
in Regional City.

Regarding the more or less flexible aspects of power, as opposed to the concept of
a fixed structure, the question would seem
to be, To what extent is any particular community issue open to genuine contest, and
to what extent is it already determined by
the structure of existing power leadership
and the attitudes of these leaders with relation to it?

Investigators have also explored other aspects of power than just the making of
decisions and obtaining of consent. These
other important leadership activities might
include initiating formal community proposals, supporting or fighting proposals
through such visible means as fund raising,
endorsing, public speaking in behalf of an
issue, mobilizing extracommunity pressures, articulating, defining, and suppressing issues, and actually making decisions as
a community official.[26]

A final question appropriate to the present discussion is that of the deliberate
development and coming prominence of
new sources of power through formal organization of such interest groups as organized labor, Blacks, and other racial or ethnic
groups. There is considerable indication
that officials of these and other voluntary
organizations, whether representing special
interests or promoting broad planning or
health and welfare goals, are exerting increasing power by virtue of their official
positions and the strength of the organizations that they represent.[27]

[25]See Alexander Fanelli, "A Typology of Com-
munity Leadership Based on Influence and
Interaction within the Leader Subsystem," *Social
Forces,* 34:4 (May 1956); Roland J. Pellegrin and
Charles H. Coates, "Absentee-Owned Corpora-
tions and Community Power Structure," *Ameri-
can Journal of Sociology,* 61:5 (March 1956);
Robert O. Schulze and Leonard U. Blumberg,
"The Determination of Local Power Elites,"
American Journal of Sociology, 63:3 (November
1957); Robert O. Schulze, "The Role of Economic Dominants in Community Power Structure,"
American Sociological Review, 23:1 (February
1958); Nelson W. Polsby, "The Sociology of
Community Power: A Reassessment," *Social
Forces,* 37:3 (March 1959); and "Three Problems
in the Analysis of Community Power," *American
Sociological Review,* 24:6 (December 1959). The
literature is, of course, too voluminous to list ex-
haustively here. Several of the above contain
additional references to other studies.

[26]Polsby, "Sociology of Community Power,"
233.

[27]More recent explorations of the "power" concept have taken three important emphases. The
first is the continued pursuit of many of the questions raised by the earlier studies. Claire W.
Gilbert made a systematic attempt to summarize
the numerous findings in "Community Power
and Decision-Making: A Quantitative Examination of Previous Research," in Terry N. Clark,
ed., *Community Structure and Decison-Making:
Comparative Analyses* (San Francisco: Chandler
Publishing Co., 1968). Willis Hawley and
Frederick M. Wirt, eds., provide a valuable collection of important articles in this field in *The
Search for Community Power* (Englewood Cliffs,
NJ: Prentice-Hall, 1968, 1974), which also contains an extensive bibliography. There is also

Cloward and Piven[28] suggest another view of the community as a distribution of power. Organizers deal with the most central facts of social life: patterns of domination and of challenges to domination. In this sense, every organizing venture is an essay on power. To initiate an organizing project is to make a statement about why particular people at a particular time may be ready to challenge power, how they can, and why they should. This statement is rarely simple, but it is crucial. Alinsky said organizers must rub raw the sores of discontent, but that does not tell us which sores or whose sores or how to inflame them or why people are ready to be activated at a given moment. Every organizing effort confronts these questions, and success depends upon seeing the answers. Were those most active in the J. P. Stevens' strike longtime workers or new workers? Were they older workers whose working conditions had deteriorated, or who had begun to think of their traditional wage and working standards as intolerable in a period of

unprecedented prosperity? Or were the activists younger workers who had absorbed new and higher expectations?

Since the reciprocal play of power is the essence of organizing, every organizing venture is based on further assumptions about the way the social or economic roles that people play can be translated into a concrete strategy for the exercise of influence by given groups at a particular time. Efforts at exerting influence will provoke responses, and organizers must also anticipate the very specific stratagems through which countervailing power will be mobilized. Then too people must be ready to believe that their resources for influence have a reasonable chance to prevail in a given contest, each of us is a political analyst—not just those who propose defiant action, but those who must risk it. People imagine the contest, think about the interplay of power, and anticipate the consequences of their actions. The analysis of power proposed by organizers must fit the sense people have of the way the world works, or else they will not join in protest. Southern blacks could not have been moved to conduct nonviolent civil disobedience in the 1920s; they would have recognized the futility of it, that they would likely be lynched. But institutional relationships change, and with them the balance of power. Agricultural modernization, migration, urban concentration, these and other socioeconomic transformations released people from old structures of domination and created new possibilities for protest. People sense these changes, and when they do, the call to action makes sense in a way it would not otherwise. Good organizers did know a lot about these matters, or they would not be able to activate people.

---

recent emphasis on multicity studies of community power configurations, especially as they affect decision-making. Clark, *Community Structure*, has this emphasis. A more recent example is Michael Aiken and Robert R. Alford, "Comparative Urban Research and Community Decision-Making," *The Atlantis*, 1:2 (Winter 1970). See also Clark's *Community Power and Policy Outputs: A Review of Urban Research* (Beverly Hills: Sage Publications, 1973). A third vein of elaboration has been associated with social action for a transfer of power from existing structures to sectors of the population who exercise little power. A popular example is Stokely Carmichael and Charles V. Hamilton, *Black Power: The Politics of Liberation in America* (New York: Vintage Books, 1967). John Walton has reviewed the development of community power studies since Hunter with a critical eye. See his "Community Power and the Retreat form Politics: Full Circle After Twenty Years?," *Social Problems*, 23:3 (February 1976).

[28]From *Roots to Power* by Lee Staples. Copyright © 1984 Praeger Publishers. Reprinted by permission of Praeger Publishers.

THE COMMUNITY AS PROBLEM

As Kramer and Specht have noted, the community may be understood, from the practitioner's point of view, as the context within which practice takes place, affecting that practice in various ways, and as vehicle or the means through which action is taken. The discussions, above, of community as place, people, shared values and social system are useful largely for their insights on the community as context. In contrast, the discussion of the community as a process of interaction and a distribution of power provides insights into ways the practitioner may use the community or various parts of it to achieve practice objectives. However, it is most often the case that a solid grasp of the components of community as context contributes to a better utilization of the community as a process of interaction and a system of power.

In this section, we consider briefly this third perspective: the community as the problem that must be solved or ameliorated by the practitioner, the target of change efforts. Warren,[29] after setting aside problems of the larger society that affect the community, such as unemployment, delinquency, or family breakdown, but which are not problems of the community, identifies two types of problems: (1) loss of community autonomy over decisions in the community (e.g., when national or multinational corporations decide to locate a plant or close down, the local community has little to say), and (2) lack of identification with the community which takes the form of (a) citizen apathy regarding community affairs and (b) loss of useful roles in the community (e.g., the social consequences of aging) and of belief in the community's dominant values (e.g., manifested in delin-

[29] *The Community in America*, pp. 14-20.

TABLE 11.1
Selected Characteristics of Moral Communities and Mass Societies

Moral Communities	Mass Societies
Identification. Members of the moral community have a deep sense of belonging to a significant, meaningful group.	*Alienation.* Members of mass society have a deep sense of being "cut off" from meaningful group associations.
Moral Unity. Members of the moral community have a sense of pursuing common goals and feel a oneness with other community members.	*Moral Fragmentation.* Members of mass society pursue divergent goals and feel no sense of oneness with other members of the mass society.
Involvement. Members of the moral community are submerged in various groups and have a compelling need to participate in these groups.	*Disengagement.* Members of mass society have no meaningful group memberships and feel no compulsion to participate in the collective activities of various groups.
Wholeness. Members of the moral community regard each other as whole persons who are of intrinsic significance and worth.	*Segmentation.* Members of mass society regard each other as means to ends and assign no intrinsic worth or significance to the individual.

quent behavior and legitimate social protest).

Poplin[30] points out that the term community may be used in a moral or spiritual sense epitomized in such terms as the quest of yearning for a sense of community or sharing. The absence of this sense has been defined as problematic. He provides the analysis shown in Table 11.1, contrasting the sense of community, which he refers to

as "moral communities," with mass society.

Indeed, as Boyte[31] has pointed out, much of the activism of the 1970s and 1980s—protest, self-help, program building, insurgency—revolved around grassroots efforts to establish moral communities. Structures of mutual aid, cooperation, and community improvement grew at an unprecedented rate. Thus has community been viewed most urgently as both part of the problem and part of the solution.

[30]Dennis E. Poplin, *Communities: A Survey of Theories and Methods of Research* © 1972. Reprinted by permission of Macmillan Publishing Company.

[31]Harry C. Boyte, *The Backyard Revolution* (Philadelphia: Temple University Press, 1980), pp. 1-12.

12.

Mayer N. Zald

ORGANIZATIONS: ORGANIZATIONS AS POLITIES: AN ANALYSIS OF COMMUNITY ORGANIZATION AGENCIES

The interdependence of subject matter in the fields of community organization and sociology has long been recognized by teachers and practitioners. Possibly to a greater extent than with any other segment of social work, the problems of this field of practice are grist for the mill of the student of society and the community. And yet there is no systematic sociology of community organization (hereinafter referred to as "CO"). Such a sociology would include

a social history of the emergence and growth of the field of practice, an analysis of its ongoing social system, and diagnostic categories and criteria for investigating community problems and structure.

This paper focuses on one aspect of the social system of the field, presenting, in particular, a set of concepts and propositions about the structure and operation of CO agencies. These concepts and propositions are designed to explain some of the determinants of agency processes and, consequently, the styles and problems of professional practice.

Source: Copyright 1966, National Association of Social Workers, Inc. Reprinted with permission, from *Social Work*, Vol. 11, No. 4 (October 1966), pp. 56-65.

Indeed, much more of the variability of practice in CO is determined by its organizational context, as compared with many professional fields. The needs and problems of the community are not funneled and defined directly between the practitioner and the community segment to which he is related; instead, needs are defined and shaped by the constitution and goals of the employing agency. Furthermore, the means selected to deal with community problems depend on organizational requirements, stances, and definitions. Whatever the practitioner's activity, he is guided by the structure, aims, and operating procedures of the organization that pays the bills.

Therefore, any useful theory of CO practice must include concepts and propositions about how CO agencies shape practice and how such organizations are themselves constrained. The question then becomes: *How are we to analyze community organization agencies?*

ORGANIZATIONAL ANALYSIS

The general approach used here is that of organizational analysis.[1] It is a form of analysis that takes the total organization, not some subpart, as its object. Typically, studies using this approach focus on the relation of goals to structure and the pressures to change goals arising from both the environment and the internal arrangements of the organization. A common focus is the allocation of power to different groups and the manner in which subgroup loyalties and power affect the operation of organizations. Furthermore, organizations are seen as developing distinctive characters—styles and strategies of coping with recurring problematic dilemmas of the organization.

Central to organizational analysis, but often only implicitly treated, is an analysis of the polity of organizations—the patterned distribution and utilization of authority and influence. The frame of reference taken in this paper is explicitly quasi-political. CO agencies are among a class of organizations in which goals are often in flux; in which the patterns of power of influence ebb and flow, but are central to understanding the problems of the organization; in which conflict is sometimes subterranean, sometimes overt, but almost always there; and in which organizations are in unstable relations to their environments. Thus, it seems warranted to give explicit attention to problems of power and the modes of binding people together for collective action. CO agencies can be analyzed as miniature polities.

Four interrelated concepts form the core of this analysis:

1. Organizations have *constitutions,* that is, they have basic zones of activi-

[1]Organizational analysis has been developed most explicitly by Philip Selznick and his students. For example, see Philip Selznick, *T.V.A. and the Grass Roots* (Berkeley: University of California Press, 1949); Selznick, *Leadership in Administration: A Sociological Interpretation* (Evanston, IL: Row, Peterson & Co., 1957); and Selznick, *The Organizational Weapon* (New York: Rand Corporation, 1952). See also Burton Clark, *The Open Door College* (New York: McGraw-Hill Book Co., 1960); and Charles B. Perrow, "The Analysis of Goals in Complex Organizations," *American Sociological Review,* Vol. 66, No. 6 (March, 1961), pp. 854-866. The following works also are informed by this perspective: David L. Sills, *The Volunteers* (Glencoe, IL: Free Press, 1957); Martin Rein and Robert Morris, "Goals, Structures and Strategies for Community Change," *Social Work Practice, 1962* (New York: Columbia University Press, 1962), pp. 127-145; and Robert D. Vinter and Morris Janowitz, "Effective Institutions for Juvenile Delinquents: A Research Statement," *Social Service Review,* Vol. 33, No. 2 (June, 1959), pp. 118-130.

ty, goals, and norms of procedure and relationships that are more or less institutionalized in the organization and that are changed only with great effort and cost.

2. Constitutions are linked to the *constituency and resource base* of the organization. The constituency is not the clientele; rather, the term refers to the groups and individuals who control the organization and to whom the agency executive or executive core is most immediately responsible—the board of directors, key legislators, officeholders, major fund-raisers or grantors.

3. CO agencies wish to affect *target populations,* organizations, or decision centers.

4. Finally, CO agencies exist among a welter of other agencies; they have foreign or *external relations* that can facilitate, impede, or be neutral to the accomplishment of their goals.

These concepts are not mutually exclusive, yet each focuses on somewhat different observations. For purposes of exposition they can be treated separately.

ANALYSIS OF CONSTITUTIONS

In a sense, the constitution of an organization represents its social contract—the basic purposes and modes of procedure to which the major supporters and staff of the organization adhere.[2] When attempts are made to change the constitution of an organiza-

tion, the agency can expect conflict and disaffection, unless clear benefits adhere to the major supporters. The constitution of an organization is made up of the agency's commitments to major programs and modes of proceeding (goals and means). This is, of course, more than just the formal or written statement of goals and procedures, for these may have little to do with the organization's actual constitution. On the other hand, many patterned aspects of agency operation may not be part of the constitution, for these patterns may not deal with basic agreements about goals and means.

Analysis of constitution and goals is important for a sociology of CO practice because it clarifies several important aspects of it—the problems agencies confront when they attempt to change goals and structure, the possibilities of effectiveness vis-à-vis specific goals, and the styles of the professional's work. To be fruitful, analysis of constitutions must be broken down into more specific analytic problems. This paper will treat two: analysis of agency goals and constituency and agency autonomy.

Dimensions of Goals

Organizations come into being to pursue collective ends. A central part of the constitution of any organization is the sets of agreements about goals that are understood by major constituents. Not only do goals represent a set of constituting agreements, they focus organizational resources on a problem field. That is, organizational goals along with beliefs about how to attain them set tasks and problems for agency personnel.

Although there are several conceptual and methodological approaches to

---

[2] Not much attention has been paid to organizational constitutions by sociologists because they often work in organizations whose constitutions are not problematic. E. Wright Bakke uses a conception of constitution or "charter" that is even broader than the author's, but has the same intent. See *Bonds of Organization: An Appraisal of Corporate Human Relations* (New York: Harper & Bros. 1950), especially chap. 6, "Organizational Charter," pp. 152-179.

the study of goals, two aspects are especially crucial here.[3] First, the goals of the organization determine some of the basic types of CO work. Second, attempts to shift the objectives of the organization can threaten its body politic. The goals of CO agencies can be classified along three analytically distinct dimensions: (1) change or service orientation (that is, according to whether the goal is to give the recipient of service essentially what he or his representative wants—information, program, and the like—or whether the community or individual is changed regardless of whether it or he initially wanted to be changed); (2) institution or individual and group orientation; (3) member (internal) or nonmember (external) orientation. The dichotomous cross-classification of these three dimensions yields the typology shown in Figure 12.1.

Of course, it is clear that some of these organizations are more likely to be sites for group work than for CO practice. But community organizers can be found in all of them.

The typology classifies organizations by their target and the ends they wish to achieve with each group. For instance, a community center (Cell D) usually offers services to individuals, rather than attempting to change them; it is oriented to groups and individuals who are members rather than to institutions (other large-scale organizations). On the other hand, in Cell B are agencies that attempt to mobilize people to change the society and its institutions.

The typology brings to the fore regularities of practice problems shared by agencies "located" in the same cell and differences among agencies in different cells. For instance, typically CO organizations aimed externally, at change, and at institutions (e.g., to change the school system) have to be able to mobilize sanctions against the target. On the other hand, those aimed at providing services to individual members (e.g., community centers) have the problem of finding attractive programs to bring people in the door—no question of conflict or of mobilizing sanctions arises in such cases.

In general, *the more change oriented the goals are, the greater the incentives needed by the practitioner and his agency to accomplish these goals.* (Of course, incentives can come from within the target or client group, e.g., an alcoholic may strongly desire to be cured of his alcoholism.) Furthermore, *the more member oriented an organization is, the greater the likelihood of a consensus on action,* because the act of joining implies some agreement about goals. Member-oriented agencies are more likely to use persuasive techniques than nonmember-oriented organizations (who must use appeals to self-interest or sanctions). Finally, *the more institution oriented the target is, the more likely the bonds of organization are not solidaristic—based on the emotional attachments between agent and client—and the more likely they are based on exchange relations, on criteria of institutional rationality.*

These dimensions also relate to the problems of organizational maintenance in the face of attempts to attain specific goals or to change goals. The constitution of the organization consists of a set of expectations that, if

---

[3]See Mayer N. Zald, "Comparative Analysis and Measurement of Organizational Goals: The Case of Correctional Institutions for Delinquents," *Sociological Quarterly,* Vol. 4, No. 3 (Summer 1963), pp. 206-230.

	CHANGE ORIENTED		SERVICE ORIENTED	
	INSTITUTION	INDIVIDUAL AND GROUP	INSTITUTION	INDIVIDUAL AND GROUP
INTERNAL (MEMBER)	**A** Regional planning groups for specific areas New-style welfare councils (planning is change oriented)	**B** Neighborhood block clubs Settlement houses	**C** Old-style welfare council (co-ordinate, no enforcement power)	**D** Community centers Adult education
EXTERNAL (NONMEMBER)	**E** Lower-class social movements Governmental community projects	**F** Agencies working with street gangs Family service agencies	**G** Regional or community research agency	**H** National health agencies (excluding research)

FIGURE 12.1
Goal Dimensions of Community Organization Agencies

violated, threaten the maintenance and stability of the organization. For example, Peter Clark has discussed the case of a local voluntary organization composed of businessmen interested in taxation and governmental efficiency.[4] The standard activity of the organization was information-gathering and education on different tax and governmental programs. Clark found that when any specific tax legislation or assessment was proposed it was difficult to get the organization to take a definite stand on the proposal. Instead, often a group of businessmen who favored or opposed the tax would form a specific ad hoc committee to lobby for or against the issue. Clark concluded that although the organization was concerned with taxation, any specific piece of legislation tended to have differen-tial effects on members and internal conflict would result if any attempt were made to take a definite stand. Instead of fighting an issue through and creating dissension, members took action outside the organization. Clark's case represents a situation in which the constitution did not allow for change attempts. Similar problems occur in other organizations. The general point is that *as an organization begins to change its basic goals, constitutional problems emerge.*[5]

The foregoing discussion of dimensions of goal analysis will also be of relevance in the discussion of constituency and target groups that follows.

---

[4]See "The Chicago Big Businessman as Civic Leader." Unpublished doctoral dissertation, University of Chicago, 1959.

[5]On the succession of goals in organizations, see David L. Sills, "The Succession of Goals," in Amitai Etzioni, ed., *Complex Organizations* (New York: Holt, Rinehart & Winston, 1954), pp. 146-158. See also Mayer N. Zald and Patricia Denton, "From Evangelism to General Service: On the Transformation of the Y.M.C.A." *Administrative Science Quarterly,* Vol. 8, No. 2 (September 1963), pp. 214-234.

Constituency and Agency Autonomy

Some CO agencies have the goals of integrating and co-ordinating major constituents. However, even when agencies have other goals, the question of constituency-agency relations is a focus of organizational constitutions. A pattern of normative expectations develops about consultation, discretion, and the locus of initiation of agency goals and programs. This pattern is largely a function of the resource dependency of the agency.[6] *To the extent that an agency is heavily dependent on its constituency it is likely to develop a constitution giving little room for discretion.*[7]

Constituency-agency relations are crucial to understanding executive roles. Professional CO role-taking varies in terms of how much and how often the executive must report to the constituency. Professional roles may vary from a situation in which the executive does little more than facilitate constituency decision-making to one in which the constituency is consulted seldom, if at all.[8] What determines these roles?

Three factors (excluding personality style) appear to be important in affecting the level of executive decision-making—the fund-raising base, the role of the constituency in accomplishing organizational goals, and the knowledge base differential between constituency and staff.

1. *The more routinized and relatively independent of the constituency the agency's fund-raising base is, the less likely the staff is to consult with and involve the constituency systematically in decision-making.* Thus, agencies that have an immediate and vital appeal to the public (such as the national voluntary health organizations) or have legal and routinized access to funds are less likely than others to have broad participation by their constituencies in decision-making.

2. *When the agency is directly dependent on its constituency for achieving organizational goals, greater attention will be paid to constituency wishes and participation.* An agency is dependent on the constituency for achieving goals when its prestige and influence must be utilized to mobilize other segments of the community. After all, the only moderate prestige and influence of CO professionals is usually insufficient to generate widespread community support. An agency is also dependent on the constituency when it is their change that is sought (when the constituency and the target group are the same).[9] Attention to the constituency may be only formal or surface; nevertheless it affects the conduct of office.

---

[6]For one treatment of the problem of organizational autonomy see Charles Perrow, "Organizational Prestige: Some Functions and Dysfunctions," *American Journal of Sociology*, Vol. 66, No. 4 (January 1961), pp. 854-866. See also, Selznick, *Leadership in Administration*, pp. 120-133.

[7]Note that the proposition does not apply to the formal or stated charter of the organization alone, but rather to the expectations that develop out of the actual dependency bases of the organization. The point is important, for many organizations, notably business corporations, formally "decentralize" and on paper sometimes resemble what are called "federated" systems. Yet through the judicious, and sometimes injudicious, use of central power these corporations never really build up a constitution of federalism.

[8]See Rein and Morris, op. cit.; and Sills, op. cit.

[9]It should be clear, however, that there is an analytic difference between a target group and a constituency. A target group or institution is the change object of the organization. The target group is not directly involved in the choosing of means, the personnel, or the goals of the agency. Target groups become part of the constituency when they become part of the decision-making apparatus of the agency.

3. *The greater the knowledge differential between staff and constituency, the more likely the staff will be given autonomy in the exercise of their work and the more likely the constituency will be consulted only on "boundary" conditions— changes that affect the relation of the agency to the community.* In general, the more decisions are defined as "professional" problems, the less likely are constituencies to be involved.

It would be wrong, however, to assume that an executive cannot influence agency-constituency relations. Constitutions are not immutable! Furthermore, the executive might not want autonomy; the constituency might represent a resource that can be cultivated usefully.

Constituency Characteristics and Agency Operation

The constitution of an organization emerges and is maintained partly to satisfy the constituency. At the same time that they give the organization its continuing mandate, the characteristics of the constituency may lead to a limit on goals and means.

Class Basis of Constituency. A large body of literature testifies to the greater difficulty of involving working-class individuals in voluntary organizations as compared to middle- or upper-class persons.[10] Extending these findings to CO agencies, the following proposition emerges: *the lower the socioeconomic status of the constituency, the more diffi-*

cult it is likely to be to maintain their interest and participation. In other words, the CO practitioner with a lower socioeconomic class constituency will devote more of his energies to motivating the constituency than he would in other organizations.

Not only is level of participation affected by the socioeconomic basis of the constituency, but there is some reason to think that the style of participation is also likely to differ. In general one would expect that *when a CO agency aimed at changing some aspect of the community has a middle- and upperclass constituency it will be more likely to attempt to gain its ends through persuasion, informal negotiation, and longrange harmonizing of interests.* On the other hand, *the more an organization has an essentially lower-class basis, the more it will resort to direct action, open propaganda, and agitation* (when it takes action at all).[11] First, the higher up one goes in the stratification system, the more likely it is that the constituency has easy access to office-holders, can command respect from them, and can threaten use of sanctions that the target person will recognize. Thus, the more élite the constituency the more likely it is that informal negotiations will take place and can be fruitful.

Second, people from higher socioeconomic groups begin having organizational experiences from an earlier age. The higher up in the status system, the more likely the constituency will have had experience in organizational nego-

---

[10]For a careful summary of much of this literature and an attempt to understand the dynamics of the phenomenon, see William Erbe, "Social Involvement and Political Activity," *American Sociological Review,* Vol. 29, No. 2 (April 1964), pp. 198-215.

[11]See the discussion in Herbert J. Gans, *The Urban Villagers: Group and Class in the Life of Italian-Americans* (New York: Free Press of Glencoe, 1962), especially chap. 5, pp. 104-120. The necessity of active and direct modes of expression in the appeal to lower socioeconomic groups is one of the essential elements in Saul Alinsky's approach to CO.

tiation, the more time they can comfortably spend in organizational participation, and the more rewarding to them is such participation.[12]

Obviously, the CO practitioner must take these factors into account. The attempt to get concrete results, the amount of time spent in agitational versus more neutral activities, and the mechanisms of involving the constituency will each differ depending on the class base of the constituency.

Organizational versus Individual Constituencies. For many CO agencies the crucial characteristic of the constituency is not so much that of its class base but whether its basis is individual or organizational. All else being equal, *the more an agency has a constituency made up of agencies, the harder it is to get commitment to an action program that does not have widespread societal consensus and the more likely the agency is to serve as a clearing-house for information and co-ordination.*[13]

One of the advantages to a CO agency of having a constituency comprised of organizations is that it then has a built-

in multiplier effect. That is, those programs that are agreed to can be disseminated through a wide range of other organizations—the population that can be reached is greater. On the other hand, a constituency made up of organizations requires the agency to work through the problem of new and extreme programs with all constituent agencies. If the new program threatens the autonomy of the organizations or challenges *their* constituencies, there will be little incentive for commitment. Because of the desire to protect organizational autonomy, agencies comprised of organizations are more likely to have a structure similar to a representative assembly, which permits veto powers, while agencies comprised of individuals are more likely to have either straight majority rule or an oligarchic structure.[14]

The "all else being equal" clause in this proposition is especially important. If the organizations have joined the CO agency with the expectation that extreme programs would be proposed, then such an agency might be as likely as one comprised of individuals to initiate new and extreme programs rapidly. Thus, some community councils organized for purposes of neighborhood protection and development have been constituted out of organizations and still have initiated "radical" action programs.

TARGET GROUPS AND CO PRACTICE

The purpose of the professional and his agency is to improve the functioning of groups, individuals and commu-

---

[12]Catherine V. Richards and Norman A. Polansky have shown that among adult women, those who participated in organizations as adolescents and whose parents also participated were more likely to participate in voluntary associations than those who did not have either of these characteristics in their background. The over-all rate of parent and adolescent participation is, of course, directly related to socioeconomic status. See "Reaching Working-class Youth Leaders," *Social Work*, Vol. 4, No. 4 (October 1959), pp. 31-39).

[13]The author has less confidence in this proposition than in the previous one. For one thing, it may cause comparison of disparate organizations, for instance, neighborhood block clubs with welfare councils. Ideally, to test such a proposition one would take CO agencies in similar types of communities with similar types of goals and see if variation in their constituencies did in fact lead to different types of action programs. Such a design might be difficult to realize.

[14]See Rein and Morris, op. cit., for a discussion of the problems of agencies whose constituencies are made up of organizations.

nities. To do this he attempts to change individuals and the relationships among individuals and groups. His goal may be reached not only by changing relationships and attitudes, but by changing the facilities—hospitals, schools, trading associations—used by people in carrying out their daily lives. Thus, he may be attempting to mobilize the community for a relatively specific substantive proposal and the target group may only be changed insofar as it has reached a fairly specific decision. Values, norms, and social relations may not be changed; only questions of efficiency may be involved. Differential diagnosis of target problems has important organizational implications. Let us examine two aspects of agency-target relations—the role definitions of line workers and the tactics of institutional penetration.

Role Definitions of Line Workers

The problem can be posed as a question: Should line workers be substantive specialists or should they be "multipurpose" workers coached by substantive specialists? Should the worker be a technical specialist, knowledgeable in the specific problems of the community, or should he be a generalist, knowledgeable about how to relate to communities?

At least partly the answer depends on the extent to which the target group accepts and is committed to the purposes of the agency. *To the extent that an organization's goals are accepted and its functions in a community understood, a specialist organization can most efficiently communicate information and methods that can then be utilized by a target group.* However, *to the extent that members of a target group are sus-*

picious of an agency, communication channels will be blocked. In such a situation a generalist will be required whose main job is to establish an organization-target group linkage. As that linkage is established, it then becomes possible to reintroduce specialists, now trading on the generalist's relations.[15]

But what of the qualifications of such multipurpose workers? Who should they be? To the extent that the target group is difficult to penetrate because of problems of distrust, and to the extent that major sanctions are not controlled by the organization, the most effective generalist is likely to be one who minimizes social distance at the same time that he represents the "ego ideal" of target group members. "Personalistic" as opposed to "professional" criteria become crucial.

As many field workers have noted in working with lower-income ethnic groups and delinquent gangs, and as Katz and Eisenstadt have suggested for Israeli administrative agencies, the overcoming of distrust may require the worker to appear to identify more with the problems and perspective of the target group than with the agency. As the level of distrust decreases, however, the target group becomes amenable to the norms and procedures of the agency and more normal agency-client relations can be established. Thus, in order to be effective, CO agencies must evaluate the extent to which target groups are

---

[15]See Albert Mayer and associates in collaboration with McKin Marriott and Richard Park, *Pilot Project India: The Story of Rural Development in Etawah, Uttar Pradesh* (Berkeley: University of California Press, 1958). See also Elihu Katz and S. N. Eisenstadt, "Some Sociological Observations on the Response of Israeli Organizations to New Immigrants," *Administrative Science Quarterly*, Vol. 5, No. 1 (June 1960), pp. 113-133; and Gans, op. cit., chap. 7, pp. 142-162.

receptive to their policies. Staff role definitions must be fitted to this diagnosis. Sometimes, however, CO diagnosis involves the question of how one makes specific decisions, not how one reaches a group. When the target question switches to penetrating institutional decision centers, a new set of diagnostic criteria becomes relevant.

Tactics of Institutional Penetration

The legacy of Floyd Hunter and C. Wright Mills to the practice field can be summed up as "to the power structure!" Many CO workers, civil rights workers, and others who are trying to change communities seem to be saying: "If you want something done you must get the power structure behind you." If community organizers followed this dictate, they would find themselves pursuing a chimera. If they tried to mobilize the same élite on every decision, they would fail both to mobilize them and to attain their objectives.

Furthermore, the power structure is often relatively irrelevant to many decisions, for it is often isolated and in an official decision center or is most sharply affected by the sentiments of that most diffuse of all decision centers, the voting populace. Thus, the job of analyzing decision centers requires the most precise diagnosis of the chain of influence and mechanism of decision-making for each specific decision.

If the decision involves a referendum, different kinds of issues appeal to different groups. Machiavellian advice to a community organizer interested in promoting school bonds is to see that the middle class is overrepresented (as it is when the turnout is low), since they tend to vote for school funds. On the other hand, when, as in some states, referenda are held on welfare matters, the

lower class should be motivated to vote, for they tend to vote "yes" on these measures.[16]

In mobilizing a target group, the CO practitioner and agency must face squarely the dilemma of their relative commitment to "the democratic process" versus their commitment to specific social values. The advice given above obviously conflicts with faith in the democratic process. This is a dilemma not only for CO practitioners, but for all advocates of social welfare. However, in part the problem of whether to pursue specific goals regardless of an idealized conception of the democratic process resolves itself according to agency goals and mandates. For instance, the more specific and concrete an organization's objectives and the greater the demands on the organization by the constituency, the more likely it is that workers' concerns about "process" will be relegated to the background.

EXTERNAL RELATIONS

In attempting to mobilize a target group, reach a specific objective, or integrate services, CO agencies must deal with other agencies. The CO agency may be but one among many and it may be without a mandate to guide, direct, or lead the other agencies. Often a CO agency has as part of its mandate the integration of the disparate institutions, but the mandate may be honored more in the breach.

One of the basic premises of organizational analysis is that only under very

---

[16]For a study that looks at the relation of income and ethnicity to "public" and "self-interest" voting on referenda see James Q. Wilson and Edward C. Banfield, "Public Regardingness as a Value Premise in Voting Behavior," *American Political Science Review,* Vol. 58, No. 4 (December 1964), pp. 876-887.

special conditions do organizations purposely attempt to decrease their scope, actually admit that they are ineffective, or willingly give up "turf." These special conditions involve low ideological or career commitment to the organization on the part of staff, an increasingly difficult fund-raising problem, and a constituency that increasingly finds better alternative uses of time and money. As a working assumption it is reasonable to assert that most organizations will attempt to maintain autonomy and increase their scope.[17] Even when it is obvious that one agency is more capable of achieving a shared goal than another, it would be rare indeed for the latter to donate its income for the expansion of the former. And it is rarely obvious that one agency has such superiority over another.

Given the assumption that agencies generally wish to increase autonomy and scope, the integration and co-ordination of agency policy and programs depends on the enlightened self-interest of the treaty signers—the independent agencies. As a general postulate, co-ordination, sharing of facilities, and proper integration are likely to take place only when both of the autonomous agencies stand to gain. Specific conditions follow.[18]

1. *If two agencies are essentially in a competitive relation to each other for funds, constituency, and staff, full-scale co-ordination and merger of programs would indeed be unlikely.* (Nor, given the nature of funding processes in which multiple appeals increase the total amount of funds available for the welfare sector, would a merger of identities necessarily lead to a more effective welfare economy.)

2. *The greater the marginal cost of co-ordination and integration or the lower the marginal profit, the less chance of integration and co-ordination of programs.* (Cost and profit do not necessarily refer to money; there can be costs of time and energy, for instance.) It follows that co-ordination will most easily be achieved on problems that are least expensive to both parties. Co-ordination is more easily achieved on a specific case than on over-all programs.

3. *The greater the organizational commitment to a fixed program or style of operation, the less likely the co-ordination and integration.* Agencies develop commitment to programs on ideological grounds and, because the programs help the agency to solve problems of identity, they thereby become part of the organizational character.[19] To the extent that a program must be changed by a merger, the costs mount.

These three propositions state the conditions that impede co-ordination and integration. Stated somewhat differently, they indicate conditions contributing to co-ordination, co-operation, and integration:

1. *The greater the symbiotic relation between agencies, the more likely the co-*

[17]In addition to Perrow, op. cit., see Norton E. Long, "The Local Community as an Ecology of Games," *American Journal of Sociology*, Vol. 64, No. 3 (November 1958), pp. 251-261.

[18]This discussion draws on the following articles, which have recently discussed problems of co-ordination and interorganizational relations: William J. Reid, "Interagency Co-ordination in Delinquency Prevention and Control," *Social Service Review*, Vol. 38, No. 4 (December 1964), pp. 418-428; Eugene Litwak and Lydia Hylton, "Inter-Organizational Analysis: A Hypothesis on Coordinating Agencies," *Administrative Science Quarterly*, Vol. 6, No. 4 (March 1962); Sol Levine and Paul E. White, "Exchange as a Conceptual Framework for the Study of Inter-Organizational Relationships," *Administrative Science Quarterly*, Vol. 5, No. 4 (March 1961), pp. 583-601.

[19]On the concept of organizational character see Selznick, *Leadership in Administration*.

ordination. For instance, interestingly enough, the police and an agency working with delinquent gangs have more to gain from co-operating than a family service agency and a street work agency. The latter agency can actually contribute only occasionally to aiding the family service agency in its work with its case load and, at best, the family service agency can help "cool out" an offender. On the other hand, the police and the street worker have a strong symbiotic relation. The street worker gains status with the boys with whom he is working by being able to negotiate with the police, while the police have fewer problems with the gang. The same principle applies to the relation of membership groups to the "Y's," of mental hospitals to general hospitals, and so on.

2. *The greater the marginal profits, the more likely the co-ordination.* Sometimes funds are granted only to co-operating agencies. If the funds are great enough they overcome the costs of integrating or joint planning. Marginal profits of co-ordination may be seen in the face of a crisis in facilities. When programs become overburdened, when facilities are inadequate and multiple expansion funds are not available, a negotiated settlement may allow specialization between agencies, reducing overall financial needs and making co-ordination profitable.[20]

There is also some evidence to suggest that overlapping constituencies contribute to such co-ordination.[21] *The less constituencies overlap, the more likely it is that the constituencies are either neutral to or distrust each other and thus the longer it will take and the more difficult it will be to gain co-operation.*

This last point suggests that external relations may also be related to the concepts discussed earlier; that is, costs and profits are defined in the context of and affected by organizational constitutions and goals, constituency, and target groups.

CONCLUSIONS

In this paper one part of a sociology of CO practice has been developed—the organizational analysis of CO agencies. In each section several testable propositions were presented about the conditions under which different kinds of CO agency problems and processes arise. However, this paper has not presented a complete analysis of CO agencies. First, there are not enough empirical studies of these agencies to permit this. Second, the internal role structure of agencies has not been dealt with. Nevertheless, the writer is convinced that analysis along these lines will be valuable for both sociology and CO practice. For sociology the reward will be rich in that studies of sets of organizations will permit an examination of problems of mobilizing support and community consensus; for community organization the reward will be rich in that an analytic and differential basis will be developed by which to assess CO agencies and evaluate practice roles.

---

[20]See Robert Morris, "New Concepts in Community Organization Practice," *Social Welfare Forum, 1961* (New York: Columbia University Press, 1961), pp. 128-146.

[21]Ibid.

PART THREE: STRATEGIES

Introduction

One day historians will record this movement as one
of the most significant epics of our heritage.
MARTIN LUTHER KING, JR., 1962

A fundamental problem for nations, for organizations, and for individuals is that of getting from where they are now to where they would like to go. The planned process by which nations and individuals (and everything in between) arrive at chosen objectives may be referred to as strategy. This sense of the word "strategy" is derived from game theory, which distinguishes games of individual skill, games of chance, and games of strategy—the last being those in which the most effective course of action for each player depends upon the actions of other players and the players' anticipation and assessment of those moves. As such, the term emphasizes the interdependence of allies' and adversaries' decisions and their various expectations about each others' behavior.

The centrality of strategy for the community practitioner is undeniable. Without it, ideology and commitment are reduced to empty rhetoric. Used by themselves, interventive actions tend to become merely forays against *ad hoc* "targets of opportunity" without any sense of how they may fit into some larger plan. The vigor with which problems of strategy are endlessly debated is but one example of their critical importance to community practice. Some have even gone so far as to suggest that strategists are born rather than made. In any case, a solid grounding in strategic thinking is a requisite for effective community practice. Only through a thoughtful and pragmatic consideration of alternatives can a reasonable evaluation of various plans of action and their respective strengths and weaknesses be made.

Just what is strategy? How may it be distinguished from tactics? When and how should one change strategies? What tools, what action "rules of thumb" are available to guide practitioner actions?

These are the questions faced by community practitioners every day. However, efforts to pose these issues sharply, or explicate them fully, are few and far between in the literature. Part Three is an attempt to do this. The articles cover a broad range of strategic approaches. Separate chapters are devoted to each of five main strategic orientations—planning, development, action, policy, and administration.

The purpose of this introduction is to present a theoretical consideration of the problem of strategy as it relates to community practice. We discuss critical contextual problems in the selection of strategies and offer a scheme to help community change agents organize their own thinking about strategy choice and implementation.

A Conceptualization of Strategy

Basically we regard strategy as an orchestrated attempt to influence a person or a system in relation to some goal which an actor desires. It is "orchestrated" in the sense that an effort is made to take into account the actions and the reactions of key allies and adversaries as they bear upon the achievement of the proposed goal. That goal may be something which relates directly to an individual actor (like a supplementary welfare check for winter clothing), or it may be much more general, such as a particular "state of the system" desired by the change agent. For example, exorcizing white racism from a big city educational bureaucracy may be a state-of-the-system goal. While most practitioners are well acquainted with thinking about strategy as influence, the notion of orchestration probably bears further attention. In a sense, it is intended to convey a dramatic "arrangement"—with different performers, each with various skills and roles, each of whom may enter and leave the scene according to some action plan. Solos articulate with the movement of the whole piece. The change agent's roles include prompter and producer-conductor. He lays out a "score" for the performance and attempts to integrate its diverse elements as the performance goes forward. In all likelihood the score itself will have to be changed—in response to shifting conditions—one or more times during any given performance.

But more is implied here than the interplay of many persons, or persons and institutions, at any given moment. There is a progression over time—as each phase of the action scheme is completed. Indeed, it suggests the notion of a "means-ends chain," where all of the simultaneous performances are at once ends in themselves, and means to a more general end. A familiar example to practitioners is the community clean-up campaign. The project is an end in itself, as well as a means to the more general goal of community cohesion and pride. Thus community strategy often involves a complex and dynamic pattern of performances within performances. However, in this general framework there are several critical issues which need to be explored in more detail.

Conflict Strategies and Consensus Strategies

The problem of strategy in the contemporary literature is often dichotomized into a choice between conflict and consensus approaches. This trend toward polarization has led some contemporary writers to offer the illusion of choice between "brave" and "cowardly" strategies, or "radical" versus "establishment" modes. While, in the terminology of the Left, this polarization may facilitate the "radicalization" of uninitiated or oppressed minorities, it also creates a new level of confusion for the practitioner. Nevertheless, these dimensions are a real and common part of everyone's daily life. As Weber points out, "Conflict cannot be excluded from social life...'peace' is nothing more than a change in the form of conflict or in the antagonists or in the objects of the conflict, or finally in the chances of selection."[1]

Yet consensus is, paradoxically, a part of conflict, as much as the converse is true. Without subsequent negotiation, agreement and some form of reconciliation, the fruits of conflict are likely to be very meager indeed. Even when total revolution or the transfer of substantial power is effected (or attempted), the "outs" who are now "in" must move to consolidate their gains through at least a modicum of consensus and reconciliation. At the same time, the current powerful thrust toward "conflict management" is also to be closely scrutinized. Any attempt to move everything by consensus and agreement, to keep everything "nice," may be used to mask significant problems and avoid the possibility of arriving at decisions on critical issues.

The inevitable coexistence of conflict and consensus has received strong support from the social science literature. Work relating to small groups is replete with comments on the task and maintenance functions which must be performed by their members. The literature which discusses task and process goals in community organization offers similar intelligence. Task goals refer to "hard" production-oriented functions in which decisions are made, individual interests neglected, feelings disregarded. Process goals involve the repair of ruptures caused by task activities and an attempt to create a higher level of group solidarity through which task business can proceed more effectively.

It has been previously pointed out that the use of conflict or consensus may be predominant in a given model of practice—such as social action in the former mode or consensus in community development. Seen more broadly, conflict and consensus are viewed as the Siamese twins of social progress. If both these task and maintenance functions are not attended to, progress toward social goals may be sharply truncated, if not halted, as William

---

[1]Lewis Coser, *Functions of Social Conflict* (New York: The Free Press, 1956), p. 21.

Gamson points out in his article on "Rancorous Conflict in Community Politics."[2]

Ideological Commitment as Goal

Most practitioners are well aware that long-term agency goals are often so vague as to be unapproachable in the real world. This problem, along with the lack of specificity about short-term or intermediate goals, is sometimes solved through goal idealization. Practitioners become "true believers" in the sense in which Eric Hoffer has suggested.[3] Since progress toward the desired goal cannot be accurately assessed, the "purity" or motivation of the practitioner becomes the foremost consideration. While not more typical of community organizers than any other group of change agents, this solution tends to move the goal out of the realm of the "practical" or empirically concrete and to develop a series of personalistic assessments. From this perspective, "commitment" becomes a culmination for the believer; without it, progress becomes impossible.

Specification of Ends and Means: A Strategy of Problem Definition

The battle over the specification of ends and means, clearly propounded by the Greeks, has been vigorously waged ever since. However, this debate has tended to obscure a perhaps more fundamental issue—that of defining the problem in such a way that means and ends may be fully articulated in designing a strategy aimed at solving or ameliorating it. Wherever possible, practitioners should attempt to select public, rather than private, means and ends. That is, the worker should choose as a means something which is concrete and subject to open verification, rather than something which is private and covert. The same can be said of ends. For example, a worker who sets as a goal the global aim of eliminating racism in a particular community is bound to be disappointed. This is not to say that the elimination of racism should not be one of his goals, but rather that it should not be *the* goal. On the other hand, if the goal is one of bringing integration to a suburban housing area, or providing new job or educational opportunities for blacks, then the results can be monitored more effectively. Without intermediate and feasible proximate goals, the worker's interventions cannot be evaluated to any significant degree and progress cannot be assessed.

The problem of means/ends specification is not limited to ends. Deciding which means and monitoring the means is also difficult. All too often it is solved by means of ritualism. Here we find, for example, the agency which relies heavily on a continuing series of meetings from which nothing ever seems to emerge. The operations of some welfare councils and human relations organizations provide excellent illustrations of this process.

[2]William Gamson, "Rancorous Conflict in Community Politics," *American Sociological Review*, Vol. 31, No. 1 (February 1966), pp. 71-81.

[3]Eric Hoffer, *The True Believer* (New York: The New American Library, Inc., 1958).

The Means-Ends Spiral

Despite some tendencies in community organization toward goal idealization and ritualistic means, most practitioners recognize both the alternation of conflict and consensus approaches and the operation of means-ends chains as common practice experiences. Putting the two notions together, strategy can be redefined as an outward means-ends spiral, alternatively emphasizing task and process, conflict and consensus modes.

The concept of strategy as an orchestrated means-ends spiral has a number of important consequences for community organization. For one thing, it suggests that total reliance on a strategy of either consensus or conflict will in most circumstances be unsuccessful. It anticipates the skill of the organizer in moving with the community or group between task and process phases. And it offers the idea of progression toward concrete intermediate objectives as a measure of strategic success. Now let us turn to an examination of the contexts in which strategic successes must be achieved.

Contextual Variables in Strategic Assessment

Strategy is not devised in a vacuum. The strategic thinker works in some specific community, with specific groups and probably for some organization. As he develops his plan, there are a number of factors which he needs to take into account.

Strategic thinking and development must begin with a consideration of the agency resources in people, money, and equipment which the agent has at his disposal. Often there are intra-agency fights over the allocation of these resources. And, whatever the level, we know that in community practice there are never sufficient amounts of any one of the resources to meet the demand. Since they are scarce, competition for them becomes intense. The more scarce the resources (and thus, the more intense the competition), the more a strategy of power-building self-help is indicated.

The resources of the broader system in which the organizer must act are another consideration. Such resources may be the availability of money, on the one hand, and that amorphous but all-important resource, public support and understanding on the other. Sometimes the agency and the system have resources differentially available to them. In some developing countries, community agents have access to expensive and sophisticated equipment which the indigenous population does not know how to use. Thus, even the presence of resources does the worker no good if they cannot be used. More frequent, and characteristic of many urban change programs in America, is the target system that has more resources than the change agency. Hence, from a strategic point of view, the system (or particular elements within that system) can "hold out" much longer than any agency-backed client organization and win most struggles. In general, when the target has more resources than those available to the change agent or agency, a social action strategy is indicated.

The amount of resistance to change objectives is a third factor of critical importance. Generally, we assume some resistance to change proposals as a matter of course. Sometimes, however, the complexity of the problem itself gives the appearance of resistance. We must be careful to distinguish between a situation where a social problem is complex, but there is no substantial resistance (for example, many public health problems fall into this category) and one where many solutions are known but there is strong resistance (for example, income maintenance). Then, too, areas where important gains can be made, and where the system is neutral to mildly opposed (for example, tutorial programs), a social planning strategy should be considered.

In modern urban America, class variables are a very strong predictor of behavior and institutional preferences, from sex habits to styles of child rearing, from religion to responses to pain.[4] It is thus with some concern that we note the absence of literature which substantially attempts to exploit these differences in the conceptualization of strategic alternatives.

Generally speaking, the change agent can represent a constituency which is of higher, equal, or lower social class than the change target. For the community practitioner this situation offers certain strategic "hints." They devolve upon the fact that change strategies are "handicapped" by their class of origin—particularly as viewed by the recipient of the change proposal. For example, a change proposal coming from a high-status change agency (or agent) to a low-status community has a good likelihood of "success," particularly if the agency is willing to utilize its prestige in achieving the desired goal over the objections of community residents. On the other hand, a change proposal coming from a lower-class constituency directed toward a middle-class formal organization is likely to be stalled, sidetracked, and indefinitely tabled or ultimately defeated. It is all too easy for the class "handicap" (either positive or negative) to obfuscate the merits of any given change proposal. Many of the demands for "power" of various sorts—as enunciated by the poor, racial and ethnic minorities, and women—can be understood as a demand for a new set of handicapping arrangements in the system. Welfare mothers, for example, suffer from the stigma of poverty and recipient status. Welfare rights organizations attempt to redress this balance and place recipient mothers on a more equal basis for negotiation with middle-class welfare bureaucrats. Problems of lower-class constituencies may be handled by developing social action strategies to build a new handicapping system (that is, causing shifts in power and/or resource allocations), followed by appropriate strategies of development and planning.

Variability in problem complexity is a relevant issue and poses questions of problem "tractability." Community problems are comprised of many unique and interrelated elements. Sometimes even the simplest technical problems—garbage collections, for example—are confounded by political

---

[4]Reinhard Bendix and Seymour M. Lipset (eds.), *Class, Status and Power* (New York: The Free Press, 1966).

complexities of great magnitude. On the other hand, problems which have substantial support across a wide range of publics—job-training projects—may falter on technical insufficiencies. Other complexities—from agency staff changes to national upheavals—also may enter the picture. Fundamentally, the change agent, taking the problem in all its ramifications, must be able to assess the degree of complexity involved, and how amenable to solution it may be. Different degrees of complexity require different kinds, timing, and sequencing of strategies.

Legitimacy—of either a target of change or a change agent—is a key variable for the community practitioner. Indeed, a change target of dubious legitimacy has a built-in vulnerability that may be exploited. On the other hand, a target with broad legitimacy in the community may be especially difficult to attack. Change agents need to make a realistic assessment of their own legitimacy and act accordingly. That is, an inadequate legitimacy must often be strengthened for effective action to take place; a charismatic legitimacy can carry the change agent a long way before an action begins.

In our modern bureaucratized society, organizational strength of either change target or change agent is often a vital contextual problem. As a change target, weaker organizations are more vulnerable to a variety of change efforts. Strong organizations, however, typically present special difficulties even for the most enterprising of change agents. Since organizations are many times vehicles through which change is carried out, their strength must be carefully appraised as part of the planning for change efforts. Six substantive problems—resources, resistance, class, complexity, legitimacy, and organizational strength—in the development of a successful community intervention strategy have been discussed.[5] There is no implication that these six are the only important factors; nevertheless they seem significant in that they cut across any functional area of community action and are common to most social change situations. How can they be dealt with conceptually in an interrelated way? One source of help is social science.

Strategy and Means of Influence

Often we become confounded by the variety of styles of influence (as well as current vogues) and fail to recognize that there are fundamentally three, and only three, core modes of influence. To get another person, group or organization to do what is desired, force, inducement, and agreement may be used.[6] These three modes occur not only on the individual level as strategies of influence, but they are main change initiators at the societal level as well. Let us consider each in some detail.

[5]For a useful consideration of some others, see Neil Gilbert and Harry Specht (eds.), *Planning for Social Welfare* (Englewood Cliffs, NJ: Prentice-Hall, 1977), and Thomas Meenaghan et al., *Macro Practice in the Human Services* (New York: Free Press, 1982).

[6]These dimensions are similar to the modes of compliance used by Etzioni. See Amitai Etzioni, *A Comparative Analysis of Complex Organizations* (New York: The Free Press, 1961), and the approaches explored in Robert Fisher, *Let the People Decide: Neighborhood Organizing in America* (Boston: Twayne Publishers, 1984).

Force, or coercive power, has been a vital concept in the analysis of human events. The possession of force, or control over the means of force, gives the change agent an important weapon. Often it is not necessary to actually use available force, but simply to make a *credible threat*. At other times, the actual application of force is necessary (for example, to establish credibility through a "show of strength"). Modes of force may range from physical violence and war on one end of a continuum, to sit-ins, confrontations, and personal harassment at the other end. Drawing on our previous distinction, force constitutes a conflict strategy, and its use typically creates resentment. The use of force also suggests the existence of resistance. Indeed, there are strong moral sanctions against using force when resistance is absent, as in the case of "shooting an unarmed man" or attacking a "defenseless" nation. In all well-integrated social systems, the subsystem which has primary responsibility for control over the use of force is the polity, or governmental structure. Agents of force, such as the police, the army, etc., are under this kind of political control. Access to certain positions in the polity are sought because of the relationship they have to the potential mobilization of force, even though the notion of force may be obscured or veiled.

The second means by which social goals may be achieved is inducement. Often, goals can be purchased or traded. Force need not be used, although value consensus may not be present. For example, people who argue that integrated housing is a "good investment" are using an inducement strategy. On a more fundamental level, the entire economic system is an inducement system. People contribute to the system and receive differential payments in return. This pay can be traded for many other goods in the system. The purchase of goods is, in turn, an inducement to the manufacturer to create new and more profitable goods.

In using coercive power, one has to control the means of force. To use an inducement strategy, one needs to manipulate the goods by which people may be induced. Money is one such "good." Interestingly, power is another. (This suggests an interaction between the three main modes which we shall discuss momentarily.) Status positions, prestigeful associations, jobs, symbols of recognition, access to personnel and equipment are also among the most desired goods. In earlier times, salvation and indulgences were coin of the realm. Increasingly, control over information is coming to be an important and negotiable commodity. As society comes to be more and more complex, more and more specialized, more and more technological, detailed information is required to solve even apparently simple problems. Hence, it becomes a desired good, and a most significant one.

Perhaps the most subtle and sophisticated method for achieving social goals is through value consensus or agreement. A consensus mode proceeds through the development of an agreement between the actors that a course of action should be followed. Typically, the consensus is based upon fundamental agreements on underlying values in the social system. Then the parties attempt to demonstrate that the position they wish to take is closely attuned with that value or operates according to it. One simple example deals with the vote. In the United States, it is common and widely accepted practice to settle matters in dispute with a vote of those present. This procedure requires a plurality achieved through the rule of one-man-one-vote. However, the strong biases inherent in this procedure are often ignored. The intensity of preference on an issue, the fact that some people may feel very strongly while others take the matter rather lightly, is simply neglected in this procedure. Similarly, with each member having a single vote, differences in knowledge, experience and analytical ability are not accorded any special weight. The presumption is made that somehow the most desirable alternatives possible will receive a full hearing.

Value consensus usually emerges through some kind of socialization process. In the most obvious case, of course, it is the socialization of infants and children to the norms and mores of the dominant culture or their own ethnic group. Less explicit, but socialization nonetheless, is a host of processes which go on in adult life—the peer group of friends, the informal "clique" at the work place or factory. Then too, many of us have a broader and more undefined group which we use as a reference point to assess our own attitudes and progress (political parties, a profession, the church, etc.).

Means of Influence and Modes of Intervention

These three types of influence have some very interesting additional properties. For one thing, each may be a goal as well as a means to the others. Thus, inducements can be used to secure power and the control over force. Force can be used to secure agreement, although in perhaps a more limited fashion. Inducements, when applied over time, tend to produce value agreement. This is the time-honored process of "cooptation."

Second, each is the basis for an important part of the stratification system in society. Certainly people possess different amounts of power and can be located somewhere on a power continuum ranging from most to least. People also have differential control over various inducements, such as money and information. A rank ordering can be done of those "commanding" salient inducements. Finally, people are closer to, or further from, valued positions in society. This is often referred to as "status." For this reason, each of these means of influence is an important "good" in the system. One might conceptualize the task of the community worker in terms of equalizing the distribution of these "goods," or improving the position of his constituency on one or more ranking scales. Often he will attempt to capitalize on the properties of one system to produce increments in another.

Third, none of these influence means can exist without the others. Not only do they interpenetrate on a goals-means basis, but they also are mutually supportive. Hence, the use of force generally exists within some context of agreement about the conditions under which force may be used and the amount of force necessary to produce certain results, etc. On the other hand, the use of force often produces a new situation with which the existing web of value agreements must cope. Both are supported by a framework of inducements. Without inducements, the potential user of force cannot often muster the necessary elements of force.

Finally, force, inducements, and value agreement are the means by which society at large insures order and stability in the social system, and the means by which the society is changed. Force, for example, can be a means by which order is maintained, or disrupted. Inducements are used to develop commitments to the system, or to lure people to other competing systems. Values are at once sources of common bonds and of great divisiveness in the society.

It might be useful at this time to relate these three means of influence to the earlier discussion of five models or modes of community intervention (Reading 1). On the intervention level, social action is most closely related to the force variable. Police, courts, and the military are typical examples of force used to maintain the system. As a change variable civil disobedience and other forms of disruptive militance are typical. Social action usually attempts to build up the pressure of cumulative force through massing large numbers of people in united and often dramatic activity. Although in a quite different fashion, policy is also related to the force variable. That is, legal and legislative machinery are often the impelling force behind the use of policy as an interventive system maintenance mode. As a change mode, the courts can be used, in this case, to support such efforts as class action suits.

Planning as an intervention technique articulates best with the inducement means of influence. Planning involves a complex of processes (which may include, as elements, development, action, policy, and administration). Fundamentally, the planner attempts to induce the system to adopt a proposed plan through a variety of techniques. Typically, the situation is one of high complexity, and the planner brings to bear significant expertise on the location and extent of the problem, past attempts to deal with it, and the most desirable alternatives in view of current circumstances.

The value means of influence best articulates with the locality development mode of intervention. In both cases, the achievement of value agreement and common orientations is a central focus of either change or system maintenance objectives.

Similarly, the value means of influence also relates to the administration mode of intervention. The achievement of value agreement is vital to system maintenance objectives (the example of cutback management comes easily to mind). The accomplishment of value consensus is a major step in working toward change objectives through the administrative model (revising such personnel policies as paternity leaves falls into this arena).

The development of these two sets of terms—one set pertaining to means of influence and the other to modes of intervention—permits us to develop a framework for considering the types of styles of strategies available to the change agent. This framework is displayed in Figure 1.

Figure 1 suggests that there are at least fifteen basic strategic themes that may be employed. While, as we pointed out, each mode of intervention is characterized by a particular means of influence (as indicated by its location on the diagonal in Figure 1), in actuality other means of influence are also typically utilized. Thus, while militance often is expressed in social action interactional schemes, inducement through negotiation takes place, as well as value consensus through moral exhortation.

MODES OF INTERVENTION

Basic Means of Influence	Action	Planning	Development	Policy	Administration
Force (Power)	Militance (1A) Disruption, sit-in, "liberation" of institutions, para-military activities	Power Elite (2B) Involve influential elites	Reconciliation (3C) (Client system with power groups)	Compliance (1D) (Legal action)	Penalty (3E) (Suspend employee)
Inducement	Negotiation (3F) Bargain, confrontation with "facts"	Expertise (1G)	Pilot Projects (2H) (Illustrative of potential gains, build to larger tasks)	Rewards (2I) (Tax Incentives)	Remuneration (2J) (Pay increase)
Value Consensus	Moral Exhortation (2K) Expose, "Radical thought"	Representation (3L) "Federation" of interests	Group Development (1M)	Recognition (3N) (Awards)	Support (1O) ("Psychic Income")

CRITICAL CONTEXTUAL PROBLEMS

	Action	Planning	Development	Policy	Administration
	Low social class High resistance	High complexity	Low resources	Legitimacy	Organizational Strength

FIGURE 1
A Matrix of Intervention Strategies, Means of Influence and Contextual Variables

In addition each mode of intervention offers special leverage on a key contexual variable or general problem situation. Thus social action is concerned especially with unequal distribution of goods and resources in the society as reflected in class stratification; planning deals with matters of high complexity; and locality development is particularly useful with a situation of limited communal resources.[7] Policy may be especially important in either augmenting or undermining the legitimacy of the political system and its institutions. Administration is likely to be particularly effective under conditions of organizational strength.

Strategy Confrontation: The Mixing and Phasing of Strategies

It is often the case, as we have suggested in the means-ends spiral notion, that the practitioner must move from one strategy to another as shifts occur in the conditions affecting his overall objectives. Figure 1 suggests a possible scheme for mixing and phasing the strategies under two fundamental problem conditions.

The first set of problematic situations requires moving horizontally across the chart. It assumes that society or some target system is using one of the means of influence to maintain a problem condition. If the change agency, for example, is dealing with a problem defined by the system as one of force and power, one begins with a militant action strategy (1A) to build power and influence, and then moves to a planning strategy to consolidate the acquired influence and build a power block (2B), to a development strategy for building value consensus and establishing channels for negotiating the allocation of scarce resources (3C), to a policy strategy for institutionalizing the newly achieved change (4D), and finally to an administration strategy for implementing the previously determined policy (5E).

In contrast, where inducement is the main mode of maintaining the status quo, one begins with a planning strategy, bringing expertise to bear on a detailed analysis of the problem (1G). Then, one can move to an illustration of the plan through small projects (2H), and subsequently to a position of hard bargaining and negotiation (3F), to provision of such policy inducements as tax incentives (2I), and subsequently to offering administrative motivators like pay increases (2J).

In the case where values form the main vehicle of conservative influence, value "liberation" needs to take place (often in small groups) (1M), followed

---

[7]Furthermore, each intervention mode is often associated with particular patterns of linkage. Thus social action typically involves local primary groups banding together to make demands upon (or link up with) formal organizations. Planning often includes a number of cross-linkages among formal organizations, as well as formal organizations tying in with neighborhood groups to improve, for example, service delivery. Locality development usually requires the establishment of good working relationships among primary groups and, at a later stage, cooperative arrangements with appropriate formal organizations. Policy usually involves the linkage between some larger aggregate (like a legislative body) that takes action for change and formal organizations through which the new mandate is carried out. For administration, the key linkage pattern begins with the formal organization and proceeds to the primary groups that are required to implement organizational changes.

by a more action-oriented strategy of moral confrontations and radicalization (2K), to a planning framework in which a number of interests are represented as negotiations take place (3L), to an administration approach for demonstrating the efficacy of the "liberated values" through testimonials of their worth at staff meetings (1O), and then to a policy initiative in which awards are publicly given to those who exemplify the new values (3N).

The second problem orientation begins not with the mode through which society maintains the status quo, but rather with the mode of intervention to which some change agent or agency is committed. This orientation helps to illustrate the type of strategic configuration which remains within one intervention mode. If an agency is committed to a social action mode, its scenario begins with militance (1A). After a militant demonstration, one moves to a position of bringing values in line with action (2K), and then to a negotiating position (3F). On the other hand, a development-oriented agency, because of its limited resources, usually begins in a group organization phase (1M) and moves through an inducement phase (2H) before coming to an action phase (3C). Planning starts with the calling together of experts (1G), moves to building a power block (2B), and concludes with some representation of all significant interests (3L). Policy typically begins with some sort of legal or quasi-legal initiative (1D), moves to consolidate the new arrangements through providing incentives for continued implementation (2I), and ends with public recognition of those who have demonstrated their commitment to the new regulations (3N). On the other hand, administration starts off with an appeal for support of organizational values (1O). Whether this succeeds or fails, the next step is often one of inducement through remuneration (2J). In the event of failure or partial failure, this approach concludes with a power induction such as suspension of employees who are not following guidelines (3E).

The main point is that one can use either the characteristics of the problem or the type of change agency (action, planning, or development policy, or administration) as a point of departure. In either case, to achieve closure on particular problems, a differential set of strategies needs to be used, perhaps relying on different agencies and different persons at different phases of action. Two elements remain constant in either departure perspective: one is the notion of the means-ends spiral, and the other is that the *beginning* strategy should be articulated with the primary maintenance means (and this initial target of change) in the system.

As always, times of great unrest and turmoil like those in which we live may be regarded primarily as either periods of great danger or of enormous opportunity for change. We are inclined to the latter view and believe that the effective use of strategy is central to the achievement of meaningful social change.

JOHN E. TROPMAN
JOHN L. ERLICH

CHAPTER I

Social Policy

INTRODUCTION

One of the new macro practice perspectives added to this volume is policy practice. For many years the study of social policy in schools of social work focused upon knowledge of extant social policies, what provisions they had, who the beneficiaries were, the history of their development and so on. In recent years, however, the concept of policy practice has developed. Three recent books have crystallized this trend. Jansson's *Theory and Practice of Social Welfare Policy* is a comprehensive discussion of policy practice. Tropman's new work, *Policy Management in the Human Services,* introduces the concept of the policy manager and suggests a range of techniques such an individual would need to have. Pierce's *Policy for the Social Work Practitioner* introduces the idea of policy practice as central to all of social work practice.[1]

These new works emphasize a common theme. First, they reaffirm the idea that policy change is an appropriate target for social work intervention. Secondly, they stress that policy exists at all levels of the social structure. Important as "social" policy has been and remains, social work practitioners should not think that influencing federal legislation is the only appropriate policy target. There is a whole spectrum of "public" policy to be influenced, ranging from the activities of state governments to boards of education, sewer authorities, planning commissions, and city councils in the local community, as well as the plethora of policies passed by other public and

---

[1]Bruce S. Jansson, *Theory and Practice of Social Welfare Policy* (Belmont: Wadsworth, 1984) John E. Tropman, *Policy Management in the Human Services* (New York: Columbia University Press, 1984), and Dean Pierce, *Policy for the Social Work Practitioner* (New York: Longman, 1984).

semipublic bodies. Increasingly, there has been a recognition that private policy is also important in the achievement of social purpose. An important aspect of this recognition has come through a study of fringe benefits. What private organizations do in the fringe benefit area is of crucial importance to the health and welfare of employees.[2] In general, as Pierce points out, policy decision making occurs in all areas where humans interact. It exists in the family (a will, for example), in formal organizations, in the community as well as at the national level. We as social workers need to take policy as a point of departure and seek to change it and improve it at whatever level it is appropriate to do so.

The emerging field of policy practice also emphasizes that policy is written. Hence, policy documents assume new importance and the ability to prepare policy documents is a crucial intellectual skill required of the policy practitioner. On a parallel note, interpersonal skill is also important. The ability to bargain, negotiate, mediate, and handle emerging situations diplomatically is part of the policymaker's stock in trade.

Policy moves through what most authors refer to as a policy cycle. The cycle begins with some kind of needs assessment and moves in a second phase through the preparation of alternatives or options for action. A third phase is often the official decision-making point (board action, for example) followed by a planning phase in which the implications of the decision and more details involving practice instructions are worked out. There is then a programming stage or actual operations period followed by an evaluation and assessment phase. It is at this point that the "loop back" to the needs assessment is completed. Hence, the policy cycle becomes the policy circle. Emphasis is placed not only on the points of crystallization in the cycle but also upon the processes involved as policy documents move through it.

It is impossible to deal with all of those elements in a few selections. Some of the more crucial aspects of the policy process are highlighted here. Pusic's piece, "Social Planning, Social Policy and Political Change," deals with policy at the highest level of society and tries to put the whole matter of social planning/social policy into a social improvement setting, while at the same time raising some questions and pointing to some difficulties in the policy planning process. It also offers an Eastern European perspective that contrasts, in important ways, with views on social policy in the West.

March's piece, "Theories of Choice and Making Decisions," goes to the heart of the policy process. Policy making is, after all, decision making. Theories of decision making or theories of choice are theories of policy making. As we indicated in the section on common elements, practitioners must be aware of the theoretical underpinnings of their work. Few authors better convey this set of theoretical underpinnings than March. It is appropriate to

---

[2]Lawrence S. Root, "Employee Benefits in Income Security: Private Social Policy in the Public Interest," and Susan M. Quattrociocchi, "Fringe Benefits As Private Social Policy," in John E. Tropman, Milan J. Dluhy, and Roger M. Lind (Eds.), *New Strategic Perspectives on Social Policy* (Elmsford, NY: Pergamon Press, 1981).

forewarn the reader that it is a difficult piece, but in our judgment well worth the effort.

Professor Dluhy, a policymaker and academic, outlines some of the key elements in local decision making. Readers will be impressed at the degree of similarity between these elements and national level activities, and will be aware of key points of influence.

In summary, policy practice is coming into its own. Its focus is on the mobilization of ideas and the targeting of new concepts and new perspectives at crucial points in the decision-making process. It deals especially with the documents of decision.[3] Policy practice does not argue that decision is everything. That is one of the reasons that planning, the development of design, monitoring, and the orchestration of citizen support are all part of the total influence process. However, we have tended to ignore, in developing those areas, the decision itself and the process by which decisions are made. Wilbur J. Cohen, former Secretary of the Department of Health, Education and Welfare (now called Health and Human Services) has often quoted his teacher and mentor, John R. Commons, to the effect that if one were forced to choose, it is better to have a poor policy administered by good people than a good policy administered by bad people. Unfortunately this dictum has caused us to focus less on the policy than we should have. The best world is one in which a good policy is administered by good people; Cohen, Commons, and all of us would surely agree with that. Thus we must continually strive.

----

[3]For an especially good discussion of decision documentation at the agency level see John Flynn's new book, *Social Agency Policy: Analysis and Presentation for Community Practice* (Chicago: Nelson Hall, 1985).

13.

Eugen Pusic

SOCIAL PLANNING, SOCIAL POLICY, AND POLITICAL CHANGE

Man's understanding of society has become increasingly free both from self-imposed or society-ordained inhibitions on his thought, and from unrealistic assessments or exaggerated expectations regarding the results of his thought. Breaking through religious dogma, man tended to see society as a free arrangement among its members who, through social contracts of one kind or another, set up the social order of their choice. The negative results of the first of these attempts at social engineering as well as the spectacular advances of the natural sciences—starting from the idea of an objective order of the universe—brought about the great reorientation during the nineteenth century. The emerging social sciences went on a voyage of discovery looking for an objective order in society, an order of "iron laws" with an objective validity comparable to the Newtonian *Philosphiae naturalis principia mathematica.* Their constructions, however dazzling by their intelligence and audacity, were disappointing in their yield of successful predictions or reliable practical applications. Probably it was not only this disappointment but also, again, the further development of the natural sciences toward a relativistic and indeterministic stance that caused the next phase in the evolution of the social sciences during the twentieth century. This phase was a movement toward acceptance of the simultaneous presence of opposites that had traditionally been considered mutually exclusive. Stability and change, differentiation and integration, freedom and regulation were now not only thought to be compatible at one and the same time; they seemed to condition each other to the point where one element of such pairs logically implies the other. To this way of thinking, the iron law and the random event seemed to be essentially of the same order.

Planning in general and social planning in particular belong to this newest epoch of thinking, where calculation and foresight as well as flexible responses to the unexpected belong; both are the essence of the operation. Social planning is pursued in the context of the political system, which is understood as the way of devising norms and methods to allocate opportunities for interest satisfaction on a society-wide basis. The political system, however, changes and some model of these changes is necessary to locate social planning on the continuum of history.

Source: This article was first presented as the Third Annual Allan T. Burns Lecture at the School of Social Service Administration, University of Chicago, October 21, 1980. From Eugen Pusic, "Social Planning, Social Policy and Political Change," *Social Service Review,* Vol. 55, No. 3, pp. 411-418. Reprinted by permission of the publisher and author.

DEVELOPMENT OF POLITICAL SYSTEMS

Simple human communities with rudimentary technology tend to be integrated by solidarity. The intense pressures of environmental uncertainty create, objectively as well as subjectively, an extreme dependence of the individual on the community. The resulting strong internal bonds complement an attitude of isolation from or absolute confrontation with the environment, including other human groups. Essentially, the posture is defensive. This keeps contact with the environment at a minimum and results in inertia, a slowness of development, as the stimulation that would provide the energy for a more accelerated differentiation is lacking.

However, differentiation *is* going on. At a certain point it evolves the specific subsystem of government, a social institution based on the monopoly of organized physical violence that can be maintained continuously over a given territory. The human community or communities living in the territory are integrated into a political commonwealth, a state, by the instrument of political power. The existence or nonexistence of solidarity among the members, or among some of them, is no longer essential to maintain integration. The attitude toward the environment, and first of all toward other states, is still one of confrontation but is no longer necessarily defensive. The system feeling stronger may go on the offensive, seek contacts with the environment—even if only to despoil it. It is turned inward toward maintaining sovereignty over its territorial domain—but also outward, seeking to expand into or to obtain advantages from the environment as well as to attack sources of disturbance to its own

ultrastability in the environment. A state will, for instance, introduce censorship of publications, or quarantine incoming ships, or establish a monopoly of foreign commerce in order to forestall the possible risks of subversion, contagious disease, or economic destabilization. It will in this way increase the frequency of its contacts with its environment, in comparison with the communities integrated on solidarity, and will thereby increase the rate of its own development. But it will also reduce these contacts indiscriminately when they seem to imply a danger to the existing order. In so doing, it will lose the potentially useful components of the banned inputs: stimulation and instruction from publications, the turnover of goods from unloaded ships, the competition from imports—to continue with the above examples.

The differentiation, however, that does take place is pushing the political system beyond integration by the monopoly of organized violence in the hands of the state. Other subsystems develop and take over parts of the task of integration by other methods. In our examples: the educational system is supposed to enable people to judge for themselves; the public health system, to get them to be inoculated against contagious diseases; the system of indirect measures of economic regulation, to protect vulnerable parts of the economy while at the same time stimulating international economic exchange. In other words, new subsystems in society are able to filter out the negative environmental influences while preserving the positive influences, thereby increasing the rate of differentiation and development of the system for a whole order of magnitude. The confrontational attitude toward the environment is gradually being replaced by a readiness for cooperation. These highly complex conditions in a society can be maintained only if a sufficient flow of energy from the environment counteracts entropic processes within the system. The energy balance of the system, however, is influenced not only by this flow inward but also by current requirements of energy expenditure. If disproportionate amounts of energy are needed to achieve the domination of one interest group in society over another, the energy balance will be negatively affected, and a return to the methods of integration by power will be the probable consequence. The whole development toward a postpower society is, therefore, reversible and depends on deliberate policy decisions.

This is where the full significance of social policy becomes apparent. From its modest beginnings in welfare efforts, social policy was oriented toward the neutralization of some of the effects of social stratification and the domination of privileged interest groups over the majority. In its newer stages, as general social policy, it pursues the more ambitious aim of minimizing stratification itself by general measures of income redistribution. This issue is, of course, highly political. In the development of political systems toward some kind of self-regulating state through a dense network of subsystems, general social policy is becoming the essentially political activity of minimizing possibilities of stable interest domination. It is a task that is likely to remain, in the foreseeable future, the key to the development toward postpower societies.

SOCIAL PLANNING WITHIN SOCIAL POLICY

What is the place of social planning within the context of this wider, and more political, understanding of social policy?

In the widest sense, planning at the level of society is a form of social regulation, that is, the exertion of systematic influence on the interests and behavior of people in accordance with socially determined standards. If society is viewed not as a steady state but as a process, planning can be understood as "the guidance of change within a social system."[1]

Social planning is a form of planning where the standards are determined by the prevailing social policy values. Values flow from the overall situation in which people find themselves for a prolonged period of time, and this situation is changing in important ways. The values, therefore, change during development. It is this change that primarily concerns us.

Planning, including social planning, at some point began to be a serious activity of government and is associated with an overall increase in government influence. This form of planning—that is, planning as an act of power, which is sometimes also called directive or normative planning—does increase considerably the already overwhelming power of the state, because it adds to its physical force the power of knowledge, the influence which essential information must necessarily give to those who control it. (In order to produce shoes, you must have leather, energy, machines, and workers. Those who know where these things can be found have information that is essential for the producer of shoes.) Interestingly, though, even in its initial power form, planning reduces the arbitrariness of government by linking governmental action to the objective regularities and material requirements of the processes with which it is concerned. (Whatever

[1] J. Friedmann, "A Conceptual Model for the Analysis of Planning Behavior," *Administrative Science Quarterly* (September 1967), p. 227.

your power, you cannot plan to produce more shoes than will be permitted by the quantity of leather, energy, machines, and workers at your disposal.)

The method used in planning at this early stage is called the method of material balances. This method lists resources and balances the total with the requirements in a process which goes from the periphery to the center in order to return again to the periphery for implementation.

However, the element of objectivity in planning, its link with material and social reality, points beyond power. After all, if it is not possible to plan beyond our resources, then our information about these resources, with all its necessary and sometimes complex details, is in itself sufficient to achieve the coordinating and regulating effect of the plan. Power seems an unnecessary addition.

There is another reason why planning seems not to fit into the structures and processes of government. In its development, for reasons well known, government differentiates into legislative, executive, and judicial functions. To legislate is to express prevailing interests, while the executive branch implements legislation on the basis of its expertise, that is, knowledge or information, without expressing judgments regarding the matters of interest dealt with in the legislative process.

Planning does not fit this distinction. In planning, interest judgments and expert knowledge are so closely interwoven that it is not feasible to separate them and allocate each to a different structure.

In sum, planning, even if born under the star of power, is really not at home in a power system. It points beyond

such a system. It is the first step toward integrating systems by control of information.

THE ROLE OF SOCIAL PLANNING

What role can social planning fill in the differentiated network of social policy instruments of an evolving social policy system?

In such a system there are, first, basic associations of interest solidarity in social matters. In the beginning, these associations are small with a mainly defensive attitude; examples that come to mind are cooperatively built and managed social institutions, and cooperative activities for the protection of children, for assistance to old and sick people, and for mutual assistance in case of need. In time, these grow stronger and are ready to confront on more equal terms those who control their interests, such as associations of small agricultural producers, trade unions, and sometimes churches. The next stage is the development of increasingly comprehensive systems of social insurance—a form of rational rather than emotional solidarity—toward a generalized background system of social security where it is assumed that the collectivity is responsible for guaranteeing the minimum requirements of existence to all its members.

Second, there are organizations of political power centered in locations around the state. The aim of social policy in relation to these organizations is to use their power, first, to maximize chances of equality, by income redistribution, financing social services, legislation of minimal wages, and by the progressive taxation of profits or of inheritance as well as by direct public economic assistance, and second, to minimize the possibilities of interest domination by administrative and court intervention in favor of widows, orphans, the unemployed, the peasants, and workers generally.

Third, developing at the same time as the measures mentioned, are social technology, professional services, and professional organizations which perform these measures on the basis of increasingly complex knowledge and skill, from psychological depth analysis to land-use planning and from the correction of speech defects in children to geriatric psychiatry. The network of organizations and institutions that offer these services is integrated mainly by the differentiated knowledge and specialized information that underlie their methods of work. That means that organizations for social research clarifying the underlying social setting and the configuration of social problems and organizations for the education and training of practitioners in the social services play more important roles in integrating services at this level than do the systems, such as government, to which the institutions may formally be attached.

Social planning may make its first appearance as planning by government, a comprehensive program of measures that the government intends to take in order to achieve social policy aims (e.g., income redistribution, housing construction, price support, public assistance, institutional care, insurance programs, and special care for vulnerable groups). Social planning by government, as does all planning, points beyond government. It has a logic of its own, based on the evolving social situa-tion, the changing needs of the population, the composition of disadvantaged groups, and new possible sources of interest domination.

With the flow of time, as the influence of government on social policy becomes less needed and the network of social service institutions and centers becomes denser, social planning increases in importance.

Large systems in an organizationally dense environment become more and more self-regulated in the sense that the maneuvering space of their elements becomes more and more restricted. That means that they need less and less regulation from the outside on the condition—and it is an important condition—that the interest implications of their self-regulating principle are acceptable to us.

To most classical and neoclassical economists, for instance, economic development from Adam Smith onward was essentially a good thing. As the interests of the entrepreneurs were in themselves conducive to economic development, regulation, as much of it as was necessary, had to follow the current. The idea of the limits of growth, however, leads to different assumptions, and the drive toward economic development is becoming problematic. Regulation based on this idea would be in the incomparably more difficult position of having to regulate "against the current," against the tendency to get richer by producing more.

Can there be a whole society, more and more worldwide, that is self-regulated on the principle of maximizing chances of interest satisfaction and minimizing possibilities of interest domination? That remains to be seen. History speaks against it, but it is a history of scarcity. In the future an economy of abundance may make systematic altruism possible. On the other hand, necessary adaptation to a global limit of resources may pose, more agonizingly than ever before, the questions of who is getting what, when, and how. Looking for a moment at the immediate future, we can see two distinct functions of a social plan. First, we see the cognitive function of collecting and presenting analytically the increasing quantity of information on social needs and available social services, on sources of inequality, and on possibilities of domination. In addition, we must devise a program of measures to relate services to needs and so help counteract the forms of inequality that are most relevant at the moment and the most dangerous tendencies toward stabilizing domination. Second, it is simultaneously the interest function that decides about the priority of needs, evaluates a situation as prejudicial to equality or leading to domination, and transfers the decision to a time when it has not yet become emotionally loaded.

The institutional structures able to carry this sort of social planning will have to perform the following functions:

to mobilize the requisite ability and expertise for the cognitive understanding of social situations and ongoing social processes;

to express adequately the interests involved, primarily the interests of disadvantaged and vulnerable groups;

to provide for a stepwise progress from special to more general levels of planning—local to worldwide, and single institution to internetwork;

to concentrate information but at the same time to decentralize maximally the taking of decisions;

to combine foresight with feedback and the possibility of reacting flexibly to unexpected developments.

All these conditions are most likely to be met at higher levels of development. They will be based on many institutions and structures that are currently in use but will also require many original solutions.

In talking about social planning, we should keep in mind the words of Francis Bacon at the beginning of modern science: "In order to achieve ends that were never before achieved, we have to use means that were never before tried."[2]

---

[2]F. Bacon, *Novum Organon,* bk. 1, aphorism 6.

14.

James G. March

THEORIES OF CHOICE AND MAKING DECISIONS

Actual decision making, particularly in organizations, often contrasts with the visions of decision making implicit in theories of choice. Because our theoretical ideas about choice are partly inconsistent with what we know about human processes of decision, we sometimes fail to understand what is going on in decision making, and consequently sometimes offer less than perfect counsel to decisionmakers. Behavioral research on how decisions are made does not lead to precise prescriptions for the management of choice. It will not tell the president of the United States, the president of Mitsubishi, or the reigning mafioso how to make decisions. Nor will it tell a headmistress of a private academy what she should do as she decides what new programs to offer, whom to hire, what kinds of staff development to authorize, what uniforms to prescribe, what new rooms to build, what kinds of disciplinary procedures to implement, and what kinds of promises to make to what kinds of patrons. However, the research results may contain a few observations that might—when combined with a headmistress's own knowledge and imagination—provide clues of how to think about decision making. In that spirit, this article attempts to summarize some recent work on how decisions are made in or-ganizations. It draws heavily on work I have done jointly with Michael Cohen, Martha Feldman, Johan Olsen, Guje Sevón, and Zur Shapira.

RATIONAL CHOICE

Virtually all of modern economics and large parts of anthropology, psychology, political science, and sociology, as well as the applied fields that build upon them, embrace the idea that human action is the result of human choice. Our theories of human behavior, like our ordinary conversations and our pop visions of ethics, present life as choice, comprehensible and justifiable primarily in terms of decisions made by human actors. Moreover, these theories of choice are theories of willful choice. They presume that choices are made intentionally in the name of individual or collective purpose, and on the basis of expectations about future consequences of current actions. If we wish to understand behavior in such terms, we ask three questions: Who made the decision? What were the decisionmaker's preferences? What expectations did the decisionmaker have about the consequences of the alternatives? If we wish to change behavior, we seek to change the decisionmaker, the preferences, or the expectations.

These two fundamental ideas—that life is choice and that choice is willful—are self-evidently useful ideas. They are as much a part of human history and human culture as the wearing of clothing. To suggest that life is more (or less) than choice and that choice is not always best understood as willful is not to propose the overthrow of Bentham or the restoration of Coleridge, but simply to argue that our ideas of choice, like our clothing, can sometimes get in the way.

Standard theories of choice view decision making as intentional, consequential action based on four things:

- A knowledge of alternatives. Decisionmakers have a set of alternatives for action. These alternatives are defined by the situation and known unambiguously.
- A knowledge of consequences. Decisionmakers know the consequences of alternative actions, at least up to a probability distribution.
- A consistent preference ordering. Decisionmakers have objective functions by which alternative consequences of action can be compared in terms of their subjective value.
- A decision rule. Decisionmakers have rules by which to select a single alternative of action on the basis of its consequences for the preferences.

In the most familiar form of the model, we assume that all alternatives, the probability distribution of consequences conditional on each alternative, and the subjective value of each possible consequence are known; and we assume a choice is made by selecting the alternative with the highest expected value.

The durability of this structure has been impressive. It is also understandable. Simple choice models capture some truth. Demand curves for consumer products generally have negative slopes, and labor unions usually are more resistant to wage cuts than to wage increases. Moreover, the core ideas are flexible. When the model seems not to fit, it is often possible to reinterpret preferences or knowledge and preserve the axioms. Finally, choice is a faith as well as a theory; it is linked to the ideologies of the Enlightenment. The prevalence of willful choice models of behavior in economics, political science, psychology, sociology, linguistics, and anthropology attests to the attractiveness of choice as a vision of human behavior.

The attraction extends to ordinary discourse and journalism. A reading of the leading newspapers or journals of any Western country will show that the primary interpretive model used by individuals in these societies is one of willful choice. The standard explanation provided for the actions of individuals or institutions involves two assertions: Someone decided to have it happen. They decided to have it happen because it was in their self-interest to do so. In cases involving multiple actors, a third assertion may be added: Different people, in their own self-interest, wanted different things and the people with power got what they wanted. Ideas of willful, rational choice are the standard terms of discourse for answering the generic questions: Why did it happen? Why did you do it?

The same basic structure underlies modern decision engineering: Operations analysis, management science, decision theory, and the various other analytical approaches to improving choices are variations on a theme of rational choice, as are standard ideas for determining the value of information and the design of information systems.

These efforts at improving the decisions of individuals and organizations have been helpful. Systematic rational analyses of choice alternatives have improved the blending of aviation fuel, the location of warehouses, the choice of energy sources, and the arrangement of bank queues, as well as providing the solutions to many other decision problems. And although it is also possible to cite examples in which the consequences of decision analysis have been less benign, a balanced judgment must conclude that these modern technologies of choice have done more good than harm.

Within such a framework, the advice we give to a headmistress is straightforward: Determine precisely what your alternatives are. Define clearly what your preferences are. Estimate the possible consequences stemming from each alternative and their likelihood of occurrence. Select the alternative that will maximize the expected value.

This basic theory of choice has been considerably elaborated over the past thirty years with the discovery of computational procedures for solving problems and the development of various more specific models within the general frame. At the same time, empirical research on the ways in which decisions are actually made by individuals and organizations has identified some problems in fitting the standard theory of choice to observed decision behavior.

UNCERTAINTY AND AMBIGUITY

Theories of choice presume two improbably precise guesses about the future: a guess about the future consequences of current actions and a guess about future sentiments with respect to those consequences. Actual decision situations often seem to make both guesses problematic.

The first guess—about the uncertain future consequences of current action—has attracted attention from both students of decision making and choice theorists. In fact, some of the earliest efforts to relate studies of decision making and theories of choice raised questions about the informational assumptions of the theories. Even if decisions are made in a way generally consistent with choice theories— that is, that estimates of the consequences of alternative actions are formed and that action is *intendedly* rational—there are informational and computational limits on human choice. There are limits on the number of alternatives that can be considered, and limits on the amount and accuracy of information that is available. Such a set of ideas leads to the conception of limited rationality for which Herbert Simon received the Nobel Prize in 1978.

The core ideas are elementary and by now familiar. Rather than all alternatives or all information about consequences being known, information has to be discovered through search. Search is stimulated by a failure to achieve a goal, and continues until it reveals an alternative that is good enough to satisfy existing, evoked goals. New alternatives are sought in the neighborhood of old ones. Failure focuses search on the problem of attaining goals that have been violated, success allows search resources to move to other domains. The key scarce resource is attention; and theories of limited rationality are, for the most part, theories of the allocation of attention.

They are also theories of slack—that is, unexploited opportunities, undiscovered economies, waste, etc. As long as performance exceeds the goal, search for new alternatives is modest, slack accumulates, and aspirations increase. When performance falls below the goal, search is stimulated, slack is decreased, and aspirations decrease. This classic control system does two things to keep performance and goals close. First, it adapts goals to performance; that is, decision makers learn what they should expect. At the same time, it adapts performance to goals by increasing search and decreasing slack in the face of failure, by decreasing search and increasing slack when faced with success. To the familiar pattern of fire alarm management are added the dynamics of changes in aspirations and slack buffers.

These ideas have been used to explore some features of adaptation to a changing environment. Decisionmakers appear often to be able to discover new efficiencies in their operations under conditions of adversity. If we assume that decisionmakers optimize, it is not immediately obvious why new economies can be discovered under conditions of adversity if they could not be discovered during good times. The explanation is natural in the slack version of adaptation. During favorable times, slack accumulates. Such slack becomes a reservoir of search opportunities during subsequent periods of trouble. As a result, environmental fluctuations are dampened by the decision process. Such a description seems to provide a partial understanding of the resilience of human institutions in the face of adversity.

Thus, in the case of our headmistress, we would expect that so long as the academy prospered, slack would accumulate. Control over the pursuit of private pleasures by staff members would be relaxed: search for improvements in existing programs would be lackadaisical; discipline would decline. If, on the other hand, a major patron were dissatisfied, or demand for the product weakened, or a loss in quality recorded, then discipline and control would be tightened and search for refinements in existing techniques would be stimulated. As a result, we would probably expect that refinements of existing techniques in the academy, or more energetic performances, would be more likely during times of adversity, but that, because of the extra slack, experiments with unusual new techniques would be more common during times of success.

Partly as a result of such observations by students of decision making, theories of choice have placed considerable emphasis on ideas of search, attention, and information costs in recent years, and these efforts in combination with concern for the problems of incomplete information and transaction costs have turned substantial parts of recent theories of choice into theories of information and attention—tributes to the proposition that information gathering, information processing, and decision making impose heavy demands on the finite capacity of the human organism. Aspiration levels, incrementalism, slack, and satisfaction have been described as sensible under fairly general circumstances.

The second guess—about the uncertain future preferences for the consequences of current actions—has been less considered, yet poses, if anything, greater difficulties. Consider the following properties of preferences as they appear in standard theories of choice:

- Preferences are *absolute*. Theories of choice assume action in terms of preferences; but they recognize neither discriminations among alternative preferences, nor the possibility that a person reasonably might view his own preferences and action based on them as morally distressing.
- Preferences are *stable*. In theories of choice, current action is taken in terms of current preferences. The implicit assumption is that preferences will be unchanged when the outcomes of current actions are realized.
- Preferences are *consistent* and *precise*. Theories of choice allow inconsistency or ambiguity in preferences only insofar as they do not affect choice (i.e., only insofar as they are made irrelevant by scarcity or the specification of tradeoffs).
- Preferences are *exogenous*. Theories of choice presume that preferences, by whatever process they may be created, are not themselves affected by the choices they control.

Each of these features of preference seems inconsistent with observations of choice behavior among individuals and social institutions: not always, but often enough to be troublesome. Individuals commonly find it possible to express both a preference for something and a recognition that the preference is repugnant to moral standards they accept. Choices are often made without much regard for preferences. Human decisionmakers routinely ignore their own, fully conscious preferences in making decisions. They follow rules, traditions, hunches, and the advice or actions of others. Preferences change over time in such a way that predicting future preferences is often difficult. Preferences are inconsistent. Individuals and organizations are aware of the extent to which some of their preferences conflict with others; yet they do little to resolve those inconsistencies. Many preferences are stated in forms that lack precision. And while preferences are used to choose among actions, it is also often true that actions and experience with their consequences affect preferences.

Such differences between preferences as they are portrayed in theories of choice and preferences as they appear in decision making can be interpreted as reflecting some ordinary behavioral wisdom that is not always well accommodated within the theory. Human beings seem to recognize in their behavior that there are limits to personal and institutional integration in tastes. As a result, they engage in activities designed to manage preferences. These activities make little sense from the point of view of a theory that assumes decisionmakers know what they want and will want, or a theory that assumes wants are morally equivalent. But ordinary human actors sense that they might come to want something that they should not, or that they might make unwise choices under the influence of fleeting but powerful desires if they do not act to control the development of unfortunate preferences or to buffer actions from preferences. Like Ulysses, they know the advantages of having their hands tied.

Human beings seem to believe that the theory of choice considerably exaggerates the relative power of a choice based on two guesses compared with a choice that is itself a guess. As observers of the process by which their beliefs have been formed and are consulted, ordinary human beings seem to endorse the good sense in perceptual and moral modesty.

They seem to recognize the extent to which preferences are constructed, or developed, through a confrontation between preferences and actions that are inconsistent with them, and among conflicting preferences. Though they seek some consistency, they appear to see inconsistency as a normal and necessary aspect of the development and clarification of preferences. They sometimes do something for no better reason than that they must, or that someone else is doing it.

Human beings act as though some aspects of their beliefs are important to life without necessarily being consistent with actions, and important to the long-run quality of decision making without controlling it completely in the short run. They accept a degree of personal and social wisdom in simple hypocrisy.

They seem to recognize the political nature of argumentation more clearly and more personally than the theory of choice does. They are unwilling to gamble that God made those people who are good at rational argument uniquely virtuous. They protect themselves from cleverness, in themselves as well as in others, by obscuring the nature of their preferences.

What are the implications for our headmistress? Uncertainty about future consequences (the first guess) and human limitations in dealing with them lead decisionmakers, intelligently, to techniques of limited rationality. But what can a sensible decisionmaker learn from observations of preference ambiguity, beyond a reiteration of the importance of clarifying goals and an appreciation of possible human limits in achieving preference orderliness? Considerations of these complications in preferences, in fact, lead to a set of implications for the management of academies and other organizations, as well as for human choice more generally.

To begin with, we need to reexamine the function of decision. One of the primary ways in which individuals and organizations develop goals is by interpreting the actions they take, and one feature of good action is that it leads to the development of new preferences. As a result, decisions should not be seen as flowing directly or strictly from prior objectives. A headmistress might well view the making of decisions somewhat less as a process of deduction, and somewhat more as a process of gently upsetting preconceptions of what she is doing.

In addition, we need a modified view of planning. Planning has many virtues, but a plan can often be more effective as an interpretation of past decisions than as a blueprint for future ones. It can be used as part of our efforts to develop a new, somewhat consistent theory of ourselves that incorporates our recent actions into some moderately comprehensive structure of goals. A headmistress needs to be tolerant of the idea that the meaning of yesterday's action will be discovered in the experiences and interpretations of today.

Finally, we need to accept playfulness in action. Intelligent choice probably needs a dialectic between reason and foolishness, between doing things for no "good" reason and discovering the reasons. Since the theory and ideology of choice are primarily concerned with strengthening reason, a headmistress is likely to overlook the importance of play.

CONFLICT

Theories of choice either ignore conflict with respect to objectives or assume that the conflict can be resolved by tradeoffs or contracts prior to the making of decisions. Actual decision making frequently involves considerable conflict at all stages.

In standard choice theory, conflict among objectives is treated as a problem in assessing tradeoffs, establishing marginal rates of substitution among goods. The process *within* individuals is mediated by the choice theory analog of the central nervous system: the process *among* individuals is mediated by an explicit or implicit price system. For example, classical theories of the firm assume that markets (particularly labor, capital, and product markets) convert conflicting demands into prices. In this perspective, entrepreneurs are imagined to impose their goals on the organization in exchange for mutually satisfactory wages paid to workers, rent paid to capital, and product quality paid to consumers. Such a process can be treated as yielding a series of contracts by which participants divide decision making into two stages. At the first stage, each individual negotiates the best possible terms for agreeing to pursue another's preferences, or for securing such an agreement from another. In the second stage, individuals execute the contracts. In more sophisticated versions, of course, the contracts are designed so that the terms negotiated at the first stage are self-enforcing at the second.

Seeing participants as having conflicting objectives is a basic feature of political visions of decision making. In political treatments of decision making, however, the emphasis is less on designing a system of contracts between principals and agents, or partners, than it is on understanding a political process that allows decisions to be made without necessarily resolving conflict among the parties. The core ideas are that individuals enter a decision with preferences and resources; each individual uses personal resources to pursue personal gain measured in terms of personal preferences. The usual metaphors are those of politics. There is a metaphor of combat. Disputes are settled by "force," that is, by reference to some measurable property by which individuals can be scaled. Collective decisions are weighted averages of individual desires, where the weights reflect the power distribution among individuals. There is a metaphor of exchange. Disputes are settled by offering or withholding resources and establishing a mutually acceptable structure of prices. Markets facilitate cross-sector-trading (e.g., bribery, blackmail) and encourage pursuit of resources with high exchange value (e.g., the taking of hostages). There is a metaphor of alliance. Disputes are settled by forming teams through exchange agreements and side payments and then engaging in combat. Outcomes are (mostly) clear once the coalition structure is given. The coalition structure is problematic.

In a conflict system, information is an instrument of strategic actors. Information may be false; it is always serving a purpose. Actors may provide accurate information about their preferences; normally they will not, except as a possible tactic. They may provide accurate information about the consequences of possible alternative decisions; normally they will not, except as a possible tactic. As a result, information is itself a game. Except insofar as the structure of the game dictates honesty as a necessary tactic, all information is self-serving. Meaning is imputed to messages on the basis of theories of intention that are themselves subject to strategic manipulation. The result is a complicated concatenation of maneuver in which information has considerably less value than it might be expected to have if strategic considerations were not so pervasive.

Alliances are formed and broken. They represent the heart of many political visions of choice, yet the real world of alliances is unlikely to be as simple as the world of the metaphor. Political alliances involve trades across time in the form of promises and implicit promises. Rarely can the terms of trade be specified with precision. The future occasions are unknown, as are the future sentiments with which individuals will confront them. It is not a world of contracts, but of informal loose understandings and expectations.

Mobilization is important. In order to be active in forming and maintaining a coalition and monitoring agreements within a coalition, it is useful to be present; but attention is a scarce resource, and some potential power in one domain is sacrificed in the name of another. Allies have claims on their time also, and those claims may make their support unreliable at critical moments. To some extent the problems of attention can be managed by making threats of mobilization, or developing fears on the part of others about potential mobilization, or using agents as representatives. However, each of those introduces more uncertainties into the process. The difficulties of mobilization, in fact, are the basis for one of the classic anomalies of organizational behavior—the sequential attention to goals. If all participants were activated fully all of the time, it would not be possible to attend to one problem at one time and another later. Since attention fluctuates, it is possible to sustain a coalition among members who have what appear to be strictly inconsistent objectives.

Political perspectives on organizations emphasize the problems of using self-interested individuals as agents for other self-interested individuals. It is a set of problems familiar to studies of legislators, lawyers, and bureaucrats. If we assume that agents act in their own self-interest, then ensuring that the self-interest of agents coincides with the self-interest of principals becomes a central concern. This has led to extensive discussions of incentive and contractual schemes designed to assure such a coincidence, and to the development of theories of agency. It is clear, however, that principals are not always successful in assuring the reliability of agents. Agents are bribed or coopted. As a result, politics often emphasizes trust and loyalty, in parallel with a widespread belief that they are hard to find. The temptations to revise contracts unilaterally are frequently substantial, and promises of uncertain future support are easily made worthless in the absence of some network of favor giving.

Such complications lead to problems in controlling the implementation of decisions. Decisions unfold through a series of interrelated actions. If all conflicts of interest were settled by the employment contract, the unfolding would present only problems of information and coordination, but such problems are confounded by the complications of unresolved conflict. For example, one complication in control is that the procedures developed to measure performance in compliance with directives involve measures that can be manipulated. Any system of controls involves a system of accounts, and any system of accounts is a roadmap to cheating on them. As a result, control systems can be seen as an infinite game between controllers and the controlled in which advantage lies with relatively full-time players having direct personal interest in the outcomes.

Such features of organizations arise from one very simple modification of classical theories of choice: seeing decisions as being based on unreconciled preferences. It seems hard to avoid the obvious fact that such a description comes closer to the truth in many situations than does one in which we assume a consistent preference function. Somewhat more problematic is the second feature of much of the behavioral study of decision making—the tendency for the political aspects of decision making to be interminable. If it were possible to imagine a two-step decision process in which first we established (through side-payments and formation of coalitions) a set of joint preferences acceptable to a winning coalition and *then* we acted, we could treat the first stage as "politics" and the second as "economics." Such a division has often been tempting (e.g., the distinction between policy making and administration), but it has rarely been satisfactory as a description of decision making. The decisions we observe seem to be infused

with strategic actions and politics at every level and at every point.

An academy, like a business firm or government agency, is a political system of partly conflicting interests in which decisions are made through bargaining, power, and coalition formation. In general, there appear to be a few elementary rules for operating in a political system. Power comes from a favorable position for trading favors. Thus it comes from the possession of resources and the idiosyncrasy of preferences, from valuing things that others do not and having things that others value. If you have valued resources, display them. If you don't have them, get them—even if you don't value them yourself. Grab a hostage. Power comes from a reputation for power. Thus it comes from appearing to get what you want, from the trappings of power, and from the interpretations people make of ambiguous historical events.

Power comes from being trustworthy. Politics is trading favors, and trading favors is a risky game. A first principle of politics is that if everyone is rational, no one can be trusted. A second principle is that someone who never trusts anyone will usually lose because although no rational person can be trusted, some people are innocent and *can* be trusted. Those who, by chance or insight, trust those who can be trusted will have an advantage over those who are unconditionally untrusting. A third principle is that all players will try to look trustworthy even though they are not, in order to be trusted by those people who might become winners (by virtue of being willing to trust some people). A fourth principle is that the only reliable way of appearing to be trustworthy is to be, in fact, trustworthy. Thus all rational actors will be trustworthy most of the time. And so on.

These complications of trust in politics are manifest in the use of that most prototypic of procedures for decision making in political systems—the log-roll. Log-rolls combine individuals with complementary interests. We solicit the support of individuals who are indifferent about a current issue by offering subsequent support on another issue. The training director supports the headmistress's project to expand the gymnasium in return for her approval of a new testing program. But log-rolls are invitations to disappointment. Support that is strategic (as most support in a log-roll is) tends to be narrow. It is possible to organize a coalition for a decision; it is less feasible to assure that all coalition members will be willing to invest equally in coping with post-decision complications that may arise. Perhaps for this reason, studies of coalition formation suggest that log-rolls occur less frequently than would be expected. Although log-rolls among individuals who are indifferent to each other's concerns certainly occur, they appear to be less common than alliances requiring more significant compromises between individuals with overlapping concerns and sentiments of trust. Moreover, when we consider more global understandings over long periods of time and across a wider range of possible agreements, the significance of trustworthiness as a source of power is further enhanced.

RULES

Theories of choice underestimate both the pervasiveness and sensibility of an alternative decision logic—the logic of obligation, duty, and rules. Actual decisions seem often to involve finding the "appropriate" rule as much as they do evaluating consequences in terms of preferences.

Much of the decision making behavior we observe reflects the routine way in which people do what they are supposed to do. For example, most of the time, most people in organizations follow rules even when it is not obviously in their self-interest to do so. The behavior can be viewed as contractual, an implicit agreement to act appropriately in return for being treated appropriately, and to some extent there certainly is such a "contract." But socialization into rules and their appropriateness is ordinarily not a case of willful entering into an explicit contract. It is a set of understandings of the nature of things, of self-conceptions, and of images of proper behavior. It is possible, of course, to treat the word *rule* so broadly as to include any regularity in behavior, and sometimes that is a temptation too great to be resisted. But for the most part, we mean something considerably narrower. We mean regular operating procedures, not necessarily written but certainly standardized, known and understood with sufficient clarity to allow discourse about them and action based on them.

The proposition that organizations follow rules—that much of the behavior in an organization is specified by standard operating procedures—is a common one in the bureaucratic and organizational literature. To describe behavior as driven by rules is to see action as a matching of behavior with a position or situation. The criterion is appropriateness. The terminology is one of duties and roles rather than anticipatory decision making. The contrast can be characterized by comparing the conventional litanies for individual behavior:

Consequential action:
  1. What are my alternatives?
  2. What are my values?
  3. What are the consequences of my alternatives for my values?
  4. Choose the alternative that has the best consequences.

Obligatory action:
  1. What kind of situation is this?
  2. What kind of person am I?
  3. What is appropriate for me in a situation like this?
  4. Do it.

Research on obligatory action emphasizes understanding the kinds of rules that are evoked and used, the ways in which they fit together, and the processes by which they change.

The existence and persistence of rules, combined with their relative independence of idiosyncratic concerns of individuals, make it possible for societies and organizations to function reasonably reliably and reasonably consistently. Current rules store information generated by previous experience and analysis, even though the information cannot easily be retrieved in a form amenable to systematic current evaluation. Seeing rules as coded information invites the questions of the long-run sensibility of rule following and its vulnerability to short-run anomalies. In this way, studies of decision making are connected to some classical puzzles of studies of culture and history, as well as population ecology.

Research on rules in decision making has examined the ways in which rules are learned, applied, and broken by in-

dividual actors, but the major efforts in studies of organizational decision making have been toward understanding some ways in which rules develop. Within this tradition, three major processes are commonly considered.

First, we can imagine an organization or society learning from its experience, modifying the rules for action incrementally on the basis of feedback from the environment. Most experiential learning models are adaptively rational. They allow decision makers to find good, even optimal, rules for most of the choice situations they are likely to face. However, the process can produce some surprises. Learning can be superstitious, and it can lead to local optimums that are quite distant from the global optimum. If goals adapt rapidly to experience, learning what is likely may inhibit discovery of what is possible. If strategies are learned quickly relative to the development of competence, a decisionmaker will learn to use strategies that are intelligent given the existing level of competence, but may fail to invest in enough experience with a suboptimal strategy to discover that it would become a dominant choice with additional competence. Although such anomalies are not likely to be frequent, they are important. They are important in practical terms because they are unanticipated by ordinary ideas of learning. They are important in theoretical terms because they make a useful link between sensible learning of rules and surprising results.

Second, we can see action as driven by an evolving collection of invariant rules. As in the case of experiential learning, choice is dependent upon history, but the mechanism is different. Although individual rules are invariant, the population of rules changes over time through differential survival and reproduction. Evolutionary arguments about the development of decision rules were originally made as justification for assuming that decisionmakers maximize expected utility. The argument was simple: competition for scarce resources resulted in differential survival of decisionmakers depending on whether the rules produced decisions that were, in fact, optimal. Thus, it was argued, we could assume that surviving rules (whatever their apparent character) were optimal. Although the argument has a certain charm to it, most close students of selection models have suggested that selection will not reliably guarantee a population of rules that is optimal at any arbitrary point in time. Not all rules are necessarily good ones, least of all indefinitely. It has been pointed out, for example, that species that disappear were once survivors, and unless selection processes are instantaneous some currently "surviving" rules are in the process of disappearing.

Third, decision making can be seen as reflecting rules that spread through a group of organizations like fads or measles. Decisionmakers copy each other. Contagion is, in fact, much easier to observe than either learning or selection. If we want to account for the adoption of accounting conventions, for example, we normally would look to ways in which standard accounting procedures diffuse through a population of accountants. We would observe that individual accountants adopt those rules of good practice that are certified by professional associations and implemented by opinion leaders.

Insofar as action can be viewed as rule-following, decision making is not willful in the normal sense. It does not stem from the pursuit of interests and the calculation of future consequences of current choices. Rather it comes from matching a changing set of contingent rules to a changing set of situations. The intelligence of the process arises from the way rules store information gained through learning, selection, and contagion, and from the reliability with which rules are followed. The broader intelligence of the adaptation of rules depends on a fairly subtle intermeshing of rates of change, consistency, and foolishness. Sensibility is not guaranteed. At the least, it seems to require occasional deviation from the rules, some general consistency between adaptation rates and environmental rates of change, and a reasonable likelihood that networks of imitation are organized in a manner that allows intelligent action to be diffused somewhat more rapidly and more extensively than silliness.

In these terms, decision making in our headmistress's academy involves a logic of appropriateness. The issue is not what the costs and benefits are of an innovative new idea, but what a good headmistress does in a situation like this. The headmistress's role, like other roles, is filled with rules of behavior that have evolved through a history of experience, New Year's resolutions, and imitation. There are rules about dress and decorum, rules about the treatment of staff members and guests, rules about dealing with grievances, rules about the kinds of equipment that should be provided and how it should be used. People in the organization follow rules: professional rules, social rules, and standard operating procedures. In such a world, some of the most effective ways of influencing decision outcomes involve the relatively dull business of understanding standard operating procedures and systems of accounting and control and intervening unobtrusively to make a particular decision a routine consequence of following standard rules.

DISORDER

Theories of choice underestimate the confusion and complexity surrounding actual decision making. Many things are happening at once: technologies are changing and poorly understood; alliances, preferences, and perceptions are changing; problems, solutions, opportunities, ideas, people, and outcomes are mixed together in a way that makes their interpretation uncertain and their connections unclear.

Decision making ordinarily presumes an ordering of the confusions of life. The classic ideas of order in organizations involve two closely related concepts. The first is that events and activities can be arranged in chains of ends and means. We associate action with its consequences; we participate in making decisions in order to produce intended outcomes. Thus, consequential relevance arranges the relation between solutions and problems and the participation of decisionmakers. The second is that organizations are hierarchies in which higher levels control lower levels, and policies control implementation. Observations of actual organizations suggest a more confusing picture. Actions in one part of an organization appear to be only loosely coupled to actions in another. Solutions seem to have only a modest connection to problems. Policies are not implemented. Decisionmakers seem to wander in and out of decision arenas. In

Ambiguity and Choice in Organizations, Pierre Romelaer and I described the whole process as a funny soccer game: "Consider a round, sloped, multigoal soccer field on which individuals play soccer. Many different people (but not everyone) can join the game (or leave it) at different times. Some people can throw balls into the game or remove them. Individuals, while they are in the game, try to kick whatever ball comes near them in the direction of goals they like and away from goals they wish to avoid."

The disorderliness of many things that are observed in decision making has led some people to argue that there is very little order to it, that it is best described as bedlam. A more conservative position, however, is that the ways in which organizations bring order to disorder is less hierarchical and less a collection of means-ends chains than is anticipated by conventional theories. There is order, but it is not the conventional order. In particular, it is argued that any decision process involves a collection of individuals and groups who are simultaneously involved in other things. Understanding decisions in one arena requires an understanding of how those decisions fit into the lives of participants.

From this point of view, the loose coupling that is observed in a specific decision situation is a consequence of a shifting intermeshing of the demands on the attention and lives of the whole array of actors. It is possible to examine any particular decision as the seemingly fortuitous consequence of combining different moments of different lives, and some efforts have been made to describe organizations in something like that cross-sectional detail. A more limited version of the same fundamental idea focuses on the allocation of attention. The idea is simple. Individuals attend to some things, and thus do not attend to others. The attention devoted to a particular decision by a particular potential participant depends on the attributes of the decision and alternative claims on attention. Since those alternative claims are not homogeneous across participants and change over time, the attention any particular decision receives can be both quite unstable and remarkably independent of the properties of the decision. The same decision will attract much attention, or little, depending on the other things that possible participants might be doing. The apparently erratic character of attention is made somewhat more explicable by placing it in the context of multiple, changing claims on attention.

Such ideas have been generalized to deal with flows of solutions and problems, as well as participants. In a garbage-can decision process it is assumed that there are exogenous, time-dependent arrivals of choice problems, solutions, and decision makers. Problems and solutions are attached to choices, and thus to each other, not because of their inherent connections in a means-ends sense, but in terms of their temporal proximity. The collection of decision makers, problems, and solutions that come to be associated with a particular choice opportunity is orderly—but the logic of the ordering is temporal rather than hierarchical or consequential. At the limit, for example, almost any solution can be associated with almost any problem—provided they are contemporaries.

The strategies for a headmistress that can be derived from this feature of decision making are not complicated. First,

persist. The disorderliness of decision processes and implementation means that there is no essential consistency between what happens at one time or place and what happens at another, or between policies and actions. Decisions happen as a result of a series of loosely connected episodes involving different people in different settings, and they may be unmade or modified by subsequent episodes. Second, have a rich agenda. There are innumerable ways in which disorderly processes will confound the cleverest behavior with respect to any one proposal, however important or imaginative. What such processes cannot do is frustrate large numbers of projects. Third, provide opportunities for garbage-can decisions. One of the complications in accomplishing things in a disorderly process is the tendency for any particular project to become intertwined with other issues simply by virtue of their simultaneity. The appropriate response is to provide irrelevant choice opportunities for problems and issues; for example, discussions of long-run plans or goals.

SYMBOLS

Theories of choice assume that the primary reason for decision making is to make choices. They ignore the extent to which decision making is a ritual activity closely linked to central Western ideologies of rationality. In actual decision situations, symbolic and ritual aspects are often a major factor.

Most theories of choice assume that a decision process is to be understood in terms of its outcome, that decision-makers enter the process in order to affect outcomes, and that the point of life is choice. The emphasis is instrumental; the central conceit is the notion of decision significance. Studies of decision arenas, on the other hand, seem often to describe a set of processes that make little sense in such terms. Information that is ostensibly gathered for a decision is often ignored. Individuals fight for the right to participate in a decision process, but then do not exercise the right. Studies of managerial time persistently indicate very little time spent in making decisions. Rather, managers seem to spend time meeting people and executing managerial performances. Contentiousness over the policies of an organization is often followed by apparent indifference about their implementation.

These anomalous observations appear to reflect, at least in part, the extent to which decision processes are only partly—and often almost incidentally—concerned with making decisions. A choice process provides an occasion:

- for defining virtue and truth, during which decision makers discover or interpret what has happened to them, what they have been doing, what they are going to do, and what justifies their actions.
- for distributing glory or blame for what has happened; and thus an occasion for exercising, challenging, or reaffirming friendship or trust relationships, antagonisms, power or status relationships.
- for socialization, for educating the young.
- for having a good time, for enjoying the pleasures connected with taking part in a choice situation.

In short, decision making is an arena for symbolic action, for developing and enjoying an interpretation of life and one's position in it. The rituals of choice infuse participants with an appreciation of the sensibility of life's arrangements. They tie routine events to beliefs about the nature of things. The rituals give meaning, and meaning controls life. From this point of view, understanding decision making involves recognizing that decision outcomes may often be less significant than the ways in which the process provides meaning in an ambiguous world. The meanings involved may be as grand as the central ideology of a society committed to reason and participation. They may be as local as the ego needs of specific individuals or groups.

Some treatments of symbols in decision making portray them as perversions of decision processes. They are presented as ways in which the gullible are misled into acquiescence. In such a portrayal, the witch doctors of symbols use their tricks to confuse the innocent, and the symbolic features of choice are opiates. Although there is no question that symbols are often used strategically, effective decision making depends critically on the legitimacy of the processes of choice and their outcomes, and such legitimacy is problematic in a confusing, ambiguous world. It is hard to imagine a society with modern ideology that would not exhibit a well-elaborated and reinforced myth of choice, both to sustain social orderliness and meaning and to facilitate change.

The orchestration of choice needs to assure an audience of two essential things: first, that the choice has been made intelligently, that it reflects planning, thinking, analysis, and the systematic use of information; second, that the choice is sensitive to the concerns of relevant people, that the right people have had a word in the process. For example, part of the drama of organizational decision making is used to reinforce the idea that managers (and managerial decisions) affect the performance of organizations. Such a belief is, in fact, difficult to confirm using the kinds of data routinely generated in a confusing world. But the belief is important to the functioning of a hierarchical system. Executive compensation schemes and the ritual trappings of executive advancement reassure managers (and others) that an organization is controlled by its leadership, and appropriately so.

Thus, by most reasonable measures, the symbolic consequences of decision processes are as important as the outcome consequences; and we are led to a perspective that challenges the first premise of many theories of choice, the premise that life is choice. Rather, we might observe that life is not primarily choice; it is interpretation. Outcomes are generally less significant—both behaviorally and ethically—than process. It is the process that gives meaning to life, and meaning is the core of life. The reason that people involved in decision making devote so much time to symbols, myths, and rituals is that we (appropriately) care more about them. From this point of view, choice is a construction that finds its justification primarily in its elegance, and organizational decision making can be understood and described in approximately the same way we would understand and describe a painting by Picasso or a poem by T. S. Eliot.

As a result, a headmistress probably needs to see her activities as somewhat more dedicated to elaborating the processes of choice (as opposed to control-

ling their outcomes), to developing the ritual beauties of decision making in a way that symbolizes the kind of institution her academy might come to be. Just as educational institutions have libraries and archives of manuscripts to symbolize a commitment to scholarship and ideas, so also they have decision processes that express critical values. For example, if an important value of an organization is client satisfaction, then the decision process should be one that displays the eagerness of management to accept and implement client proposals, and one that symbolizes the dedication of staff to principles of availability and service.

INFORMATION AND IMPLICATIONS

These observations on decision making and theories of choice are not surprising to experienced decision-makers. But they have some implications, one set of which can be illustrated by examining a classical problem: the design of an information system in an organization. In the case of our headmistress, there are issues of what information to gather and store, which archives to keep and which to burn, what information to provide to potential contributors, and how to organize the records so they are easily accessible to those who need them.

In most discussions of the design of information systems in organizations, the value of information is ordinarily linked to managerial decision making in a simple way. The value of an information source depends on the decisions to be made, the precision and reliability of the information, and the availability of alternative sources. Although calculating the relevant expected costs and returns is rarely trivial, the framework suggests some very useful rules of thumb. Don't pay for information about something that cannot affect choices you are making. Don't pay for information if the same information will be freely available anyway before you have to make a decision for which it is relevant. Don't pay for information that confirms something you already know. In general, we are led to an entirely plausible stress on the proposition that allocation of resources to information gathering or to information systems should depend on a clear idea of how potential information might affect decisions.

A notable feature of the actual investments in information and information sources that we observe is that they appear to deviate considerably from these conventional canons of information management. Decisionmakers and organizations gather information and do not use it; ask for more, and ignore it; make decisions first, and look for the relevant information afterwards. In fact, organizations seem to gather a great deal of information that has little or no relevance to decisions. It is, from a decision theory point of view, simply gossip. Were one to ask why organizations treat information in these ways, it would be possible to reply that they are poorly designed, badly managed, or ill-informed. To some extent, many certainly are. But the pervasiveness of the phenomenon suggests that perhaps it is not the decisionmakers who are inadequate, but our conceptions of information. There are several sensible reasons why decisionmakers deal with information the way they do.

Decisionmakers operate in a surveillance mode more than they do in a problem-solving mode. In contrast to a theory of information that assumes that information is gathered to resolve a choice among alternatives, decisionmakers scan their environments for surprises and solutions. They monitor what is going on. Such scanning calls for gathering a great deal of information that appears to be irrelevant to "decisions." Moreover, insofar as decisionmakers deal with problems, their procedures are different from those anticipated in standard decision theory. They characteristically do not "solve" problems; they apply rules and copy solutions from others. Indeed, they often do not recognize a "problem" until they have a "solution."

Decisionmakers seem to know, or at least sense, that most information is tainted by the process by which it is generated. It is typically quite hard to disaggregate social belief, including expert judgment, into its bases. The social process by which confidence in judgment is developed and shared is not overly sensitive to the quality of judgment. Moreover, most information is subject to strategic misrepresentation. It is likely to be presented by someone who is, for personal or subgroup reasons, trying to persuade a decisionmaker to do something. Our theories of information-based decision making (e.g., statistical decision theory) are, for the most part, theories of decision making with innocent information. Decision information, on the other hand, is rarely innocent, and thus rarely as reliable as an innocent would expect.

Highly regarded advice is often bad advice. It is easy to look at decisionmaking and find instances in which good advice and good information were ignored. It is a common occurrence. Consequently, we sometimes see decisionmakers as perversely resistant to advice and information. In fact, much highly regarded advice and much generally accepted information is misleading. Even where conflict of interest between advice givers and advice takers is a minor problem, advice givers typically exaggerate the quality of their advice: and information providers typically exaggerate the quality of their information. It would be remarkable if they did not. Decisionmakers seem to act in a way that recognizes the limitations of "good" advice and "reliable" information.

Information is a signal and symbol of competence in decision making. Gathering and presenting information symbolizes (and demonstrates) the ability and legitimacy of decisionmakers. A good decisionmaker is one who makes decisions in a proper way, who exhibits expertise and uses generally accepted information. The competition for reputations among decisionmakers stimulates the overproduction of information.

As a result of such considerations, information plays both a smaller and a larger role than is anticipated in decision theory-related theories of information. It is smaller in the sense that the information used in decision making is less reliable and more strategic than is conventionally assumed, and is treated as less important for decision making. It is larger in the sense that it contributes not only to the making of decisions but to the execution of other managerial tasks and to the broad symbolic activities of the individual and organization.

If it is possible to imagine that life is not only choice but also interpretation, that they are heavily intertwined, and that the management of life and organizations is probably as much the latter as the former, it is possible to sketch some

elements of the requirements for the design of useful management information systems.

We require some notion of the value of alternative information sources that is less tied to a prior specification of a decision (or class of decisions) than to a wide spectrum of possible decisions impossible to anticipate in the absence of the information; less likely to show the consequences of known alternatives for existing goals than to suggest new alternatives and new objectives; less likely to test old ideas than to provoke new ones; less pointed toward anticipating uncertain futures than toward interpreting ambiguous pasts. Such a view of information is associated classically with literature, art, and education; and if there are appropriate models for a management information system of this sort, perhaps they lie in discussions of education and criticism rather than in theories of decision.

To describe information management in such terms is, of course, to glorify it. It suggests that office memoranda might be viewed as forms of poetry and staff meetings as forms of theater, and we may perhaps wonder whether it would be better to admit a distinction between a sales chart and a Van Gogh painting—if only to assure that each may achieve its unique qualities. Yet the vision has a certain amount of charm to it. At least, it seems possible that with a little imagination here and there, educational philosophy and literary criticism might be used to help management information systems achieve a useful level of irrelevance.

More generally, research on how organizations make decisions leads us to a perspective on choice different from that provided by standard theories of choice, and may even provide some hints for an academy headmistress. The ideas are incomplete; the hints are rough. They point toward a vision of decision making that embraces the axioms of choice but acknowledges their limitations; that combines a passion for the technology of choice with an appreciation of its complexities and the beauties of its confusions; and that sees a headmistress as often constrained by sensibility and rules, but sometimes bouncing around a soccer field.

15.

Milan J. Dluhy

HOMELESSNESS AS A PUBLIC CONCERN: HOW TO DEVELOP A COMMUNITY APPROACH TO SOLVING THE PROBLEM

Historically, the 1980s will be remembered as the decade when substantial economic and social transformations took place in the United States, but it will also be remembered as a time when the problem of homelessness resurfaced as a major social concern just as it had been in the Great Depression.[1] There has been a mythology developed about who the homeless are and these images have persisted well beyond the reality of the actual situation of the homeless today. The stereotype is that the homeless are derelicts, end-stage alcoholics, lazy, crazy, or doped but, above all, individuals who freely choose their lifestyle to avoid the responsibility of the real world.[2] Today, they seem to be everywhere; in doorways, sleeping in the parks, wandering around in the public libraries, pushing shopping carts around in the street, and even roaming around the suburban shopping malls. Most of us avoid them physically while putting them out of our minds psychologically. We even try to rationalize away the conditions which cause their existence. In short, the image is a negative one and the individual, for the most part, is viewed as "undeserving" and worthy of only modest charity. If charity is given, it must be accompanied by the appropriate behavior on the part of the homeless individual. This behavior must demonstrate docility, gratefulness, guilt, politeness, and above all passivity.[3] Those who are assertive, loud, nondeferential, and bold will be denied the charitable gift.

Today's reality, however, is that many homeless do not fit this image because they may be: young, economically dis-

Source: This article was written expressly for this book and is reproduced by permission of the author.

[1]M. Robertson, *The Homeless of Los Angeles County* (Los Angeles: U.C.L.A. Press, 1985).

[2]R. Caulk, *The Homeless Poor* (Multnomah County, OR, 1984).

[3]M. Stern, "The Emergence of the Homeless As A Public Problem," *Social Services Review* (June 1984), pp. 291-301.

placed workers; women and children who have been victims of domestic violence or family breakups; severely mentally incapacitated individuals who have had periodic contacts with psychiatric facilities; or individuals and families who merely have insufficient resources to secure affordable housing.[4] In these cases, the images are more positive in that the individuals or families are more "deserving" and perhaps even entitled to help. The conditions which produced their homelessness may even be beyond their control. If the conditions are viewed in this way, help could be immediate, swift, and with no strings attached.

There is no doubt that the level of interest in the homeless today is high and most experts agree that the number is growing.[5] Because of these growing numbers and because some of the homeless appear to be more "deserving" than those of the past, communities show signs of being more interested in solving the problem than ever before. Major efforts to solve the problem have been undertaken in the last five years in such cities as Baltimore, Boston, Chicago, Detroit, Los Angeles, Milwaukee, Minneapolis, New York, Philadelphia, Phoenix, Pittsburgh, Portland, San Diego, the state of Ohio, and Washington, D.C. (See References at the end of the article). Partly because the issue of homelessness is so emotionally charged and value laden, communities need to develop a sound approach for solving the problem. The approach should be one which is deliberative, well informed, and part of a larger attempt to increase the community's understanding and awareness of this vexing problem. The purpose of this article will be to provide the reader with some background information on the problem of homelessness, but the central concern will be to outline how human service professionals can organize and present information to communities struggling with the problem so that these communities can develop the most reasonable solutions to fit their local circumstances. If there is any one overall observation about the problem of homelessness in the United States, it is that the problem and its causes vary enough across communities to justify a strategy that carefully assesses and evaluates the local situation and develops solutions which are responsive to local reality and not national stereotypes of the problem and its causes.

THE CONTEXT OF THE PROBLEM

A number of important trends in the 1980s in American society have contributed to the increases in homeless individuals and families. While there has been some disagreement about which trends have been the most pervasive, most commentators agree that in the last decade there has been:

1. An acute shortage of rental housing for low income people.
2. A steady deinstitutionalization of people from state mental hospitals and correction facilities who have not found permanent homes.
3. Major cutbacks in housing and social services programs that would

---

[4]U.S. Department of Housing and Urban Development, *Report to the Secretary on the Homeless and Emergency Shelters* (Washington, DC: GPO, 1984).

[5]E.L. Bassuk, "The Homeless Problem," *Scientific American,* 251 (1984), pp. 40-45.

have kept many people off the streets.

4. A continued increase in the number of family breakups and the number of victims of domestic violence and these groups are continually searching for low cost housing.

5. A consistently high unemployment rate among minorities and low skilled workers which has caused many to live on the streets for longer periods of time.[6,7,8]

Public concern with the homeless began to crystallize in the early 1980s. The establishment of the National Coalition for the Homeless in New York and the 1981 court decision which forced localities in New York State to provide decent shelters for the homeless gave advocates in the political arena new hope.[9] In December 1982, the U.S. House Subcommittee on Housing and Community Development convened comprehensive hearings on the problem and received testimony from across the country. Because of the national interest in the issue, the U.S. Department of Housing and Urban Development completed a major national study of the problem in 1984. As noted above, many of the larger cities also set up Task Forces to study the problem and bring back recommendations. By 1985, the homeless issue was clearly on the political agenda. Each winter, most newspapers ran accounts of the homeless and brought their plight to the attention of the public.[10,11,12] With the escalation of the issue came some troubling, and to date, unanswered questions. First, do we have an accurate count of how many homeless there are and what the major causes of their situation are? Second, who should take responsibility for the homeless: the federal government, state governments, local governments, nonprofit organizations, others? Third, are the homeless "deserving" or "undeserving" and how much help should they be given? In this context, the critical question is whether they are entitled to help, as we do with other government entitlement programs, or whether the help should follow the traditional norms of charity and the gift relationship[13]? Finally, and most importantly, are the solutions we are seeking short term and temporary or long term and permanent?

In 1986, these questions remain with us and while there has been some attention to the problem at the national level, it is more reasonable to expect that the major initiatives will come from local communities. This is the case largely because in an era of shrinking federal resources and large public deficits, it is perhaps unrealistic politically to expect major national action. Accepting this premise, the critical concern then is how communities can intelligently develop an approach to solving this problem.

[6]K. Hopper, *One Year Later: The Homeless Poor in New York City* (New York: Community Service Society of New York, 1982).

[7]S. Kondratas, *A Strategy for Helping America's Homeless* (Washington, DC: The Heritage Foundation, 1985).

[8]U.S. Department of Housing and Urban Development, op. cit.

[9]T. Main, "The Homeless of New York," *The Public Interest,* 72 (1983), pp. 33-38.

[10]T. Fitzgerald, "Unmet Needs of the Homeless," *The Ann Arbor News* (Feb. 10, 1985).

[11]J. Leen, "Miami Doesn't Spare A Dime for the Homeless," *The Miami Herald* (Jan. 5, 1986).

[12]E. Zorn, "Headaches and Heartaches," *The Chicago Tribune* (Jan. 18, 1985).

[13]Stern, op. cit.

ORGANIZING AND PRESENTING INFORMATION TO COMMUNITIES

Increased community awareness and education is the fundamental goal underlying the following approach. To facilitate this goal, the approach should:

1. Identify critical assumptions.
2. Clarify key terms and concepts.
3. Review research findings on the problem.
4. Conduct a population count and develop a useful typology of the homeless.
5. Isolate key issues that need to be resolved.
6. Array a set of options or solutions for solving the problem.
7. Suggest a process for developing a comprehensive community response to the problem.

The human service professional's role in this approach is to help communities make a decision, not make the decision for them. Therefore, the professional should take the position that developing accurate information about the problem and facilitating an open community debate about it will produce the best results in the long run.

Identify Critical Assumptions. It is essential to convey to the community that some assumptions about the problem and its solution should be made from the beginning so that only constructive solutions are developed. The most important assumptions are that:

The homeless contain various subpopulations which need different facilities and services; therefore no single strategy will work.

The homeless do not prefer the street to coming indoors; therefore strategies which facilitate street life should be avoided.

There is a need for outreach to help the homeless since many will not voluntarily seek treatment; therefore strategies which emphasize trust and rapport over many months are preferred.

The goal of permanent placement of the homeless should be pursued under all circumstances; short-term strategies should be integrated into a long-term plan for the resolution of the problem.

A community-wide solution is always preferable; no single agency, organization, or church should be expected to solve the problem on their own.

It is wise to review these assumptions with community groups and key actors so that there is a common understanding about how solutions will be developed. In this case, only solutions which are multifaceted, aimed at getting people off the streets, oriented toward treatment and permanent resolution of the problem, and community wide in scope will be considered. In short, the community should buy into these assumptions right from the start.

Clarify Key Terms and Concepts. A homeless person is by choice or circumstance an individual who is without a permanent residence at any one point in time. A critical distinction, however, is whether the homeless individual is a long term, episodic, or transitional one. It is important that communities understand how many of the homeless population can be defined as:

Long-term homeless, with no permanent residence, and where the condition of homelessness persists for more than a year.

Episodic homeless, where the condition of homelessness is less than a year but it happens one other time during the year.

Transitional homeless, where the condition of homelessness is less than a year but there is no previous history of it.

The reason this distinction is critical is because each type of situation will require a somewhat different combination of strategies for solution. The long-term homeless person is often in the final stage in a lifelong series of crises and missed opportunities which culminate in a gradual disengagement from supportive relationships and institutions.[14] This group is hard to reach and difficult to rehabilitate. The episodic and transitional homeless represent groups which are easier to reach, and, in most cases, easier to help. The key is to get community groups to differentiate between the kinds of homelessness that occur. Beyond this, there is a whole vocabulary that a community and its leaders must master to be able to develop constructive solutions. This vocabulary includes many of the governmental and nonprofit programs that currently exist and could be used to help the homeless. A selected glossary with some of these key terms is included as an appendix to this article. The community groups and key actors dealing with the problem should be given this glossary of terms and it should be reviewed with them so that the existing safety net of programs and services is well understood. Further, the options section discussed below as-

sumes an understanding of these basic terms and programs.

Review Research Findings on the Problem. Most community groups and key actors at the outset will ask what is known about the problem, given the experiences of other communities and research on the topic. Below are some of the consistent findings on the homeless. It should be emphasized that each community is likely to deviate somewhat from the core knowledge and description we have of the homeless because of local circumstances. For example, New York appears to have a higher percentage of deinstitutionalized mentally ill than most cities, Phoenix and Portland have homeless populations which contain high percentages of people from other parts of the country, while Pittsburgh, Philadelphia, Minneapolis, and Baltimore have homeless who are predominantly indigenous, and Los Angeles and Chicago contain higher percentages of homeless who are minorities and who are also looking for employment. These kinds of variations make the subpopulations to be helped quite different and skew the solutions toward strategies that work best with each type of group. Beyond stressing the important deviations, it is essential to review the core knowledge we do have about the homeless in this country. Some of the more important findings to share with the communities working on the problem are:

The number of homeless is on the rise nationally and no major city seems to be immune from the problem.

Accurate estimates of homeless are hard to come by, but some research indicates that shelters only serve about 10% of the estimated need and therefore only a small number of

---

[14]Bassuk, op. cit.

homeless come into contact with shelter programs.

Most organized programs seek permanent placements for the homeless.

The probability for successful placements are higher for: economically indigent but high functioning people; the elderly, chronically mentally ill or physically disabled who qualify for AFDC, SSI, or Social Security; younger alcoholics/drug dependent under 30; and women who have been victims of domestic violence. In turn, the probability for successful placements are lower or close to zero for: former mental patients who are not in contact currently with the Community Mental Health (CMH) system and who do not qualify for any benefits except general assistance (GA); older alcoholics/drug dependent; and the classic street person who by choice avoids any structured living environment and can be labeled as the long term homeless.

The hardest to place do not like to use formal referral systems, they prefer to use an informal referral network or grapevine. They generally avoid bureaucracies and any situation they view as a hassle.

The homeless are more likely to be men than women (80% vs. 20%).

The homeless who are victims of natural disasters, sexual assaults, or other temporary hardships are generally served quite well by the existing social service system.

The homeless indicate few social supports that they can rely on.

The homeless indicate higher use of alcohol and drugs than the normal population.

The homeless report poorer physical health and mental health than the normal population.

The homeless are more dissatisfied with life than the normal population.

The homeless are fairly young; a substantial majority are under 40 and many are under 25.

Conduct a Population Count and Develop a Useful Typology. The next step for a community is to examine its own circumstances carefully. While some communities have devised elaborate schemes for measuring the extent of the problem,[15] most communities have used a combination of techniques to identify the number and causes of homelessness. The most frequently used techniques are:

Interviews and counts within shelters.

Interviews with social service providers and other key informants.

Participant observation.

Single day counts and interviews on the street.

Sample counts and interviews in a combination of places the homeless are thought to be, like shelters, jails, hotels, flophouses, soup kitchens, parks, streets, bars, libraries, etc.

Once the survey of the homeless population has been completed, a carefully constructed typology of the subpopulations should be developed for service planning purposes. Based on already published studies, the typology in Table 15.1 demonstrates the way in which information can be presented to a community. Table 15.1 gives rough estimates of the percentages of homeless in each category, but it should be stressed that while each community

---

[15]C. Concord, *Listening To The Homeless* (Milwaukee, WI: Human Services Triangle, 1985).

TABLE 15.1 - TYPOLOGY OF "HOMELESS"
Individuals Based on Shelter Population Counts
(These are rough estimates only from research studies)

Category By Primary Problem	Characteristics	Possible Solutions	Estimated Percentages
Psychiatric Disorder	low/moderate functioning mean age 35 disproportionately men past hospitalization behavioral problems unemployable	County Infirmary Foster Care Social Services	34%
Alcohol or Drug Dependent	low/moderate functioning mean age 40 disproportionately men physically violent contacts with law marginally employable	County Infirmary Foster Care Social Services	8% (hard core) higher if usage is criteria

Economically Indigent	high functioning
	mean age 31, although
	  large % 18-25
	employment histories
	  (discouraged workers)
	family connections
	minority
		Vouchers
		Home sharing
		Social Services
		Permanent
		  placement
			19%

Physical Disability	moderate functioning mean age 49 disproportionately men few family connections unemployable	Foster Care County Infirmary Home sharing Social Services	3%
Runaway Youth	high functioning 13-18 estranged from family little employment history contacts with law	Shelter Social Security Foster Care Permanent placement	1% but varies by availability of youth group homes
Victims of Domestic Violence	high functioning mean age 28 women little employment history few family connections	Shelter Social Services Vouchers Home sharing Permanent placement	1% but varies by availability of women's shelters
Classic Street Person or Other (Unclassified)	moderate functioning alcohol/drug use disproportionately men nomadic by choice no family connections employable but irregular history mean age 35; anti-rules	Shelter Voucher Social Services Home sharing?	34-40% estimates vary considerably, hardest to classify

may have some of each type, the actual percentage in each category will vary from community to community. The purpose of the typology is to get the community to think about possible combinations of solutions for each subpopulation.

Isolate Key Issues That Need to be Resolved. While there will be many issues that the community will confront in developing solutions to the problem, the experience of other communities suggests that certain issues inevitably surface. These issues are indicated below so that the human service professional can help the community to resolve them.

Does the community want to use a rehabilitation strategy or a traditional welfare strategy? The former seeks to change the potential functioning of individuals and is always aimed at promoting independent living. The latter is a maintenance strategy which accepts current lifestyles and does not seek to change people.

Since the homeless population is heterogeneous, what mixes of these individuals in living situations should be avoided or how many different types of facilities/placements are necessary to avoid the negative consequences of mixing?

How much time should elapse before someone is classified as long-term homeless, opposed to temporarily homeless? This will establish the kind and amount of assistance someone may receive.

Should temporary shelters and other longer term placements have work requirements for those capable of working?

The resolution of these issues will allow the community to design a reasonable strategy. Therefore, substantial dialogue on each issue should be encouraged. The professional should seek clarity and ultimately resolution of these issues before proceeding with the development of options.

Array a Set of Options or Solutions for Solving the Problem. Now the construction of alternatives or solutions to the problem can take place. Table 15.2 illustrates a format for laying out some of the options. Each option should be described, its cost estimated, its advantages and disadvantages discussed, and finally the subpopulations that would benefit from each option should be made clear.

Suggest a Process for Developing a Comprehensive Response to the Problem. The final step is to lay out a time frame for problem resolution. To this point, the steps indicate the organization and presentation of information to the community and its key actors. Most communities are likely to establish a special task force to work on the problem. Assuming that the preceding steps and sharing of information discussed above has been done with the task force, the final step should be involvement of the broader community. In order to do this, the task force should produce a report which includes information on: assumptions; key terms and concepts; research findings; a typology of the homeless; key issues; options and solutions; and recommendations.

At this point, a community-wide forum for discussion of the report should be planned. Reactions to the report should be encouraged and testimony should be recorded. Next a new

TABLE 15.2 - CRITICAL OPTIONS TO CONSIDER IN RESOLVING THE PROBLEM

Option	Brief Description	Cost	Advantages/ Disadvantages	Potential Beneficiaries
County Infirmary	Highly structured environment For ambulatory persons Some social services Serves semi-permanent group Half self paying or GA	Estimated to be about $6000-$9000 per bed per year	Location is problem Heavy initial capital needed Compete with nursing homes Population mix problematic	Psychiatric disorders Drug dependent Aged Physical disability
Emergency Shelter	Moderately structured environment For ambulatory persons Some social services Serves transient, chronic homeless	Comparable to infirmary depending on services offered	Separating people who are temporarily homeless from those who are chronically homeless	Street people Runaways Economically indigent
Discretionary Grant Program	Entertain proposals from agencies who will either run a shelter program or administer a voucher system	Estimated to be $2000-$3000 per person per year	Can be coordinated with FEMA, city, other funds. Provides incentives to voluntary sector to develop programs	All types if programs develop to serve different population groups
Reference or Counseling Bureau	Individual calls hotline for wide range of housing assistance, screening is done, referral is made to appropriate agency, program, shelter. Also advocate for increased housing in community.	$100,000 per year but HUD may pay 25% of cost	Can expedite a person qualifying for entitlements or other aid. Can screen and make referral in centralized, efficient way.	All types
Home Sharing Program	More limited version of the Reference Bureau Focused only on high functioning people who seek shared living situation	$30,000 per year	Can potentially be useful but never for more than a small % of the "Homeless" population	High functioning, willing to share a home

group should be established to implement the recommendations of the report and any changes in the report stemming from the community-wide forum. This implementation group consisting of community people should include decision makers from the government and the nonprofit sector as well as community influentials generally. The composition of the implementation group should be carefully thought through, and it should include people who have the capacity to deliver the resources necessary to implement the recommendations. The implementation group should stress implementing deadlines. Finally, a watchdog advocacy group should remain in existence in order to monitor progress.

CONCLUSION

This article has stressed how information can be organized and presented to a community in order to help that community solve the problem of homelessness. The key points are that a community-based approach should be knowledge-driven in order to maximize community awareness and understanding. A knowledge-driven approach will also minimize, though perhaps not eliminate, conventional and traditional stereotypes of the homeless problem and its solution. Second, the community-based approach should set up a deliberate timetable and a plan for the resolution of the problem. Finally, the human service professional can aid in this community-based approach by providing accurate information, organizing it in a way that facilitates decision making, and by following up and following through on the implementation timetable. In the end,

communities can take pride in solving their own problems rather than passing the problems on to another level of government or by passing the responsibility for those problems back to the victims of homelessness themselves.

GLOSSARY

Homeless. Whether by choice or circumstance, an individual without a permanent address or residence.

Expediter. Person, organization, or governmental unit which speeds up the progress or hastens the solution of the problem.

Ambulatory. Capable of walking or using a wheelchair, not confined to bed.

County Infirmary. Used to be county poorhouses or farms in 19th century. Today they may house the homeless in many communities. Some are relatively new, while others are renovated and very old buildings.

General Assistance. Totally state and local funded program for the indigent who do not qualify for other entitlements.

FEMA. Federal Emergency Management Assistance. Program gives money for emergency food and shelter to the nonprofit sector for distribution.

Adult Foster Care. Federal/state program which provides financial support for adults who are aged, blind, or disabled.

Section 8. Major federal housing program for low-to-moderate income people in addition to public housing. Subsidies are available for new construction, rehabilitated units, and tenants directly.

Housing Voucher. Reform of 1983 which gives federal voucher directly to the tenant to compensate for the difference between their income and prevailing market rents.

Housing Counseling Assistance Program. Federal program giving funds to local agencies to provide counseling for individuals and families in the areas of delinquent mortgages, tenant/landlord problems, security deposits, etc.

REFERENCES

APA. *The Homeless Mentally Ill.* H. Lamb (Ed.). Washington, DC: American Psychiatric Press, 1984.

Baltimore City Health Dept. *Report on the Homeless.* Baltimore, MD, 1985.

Baxter, E., & Hopper, K. *Private Lives/ Public Spaces.* NY: Community Service Society of New York, 1981.

Chicago Coalition for the Homeless. *When You Don't Have Anything.* Chicago, 1983.

Downtown Homeless, *Final Report to the Mayor.* San Diego, 1984.

Emergency Shelter Commission of Boston. *Seeing the Obvious.* Boston, 1984.

Fox, E. *Report to the Task Force on the Homeless.* Philadelphia, 1984.

League of Women Voters of Minneapolis. *Home Sweet Home.* Minneapolis, 1984.

Milwaukee Task Force on Emergency Shelter and Relocation Services. *Homelessness in Milwaukee.* Milwaukee, 1984.

Ohio Office of Mental Health. *Homelessness in Ohio.* Office of Program Evaluation and Research of the Ohio Dept. of Mental Health, 1984.

Stark, L. *A Day in June.* Coordinating Committee on the Homeless in Phoenix, AZ, 1983.

U.S. Congress. Subcommittee on Housing and Community Development. Hearings on Homelessness, Dec. 1982. Washington, DC: GPO, 1982.

U.S. Congress. Subcommittee on Housing and Community Development. Hearings on Homelessness. June 1984. Washington, DC: GPO, 1984.

Winograd, K. *Street People and Other Homeless, A Pittsburgh Study.* Allegheny County, PA, 1983.

CHAPTER II

Social Planning

INTRODUCTION

Social planning continues to be among the most articulated and certainly the most tumultuous change approaches. Not only has new technology made it possible to predict and project social trends which a few short years ago would have been regarded as guesswork, but that same technology has made assessment and evaluation more prominent and more pressing. Further, social planning was itself a rubric which contained within it elements of policy making, research, and political action. As differentiation among these action approaches emerged, a range of complex policy, planning, and advocacy efforts emerged at all levels of American society.

Historically, planning has something of an "image" problem, at the community level certainly. Many people associate "planning" with some sort of "foreign" political ideology or assume that it will require unacceptable levels of constraint. Somehow planning equals "control" and "control" is antithetical to "independence." We are caught between the conflicting pressures of increasing complexity and the tradition of self-determination. When one adds the rise in societal-wide distrust of authority manifest in recent years, the resulting community response to planning is often profoundly ambivalent.[1]

There is considerably less objection to planning which the individual, private corporation, labor union, or other private group applies to its own activities. Certainly, corporate strategic planning, financial planning for per-

---

[1]See, for example, S. M. Lipset and W. Schneider, *The Confidence Gap* (New York: Free Press, 1983).

sonal and family needs, and, perhaps to a lesser extent, in some circles, family planning to control the number, timing, and spacing of children have fairly wide acceptance. It is planning done by the state which is imposed on individuals, restricting their freedom of action, which arouses the ire of considerable numbers in the United States. From a community organization and macro practice perspective, it is best to understand planning as existing within a contentious context, and to make the management of that context part of the skills required of the planner whether she or he be a physical planner, a social planner, or strategic planner.

In our view, the best planning comes after the policy-making process has reached at least the official decision phase. Planning without policy means that there is no framework of values, decisions, or priorities to guide the planner. The absence of these structures has often meant, in the social service field at least, that plans have developed for actions in advance of agreement upon policies to legitimize that action. The fact that these plans were often in the public interest (broadly conceived), made with good intentions, and encompassing good themes and appropriate values does not diminish the fact that without prior agreement on a general policy direction a set of plans lacks the legitimacy needed for implementation.

It is important to recognize that the social policy planning process involves a set of general decisions for the establishment of a set of general guides to action on the one hand (policies), and a set of more specific detailed operational guidelines (plans), on the other.

Conceptually, at least two themes run through the planning literature (much as is true for the policy literature). One views planning as a rational technical skill requiring special training and often a professional jargon unintelligible to the uninitiated. Rhetoric here emphasizes neutrality and impartiality, "the facts" and "the public interest." The other theme describes planning as a political process in which the planner pursues goals that are often not widely shared (the advocate or the partisan fits this view). Part of the planner's task is to persuade the community to accept these goals; her or his job is to "engineer consent." This kind of planning might be seen more as an art than a profession. Furthermore, it is the art of the possible rather than the profession of the desirable. The contributions in this chapter demonstrate both approaches and provide some attempts at amalgamation.

Armand Lauffer offers a broad perspective on social planning. He reviews several definitions of planning, the types of problems addressed by planners and the settings and structures through which planning is carried out. The significance of the planner's view of the community is also addressed. In looking toward the future he considers the possible effects of planning on emerging social policy.

Barry Checkoway examines the political aspects of planning, the skills required for planning with particular attention to building support for plans. His review includes a rather full survey of the recent literature, and will lead the reader to many other articles that may be important in developing her or his own planning practice. Finally, Carl Patton's piece, "Citizen Input and Professional Responsibility," deals with the issue of citizen participation. While the rhetoric of participation may not be as strident as in the past the issue nonetheless remains politically potent and theoretically essential to the planner. Policies and plans which do not have public support will not be effectuated regardless of how appropriate or wonderful they may be. But the difficulties of involving people are legion and this piece seeks to consider some of those issues.

Planning, then, is the specification of a line of action within the framework of policy. Though often confused with policy it is a derivative process and one which follows after policy architecture has been laid out.

JOHN E. TROPMAN

16.

Armand Lauffer

SOCIAL PLANNERS AND SOCIAL PLANNING IN THE UNITED STATES

A chicken is just an egg's way of making another egg.
Samuel Butler

A difference that makes no difference is no difference.
Josiah Royce

The dogmas of a quiet past are inadequate to the stormy present. Let us disenthrall ourselves.

Abraham Lincoln

Professional social planners work under a variety of auspices. Their training may have been in any of several dozen professional schools or academic disciplines. Their ideological commitments may vary from conservative to radical. Despite this heterogeneity, their work shows considerable similarity when broken down into its operational components.

Nearly all social planners are engaged in such activities as (1) fact-finding and problem definition, (2) building communication networks or operating structures, (3) selecting and determining social goals as reflected in the policies and designs of action strategies, (4) some aspect of plan implementation, or (5) monitoring the resultant change, assessing feedback information, and evaluating impact or process. Together, these activities may be considered the stages of a planning process. A planner's power to influence change may be diminished to the extent that he or she may not be involved in any of

these sets of activities and that other key publics are either not involved or actively opposing the planner's efforts.

Social planners are found in grassroots and advocacy groups; in direct-service agencies; in coordinating and allocating organizations; in planning units at the local, state, regional, or national levels. They are employed in the private, voluntary, and public sectors. In contrast with others, "social" planners focus on "social" programs and services. But what they do may not be so easily distinguished from the work of urban, regional, or health planners who also advocate for the most needy and deprived and who use a more comprehensive approach to integrating economic, housing, transportation, and social service programs (Krumholz, 1982).

Planning is based on the assumptions that the aggregate of individual and group activities does not adequately distribute resources or opportunities, and that preferable conditions may be accomplished (Warren et al., 1974) by means that are thought through both

Source: This is an unpublished article reproduced by permission of the author.

systematically and carefully. Some opponents to planning, however, argue that men do not have the means or the wisdom to achieve planned results that are more beneficial than those that do, in fact, emerge from the marketplace. Planned change, they argue, is not only inefficient, but may pose dangers for the democratic values we cherish in this country.

This points up the central dilemma in planning (Michaels, 1973; Barfield, 1970; Wildavsky, 1981; Clark, 1981). Opposition to planning in the name of freedom is self-defeating. Social change continues at an ever-accelerating rate regardless of planned intervention. Man's freedom of choice can only be preserved by choice. Without control over the direction of change, man is at the mercy of his social environment, much as in an earlier day he was the victim of a harsh physical environment. Nevertheless, complete centralization would undermine effective participation and remove from the citizenry control over the directions of their lives.

The unanswerable or perhaps multianswerable question is, how much and what planning is desirable? The question becomes somewhat less intolerable when we accept the fact that the outcome of a planning effort is rarely known in advance. Planning is still a system of interaction and adaptations whose outcome is never fully predictable. In practice, planning goals are hardly fully fixed, are never completely calculable, and are ever moving and changing.

THE SOCIETAL CONTEXTS OF SOCIAL PLANNING

American social planning is by its very nature an attempt at *ad hoc* solutions to specific problems. Suffering from a lack of comprehensiveness, it serves primarily as a corrective device for deficiencies in a welfare system whose services are neither equitably distributed nor necessarily effective. Although these services themselves evolved in order to compensate for the wastage and breakage of a competitive, industrial, urban society in which individuals and groups are frequently cut adrift or left behind, the evolutionary process is not yet complete. Some services must be helped to grow or to change directions; others may have to be nudged out of existence because they are neither effective nor any longer relevant.

In the United States, planning has been largely an attempt to introduce order at the local or community level and in the midst of generally uncoordinated efforts to influence the direction of economic growth, physical and urban development, and income and power redistribution. Although a serious effort towards centralized decision making at the national level was in evidence during the heyday of the "Great Society" in the late 60s and early 70s, for the moment the locus of authority for planning and resource allocation has been obscured. An earlier myth about the countervailing power of the federal government has been shattered as little evidence was found (in certain sectors, at least) that federal bureaucracies could redistribute goods equitably, control that distribution, or guarantee adequate welfare for the citizenry. Today, a broad consensus exists that societal level planning is neither likely nor (for the moment) desirable. The arguments against central planning run as follows: (1) the growth of vested or configurational interests has obscured the more universal public interest; (2)

local involvement in decision making contributes to democracy and freedom, while reducing the intrusiveness of the bureaucracy; (3) neither the knowledge nor the technology available to planners have demonstrated themselves to be superior to the decisions made by ordinary citizens (Lauffer & Newman, 1981). Let's take these arguments one at a time.

There has indeed been a decline in consensus over what is in the public interest; and this decline parallels the growth of special interest groups that press for changes on behalf of various populations (the elderly, children-at-risk, the disabled, ethnic minorities, etc.) or that focus on specific issues (the environment, family planning and abortion, pornography). Sometimes these interest groups are at odds with each other, whereas at other times they may collaborate around limited concerns. These interest groups and the relationships between them are in an ever-moving state of flux, with new configurations emerging continuously.

In recent years, we have also witnessed a return to the more proximate geographic unit as the locus of decision making. In some ways this seems anachronistic in an age of multinational corporations, and at a time when most of the problems that are manifested at the local level did not originate there. Yet there clearly exists a sentiment in favor of increased state, substate, and local decision making that supports Washington's emerging "New Federalist" orientation. Rather than reflecting nineteenth century thinking, as the critics of the New Federalism argue, it may well reflect a twenty-first century orientation in its recognition of the complexity of social reality. At least part of that complexity may best be confronted at the more

proximate levels of social organization ... the neighborhood, the community, and the state.

The more local the locus of decision making, it can be argued, the more likely that decisions are going to be relevant and responsive to local needs and interests. "Smaller is better" because it is close to home, more manageable, more personal, and probably less wasteful of resources. The greater the diversity of local responses to locally felt needs, the greater the freedom of choice. Getting (big) government "off our backs" restores responsibility to the individual and to the locale where it truly belongs. In effect, what is being proposed is a redistribution of responsibility for decision making and action.

Such redistribution is not likely to take place without considerable conflict and without danger to populations that have traditionally concerned and involved social planners. It is likely to result in new and unaccustomed alliances. And it retards efforts to plan on a more comprehensive basis. In part, however, the problem lies in our unwillingness to specify national social priorities and in our reliance on the counterbalance of vested interests. This unwillingness is not accidental. It is the effect of these vested interests.

It has been possible for the nation to harness scientific and technological know-how of gigantic proportions to reach the moon. Hundreds of professional specializations and scientific disciplines were coordinated in one of mankind's most spectacular collective achievements. A number of different but complementary interests were brought into play in that effort. It seems unlikely that similar resources or concentration of efforts will be directed at the resolution of urban problems. Could the various vested interests be coordinated in one urban NASA? *The dogmas of a quiet past* still prevail upon us, *inadequate* as they may be *to the stormy present.*

The difficulties faced by those who attempt to plan centrally stem in part from the inadequacies of planning theories and planning instruments. This is, itself, an accident of history. The physical sciences like engineering technology have progressed much more rapidly than knowledge in the social sciences. And little has been done to translate such knowledge into "social engineering" technology.

THE ORGANIZATIONAL CONTEXTS OF SOCIAL PLANNING

Planners are seldom, if ever, free agents. They are employed by organizations with limited mandates and limited power to affect the course of social change and the arrangements of social institutions. The freedom to maneuver in these organizations is constrained by tradition, mandate, and vested interests. Even venturesome organizations and social movements become institutionalized at the point at which they settle on the provision and maintenance of a service perspective. Planning organizations, like all other organizations, are dependent on exchanges with "input" and "output" constituencies (Lauffer, 1978, 1984; Warren, 1967). Input constituencies provide them with legitimation, community support, staff, financial revenue, knowledge, and other resources. Output constituencies are those that are the recipients or beneficiaries of the planner's or organization's interventions.

Input constituencies generally exercise more control over the planner or

the planning organization than do output constituencies. For this reason, planning efforts may be biased towards the provision of services and the establishment of programs aimed at changing individuals rather than changing the basic structural arrangements of society. It is easier to develop a job-training program that experiments with new educational technologies than to intervene at the causal level of structural unemployment. It is also less risky in terms of one's employment or one's agency's sources of support.

When planners' efforts are aimed at basic structural changes, at least some powerful input constituencies will be threatened. Even apparently secure and independent sources of funding may dry up if the planner appears to threaten entrenched and powerful interests. For that reason some planning efforts that begin by aiming at changing structure of institutional relationships shift so in orientation that they soon focus on the provision of new or expanded services aimed at changing individuals. This process of goal distortion has received increasing attention by theoreticians and practitioners alike (Schone, 1983; Rein and Rabinowitz, 1977; Elmore, 1980; Lipsky, 1980).

DEFINING SOCIAL PLANNING

Efforts to define social planning, or for that matter, any form of planning, have sometimes generated more confusion than clarity. One problem with definitions is that they tend to be more prescriptive than descriptive, specifying what the analyst thinks planners *ought* to do, rather than describing the great multiplicity of tasks they *perform.* Interestingly, whatever the definitions used, they tend to be equally applicable to planning conducted by professionals trained in a variety of occupations: social work and other human service professions; urban and regional planning, health, environmental affairs, education, and so on, suggesting that there may be something "generic" that unifies all planning.

Friedmann and Hudson (1974) define planning as the "linkage between knowledge and organized action," but this definition without qualification is so inclusive as to make it relatively useless. More typically, we find planners defining their work in terms of processes or method, for example:

1. A rational method of problem solving and decision making;
2. Program development based on a process of goal and means selection, the concerting of necessary resources, and the progressive overcoming of resistances to goal attainment;
3. A process whereby policy, determined by a separate political process, is translated into a set of operational steps or procedures for the execution of that policy;
4. The feeding of information and explanatory concepts into the decision-making system;
5. A transactive process through which consensus is gradually arrived at and plans of action developed, implemented, and adjusted; in effect, a way of concerting community influence towards achievement of common or complementary goals.

What is one to make of this somewhat contradictory array of definitions? The first focuses on rationality while another (#5) emphasizes the interactional nature of planning. A third sounds suspiciously like a defini-

tion of social policy analysis (#4), while two others combine elements of the political and administrative processes (#2 and #4). Hudson (1979), in what has since become a seminal article, attempted to deal with these differences by comparing alternative theories of planning. His typology begins with an examination of what he terms *synoptic* or rational and comprehensive planning, and then goes on to examine other approaches: *incremental; transactive; advocacy;* and *radical* planning. None of these is entirely distinct from the others; in fact, the latter four draw on the rational model as they attempt to distinguish themselves from it.

The *synoptic* model presumes a rational sequence that flows from problem identification and goal selection, through the design of a writing or planning "structure," to the evaluation of policy alternatives and the elaboration and evaluation of means and ends, through implementation, and finally to some form of monitoring and evaluation. It is both data and concepts based, generally drawing on an open systems perspective. It often attempts to deal with problems comprehensively. In contrast, the *incrementalist* approach, most eloquently described by Lindblom and Braybooke (1963), presumes neither rationality nor the possibility of comprehensiveness.

For them, the rational approach is a normative prescription of what some planners think they *ought* to do rather than a description of what they actually do. What they perceive to be the reality is that planning is a disjointed process of mutual adjustment that takes place because the protagonists for one or another course of action take advantage of accident and circumstances. York (1982), drawing on earlier work done by Etzioni (1970), tries to reconcile both approaches by describing a "limited rational planning approach" that uses the most advanced knowledge and techniques available, but that recognizes both their limitation and the likelihood that choices by decisionmakers may ignore the planner's data or recommendations.

This is precisely the point that troubles Friedmann (1973) whose *transactive approach* draws on insights from the human "potentials" movement and the fields of organizational and community development. Like Geoffrey Vickers (1963), he argues that differences among people cannot all be resolved by references to matters of fact. The most appropriate decisions are those that are made through face-to-face interactions by those most directly affected by decisions ... administrators, staff, consumers, ordinary citizens. For Friedmann, the arrival at consensus is more dependent on interpersonal dialogue than on the gathering and manipulation of data.

Advocacy planners might assume a rational, transactive, or incrementalist style, but unlike other planners they will be less likely to be concerned with the public good than with the good of a particular public. The same may be true of some radical planners, especially those who emphasize self-reliance and mutual aid, grass roots activism, and locality development.

Interesting as these distinctions may be, they still don't adequately define what social planning is. It might, in fact, be wiser to describe what planners do than attempt an all-encompassing definition. What planners do is perform a variety of interactional and analytic tasks at various stages in the planning process (Perlman & Gurin, 1971; Lauffer, 1977). Thus they are involved in both "rational" as well as "transactional" activities. To better understand this, it may be helpful to follow the steps noted earlier in the description of rational or synoptic planning, but expand them to accommodate some to the other approaches described by Hudson.

ANALYTIC AND INTERACTIONAL ACTIVITIES IN THE SOCIAL PLANNING PROCESS

At the point of *defining a problem* to be acted on, or on choosing an objective or intervention, the planner and others involved in the planning process must often choose from among a number of competing problem definitions each leading to different goals. Such choices are not made on the basis of information about the problem or considerations of cause-effect relationships alone. Problem definition and tentative goal selection are influenced as much or more by those with whom the planner interacts as by data and analyses. In fact, the most pertinent aspect of a planner's analysis may be of the individuals and groups that have influence over planning outcomes, rather than of the problem situation around which a planning effort is to be undertaken.

Often, the process of problem identification flows directly into *the establishment of a working structure* to deal with the problem. Planning, at this stage, is essentially an art of choosing and guiding coalition partners. The planner is generally involved in the establishment of communication and interactional patterns that will extend over time, long enough to achieve some desired end. This end may be intermediary — as in determining a policy direction, or more long-term, as in achieving a specific goal.

Policy formulation and means-end elaboration are as much an interactional as an analytic process. On the analytic end of the continuum, the planner may bring to bear insights drawn on former experience (those of the planner and others). He or she may utilize knowledge of the political process to assure selection of feasible objectives. While situational logic may dictate the specifics of a plan and its objectives, this logic often emerges from the interactional process in which the planner elicits and examines the interests and preferences of fellow staff members, constituents, powerful community figures, target populations or organizations, and members of a sponsoring or auspice-providing organization.

Plan implementation[1] may also require a variety of analytic and interactional tasks. While implementation requires careful specification of the tasks to be performed at every step in the process, it may also require managing the relationships with and between relevant actions. Although implementation tasks are often thought of as interactional only, they also require careful reading (analysis) of the consequences of every action undertaken.

The design of a *monitoring, feedback, and evaluation* system requires the receiving and elicitation of information based on the experiences of relevant actors, and the analysis of the consequences of plan implementation. How the emerging and resulting data will be

used and by whom (transactive issues) are as important as the analytic aspects.

While this sequence is logical enough, in actual practice the order of activities undertaken may not follow a temporal logic. In one project, the real problems to be addressed may be uncovered only at the point of evaluating the outcomes achieved. In another, goals might become clear through action, in the process of implementation. In a third, the process of structure building will become an end in itself, subsequent thought and energy going into the maintenance and expansion of the structure.... in effect suggesting an incrementalist approach that builds on opportunity as it presents itself. In some settings, policy program options, backed by extensive information and analysis, may be presented by the planner for decisions by policymakers; whereas in others, decisions may evolve out of the interaction of various key protagonists, only later generating a demand for data.

LIMITS ON RATIONALITY

While the different emphases on one or another of these steps, or on analyses or interaction, may depend on a planner's ideological perspective, it is more likely to be the result of the settings in which planners operate. The organizations in which they are employed are impacted upon by market forces that shape options and define the organization's and the planner's mandates. The market is composed of various publics, each of which may demand one or another planning product, while being indifferent or opposed to others (Lauffer, 1984).

---

[1]The planner's involvement in implementation is what most distinguishes planning from the field of policy analysis which has emerged as a separate discipline during the past 10-15 years (Quade, 1975; Alexander, 1982).

A planner, his or her constituents, the sponsoring organization, and its publics must make choices at every stage in the planning process. These choices are frequently made on the basis of: preferences, value commitments, and available information. Preferences are expressions of wants (Galloway & Edwards, 1982) that can never be fully ordered; nor are they ever entirely satisfied. Values are by their nature too general to ever be fully realized. Information is rarely adequate. Successful accomplishment of planning goals may result in the recognition of new wants, the identification of different value commitments, and the reordering or uncovering of new information. Does this mean that planning can never be fully rational?

Undoubtedly that is the case. Yet whatever its limitations, rationality in social planning aims at producing the greatest return for the efforts expended. It chooses a middle ground between effectiveness, efficiency, and feasibility. It aims at what Herbert Simon (1958) and other administration theorists have termed "optimization" rather than "maximization."

The emphasis on planned change gives order to the otherwise technological or essentially political processes of attempting to influence social change. A new birth-control device, a new fuel, a surgical technique, or a new data-processing system are examples of technological innovations that create social change. *Quid pro quo* agreements, the use of coercive power, or an appeal to public opinion are examples of political efforts to influence the direction of change.

Planners certainly utilize technological innovations and political tactics.

What distinguishes planning from other processes, however, is its attempt at a balanced ordering of feasible objectives and/or the use of analytic tools to determine the efficacy of various means to overcome resistance to desired change — that is, to replace the irrational forces of the market with rational, calculated change strategies, even when these are heavily transactive in style.

A caution: the foregoing might suggest that engineering solutions to all social problems might be possible; that "correct" solutions might be engineered if only the relevant facts are known and the appropriate techniques used, and the right "proper management" techniques employed. But as Klosterman (1983) points out, when dealing with social problems factual questions are not easily distinguished from questions of value, and the methods of science cannot be used to resolve empirical questions of fact without relying on individual or collective values or preferences and few of these can ever be rationally supported or defended. The very act of planning already demonstrates a value preference. And some people are more able to enforce their values and preferences than others. Perhaps, as Davidoff argues, the "right course of action is always a matter of (some people's) choice, never of fact" (Davidoff & Reiner, 1962).

PLANNING AS A CORRECTIVE IN THE SERVICE-DELIVERY SYSTEM

We noted earlier that most American social planning activities are directed towards creating changes in service organizations and in the relationships between them (Rich, 1982). In general, they are not aimed directly at the amelioration or eradication of social problems and social ills. Instead, they attempt to deal with the effects of social problems by altering the processes of resource allocation, service delivery, and program development in those systems currently or potentially charged with supplying appropriate social provisions.

In practice, American planners have neither the mandate nor the tools to influence or direct basic changes in the fabric of society. Their planning activities are generally aimed at (1) provision of new or extended services to populations that have been rejected for service or that have never been appropriately served (Lauffer, 1983), and (2) reexamination of the linkages between service agencies and between service systems and relevant community groups such as resource allocators, clients, and consumers.

When planning proceeds from the assumption that services are deficient, five kinds of problems may be focused on:

1. *the quantitative lack of services or resources* (assumes that the means for dealing with actual or potential social problems are known but they are not available to a population in need);
2. *the inaccessibility of services* (assuming availability, but inaccessibility due to such barriers as location, psychological or other costs, scheduling, and so on);
3. *ineffectiveness* (i.e., changes sought are not achieved — *a difference that makes no difference is no difference);*

4. *inefficiency* (whereby costs may outweigh benefits, where with proper design one might be able to get a "bigger bang" for the same "buck," or spend fewer dollars to achieve a similar result);
5. *lack of responsiveness to needs and wishes of some key input or consumer public* (in effect no accountability or accountability to the wrong publics).

When planning focuses on the linkages between service providers, between providers and consumers, or providers and resource suppliers, the planning problem may be defined as:

1. Lack of *continuity* (e.g., one service cannot be effective without leading to another as in hospital discharge and community-based care);
2. Lack of *comprehensiveness* (dealing with multiple aspects of a problem; or
3. Lack of *compatability* (one service component complements another).

Without distinguishing between these deficiencies, otherwise competent planners may apply unsuitable tactics in their efforts to produce changes in target organizations. An effective strategy aimed at a service organization that is inappropriately structured to deliver its services would be quite different from a strategy aimed at linking organizations into a more effective network. Careful analysis of the presenting problem and its contextual elements is required. Both the presenting problem and the context will differ if the planning activity is sectoral or intersectoral in focus.

SECTORAL PLANNING

Sectoral planning takes place within a specialized problem or program arena (e.g., mental health, child welfare, aging, disabilities). It involves promoting the interest of a particular population, service agency, or service network organized on behalf of that population. Sectoral planning has frequently been spurred by federal or voluntary appropriations or by the interests of existing agencies to expand their domains.

All direct service agencies are dependent on external sources of financial support and good will. For this reason, their planning efforts are often directed more at resource acquisition ("getting the money we need") than on service distribution ("getting the right services to clients"). Planners employed by direct service agencies generally perform three functions: (1) they mobilize support for the agency's ideology, program, or financial needs; (2) they guide the process of interorganizational exchanges of such resources as personnel, specialized expertise, facilities, funds, and influence; and (3) they direct their efforts at changes in community resources and programs outside the direct jurisdiction of their agencies but necessary to the welfare of their clients and constituencies (Dumpson, 1964).

Mobilization of community support assures that the agency can maintain viable programs through: (a) the winning of public acceptance, (b) the recruitment of clientele, and (c) securing of adequate financing. If there is a lack of adequate support, the planner may attempt to isolate or nullify external threats or to reexamine the very nature of the agency's services with the view of rectifying inadequacies.

Just as these agencies are dependent on external services, so are they looked upon for support by other organizations. Frequently, the planner in the direct service agency enters into: (a) collaborative exchanges with other organizations through the coordination of services or responsibilities for mutual client systems; or (b) joint-action efforts aimed at community education, the passage of new legislation, or the securing of new resources to be shared. Such exchanges depend on a mutual (although not necessarily equal) sharing of benefits.

Agency planners may also attempt to change the directions of other service systems or influence the general direction of community resource allocation. Their efforts may result in the creation of new services that are autonomous, jointly sponsored with other agencies, or, in some cases, developed within their own agencies. Success will depend on the values attached to planners' efforts by their own and other existing service agencies. It will also depend on the administrative and other supports received within the host agency.

The press of ongoing administrative and maintenance responsibilities makes it unlikely that direct service agencies can adequately plan for sectoral needs apart from their immediate clientele. Case management has, during the 1980s, emerged as the principal method through which individual case planning is conducted on behalf of clients who are seen by more than a single agency. Nevertheless efforts at more comprehensive or intersectoral planning are still very much in evidence.

INTERSECTORAL PLANNING

The proliferation of social programs poses the problem of coordination and the need for more comprehensive approaches that cut across sectors. Accordingly, a number of coordinating, allocating, and intersectoral planning bodies have grown up during the middle decades of the twentieth century. At the local level, these have included welfare councils, sectarian federations, community mental health boards and, more recently, community development corporations.

Welfare councils have had the longest standing relationship to social work and social welfare agencies. Their major contributions have been to further cooperative relationships between voluntary social agencies, to raise the standards of professional practice, and to stimulate the planning and coordination of new services. Today most welfare councils have been "folded" into local United Ways which raise funds and allocate them. Their involvement in the planning and coordinating of services is a supportive function.

Sectarian federations have played similar roles within ethnic or religious communities, notably among Catholics and Jews. In addition, "functional" federations, limited to particular fields, have coordinated and planned for other services. Examples are hospital associations, local urban leagues, various health or education associations, and advocacy coalitions that have assumed planning and coordinating functions as a byproduct of successful political and educational activities.

During the 1960s, under President Johnson's Great Society initiative, the federal government entered the intersectoral arena with a number of innovative structures. Among them were community action agencies (CAAs) funded by the Office of Economic Opportunity, and Model Cities programs funded by the Department of Housing and Urban Development. CAAs were organized with the objective of stimu-

lating existing agencies and councils to participate in the national antipoverty effort, while providing a voice to the disenfranchised poor. CAAs spawned a number of new programs, particularly in the area of youth services and job training. Model Cities agencies performed similar functions, but added housing and neighborhood rehabilitation services. Later, Area Agencies on Aging represented, as they still do, a cross between sectoral and intersectoral planning at the locality level.

Today's citizen involvement in health planning (Checkoway, 1980) draws in part on the earlier experiences of CAAs, Model Cities and of the community mental health boards that undertook to stimulate the growth of county- or region-wide, community-based, comprehensive care to populations with mental health needs. The human resource commission (HRC) is still another form of a service-coordinating agency that emerged in the late 1960s. Generally under local governmental auspices, the typical HRC was established by local mayors or city councils to integrate governmental and private services at the local level.

Until the early 1970s many of the federal dollars coming to local communities were "categorical," that is, earmarked for certain categories of programs, often aimed at specific populations. . . .the aging, the poor, children-at-risk. A shift towards local decision making unencumbered by federal government categorical programming began during the Nixon presidency, expanded under Carter, and has accelerated during the Reagan years. Federal revenue sharing with local municipalities signaled the demise of Community Action and Model Cities programs. The use of block grants to state and local governments increased the importance of planning and coordination at state and local levels. For example, Title XX gave state departments of social services responsibility for planning programs for children and families at risk.

A particularly interesting manifestation of what is commonly referred to as the "New Federalism" was the "Community Development Block Grant Corporation" (Plan & White, 1981) which was given responsibility for coordinating the activities of municipal line agencies. In the interest of better management, they generally required the input of local business enterprises and neighborhood citizen groups. While Reagonomics has virtually eliminated block grants themselves, community development corporations are still very much in evidence and are likely to continue in modified form throughout the century. They represent a prototype of citizen involvement in subarea planning that, by including the private and public sectors, is increasingly characteristic of efforts to decentralize service planning in most industrialized nations (Checkoway, 1984; Lauffer, 1986; Warren, 1985).

THE PLANNER'S PERSPECTIVE

Questions of consumer control or citizenship involvement vary according to whether the planning unit operates at the locality level or is extracommunity in locus and scope. At the community level, planners often give high priority to consumer involvement and citizen participation. In fact some planners envision planned change as emerging from the bottom and moving upwards. The general citizenry or a specific population may be involved in the process of both goal formation and task accom-

plishment. For some of these planners, the process of community involvement may take higher priority than the service goals of a particular project. Other planners place greater emphasis on attaining specific program or service objectives.

Planning efforts may vary in accordance to the value placed on mutuality of goals and cooperative strategies, in contrast with the utilization of contest and conflict strategies. This, however, may be neither a political nor an ideological consideration. Warren (1967) has observed that in an environment in which there is consensus on goals and means, collaborative and cooperative strategies may be the most effective. In an environment where differences of opinion or plain indifference exists, the more effective strategy may be one of persuasion. Where differences of opinion are strong, leading to conflict over means or ends, contest strategies may be the most effective.

Despite the influence of setting and environment and the constraints imposed by funding sources and other constituencies, a good part of what a planner chooses to do may be influenced by his or her characteristic manner of looking at problems. Cognitive styles may be as influential as ideological perspectives.

A number of planners function in much the same manner that the "operationalist" does in the social sciences. In examining a presenting problem, the planner may begin with the following observations. "These are the skills I possess (for example, negotiating skills or the use of cost-benefit analysis), and these are the problems I observe that are within the scope or domain of my agency." The planner then asks: "Which of the problems I observe are amenable to intervention and what goals can I accomplish within the constraints of my organization and with the skills I have at my disposal?" Taken to the extreme, this position may suffer from what Abraham Kaplan (1964) calls "the law of the instrument" (discussed in Lauffer, 1975). "Give a small boy a hammer, and he may find that everything in sight needs pounding."

Other planners put implicit faith in the utilization of data and theory for the formation of goals. The gathering of relevant data and the analysis of facts become the guiding criteria for action. In positivist tradition, they may begin the planning process by asking themselves, "If this were so, what must I do?" They gauge the distance between some normative ideal and the observation and measurement of conditions as they perceive them to exist. There is a tendency for these planners to state objectives in terms of ideal goals and to assume implicitly that by pursuing some immediate and measurable objective, movement towards the more distant objective has been demonstrated.

For still other planners, the meaning of current situations and observed social problems lies in their implications. In pragmatist fashion, they ask, "What difference does it make if this is so, and what difference would it make if it were altered in this manner or that?" Planners of this persuasion tend to be less selective about ends and more apt to see the interconnectedness of ends and means. They aim toward optimization and let their actions be dictated by their interpretations of what is and what is not feasible.

Planners also differ to the extent that they are willing to take risks. The planner who does not take risks may face a secure if dull future. Many good planners do take risks. An experienced city planner confides that to be effective he stirs up so much trouble that he must move on every few years. "It's my job to open up the community. Other people can then come in to consolidate actions." Another planner calls himself a "social-work bum," and still another decries her position at the end of an "occupational yo-yo." Students who graduate from schools of social work and other graduate professional programs in which planning is taught report that they are not always able to find a job that is initially defined as planning, but that they soon find themselves engaged in planning activities or helping to professionalize others in their agencies or within placements who perform planning functions. Staking a claim and defining one's mandate is of critical importance.

GENDER DIFFERENCES IN PLANNING

The planning literature is strangely silent on the impact of gender differences on planning (i.e., who plans or with whom they plan). Perhaps this is because the vast majority of planners and writers about planning are male. There are two notable exceptions. Ruth Brandwein (1981) notes that the collaborative, facilitative, and enabling orientations associated with women have given way to more male-oriented directive and controlling planning orientations. Although not limited to either males or females, Brandwein defines female-style roles as facilitating, enabling, and coordinating, with a win-win orientation and participatory decision making in informal settings.

Male style roles tend to be more in the nature of adversarial, technocratic, and managerial roles. Masi (1981) is less concerned with differences in roles than with differences in issues addressed. She suggests that concern with what are sometimes seen as women's issues (rape, domestic violence, addiction) may better distinguish male from female planners' work than the how of planning. There seems to be some evidence in favor of Masi's argument. Similar conclusions might be made about planners who come from racial or cultural minorities and others who represent special interests and whose motivations may stem in part from the populations with which they identify. Again, the empirical evidence is slim.

PLANNING OF THE FUTURE

Where does planning go from here? Will planning take us into the future, or will we drift aimlessly forward, allowing the currents of time and the uncontrolled forces of change to take us in directions over which we have no control? Will planners assume greater responsibility in steering a course through the stormy present?

Despite the haze that obscures every planner's crystal ball, some trends emerge relatively clearly. First, as unplanned or partially planned service systems become increasingly more complex and as new types of services are developed, planning will continue to be an important corrective device. One can expect that planners with whatever job title will be employed in larger numbers by a greater variety of service systems, in evolving and newly developing welfare sectors.

The intersectoral nature of planning will increase in importance in direct proportion to the increasing importance of the sectoral aspects of planning. Changes in one sector will increasingly be felt in others. Planning in one part of the system will result in the necessity for planning in another part of the system.

Social planners will be expected to share responsibility with other professionals from public and voluntary agencies and with representatives of the private sector. Relationships established in one planning effort need not lead to permanent structures. Rather planning structures will shift in both form and focus as new configurations of interest shape planning actions.

The increasing complexity of bureaucratic structures will require planners to advocate on the behalf of individuals and groups who might otherwise be ignored, misprocessed, or stripped of their dignity as they attempt to maneuver through the intricate maze of services, requirements, and regulations.

The growth in information technology and of sophisticated predictor models will require that some planners become technical experts. In fact, their power may be in direct proportion to their technical competence (Ellul, 1965). Yet no amount of technical wizardry is likely to be sufficient without equal skill in communication and consensus building (Bachrach & Lawton, 1981).

David Loye (1978) points out that the early enthusiasm for econometric and other forecasting techniques, developed by Kahn, Helm, and deJouveral and other futurists in the early 1970s, has since been tempered with a dose of reality. Nevertheless, by focussing on changes in social knowledge and in the ways in which ideas are treated in society, it becomes possible to predict the issues that will frame planning problems, and the likely responses by the public to those issues (Lindblom & Cohen, 1979).

And what of planning theories? Are these to become more technical or more transactive? Will they become sufficiently grounded in experience to provide relatively value-free guides to action?

The answers are not clear. Rothman (1984) has proposed an approach to "social R and D" that makes it possible to abstract from science and translate scientific propositions into action guidelines. Yet many would argue that the logic of science and of scientific inquiry is not the same as the logic of practice (Bolan, 1980). Practitioners confront the uniqueness of the actual situations in which they find themselves. Theorists attempt to abstract and generalize from experience. Although at the core of professional behavior is the conviction that action must be guided by knowledge, practice knowledge is derived more from action and experience than from theory. Donald Schone (1983) also makes this point. An epistemology of practice, he suggests, should include normative analyses grounded in experience. The reflective planner is one whose knowledge grows and expands in practice. As the cumulative experiences of reflective planners are shared, a new planning theory may emerge. *A chicken is, after all, an egg's way of creating another egg.*

REFERENCES

Alexander, Ernest. "Implementation: Does It Add Up to a Theory?" *Journal of the American Planning Association,* 48 (1982): 1.

Bachrach, Samuel & Edward Lawler. *Bargaining: Power, Tactics and Outcomes,* San Francisco: Jossey-Bass, 1981.

Banfield, Edward C. *The Unheavenly City,* Boston: Little, Brown & Co., 1970.

Bolan, Richard S. "The Practitioner as Theorist: The Phenomenology of the Professional Episode," *JAPA,* 46 (1980): 3.

Brandwein, Ruth. "Towards Feminization of Community Operation Practice," In Lauffer & Newman, *Community Organization for the 1980s, SDI* Special Double Issue, 5 (1981): 2-3.

Checkoway, Barry, ed. *Citizens and Health Care: Participation and Planning for Social Change.* New York: Pergamon Press, 1980.

Checkoway, Barry. "Two Types of Planning in Neighborhoods." *Journal of Planning Research and Education,* 3 (1984): 102-109.

Clark, Terry, ed. *Urban Policy Analysis: Directions for Future Research.* Beverly Hills, CA: Sage, 1981.

Davidoff, Paul & Thomas A. Reiner. "A Choice Theory of Planning," *Journal of the American Institute of Planners,* 28 (1962): 103-115.

Dumpson, James R. "Planning by Social Agencies." *Social Progress through Social Planning.* Proceedings of the 12th International Conference of Social Work, Athens, Greece, 1964.

Ellul, Jacques. *The Technological Society,* U.S. ed. New York: Victory Books, 1964.

Elmore, Richard. *Complexity and Control.* Washington, DC: U.S. Department of Education, 1980.

Etzioni, Amitai. "Mixed Scanning." In Andreaus Faludi, ed. *A Reader in Planning Theory.* New York: Pergamon Press, 1973.

Forester, John. "Critical Theory and Planning Practice," *JAPA,* 46 (1980): 3.

Friedmann, John & Barclay Hudson. "Knowledge and Action: A Process of Paradigm Change," *Journal of the American Institute of Planners,* 43 (1974): 1.

Friedmann, John. *Retracking America.* New York: Anchor Books, 1973.

Galloway, Thomas D. and J. Terry Edwards. "Critically Examining the Assumptions of Espoused Theory." *JAPA,* 48 (1982): 2.

Hudson, Barclay. "Comparison of Correct Planning Theories: Counterparts and Contradictions." *JAPA,* 45 (1979): 4.

Kaplan, Abraham. *The Conduct of Inquiry.* San Francisco: Chandler, 1964.

Klosterman, Richard E. "Fact and Value in Planning." *JAPA,* 49 (1983): 2.

Krumholz, Norman. "A Retrospective View of Equity Planning: Cleveland 1969-79." *JAPA,* 48 (1982): 12.

Lauffer, Armand and Edward Newman. "From the 1980s to Century 21." In

Lauffer and Newman, eds., *Community Organization for the 1980s, SDI Special Issue,* 5 (1981): 2-3.

Lauffer, Armand. "Planners, Planning Settings and Planning Choices." In Gerald T. Horton, ed., *Readings on Human Services Planning.* Arlington, VA: Human Services Institute, 1975.

Lauffer, Armand. *Social Planning at the Community Level.* Englewood Cliffs, NJ: Prentice-Hall, 1977.

Lauffer, Armand. *Grantsmanship,* 2nd ed. Beverly Hills, CA: Sage, 1983.

Lauffer, Armand. "Community Self-Help as Strategy and Outcome." Jerusalem: Brookdale Institute, 1986.

Lindblom, Charles and David Braybooke. *A Strategy of Decision.* New York: Free Press, 1963.

Lindblom, Charles and David Cohen. *Useable Knowledge.* New Haven: Yale University Press, 1979.

Lipsky, Michall. *Street Level Bureaucracy.* New York: Basic Books, 1980.

Loye, David. *The Knowledgeable Future: A Psychology of Forecasting and Prophecy.* New York: Wiley Interscience, 1978.

Masi, Dale. *Organizing for Women.* Lexington, MA: Lexington Books, 1981.

Michaels, Donald. *On Learning to Plan and Planning to Learn.* San Francisco: Jossey-Bass, 1973.

Plan, Jeremy and Louise G. White. "Planning Under the New Federalism." *JAPA,* 47 (1981): 2.

Quade, Edward. *Policy Analysis for Public Decisions.* New York: Elsevier Press, 1975.

Rein, Martin and Francine Rabinowitz. *Problem Analysis in Policy Research.* Cambridge, MA: Harvard-MIT Joint Center, 1977.

Rothman, Jack. *Social R and D.* Englewood Cliffs, NJ: Prentice-Hall, 1984.

Schone, Donald. *The Reflective Practitioner.* New York: Basic Books, 1983.

Simon, Herbert. *Administrative Behavior.* New York: Free Press, 1958.

Vickers, Geoffrey. *The Art of Judgement.* New York: Basic Books, 1963.

Warren, Donald. "On the Role of Neighborhood Mediating Structures in Restructuring of the Welfare State." Ann Arbor: University of Michigan Press, 1985.

Warren, Roland. "Interaction of Community Decision Organizations; Some Basic Concepts and Needed Research." *Social Service Review,* 41: 3 (September 1967): 261-70.

Wildavsky, Aaron. *Speaking Truth to Power: The Art and Craft of Policy Analysis.* Boston: Little, Brown & Co., 1981.

York, Reginald O. *Human Services Planning: Concepts, Tools, and Methods.* Chapel Hill: University of North Carolina Press, 1982.

17.

Barry Checkoway

POLITICAL STRATEGY FOR SOCIAL PLANNING

Social planning operates in an imbalanced political arena. Private groups blame government for economic problems and planning agencies for a variety of ills. They mobilize substantial resources, mount campaigns to shape attitudes, and elect representatives who target agencies with reductions and cutbacks. In the recent history of health planning, for example, American Hospital Association leaders pledged to "square off at the regulators" and "beat the system" (McMahon, 1978, p. 113). American Medical Association leaders vowed to "obstruct"

Source: Reprinted with permission from Barry Checkoway, ed., *Strategic Perspectives on Planning Practice,* scheduled for publication by Lexington Books.

planning agencies, and urged doctors "to roll up their sleeves and apply the political pressure of organized medicine" (Lipschultz, 1980, p. 1). In Iowa and Texas, physicians and hospitals mobilized letter-writing campaigns against federal planning guidelines (Danaceau, 1979). In Rhode Island, they aroused citizens and defeated plans for medical manpower and hospital beds (Rosenberg, 1980). In Illinois, they assigned staff to political campaigns, bussed voters from hospital wards to the polls, and elected slates to planning boards (Checkoway, 1982). Planners no longer expect to generate widespread support, but instead may struggle for survival in the face of power.

It thus is no surprise that planning agencies may not implement their plans. Analysts have documented the impacts of power imbalance and problems of implementation for years (Alterman, 1983; Bardach, 1977; Barrett and Fudge, 1981; Larson, 1980; Lynn, 1980; Mazmanian and Sabatier, 1981; Palumbo and Harder, 1981; Pressman and Wildavsky, 1973; Thompson, 1981). The surprise for many planners today is that the problem is neither power imbalance nor implementation alone, but also their very future in the community. Austerity policies and adversarial power challenge planners to recognize political change and develop capacity for the years ahead.

This paper analyzes political strategy for social planning. It draws on research and practice in several fields and includes cases of planners and agencies that apply innovative methods to formulate strategy. It does not suggest that these planners are typical in the field, or that these methods alone are sufficient to alter the context of practice, or that

this approach contradicts the drive for efficiency or effectiveness. It does suggest that planning operates in a political context, and that political strategy can serve as a source of power for planners who want to influence implementation.

PERSPECTIVES ON STRATEGY

Social planning is a process to develop policies, plans, and programs for human services. Practitioners work in public or private settings; in functional areas such as health, housing, or welfare; and in territories ranging from neighborhood to nation. They play various analytical and interactional roles; espouse equity, justice, or other social values; and hold ideologies from conservative to progressive. Some analysts view social planning as means to assess the social impacts of land use and other planning decisions, others as means to create social change in society overall. These views are important to consider, although the emphasis here is on human services. It would be as mistaken to place all burden for social impacts on social planners as it would be to excuse any planner from responsibility to consider social values in his or her work. There is no single notion of planning that characterizes all forms of practice.

Social planning practice is changing. Previous years of economic growth contributed to an increase in federal, state, and local planning agencies, in addition to regional and special purpose bodies with territorial or functional responsibilities. In times of growth, planning was viewed as a type of social engineering characterized by objective fact-finding and the so-called rational model. Leading texts emphasized technical research and "hard data," while government guidelines described scientific application of facts (Krueckeberg and Silvers, 1974; Spiegel and Hyman, 1978). Planners were akin to technical experts who analyzed data for people who considered alternatives and made decisions. If some planners criticized contradictions between the rational model and actual practice, or used planning as a vehicle for power redistribution and social change, they were by no means typical in the field (Baum, 1983; Beyle and Lathrop, 1970; Boyer, 1983; Burchell and Sternlieb, 1978).

Today economic recession has replaced growth and reduced development. This has exacerbated conditions in central cities and metropolitan areas, some of which are slowing or declining in population and other measures of urban activity. Private groups mobilize against social programs and target agencies with reductions. Budget cuts have worsened conditions for poor people, minorities, and other disadvantaged groups who had depended on social programs because they perceived few other possibilities. Soup kitchens, housing shelters, and health clinics report requests for emergency services. The future of social planning is uncertain at a time when social programs are more important than ever (Hasenfeld, 1983a).

Previous planning agency attempts to operate in a political context have tended to produce uneven results. Some agencies have advocated the interests of disadvantaged groups, but they have not always built sufficient support to withstand opposition and implement plans (Davidoff, 1965; Heskin, 1980; Krumholz, 1982). Others have established programs to involve citizens in planning, but they have not always ensured the quality or

impact of participation (Arnstein, 1969; Checkoway, 1982b; Rosenbaum), yet others have adopted subarea programs to involve territorial subunits in planning, but this has often deconcentrated functions without decentralization to local residents (Checkoway, 1984). Exceptional agencies *have* formulated strategy, but they are not typical in the field.

Political strategy can serve as a resource for social planning at the community level. Strategy is the science and art of mobilizing resources towards goals. It involves choice and sequence, staging and timing, and some combination of roles and styles. Strategy shows commitment to think ahead, anticipate alternatives, and achieve results (Booth, 1977; Bryson and Delbecq, 1979; Staples, 1984; Steiner, 1979).

Corporate leaders formulate strategies with fervor. For example, the U.S. Chamber of Commerce (1979) publishes "action plans" to help members serve on planning boards. Medical construction, equipment and supply industry trade associations join local interests to support legislation favoring expansion of facilities (Glenn, 1979; McKinlay, 1984; Relman, 1980). Long-term care industry provider organizations prepare legislation representing local operators and strategies advising them how to prepare for actions by reform groups (Norville and Modrow, 1978).

Planners in public agencies tend not to think or act strategically. Studies suggest that although planners once may have emphasized broad strategy and long-range plans, many have become preoccupied with applying instrumental rationality and short-range expediency (Dyckman, 1983; Marcuse, 1983). They often train in schools in which strategy is not central, and subsequently lack skills to operate strategically

(Baum, 1983a; Hemmens, Bergman, and Moroney, 1978; Schon, Cremer, Osterman, and Perry, 1976). Other studies suggest that social administrators should consider playing a more powerful political role, but they often raise legal, ethical, or professional questions about practice (Alexander, 1982; Stewart, 1981; Walter, 1973). Increasing numbers of them *do* participate in politics, but tend to lack influence in decisions (Mathews, 1982; Wolk, 1981).

However, there is evidence of increasing efforts to develop strategic social planning practice. For example, Bleiker (1978) instructs planners to develop support for plans that are difficult to implement. Bryson, Freeman, and Roering (1985) describe a health service, county government, and other agencies which formulate plans with implementation in mind. Gummer (1984), Hasenfeld (1983b), and Patti (1983) cite literature on social administrators who recognize the importance of political influence in organizational relationships affecting effectiveness. Mahaffey and Hanks (1982) edit studies of strategy and politics with accounts by practitioners who run campaigns and win elections.

Should social planners formulate political strategy? Some analysts argue that public, nonprofit, or voluntary agencies are strategically weak and would benefit from strategy developed in business (Newman and Wollander, 1978; Wortman, 1981). Others warn against application of corporate models to agencies where strategy might violate norms or undermine trust on which public practice presumably depends (Walker, 1983). The issue is not whether planners should act more like business, but whether they will develop strategy at all. Meanwhile, corporate groups *will*

continue to formulate strategy and influence agencies.

SKILLS IN POLITICAL STRATEGY

Political strategy involves several skills which are possible to place in sequence and consider in order, although no single notion of process characterizes all approaches to practice. The following are not the only skills, but they are among the most important.

Set Goals

Goals are statements of general social concern toward which action is directed. They provide an expression of vision and a sense of direction. They provide a proclamation of domain and a platform on which to campaign in the community. Ideally they result from a process that gives them legitimacy and represents those who participate in their formulation.

Goal setting can build support for plans, but also can engender controversy and evoke opposition. In Winnetka, Illinois, citizens hold annual meetings to discuss issues, mail questionnaires with utility bills, and formulate platforms for public officials. In Dallas, citizens hold small group meetings to discuss problems, convene citywide conferences to set goals, and form committees to draft plans for implementation (Goals for Dallas, 1982). In Alameda, California, committee members conduct interviews and surveys, organize task forces, and draft goals for implementation by officials. In Raleigh, North Carolina, city councilors used study groups, training workshops, and issue-balloting techniques to expand participation and set goals in a city dominated by development interests. The program was so influential that private powerholders formed an opposition group and elected representatives committed to private ends (Smith and Hestor, 1982).

However, goals often originate outside the community. They may come from earlier mandates, higher authorities, or emergency events which require quick action. The issue is not that such goals are necessarily inappropriate for local action, but rather that they may limit the process in which people set goals for themselves. Goal setting can activate citizens, but this is not necessarily typical of practice today.

Identify Issues

Issues express specific social concerns and affect people in deeply felt ways. They appeal to particular constituencies with concrete proposals, and provide tactical handles for practice. Which is the most salient issue? Who are the constituencies? What tactics apply? Booth (1977) instructs practitioners to "cut" issues in ways which relate to constituencies, although many planners produce plans with broad goals for some general public. Such plans may serve functions but diffuse constituencies and exacerbate implementation. Such goals may be valuable but too vague to move constituents to action.

How can planners cut issues which build support? Lancourt (1979) challenges planners to consider salience in identifying issues for implementation. She assumes that people will act in the name of public responsibility when it is in their interest to do so. Roche (1981) describes planners who take goals from agency plans, list groups with identifiable stake and political strength, define issues

in terms of target groups, and use media to make issues come alive to these groups. They engaged labor leaders by seeking their input and showing how plans would maintain wages and minimize disruption to employees. They did not justify esoteric formulas or sell rationality, but appealed to their interests and finally won their endorsement.

However, issues alone will not generate support. On the contrary, Krumholz (1982) describes planners who frame plans in terms of specific issues, but still lack resources to overcome opposition in the community. Issue identification is important but insufficient to build support in the absence of other skills.

Develop Constituencies

Building an organization involves caring about those who are affected. Whose issue is it? What do they see as their stake? What power do they bring? Constituencies are those who are affected by issues and potential supporters of an organization. They can provide a membership base and show strength in the face of power. Planners who represent the public interest rather than specific constituencies may do so at risk to themselves.

Planners usually do not view planning agencies as constituent organizations with a membership base. Instead, they often take the general public as their constituency, develop plans for all interests within their jurisdiction, or remain aloof from the influence of particular groups. However, agencies that try to represent the interests of everyone represent no one, reduce their accountability, and open themselves to dominance by those already organized in the community. Strategic representation of constituencies requires "mechanisms of accountability," but many agencies lack such mechanisms and thus may benefit groups with concentrated interests and ongoing organizations over individual citizens representing no particular interest or some diffuse public interest (Marmor and Morone, 1980; Pitkin, 1967).

Who are the constituencies? There is reason to expect planners to engage constituencies with commitment to planning. But planning has many participants who are skeptical of the enterprise. It would be ironic if agencies involved individuals or groups with relatively little commitment to the activity, although this happens in some communities.

Constituencies are not random relationships but may result from efforts to identify and develop them (Barkdoll, 1983; Beneviste, 1977; Lipschultz, 1980). In one agency, for example, planners identify major constituency groups, invite them to select representatives to the governing body, and assist them in building support in the community. In another they create an independent constituency organization with business, labor, professional, and consumer group members who build support beyond the governing body (Checkoway, 1981). In yet another they analyze agency goals in terms of key individuals and then develop relationships and provide services to selected ones in expectation of loyalty in return (Roche, 1981). Successful politicians have long received rewards from responding to their constituents (Johannes, 1984; Riodan, 1963). Constituents are too important to withdraw from the matter, or to leave them to traditional mechanisms of representation alone.

Select Tactics

Political strategy can involve a series of "campaigns" or planned activities in sequence which build on the success of the one before. Each campaign in turn can involve a series of "tactics" or particular actions which focus on issues. Which tactics will work? What resources will they require? Where will they lead? Selecting tactics is a systematic activity informed by strategic objectives. They also can engender commitment from individuals who derive psychosocial benefits from involvement in them (Linton and Witham, 1982), but therapy is not usually a principal end of political strategy.

Private economic groups employ tactics to build power. Feldstein (1977) describes health associations that prepare legislation, provide information to regulators and legislators, and deliver benefits for their members. Pines (1982) describes business groups that send sample editorials to local newspapers for publication, conduct opinion surveys and legal analysis, pack hearings with witnesses and lengthy testimony, write speeches for legislators, prepare amendments and influence regulations.

However, planners often apply "safe" tactics without strategy in mind. Studies show that in citizen participation programs, they distribute plans to libraries, publish legal notices of meetings in newspapers, conduct formal public hearings, publish newsletters, and convene boards and committees rather then to apply more powerful methods. In political action, they play conventional roles in which they are more likely to discuss issues, write letters, and join political organizations rather than to attend political meetings, participate in political campaigns, contribute money to candidates, or run for office (Mathews, 1982; Wolk, 1981). Exceptional practitioners may become political gladiators, but they are not typical in the field.

Tactics are not strategy but ideally flow from it. They can cause changes, to be sure, but they also can provoke countertactics which jeopardize the agency. The issue is not whether to select tactics but rather to assess the agency situation and select ones that work.

Build Organizational Structure

Structure refers to institutional means which involve some combination of established policies and procedures, roles and responsibilities, mechanisms and methods toward goals. What structure and process will generate ideas and solve problems? How should participants make decisions, divide responsibilities, and implement plans? What are the roles of boards and committees, chairpersons and staff members? The challenge is to fit structure to situation.

More research is needed on organizational structure for political strategy, but lessons can be learned from innovative agencies. These include an agency which centralizes governance in a representative board and forms an independent organization to expand participation; deconcentrates functions to subarea councils with staff and facilities to address local concerns; forms committees and task forces to involve individuals and channel adversaries. Studies suggest that the organizational or structural correlates of practice in agencies include community leadership, executive management, staff

skills, and resources in time and money in addition to sociopolitical context and commitment to goals (Checkoway and O'Rourke, 1983; Mayer, 1984; Tropman, 1984). Structure is not strategy but can facilitate its practice.

Activate People in Planning

The benefits of citizen participation are well known. For agencies, participation can provide information, improve communications, and fulfill legislative mandates. It also can open up the political process, involve low income and minority citizens, and develop community organizations. For citizens, participation can offer opportunities to gain representation, exercise legal and political rights, and influence policy decisions. Done with knowledge and skill, participation can improve planning and build support for change.

Recent years have witnessed an increase in participation methods employed by agencies, although the overall record has been uneven. Many agencies have expanded the scope of participation, and exceptional ones have sought participation with fervor. But few agencies have adopted strategic objectives for participation or employed methods that activate citizens. Analysts have criticized shortcomings of agencies that use participation to serve administrative ends rather than to transfer power to citizens, but have not shown that support has been built (Arnstein, 1965; Checkoway, 1981b).

Knowledge of participation has increased over time. Agency catalogues count more than fifty current or emergent methods; analyze selected methods according to function; and rationalize the design, implementation, and evaluation of practice (Advisory Com-

mission on Intergovernmental Rela
tions, 1979; Community Services Ad
ministration, 1978; U.S. Department
of Transportation, 1976). Analysts
study methods and factors influencing
the field (Burke, 1979; Gil and
Lucchesi, 1979; Glass, 1979;
Rosenbaum, 1983; Rosener, 1979).
Reflective practitioners provide lessons from experience. For example,
Creighton (1981) describes programs to
identify objectives and publics, formulate alternatives, assess internal and
external resources, and match methods
to purpose at each stage of planning.
However, others suggest that formal
methods alone do not assure the quality or impact of participation, while
other factors such as organizational
leadership and commitment do foster
quality participation (Checkoway and
O'Rourke, 1983; Schon, 1982). Methods serve functions but themselves
alone appear insufficient to activate
citizens or support agencies.

Find and Make Leaders

Citizen leaders ideally show commitment to goals and develop a following
in the community. They also attend
board meetings and chair committees,
but these are vehicles for leadership
rather than leadership itself. Many
planners retreat from the process by
which leaders are selected or developed. Instead they view leadership in
the narrow context of committees or
meetings, or consider selection and representation process beyond their domain, or "appropriate" leadership by
promoting people who hold positions
in established institutions. However,
leadership appropriation also may promote people who are unrepresentative
of the community or too busy to give

time to the agency. There is reason to
expect leaders to have commitment to
their agencies, but planning has many
participants who are skeptical of the enterprise. It would be ironic if agencies
appropriated leaders with relatively little commitment to planning, although
this happens in some communities.

How can planners find and make
leaders? Neven (1981) describes a process of searching for people with few
credentials but with demonstrated capacity for personal initiative and community problem-solving. Max (1973)
describes steps to find persons who
have shown talent for organizational
activity but never considered themselves as leaders. He directs staff to help
create a context where individuals can
recognize their abilities, and view
themselves as leaders. Bradley (1981)
describes an agency that seeks to identify potential leaders and develop their
skills. He assumes that any citizen can
function well with proper support, that
planners have responsibility to foster
development, and that if citizens are
not acting like leaders, planners may
not be doing their job properly. Dale
(1979) and Leinberger (1978) describe
curricula to teach board members how
to consult with citizens and enlist their
participation. There is no science of
leadership development in planning,
but if planners themselves do not take
responsibility, then who will?

Educate the Public

Citizens cannot be expected to support social planning without understanding their own problems and their
stake in the agency addressing them.
Why is planning important? Whose interests does it serve? The challenge is
not public relations but popular educa-

tion and community development. It is an older conception of planning in which planners help people learn about themselves, the forces that affect their lives, and possible actions against their problems (Friere, 1970; Goulet, 1973; Michael, 1973).

Private economic groups recognize popular education as a social force. They advertise to build their reputation and persuade others of their positions. They prepare programs for the workplace and classroom, publish curricula and textbooks, and establish research centers for strategic analysis and dissemination throughout society (Pines, 1982). Media officials respond to the most powerful inputs they receive, and these often come from private interests who may own or control information networks and communications channels. They thus may accept private notions of public planning, emphasize shortcomings of agencies, and present clients in a negative light. They can exert powerful influence on public understanding.

Planners also recognize the importance of popular education, but often employ public hearings and other low visibility approaches to inform the general public rather than specific constituencies (Texas Municipal League, 1975; Winholz, 1968). Others lack educational objectives or rely upon obscure media-like legal notices in newspapers, although studies show that these are among the least effective ways to communicate with the public (Rosener, 1975; Sinclair, 1977). Yet others use technical language which exacerbates difficulties in understanding and gives the impression that only professionals can present an adequate response (O'Rourke and Forouzesh, 1981). Low income and minority citizens may have

particular problems in understanding (Mueller, 1973). No wonder many people lack understanding of agencies, know little about the people served by them, or withdraw their support (Patti, 1983).

New initiatives are needed to expand public understanding of social planning. Who are the people to be reached? What issues will develop constituencies? What media and language will communicate? Joslyn-Scherer (1980) provides perspectives on problems and issues related to communications in the human services. Gordon (1978) formulates strategy for using newspaper, radio, and television media for social change. Brawley (1983) presents ways human service organizations can use mass media to communicate their message. Lauffer (1984) analyzes marketing methods for social agencies to sell services to target groups. Glenn (1947) describes agencies which produce planning exhibits for shopping centers and popular publications for mass distribution. There are innovative agencies that provide direct mail and personal outreach by staff and board members, conduct education and leadership training programs, publish educational guides to activate citizens, and reach the public through newspaper columns and television and radio appearances (Checkoway, 1981). These agencies view public understanding as central to their mission, and work to bring planning closer to the community.

Establish Relations with Influentials

These key actors are able to influence decisions that affect the agency. Who are the influentials? What are their political resources? What is their place in various institutions? What are the possible paths of influence? These are not random relationships but result from a plan for establishing and maintaining them.

How can planners identify and develop relations with influentials? Tait, Bokemeir, and Bohlen (n.d.) and Trounstine and Christensen (1982) describe positional, reputational, and other methods to identify influentials in the community. Roche (1981) analyzes ways to cultivate relationships through issue-based appeals to self-interest, special efforts to involve influentials in decisions, or priority responses to requests from government, business, and media. He describes planners who confer with influentials to explain their stake, and who participate in elections for officials in return for support. There is no lack of published advice on how to win friends and influence others.

Strategic analysis and tactical research are forms of intelligence which produce knowledge for neither general reference nor academic study, but for actual practice (Greever, 1972; Katz, 1980; Nix, 1977). Planners respect research but few employ strategic analysis with implementation in mind. Traditional planning studies serve functions but contrast with strategic studies which may influence implementation (Henderson and Thomas, 1980).

Build Coalitions

Coalitions are working relationships which unite individuals or groups around a common purpose. They may be short-term or relatively permanent, voluntary and occasional, or professionalized and staffed. They are important for individuals seeking to share resources and generate power beyond

reach of what each could accomplish alone (Dluhy, 1981; Schakowsky, n.d.).

Coalition-building varies from one case to another. On the local level, for example, an agency covering a large rural area applies "coalitional planning" among public officials and community leaders. Agency staff identify influentials and include them on governing boards as means to build support. Another agency creates councils which identify local problems, lobby legislators, and support implementation at the subarea level (Roche, 1981). Yet another agency targets underserved groups, and develops a coalition which has impact on agency activities (Glenn, Lipschultz, and Sherry, 1981).

On the state level, Dear and Patti (1981) show how groups build coalitions and influence legislation. Dluhy (1981) describes how professionals organize statewide political structure, take formal positions, and target bureaucrats and politicians. Berry (1981) analyzes how national coalitions conduct research for release to media, contact constituents, and advocate in legislative and administrative arenas. Coalitions face obstacles and have costs, but the costs should be weighed against benefits during turbulent times.

Advocate for Political Change

Advocacy is the practice of representing interests in legislative, administrative, or other established arenas. It assumes that existing institutions are capable of serving interests in society, that some interests mobilize more resources than others, and that practitioners can compensate for political imbalance by representing less powerful interests rather then special economic ones.

There is nothing new about planning as a form of advocacy. Early twentieth century planners applied rudiments as part of social reform movements intended to improve conditions in large cities and poor neighborhoods. In the 1960s and 1970s, planners openly advocated the interests of poor people and minorities in order to give them a voice in the planning process. They worked with community groups, contended with adversaries in the political arena, and sought to overcome the effects of public and private institutional decisions. They represented clients against bulldozers of urban renewal, routes of proposed expressways, and intrusion of facilities into nearby areas.

Today practitioners apply diverse advocacy roles. For example, legislative advocates lobby legislators to see things their way in policy decisions. Administrative advocates hold agencies accountable for compliance with mandates and regulations. Legal advocates represent classes of people in judicial arenas. Educational advocates build arenas around practice through popular education and media campaigns. Electoral advocates educate and turn out voters through political appeals connecting social issues to specific constituencies and agency programs (Newman, 1983).

There is growing knowledge of social practice as political advocacy (Patti, 1983a). Bell and Bell (1982) describe ways to monitor the bureaucracies responsible for implementation of social legislation. Dluhy (1981) and Whitaker (1982) analyze approaches to build coalitions to achieve social welfare objectives in the face of opposition. Salcito (1984) and Whitaker and Flory Baker (1982) analyze methods to participate in political campaigns to elect representatives supportive of social values. Messinger (1982) describes her campaign for political office and service as an elected official in New York City. Mahaffey (1982) analyzes her role as a city councilor in establishing a new service in Detroit. Political participation is a practice skill which directly affects the context of planning, a lesson which private economic interests learned years ago.

WHAT ARE THE OBSTACLES?

There are obstacles to political strategy for social planning at the community level, although this is not my primary purpose here. However, it is important to recognize reality while also embracing the possibility of change.

It is difficult to formulate political strategy when planning agencies lack legitimacy in the community. Private economic interests exercise power in planning decisions and resist efforts to share this with others. Citizens may accept the notion of private power over planning for public intervention. Only some of the general public perceive planning as an activity in which they could participate or know of the functions of planning agencies, or think that social programs "work" (Foley, 1955; Lipsky and Lounds, 1976; Riska and Taylor, 1978). Citizens often receive information through networks influenced by private interests and hesitate to "intrude" in areas involving private power. The lack of public knowledge tends to lower expectations and reduce incentives for planning. This is not to suggest that public attitudes toward planning necessarily arise from some independent consciousness to be taken as given. On the contrary, it would be as mistaken to take public attitudes as given as it would be to ignore private efforts to shape them or to reject the possibility that new initiatives could alter the situation. Intervention *can* make a difference, as private interests have shown for years.

It is also difficult to formulate political strategy when planners lack knowledge, skills, or attitudes conducive to practice. Baum (1980) finds only a minority of planners who regard their work as properly or inevitably political, a majority of straightforward technicians who believe they are or should be concerned with objective fact-finding and rational analysis of information, and a substantial group who are ambivalent about acting political and who tend to emphasize technical skills as a result of this ambivalence. There are exceptional practitioners who think and act politically, but they appear neither typical of practice nor influential in decisions nonetheless (Mathews, 1982; Wolk, 1981).

This image has implications for planning education. First, most planners do not perceive themselves as political, a situation which could be defined as a problem for education to address. Second, a minority of planners are political and their work could provide lessons for others. Third, a substantial group of planners are ambivalent and could be viewed as possible allies in changing practice. There is no *a priori* reason why planners could not develop skills to build political support in the community. Education could find excellent opportunities here.

But education does not always prepare people for effective practice. De Neufville (1983) contends that planning schools have no common litera-

ture, raise questions which have no answers, and provide poor instruction to make planning work. She argues that theory is inconsistent with experience, irrelevant to application, and frustrating to practitioners. Schone, Cremer, Osterman, and Perry (1976) find graduates who report that skills in negotiating, influencing, and consulting with clients are not usually available in planning curricula. Hemmens, Bergman, and Moroney (1978) find graduates who report that their jobs require skills different from training received in the schools. Some schools place students in political settings with elected officials and legislative representatives, but this has done little to strengthen subsequent political practice (Campfens and Loach, 1977).

But it would be as mistaken to blame scholars and educators for not bridging the gap between knowledge and action, as it would be to excuse practitioners from their responsibility to apply knowledge that is already available. The issue is not necessarily the continuing need to improve knowledge and education, but whether practitioners are willing or able to apply what is already known. Some planners have effectively influenced implementation, but others have opted to sit tight and wait for earlier times to return rather than to play a more active role. Despite technical innovations in planning, most planners have not adopted behavior conducive to agency survival.

In the final analysis, planning agencies face the power of private economic interests. Public participation has increased in scope and quality, and some citizens have organized around planning agencies, but private interests remain the most active, organized, and influential participants. They challenge planners to respond, but even exceptional practice would still operate in the face of this power.

WILL STRATEGY CREATE CHANGE?

Planning operates in a political context, and planners who want to influence implementation can benefit from political strategy. There are obstacles to political strategy for planning practice, but exceptional agencies show possibilities and provide lessons nonetheless. This does not suggest that the answer to implementation is in political strategy alone, for planning operates in an arena which requires more than the skills described here. Nor does it deny that this approach might engender controversy and arouse reaction by groups that may emerge as more powerful than before. Nor does it neglect that planning agencies offer only one of several means to act politically and create change in the community. There are other means, used as one or a combination, which may better create change. In the final analysis, political strategy for planning practice might not make much difference. But then again it might.

REFERENCES

Advisory Commission on Intergovernmental Relations. *Citizen Participation in the American Federal System.* Washington: Advisory Commission on Intergovernmental Relations, 1979.

Alexander, Chauncey. "Professional Social Workers and Political Responsibility." In *Practical Politics: Social Work and Political Responsibility,* eds., Maryann Mahaffey and John W. Hanks. Silver Spring: National Association of Social Workers, 1982.

Barkdoll, Gerald L. "Involving Constituents in Agency Priority Setting: A Case Study." *Evaluation and Program Planning.* 6 (1983): 31-37.

Barrett, Susan and Colin Fudge, eds. *Policy and Action: Essays on the Implementation of Public Policy.* New York: Methuen, 1981.

Baum, Howell S. *Planners and Public Expectations.* Cambridge, MA: Schenkman, 1983.

Baum, Howell S. "Politics and Ambivalence in Planners' Practice." *Journal of Planning Education and Research.* 3 (1983a): 13-22.

Bell, William G., and Budd L. Bell. "Monitoring the Bureaucracy: An Extension of Legislative Lobbying." In *Practical Politics: Social Work and Political Responsibility,* eds., Maryann Mahaffey and John W. Hanks. Silver Spring: National Association of Social Workers, 1982.

Benveniste, Guy. *The Politics of Expertise.* San Francisco: Boyd and Fraser, 1977.

Berry, Jeffrey M. "Beyond Citizen Participation: Effective Advocacy Before Administrative Agencies." *The Journal of Applied Behavioral Science.* 17 (1981): 463-477.

Booth, Heather. *Direct Action Organizing.* Chicago: Midwest Academy, 1977.

Bradley, John. "An Educational Approach to Health Planning." In *Citizens and Health Care: Participation and Planning for Social Change,* ed., Barry Checkoway. New York: Pergamon, 1981.

Brawley, Edward A. *Mass Media and Human Services: Getting the Message Across.* Beverly Hills: Sage Publications, 1983.

Brown, L. David. "Organizing Participation Research: Interfaces for Joint Inquiry and Organizational Change." *Journal of Occupational Behavior.* 4 (1983): 9-19.

Bryson, John M. and Andre L. Delbecq. "A Contingent Approach to Strategy and Tactics in Program Planning." *Journal of the American Planning Association.* 45 (1979): 167-179.

Bryson, John M., R. Edward Freeman, and William D. Roering. *Strategic Planning in the Public Sector: Approaches and Future Directions.* Minneapolis: Strategic Management Research Center, University of Minnesota, 1985.

Burke, Edmund M. *A Participatory Approach to Urban Planning.* New York: Human Sciences Press, 1979.

Campfens, Hubert and Fred Loach. "Political Placements in Social Work Education: The United States and Canada." *Journal of Education for Social Work.* 13 (1977): 11-17.

Chamber of Commerce of the United States. *A National Health Care Strategy.* Washington: National Chamber Foundation, 1979.

Checkoway, Barry. "Citizen Action in Health Planning." In *Citizens and Health Care: Participation and Planning for Social Change,* ed., Barry Checkoway. New York: Pergamon Press, 1981a.

Checkoway, Barry. "The Empire Strikes Back: More Lessons for Health Care Consumers." *Journal of Health Politics, Policy and Law.* 7 (1982a): 111-117.

Checkoway, Barry. "Citizens on Local Health Planning Boards: What Are the Obstacles?" *Journal of the Community Development Society.* 10 (1979): 106.

Checkoway, Barry. "Public Participation in Health Planning Agencies: Promise and Practice." *Journal of Health Politics, Policy and Law.* 7 (1982b): 122-133.

Checkoway, Barry. "Consumerism in Health Planning Agencies." In *Health Planning in the United States: Selected Policy Issues.* Washington, DC: National Academy of Sciences Press, 1981b.

Checkoway, Barry. "The Politics of Public Hearings." *The Journal of Applied Behavioral Sciences.* 17 (1981c): 566-582.

Checkoway, Barry. "Two Types of Planning in Neighborhoods." *Journal of Planning Research and Education.* 3 (1984): 102-109.

Checkoway, Barry and Thomas O'Rourke. "Correlates of Consumer Participation in Health Planning Agencies." *Policy Studies Journal.* 3 (1983): 296-310.

Checkoway, Barry and Jon Van Til. "What Do We Know About Citizen Participation? A Selective Review of Research." In *Citizen Participation in America: Essays on the State of the Art,* ed., Stuart Langton. Lexington: Lexington Books, 1978.

Community Services Administration. *Citizen Participation.* Washington, DC: Community Services Administration, 1978.

Creighton, James L. *The Public Involvement Manual.* Cambridge, MA: Abt Associates, 1981.

Dale, Duane, with David Magnani and Robin Miller. *Beyond Experts: A Guide for Citizen Group Training.* Amherst: Citizen Involvement Training Project, 1979.

Danaceau, Paul. *The Health Planning Guidelines Controversy: A Report from Iowa and Texas.* Hyattsville: Health Resources Administration, 1979.

Davidoff, Paul. "Advocacy and Pluralism in Planning." *Journal of the American Institute of Planners.* 31 (1965): 596-615.

Davies, James C. *Politics of Pollution.* Bloomington: Indiana University Press, 1975.

Dear, Ronald B. and Rino J. Patti. "Legislative Advocacy: Seven Effective Tactics." *Social Work.* 26 (1981): 289-296.

Dluhy, Milan. *Changing the System: Political Advocacy for Disadvantaged Groups.* Beverly Hills: Sage Publications, 1981.

Dyckman, John. "Planning in a Time of Reaction." *Journal of Planning Education and Research.* 3 (1983): 5-12.

Feldstein, Paul J. *Health Associations and the Demand for Legislation: The Political Economy of Health.* Cambridge: Ballinger, 1977.

Feshbach, Dan, and Takuya Nakamoto. *Political Strategies for Health Planning Agencies.* In *Citizens and Health Care: Participation and Planning for Social Change,* ed., Barry Checkoway. New York: Pergamon Press, 1981.

Foley, Donald. "How Many Berkeley Residents Know About Their City's Master Plan?" *Journal of the American Institute of Planners.* 21 (1955): 138-144.

Friedman, John F. *Retracking America: A Theory of Transactive Planning.* Garden City, New York: Anchor, 1973.

Friere, Paulo. *Pedagogy of the Oppressed.* New York: Seabury Press, 1970.

Gil, Efraim and Enid Lucchesi. "Citizen Participation in Planning." In *The Practice of Local Government Planning,* ed., Frank So. Washington, DC: Interactional City Management Association, 1979.

Glass, James J. "Citizen Participation in Planning: The Relationship between Objectives and Techniques." *Journal of the American Planning Association.* 45 (1979): 180-189.

Glenn, Karen. *Planning, Politics and Power: A User's Guide to Taming the Health Care System.* Washington, DC: Consumer Coalition for Health, 1979.

Glenn, Karen, Claire Lipschultz, and Susan

Sherry. "The Consumer Health Advocacy Project." In *Citizens and Health Care: Participation and Planning for Social Change,* ed., Barry Checkoway. New York: Pergamon Press, 1981.

Goals for Dallas. *Goals for Dallas.* Paper presented at the Annual Conference of the American Planning Association, Dallas, 1982.

Gordon, Robbie. *We Interrupt this Program . . . A Citizen's Guide to Using the Media for Social Change.* Amherst: Citizen Involvement Training Project, 1978.

Goulet, Denis. *The Cruel Choice: A New Concept in the Theory of Development.* New York: Atheneum, 1973.

Greever, Barry. *Tactical Investigations for People's Struggles.* Chicago: Midwest Academy, 1972.

Gummer, Burton. "The Social Administrator as Politician." In *Human Services at Risk,* ed., Felice Davidson Perlmutter. Lexington: Lexington Books, 1983.

Harty, Sheila. *Hucksters in the Classroom: A Review of Industry Propaganda in Schools.* Washington: Center for Study of Responsive Law, 1979.

Hasenfeld, Yeheskel. "The Changing Context of Human Services." In *Human Services at Risk,* ed., Felice Davidson Perlmutter. Lexington: Lexington Books, 1983a.

Hasenfeld, Yeheskel. *Human Service Organizations.* Englewood Cliffs, NJ: Prentice-Hall, 1983b.

Hasenfeld, Yeheskel. "The Implementation of Change in Human Service Organizations: A Political Economy Perspective." *Social Services Review.* 54 (1980): 508-520.

Hemmens, George C., Edward M. Bergman, and Robert M. Moroney. "The Practitioner's View of Social Planning." *Journal of the American Institute of Planners.* 44 (1978): 181-192.

Henderson, Paul, and David N. Thomas. *Skills in Neighborhood Work.* London: George Allen & Unwin, 1980.

Heskin, Allan. "Crises in Response: A Historical Perspective on Advocacy Planning." *Journal of the American Planning Association.* 46 (1980): 50-63.

Johannes, John R. *To Serve the People: Congress and Constituency Service.* Lincoln: University of Nebraska Press, 1984.

Joslyn-Scherer, M. S. *Communication in the Human Services.* Beverly Hills: Sage Publications, 1980.

Katz, John. *Action Research: A Guide to Research.* New Orleans: The Institute, 1980.

Kimmey, James R. "Technical Assistance and Consultation for Consumers." In *Citizens and Health Care: Participation and Planning for Social Change,* ed., Barry Checkoway. New York: Pergamon Press, 1981.

Klein, Ted, and Fred Danzig. *How to be Heard: Making the Media Work for You.* New York: Macmillan, 1974.

Krueckeberg, Donald A., and Arthur L. Silvers. *Urban Planning Analysis: Methods and Models.* New York: John Wiley, 1974.

Krumholz, Norman. "A Retrospective View of Equity Planning: Cleveland 1969-1979." *Journal of the American Planning Association.* 48 (1982): 163-184.

Lancourt, Joan. *Confront or Concede: The Alinsky Citizen-Action Organizations.* Lexington: Lexington Books, 1979a.

Lancourt, Joan. *Developing Implementation Strategies: Community Organization Not Public Relations.* Boston: Boston University Center for Health Planning, 1979b.

Larson, James S. *Why Policies Fail: Improving Policy Implementation.* New York: Praeger, 1980.

Leinberger, Paul, ed. *How to Be a More Effective Commissioner or Public Board Member.* Berkeley: Continuing Education in Environmental Design, University of California, 1978.

Linton, Rhoda and Michele Whitham. "With Mourning, Rage, Empowerment and Defiance: The 1981 Women's Pentagon Action." *Socialist Review.* 62-63 (1982): 11-36.

Lipschultz, Claire. *Political Action in Health Planning: Building a Consumer Constituency.* Bethesda: Alpha Center for Health Planning, 1980.

Lipsky, Michael and Morris Lounds. "Citizen Participation and Health Care: Problems of Government Induced Participation." *Journal of Health Politics, Policy and Law.* 1 (1976): 85-111.

Lynn, Laurence E. *The State and Human Services: Organizational Change in a Political Context.* Cambridge: MIT Press, 1980.

Mahaffey, Maryann. "A Social Worker-

Politician Creates a New Service." In *Practical Politics: Social Work and Political Responsibility,* eds., Maryann Mahaffey and John W. Hanks. Silver Spring: National Association of Social Workers, 1982.

Marcuse, Peter. "The Feeble Retreat of Planning." *Journal of Planning Education and Research.* 3 (1983): 52-53.

Marmor, Theodore R. and James A. Morone. "Representing Consumer Interests: Imbalanced Markets, Health Planning and the HSAs." *Milbank Memorial Fund Quarterly/Health and Society.* 58 (1980): 125-165.

Mathews, Gary. "Social Workers and Political Influence." *Social Services Review.* 58 (1982): 617-628.

Max, Steve. *Four Steps to Developing Leaders.* Chicago: Midwest Academy, 1973.

Mayer, Neil S. *Neighborhood Organizations and Community Development.* Washington: Urban Institute Press, 1984.

Mazmanian, Daniel and Paul A. Sabatier, eds. *Effective Policy Implementation.* Lexington: Lexington Books, 1981.

McKinlay, John B., ed. *Issues in the Political Economy of Health Care.* New York: Tavistock Publications, 1984.

McMahon, J. Alexander. "The Perspective of the American Medical Association." In *Effects of Payment Mechanisms on the Health Care Delivery System,* ed., W. R. Roy. Washington: Department of Health, Education and Welfare, 1978.

Mendeloff, James. *Regulating Safety: An Economic and Political Analysis of Occupational Safety and Health Policy.* Cambridge, MA: MIT Press, 1979.

Messinger, Ruth W. "Empowerment: A Social Worker's Politics." In *Practical Politics: Social Work and Political Responsibility,* eds., Maryann Mahaffey and John W. Hanks. Silver Spring: National Association of Social Workers, 1982.

Michael, Donald J. *On Learning to Plan and Planning to Learn.* San Francisco: Jossey-Bass, 1973.

Mueller, C. *The Politics of Communications.* New York: Oxford University Press, 1973.

Neven, David. *Left-Handed Fastballers: Scouting and Training America's Grass-Roots Leaders 1966-1977.* New York: Ford Foundation, 1981.

Newman, William H., and Harvey W. Wallender. "Managing Not-For-Profit Enterprises." *Academy of Management Review.* 3 (1978): 24-31.

Newman, Sanford. "Project VOTE! Tapping the Power of the Poor." *Social Policy.* 13 (1983): 15-19.

Nix, Harold L. *The Community and Its Involvement in the Study Planning Action Process.* Washington: Department of Health, Education and Welfare, 1983.

Norville, Jerry L., and Robert E. Modrow. "Preparing for Potential Actions by Nursing Home Reform Groups." *Nursing Homes.* March-April (1978): 4-11.

O'Rourke, Thomas W., and Mohammed Forouzesh. "Readability of HSAs' Plans: Implications for Public Involvement." *Health Law Project Library Bulletin.* 6 (1981): 23-26.

Palumbo, Dennis J., and Marvin A. Harder, eds. *Implementing Public Policy.* Lexington: Lexington Books, 1981.

Patti, Rino J. "Political Action." In *1983-84 Supplement to the Encyclopedia of Social Work.* Silver Spring: National Association of Social Workers, 1983a.

Patti, Rino J. *Social Welfare Administration: Managing Social Programs in a Developmental Context.* Englewood Cliffs: Prentice-Hall, 1983b.

Pines, Burton Yale. *Back to Basics: The Traditionalist Movement That Is Sweeping Grass-Roots America.* New York: William Morrow, 1982.

Pitkin, Hannah F. *The Concept of Representation.* Berkeley: University of California Press, 1967.

Pressman, Jeffrey L., and Aaron B. Wildavsky. *Implementation.* Berkeley: University of California Press, 1973.

Relman, Arnold S. "The New Medical-Industrial Complex." *The New England Journal of Medicine.* 303 (1980): 963-970.

Riordan, William L. *Plunkett of Tammany Hall: A Series of Very Plain Talks on Very Practical Politics.* New York: E. P. Dutton, 1963.

Riska, E., and J. A. Taylor. "Consumer Attitudes Toward Health Policy and Knowledge and Legislation." *Journal of Health Politics, Policy and Law.* 3 (1978): 112-123.

Roche, Joseph L. "Community Organization Approach to Health Planning." In *Citizens and Health Care: Participation and Planning for Social Change,* ed., Barry Checkoway. New York: Pergamon Press, 1981.

Rosenbaum, Nelson, ed. n.d. *Citizen Participation: Models and Methods of Evaluation.* Washington: Center for Responsive Governance.

Rosenberg, Charlotte. "These Doctors Head Off a Health-Planning Debacle." *Medical Economics.* 27 (1980): 33-35, 42, 47, 51.

Rosener, Judy B. "Citizen Participation: Tying Strategy to Function." *Public Management.* 12 (1975): 16-19.

Salcito, Ramon M. "Social Work Practice in Political Campaigns." *Social Work.* 29 (1984): 189-191.

Schone, Donald A. *The Reflective Practitioner: How Professionals Think in Action.* New York: Basic Books, 1983.

Schone, Donald A., Nancy Sheldon Cremer, Paul Osterman, and Charles Perry. "Planners in Transition: Report on a Survey of Alumni of MIT's Department of Urban Studies, 1960-1971." *Journal of the American Institute of Planners.* 42 (1976): 193-202.

Sinclair, Michael. "The Public Hearing as a Participatory Device: Evaluation of the IJC Experience." In *Public Participation in Planning,* eds., W.R.D. Sewell and J. T. Coppock, New York: John Wiley, 1977.

Smith, Frank J., and Randolph T. Hester. *Community Goal-Setting.* Stroudsburg, PA: Hutchinson Press, 1982.

Sosin, Michael, and Sharon Caulum. "Advocacy: A Conceptualization for Social Work Practice." *Social Work.* 28 (1983): 12-19.

Staples, Lee. *Roots to Power: A Manual for Grassroots Organizing.* New York: Praeger, 1984.

Tait, John L., Janet Bokemeir, and Janet Bohlen, n.d. *Identifying the Community Power Actors: A Guide for Change Agents.* Ames: Iowa Cooperative Extension Service.

Texas Municipal League. *Building Citizen Support in Texas Cities.* Austin: Texas Municipal League, 1975.

Thompson, Frank J. *Health Policy and the Bureaucracy: Politics and Implementation.* Cambridge: MIT Press, 1981.

Tropman, John. *Policy Management in the Human Services.* New York: Columbia University Press, 1984.

Trounstine, Philip J., and Terry Christensen. *Movers and Shakers: The Study of Community Power.* New York: St. Martin's Press, 1982.

U.S. Department of Transportation. *Effective Citizen Participation in Transportation Planning.* Washington, DC: Government Printing Office, 1976.

Walker, J. Malcolm. "Limits of Strategic Management in Voluntary Organizations." *Journal of Voluntary Action Research,* 1983.

Walzer, Michael. "Political Action: The Problem of Dirty Hands." *Philosophy and Public Affairs.* 2 (1973): 160-180.

Whitaker, William H. "Organizing Social Action Coalitions: WIC Comes to Wyoming." In *Practical Politics: Social Work and Political Responsibility,* eds., Maryann Mahaffey and John W. Hanks. Silver Spring: National Association of Social Workers, 1982.

Whitaker, William H., and Jan Flory-Baker. "Ragtag Social Workers Take on the Good Old Boys and Elect a State Senator." In *Practical Politics: Social Work and Political Responsibility,* eds., Maryann Mahaffey and John W. Hanks. Silver Spring: National Association of Social Workers, 1982.

Winholz, William G. "Planning and the Public." In *Principles and Practice of Urban Planning,* eds., William I. Goodman and Eric C. Freund. Washington: International City Managers' Association, 1962.

Wolk, James. "Are Social Workers Politically Active?" *Social Work.* 26 (1981): 283-288.

Wortman, Max S. "A Radical Shift from Bureaucracy to Strategic Management in Voluntary Organizations." *Journal of Voluntary Action Research.* 10 (1981): 62-81.

18.

Carl V. Patton

CITIZEN INPUT AND PROFESSIONAL RESPONSIBILITY

INTRODUCTION[1]

Many planners believe that the quality of planning decisions relates substantially to the similarity between actual citizen desires and desires as revealed through public hearings, citizen surveys, and other sources of public input. Political scientists, organizational theorists, and other scholars have developed perspectives on decision making relating to the motivation to participate and the mode and the quality of participation.

Planners must use these concepts in a very practical way as part of the plan-making process. How much weight should be given to competing viewpoints? Which citizen opinion poll is correct? Which citizen group truly speaks for the community? Which data sets about opinions, attitudes, and beliefs are indeed representative? How should decisions between technically superior and politically feasible alternatives be made, especially when staff recommendations support a technically superior alternative that does not have public support?

In order to improve the quality of citizen input, planners have increased the quantity and sources of this input by expanding the number of public hearings, by conducting public opinion surveys, and by collecting policy-relevant data from decisionmakers and other public officials.

The public hearing has long been widely used for collecting citizen opinion, although not without problems. As both a practicing planner and a citizen member of several boards and commissions, I have observed citizen opinion on a particular topic at public meetings change over time. This was due not so much to specific individuals changing their minds as to the changing composition of the group of citizens attending the public meetings. Who can be certain that the citizens *attending* a public hearing are a representative sample of the relevant community, and who can be certain that those people *voicing* their opinions at public meetings are a representative sample of the community or even of the persons attending the given public meeting? Not only may citizen opinion at public meetings change over time, but this opinion may also differ from opinion collected from other sources at the same time. In particular, it may differ from opinions expressed through citizen surveys.

Source: Carl V. Patton, "Citizen Input and Professional Responsibility" in *Journal of Planning Education and Research* (Summer 1983), pp. 46-50.

[1]An earlier version of this article appeared in *Planning and Public Policy,* Vol. 7, No. 3 (August 1981), as "Testing Citizen Input to Planning Decisions: Some Observations."

TESTING THE REPRESENTATIVENESS OF CITIZEN INPUT

Through my involvement with a community development (CD) program, I had the opportunity to compare the majority opinion expressed at public meetings for development policies with the opinion of a representative sample of heads of households of the same area. Comparisons were made for two community development target areas within the same city.

Three types of differences in opinion were considered: (1) differences between group opinion expressed at two public meetings; (2) differences between group opinion expressed at public meetings and majority citizen opinion as revealed through a sample survey; and (3) differences in opinion between the majority opinion of development site residents and that of nondevelopment site residents.

For both CD target areas, comparisons were made between majority opinion expressed at two different public meetings, and majority opinion at public meetings was compared with majority opinion generated through a random sample of target area households. Substantial differences were found between the majority opinion expressed at different public hearings and that obtained through the sample survey.[2]

Within one of the target areas, additional information was collected about the attitudes toward a proposed redevelopment scheme for a particular site. Opinions of the *residents* who would be *directly* affected by the proposal were compared with opinions of the surrounding *neighbors* who would be *indirectly* affected by the proposal. Substantial differences were also found between the opinions of these two groups.

It is important to note that the differences between the *opinions of groups* were able to be measured in this study, not the change in the opinion of specific *individuals.* The shift in opinion at public meetings is likely attributable to the changing composition of the group in attendance. The difference between majority opinion expressed at public meetings and majority opinion gathered through citizen surveys may also be attributable to the different composition of the two groups.

Since groups are comprised of individuals, changes in group opinion may also be attributable to changes or differences in individual opinions. For example, there is the possibility that differences exist between an individual's public and private opinions. We may argue one way in public and act the opposite way in the privacy of our home or in the secrecy of the voting booth. It is conceivable that an individual's public statement on an issue might be influenced by the composition of the audience or that the anonymity of a survey might allow one's subconscious attitudes to surface. One might even consider an extreme situation in which individuals make certain public statements because they feel threatened or are otherwise coerced. Is not the desire to express one's individual beliefs without fear of consequence the foundation upon which the secret ballot is based?

---

[2]For a description of the survey see Thomas E. King, "Neighborhood Renewal: A Case Study of Citizen Views," Graduate Master's Project, Urbana: University of Illinois at Urbana-Champaign, Department of Urban and Regional Planning, 1981, mimeographed.

Perhaps the assurance of anonymity would benefit planning decisions when representative citizen opinion is sought.

Opinion Conflict in Two Case Areas

Located within the same middle-sized, midwestern town, one community development target area was predominantly black, the other was virtually all white. The black area was the initial CD target area. The program was extended to the white area after it had operated for several years in the black area.

The issue of shifting citizen priorities was brought to my attention during the early days of my involvement with the commission. At the first CD meeting I attended, the audience spoke at length about support for the expenditure of CD funds on street reconstruction, sidewalk construction, and streetlight updating and installation. At my second CD public meeting several members of the audience voiced opposition to the above expenditures, arguing that funding priority be given to housing rehabilitation. Other members of the audience did not reaffirm or reject the earlier position.

Conflict in citizen opinion again surfaced when hearings were held about a possible application for unallocated federal funds. Based on input at earlier public meetings, the CD commission (and CD division professional staff) felt that residents favored the redevelopment of a particular blighted site within the larger target area. The site was proposed for redevelopment through an acquisition, demolition, and housing reconstruction program. Single family homes and low density apartments and townhouses were proposed for the site.

A grant request was prepared for the unallocated funds but was not supported by persons attending the public hearing. Those speaking against the proposal argued that it would deprive the affected population of homes that they did not want to leave. These continuing conflicts in opinion led the CD division to arrange for a random sample survey of resident attitudes toward various redevelopment options.

The survey results provided an additional source of opinion about development schemes. Two comparisons were made possible: extent of support for development options expressed at the public meetings was compared with that expressed through the survey, and attitudes of redevelopment site *residents* were compared with the attitudes of their *neighbors.*

Residents versus Neighbors

The sample survey revealed opinions about overall target area development that were generally consistent with those expressed throughout the two public meetings. However, the survey did not reveal widespread opposition to capital improvements as might have been concluded from the second public meeting.

The sample survey also revealed a major difference of opinion between residents and neighbors. Both groups favored public improvement, but a greater percentage of residents felt change was needed. The residents of the proposed redevelopment site were overwhelmingly in favor of the proposal for the acquisition of their homes and relocation elsewhere in the target area or in the larger community. The neighbors, on the other hand, tended to oppose these measures on the basis that it would not be good for the residents of the proposed redevelopment site, who, the neighbors believed, wanted to remain in their present homes. The report of the survey of residents and neighbors summarized this contradiction.

The residents feel change is needed even more strongly than the neighbors. The residents of the area recognize that the majority of houses are beyond repair and that the situation is severe enough to warrant demolition of the area and replacement with new development. The neighbors were protective of the residents and did not want them to be forced out of their houses. The actual case seems to be, however, that the residents are presently unhappy with the area and most households would take advantage of an opportunity to leave.[3]

Neighbor opposition may have resulted from one or more factors. Neighbors may have felt that the residents would have been relocated against their wishes or in undesirable housing, they may have wished to see a redevelopment plan that encompassed more of the target area, they may have felt the expected funds could have been better spent on other improvements, or they may have feared that a developer would receive a windfall. Later personal interviews also lend credence to the possibility that neighbor opposition grew in part from envy over the benefits that would be received by the residents. The homes of these persons would have been purchased at fair market value and the households would have received up to an additional $15,000 for relocation.

---

[3]Ibid., p. 60.

Focusing on Specifics
Can Switch Preferences

Wishing to avoid similar ambiguity of opinion in a second target area, the CD division combined a sample survey with public meetings from the outset of its involvement in the second target area.[4]

Conflict between citizen opinion derived from public meetings and that derived from the sample survey was revealed in two ways. Early public meetings in this target area were dominated by one group that "got its members out." A church congregation sought the reconstruction of the street on which its physical facility fronts. Members of the church who lived outside the target area joined the members who lived in the target area at public hearings. Thus the majority opinion at public meetings favored reconstruction of the street. The sample survey of resident opinion, however, revealed a low ranking for this street.

In regard to a second issue, citizen opinion at public meetings favored capital improvements such as street reconstruction, sidewalk rehabilitation, storm drainage system repair, *and* grants and loans for home rehabilitation. But as was to be found through the sample survey, respondents wanted minimum home improvement grants essentially for low income and older persons and loans for *others,* not for themselves. This finding underscores a position found in the first target area, that "private homes are not a govern-

---

[4]For a description of the survey see Janet Jaross-Arbies, "A Survey and Analysis of the Community Development Needs of the ... Neighborhood ...," Graduate Master's Project, Urbana: University of Illinois at Urbana-Champaign, Department of Urban and Regional Planning, 1981, mimeographed.

ment concern." It also suggests that public opinion may differ from private opinion or at least that a survey may be able to reveal a fuller dimension of general public opinion.

This is not to say that surveys necessarily reveal consensus among residents. For example, a majority of respondents favored the reconstruction of a particular street, but there was disagreement about the *mode* of repair. Half of the respondents in favor of reconstruction wanted the brick street rebuilt in its original style as an "aesthetically pleasing" brick street; the other half wanted it reconstructed as a smooth, modern concrete street. Consequently, neither *specific* option was supported by a majority of respondents, although a majority of respondents favored the reconstruction of the street *in general.*

Such a dilemma may encourage an option to be selected which is supported by a smaller percentage of the population than another option. This can occur when it is necessary for one of the *general* options to be restated in more *specific* terms. Thus the support may be split so that the top-ranked alternative loses support, permitting another option to receive a plurality of votes. In a case such as that above, a street rated second in need of repair might move to first place because residents support the details of its reconstruction.

Support for particular development options may also be influenced by respondent perception of who will benefit and who will bear the costs of the proposal. A conflict of opinion similar to that between residents and neighbors in the first target area appeared between renters and owners in this second target area. Residents along certain

streets opposed reconstruction of their streets, while neighbors on other streets supported the reconstruction. Examining specific streets, it was found that opposition tended to come from renters and support tended to come from home owners. Although our evidence is limited, it appears that these differences derive from a perception by renters that the property owner will receive the benefit of the increased property value brought about by the street improvement while they (the renter) will bear through their rents the cost of possible higher property taxes resulting from increases in property assessment. Owners, on the other hand, perceive that they will bear both the costs and benefits but that the benefits will outweigh the costs.

IMPLICATIONS FOR PLANNING EDUCATION AND PRACTICE

Citizen action, planning decisions, community development allocations, and urban change have been explained by theories of political power, voting patterns, social and economic status, and similar sociocultural phenomena. Also, every participant presumably is motivated by some vision of the public good. Such visions are expected to differ, but they are usually assumed to be high-minded. Seldom are less public-spirited emotions presented as the driving force behind planning and development decisions.

The cases suggest that planning theory which addresses citizen input, development decisions, and the public interest may need to be modified. Required is explicit recognition that commonplace human motives and emotions, such as personal interest, self-aggrandizement, and envy may underlie citizen positions, may thwart ideas, and may affect the decision-making process. It is possible that these motivations may even increase in the future as budgets constrict. Those who will benefit from a program may be opposed more and more by their neighbors who do not qualify for the program. To those excluded (sometimes merely because they live across a census tract boundary), the benefits to the neighbors may appear to be windfalls.

Planners need to recognize these issues. At a minimum, the benefits program participants will receive and why *they* will receive them must be clearly presented. It may also be helpful to explain carefully the concepts of indirect economic benefit, externalities, and spillover effects. It may be that neighbors will receive more than they think they will from the programs they oppose. Furthermore, planners may need to design programs and activities that will directly benefit neighbors as well as residents.

A related issue is the domination of public hearings by especially vocal individuals. Those who have been involved as professional planners or who have served on citizen boards, planning commissions, and the like are aware that aggressive people exert more than their share of influence over public decisions. The possible biases resulting from this dominance should also be recognized.

Although the evidence from these two cases is far from conclusive, it suggests that there is much to be said for using multiple sources of citizen opinion, for avoiding the complete reliance on public hearings, and for including sample surveys as an integral part of the citizen input process. This point was made by the analyst who examined the citizen opinion data from the meetings and surveys in the second target area.

. . . At public meetings, the most outspoken people are heard while others sit and listen . . . In addition, community socioeconomic data cannot be gathered at a public meeting . . . due to the biased representation of the community. In contrast, a well-designed household survey gets responses from many different people of a wide variety of socioeconomic backgrounds . . . this type of survey can gather information about the severity of problems in the community and about changes residents would like to see, as well as determine the climate for public agency proposed changes. The survey can also stimulate additional community interest in the proposed projects . . . [5]

Surveys have limitations, of course. "Standard" surveys may be forced to fit "nonstandard" neighborhoods, may achieve a low response rate, and may not reveal important cyclical changes. Surveys also may require talent and money that are not available. These limitations can be overcome through the use of proper survey research methods that capitalize on the efficiency of sampling, the effectiveness of longitudinal surveys, and the parsimonious use of talent in neighboring governmental units and nearby universities.

The cases also suggest that planners need to be aware that technically superior alternatives may not be politically acceptable and that alternatives generated through public input may not be technically feasible. In some instances technically feasible alternatives may be known and the planner's task may be to assist relevant actors in deciding among the alternatives. Planners have long recognized the need for political analysis, but how the political analysis is conducted is still being debated. One

---

[5]Ibid., pp. 1-2.

view is that after the proper policy has been identified we need to figure out how to obtain it. This approach holds when planning and analysis is seen as a sequential process in which the problem definition leads to the specification of alternatives, and then the preferred alternative is implemented. Political factors are thus considered at the end of the analytical process. Another approach is to introduce political analysis at each step of the planning process, in order to reconcile differences between technical and political feasibility while changes can be made with less disruption. Under this conceptualization political feasibility is considered during problem definition and alternatives generation, analysis and evaluation. In the linear approach politics is simply one of the criteria used to select the preferred technical alternative. In the iterative approach there is a continuous interaction between political and technical considerations as new technical information is discovered and as individuals and groups specify their preferences.

For citizen input to contribute to better plans, planners need to recognize political concerns as an integral part of the planning process, learn terminology to communicate about political factors, and use consistent methods to report, analyze, and display political issues and their planning ramifications. Recognizing the importance of political issues means more than acknowledging that designing and implementing plans involves politics. It means actively seeking out and analyzing political issues, determining the stakes of political actors, and designing politically acceptable alternatives. Too often we so strongly desire to identify the technically superior alternative, and we become so

engrossed in calculating economic costs and benefits, that we postpone the political analysis. Instead of tacking political analysis onto the end of analysis by means of a public hearing, we must begin as early as the problem definition stage to ferret out both the technical and political aspects of the problem and the technical and political goals and objectives of the client and interested and affected groups. The planner must ask whether he or she is dealing with a technical or political problem or both and determine the purposes of the analysis and citizen input efforts. Are the citizen input activity and political analysis intended to get the public to recognize the problem, to have a client or superior to accept the analysis, or to garner votes? If we want the public to recognize the problem, we might concentrate on ways to cause important public groups to increase their stakes in the problem. If we want our superior to accept the analysis, we might focus on office or agency politics. If we want to obtain a majority vote for a technical solution, we might think of alternative means of introducing the policy and the impact of timing of the introduction.

CONCLUSION

There may be differences between the public and private opinions of individuals as well as between groups. Planning decisions must be based to a substantial degree on citizen values and objectives, but planners must be certain that the publicly voiced opinions are indeed the true and full positions of the respondents.

Use of either a public meeting or a citizen survey should depend on the purpose. Public meetings are best when the purpose is to inform, to generate ideas, and to let people express their viewpoints, even to the extent that they attempt to convince other citizens. Sample surveys are best for collecting factual data about potentially sensitive topics and for obtaining a sample of representative citizen opinions. They are also useful for generating ideas and for informing people about options. Surveys obviously are not a substitute for public forums.

Nor are surveys and meetings a substitute for decision making by public officials. The cases show that often there may be no clear-cut solution that can be derived from either a survey or a public meeting. Professional judgment will have to be used in the interpretation of data from public meetings and citizen surveys, and planners will have to judge the *quality* of the citizen input. Is the participant responding as a self-interested citizen or as a citizen in the role of planner? It may be that sample surveys are better at eliciting the self-interest response and that properly conducted public meetings may be able to generate the citizen-as-planner response. However, it is not always clear which of these types of responses the planner needs. Sometimes the planner may want to discover what individuals seek for themselves; at other times the planner may want to guide people toward what he or she believes is in the public interest.

Even when planners use alternative methods to obtain citizen input, these efforts will not replace the political process. Some planners have tended to eschew the political process, and others continue to seek "objective" ways to decide among competing alternatives. The cases discussed here suggest that alternative citizen input methods can generate conflicting input, that these methods do not replace the political process, that planners must be actively involved in the decision process, and that good decisions require input from multiple sources.

Findings from both public meetings and citizen surveys must be integrated with other information such as census data, engineering analyses, and opinions of public officials. Certainly surveys should not be used as a shield from public debate, and public input in general should not be used as a way to derive an average answer and thus provide an escape from the responsibility of making tough, sometimes unpopular, planning and development decisions.

CHAPTER III

Locality Development

The crux of locality development is citizens from all walks of life learning new skills and engaging in a cooperative self-help process to achieve a wide variety of community improvements. It implies a condition of limited resources and an effort to increase and expand such resources for mutual benefit. As Arthur Dunham puts it, this approach involves—

...helping people to deal more effectively with their problems and objectives, by helping them develop, strengthen and maintain qualities of participation, self-direction and cooperation....[1]

Moreover, this strategic orientation is optimistic and positive about people's ability to work with each other around common concerns.

Khinduka highlights some of the positive features of locality development, and points out some limitations as well. He comments on its lofty aims in educating and motivating people in the direction of self-help, its efforts to develop local leadership and enhance a sense of citizenship and civic consciousness, and its attempts to strengthen local democracy. The broad and diverse purposes and wide scope of community involvement embodied in the approach also receive favorable evaluation. Khinduka characterizes locality development as reflecting the virtues of "citizen involvement, consensus, localism, and gradualism." Locality development, however, he points out is not always carried out in an ideal fashion. There may be an insufficiency in qualified staff to implement its goals. Staff specialists may work at cross purposes. Adequate funding may be lacking. Beyond that, Khinduka states, locality development may put excessive emphasis on proc-

---

[1]Arthur Dunham *The New Community Organization* (New York: Thomas Crowell, 1970), p. 4.

ess goals at the expense of material task goals. In that sense, he sees the strength of locality development in terms of social service objectives. As a method of broad social change, he feels it is a less desirable strategy.

The article by Martí-Costa and Serrano-García incorporates an interesting blend of research and practice. The authors define community (locality) development as a process of consciousness-raising whereby local citizens are empowered to deal with local concerns in a more competent fashion. Consciousness-raising includes the ability to make critical judgments on local situations, to understand the causes of problems, and to take an active role in reform and transformation. Needs assessment is viewed as a valuable tool in this process, because, the authors state, any social movement must start with an appreciation of the felt needs of the residents of a community. Needs assessment, in this formulation, is not merely a device for gathering information; it is also a political mechanism for informing, organizing, and mobilizing people. According to the authors, needs assessment should be embedded in a group process at the local level. It is not a procedure to be used in isolation by research experts, rather it should be employed by local citizens through a core planning group and task forces. In this way, the citizenry becomes knowledgeable about the use of the method, sensitive to community problems, and through the information-gathering process becomes organized into groups that can take action to attack the problems that they discover through doing research.

The experience of Milwaukee in implementing desegregation is portrayed by Harris. Two citizens' groups, the Committee of 100 and the Coalition for Peaceful Schools, are described concerning their actions and impact on the desegregation issue. The Committee of 100 is shown to take a course fairly consistent with locality development. They had close ties to the power structure in the situation, e.g., the school board, and they used existing channels to make their wishes felt. The Coalition acted more as an advocacy group, going outside of existing channels and using pressure tactics. In part this was because of the inhospitable attitude of the school board toward them. This case analysis shows clearly that the appropriateness of the local development approach is contingent on the kind of response by decisionmakers. The approach will show positive results mainly when there is receptivity and cooperation on the part of those who "call the shots." The case study demonstrates the value of citizen participation in affecting community policy, in this instance in areas of curriculum reform.

In the crosscurrents of the turbulent sixties, social change approaches with modest objectives and consensus-based means were attacked and belittled. However, unlike some of the more radical departures locality development has stood the test of time. Accepted for what it is—a modest means of achieving community improvements—locality development can make an important contribution to enhancing community life.

JACK ROTHMAN

19.

S. K. Khinduka

COMMUNITY DEVELOPMENT:
POTENTIALS AND LIMITATIONS

Despite numerous definitions by conferences, international bodies, and writers, the concept of community development remains vague. This vagueness has evoked two entirely different reactions. Some social scientists tend to dismiss community development as a totally "knowledge-free" area, remarkable for "the murky banalities, half-truths and sententious nonsense that abound" in its literature.[1] Other writers maintain that community development is the only key to the modernization of traditional societies.[2]

Community development includes a composite process and program objectives. As a process, it aims to educate and motivate people for self-help; to develop responsible local leadership; to inculcate among the members of rural communities a sense of citizenship and among the residents of urban areas a spirit of civic consciousness; to introduce and strengthen democracy at the grass-roots level through the creation and/or revitalization of institutions de-

signed to serve as instruments of local participation; to initiate a self-generative, self-sustaining, and enduring process of growth; to enable people to establish and maintain cooperative and harmonious relationships; and to bring about gradual and self-chosen changes in the community's life with a minimum of stress and disruption.

The multipurpose, intersectoral character of its program is the other major feature of community development. In rural areas, agriculture, irrigation, rural industries, education, health, housing, social welfare, youth and women's programs, employment, cooperatives, and training of village leaders constitute important components of community development. In the urban areas, community development covers a wide array of similar activities.

It is inevitable that such a gigantic international movement, which has received official sanction and support from governments in Asia, Africa, and Latin America and which is viewed by many as a cure for the riot-torn cities of this country, should encounter difficulties in achieving its goals. Problems of manpower, training and organization have proved formidable barriers to the realization of its objectives in some nations. Inadequate staff, indifference in national bureaucracies, and lack of coordination and communication among specialists at the local level have often

Source: Reprinted from S. K. Khinduka, "Community Development: Potentials and Limitations," in *Social Work Practice, 1969,* © National Conference on Social Welfare, New York: Columbia University Press, 1969, by permission of the publisher and the author.

[1] David Brokensha, "Comments," *Human Organization,* XXVII, No. 1 (1968), 78. See also Charles J. Erasmus, "Community Development and the *Encogido Syndrome,*" ibid., pp. 65-74.

[2] See, for example, B. Mukerjee, *Community Development in India* (Calcutta: Orient Longmans, Ltd., 1961), p. vii.

combined to create bottlenecks in the implementation of programs. Some governments have paid lip service to community development, but have not earmarked adequate funds for the projects. In a number of instances, community development programs have created adverse side effects which were neither intended nor anticipated. Moreover, accentuation of intergroup tensions instead of a strengthened community solidarity and the rise of an opportunistic type of party politics instead of a widespread consciousness of people's rights and responsibilities have not been altogether absent. In some situations, the equalitarian rhetoric of community development has infuriated the rich, while the unequal distribution of its benefits has frustrated the poor.

However serious these may be, neither the flaws in implementation nor the possibility of undesirable consequences reflects the real weakness of community development. With a better trained cadre of workers, a stronger commitment by governments, and a more efficient pooling of international experience, many of these deficiencies can be substantially rectified. What is more difficult—and more important—to change, is the basic ideology of community development; for, more than anything else, the ideology of community development has definite assumptions and biases in favor of citizen involvement, consensus, localism, and gradualism. In its extreme form, this ideology prefers nonmaterial goals to tangible ones. It holds that change in the individual's values, motivation, attitudes, and aspirations is a necessary precondition for any worthwhile alteration in the society. Although some

theorists recognize the significance of accomplishing physical tasks,[3] the community development approach to social change, by and large, is still dominated by a process orientation which evaluates the actual outcome of a community project primarily in terms of what happens in the minds of men rather than in terms of its impact on the social structure.

It is the thesis of this paper that community development is a rather soft strategy for *social change.* As a method of *social service,* however, its contribution can be very significant.

Community development has a latent propensity for delaying structural changes in the basic institutions of a society. Nowhere does this become clearer than in the familiar strain for precedence between its process and task-accomplishment goals.[4] In such a conflict, the community developer typically upholds the process aspect, which stresses citizen involvement, consensus, localism, and change in the attitudes and values of people as a necessary condition for effecting institutional changes.

There is no doubt a great deal to commend in community development's concern with human values and aspirations. As an antidote to some experts' penchant for explaining all industrial backwardness in purely economic terms, and to the equally unwise preoccupation of some governments with narrow models of economic growth,

---

[3]Arthur Dunham, "Community Development — Whither Bound?" *Social Work Practice, 1968* (New York: Columbia University Press, 1968), pp. 48-61.
[4]Melvin M. Tumin, "Some Social Requirements for Effective Community Development," *Community Development Review,* No. 11 (1958), pp. 3-4.

community development's wholesome attempt to underline the human factor and to plead for balanced social and economic progress has indeed had a salutary effect. No wonder that recent approaches to national development have turned away from exclusively economic models.[5] An increasing number of economists now appreciate the significance of noneconomic variables in economic development. "Economic development," two economists observe, "is much too serious a topic to be left to economists."[6]

While community development and social welfare workers have been among the first to recognize the lopsidedness of many prevailing models of economic growth, they have made the reverse error of overstressing the culturally and psychologically propitious preconditions for development. Ever since Max Weber suggested a positive correlation between a people's value system and their economic development,[7] it has become commonplace in many circles to attribute the poverty of a people to their otherworldliness, fatalism, lack of thrift, industry, and entrepreneurial aptitude, and, more recently, to their low achievement motivation. Weber's thesis is now being used not only as counterpoint to the Marxian theory of economic production and social classes, but also as spurious anthropology that overlooks internal and external exploitative economic relationships and explains economic backwardness as if its causative factors were located entirely within the individuals who suffer from it. In embracing this theory, community development, like much of professional social work, leaves itself vulnerable on scientific as well as on strategic grounds.

Attitudinal and value modifications do not necessarily precede behavioral or structural changes; they may often follow them. It is not necessary, for example, to wipe out prejudice (an attitude) in order to eradicate segregation (a behavioral practice). Modifications in individual and group behavior can be brought about by a change in the social situation in which people function.[8]

Festinger's theory of cognitive dissonance holds that, under certain conditions, behavior can produce cognitive and attitudinal realignments in the person. When a person commits an act which is contrary to his beliefs, he is in a state of dissonance, which is unpleasant to him. Reduction of this dissonance is achieved mainly by changing his beliefs, since the "discrepant behavior" has already taken place and cannot be undone.[9] Epstein's study of two Indian villages showed that it was economic development that led to behavioral changes, not vice versa. She reports:

Whenever there was ... economic change we also found corresponding changes in po-

---

[5]See, for example, Gunnar Myrdal, *An Asian Drama: An Inquiry into the Poverty of Nations* (New York: Twentieth Century Fund, 1968).

[6]G. M. Meier and R. E. Baldwin, *Economic Development* (New York: John Wiley & Sons, Inc., 1957), p. 119.

[7]Max Weber, *The Protestant Ethic and the Spirit of Capitalism*, H. Talcott Parsons (London: George Allen & Unwin, Ltd., 1930).

[8]Kenneth B. Clark, "Some Implications for a Theory of Social Change," *Journal of Social Issues*, IX, No. 4 (1953), 72.

[9]Leon Festinger, *A Theory of Cognitive Dissonance* (Evanston, Ill.: Row, Peterson & Co., 1957). See also Albert O. Hirschman, "Obstacles to Development: A Classification and a Quasi-vanishing Act," *Economic Development and Cultural Change*, XIII (1965), 391.

litical and ritual roles and relations as well as in the principles of social organization. Thus we have established a positive correlation between economic, political, ritual, and organizational change, with economic change being the determining variable.[10]

It is an oversimplification to attribute all or most of the difficulties in development to people's mental outlook. It will not do to invoke values to explain economic underdevelopment without referring back to the social structure and economic processes which permit some values to persist and others to change.

One might add that even if modification of attitudes and values is considered a necessary precondition for structural social change, community development has chosen an incomplete, if not an inappropriate, target group. Although it may be important to change the attitudes of the victims of social and economic injustice, it may be more useful to bring about a shift in the attitudes and values of those sections of the population who are its principal beneficiaries. That is why concentration of community development programs among blacks, Puerto Ricans, Mexicans, and Indians will not be enough unless they are accompanied by a similar educational effort to resocialize the privileged, affluent, and suburban segments of the society.

Once it is recognized that values, beliefs, and aspirations are not in every circumstance the optimum locus of professional intervention for social change, the strategic weakness of the community development approach becomes clear. The strategy of concentrating on a group's outmoded attitudes

which are assumed to constitute the principal obstacle to its growth does not recognize that there may be legitimate reasons for people not to take the initiative or the necessary risks in the adoption of new practices. Where benefits are apt to be absorbed by middlemen or moneylenders, for example, it would be unrealistic to expect the villagers to venture the investments or muster the enthusiasm for a new project.[11]

Since a change in value systems of tradition-haunted societies is a matter of generations, such an emphasis on changing the value system may have a pessimistic and despairing implication for the rapid socioeconomic development of the "third world." The assumption that a man's activities cannot be changed without altering his values may result in neglect of the appropriate targets of intervention. A psychologist observes:

An effective strategy for inducing social change would consist of bringing about change in the societal system—and its reinforcing mechanisms—and the development of the appropriate patterns of motivation—and expectancy—through suitable programmes. For any social change, the primary condition is a change in the societal system without which appropriate changes cannot be introduced or, if introduced, cannot be sustained.[12]

If the planners and policymakers wait for attitudes to change and do not intervene at the structural level with social

---

[10]T. Scarlett Epstein, *Economic Development and Social Change in South India* (Calcutta: Oxford University Press, 1962), p. 334.

[11]United Nations, Department of Economic and Social Affairs, *Local Participation in Development Planning: A Preliminary Study of the Relationship of Community Development to National Planning* (New York: United Nations, 1967), p. 27.

[12]Udai Pareek, "Motivational Patterns and Planned Social Change," *International Social Science Journal*, XX (1968), 465–66.

policy and legislation, then achievement of economic development in the third world and of social justice in the "first world" is likely to take a hopelessly long time.

Another dimension of the inadequacy of community development as a strategy for large-scale social change is concerned with the time and rate of change. In the belief that far-reaching social change produces tensions and maladjustments—which are to be avoided at all cost—community development has put great emphasis on moving at a slow pace. Time, it is suggested, should not be allowed to become a major factor in the process of community growth.[13] Here, again, community development has aligned itself with only one school of thought in the social sciences. Heilbroner, however, states that the world political situation enjoins the speediest possible time table for development.[14] Under some circumstances, notes Margaret Mead, the least dislocating change is one which is introduced rapidly.[15] A social scientist from the third world, Guillermo Bonfil Batalla, of Mexico, makes another point clear:

Sometimes it looks as if those who work along the road of slow evolution intend to achieve only minimal changes, so that the situation continues to be substantially the same; this is, in other words, *to change what is necessary so that things remain the same.* Those who act according to such a point of view may honestly believe that their work is useful and transforming; however, they have in fact aligned themselves with the conservative elements who oppose the structural transformations that cannot be postponed in our (Latin American) countries.[16]

Community development's insistence on consensus as the only satisfactory basis for major community decisions provides another example of its limitations. It is, of course, more pleasant to work in an atmosphere of consensus than in one of contest, controversy, or conflict. However, it is easier to obtain near-unanimity on superficial and innocuous matters; issues of substance, which affect the diverse subgroups of the community in different ways, often generate controversy as well as a clash of interests.

Major structural reforms have rarely been instituted with the enthusiastic consent of those who are most likely to lose as a result of those reforms. A certain modicum of legal coercion is a necessary component of any effective strategy of social change. Community development has been rather slow to appreciate this elementary principle. This may in part account for the more or less peripheral role that it has played in movements for rural land reform in most Asian nations.

Its fondness for consensus, however, is only an extension of community development's faith in the desirability and efficacy of citizen involvement. Here, it seems, an essentially instrumental value has been converted into an ultimate value. Citizen participation takes various forms; each form, in turn, rests upon certain assumptions and conditions peculiar to itself. It cannot be assumed that all types of citizen participation are appropriate for all occa-

---

[13]Murray G. Ross, *Community Organization: Theory and Practice* (New York: Harper & Brothers, 1955), p. 22.

[14]Robert L. Heilbroner, "Counterrevolutionary America," *Commentary*, XLIII, No. 4 (1967), 33.

[15]Margaret Mead, *New Lives for Old* (New York: William Morrow & Co., 1956), pp. 445-47.

[16]Quoted in Gerald D. Berreman, "The Peace Corps: A Dream Betrayed," *The Nation*, February 26, 1968, p. 266.

sions or for all organizations.[17] Excellent participation is not sufficient to introduce major changes into a community,[18] nor is voluntary participation always a prerequisite for rapid, extensive cultural change.[19] The principle of citizen participation has been advanced on ethical grounds: people are intrinsically good; given an opportunity, they will do the "right thing." As a technique, it is not backed up by unequivocal evidence that it is indeed as crucial a mechanism for the success of a community development project as has been so frequently suggested.[20]

A noteworthy feature of community development is that it seeks to promote an identification with, and a loyalty to, the local community. The locality is the key unit around which people are to be mobilized for community development projects, and a locality-centered strategy for social change has to face certain problems.

In the first place, the local community no longer exercises decisive control over the lives of an increasingly mobile population. Due largely to the population explosion, implosion, and diversification, and the accelerated tempo of social and technological change — factors which constitute the "morphological revolution"[21] — the local communi-

[17]Edmund M. Burke, "Citizen Participation Strategies," *Journal of the American Institute of Planners*, XXXIV (1968), 293.

[18]See Peter H. Rossi, "Theory, Research and Practice in Community Organization," in Charles R. Adrian et al., eds., *Social Science and Community Action* (East Lansing, Mich.: Michigan State University, 1960), pp. 9-24.

[19]Alex Weingrod, *Reluctant Pioneers: Village Development in Israel* (Ithaca, N.Y.: Cornell University Press, 1966), pp. 197-203.

[20]Gilbert Kushner, "Indians in Israel: Guided Change in a New-Immigrant Village," *Human Organization*, XXVII (1968), 359-60.

[21]Philip M. Hauser, "The Chaotic Society: Product of the Social Morphological Revolution," *American Sociological Review*, XXXIV (1969), 1-19.

ty does not offer any realistic possibilities of a genuine *Gemeinschaft* environment dictated by natural will and characterized by intimate, spontaneous, inclusive, and enduring personal relationships. Even if the morphological revolution could be halted, it would require all the power and resolution of a sovereign world organization; local communities are too feeble to effect such a reversal.

Local institutions can no longer remain unaffected by the extra-community system. Local destinies, for the most part, cannot be decided locally. Nor can the major problems of a locality — poverty, unemployment, housing, and discrimination — be solved merely or mainly by mobilizing local efforts.

History is replete with examples showing that some of the most progressive policies have emanated from the legislative, executive, and judicial branches of a national government. Untouchability would never have been proscribed in India if each local community had been allowed to fashion its own rules. Nor would much progress be made in the United States in establishing racial equality if the decision-making power were vested entirely in the local political institutions. Paradoxically, an indiscriminate application of the seemingly sound principle of local self-determination is at times incompatible with the tenets on which a democracy rests. The fact that it is not possible today to preserve total local autonomy is thus a cause for optimism, not for alarm.

A complicating factor is that the idea of local autonomy is used for two quite conflicting purposes. On the one hand, there are champions of local rights who oppose federal intervention so that they can perpetuate the injustice of the local political and economic arrangement.

The principle of local rights is thus invoked mainly to defeat, delay, or dilute national policies designed to correct the inequities of the local system. An entirely different and socially much more justifiable demand is also couched in the idiom of local self-determination. When the blacks in the ghettos ask for control over local institutions, they are, in effect, saying that they no longer want white domination of their lives and institutions. This is a demand for self-determination, *not* local self-determination. Despite their superficial and deceptive similarity, these demands represent two diametrically divergent objectives: the latter seeks to restore respect for a group often subjected to conscious and unconscious indignities; the former is calculated to deny precisely this egalitarian end.

It has often been assumed that local development and national development always proceed hand in hand. However, community development may inadvertently reinforce economically inefficient customs and practices which prolong the hold of growth-resisting tradition. The desire for local autonomy may create distrust of the national government, its central bureaucracy, and those federal laws which curb a locality's power to manage its own affairs. Recognition of this dilemma has led some community development advocates into an even less tenable position: they will have nothing to do with national development and focus all their efforts on the local community.[22]

The besetting limitation of community development as a strategy for social change is its psychological rather than socioeconomic approach to social problems. Community development programs aim at revolutionary change in the people's psychology without bringing about an actual revolution in their socioeconomic relations.[23] They are concerned with people's psychological capacity to make decisions, not with their economic power to do so. By encouraging them to participate in community activities, community development seeks to give them a feeling that they count and they are competent, but it stops there. Community development will do practically everything to improve the psychological lives of the poor: it will create among them a sense of self-respect and confidence, of civic pride, and identification with their locality—which may be an uninhabitable slum; it will provide recreational programs; it will even organize courses and encourage handicrafts to increase their earning capacity. But it will not usually question the economic system which permits the coexistence of poverty and plenty. And when poverty is at least as much a function of social injustice as it is of individual ineptitude, it is questionable if psychological repair of an individual can accomplish what requires a fundamental rearrangement of economic and social institutions.[24]

Some community developers are really caseworkers practicing in a community setting. They use the community development method for expediting the personality growth of the members of the community. According to William and Loureide J. Biddle, per-

---

[22]William W. Biddle, "Deflating the Community Developer," *Community Development Journal,* III (1968), 191-94.

[23]Charles Madge, "A Sociologist Looks at Social Education," *Community Development Bulletin,* XII, No. 1 (1960), 23.

[24]Simon Slavin, "Community Action and Institutional Change," in *The Social Welfare Forum, 1965* (New York: Columbia University Press, 1965), pp. 155-57.

sonality growth, through responsibility for the local common good, is the focus of all community development.[25] No wonder economic improvement is dismissed as a "materialistic measure" not quite fit to become a community development goal. "If economic betterment is not an extravagant hope, it is an inappropriate one," writes William Biddle.[26] It is just this preoccupation with process and with personality that keeps community development from becoming an effective instrument for large-scale institutional change.

We do not deny the value of community development as a program of social service or its validity as a response to specific local situations. By stressing the crucial role of the human factor in national development, community development has done a great service to mankind. Its integrated and holistic concept of development is, similarly, a refreshing improvement over the narrow, sectoral approaches to national planning.

For certain types of goals and within a certain sphere, community development can be a very effective strategy. Community development is a gentleman's approach to the world. It brings people together; it helps them live and reason together. By involving them in the local decision-making process in the community, it aims to strengthen participatory democracy. If some values and attitudes are detrimental to social progress, it attempts to modify them gradually, with the least disruption and maximum voluntary cooperation, without conflict or contest, shun-

ning bitter controversy, seeking better consensus. Perhaps it does not recognize the existence of classes; it sees only a community. Where this community has "eclipsed," it seeks to resuscitate it. Where it is disintegrated, it reorganizes it. When passions run high and factions grow intolerant of one another, it applies the healing touch of understanding and empathy. In this sense, community development is an extension of group work to the community setting; both processes are dedicated to helping people live harmoniously with fellow human beings.

Essentially, community development is a humanistic and humanizing method. The promise and potentials of such a method are almost self-evident in an age when much of what we call "progress" conceals widespread alienation, apathy, antagonism, cynicism, impersonal bureaucratization, and self-centered pursuit of purely hedonistic ends. The only problem is that community development's relative neglect of such equally humanizing principles as equality, justice, and material well-being are apt to create an uncomfortable gap between its intent and its effect.

Community development can be a potent program for mental health. Students of urban life have noted with dismay the strong feelings of anomie, dependency, and personal worthlessness among the residents of urban slums. Many of these people feel uprooted and marginal; they do not identify with, or belong to, communal organizations. Community development programs can meet the socialization needs of such people.[27] These programs can also be used, as they have

[25]William W. Biddle and Loureide J. Biddle, *The Community Development Process: The Rediscovery of Local Initiative* (New York: Holt, Rinehart & Winston, 1965), p. 78.

[26]William W. Biddle, "Deflating the Community Developer," p. 192.

[27]Lloyd E. Ohlin and Martin Rein, "Social Planning for Institutional Change," in *The Social Welfare Forum, 1964* (New York: Columbia University Press, 1964), p. 87.

been in many countries, to educate people in the art and intricacies of the democratic processes of participation and persuasion. Community projects can likewise strengthen the spirit of unity in a community. Community development activities, which create linkages between various communities, can, similarly, be helpful in improving intercommunity relations. By successfully completing even relatively inconsequential community projects, the participants may develop a sense of competence, a new faith in their ability to overcome forces of nature. This faith in their capacity may be very important for people who live in small, rural areas of traditional societies.

Community development stands for cooperation between public and private effort. Problems sometimes arise in working out arrangements between governmental and voluntary agencies. The idea of "maximum feasible participation" of the local people, for example, may at times result in "maximum feasible misunderstanding." Nevertheless, community development presents a fairly workable model for combining outside technical assistance with indigenous enterprise. As a strategy for mobilizing voluntary efforts at the local level, it is particularly applicable in those communities where people have become excessively dependent on government and community initiative has more or less atrophied.

Although community development is generally viewed as a program designed to strengthen the horizontal pattern of a community,[28] its great potential consists, especially for the third world, in its ability to help weld numerous small localities into a large national polity. Community development can

make a significant contribution to the political development of the third-world nations if it puts greater emphasis on inculcating a sense of national purpose and national identification than on merely identifying with the local community. Equally valuable is its potential as a feedback mechanism. In many countries community development programs have resulted in a better understanding of local problems by higher government officials.[29] Community development can thus provide two-way communication between the local community and the state or national government. Such channels are particularly important in newly independent countries where long periods of foreign rule have created a hiatus between the people and their governments.

Even at the local level, community development is capable of making a more significant contribution if it deemphasizes its earlier self-help orientation and boldly but discriminately incorporates in the mainstream of its ideology some of the features of recent attempts to organize the urban poor. The main objectives of the former model are: creation of community feeling, self-reliance, local leadership, and cooperation between the government and the people in the use of services.[30] The latter model extends the goals of community development to include economic and political objectives, such as the realignment of power resources in the community.[31] The community

---

[28]Roland L. Warren, *The Community in America* (Chicago: Rand McNally & Co., 1963), p. 324.

[29]Irwin T. Sanders, "Community Development," in David L. Sills, ed., *International Encyclopedia of the Social Sciences* (New York: Macmillan Co. & Free Press, 1968), III, 172.

[30]For an example of this model, see Marshall B. Clinard, *Slums and Community Development* (New York: Free Press, 1966).

[31]Charles Grosser, "Community Development Programs Serving the Urban Poor," *Social Work*, X, No. 3 (1965), 15-21.

developer following this model does not fight shy of using negotiation, bargaining, advocacy, protest, noncooperation, and other forms of nonviolent social action[32] in order to help the community attain a composite of social, psychological, and political-economic objectives.

Community development is no substitute for centrally planned changes in

the institutional structure of a society. However, one should not downgrade the services of the thousands of dedicated community development workers who quietly help bring about slow, incremental adaptations in the social system. Within this less ambitious sphere, community development is potentially quite a powerful social invention. Its effectiveness will perhaps increase if it modifies the locality-oriented, enabling model and recognizes the legitimacy of other nonviolent approaches to organizing people for redressing their grievances.

[32]See George Brager, "Organizing the Unaffiliated in a Low-Income Area," *Social Work*, VIII, No. 2 (1963), 34-40; George Brager and Harry Specht, "Mobilizing the Poor for Social Action," in *The Social Welfare Forum, 1965* (New York: Columbia University Press, 1965), pp. 197-209.

20.

Sylvia Martí-Costa

Irma Serrano-García

NEEDS ASSESSMENT AND COMMUNITY DEVELOPMENT: AN IDEOLOGICAL PERSPECTIVE

Community development is a process which, through consciousness-raising, promotes and utilizes human resources, leading to the empowerment of individuals and communities so that they can understand and solve their problems and create new circumstances for their livelihood. As part of this process, needs assessment may be utilized as a central method to facilitate the modification of social systems so they become more responsive to human needs.

Source: Sylvia Martí-Costa and Irma Serrano-García, "Needs Assessment and Community Development: An Ideological Perspective," in *Prevention in Human Services* (Summer 1983), pp. 75-88. Reprinted with permission of the authors and the publisher.

At the individual level, community development promotes psychological growth and enhancement by channeling energies into self-help projects and through the genuine participation of individuals in those decisions that affect their lives. The basic assumption that underlies this reasoning is that most human beings can solve their problems when they obtain access to resources and create alternatives. The emphasis is on their strengths and their development (Rappaport, 1977).

Awareness of problems and of change possibilities is achieved by raising an individual's consciousness from its current or real level to its possible capacity.

Real consciousness is defined as an individual or groups' understanding of reality at a given time. Possible consciousness is the maximum understanding that can be achieved by an individual or group according to its material circumstances at a given historical moment (Goldman, 1970).

Consciousness-raising includes critical judgment of situations, the search for underlying causes of problems and their consequences, and an active role in the transformation of society (Ander-Egg, 1980). It is an awareness of human dignity and is essential in the exploration of the relationship between the social order and human misery and in the discovery of the shortcomings inherent in our society (Freire, 1974). It facilitates individual and collective participation in building a new and less oppressive social order, thus affecting the general well-being of the population by enhancing the relationship between individuals and society. Needs assessment is valuable in the consciousness-raising process, because any social movement should start from and respond to the felt needs of the population, in other words, their real consciousness.

Community development can foster consciousness-raising through the involvement of individuals in change efforts. Community development activities need to be grounded in a specific political commitment that responds to the liberation of the powerless groups of society. This does not ignore the participation of the powerful in the maintenance or change of the present social order. It does, however, require a personal and professional commitment to the oppressed because of the mission of prevention—understanding and relieving human suffering.

Contrary to this view, many social scientists have fostered the value-free, apolitical, and ahistorical character of their disciplines throughout several decades (Moscovici, 1972; Weimer, 1979; Zuñiga, 1975). This position, which may be referred to as "the myth of neutrality," distorts the real value-laden and political nature of theory, methods, and practices and thus serves to alienate us from ourselves and others (Ander-Egg, 1973). It creates divisions and distrust within our ranks and resentment from those that participate as "subjects" or recipients of our work, feeling used, manipulated and misunderstood. Thus, it is necessary to examine this myth which has resulted in the social sciences serving the dominant groups of society.

The "myth of neutrality" has reasons for its existence. In some cases it has been sponsored by individuals who clearly believe in it, but in most cases, it has been accepted inadvertently by social scientists. One of the ways in which this occurs is by considering objectivity and neutrality as synonymous and inseparable concepts which are highly desirable in social scientific endeavors.

Those that hold that neutrality and objectivity must go together state that social scientists should not take political stances toward the object of their studies because this will hamper their research efforts (Myrdal, 1969). To them objectivity is defined as the capacity to study facts as they occur, without adhering to previously formed opinions and judgments and with the willingness to abandon positions that are proven false, inadequate, and unsatisfactory (Ander-Egg, 1977). Neutrality, its inseparable counterpart, is defined as a valueless stance before the objective reality (Martí, Note 1).

It is said that if researchers are not neutral, they cannot be objective (Martí, Note 1). This does not ring true as both concepts are different and clearly distinguishable, and while the pursuit of objectivity is desirable and necessary, the search for neutrality is not only impossible, but unwarranted. Objectivity is desirable because its definition implies the existence of defined values and positions which one is willing to change when an examination of reality requires it. Neutrality is impossible because every activity takes place in a particular political context.

If the political nature of the social sciences is recognized and accepted then an explicit definition of social scientists' values is necessary. It is our position that this value stance must be characterized by a commitment to the disadvantaged and powerless groups within a given society. This commitment is to the abandonment of a spectator role and the activation of a professional's mind and art to the service of a cause (Palau, Note 2). This cause should be the significant transformation of inequities in society which implies activism, risk, initiative, and a willingness to fight for clearly defined points of view.

To summarize, needs assessment is an integral part of community development, the process of consciousness-raising. It implies a political commitment which undermines the traditional view of a neutral science and a firm commitment to the exploited, underprivileged and powerless groups in society.

This paper will show that needs assessment is a political process that can be conceptualized as a tool for the organization, mobilization and consciousness-raising of groups and communities. This implies (1) that the diverse uses of needs assessment methods be placed on a continuum, ranging from the perpetuation of control and the maintenance of the social system to the achievement of radical social change; (2) an emphasis on multiple techniques of needs assessment that facilitate collective activities, leadership development, growth of organizational skills, and participation of community members in interventions within research (Irizarry & Serrano, 1979); and (3) the belief that it is necessary to examine ideologies and values as they influence objectives, the selection of needs assessment techniques, intervention strategies, conceptual frameworks, and the utilization of obtained data.

NEEDS ASSESSMENT

Purpose

Needs assessment is part of a process used to plan social service programs (Pharis, 1976; Siegel, Attkisson, & Cohn, 1977). It is used to determine the problems and goals of the residents of a given community to assure that an intervention will respond to the needs of the population that is being sampled (Warheit, 1976).

The purposes that sustain the use of needs assessment methodology can be placed on a continuum (Table 20.1) according to their political roles. Towards the top of Table 20.1 are purposes that foster system maintenance and control; towards the bottom are ones that promote social change and consciousness-raising. Social system maintenance and control efforts include those activities which are carried out to maintain and/or strengthen the status quo. They also include first order change efforts which

TABLE 20.1. CONTINUUM OF NEEDS ASSESSMENT PURPOSES

Political Role	Purpose
Control System Maintenance	Guarantee the economic survival of service programs
	Respond to interest group pressures
	Provide services required by communities
	Program evaluation
	Program planning
	Public policy decision making
Social Change	Measure, describe, and understand community life styles
	Assess community resources to lessen external dependency
	Return needs assessment data to facilitate residents' decision making
	Provide skill training, leadership, and organizational skills
	Facilitate collective activities and group mobilization
	Facilitate consciousness-raising

alter some of the ways in which the system functions but not the ideology on which it is based (Watzlawick, Weakland, & Fisch, 1974). Radical, or second order, social change efforts imply consciousness-raising and structural and functional alterations.

In consonance with these definitions, the very bottom of the continuum shows needs assessment as a mechanism used by community residents for participation and control in decision making. Needs assessment becomes a technique that facilitates second order social change.

The very top of the continuum lists purposes that foster system maintenance and control, including those that are used to obtain additional funding for already established community programs (Siegel et al., 1977) so as to guarantee their continuation. In the middle of the continuum, but still focusing on maintenance and control

efforts, are included purposes such as (a) planning for decision making and program evaluation (Murell, 1976); (b) gaining additional input toward personnel recruitment; (c) describing, measuring and understanding different aspects of community life (Siegel et al., 1977); (d) determining discrepancies between residents' and professionals' points of view (Ronald, Titus, Strasser, & Vess, Note 3); and (e) obtaining knowledge about community resources so as to link these to agency services.

In analyzing this continuum it is important to notice that most needs assessment efforts are directed towards consumer satisfaction and agency survival. These are legitimate and necessary goals; however, if technique development is limited to these goals, it will be incomplete and unsatisfactory. Needs assessment methodology, if it is to respond to a commitment to the powerless and to the fostering of social change, must (a) emphasize techniques that, singly or in combination, facilitate grouping and mobilizing people; (b) foster collective activities; (c) facilitate leadership development; and (d) involve residents in the entire research process. These characteristics are essential so that the technique can facilitate consciousness-raising.

Categorization and Evaluation of Techniques

At present there is a great diversity of needs assessment techniques. In some instances it is suggested that different techniques be combined focusing on diverse kinds of interventions (Aponte, 1976; Pharis, 1976; Siegel et al., 1977). Others suggest that only one technique be used with one line of intervention preferred (Clifford, Note 4; Evans, Note 5; Zautra, Note 6). In order to respond to the goals of organization, mobilization, and consciousness-raising in communities, the multiple technique approach is more desirable since a more precise view of reality is obtained. More data are gathered which will vary quantitatively and qualitatively, thus providing a thorough appraisal of community needs. Another reason for the combined use of techniques is that their limitations and deficiencies can be balanced. However, it is also important to study how each individual technique contributes to the goal of greater mobilization.

Needs assessment techniques can be grouped in three different categories defined by the contact they provide between the researcher and community residents. This contact is extremely important as it may be used to foster collectivization, mobilization, leadership development, and resident involvement (Ander-Egg, 1980; Sanguinetti, 1981), characteristics that are essential to a new focus on needs assessment goals.

No contact with participants. In this category, techniques permit no relationship between the intervener and the participants. These techniques are rates or percentages under treatment, social indicators, social area analysis and dynamic modeling (Kleemeir, Stephenson, & Isaacs, Note 7; Bell, 1976; Murell, 1976; Pharis, 1976). In general terms, these methods try to determine community needs by utilizing qualitative and quantitative data from several sources, such as demographic records and other social indicators. They are based on the assumption that community needs and problems that appear in official statistics are representative of community problems. The major limitation of the "non-contact with the participant" techniques lies in their absolute lack of direct mobilization potential. Since the residents are not involved in the needs assessment project—in fact, it can even happen without their knowledge—their involvement in social action efforts is not to be expected.

Contact with the agency or community. The "contact with the agency or community" category includes observation (Ander-Egg, 1978), service provider assessment (Kelly, Note 8), key informants (Pharis, 1976), behavioral census (Murell, 1976), surveys (Clifford, Note 4; O'Brien, Note 9), nominal groups (Delbecq, Van de Ven, & Gustoffsen, 1976), and community forums (Kleemeir et al., Note 7) among other techniques. The interaction that these techniques allow for takes place basically through three means: observations, interviews, and group meetings.

Observation facilitates interaction by the observer's mere presence in the setting. Interviewers interact individually and in groups with community residents, service providers, or other key informants to directly obtain data. This interaction takes place openly, as in community forums, or in a more controlled manner, as in nominal groups.

Key informants, nominal groups, community forums, and surveys respond to the goals of mobilization and consciousness-raising in the community. The first three techniques encourage community input by eliciting residents' discussions and introspections about the collective nature of their problems and needs. They serve to strengthen communication networks in the community and they facilitate the process of program planning. Survey techniques share some of these qualities if the survey is constructed, coordinated, and administered by community members. This process generates great involvement and knowledge and the ready acceptance of results by the rest of the community (Sanguinetti, 1981).

The nominal group technique has these, and other, advantages. Because of the structured nature of its process (Delbecq et al., 1976), it (1) maximizes the amount, diversity, and quality of the problems and alternatives proposed; (2) inhibits the control of the group by a few vocal persons (Siegel et al., 1977); (3) allows conflicting opinions to be tolerated; (4) fosters creativity; (5) facilitates attention to the contributions of marginal group members; and (6) emphasizes the role of needs assessment as the basis for program creation and planning. These four techniques have the highest mobilization potential.

Combined techniques. This category includes convergent analysis (Bell, 1976), community impressions (Siegel et al., 1977), community meetings/surveys (Kleemeir et al., Note 7), and others. Convergent analysis techniques include techniques of service utilization, social indicators, and surveys. Each technique is used with a specific objective in mind and it is expected that, overall, the information offered by the techniques should give an estimate of those persons whose needs are not being satisfied.

Community impressions and community meetings/surveys have several common elements. The former include the techniques of key informants, data revision, and community forum. The latter includes the first two steps in addition to a survey, allowing the data to be validated and permitting additional verbal input from participants. Although all these techniques require a lot of energy and effort, they are the best alternative in the needs assessment process because they combine high mobilization potential with the more traditional criteria of representativeness, validity, and reliability.

Criteria to Judge the Adequacy of Techniques

Given the diversity of techniques, it is necessary to develop specific factors or criteria that should be considered in judging the adequacy of a technique. Some authors have examined this issue and have proposed criteria for the selection of techniques. These criteria include: the nature of the problem, the skills of both the researcher and the participants, available resources (League of California Cities, 1979), representativeness, the specificity required of the information (Murell, 1976), and the amount of political risk that the sponsoring group desires to tolerate (Aponte, 1976).

Although all these criteria are useful, additional criteria should be considered if the needs assessment effort is to contribute to community organization and mobilization. These criteria are presented in Table 20.2 and contrasted with more traditional views. The following dimensions are used as a guideline for this comparison: the goals, sources, content, and processes of the assessment.

A major distinction between the two sets of criteria is their goals. One set emphasizes prevention and promotion and the awareness of the collective nature of needs. The other works from a remedial perspective which focuses on the individual and on fostering dependency on external resources. The impact of these differences is most noticeable in the assessment process since a collective focus requires a collective in-

TABLE 20.2. SUGGESTED CRITERIA TO EVALUATE THE ADEQUACY OF NEEDS ASSESSMENT TECHNIQUES

Dimensions of Needs Assessment Process	Criteria	
	Criteria That Foster Mobilization	Traditional Criteria
Goals of Assessment	Prevention and promotion	Treatment
	Awareness of collective nature of needs	Individual focus
	Encourage collective action	Foster dependency on external resources
Source of Input	Community residents Marginal groups	Service providers Total population
Content of Assessment	All perceived needs Internal community resources	Assessment of needed services
Processes of Assessment	Facilitate community involvement and control of process	Assessment carried out by "experts"
	Facilitate face to face interaction between intervener researcher and participants	Lack of community participation Interaction highly controlled by scientific standards
	Data belong to participants	Data collection and future planning controlled by agencies
	Planning and collective action carried out by intervener-researcher and participants	

tervention and an individual focus does not.

An evaluation of previously mentioned techniques according to the community organization and mobilization criteria appears in Table 20.3. As can be seen, key informants, surveys, nominal groups and community forums are the most adequate techniques. It is important to stress, however, that no single technique can be seen as valid for all times and circumstances; therefore, they should be tailored to the particular situation in which the needs assessment is conducted.

NEEDS ASSESSMENT AND COMMUNITY DEVELOPMENT

Irizarry and Serrano (1979) have developed a model, Intervention within Research, which integrates needs assessment into a community development approach. It uses needs assessment as its methodological foundation and the concept of problematization as its ideological guideline (Freire, 1974). Problematization, our translation for the term *problematización,* refers to the process whereby consciousness-raising takes place. If the latter is seen as the goal, then problematization involves the different strategies whereby it can be achieved.

The model conceptualizes the processes of intervention and research as simultaneous and interdependent. It also assumes that all phases of the model should be permeated with explicit ideological inputs that lead to consciousness-raising.

The objectives suggested for this model include: (1) the creation of collective efforts to solve community problems as defined by community res-idents; (2) the achievement of individual and group participation in the analysis of social reality; (3) the creation of grass-roots organizations; and (4) the development of political skills among participants, resulting in their increased involvement in public affairs.

The model includes four phases. The first phase, familiarization with the community, includes a review of all written and statistical material regarding the community, and several visits to the same. This approach provides knowledge regarding the community's history, its structures, and the processes which facilitate the intervener's entry into the community. It should emphasize the early identification of key persons in the community through informal communication or through more structured means.

The second phase, which arises from a later revision of the original model (Martí, Note 1), is characterized by the creation of a core group that must be composed of both key community persons and interveners. This core group has planning, coordination, and evaluation responsibilities throughout the entire process of intervention within research.

The creation of this core group has positive psychological and operative repercussions. Since the group is formed with community people, a more effective dialogue can take place. It is also possible to increase their commitment and guarantee the group's continuance in this way. In addition, the key person can acquire skills through modeling or training that will be useful to future community work.

One of the most important tasks of this group is the direction and coordi-

TABLE 20.3
Evaluation of Needs Assessment Techniques According to their Potential for Mobilization
Organization and Consciousness-Raising

Techniques

Criteria	Social Records	Computer Use	Observation	Social Indicators	Dynamic Modelling	Systems Model	Surveys	Key Informants	Forum	Nominal Group	Service Provider Assessments	Behavioral Census	Key Persons
Obtains information from community residents							X		X	X			X
Obtains information from marginal groups	X						X		X	X			X
Achieves change in services provided			X				X	X	X	X	X	X	X
Facilitates identifying a wide range of needs		X	X	X			X		X	X			
Facilitates development of internal resources								X	X	X		X	X
Control of information by residents			X	X			X	X	X	X		X	X
Oriented toward prevention			X						X	X			
Collective view of problems									X	X			
Commitment to residents' participation in general									X	X			
Commitment to residents' participation in research							X		X	X			
a. data collection							X		X	X			
b. instrument construction							X		X	X			X
c. data analysis							X		X	X			X
d. data returns									X	X			X
Fosters relationship between residents and intervener								X	X	X			X
a. more time together								X	X	X			X
b. dialogue								X	X	X			X
Facilitate collective activities									X	X			X
a. two or more persons									X	X			
b. two or more persons regarding common problems									X	X			
c. adding the discussion of possible solutions									X	X			
d. initiate collective action									X	X			

nation of the needs assessment. This begins with the core group taking an active role in evaluating the relevance of the different needs assessment techniques to their particular community. The group's next step is the consideration of alternative actions to develop an effective propaganda campaign to inform residents of the needs assessment. In this effort it is essential to obtain the support of other organized groups in the community.

The core group should direct the needs assessment process per se as well as the process of returning the analyzed data to community residents. This can be done through letters, individual visits, group meetings, or community assemblies. The method used will be determined by the needs assessment technique previously used, by the number of participants it entailed, and by the number of human resources available. The data should be returned promptly and should be explained in simple terms.

The third phase, formation of task groups, includes group activities suggested by the needs assessment. In this phase, short- and long-term goals are defined and further action plans developed. To carry out these activities an organizational structure must be created. It is suggested that for this purpose a general community meeting should be held where task groups are formed around the needs assessment priorities. This general meeting should be planned and conducted by all participants with the support and guidance of the core group.

In addition to the task groups, workshops and other social, cultural, educational, and recreational activities must be fostered. Workshops should concentrate on the development of skills so as to help community groups deal effectively with outside forces that rally against their efforts. Some possible topics for the workshops are leadership, skills to deal with service agencies, interpersonal communication, propaganda, and organizational skills. Particular attention should be given to internal group processes so that the task groups' decision making will improve, their leadership struggles diminish, and their cohesiveness increase. We believe that this last characteristic is particularly important and that both the workshops and group tasks should emphasize cohesiveness.

The last phase in the model, involvement of new groups, is initiated after some of the short- and long-term goals of the task groups are achieved. This involves the development of new goals which should help in bringing together other community groups. The steps described should be repeated in a cyclical manner because needs change throughout the process and the community may develop other goals and interests.

CONCLUSION

This paper has presented an alternative ideological framework to evaluate and direct needs assessment efforts. It has also presented a model for its use for community development. Community residents can and should control intervention within research efforts that directly or indirectly involve them and scientists should facilitate this control. If some of these changes are incorporated into current needs assessment efforts, scientists will be more responsive to the people to whom their major efforts should be directed.

REFERENCE NOTES

1.Martí, S. *Hacia una identificación de necesidades en el sector femenino del Barrio Buen Consejo.* Unpublished M. A. thesis, University of Puerto Rico, 1980.

2. Palau, A. *La investigación con la técnica de observación: ¿Para quién y desde dónde?* Unpublished manuscript, 1977. (Available at Sociology Department, University of Puerto Rico, Río Piedras, P.R.).

3. Ronald, L., Titus, W., Stasser, G., & Vess, J. *Views of mental health: A first step in needs assessment.* Paper presented at the 87th Annual Convention of the American Psychological Association. New York City, 1979.

4. Clifford, D. L. *A critical view of needs assessment in community mental health planning.* Paper presented at the Second National Conference on Needs Assessment in Health and Human Services, Louisville, Kentucky, 1978.

5. Evans, P. *A model for conducting needs assessment and a report on national ratios.* Paper presented at the 87th Annual Convention of the American Psychological Association, New York City, 1979

6. Zautra, A. *Quality of life determinants: Some guidelines for measuring community well-being.* Paper presented at the Second National Conference on Needs Assessment in Health and Human Services, Louisville, Kentucky, March, 1978.

7. Kleemeir, C. P., Stephenson, D. P., & Isaacs, L. D. *Developing a needs assessment approach for community consultation and education.* Paper presented at the 87th Annual Convention of the American Psychological Association, New York City, 1979.

8. Kelly, M. *Halton region services for children: A needs assessment.* Unpublished manuscript, 1978. (Available at Faculty of Social Work, Wilfrid Laurier University, Waterloo, Ontario, Canada.)

9. O'Brien, D. *Merging the technical and community catalytic functions of citizen surveys: Toward a theoretical framework.* Paper presented at the Second National Conference on Needs Assessment in Health and Human Services, Louisville, Kentucky, 1978.

REFERENCES

Ander-Egg, E. *Hacia una metodología de la militancia y el compromiso.* Buenos Aires: Ecro, 1973.

Ander-Egg, E. *Diccionario del trabajo social.* Barcelona: Nova Terra. 1977.

Ander-Egg, E. *Introducción a las técnicas de investigación social.* Buenos Aires: Humanitas, 1978.

Ander-Egg, E. *Metodología del desarrollo de comunidad.* Madrid: UNIEUROP, 1980.

Aponte, S. F. Implications for the future of needs assessment. In R. A. Bell, M. Sundel, S. F. Aponte, & S. A. Murell (Eds.). *Needs assessment in health and human services.* Louisville: University of Louisville, 1976.

Bell, R. A. The use of a convergent assessment model in the determination of health status and assessment of need. In R. S. Bell, M. Sundel, J. F. Aponte, & S. A. Murell (Eds.). *Needs assessment in health and human services.* Louisville: University of Louisville. 1976.

Delbecq, A., Van de Ven, A., & Gustoffsen, D. *Group techniques for program planning: A guide to nominal group and Delphi processes.* Chicago: Scott, Foresman, & Company. 1976.

Freire, P. *Pedagogía del oprimido.* México: Siglo 21, 1974.

Goldman, L. Conciencia adecuada, conciencia posible y conciencia falsa. In L. Goldman (Ed.), *Marxismo y ciencias humanas.* Paris: Galiemard, 1970.

Irizarry, A., & Serrano-García, I. Intervención en la investigación: Su aplicación al Barrio Buen Consejo. *Boletín AVEPSO,* 1979, *2,* 6-21.

League of California Cities. Social needs assessment: A scientific or political process. In F. Cox, J. Erlich, J. Rothman, & J. Tropman (Eds.), *Strategies of community organization.* Itasca, Illinois: F. E. Peacock, 1979.

Moscovici, S. Society and theory in social psychology. In J. Israel & H. Tajfel (Eds.), *The context of social psychology.* New York: Academic Press, 1972.

Murell, S. A. Eight process steps for converting needs assessment data into program operations. In S. A. Bell, M. Sundel,

J. Aponte, & S. Murell (Eds.), *Needs assessment in health and human services.* Louisville: University of Louisville, 1976.

Myrdal, G. *Objectivity in social research.* New York: Random House, 1969.

Pharis, D. B. The use of needs assessment techniques in mental health planning. *Community Mental Health Review,* 1976, *1,* 4-11.

Rappaport, J. *Community psychology: Values, research and action.* New York: Holt, Rinehart, & Winston, 1977.

Sanguinetti, Y. La investigación participativa en los procesos de desarrollo de américa latina. *Revista de ALAPSO,* 1981, *1,* 221-238.

Siegel, L. M., Attkisson, C. C., & Cohn, I. H. Mental health needs assessment: Strategies and techniques. In W. A. Hargreaves & C. C. Attkisson (Eds.), *Resource materi-*

als for community mental health program evaluation. Rockville, Maryland: National Institute of Mental Health, 1977.

Warheit, George J. The use of field surveys to estimate health needs in the general population. In R. A. Bell, M. Sundel, J. Aponte, & S. A. Murell (Eds.), *Needs assessment in health and human services.* Louisville: University of Louisville, 1976.

Watzlawick, P., Weakland, J., & Fisch, R. *Change: Principles of problem formation and problem resolution.* New York: Norton, 1974.

Weimer, W. *Notes on the methodology of scientific research.* New York: Wiley, 1979.

Zuñiga, R. The experimenting society and radical social reform. *American Psychologist,* 1975, *30,* 99-115.

21.

Ian M. Harris

COMMUNITY INVOLVEMENT IN DESEGREGATION: THE MILWAUKEE EXPERIENCE

Since January 19, 1976 the Milwaukee Public School District has been under court order to desegregate its schools. The School Board in this city of 600,000 has fought this order all the way to the U.S. Supreme Court, and finally in the spring of 1979 agreed to an out-of-court settlement which would require two-thirds of the 90,000 pupils in Milwaukee to attend desegregated schools. In the fall of 1978 and 1979 the School Board has

met this requirement, and increased the percentage of pupils attending desegregated schools (a desegregated school is defined by a 25 to 50 percent black student population) from 16% in 1976 to 69% in 1979. This change has occurred peacefully in a northern industrial city approximately the size of Boston and Louisville. John Gronouski, a former U.S. ambassador to Poland and Postmaster General, who served as a special master to the courts in Milwaukee, has been quoted as saying that the Milwaukee desegregation plan was "an immense success, a model with national

Source: Published by permission of Transaction, Inc. from *Journal of Voluntary Action Research,* Vol. 9, Nos. 1-4, copyright ©1980 by Transaction, Inc.

ramifications. This community has gone through an enormous transition without a ripple. I think the desegregation plan will go down in history as a model of human relations for the nation, not just human relations, but desegregation and quality education as well" (*The Milwaukee Journal*, July 23, 1977: 1).

The struggle to desegregate Milwaukee's schools has not been easy. The original suit to desegregate the schools was filed in June of 1965 by attorney Lloyd Barbee, and it took 14 years just to resolve the legal complications of this suit.[1]

In 1985 the original court order expired, and school officials are planning how they want to continue this effort. One recent complication is that in 1984 the Milwaukee School Board sued the suburbs to get them to participate in school desegregation efforts.

In the twenty years between 1960 and 1980 thousands of parents, students, and citizens have been active, demonstrating both for and against desegregation. One of the hallmarks of the "Milwaukee Plan," that distinguishes the effort to desegregate in Milwaukee from those in other cities, has been an attempt to solicit volunteer involvement in planning for desegregation. Some people have been involved in ad hoc formulations—rallying to a particular cause, or participating in a demonstration. Others have been active in organizations such as the NAACP, which has worked on this issue throughout these years. This article will discuss the role of two organizations— the Committee of 100 and the Coali-

tion for Peaceful Schools—that were created in 1976 specifically to work on desegregation in Milwaukee. These organizations have been widely heralded for their contribution to the policies that have made Milwaukee's desegregation so successful.

Information for this study has been gathered from personal observation, from interviews, and from surveys. The author was an original member of the Committee of 100 and was a board member of the Coalition for Peaceful Schools from 1977-1979. In 1976 he conducted a survey of the Committee of 100 and in 1977 a survey of the Coalition for Peaceful Schools. These surveys determined various aspects of the membership of these committees and their attitudes towards desegregation.

THE COMMITTEE OF 100

The Committee of 100 was created by the Milwaukee School Board on February 8, 1976 "to provide a forum for the community to be involved in the discussions and decisions on alternative school planning and integration" (Milwaukee School Board of Directors Meeting, Feb. 8, 1976). The School Board created this committee by advertising in newspapers and television to encourage parents and citizens to go to their local schools on the evening of March 8, 1976 to volunteer to serve on the Committee of 100.[2] At these local schools parents elected 10 representatives who went to a meeting the next week at the high schools that students from those local schools attended. In this manner each high school constitut-

---

[1]For a complete history of this struggle see Lloyd A. Barbee, "Milwaukee School Desegregation: A History," published in a four-part series by the *Milwaukee Community Journal*, starting with Volume 5, #9, December 20-27, 1978.

[2]For further discussion of the Committee of 100, see Ian M. Harris, "The Citizens' Committee in Milwaukee," *Integrateducation*, July/August, 1978: pp. 35-41.

ed a "cluster," which included itself and all the feeder schools that sent students to that high school. At these high schools the elected representatives chose seven people to represent that cluster on the Committee of 100. With 15 high schools in Milwaukee, these representatives—five parent/citizens, one staff, and one student—constituted a committee of 105 people.

At its first meeting on April 6, 1976, the Committee elected a steering committee that consisted of one person from each cluster. For three years this steering committee provided a core group of dedicated individuals who kept the Committee alive by developing agendas and by setting issues for the deliberation of the larger body.

The Committee of 100 met once a month at the beginning of each month. Members of the Committee were also supposed to meet on a monthly basis at neighborhood schools with parents and concerned citizens to report back and consult with them about directions for the Committee of 100. In this way the Committee of 100 established ties into every neighborhood in Milwaukee, which gave school officials informal channels to dialogue with parents and citizens about desegregation in Milwaukee.

The original Committee of 100, elected in 1976, accurately reflected the racial composition of the schools— 35% Black, 60% White, and 5% Hispanic and Native American. Eighty-three percent of the Committee had school age children, and sixty percent were women. The median education level was 16.2, and the average income per family was slightly over $15,000. The Committee of 100 has always supported desegregation. On a survey 90% of the respondents agreed with the state-

ment, "I feel that public schools should be desegregated." Fifty-three percent agreed with using forced busing to achieve desegregation.

The Committee of 100, functioning as an advisory group to the Milwaukee School Board, made a series of recommendations on how to proceed with desegregation. Their recommendations asked for alternative schools and specialty programs; advised the Superintendent as to what schools to close as enrollments have declined; established human relations training for parents, students, and staff; forwarded desegregation related complaints to the School Board; and made specific suggestions concerning instructional programs throughout the city. For the first two years of the court order, the plan for desegregation ultimately adopted by the school district originally came from the Committee of 100.

THE COALITION FOR PEACEFUL SCHOOLS

The Coalition for Peaceful Schools originated in the private sector. In May of 1976 the Public Education Task Force of the Greater Milwaukee Conference on Religious and Urban Affairs sent invitations to business, church, labor, and community groups. Members who attended that first meeting were various community leaders concerned about desegregation who wanted to assist the School Board meet the mandates of the Judge's order. This group incorporated as a Coalition to:

Support and facilitate peaceful, humane desegregation of the Milwaukee Public Schools, to increase community understanding of the desegregation process in Milwaukee, to open and maintain communication among community groups working for peaceful implementation of school de-segregation, and to assist the Milwaukee Public School System in the implementation of desegregation (Coalition for Peaceful Schools, Proposal Submitted to the U.S. Office of Education, July 15, 1978).

The Board of Directors of the Coalition for Peaceful Schools consisted of approximately 50 civic and religious organizations. For its first year of operation the Greater Milwaukee Conference for Religious and Urban Affairs, an interdenominational organization composed of the judicatories of the major religious denominations in Milwaukee, provided an office, secretarial help, utilities, and a staff person. In 1976 a successful proposal was submitted to the U.S. Office of Education under Title VII of ESAA which allowed the Coalition to open offices of its own and hire four staff. That grant has been renewed for the school years 1977-1979, 1979-1980, and 1980-1981, and finally terminated at the end of 1981.

The Coalition consisted of a Board of Directors, staff and 100 community leadership specialists. The executive director met monthly with the Board to determine direction and goals for the Coalition, and staff worked closely with the community leadership specialists to carry out the work of the Coalition in community settings throughout Milwaukee.

The membership of the Coalition for Peaceful Schools consistently supported desegregation. The slightly lower income level of its membership reflected the involvement of grass roots volunteers actively solicited by the Coalition. Forty-two percent of the members had children, and 78% of those sent their children to desegregated schools. Ninety-three percent of those polled agreed with the statement that

the public schools should be desegregated, while 95% believed that school children profit from interracial relationships. Eighty-six percent thought that desegregation will lead to an improvement in education. The original membership of the Coalition—45% Caucasian, 43% black, and 2% from other ethnic groups—represented a multi-racial collection of community leaders who came together to make desegregation peaceful.

The Coalition for Peaceful Schools worked with the School Board and school administration to inform the public about what desegregation would imply in Milwaukee, and to assist them in various aspects of their planning. To do this the Coalition published a monthly newsletter on desegregation, held a variety of workshops on different desegregation topics, sponsored city-wide parent-teacher conferences, and met informally with the superintendent and his staff to represent community concerns about desegregation. Once the federal grant ran out in 1981 the Coalition ceased functioning.

ASSESSMENT

In evaluating these committees two variables will be examined: function and membership. "Function" refers to the activities of these organizations. What have they been doing? "There is a way to measure citizen involvement that yields a better picture of its impact than does the counting method. This way is to examine participation in the context of the functions it performs, not only for citizens, but for elected officials and professionals as well" (Rosener, 1977: 58). Functions that these committees have served in Milwaukee include making recommendations on school desegregation policy, providing official channels of communication, and offering some accountability mechanisms for school policy. An evaluation of these functions will determine how well these groups have been able to accomplish their goals and influence desegregation policy in Milwaukee.

"Membership" concerns the type of volunteers that have been working on desegregation through these organizations. It is important to ask when evaluating citizen groups how representative they are of the larger community. "Unless an advisory committee represents its community, it is not a voice for the community but speaks only for itself" (Wireman, 1977: 4). A factor that will be considered with this variable is how membership has changed over the years.

FUNCTION

Mele Koneya (1978) has suggested a seven stage continuum to evaluate the functions of citizen participation. The continuum goes from government-centered to citizen-centered, and describes the degree to which a governing body allows a citizen group to exercise authority. The categories detail how the governing body relates to citizen organizations:

1. Decides, announces decision through bulletins.
2. "Sells" decision to citizens.
3. Announces decision, permits questions.
4. Presents tentative decision, consults citizens, and then decides.
5. Presents problems, asks for ideas, then decides—by using the ideas.

6. Presents problems and boundaries, but citizens decide.
7. Citizens have as much freedom as government leaders to define the problem and to decide action.

Point 1 on this continuum suggests a position of government autocracy where the governing body has complete power using the citizen participation mechanism only to announce its decisions. Point 7 suggests that citizens have a say in determining policy and can bring about what they value. Each one of these categories describes different functions performed by citizen groups.

The Committee of 100 never did occupy positions 6 and 7 on this continuum, where its membership had the power to decide school policy concerning desegregation. Its function as an advisory group was thwarted by a School Board that rejected some of its recommendations. From its inception the Committee strongly supported desegregation, while the School Board resisted the court order by appealing it all the way to the United States Supreme Court. "Citizen involvement programs must be closely related to actual decision making" (Priscoli, 1978: 104). This hostility of the School Board towards some of the recommendations of the Committee of 100 has hindered what it has been able to accomplish. Since the ultimate power for decision making rested with the School Board whose majority opposed desegregation, the Committee of 100 had a great deal of difficulty functioning as a policy making board. However, most of its decisions were ultimately adopted because of the power of the federal court, where Judge Reynolds mandated, over the objections of the School Board, that the recommendations of the Committee become school policy.

Just because some of its strongest pro-desegregation recommendations were rejected by the School Board does not mean that the Committee was a failure. The Committee did function well in categories 1 through 5 mentioned above, where it allowed school officials to dialogue with parents and citizens about desegregation in Milwaukee. It has provided the parent participants a forum for their views about public schools. It provided the School Board with a pro-desegregation voice with which it has had to contend. It provided the administration a sounding board for announcing new policies, and getting information out into the community. It provided the Superintendent with a showcase that he can point to nationally, where Milwaukee is gaining a reputation for solving some of the problems facing northern industrial school districts undergoing desegregation. It also provided the press with a visible body of citizens whose opinions they could elicit in discussing the many confusing aspects of this issue.

The Coalition for Peaceful Schools has likewise had a hard time influencing official school policy. It has operated almost exclusively on categories 1 through 5, although over the three years of its existence it has drastically changed its functions. Originally the Coalition consisted of "desegregation boosters," citizens and parents who wanted to work through the Coalition to make desegregation successful. In its attempt to serve a multi-racial population, it hired organizers who had deep roots in the black community. These organizers developed a community involvement structure with community leadership specialists placed in many

neighborhoods throughout the city. When these community people brought forth a variety of complaints about the way desegregation was being handled, the Coalition became an advocacy organization, advocating for the interests of parents and citizens against some of the recommendations and policies of the school district.[3] In this new function it became a vehicle to articulate concerns about desegregation for many citizens who traditionally have no representation in determining public policy. The Coalition supported desegregation but tried to make desegregation fair or just, so that implementation of desegregation plans did not create undue burdens and hardships. (An example of injustice is that 80% of the busing to achieve desegregation in Milwaukee has been done by black children.)

The Coalition for Peaceful Schools, as a private citizen's group, had no direct channels to affect school policy related to desegregation. It functioned most effectively behind the scenes, where Coalition staff and board members used their contacts to influence the behavior and decisions of School Board members. An example of how it has had to operate concerns the Coalition to Save North Division. This Coalition consists of black parents who were outraged that the school board was going to turn a brand new multi-million dollar high school into a specialty school, and not allow local black youth to use it as a neighborhood school. The Coalition

---

[3]In a conversation, Carolyn Andrews from the Title VII office in Washington mentioned that this is the only Title VII funded organization in the country to take such a strong advocacy stance. Other Title VII funded agencies have served as a public relations vehicle and a support group for the local educational agency undergoing the attempt to desegregate.

for Peaceful Schools joined this coalition and supported the efforts of black parents to keep the school open by participating in a year-long campaign of street demonstrations and protests which finally changed the School Board's position. In this new function, as a representative of people who felt they were discriminated against by desegregation policies, the Coalition has worked effectively outside official channels to have its recommendations incorporated in school policy.

Both of these community groups have served an important function in providing administrators, many of whom do not have channels of communication with the broader public, important contacts through which they could discuss policy related to school desegregation. "Between the authority of the Board to operate schools and the types of major decisions left to the voters, there is a tremendous void of formal structures for examining the issues and making decisions about education" (Bloomberg and Sunshine, 1963:8). One of the major accomplishments of the Committee of 100 and the Coalition for Peaceful Schools has been to allow parents and citizens to become active in school affairs in a way that was never possible under the PTA format, where parents serve, at best, as boosters for their local schools.

These groups have suggested whole new accountability mechanisms for school districts, where they can negotiate with an organized body of citizens about school-related policy, but have not lived up to their promise in this area. Although the School Board did adopt some of the recommendations of the Committee of 100, it failed to respond to some of the demands citizens placed before it. In a similar manner

the Coalition for Peaceful Schools has found many things wrong with desegregation practices, but has not been able to influence school policy by going through official channels. Once it sensed that school officials were not going to respond to its demands that minority children be treated fairly, it took to the streets to build up support for its activities through direct action campaigns. These campaigns, in turn, received support of notable officials in the community, and ultimately pressured the School Board to change some of its policies. Because of School Board resistance, these organizations have not functioned smoothly as accountability vehicles for school policy. These groups did get the Milwaukee School Board to respond to their demands but not in a cooperative way, where the School Board welcomed the suggestions offered by the groups. The potential for accountability suggested by these groups would have been considerably improved if the School Board had taken more seriously the recommendations they offered.

MEMBERSHIP

The membership of both the Committee of 100 and the Coalition for Peaceful Schools did not accurately reflect the general population of Milwaukee. As can be seen from the table below, these organizations have reproduced a common characteristic of citizen advisory groups: They are elitist with a better educated and more affluent membership than the public at large (Checkoway and Van Til, 1978).

The stronger acceptance of desegregation and forced busing on the part of the membership of the Coalition for Peaceful Schools can be understood by

TABLE 21.1. COMPARISON OF COMMITTEE OF 100 AND COALITION FOR PEACE-
FUL SCHOOLS WITH GENERAL POPULATION OF CITY OF MILWAUKEE

	Family Income	Education	Favor Desegregation	Favor Forced Busing
General Population*	$11,500	11.9	46%	29%
Committee of 100	$15,000	16.2	90%	53%
Coalition for Peaceful Schools	$13,000	16.5	93%	68%

*Information on the general population was provided by *The Milwaukee Journal* through a scientific poll conducted in March of 1976.

the fact that the membership of the Co-alition for Peaceful Schools volunteered to make desegregation a success, while the membership of the Committee of 100 came from citizens and parents who were concerned about desegregation, and wanted to use the Committee of 100 as a public vehicle to express their opinions. Some of the membership elected to this committee opposed desegregation.

Strong support for desegregation created problems for the Committee of 100. Not only did enthusiasm for desegregation antagonize a School Board that was originally opposed to desegregation, but it also alienated those volunteers who had hoped to represent people in the community who did not want to desegregate the schools. A white cluster from the working class community resigned after the first year because it did not feel that its wishes were being attended. Likewise, many members of the black community who became involved in the Coalition to Save North Division withdrew from the Committee of 100 when they felt that the Committee was not responsive to their needs.

The people who remained on the Committee of 100 worked hard to develop plans that finally provided the policies that led to the successful desegregation of the schools. This Committee has lost its membership over the years, and by the third year folded because it no longer attracted a quorum. This lack of interest can be explained by two factors. First, the Committee spent all its time on desegregation. As the desegregation plans were implemented, it chose no further issues to work on. When there was a sense of urgency provided by the need to desegregate, the membership was active on the Committee, but as desegregation proceeded the membership lost its sense of mission and failed to attract a quorum. Secondly, the attitudes of the School Board, which constantly opposed the recommendations of the Committee of 100, discouraged Committee members. When their plans were rejected by the School Board, these volunteers felt they were wasting their time and became discouraged.

The membership of the Coalition for Peaceful Schools changed drastically over its four years of existence. As the Coalition became an advocacy organization, it began to attract many grass-roots members. Whereas before it consisted of business and community leaders from such organizations as the Parent Teacher Association and the League of Women Voters (both of these organizations have withdrawn their support from the Coalition), during its last year its membership consisted of community people who do not represent such a middle-class base.

When both of these committees were first formed, there was considerable overlap in their membership. Volunteers on both committees provided a small core of about twenty people who were involved in all aspects of desegregation. This group of professionals demonstrated their civic concern by volunteering for these organizations. Their contributions were valuable, but their strong middle-class background represented a weakness that plagued the Committee of 100. It did not attract or retain membership that was lower class, new, or different from middle-class interests expressed by this core. As the Coalition pursued activities geared more towards representing parents and citizens often opposed to school board policy, many of the original middle-class core resigned from the Coalition. Now that the Committee of 100 no longer meets, this core has lost its organizational base for working on school issues.

CONCLUSION

The United States Commission on Civil Rights in its report, *Desegregating the Nation's Schools,* stated that "School desegregation impacts at many different points in public education and community life. The experiences described here clearly indicate that, in the last analysis, whether the impact is generally beneficial or adverse depends in large measure upon the determination and the planning of school and community leaders" (1976: 173). Citizen participation in the desegregation activities in Milwaukee has enabled parents, students, and teachers to help formulate desegregation policy. These citizens have had the opportunity to develop one of the most successful school

desegregation strategies in the country. The impact of the two groups I have described in this paper has been tremendous. Basically they have pushed for equity, so that blacks and whites get treated equally, and for school reforms.

The most profound and lasting contribution of these groups has been in the area of curricular reform. Prior to the court order, many parents had tried for years to reform the Milwaukee Public School System. Now, after working through these organizations, many concerned parents have been able to establish in Milwaukee a wide variety of specialty schools and magnet programs, such as Montessori schools, open education classrooms, career specialties, and individually-guided instruction that have improved the quality of educational offerings in the school district. Without a court order, or without the type of city-wide base that these organizations represent, many of these parents would have continued to work in frustration at the local school level to reform the school system. Both of these groups have given parents a political base from which to launch their ideas for educational improvements of the public schools.

Community involvement in desegregation is a new area of voluntary action. In the late 1970s committees similar to those described in this paper have appeared in Los Angeles, Chicago, Seattle, Denver, and Dayton. Experiences in Milwaukee indicate that the potential success of these organizations depends upon the following factors:

1) The Relationship with the School Board. Both citizen groups in Milwaukee have been hindered by the hostility of the local school board. In

Seattle a citizen's group worked closely with the school board to draw up a plan that led to successful voluntary desegregation. The work of these organizations in Milwaukee would have been greatly improved if the Milwaukee School Board had enthusiastically endorsed their recommendations.

2) Proceedings. The original Committee of 100 contained many grass roots members who were quickly alienated from the formality of its proceedings, which were run strictly according to Robert's Rules of Order. These people expressed on the floor a desire to talk informally about issues, and quickly left when they could not express their interests through the rigidity of Parliamentary Procedure.

3) Funding. The Coalition for Peaceful Schools had a Title VII federal grant which provided four staff positions, secretarial help, and enough money to give community leadership specialists a small stipend for attending meetings. These funds have made it easier for people in this organization to devote their energies to the causes taken on by the Coalition. Nobody was ever paid for the long hours volunteered for the Committee of 100, nor was there any training money which could have been used to educate citizens about the complexities of school board policy determination and provide human relations training to mold the organization into a more coherent group.

4) Special Accommodations for Membership. If committees such as these are to retain volunteers who are poor, they should provide child care and transportation. Many of the lower income members of the Committee of 100 left because they could not leave their children alone, and they did not have cars to drive all over town to the meetings.

5) Incorporating Hostile Elements. One of the great problems in planning for desegregation is overcoming resistance to the idea of desegregation. The Committee of 100 originally contained volunteers opposed to desegregation, but these people left when their views were denied an audience. Working with hostile elements can help incorporate some of their concerns in planning for significant social change. The School Board went ahead without incorporating the wishes of these groups, and later ran into some opposition in such cases as the Coalition to Save North Division.

The history of desegregation in Milwaukee has not been easy. Fifteen years after the original court case was filed, 70% of the students in Milwaukee's schools are attending desegregated facilities. Citizens have mobilized both for and against desegregation. In addition to providing some important structural changes in the operation of schools, citizens have been able through their involvement in the desegregation decision to exercise their potential for leadership. Few Americans have a chance to experience leadership, because there are so few vehicles for them to express their opinions publicly. By providing a public forum for matters related to desegregation, both the Committee of 100 and the Coalition for Peaceful Schools have given citizens and parents an experience of participation within a society that expresses a commitment to democratic management of its affairs.

Furthermore, in planning these reforms the volunteers and paid staff have worked in multi-racial settings that have provided cross-cultural experiences for the participants. All of these groups are at least bi-racial (black and white), and often include Hispanics, Native Americans, and people with Oriental backgrounds. Working within such diversity has given the participants personal experience with what it means to live within a desegregated society, and has helped break down many of the stereotypes that make desegregation so difficult. If this work could be expanded to reach other populations, more citizens of the United States might move closer to the goal of equal protection under the law, which provision marked the initial legal impetus for desegregation.

REFERENCES

Bloomberg, Warner Jr. and Morris H. Sunshine. *Suburban Power Structures and Public Education.* Syracuse, N.Y.: Syracuse University Press, 1963.

Checkoway, Barry and Jon Van Til. "What Do We Know About Citizen Participation? A Selective Review of the Research." In Stuart Langton (ed.), *Citizen Participation in America.* Lexington, Mass.: D.C. Heath and Company, 1978, pp. 25-42.

Harris, Ian M. "The Citizen's Committee in Milwaukee." *Integrateducation,* 94 (July/ August 1978): pp. 35-41.

Koneya, Mele. "Citizen Participation Is Not Community Development." *Journal of the Community Development Society,* 9 (Fall 1978): pp. 23-29.

Priscoli, Jerry Delli. "Implementing Public Involvement Programs in Federal Agencies." In Patricia Marshall (ed.) *Citizen Participation Certification for Community Development: A Reader on the Citizen Participation Process.* Washington, DC: National Association of Housing and Redevelopment Officials, 1977.

Rosener, Judy B. "Citizen Participation: Tying Strategy to Function." In Patricia Marshall (ed.), *Citizen Participation Certification for Community Development: A Reader on the Citizen Participation Process.* Washington, DC: National Association of Housing and Redevelopment Officials, 1977.

U.S. Commission on Civil Rights. *Desegregation of the Nation's Public Schools.* Washington, DC: U.S.C.C.R., 1976.

CHAPTER IV

Social Action

Observe the smallest action, seeming simple,
with mistrust.
Inquire if a thing be necessary
especially if it is common.
We particularly ask you—
when a thing continually occurs—
not on that account to find it natural.
Let nothing be called natural
in an age of bloody confusion,
ordered disorder, planned caprice
and dehumanized humanity, lest all things
be held unalterable.

BERTOLT BRECHT
The Exception and the Rule

Is it really that quiet on the social action front, or does it just appear to be that way? Perhaps the answer depends most on when and where and how one looks at what is going on in neighborhoods and communities around the country (indeed, around the world). The provocative rhetoric, protracted hostilities, and mass confrontations of the 1960s and 1970s may be gone. But the quest of America's poor and oppressed minorities for social, economic, and political justice continues. Newer action organizations (like The Association of Community Organizations for Reform Now [Acorn] and Massachusetts Fair Share) have emerged to replace those that have gone under or receded in our consciousness. Many efforts—born of the upheavals of the last quarter century—are flourishing. Rather than dying out, the neighborhood movement is alive and vibrant.[1] The profile may be lower, but

---

[1]For example, see Robert Fisher, *Let the People Decide: Neighborhood Organizing in America* (Boston: Twayne Publishers, 1984).

the struggles for the rights of disenfranchised people—gays, the aging, the handicapped, tenants, single parents, ex-offenders, low wage workers, new immigrants, political refugees, and the like remain. No less in communities across the nation, the battle for equal opportunities for racial and ethnic minorities is still in motion. Foundations, labor unions, churches, numerous community organizations, and people themselves have provided personnel and funding for these efforts.

The initial article by Robert Fisher provides a historical orientation to the emergence of "three dominant traditions" in community organizing— "social work," "political activist," and "neighborhood maintenance." He also discusses the "backyard revolution," a turning toward community-based solutions by city dwellers who want more control over the decisions that affect their lives. The conservative implications of this movement, along with liberal and radical ones, are not neglected. Illustrations are drawn from a range that includes Houston's The Metropolitan Organization (TMO) and Students for a Democratic Society (SDS) to The Association of Community Organizations for Reform Now (ACORN) and Boston's Restore Our Alienated Rights (ROAR).

Probably nothing is more important in social action organizing than having clear guidelines about how to proceed. Most of the available materials in this area are either elaborate case studies or a series of theoretical propositions barely tested out (if at all) in the real world. Lee Staples lays out a basic and vital set of methods and functions for establishing an effective grass-roots organizations—based on the work of experienced organizers. Constituency, membership, leadership, structure, finances and staff are explored. What is the process by which a multi-constituency, multi-issue, self-funded, democratically led, membership organization may be established?

One of the things that has been most lacking in the social action literature is a clear exploration of the relationship between who an organizer is and what she or he does. In Warren Haggstrom's article, the moral and ethical dilemmas of everyday organizing are addressed head-on. The knowledge base that informs the organizing effort is also explored. Based on Haggstrom's extensive experience as an organizer, this chapter also draws on his knowledge of the Industrial Areas Foundation founded by Saul Alinsky. The medium and long-range demands of organization building are discussed. Emphasis is also laid on the hard political and personal choices that confront social action organizers.

Taken together, these articles suggest a range of possible value stances regarding social action for the community practitioner. In addition, a series of potential intervention roles is clearly delineated. While the emphasis is, as it must be, on conflict-based strategies, the authors also direct attention to the bargaining, negotiation, and cooperative aspects of these efforts. Some of the newer organizational auspices under which various social action modes might be most effectively employed are considered.

The components of successful action organizing are delineated along with the vital steps that make it possible. For the careful reader, a number of points of attack are posited. But no final or complete "answers" are offered and this is as it should be. As Haggstrom notes, the world of the social actionist is a place where ". . .complex structures constantly dissolve and reform before him," a world ". . .of possibility in which he takes a hand to reshape the future."

JOHN L. ERLICH

22.

Robert Fisher

COMMUNITY ORGANIZING IN HISTORICAL PERSPECTIVE: A TYPOLOGY

The rebirth of interest in neighborhoods and community organization during the 1960s and 1970s is readily apparent in Houston and throughout the United States today. A recent Gallup poll indicated, for example, that 42 percent of the people interviewed belong or would like to belong to a neighborhood organization and that a majority of citizens are willing to take direct action in defense of their neighborhood.[1] Many of our nation's large cities have neighborhood crime prevention programs and health centers, food and day care cooperatives, community development corporations, little city halls, community action programs, tenant and homeowner organizations, and other neighborhood-based social service and political-action organizations. Signs on buildings and storefronts announce these projects, and advertisements, like the billboard along I-10 in Houston which reads, "Come See, Come Sigh ... Great Neighborhoods from the 50's," indicate that realtors and land developers believe money can be made from this renewed interest in neighborhood life.

Politicians in Washington have also taken note. The federal government's National Neighborhood Policy Act of 1976 attempted for the first time in the ten years since the Model Cities Act to articulate the needs of our neighborhoods, and Carter's Urban Policy of 1978 noted the importance of neighborhood organizations in the city building and revitalization process. The Republican Party, traditionally aloof from grass-roots issues since the days of Reconstruction, included in its national platform of 1980 strong emphasis on the value of neighborhoods and neighborhood organizations. On a more local level, the Houston Planning and Police Departments recently cosponsored a "Building Better Neighborhoods" fair, with exhibits and workshops on neighborhood concerns. "Small is beautiful" appeals to a citizenry alienated from its economic and political power centers, and now those centers are moving to acknowledge, coopt, and profit from this impulse.[2]

Turning inward into community-based solutions is clearly a conservative act for many—a retreat from urban and national problems, a reaction against

Source: Robert Fisher, "Community Organizing in Historical Perspective: A Typology" in *The Houston Review* (Summer 1982), pp. 75-87. Reprinted by permission of the author and the publisher.

[1]Stewart Dill McBride, "A Nation of Neighborhoods." *Christian Science Monitor* Reprint (articles originally appeared September-December, 1977).

[2]For information on this renewed interest, see Rachelle B. Warren and Donald I. Warren, *The Neighborhood Organizer's Handbook* (Notre Dame: University of Notre Dame Press, 1977); Harry C. Boyte, *The Backyard Revolution: Understanding the New Citizen Movement* (Philadelphia: Temple University Press, 1980).

minority group demands for a social change, and a nostalgic harkening for a simpler, mythical age.[3] But the overriding sentiment behind neighborhood organizing is a positive response on the part of city dwellers who want to get control of the institutions that affect their lives. Where such neighborhood organizations are committed to political and economic democracy, they reflect an emerging opposition in the nation to corporate control of people's lives and unresponsive government. Heirs of the social change movements of the 1960s, these urban residents have combined to fight real estate speculation, absentee home ownership, redlining*, high rents and taxes, racism, sexism, and insufficient public services.[4]

This "backyard revolution" is in many ways less obvious in the South and the sunbelt, where sprawling cities traversed by freeways seem, at first glance, to lack neighborhoods, let alone the time to have developed the strong neighborhood tradition one would find in Boston, Chicago, or Philadelphia. "Smaller is better" appears to make little sense in a region where expansion and growth, fueled by a "laissez-faire" political climate, are the hallmark. Texas and Houston epitomize this bigger is better, biggest is best ethic.

Nevertheless, a turning inward to "mediating institutions"—institutions at the local level like neighborhood organizations which can enable people to address local problems—is readily apparent here.[5] As the uses of "smaller is better" reflect a city's political climate, Houston's neighborhood organizations tend to be more conservative than programs in the North or on the West Coast. Houston has food cooperatives, tenant organizations, and social action neighborhood programs, though far fewer than Minneapolis or San Francisco where social change groups are stronger and more accepted. Instead, Houston abounds with more than six hundred improvement associations.[6]

A vast literature on neighborhood organizing appeared almost simultaneously with this nationwide community movement. Urban planners, social workers, sociologists, and political scientists saw neighborhood-based organizations as a solution to the "urban crisis" of the 1960s. They wrote theoretical analyses on the nature of community organization efforts and described in case histories the efforts of widely diverse community-based organizations.[7] This literature provides a

---

[3]Zane L. Miller, "The Role and Concept of Neighborhood in American Cities," in Robert Fisher and Peter Romanovsky, eds., Community Organization for Urban Social Change: A Historical Perspective (Westport: Greenwood, 1981).

*Editor's note: Redlining means the demarcation of urban areas by banks and insurance companies to indicate where mortgage loans and real property insurance will not be issued. The practice is generally not made public.

[4]See Robert Cassidy, Livable Cities: A Grass-Roots Guide to Rebuilding America (New York: Holt, Rinehart, & Winston, 1980), which includes a good bibliography.

[5]Peter Berger and Richard Neuhaus, To Empower People: The Role of Mediating Structures in Public Policy (Washington, DC: American Enterprise Institute for Public Research, 1977).

[6]Roberta Burroughs, Director of Neighborhood Revitalization Section of Houston Planning Department, interview with author on June 26, 1981.

[7]A representative sample could include George Frederickson, ed., Neighborhood Control in the 1970s (New York: Chandler, 1970); Hans Spiegel, ed., Citizen Participation in Urban Development, two volumes (Washington, DC: Center for Community Affairs, 1968); David Morris and Karl Hess, Neighborhood Power: The New Localism (Boston: Beacon Press, 1975); Jack Rothman, Planning and Organizing for Social Change: Action Principles from Social Science Research (New York: Columbia University Press, 1974).

rich, if incomplete, picture of the community movement of the last fifteen years. But these materials share an obvious failing: all are ahistorical and all ignore the historical experience of the urban South. The description and evaluation of community organization efforts proceed as if neighborhood-based solutions to problems in the United States are unprecedented, as if the issues faced by organizers are unprecedented, as if historical roots can offer little to our understanding of current and future efforts.[8] This is not so.

The history of community organizing illustrates nicely how neighborhood efforts originate and change over time, why they succeed and why they fail, and where they fit into the scheme of events and developments.[9] It can also reveal, and this is the more limited subject of the article, the connecting threads and recurrent themes in the history of community organizing that exist despite the unique historical circumstances and conditions that produce each effort. Historically, there appear to be three dominant, distinctive, and relatively exclusive approaches to community organization, which we can label the social work, political activist, and

---

[8]Milton Kotler, "The Purpose of Neighborhood Power," in *South Atlantic Urban Studies* IV (1979), p. 29, states that "we must remember where the neighborhood movement came from and what happened to create the present situation. The neighborhood movement did not fall from heaven yesterday. It began in the 1960s."

[9]For further information on the history of community organizing, see Fisher and Romanovsky, *Community Organization for Urban Social Change*. It is difficult enough for people today to agree on a definition of community organizing, let alone agree on one for all the various types of efforts since the 1890s. In the interest of inclusiveness, let us define it as the act of involving residents in a neighborhood or community organization which subordinates other forms of activity to the priority of neighborhood concerns.

neighborhood maintenance traditions (See Table 22.1).[10]

The social work tradition views the community essentially as a social organism; it focuses on social issues such as building a sense of community, gathering together social service organizations, or lobbying for and delivering social resources. It assumes that basically the community's problem is social disorganization. The organizer functions either as an "enabler" to help the community gather itself together or as an "advocate" to secure additional services for the community. The strategy is gradualist and consensual, which means that organizers assume a unity of interest between the power structure and the neighborhood and assume a willingness of at least some in power to meet community needs. The structure of organizations in this tradition tends to be more formalized and led by professionals trained in schools of social work. Organizations in this tradition vary in the extent of indigenous participation and grassroots leadership, but the professional community worker is almost always the core of the program. She or he provides at least the initial stimulus program, and, quite often, the focus and personality of the organization. Most important, in the social work approach the community organization sees itself as a social enterprise and operates within the general orientation of the social work profession.

The political activist approach, on the other hand, sees the community as a political entity. It focuses on obtaining, maintaining, or restructuring power.

---

[10]This typology is influenced by a number of others, especially Jack Rothman, "Three Models of Community Organization Practice," in Fred Cox et al., eds., *Strategies of Community Organization* (Itasca: F. E. Peacock Publishers, 1974).

TABLE 22.1. HISTORY OF COMMUNITY ORGANIZING:
THREE DOMINANT TRADITIONS

	Social Work	Political Activist	Neighborhood Maintenance
Concept of Community	social organism	political unit	neighborhood residence
Problem Condition	social disorganization	powerlessness exploitation	threats to community permanence
Role of Organizer	professional social worker enabler and advocate coordinator and planner	political activist mobilizer educator	elected spokesperson
Role of Neighborhood Residents	partners with professional recipients of benefits	fellow activists indigenous leaders mass support	organizers leaders members
Strategy	consensual gradualist work with power structure	conflict mediation challenge power structure provide alternative services	consensual peer pressure political lobbying legal action
Goals	group formation social integration service delivery	obtain, maintain, or restructure power develop alternative institutions	improve property value maintain neighborhood deliver services enrich sense of community
Examples	Social Settlements Community Centers Cincinnati Social Unit Plan Community Chests United Community Defense Services United Way Community Action Program	Unemployed Councils Tenant organizations Alinsky programs White Citizens' Councils Student Non-Violent Coordinating Committee (SNCC) Students for a Democratic Society (SDS) Association of Community Organizations for Reform Now (ACORN) Communities Organized for Public Service (COPS) Restore Our Alienated Rights (ROAR)	Neighborhood Preservation Associations Neighborhood Civic Clubs Property Owners' Associations

Or, if it does not seek to empower community residents, it is political in that its goal is to develop alternative institutions. The community's problem as defined by organizers is the absence of power needed to give people more control over their lives. The organizer's role is to educate and mobilize the community to understand its problem and its potential power. The strategy of the political activist ranges from consensual to confrontational, but in all cases it is rooted in an understanding of the conflict of interest between the community and those in power. The organization usually has a less professional and less formal structure than groups in the social work tradition, and initiators and leaders come more often from the neighborhood. Where the organizers focus solely on their own goals rather than on meeting community needs and developing democratic participation, the political activist approach, like its social work counterpart, takes on an externally-led and autocratic posture.

A third tradition, less commonly thought of as community organizing, is the neighborhood maintenance approach. Here the community is defined as a residential area. The problem is maintaining and improving the neighborhood while opposing external and internal threats to its permanence and commercial value. The organizer serves as an elected representative and spokesperson of the association; the neighborhood residents act as organizers, leaders, and members of the organization. The strategy is generally one of consensus, wherein the association first applies neighborhood peer pressure to resolve problems and then, if necessary, resorts to political and legal channels. Unlike the political activist approach, which will publicly confront local officials, neighborhood maintenance associations most often work quietly behind the scenes in cooperation with their elected representatives. The goal is to promote the neighborhood status quo, focusing essentially on maintaining, if not improving, property values. Unlike the social work and political activist approach, the neighborhood maintenance tradition is most often found in outer city neighborhoods and suburbs where resi-

dents own single-family homes and where they have a vested property interest in protecting their neighborhood. Such neighborhoods have relatively few problems obtaining public services or convincing local power brokers of their needs, issues which plague neighborhoods where organizations in the social work and political activist traditions are most active. The neighborhood maintenance association, in fact, is usually free of major problems or pressing concerns, except when accepted practices are threatened by forces of commercial development or social change.

The social settlement movement of the early twentieth century is a good historical example of the social work approach. In the first decades of this century a number of social reformers saw neighborhood organization as the most progressive and effective response to the problems besetting America's large urban/industrial centers. Generally liberal, upper-middle and upper-class, and white Anglo-Saxon Protestant, these activists—Jane Addams, Lillian Wald, Robert Woods and hundreds of others—moved into working-class, immigrant neighborhoods in the nation's largest cities and established neighborhood centers offering a wide range of programs and activities. Initially their objective was to counteract the ills of urban poverty and disorganization, especially the threat of social disorder, by encouraging active participation of the neighborhood residents in the life of the settlement. This was as true for Houston as it was for New York City and Chicago. The first Houston settlement, Rusk Settlement, begun in 1907 in a small cottage near Rusk School in the Second Ward, was led by "men and women of education and culture" who sought to offer

constructive programs in clubs, in discussion groups, in recreation . . . to stimulate in residents of a community an awareness of their needs, a desire to meet them, to develop their potential leaders, and their own sense of responsibility.[11]

In practice, however, settlements developed more as social service centers than as vehicles for developing community leaders or neighborhood self-empowerment. The class condescension and social control evident in the early leadership prevented effective resident involvement in decision making at these neighborhood centers. Reflecting this problem, Corrinne Tsanoff, one of the leaders in the social welfare and social settlement community in Houston, noted in 1938 that community health centers could keep neighborhoods "not only physically sound but also mentally and morally and socially sound," and could "transform the entire life of the masses in Houston."[12]

Given this perspective of working for, not with, the people, settlements, like the social work profession in general, concerned themselves with delivering health, educational, and recreational services to poor neighborhoods which needed such programs. Thus, from its inception, the social settlement movement functioned within the "social work tradition" of community organizing, even though it actually pre-ceded the development of the social work profession. The focus was to build social unity and deliver social services in an effort to ameliorate problems caused by "social disorganization" in working-class communities. As Jesse Steiner, the author of the first text in community organization in 1925, described this approach: "The modern community movement is essentially an insistence upon the community as a *social unit* to be given first consideration in dealing with *social problems*."[13]

This orientation of the social work tradition of community organizing to identify their work in terms of social disorganization, social problems, and social reform, and to seek solutions through improving social relationships and delivering social services continued from the 1930s through the Great Society programs of the 1960s and the community-based social welfare programs of today. Programs as different as the United Community Defense Services during the Korean War, Community Action Programs in the 1960s, and current efforts of a host of neighborhood centers, settlements, and clubs continue to function within the social work tradition of community organizing.

Some settlement leaders always understood the value of using neighborhood centers as vehicles of social change as well as for service delivery. Franklin Harbach, the leading figure in the neighborhood center movement in Houston since the 1940s, who also served for a time as president of the Na-

---

[11]Corrinne S. Tsanoff, *Neighborhood Doorways* (Houston: Neighborhood Centers Association of Houston and Harris County, 1958), p. 2.

[12]Corrine S. Tsanoff to W. D. Cleveland, Jr., May 26, 1938, United Neighborhood Houses Collection, Social Welfare History Archives, University of Minnesota.

[13]Jesse Steiner, "Appraisal of the Community Movement," *Social Forces* VII (March 1929), p. 337. For more information on the social center movement, see Robert Fisher, "Community Organizing and Citizen Participation: The Efforts of the People's Institute in New York City, 1910-1920," *Social Service Review* LI (Sept. 1977), pp. 474-490.

tional Federation of Settlements and Neighborhood Centers, cited the need for social change when he remarked that neighborhood organization would always be needed "because there'll always be people on the bottom trying to move up the ladder and people on the top trying to hold them down."[14] But community organization in the social work tradition in Houston and throughout the nation has remained limited in its ability to do much more than offer social services—valuable and necessary services—at the neighborhood level. As the current director of Ripley House, Felix Fraga, noted recently, community neighborhood centers have dropped because, among other reasons, funding sources prefer to sponsor direct services, that is, programs that can show more concrete results.[15]

The political activist approach is most often associated with the work of Saul Alinsky. Using the lessons and practice of Congress of Industrial Organization organizers active in Chicago in the 1930s, Alinsky sought to organize a democratic "people's movement" at the grass-roots level. He began his work in the Back of the Yards neighborhood in Chicago, described decades earlier in Upton Sinclair's *The Jungle.* Over the course of a generation of forming organizations and training organizers, he and others spread his method to dozens of cities and rural areas throughout the nation. The framework for all of this activity was that the community was a political unit, that obtaining power was

the objective, and that confrontation with existing powers was to be expected and encouraged. In his earlier and more militant *Reveille for Radicals* (1946), he called for a "new power group . . . dedicated to an eternal war." Some years later in *Rules for Radicals* (1971), Alinsky, tempered by his experiences with McCarthyism and the New Left, said the goal was to enable the "have nots" and the "have nots, want mores" to take power from the "haves."[16] But always, whether organizing in churches or the fields of California, community organizing in the Alinsky style was political and sought to obtain power.

Ernie Cortes, one of the more successful contemporary community organizers in the nation and currently active in Houston with The Metropolitan Organization (TMO), defines his efforts in typical Alinsky terms: "Organization means hope for people. It means making their institutions relevant. But most of all, organization means power. It means being able to do something about things they've been frustrated about all their lives."[17] The Association of Community Organizations for Reform Now (ACORN), active nationally and in Houston as well, shares a similar perspective. For ACORN, like Alinsky and Cortes, the delivery of social services is a means to gaining more power for community residents, not simply an end in itself as is often the case in the social work tradition. "The major ques-

---

[14]Harbach quoted, Houston *Chronicle,* September 19, 1966, United Neighborhood Houses Collection, Social Welfare History Archives, University of Minnesota.

[15]Felix Fraga, interview with author in fall 1980.

[16]Saul D. Alinsky, *Reveille for Radicals* (New York: Vintage Books, 1969), pp. 132-133; Saul D. Alinsky, *Rules for Radicals* (New York: Vintage Books, 1972), p. 3. For more information, see Michael Connolly, "A Historical Study of Change in Saul D. Alinsky's Community Organization Practice and Theory, 1939-1972" (Ph.D. diss., University of Minnesota, 1976).

[17]Ernie Cortes quoted in Boyte, *Backyard Revolution,* p. 44.

tion," an ACORN organizer put it, "is not whether we can adequately deliver social services, but how can we build the power of ordinary people to decide what services should be provided and how they should be delivered."[18]

But Alinsky practice, past and present, is only one type, be it the most noted one, in the political activist tradition. Community organizing efforts of the Communist Party (CPUSA) in slum and working-class neighborhoods in the 1930s, of tenant organizers in New York and other cities dating back as early as the 1890s, and of the Student Nonviolent Coordinating Committee (SNCC) in rural southern communities and Students for a Democratic Society (SDS) in northern urban neighborhoods in the 1960s are other important precursors to current neighborhood programs.[19] Despite their vast differences, all of these efforts, from the CPUSA through Alinsky, TMO and ACORN, are clearly rooted in this political activist approach to community organizing.

It would be inaccurate, however, to give the impression that all efforts in the political activist tradition share a progressive or radical critique of American society. Unlike the social work tradition, which is rather firmly rooted

in a liberal, social welfare vision of community organization, efforts in the political activist tradition run the ideological gamut from revolutionary to reactionary. Right-wing historical examples in this tradition include segregationist efforts like the Citizens' Councils in the 1950s and Restore Our Alienated Rights (ROAR)—an antiabortion, antibusing, anticommunist effort—in white, ethnic neighborhoods in Boston in the 1970s.[20]

It is ironic that the neighborhood maintenance tradition, with the deepest historical roots, is the least recognized type of community organization. Community organizing is most often thought of in relation to community work in working-class and racial and ethnic minority neighborhoods, where both the social work and political activist tradition focus most of their attention. But the neighborhood maintenance approach predates the other traditions, and according to historian Joseph Arnold, is more common, lasts longer, and tends to have more clout at city hall than comparable working-class and lower-class groups. In Baltimore, for example, there were more than thirty neighborhood associations covering the entire city and its suburbs by 1900. City services were sparse in the outlying middle-class neighborhoods of Baltimore so the residents of these areas organized, as early as 1880, to pressure local officials for better roads, lighting, drainage, police protection, and schools.[21]

[18]Ibid., p. 41.
[19]On Communist Party efforts see Mark Naison, "The Communist Party in Harlem, 1928-1936" (Ph.D. dissertation, Columbia University, 1976); and Frances Piven and Richard Cloward, *Poor People's Movements: Why They Succeed, How They Fail* (New York: Random House, 1979). On tenant organizing, see Joseph Spencer, "Tenant Organization and Housing Reform in New York City, 1936-1943" (Paper delivered at meeting of Organization of American Historians, April 1978). On Students for a Democratic Society organizing strategy, see Sara Evans, *Personal Politics: The Roots of Women's Liberation in the Civil Rights Movement and the New Left* (New York: Alfred Knopf, 1979).

[20]On the Citizens' Council, see Neil R. McMillen, *The Citizens' Council Organized Resistance to the Second Reconstruction, 1954-1964* (Urbana: University of Illinois Press, 1971).
[21]Joseph Arnold, "The Neighborhood and City Hall: The Origin of Neighborhood Associations in Baltimore, 1880-1911," *Journal of Urban History* VI (November 1979), pp. 6-14.

Houston's experience with neighborhood maintenance associations is tied more to the issue of land use management than public service delivery. By 1980 there were an estimated six hundred clubs and homeowners' associations in the city with the expressed purpose of enforcing deed restrictions, Houston's neighborhood-based alternative to zoning. These civic clubs, organized and run by neighborhood residents, perform functions other than deed restriction enforcement. The Southwest Civic Club, for example, begun in 1951 in the Braeswood area, has provided a number of services in its thirty-year history, including mosquito fogging, security patrols, and recreational activities for children and adults. Most well-established civic clubs offer similar services and work to secure better services from the city. But the essential function is to enforce deed restrictions in the subdivision, "to defend the neighborhood against anything that threatens its attractiveness and the stability of property values."[22] Such threats range from messy front lawns, cluttered driveways, and nonconforming new construction to commercial development, multi-family use of property, and minority group members moving into the neighborhood.[23]

---

[22]Southwest Civic Club leaflet in Houston Chamber of Commerce, *Handbook for Civic Club Leaders* (Houston: Houston Chamber of Commerce, Civic Affairs Committee, 1979). Reference #9.

[23]See Clement C. Vose, *Caucasians Only: The Supreme Court, the NAACP, and the Restrictive Covenant Cases* (Berkeley: University of California Press, 1959) for information on the role of neighborhood associations in excluding blacks from suburban neighborhoods. Many civic clubs in Houston were dues-paying members of the Allied Civic Club, an umbrella organization which helped neighborhood associations in the 1960s oppose integration and panic selling.

The neighborhood maintenance tradition shares much in common with the other two approaches. Like the social work approach it concentrates on providing services to the neighborhood; like the political activist type its function is essentially para-political—lobbying city hall or enforcing deed restrictions—though most civic clubs in Houston do not think of themselves as being political, which they define in electoral or partisan terms. The neighborhood maintenance tradition is different, however, because its leaders and organizers are always neighborhood residents, never outsiders as is often the case in the social work and political activist approach, and most especially, because it seeks to maintain the status quo. Neighborhood associations generally ignore social change efforts, unless they threaten the community. The goal is not to ameliorate the problems of society as is true in the social work approach or to empower people as is the political activist's want. Rather the conservative objective is to get neighborhood residents to participate in protecting the value of their property and, relatedly, to maintain the standards of the neighborhood, as defined first by the developer in the initial deed restriction and later by a majority of neighborhood residents.

These three traditions in community organizing have largely been isolated from each other. Practitioners and writers using the social work approach prior to the 1970s would not have considered the Communist Party's Unemployed Council movement of the 1930s or the Citizens' Councils of the 1950s as community organization, let alone civic clubs designed to protect property values and neighborhood homogeneity. They might briefly note the work of

Saul Alinsky, primarily because Alinsky began his work within the social work tradition and because he continued to use much of his earlier-learned practice. The same isolation is true for those using the political activist approach. That tradition traces its roots back to the political protest movements, not the origins of social work practice. Political activist organizers trace their heritage to prior political efforts, like the populist movement. They do not recall efforts of social settlements and neighborhood councils developed by professional community workers, or neighborhood protection and associations organized by homeowners. Most often, those in the neighborhood protection maintenance tradition do not think of themselves as part of a larger community organization movement or heritage. Their historical roots are identified solely in terms of the history of the neighborhood and the improvement association.

It would be an error, however, to paint these traditions into exclusive corners. In the decade preceding the First World War, the social work and political activist traditions overlapped in the more progressive settlements like Hull House and Chicago Commons in Chicago and New York City's Henry Street Settlement. These settlements were pioneers in the social work tradition of community organization, but they also were sensitive to the needs of their constituents and thus at times sought to mobilize neighborhood residents in political struggle against local political bosses and industrial sweatshops. As Mary Follett, a settlement worker and activist in the community center movement, proclaimed in 1918:

Politics can no longer be an extra-activity of the American people, it must be a means of satisfying our wants . . . Our proposal is that the people should organize themselves into neighborhood groups to express their daily life, to bring to the surface the needs, desires, and aspirations of that life, that these needs should become the substance of politics, and that neighborhood groups should become the recognized political unit.[24]

In the 1960s the two approaches overlapped again as the decade's political ferment forced them together. Activist organizers and the organizations they were involved with—SNCC, SDS, and a host of other programs spawned by the black struggle and new left protest, for instance—forced those in the social work tradition to reexamine their reformist and social service approach to community organizing. At the same time the Great Society co-opted many activists into an approach to community organizing which straddled both traditions, but as exemplified by Manpower and the Community Action Program (CAP), was rooted in the social work approach.[25] Only during these two periods of heightened community organizing activity—1900-1920 and since the 1960s—have these two traditions, while maintaining distinctive approaches, overlapped and been aware of each other.

Since the early 1970s both traditions, but especially the political activist approach, have begun to use elements of the neighborhood maintenance prac-

---

[24]Mary P. Follett, *The New State* (New York: Longmans, Green, 1926), pp. 189-192.

[25]Charles Grosser, *New Directions in Community Organization: From Enabling to Advocacy* (New York: Praeger, 1973) and Jeffrey Galper, *The Politics of Social Services* (Englewood Cliffs: Prentice-Hall, 1975) reflect changes in the social work profession during the late 1960s and early 1970s.

tice. Increasingly, organizers realize that when you "let the people decide," one of the key concerns of residents is protecting their neighborhood against outside threats. At times neither the problem nor the solution as defined by community residents is one with which the organizer agrees. But organizers in the political activist tradition are learning to understand and respect this protectionist impulse, as well as others found in the neighborhood maintenance tradition. Reflecting this new trend, Harry Boyte notes in his *The Backyard Revolution:*

Contemporary citizen organizing is more down to earth, more positive, above all more enduring and rooted in the social fabric ... It is accompanied by a sense of the richness, creativity, and vitality in people's traditions, folkways, and culture that sixties radicals were prone to scorn or dismiss.[26]

This typology of community organizing methods raises as many questions as it answers, but it does underline some important points about the nature of local-based organizing efforts. First, community organizing is a child of diverse origins and of varied inclinations.

---

[26]Boyte, *Backyard Revolution,* xii.

Historically and currently there are numerous types of community organizing practices. Neither the social work profession's practice of community organization, the Alinskyite organizer's method of community organizing, or the civic club member's efforts at neighborhood maintenance has a monopoly on neighborhood organizing. It is a method, an approach widely used by various segments of society to achieve specific goals, to serve certain interests, and to advance often well-defined political perspectives. It is neither inherently progressive and positive, nor fundamentally parochial and exclusionary. Second, community organizing has long, if overshadowed, roots in the American experience. While the dominant trend in the United States during the last century has been toward centralization and concentration—"bigger is better"—efforts at decentralization and local control—"smaller is better"—are apparent as well, even in Houston. With roots dating back at least to the late nineteenth century, community organizing is obviously more than a phenomenon of the 1960s. As our society becomes increasingly fragmented and decentralized, we should expect the interest in community organizing, so visible in the 1970s, to continue to grow.

23.

Lee Staples

"CAN'T YA HEAR ME KNOCKING?":
AN ORGANIZING MODEL

COMMUNITY ORGANIZATIONS

Building an effective community organization requires a systematic approach. An organizing model serves as the blueprint. The one described in this article has evolved over the past 16 years from my experiences working with the National Welfare Rights Organization, doing neighborhood organizing with Warren Haggstrom in Los Angeles, California, and as an organizer and regional staff director for Massachusetts Fair Share.

Few of the techniques set forth here were developed solely by me. Rather, they represent an amalgamation of the ideas and methods of a number of highly skilled organizers with whom I've had the opportunity to work.[1] Thus, this organizing model bears a strong resemblance to a number of others which also work very well. While the specifics may vary, the basic principles of organizing and moving people into action are common to all successful models. Therefore this article can be read on two levels—as a general outline of key principles or as a step-by-step manual

for a particular proven organizing model.

Just as an architectural blueprint is drawn with definite functions in mind, the methods used in any organizing drive are tailored to the kind of organization one is attempting to create. Much of this model could be applied more broadly, but it's designed to build community organizations with the following prescribed characteristics.

Constituency

This model generally has been used to organize low- and moderate-income people. While many of the methods could be utilized to organize in higher-income neighborhoods, the conflict methods it features are geared to situations in which a constituency is in a relatively powerless position vis-à-vis other segments of society. In addition, the organizing described here is done on a geographic or "turf" basis rather than by specific issue or constituency. This multi-constituency approach includes all the low- and moderate-income people in a particular neighborhood, not just one group such as tenants, homeowners, welfare recipients, women, senior citizens, or Hispanic residents. However, I can attest from personal experience that all the principles and most of the specific

Source: From *Roots to Power* by Lee Staples. Copyright © 1984 Praeger Publishers. Reprinted by permission of Praeger Publishers.

[1]The partial list includes: Bruce Thomas, Bill Pastreich, Wade Rathke, Kris Ockershauser, Warren Haggstrom, Mark Splain, and Barbara Bowen. And most importantly this model flows from the knowledge and techniques developed by the legendary Fred Ross.

methods and techniques of this model are directly applicable to single-constituency organizing as well.

Issues and Tactics

Perhaps the most fundamental principle of organizing is that issues should arise from the people one is organizing, not from the organizer. People become involved when they're convinced that the organization can produce a change on some issue which is important to them. Thus, people join organizations, as they do other things, because they are motivated by a perceived self-interest. Since there are multiple interests within any low- or moderate-income neighborhood constituency, it follows that there will be multiple issues. Different issues suggest a multiplicity of tactics, and the nature of the constituency and its concerns dictate a high level of conflict. This organizing model is designed on a multi-issue, multi-tactic basis, emphasizing direct action.

Membership

I'm laying out a method for building what can best be described as a direct membership organization that people join as individuals or families, usually by paying some sort of membership dues. This is in sharp contrast to the type of organization developed by Saul Alinsky that features the formation of a permanent neighborhood coalition—an organization composed of pre-existing organizations. In the Alinsky model, individuals become part of the larger organization by virtue of their membership in one of the participating groups. Thus, the building blocks of

an Alinsky organization are smaller organizations, while the direct membership organization, like a labor union, has as its basic unit the individual or the family.

Without debating the merits of these two general organizational models, it should be pointed out that there are significant differences in the processes for building each type. The formation of an Alinsky organization involves a series of steps designed to entice pre-existing organizations to buy into a new coalition organization and to participate in the formation of that entity through a "people's convention" or "community congress." A direct membership organizing drive features systematic recruitment of individuals and families, usually through door-to-door contacts, leading to an organizational formation meeting. While most of the basic organizing principles are the same for both types of organization, the particular methods and skills utilized obviously will vary. This chapter is confined to the direct membership model.

Leadership

As in most, if not all, community organizing models, there's an emphasis on producing indigenous leaders who will operate through democratic decision-making structures. The development of such leaders is critical to the membership's sense of their own power and feeling of organizational ownership. These concerns profoundly affect each step of the organizing process and should be borne in mind throughout this chapter. Indeed, the amount of space allocated here for this discussion is by no means commensurate with the importance of leadership development.

While the Alinsky coalition model draws experienced leaders from pre-existing groups, the direct membership model tends to produce leaders who've had little prior organizational involvement. Thus leadership development is critical to this model. The general philosophy expressed here is that leaders learn through direct experience. This involves a three-part process of planning strategies and specific tactics (featuring lots of meetings, role playing, and other advance preparation), executing the plans, and assessing the results during and after the issue campaigns.

Structure

This model produces a neighborhood-wide organization in which the members choose their leaders directly through democratic elections. The neighborhood organization could exist as a separate entity, but because most social problems flow from political and economic policies that are made far above the neighborhood level, this model is consciously designed to create local "chapters" of citywide, statewide, regional, or national organizations as well. Thus, it's deliberately simple and universal enough to be easily replicated.

The organization should be governed by a formal set of bylaws that define the rights and responsibilities of members and leaders. These should cover the purpose of the group and the definition and powers of members. There should be a clear indication of how often general membership meetings should be held, of quorum requirements, and of the kinds of decisions to be made by the whole membership. Provisions for forming and dissolving committees and choosing their leaders should be specified clearly. The elected officers, their duties, and their powers also should be listed, as well as the group's mechanism for selecting them. Other subjects that should be covered include conflict of interest, financial guidelines, staff responsibilities and rights, and the process for amending the bylaws. The goal is an organizational structure that builds ownership and control while maintaining an open, flexible direct action focus.

Finances

Grass-roots organizations need money to operate, for expenses such as supplies, mailings, actions, an office, and paid staff. How and where an organization gets funding will influence every facet of its operation.

This model is based on the premise that an action organization should not accept funding that compromises its ability to push for maximum social change. Funds from sources that are potential targets come with "strings attached" that can be used to leverage control, containment, and cooptation. Whoever pays the piper calls the tune. Generally speaking, that eliminates most government and corporate sources. Exceptions might occur when an organization receives funding that is insulated from interference and largely paid in advance, but even then an organization shouldn't be seduced into significant dependence on such funds. Rather, it should immediately make plans to replace these monies with more independent and stable sources. With this kind of insurance against the loss of funding, the organization is free to run as far and as fast with the money as possible, while it's still available.

Social action organizations receive most of their funding either from external sources such as foundations, churches, and wealthy individuals or from internal sources including dues, door-to-door canvassing for contributions, and a variety of grass-roots fundraising projects (such as raffles, dances, carnivals, bake sales, ad books, and potluck suppers). It's desirable to raise as great a portion of the budget as possible internally. Internal fundraising not only protects the organization from external interference but, more importantly, gives the membership a greater sense of ownership. It's worth remembering though, that even internal fundraising has profound effects on the functioning of the organization. An emphasis on membership dues, for instance, necessitates stressing collection techniques and quotas; canvassing requires issues and a style appealing to a wide range of potential contributors (often middle class); and grassroots fundraising projects may monopolize large blocks of staff and leadership time.

Staff

This organizing model relies heavily on door-to-door recruitment, which requires major amounts of time. Organizers should be prepared to commit 60 to 80 hours per week for six weeks, and ideally should have some supervised training in organizing methodology. It will be difficult to find unpaid volunteers with the time, commitment, and skill to organize this intensively. Though part-time volunteer organizers could make adjustments to this model to fit their own situations, an experienced, full-time staff worker will make the job infinitely more manageable.

There are many possible variations that work well, including one organizer working alone, a team of organizer trainees moving as "floating doorknockers" from drive to drive, or a more permanent intensive staff. Since staff salaries are usually the largest organizational expense, key decisions must be made regarding the utilization of an organizing staff within the confines of the budget. These decisions usually focus on the age-old problem of "breadth versus depth"; that is, how can the organization be in enough places to have clout at its highest level of structure (whether citywide, statewide, regional, or national) without spreading itself so thin that it becomes merely a "paper" organization with no significant base of active leaders and members?

The optimum situation would feature an experienced lead organizer supervising a new trainee during the organizing drive, thereby simultaneously nearly doubling the amount of turf covered and developing new staff. This model provides enough depth with a neighborhood to be effective, while maintaining a lean enough staff intensity to allow maximum spread.

THE ORGANIZING PROCESS

These seven elements together help define an organization. By analyzing them, it should be possible to gain at least a rudimentary understanding of any social action organization. In this instance, it should be clear that the model I'm describing is designed to build a multi-constituency, multi-issue, action-oriented, self-funded, democratically led, membership organization. With that as the objective, the organizing process unfolds in four distinct phases:

1. Groundwork: During the initial phase of the organizing process, the organizer gathers basic information about the community and begins to analyze the power dynamics at work within it.
2. Developing an Organizing Committee: A two-step phase follows during which the organizer first talks with key "gatekeepers" in the community, who, once convinced of the merits of the organizing effort, provide a "contact list" of potential members for the organizer to visit. The organizer then meets with those contacts (adding new ones in snowball fashion as s/he goes along) and pulls together an organizing committee that provides the initial core group for the organizing drive.
3. General Recruitment Drive: A systematic recruitment is launched with the active support and participation of the organizing committee members.
4. Formation Meeting: The organizing drive culminates with a formation meeting where temporary leadership is elected and organizational action is planned.

The general recruitment phase, which is the heart of the organizing drive, will cover about six weeks while another four to six weeks should be spent doing the preliminary work. These figures are somewhat flexible; however, six weeks of doorknocking seems to be the maximum time that an organizing drive can continue without the loss of critical momentum.

Most organizers will be able to average between 30 to 40 doors per day, or roughly 1000 to 1500 doors during the course of a six-week drive. The neighborhood size, of course, will vary, although areas of more than 4000 doors usually don't hang together well and pose the danger of becoming "paper organizations" unless there's more staff for ongoing door-knocking. On the other hand, neighborhoods of less than 500 doors are generally too small to produce adequate leadership numbers, membership dues potential, and variety of issues.

The amount of turf covered during the drive is a simple function of the number of doors a person can cover in an average day times the number of people doing the doorknocking and the number of days that the drive lasts. All things being equal, I favor the above range of neighborhood size and a six-week timetable with a team of an experienced organizer and a trainee as the ideal combination of cost efficiency plus staff training and support.

Again, while this model is clearly designed to produce direct action, conflict oriented organizations, the techniques are widely applicable to most types of community work. The initial organizing steps, in particular, are critical to the success of any organizing effort, providing legitimation, an initial leadership core, an understanding of key issues in the neighborhood, and an opportunity to identify and perhaps neutralize opposition.

Groundwork

Before beginning the process of organizing in a neighborhood, it's wise to gather some very basic information. Many organizers call this process a "power analysis." Of course, the most critical information will come later when the organizer talks directly with neighborhood people, and it's important to avoid the danger of falling into an "analysis paralysis" that delays actual organizing. Nevertheless, by gaining a good initial understanding of the dynamics of the neighborhood, the organizer will be able to ask more sophisticated questions and avoid obvious mistakes during the early phases of the organizing drive. The key is to see what can be, not simply what *is.* During the Groundwork phase, I attempt to gain basic information about the following areas.

Turf. What are the natural boundaries of the potential neighborhood? Using maps and both driving and walking tours I try to get an initial feel for the turf and how it meshes with the rest of the city. Are there obvious physical boundaries such as a highway, major street, railroad track, or industrial area? What are the church parish boundaries or the areas designated for various government programs and development projects? Political jurisdictions (congressional, state legislative, ward, precinct, city council, etc.) also may be relevant, although such districts frequently are gerrymandered contrary to neighborhood lines. Ultimately these criteria will have to be squared with how the residents themselves define "the neighborhood" but a lot can be determined with a little initial work.

Constituency. Using basic statistics, doing some reading (both current and historical), and talking with people I already know, I try to get a sense of basic demographic trends and characteristics. Obviously, I want to know who lives there now—race/ethnicity, age, sex, religion, educational levels, income, and so on. But I also want to know how these statistics have changed over the years and are likely to change

in the future. Are large numbers of a particular racial/ethnic group moving in or out of the neighborhood? Is the area becoming gentrified or are more low-income people moving in? What is the mix of tenants and homeowners and is it changing? Do landlords tend to occupy their own properties or are they increasingly absentee? Dozens of such questions should be asked and answered in order to understand the potential constituency and the implications for organizing.

Key Institutions. A partial list of institutions includes local government bodies, large businesses and employers, banks, hospitals, educational institutions, churches, newspapers, and other media outlets. It's impossible to construct an exhaustive list of standard questions about key institutions. Each organizing situation is unique and one question invariably leads to another. My primary interest is in finding potential organizing issues and targets or possible sources of support.

Existing Organizations and Social Service Agencies. Including unions, church groups, senior citizens clubs, various issue or constituency groups, turf organizations (block clubs), political organizations, social groups, and the multitude of service agencies, the list of organizations may be quite extensive. Here again I'm looking for potential support as well as possible competition in various forms. As with the institutions, this information is gathered primarily by reading, especially local newspapers, and by talking with people I already know and trust.

Powerful Actors. I'm looking for movers and shakers, the variety of people who head up key institutions and organizations or who fill various roles as brokers, gatekeepers, leaders, and people of influence. Examples include politicians, key business and civic leaders, clergy, community leaders, and other power brokers. From this list will come potential opponents, allies, people to neutralize, and perhaps even some participants in the organization.

Existing Issues. Usually a new organization won't get involved in a longstanding issue which already has produced leaders and some measure of organization. Exceptions are possible here, but the main purpose in studying these issues is to learn more about who and what are the major forces in the neighborhood.

Potential Issues. People will be recruited largely around specific issues. These issues invariably spring from social problems which produce hardship, injustice, dissatisfaction, and anger. The organizer helps people create a structure and a strategy to overcome these problems. During the Groundwork stage, the organizer looks at social conditions in an attempt to find problems that can be remedied by future organizational campaigns.

The best organizer can spot the contours of future issues on a political landscape that are indistinguishable to the untrained eye. As the organizing drive progresses, the organizer sharpens and tests these issues with the emerging leadership who make the final decisions for action.

Objective Conditions and Political Trends. This is a very broad area covering every level of influence, from the impact of new development projects in the neighborhood to the national political climate. The analysis aims to determine what is possible for the organization to accomplish given conditions and trends at the different levels over which it will have little or no control. These conditions make it possible to accomplish more in certain spheres of activity and less in others at any given time. Thus, an organizational campaign to expand city services in a neighborhood might be less than successful if conducted in the face of a 25 percent cutback in city expenditures. Conversely, the local branch of a corporation that's been cited for violations of affirmative action guidelines might be vulnerable to an organizational campaign to win jobs for minority residents. Some examples are obvious and others more subtle. During the Groundwork phase the organizer begins the neverending process of analyzing these conditions and trends and projecting the potential issue campaign possibilities.

Conceivably, this Groundwork stage could literally take months to complete. Indeed, communities are dynamic entities and as such constantly must be re-examined and re-analyzed. However, most organizers operate under the realities of tight scheduling and don't have the luxury of long periods of study. In any case, the most relevant knowledge about a community will come as the organizer interacts with residents and starts to understand how they see the world. Thus, the Groundwork stage can be completed in two weeks when necessary and the need to gather more information shouldn't become a reason for postponing organizational activity much beyond one month's time.

24.

Warren C. Haggstrom

THE TACTICS OF ORGANIZATION BUILDING*

The organizer lives in a world in which everything is called into question, subject to change, where half-perceived and complex structures constantly dissolve and reform before him, a world of possibility in which he takes a hand to reshape the future. . . .

The organizer cannot afford to believe that he knows his world well because he is engaged in a course of action under barely tractable, constantly changing, and mostly invisible circumstances which contrast sharply with the neat flatland of the sociological theorist.

To build organization in low-income areas is something like playing a long game of blindfold chess in which no player is sure of the rules. The chess pieces move by themselves; skillful players help get this movement channeled into planned patterns, strategies, and tactics. There are standard beginning lines (e.g., house meetings vs. dramatic large public meetings) and some established principles of play ("rub raw the sores of discontent," "the social situation sets the limits for moves"), but much depends on atten-

tion to detail, immense energy, and individual brilliance in capitalizing on whatever happens. Finally, these chess pieces can throw an ineffective player right out of the game.

It follows that the question, "How does one build an organization of the poor?" cannot be answered in the same way as the question, "How does one build a house?" or "How does one build a great football team?" One can only relate a history of past organizations of the poor, a description of those currently functioning, and principles to which some able organizers more or less adhere. The following remarks are directed to the [last-named] task.

THE STARTING POINT

The physical structure and location of a low-income area carry collectively held meanings to the people of the area, meanings which affect the relevance of the physical context to their lives. For example, a hospital may carry the meaning of being a slaughterhouse or of a place in which patients are "treated like dirt." A row of slum houses may mean at once inferiority and deprivation and reassuring familiarity to slum dwellers. Of seven unmarried mothers living in public housing, six may be respectable women and the seventh a scandal—all in accordance with criteria which are not known outside the neighborhood in question. . . .

The social situation in low-income areas, consisting of such collectively

*The following paper is a revised version of one read at the Annual Conference of the Greater Washington Chapter of Americans for Democratic Action on September 18, 1965. The content of the paper stems primarily from my own organizational experience. I am also particularly indebted to Fred Ross for helpful reactions to many of these ideas, and have benefitted from conversations with Saul Alinsky and Tom Gaudette.

Source: Warren Haggstrom, "The Organizer." Previously unpublished. Reprinted by permission of the author.

held sets of meanings, can vary tremendously around any physical situation. It is a key responsibility of the organizer to come to know the social situation and, further, he must consider as well his own meaning as a stranger in the neighborhood. He starts work where he and the people of the neighborhood are in a social situation which slowly becomes intelligible to him. If people want their windows fixed and the welfare check increased, the organizer helps them to begin to act on these problems even though he may privately believe they would be better off working to open up additional jobs. He is limited by the fact that people consciously and unconsciously misrepresent where they are, and, sometimes, they do not understand how to be relevant to the organizer since he has not clearly defined himself and his purpose in the neighborhood. One can come closest to starting where the people are when one begins in an atmosphere of mutual trust which develops when the organizer places himself clearly on the side of the people with whom he is working and states as plainly as possible his purpose in the neighborhood, but does not presume to define for them their problems or the solutions to their problems.

The people, with the help of the organizer, start to work on problems. Very shortly, their action is contested and the problems are transformed into issues with established institutions opposing the action of people in low-income areas. For example, when a number of people in one city began to seek additional money for school supplies for their children, the Commissioner of Welfare at first acceded to the request. When the number of people making such a request becomes large

enough, the commissioner began to deny many of the new requests. At that point, the requests became demands and the resulting struggle drew an increasing number of people into sustained activity of value in building organization. Through a process of struggle around issues perceived in the neighborhood as central the organization develops power which can be used to resolve problems of many varieties.

When an organizer helps people to begin to act on central problems, that is, to make their own decisions about resolving their own problems and to begin to implement those decisions, by that very fact the organizer deliberately creates conflict since the problems of low-income areas cannot be resolved without negative consequences for the self-perceived self-interest and traditional ways of thinking and acting of various advantaged minorities. Until the problems are resolved, so long as the organizer maintains neighborhood action he will by that fact maintain conflict, and requires no artificial strategies leading to artificial confrontations.

THE WAY TO BEGIN

People are usually immersed in private lives centered about work and home. The organizer pulls and jolts them into the public arena.

In the beginning, the organizer is simply another stranger trying to convince people to do something. He is like a salesman—and is met by the evasive tactics which people use to ward off salesmen. A salesman has only to persuade people to one act, to make one purchase. An organizer has the more complicated job of pulling people into new lives, into long-extended alternative lines of action. . . .

Because people do not yet know him, the organizer has to be credible, creating a convincing picture of what might be, relying on the emotional contagion produced by fire and enthusiasm as well as on the factual account that he gives. Since all this should be appropriate to the people with whom he is talking, he modifies his presentation at first as he talks with different persons and groups until working out an approach which is most effective for him (although not necessarily for other organizers) in the neighborhood in which he is working (although not necessarily in the other neighborhoods).

The organizer starts by persuading people to come to a meeting or begin action. He listens, describing the meeting or action as it is relevant to the situation of those with whom he is talking. He appeals to self-interest, builds anger, works along friendship and relationship networks and other formal and informal social structures. He recruits members without appearing too eager to recruit members; they must see themselves as acting on their own initiative. When people have decided to attend a meeting, join a delegation, etc., then an organizer does his best to make certain that their intention is carried out. People may be reminded again and again of the event, some are provided with transportation, etc.

Once at a meeting an organizer concentrates on moving those attending into decision and action through whatever formal structure may exist. He may make certain that decisions are made to do something concrete about sore points of acute concern: the speeding car that killed Bobby Smith, the lack of a policeman to protect Mrs. Jackson, the slum landlord who runs down the neighborhood, etc. He may ask action-oriented questions, or he may suggest alternatives by describing what other organizations have done in similar situations or on similar problems.

From the point of view of the organizer, the sole point of meetings is to prepare for action just as the sole point of organization is to provide a structure through which action takes place. Thus, he helps to clarify alternatives around concrete and immediate courses of action, makes certain that whatever process results in decisions is both legitimate (in accordance with the rules) and efficient (a course of action is undertaken which is likely to attain the objective intended or otherwise to build the effectiveness of the organization).

At first, people defend themselves against accurately seeing their position in the community and against admitting their discontent to themselves and others. An early objective of action is to provide people with experiences which destroy these defenses. A second early objective is to provide people with experience in responsible planning in defining social paths along which they can make actual gains. . . .

The legitimation for action is provided in meetings, but specific action events may develop from the general responsibility of a committee or other group of work in some area, and not directly from meetings. . . .

For example, in one city, people representing a small neighborhood, with the help of the organizers of a large organization, went to a district sanitation inspector to appeal for better street cleaning. During the course of the discussion the supervisor mentioned that there was no point in putting additional equipment into such neighborhoods since the residents didn't care whether their streets were clean or dirty. When the story of this insult was widely reported (the organizer helping the report along), a large number of people wanted to do something to change street-cleaning practices which they had never before clearly understood to be deliberately discriminatory. They planned a series of actions, including sweeping their own streets while newspaper reporters recorded the event, had the implied backing of the large organization, and several times carried the debris to the homes or businesses of politicians who were responsible. They picketed the district sanitation office and protested at the central sanitation office of the city. Since the city had received national beautification awards and the mayor wanted to maintain its reputation and since the various politicians involved feared that their reelection would eventually be jeopardized, the embarrassment was enough to end the discrimination. . . .

During the course of the several actions, people for the first time saw their relationship to one city service with stark clarity; this alone drove them to action. The insights provided through the experience of people in action are the fuel for a dramatic and broadening rhythm of action. The landlord who denies that blacks are good tenants; the school principal who "confesses" that neighborhood parents do not want their children to get an education—both can become focal points around which a good organizer builds action. As groups of people become drawn into a series of actions, each group working on its own problems but in relation to a common organization, there develops a body of accurate knowledge, enhanced levels of skill, and a larger number of active persons. Together, these enhance to the greatest extent possible the opportunity for each member to resolve his problems through the organizational structure.

ORGANIZER RESPONSIBILITY

An enabler is relatively passive, accepting the prevailing views, and helping people with their problems as defined by current neighborhood perspectives. An organizer is sensitive to current neighborhood perspectives, but may disagree aggressively with people while he remains clearly on their side.

For example, it is common in low-income areas for people to scapegoat their neighbors: "they don't care," "they run down the neighborhood," "people around here will only complain, they never do anything," etc. In this fashion, people repeat the outside stereotypes of low-income areas and develop a rationale for not themselves venturing into organizational efforts. An organizer who agrees with the condemnation not only undercuts neighborhood confidence in the possibility of organizing, but also finds himself rejected as possibly concealing a negative opinion of *everyone* in the neighborhood. Or, the members of an organization may decide on an action that is certain to fail, or which is clearly in violation of the constitution of the organization, or clearly leads to violence, to a collapse of democratic process, etc.

In all these cases, an organizer may find it necessary to disagree aggressively with the members, not to convince people of his own point of view on issues, but rather to make it possible to organize, to build effective organization. The people provide the content of action. The organizer has the responsibility to create and maintain the effective democratic structure of action, that is, a structure through which each neighborhood person has as nearly as possible an equal opportunity effectively to secure self-realization. The organizer, thus, must sometimes assert vigorous, aggressive leadership, even though he is not a member of the organization, and although such leadership should never include projecting his own substantive orientations upon the neighborhood.

On the other hand, the organizer should always refrain from leadership or participation when his intervention is not clearly necessary. For example, when a delegation visits a city official, the preparation ahead of time may not have been enough and the meeting may threaten to dissolve into confusion. An organizer has the responsibility to intervene forcefully to ensure that an effective case is presented. Such intervention should occur rarely, and the organizer should refuse to participate above that minimal level even when urged to do so. To the extent that an organizer has to intervene, to that extent the members will not see the victories as *their* victories, will not maximally acquire knowledge and skills themselves, and will not develop effective organization.

Thus, the role of the organizer is extremely complex. He must stand by the side of the people and see the world from their perspective. But he must also be able to go outside that perspective to analyze and decide accurately what he should do in order to build organization. He should never be a member of the organization and should place the organization in the hands of the membership, but he also should know when and how to intervene to protect the essential characteristics which he is responsible for ensuring in the organization. He must be a passive enabler and an aggressive leader at the time when each is required of him, must use his own judgment to determine when he should do either, and therefore must not *need* to play either role.

In his role of energetic intervener, an organizer does not actually place himself in opposition to the neighborhoods. Instead, he allies himself with the long-term objective self-interest of the people in building organization through which they can act effectively, and he seeks to break up collective distortions and orientations which make impossible the creation of such an organizational structure. With this one exception the organizer stays as close as possible to present neighborhood points of view. By this strategy he makes certain that it will be very difficult for enemies of the organization to isolate him from the neighborhood by attacking him as an outsider, as being on someone else's side, etc. Further, the gradual identification of neighborhood persons with their organization makes it increasingly likely that through, rather than outside of the organization, they will seek solutions to problems which for the first time become perceived as problems rather than as conditions of existence.

For example, where there is no organization, children playing on busy streets may be injured or killed without any response in the neighborhood. People assume that nothing can be done except, maybe, to watch the children more closely. "Life is like that." The presence of an organization provides a new remedy: "We can get a traffic light." Thus, getting a traffic light becomes a problem which, in the resulting struggle with the relevant city department, is itself transformed into an issue.

The organizer, therefore, not only creates issues and conflict; prior to that he creates problems where none were perceived before by creating opportunities where none had been before.

Inexperienced organizers typically fail to understand the necessary self-discipline, the requirement to act (or not) always to build organization and never through needs of the organizer which are irrelevant to or destructive of the building of organization. An organizer who is committed to racial integration cannot organize for racial integration in a community in which people oppose or are indifferent to this stance. . . . An organizer who admires a certain neighborhood leader cannot remain passive while that leader transforms the organization into his own political organization or social club. . . .

The people in a low-income neighborhood may decide not to adopt the kind of organizational structure recommended by an organizer. What then? Should the organizer try to manipulate or coerce the people into accepting what he recommends?

An organizer does not seek to impose himself on a neighborhood; instead he offers his services on the clearly stated basis that he will help build organization with certain characteristics, with the clear understanding that the organizer has responsibility to ensure that the organization meets certain criteria and that the organization belongs and will belong to the members. At first, the members do not yet understand the requirements of organization very clear-

ly; they must be helped to clarity as rapidly as possible and should be made aware that at any time they can discharge the organizer. In short, the organizer must have a legitimated and mutually agreed upon relationship with the organization, a relationship which the organization can cancel whenever it may wish. When the organization achieves permanent status, it may be wise to outline in a written agreement the rights and responsibilities of the organizer and of the organization with respect to each other. . . .

THE STRUCTURE OF SOCIAL ACTION

Any structure through which the poor act on the sources of their problems will be under attack from local governmental and other established institutions. The attack may not be direct; it may consist of subtle attempts to talk organization members out of their concerns, to divert attention to other questions, to ridicule the organization in informal discussions, etc. Attacks by established institutions on an organization of the poor tend to be indirect as much as possible, while it is to the advantage of an organization of the poor to bring these subtle, half-concealed attacks into the arena of open confrontation.

An open attack on the organizational effort in low-income areas usually sharpens the issues and can be used to quicken the pace of organization. Established institutions, realizing this, may choose to attack the sponsors of organization (whoever pays the salary of and supervises organizers) rather than the organizational effort itself. . . .

The sponsor of organization may have any of a wide variety of structures providing only that it is able to refrain from emasculating the work. However, there are fewer alternatives for the structure of the organization being built. It may be a direct membership neighborhood council or an organization of previously existing organizations. In any case, the point is to build a clearly defined structure through which people in low-income areas can act. Thus, although the organization of the poor may carry on social activities, provide services to members, and constitute a forum for militant rhetoric, the basic orientation has always to be the expression of power through the greatest possible number of members acting together to resolve the central problems of their lives.

For people to be able to act through a structure, it must be democratic. Any large number of people can act together democratically in complex activities only when the rules for their participation are clearly stated and equally applied to all members. Complex activities also require specialization of roles (e.g., the spokesman, the chairman, the secretary, the committee member, etc.) and a clear definition of the relationships among the roles. Thus, rules must be explicit and generally accepted in accordance with which members of the organization have a formally equal opportunity to participate in decisions and occupy various positions. The organizer is responsible to ensure that such a structure is developed and that formal equality is reflected as far as possible in actual practice. Since many low-income people are learning for the first time to maintain organizational roles, these structural requirements must be communicated and legitimated more vividly than would be necessary with memberships with more organizational experience.

It is common for an inexperienced organizer to attempt to develop movement through the natural relationships among people rather than to create an explicit structured set of interpersonal relationships and decision processes. The movement which results from the former course either is temporary and effective only in carrying out simple activities, or it becomes complex but the instrument of one person rather than of the widest possible portion of the general membership. In either case, the resulting organization is a relatively ineffective structure, relatively unavailable for collective action by the poor. . . .

One way to create [an effective] structure is to hold a series of preliminary unstructured small or large meetings with people in the neighborhoods in which organization is being developed (after organizers have been invited in by neighborhood persons and institutions). In those preliminary meetings issues can be clarified, leadership can become visible in the neighborhood, and a general interpretation can be made by the organizer of the nature of such a proposed organization. Then, an initial general meeting can decide whether to organize, can elect temporary officers, and provide preliminary committees (to develop a constitution, begin action, etc.). A permanent structure (officers, committees, constitution, by-laws, etc.) can be adopted at a later meeting. After such a beginning, there is a legitimated democratic process for replacing persons in various positions, a process which makes it less easy for the organization to become the captive of a single leader, and less likely that the organization will dissolve, turn into a social club, or meet others of the usual disastrous fates of democratic organizations.

THE SOCIAL SITUATIONAL CONTOURS OF CONFLICT

... The meaning of a move in a conflict depends on the nature of the move, its context, and may also vary to different audiences. For example, depending upon the context, when a Commissioner of Public Welfare increases clothing allotments this may be understood by everyone as an act of generosity or, alternatively, of weakness. Or, it may be perceived as an act of generosity to members of the welfare establishment *and* as an act of weakness to members of the organization demanding the increase. Further, the divergence of interpretations of the same public act in a conflict situation tends to make the reactions of each side incomprehensible to the other. When the organization renews its pressure, persons in the welfare establishment may believe that the organized welfare clients are simple-minded puppets of organizer manipulation and agitation, and also amoral and naturally parasitic. The organized welfare clients, on the other hand, may believe that the commissioner is trying to deprive them of their rightful allotments, that this is why he is not giving straight answers to their questions.

In a conflict situation the objective consequences of an act by one side or by another, or the intentions behind the act, may be almost irrelevant. The act is one point around which conflict swirls,

and a common interpretation may eventually be made as both sides, usually first really brought together by the conflict, begin to know one another better. ...

SOCIAL ACTION AS MORALITY DRAMA

The organizer conducts the conflict which draws to itself the fascinated attention of a large portion of the entire community. The public conflict creates an audience and actors who play to the audience. The actors invent their own lives in a performance not to be repeated. The organizer ensures that the play is seen as a struggle between the forces of good and the forces of evil (although there will be no consensus concerning which side is which). Through helping keep the initiative with the organization of the poor, through breaking up existing perspectives by unforeseeable improvisations, through drawing the powerful into a conflict in the spotlight of public attention, the organizer enables that organization to begin to control the opponents, thus creating the first interdependency for previously dependent people. From that point, the organizer works with a process which includes the opponents; no longer does he work *only* with the organization of the poor. He conducts the play in which one group of actors (the organization of the poor) creates and controls the conflict, and in which the other mainly responds and attempts to avoid the conflict. The actors write their own lines, but the organizer helps them to improve the performance. There is rehearsal prior to a public event (role-playing) and an analysis afterward. As the play continues, the skills of the poor begin clearly to rival, and then to outstrip, those of the opposition. The public conflict then communicates the ability of the poor to the community which had previously depreciated that ability. . . .

Besides achieving a diminution in dependency and a lesson in equality, the organizer has the task of institutionalizing the new relationships so that, as the audience departs, the poor find themselves with a stable level of power, greater than before, and incorporated into the new community status quo.

The institutionalization of a new social position for the poor is possible because, although the conflict may subside, and the audience may leave, the ability of the organization to create the conflict and draw the audience has been established. Thus, the actions of the poor now acquire a new meaning. . . .

SYMBOLIC CONCESSIONS

When the organization becomes powerful enough, it will force concessions from opponents. The mayor will appoint a Human Rights Commission, the urban renewal agency will agree to more citizen involvement in relocation of people from the demolition area, the state legislature will pass a resolution setting forth state policy on housing code enforcement, the public education system will announce classes for adult poor, trade unions will state that they no longer exclude anyone from apprenticeship programs on racial grounds, public welfare publicly decides no longer to support slum landlords by paying rent for welfare recipients in slum hous-

ing, the police chief assures the organization that there is now a new complaint process to which he pays personal attention, etc.

All these are promissory notes, issued under pressure. It is a responsibility of the organizer to make certain that they are converted into the legal tender of actual changes in practice which benefit the people in low-income areas, that they are not merely used as symbolic substitutes for the actual resolution of problems. When the leaders of an organization of the poor are appointed to this committee and that board, the result is usually that they become part of the opponent apparatus by which the lives of the poor are controlled. Until enough experience develops in the organization it is often possible for opponents to take the edge off campaigns against them by making agreements which they intend never to keep. Especially in the early stages of organization, the organizer helps keep attention focused, not on promises and agreements announced with however much fanfare, but on whatever actually occurs in the lives of people in the low-income areas as a consequence of such announcements. When an opponent has agreed to a concession, a new line of action must usually soon be directed to force the opponent to carry out his agreement. Only after a period of time does it become clear to everyone concerned that agreements must be kept or painful sanctions will be imposed by the organization. The organizer repeatedly calls the attention of members, often by Socratic questioning, to what is actually happening within the low-income area, and brings out discrepancies between opponent promises and performances. The organizer agitates; the organization acts; a reluctant opposition is coerced into honesty.

KNOWING OPPOSITION TACTICS

Persons in positions of power have long experience in frustrating opposition to them. An organization of the poor gradually develops equivalent or even superior expertise through its own experience. The organizer helps members, and especially leaders, to think through the strategies and tactics of opponents.

He must, for example, understand the usual initial "cooling out" approach in which someone with a friendly and disarming manner attempts to persuade the neighborhood to accept something other than what is being demanded. He must know that opponents may replace an old and hated injustice with a new injustice about which anger has not yet been developed, as happened, for example, when alienation in public housing was substituted for exploitation by private slum landlords. He must be alert to the use of rules and regulations to confuse critics. For example, when a delegation went to talk with a welfare commissioner, the members were told that their demands could not be met because everything in welfare is done according to the rules— federal rules, state rules, county rules— and pointed to a huge manual to support his statement. If they had not been prepared the members would not have been able to describe numerous instances in which public welfare workers used wide discretion in interpreting and applying the rules.

The organizer must know the divide-and-conquer techniques, as, for example, when concessions are offered to leaders or to some portion of an organization in order to create illegitimate advantages and unfair disadvantages within the organization.

Opponents typically portray the organization to the rest of the affluent community as threatening some revered symbol: the nation, the American way of life, law and order, and the appeal for unity against subversion, for harmony rather than disruption, etc. They taunt the people for needing organizers, offer concessions provided the organizers are discarded, praise the people while attacking the organizers as outsiders trying to tell the people what to do. The organizer helps the people to understand the nature of the attack and to turn it back on the attackers in various ways. For example, the organization may publicize the extent to which the opponents violate other symbols: the right to equal opportunity, the value of self-help, the defense of mother and children. . . .

The current action requires development of moves against the vulnerable points of opponents. The organizer jogs members into thinking through what the opponent needs that the organization can provide, interrupt, or otherwise affect. Does a public agency fear public scrutiny? An organization of the poor can draw public attention to it. Does a city councilman need a thousand additional votes? An organization of the poor can affect many more than that number. Does a department store need a positive image? A margin of profit? A mass organization may be able to affect the one by bringing employment discrimination into the open; the other by a combination of picket lines and boycotts. Does a social agency need to pretend that it is meeting needs? A people's organization can demonstrate unmet needs by helping ten times as many people with legitimate need to apply for help as the agency has openings. Does a school claim that the parents of the neighborhood are not interested in education? The parents can seek public funds to sponsor their own school, picket and boycott the existing school, make it clear that their interest in education is as intense as their opposition to the existing school. Do a variety of people and organizations want to avoid the fray, to stay neutral? The organization can focus public attention on their neutrality, force them to examine the issues, force them to take sides. Since most people with detailed understanding of the issues will agree with the orientation of a mass organization of low-income people, or at least do not want the opposition of such an organization, forcing neutrals to take sides will result in increasing support for it in the affluent community.

Since low-income people lack resources, it is useful to get opponents to work for the organization. If persons in authority are drawn into attack on the low-income people or on the symbols dear to them, the attack itself will build organization more quickly than any number of organizers could do by themselves.

An organization has often to map possible lines of action by opponents in order to make it easiest for them to meet organizational demands. It is not enough only to attack the destruction by urban renewal of low-income neighborhoods; the organization may have to secure competent technical counsel to prepare alternative feasible plans for neighborhood rebuilding, plans which will not violate the professional stan-

dards of city planners while having the advantage of support by the people of the neighborhood. . . .

All the moves mentioned above have been tried and found useful in one or another context. No one can say whether they would be useful again in other contexts. One could also consider modifications. Could clients or tenants engage in collective bargaining in order to work out new contractual agreements with a public welfare agency or a public housing authority? Could a low-income area organize to spend the bulk of its entire income in accordance with organizational decisions? What would happen if the poor used cameras and tape recorders to create a record of their treatment compared with that given affluent persons in shops, public offices, banks? Can low-income areas organize a "hiring hall" for jobs of all kinds, the analogue of industrial unionism on a community basis? . . .

THE KNOWLEDGE BASE OF ACTION

In a conflict situation, the organization does what is unexpected, dividing and confusing opponents, keeping them off balance. It seeks out and tackles points of weakness: the fact that bureaucratic organizations depend on clients or customers or constituents, provisions and communication, all of which may be affected at unpredictable times in unpredictable ways; the fact that powerful persons usually need to be jolted before they even begin to take seriously the lives of low-income people; the fact that people and organizations operating on routines cannot tolerate disruption. . . .

The knowledge base of social action must constantly be reformed; the organizer senses changes needed, inspires daily examinations and theoretical reanalyses of the event process. A series of demonstrations which had been projected for weeks may be abandoned without notice; an enemy of years' standing may become a friend; the major issue of one day may have been entirely replaced by another the next day; a drive to force landlords to repair housing may be replaced by a plan for public housing operated by the tenants. Academic observers may be surprised at the apparent lack of a predictable, consistent set of alliances, tactics, orientations, by the organization. However, the organization learns to follow the single principle of building power in the low-income area; it would be disastrous to that ambition if the organization were to become predictable to academic observers. . . .

CAMPAIGNS

The organization grows through actions and activities. Either is carried on by a series of campaigns of strictly limited duration. The actions may include a month of daily picket lines around city hall to protest police brutality, or a two-month period of voter registration and voter education ending in a massive directed vote, or a six-hour sit-in at a public official's office, or a two-hour play-in by children at city hall. The activities may consist of a two-day fund-raising barbecue, a week-long fund-raising carnival, a two-week chest X-ray campaign, a monthly tour of scenic places for elderly persons in the neighborhood, an annual one-day fashion show. Actions are directed toward securing change in the relationship of the low-income area to the affluent community; activities contribute only

indirectly to this outcome: directly they occur within established inside-outside relationships. However, in either case, a large number of people will only become involved for what is known in advance to be a limited period of time after which there will be a time of relative quiescence. It is a responsibility of the organizer to make certain that a series of campaigns is developed, involving the problems and issues and interests and skills of the widest possible number of persons in the area being organized. And, since the organization exists primarily for action, the organizer should ensure that campaign *activities* do not come to occupy the major attention of the membership.

Through such a series of campaigns, the number of persons identified with the organization continues to increase. Provided there is maintained an action emphasis, the pressure on the opponents of the organization will continue to mount. . . .

SERVICES

To some extent, outposts of the affluent community in areas of poverty (welfare, medical care, public housing, private business) are not likely to be responsive enough to organizational demands to supply adequate services sensitively tailored to the self-perceived needs of low-income people. To that extent, the organization can itself sponsor temporary services which will eventually disappear when the area being helped is no longer one of poverty. From the point of view of the affluent community it is prudent to spend a given sum of money (a) more efficiently than it is now spent, and (b) without being open to blame for the inadequacies and inequities involved in the extension of services to a dependent and hostile population. It will therefore become attractive for the affluent community to finance services which will be operated under the direction of organizations of the poor. The organizer will need to acquire some understanding of the pitfalls and advantages of this eventual outcome, and help the organization to secure needed services in such a way that the organization is strengthened and retains its action orientation and in a way that avoids the stigma which attaches to many service programs operated by low-income people. . . .

The organizer should not get so involved in the tough daily struggle of creating organization that he loses sight of the minimum long-range outcomes which will validate the amount of effort by the organization.

WHAT WILL NOT WORK

. . . First, there is no easy or quick way to build powerful organizations in low-income areas. Power only comes to an organization after a large number of people have acquired the skill to work efficiently through the organizational structure. It takes several years to meet these conditions. Building mass demonstrations in a short-lived movement or campaign may leave a residue of change, but they do not provide a structure through which power is exercised. Or, one can pull together existing organizations and groups into an organization of organizations in a convention with mass attendance, but the people who attend such a convention are not yet organized. All that has happened is that groups which previously met separately now meet once together and maintain some subsequent communi-

cation. The long, hard work of building a single powerful organization will require additional years. It is important in organizational work that some power be exercised very nearly at the beginning, but the early exercise of power does not mean that a structure has yet been created through which the exercise of power is effective and routine.

Second, an organizer can "look good quick" by organizing at once a mass action effort. However, if he does not also concentrate on creation of a structure and decision process through which people themselves can act effectively, his flash flood of action will soon disappear or leave behind an organization run by one person or a clique, not a structure through which the neighborhood can act.

Third, an organizer may have made a brilliant analysis of the need for a revolutionary social transformation, or he may have a beautiful vision of participatory democracy. But, if he projects these perspectives of his upon a low-income population with immediate and concrete problems, even if he also pays attention to these latter problems, he will find that his organization will be small, weak, sectarian, and easily isolated. An organizer must always be directly relevant to present neighborhood perspectives.

Fourth, it is sometimes argued that the appropriate structure for organizational work is that of the storefront church or some other type of organization [of] which low-income people are already members. This argument takes the culture of the poor into account, but not the fact that storefront churches and other organizations in low-income areas do not *do* much, do not perform complex tasks. In addition to the requirement of conforming to neighborhood traditions there is the other requirement of creating a structure adequate to carry on action and activities and operate services simultaneously and efficiently on a wide variety of problems and issues. Over any length of time this requires a division of labor, specialization, differentiated explicit role structures. Primitive structures do primitive tasks.

Fifth, existing social welfare institutions usually cannot sponsor organizational work in low-income areas because they cannot tolerate the conflict, because they define the problems of low-income people from outside rather than working with the definitions of low-income people, because they start from a position above the poor and reach down rather than starting with a working respect for low-income people.

Sixth, an organizer cannot follow a political organizational model since such models are developed solely to deliver votes and since they deliver votes by the politician doing things for people rather than by people doing things for themselves. A neighborhood acts through a political organization only in a very limited way. . . .

AWARENESS OF CHANGE

. . . In social action, the power of the poor shifts imperceptibly through their efforts. The public welfare worker is a little more alert to guard their rights, the politician a little more concerned about their opinion, the police officer less inclined to acts of brutality or corruption in the low-income neighborhood and a little more inclined to protect the rights of the people. The neighborhood continues to see the public welfare worker, the politician, the police officer, on the basis of years of

experience. It is one task of the organizer to arouse the people from their bad dream which includes an underlying fear of their own weakness and inferiority, to point out and describe the changes which are taking place even outside the areas of concrete actions by the neighborhood organization. It is a task of the organizer to go beyond the creation of an account of neighborhood action to helping the people in the organization create an alternative and more accurate view of their world and of their position in it. The assumption that blacks and women are excluded from an apprenticeship training program may be generally believed, no longer true, and an important belief for the behavior of young blacks and women. The assumption that the barriers to professional education are fixed and unchangeable may be important and no longer accurate. The organizer points out changes [and] possibilities and helps an appreciation of them to become incorporated in the everyday thinking of most people in the areas of poverty in which he is working.

THE NEW TRADITION

An organizer helps an alternative account of the world to develop in the organization. He may relate the story in detail again and again of how this leader stood right up to the commissioner and told him the truth, or how that demonstration led to an increase in police protection or how the voting power of the organization has the council passing ordinances which they never considered before. The action of neighborhood people becomes fixed in a positive account which creates a clear context whereby people can gain self-esteem through action, whether or not individual employment or other opportunities are open to them. . . . A positive collective identity becomes rooted in the past, and no longer subject to the vicissitudes of an uncertain world. This identity is publicly known throughout the neighborhood; it can be revived at any time as it bolsters self-esteem in contemporary actors.

An organizer who recounted traditions would normally be merely a neighborhood bore. But when the account is credible and about what neighborhood people have accomplished in combat on crucial issues against great odds, the account is often quickly grasped and long relished.

Thus, an organizer not only learns to listen carefully when he talks with people, but also learns to provide through his words a concrete, vivid, compelling, and credible picture of the situation, a picture that is intended to upset the existing definition, force people to take sides about a proposed course of action, and outline such a course with clarity. This concrete, vivid, compelling and credible picture is often essential for getting movement under way, even though it stereotypes a wide variety of people and events under single labels and thus distorts reality through oversimplification and selection. People learn first to think about action while making only the major distinctions. Later, and through their own experience, people make the exceptions and fill in the details. . . .

The fact that an organizer creates an oversimplified sketch of action space should not be taken to mean that the people of low-income areas think in simple terms. Rather, just as the first knowledge of university students about a new area is stereotypic, for the same reason people who begin collective ac-

tion must begin on the basis of the major relevant ideas and would be immobilized by a complete and detailed account which would not be easily incorporated in action.

THE LOCUS OF RESPONSIBILITY

The success of action can be undermined in two major ways: (1) it does not attain its objectives and, (2) it attains its objectives, but someone other than members of the organization is seen as responsible for the result. If the enemy is perceived in the neighborhood as having simply decided to give the people what they want, the action may be seen as ending well, but it is a failure as social action. It only becomes a social action success when the outcome is understood in the low-income area to be a direct consequence of organizational activity. Similarly, if the intended outcome is perceived in the low-income area as directly due to the intervention of the organizer, it is a social action failure. The organizer must ensure that the responsibility for securing an intended outcome is always placed squarely on the organization membership. Thus, the organizer typically ensures that meetings are well attended, that the necessary work gets done, that the organization holds such an initiative that an action favorable to the organization by an opponent is perceived as stemming from this initiative. But, the organizer accomplishes these ends as unobtrusively as possible in view of the fact that he may sometimes need conspicuously to intervene and that he must maintain a relationship of candor and responsibility with the people he helps. He interprets his role: "It is your organization, you will call the shots, do the work (and it's hard work)!" . . . Constant attention to placing responsibility with the people of low-income areas not only ensures that action has the most positive outcome for the skills and self-concept of the people involved, but also more people are more likely to become and remain active in an organization structured to increase their self-responsibility.

DEVELOPING THE PERSPECTIVES OF THE PEOPLE

People begin to act for themselves rather than have someone act for them. This requires that people also learn to think for themselves and not merely rely on the organizer's thinking. As much as possible, the organizer helps develop from the action itself a tradition of success; he does not only create the tradition and tell it to the people. . . .

Instead of outlining action possibilities for organization members, the organizer will often ask questions which help people to think through action alternatives for themselves and strategies of action by their opponents. Insofar as efficiency is not too greatly reduced, responsibility for thought as well as for action is placed in the neighborhood, not merely with leaders or with organizers.

For example, suppose that an organization is trying to stop the illegal distribution of narcotics by licensed pharmacists in its neighborhood. After learning that state officials will do nothing, the members begin to think of securing legislative remedy. The organizer could simply explain the difficulty of getting legislation, especially in the face of well-financed opposition. But this approach would leave him more vulnerable to the constant attack by opponents: "The idea behind your organization is a fine thing. But aren't you people grown up yet? Do you need an organizer to do your thinking for you?" It would also mean that members may agree, but would not act with much conviction on the basis of ideas that were not their own. An alternative is preferable. The organizer may ask a series of questions about exactly how the organization can use its energy most effectively. Can you put much pressure on the legislature at this stage? Are there any other ways to act? What about direct pressure on druggists in the neighborhood? What has the best chance to succeed? The organization may in any case seek legislation, but the decision will be made after a realistic examination of alternatives and will clearly be that of the organization itself.

A more complex problem arises when the organizer must respond to attempts (very common in organizational work) to isolate him from the members. For example, suppose that opponents of the organization spread the word that, although the organization itself is basically a good idea, it is hurt by the presence of an organizer who is a "communist." The line of questioning by the organizer must help the members to an accurate appraisal of the attack: that the allegation is false and that it is an attempt to weaken the organization. . . .

It is not easy to help people to think for themselves in areas outside their usual experience. The organizer can only do it well through self-discipline and great respect for the people (to prevent manipulation in . . . the direction of organizer biases) and through having become perceived in the neighborhood as responsible and trustworthy. People are often afraid to act, uncertain about whom they can depend on, ignorant of the extent to which they are vulnerable to one or another disastrous outcome. The organizer must be the kind of person who can be counted on. He helps them undertake actions on the basis of assumptions which, through their own experience, people discover to have been valid. Even when it would be easier to agitate people by building up unfounded fears, the organizer maintains a relationship of honesty with neighborhood people, helping them to see accurately the possible disasters as well as limitations in the successes before them. Any other approach would lead to initially dazzling demonstrations or other actions followed by a decline in the organization as its members lost confidence in the organizer. For example, suppose people in one area are considering a rent strike to force landlords to fix up slum dwellings. The rent strike would get started very quickly if the organizer stressed only the facts that attorneys will represent the tenants, that money is available for legal expenses, that rent strikes do not appear to be illegal, etc., but did not mention the fact that tenants could probably be evicted after thirty days for nonpayment of rent. After the first few evictions, the reputation of the organizer and of the organization would have been destroyed beyond recovery. Over time, a self-confident critical elaboration of an adequate neighborhood perspective stems from the experience of having acted on a reasonable appraisal of alternatives and possibilities with the help of an organizer who is responsible and honest.

TRANSFORMATION OF RELATIONSHIPS

The relationships in a low-income area are primarily: (a) friendship, familial, or neighbor relationships, all object relationships with persons within the area, and (b) ecological dependency relationships with persons and institutions outside. In the beginning, to some extent people simply shift their dependency from other persons and institutions to organizers. When an organizer first appears he is interpreted within the context of usual ways of relating. He is an outsider on whom people depend for the provision of skills and resources. He is also like a friend. Therefore, at first, he is likely to be loved, at the same time hated, deferred to, and depended on. One task of the organizer is to transform this personal relationship (in which people find it difficult to accept a substitute for him) into a role relationship in a structure with which people identify. He is successful (a) to the extent that members value him as a resource, but in relationships of interdependence in which members make the important decisions and do much of the work; and (b) to the extent to which members want an organizer without needing a specific organizer, and (c) value him for his contribution to the organization rather than for the broad range of his unique personality characteristics. In other words, the relationship of an organizer to the organization becomes gradually depersonalized and egalitarian from a beginning point of personalization and dependency. . . .

SUCCESS

Success occurs when the people in low-income areas can, through organization, solve a wide variety of central problems which they could not solve before, when through organization they can become effective acting persons rather than passive objects of action. Many people are swept into action, not by direct active membership in the organization, but through identification with an acting neighborhood-based mass organization. The organizer has succeeded when he has ensured the creation of such a structure which expands the area of freedom for persons in the action area. . . .

As an organization accomplishes a number of things over a period of time, an organizer has to work actively against its decline into a bureaucratic skeleton going through routine motions while major collective problems remain unresolved. Because of the tendency of organizations to fossilize, organizers will very likely be needed to maintain an action emphasis for as long as one can plan ahead. . . .

CHAPTER V

Administration
and Management

One perspective from which to view the methods of delivering human services that do not focus on helping the individual client or family is that of administration. The central focus of the administrative method is the development and maintenance of the organization whose staff members engage in policy, community practice, or in the delivery of some form of human service. The functional equivalent of such services is provided by families and neighbors, but with industrialization and urbanization, these primary group sources of help often do not serve. Thus formal organizations are required to take up the slack.

Those who administer are charged with providing the necessary resources, including moral support and recognition from the community, creating the conditions that motivate devotion to the work of the organization, coordinating the activities of those whose work is required to achieve the organization's purposes, and resolving conflicts that arise within the organization for competing goals, resources, etc.

However, administration is not merely "housekeeping," as some would have it. What often appear to be routine actions, such as employing or training staff, searching for and accepting financial support, etc., commit the organization and other staff members to the constraints inherent in such decisions. Accepting support often commits an organization, at least in part, to the interests of those providing the support. Likewise, in hiring staff, particularly professional staff, an organization "buys" the commitments of those staff members to professional and personal values that may have an important impact on the way they do their work, the clientele they seek to serve, and the goals they pursue. Other decisions, such as the location of offices, the nomination and election of board members, and rules about the freedom (or lack of it) for line staff to make decisions without consulting with supervisors may have equally significant implications for the character and competence of the organization as well as its mission and goals.

Administration, or at least what is often called management, is not exclusively the work of organizational leaders, executives, and high bureaucrats. Lower echelon employees, including line workers, can have an important impact on the goals and values of the organization, as implied in the previous paragraph. Elsewhere (Cox, et al., *Tactics*, 1984, p. 253ff.) we have made the point that true leadership involves careful, albeit constrained, choices that transform the organization into an institution, infusing it with value, defining its mission and role, its character and competence through decisions that shape organizational structure and capability. But such decisions are not made exclusively by executives. A receptionist who presents a warm and welcoming attitude toward people in a neighborhood helps greatly to give an organization the character of a place that cares about community problems. An organizer who refuses to become involved in confronting public officials who are misusing their authority goes a long way toward defining the organization as one that is incapable of dealing with conflict. Granted, the decision to employ the professional and the training provided the receptionist are the responsibility of the organization's leadership, but once employed and trained, line staff exercise considerable influence in defining the character of the organization.

Another misconception is that administration is focused entirely upon the organization and its operations. Although administrators are called upon to attend to the coordination of activities, the resolution of internal conflicts and the allocation of scarce resources, they are also required to obtain financial resources and staff, as noted earlier. Clearly, these come from outside the organization. What may not be quite so evident is that goals are normally "imported" from the environment, from those who create and maintain the organization, its constituents, as it were. In addition, those that send clients or agree to participate in the organization must acknowledge, at least tacitly, that it has the "right" to do what it claims to be doing, has competent staff with the requisite skills and values to achieve the goals which are desired by those who interact with the organization, granting the organization the right to its domain. Administration must come to grips with these outside forces if the organization is to prosper.

Likewise, the demands of the tasks the organization is called upon to perform shape the technology it uses. Must three community agencies and a state agency combine resources and agree on a common plan to achieve some purpose? Then the administration must organize the agency to make this possible. It must agree on what resources it can commit to the common effort, what concessions it will make to gain agreement, and grant considerable latitude to those negotiating on its behalf. Can the task be accomplished by the elaboration of detailed rules applied uniformly to every situation, as, for example, in determining eligibility for public assistance? Then the organization can be structured in a hierarchical bureaucratic fashion with very limited latitude for employee discretion.

Some are under the impression that administration is all "head" and no "heart," a question of carefully calculated effectiveness and efficiency in obtaining predetermined goals. For the most part, this is nonsense. Many administrative choices have no "scientific" basis, but rather reflect value preferences which may be drawn from a widely shared framework of values but cannot be "proven" in any positive sense. Furthermore, full rationality in administration is virtually impossible because such rationality implies (1) completely articulated goals and values which are measurable and weighted, (2) stability of such preferences over time, (3) consideration of every possible means of achieving such goals and values, (4) selection of the method that achieves these values at the least cost. Except in trivial cases, or perhaps in certain fields of engineering, these conditions can never be met. Further, it has been observed, repeatedly, that administrators do not work like that. They try to find an acceptable choice, perhaps considering several options but never being sure about the exact outcomes of their choices in advance, or whether "unanticipated consequences" might appear and change their preferences at a later time.

In the articles we have selected, it has not been possible to cover every aspect of administration. The best we could do was to choose a few pieces that introduce the reader to some of the more important topics. The first paper is an excellent review of organization theory as it bears upon administration. In this article Gummer reviews organizational theory from the perspective of three models applied to an understanding of organizations, each of which has some relevance to administration.

The first views organizations as rational instruments for achieving goals. It raises questions about the effectiveness and efficiency of the means chosen to achieve goals, and the technology required by the nature of the task environment. Important variables for the administrator to take into account are (1) the extent to which goals are concretely or abstractly defined, (2) the degree of uncertainty about goals and the means for achieving them including the extent to which the organization is able to control the necessary means, and (3) the degree of consensus on goals among those in the organization and others who control needed resources.

A second approach is to view organizations as natural systems, with system maintenance and enhancement as well as the production of some product or service as goals of the organization. The importance of various subsystems and informal structures that pursue norms, or goals that diverge from or reinforce the formal goals of the organization (or reinforce or conflict with one another), are among the important considerations for the administrative staff.

Organizations are viewed from the perspective of what Zald calls "polities," responding to internal and external influences on goals and values, particularly with respect to various constituencies controlling the acquisition of resources. This perspective is particularly important when trying to understand how basic changes in organizations take place, a fundamental issue in administration.

Hasenfeld discusses program development from the perspective of organization theory seen from a systems perspective. He reviews in some detail the tasks and skills required by the practitioner in developing and implementing new programs.

Finally, Morris focuses on a new role for human service administrators that is particularly applicable to the smaller cities and towns found in thinly populated areas of the country. In recent years, the population of such places has grown, often resulting from the decentralization of employment and the movement of suburban people into such places, further removed from the services offered by major cities. These new arrivals demand high quality services comparable to those found in urban areas, and small towns and sparsely settled counties have often lacked the human and financial resources to meet these demands. Morris' "circuit riding administrator" is one approach to meeting this growing need. She offers us a description of the role and a case illustration.

FRED M. COX

25.

Burton Gummer

ORGANIZATION THEORY
FOR SOCIAL ADMINISTRATION

This article presents an overview of the major theoretical approaches used to explain the behavior of formal organizations. The rationale for the inclusion of this material in the present volume proceeds from the assumption that an understanding of relevant theories is as important for the practitioner of administration as it is for practitioners of other social work methods. In much the same way that personality theory offers the caseworker a framework for understanding and analyzing individual behaviors, organization theory provides the administrator with a conceptual device for comprehending organizational behaviors. Without some coherent perspective from which to view things, the day-to-day activities of a complex organization would appear unrelated, random, and beyond comprehension. In the same way that personality theory enables the counselor to look beyond the endless array of behaviors presented by the client and get at the underlying personality structures upon which these behaviors are predicated, organization theory offers the administrator a way of understanding the events and activities of organizational life as a function of the underlying structures and environmental conditions which, in Selznick's (1960, p. xi) words, "constrain and summon" behavior.

The framework used for examining these perspectives is an extension of a scheme first developed by Gouldner (1959). Gouldner sees theories of organizations falling into two broad categories. In the first, the organization is seen as a "rational instrument" for accomplishing some specific purpose, while in the second it is seen as a "natural system" that has the same system maintaining and enhancing requirements of any other social system. A third perspective, the organization as an arena for the exercise of "power-politics," will be added to draw attention to the importance for organizational structure and behavior of the way in which resources are obtained and the internal mechanisms for their allocation (Gummer, 1978; Wamsley and Zald, 1976). The three models will be analyzed by first looking at the major variables that make up the model, and then examining the dynamic processes that connect these variables with each other (see Table 25.1).

THE RATIONAL MODEL

The oldest, and consequently most venerable, approach to the study of organizations is the rational model in

Source: Burton Gummer, "Organization Theory for Social Administration," in Felice D. Perlmutter and Simon Slavin (eds.), *Administration: Perspectives for the 1980s.* Philadelphia: Temple University Press, 1980, pp. 22-49. Reprinted by permission of the author and the publisher.

TABLE 25.1. MAJOR VARIABLES AND DYNAMICS IN THE RATIONAL, NATURAL-SYSTEM, AND POWER-POLITICS MODELS OF ORGANIZATIONS

	Rational	Natural-System	Power-Politics
Variables	Production goals	Subsystem goals	Resource characteristics
	Technologies	Informal structure	Control structure
Dynamics	Maximization of rationality	Management of internal conflict	Adaptation to changes in resource availability
	Reduction of uncertainty	Maintenance of the character of the system	

which, as Gouldner (1959, p. 404) observes, the organization is conceived as an "instrument"—that is, as a rationally conceived means to the realization of expressly advanced group goals. Its structures are understood as tools deliberately established "for the efficient realization of these group purposes." This approach is predicated on the assumption that the *raison d'être* of an organization is that it is the best (i.e., the most efficient) means for achieving a goal. This model has its roots in the writings of Max Weber (1964), who developed the classic conception of the rational organization in his work on bureaucracy.

Organizational Goals

Two organizational variables central to the rational model are the goals of the organization and the technologies employed to pursue those goals. Within this model goals are usually defined in product terms. That is, the primary concern of an organization is the production of a product or service, and the organization exists exclusively for that purpose. Since the efficient attainment of goals is the central purpose of an organization, the identification and specification of goals becomes critical since all other organizational activities are dependent upon them. Selznick (1957,

pp. 61-64), for instance, considers the setting of goals ("the identification of institutional mission and role") as one of the major functions of leadership in an organization.

One aspect of organization goals of particular concern here is the degree to which they can be specified. That is, organizational goal statements can vary along a dimension that goes from concrete, specific goals to abstract, general goals. An example of the former would be Day Care Agency X, which states that its goal is to serve 100 children (from specified socioeconomic backgrounds, and with certain family characteristics) per week, with a program that is an equal mixture of socialization and educational components, with the intention of developing specific educational and interpersonal skills within the child during a set period of time. Day Care Agency Y, on the other hand, has as its goal a statement that the purpose of the agency is to "enhance the growth and development of children through the provision of quality day care services." The latter statement offers little in the way of guidance as to how one should structure activities to achieve that goal. Within the rational model the goal of the organization is the keystone to the entire structure. It is the source of the major criterion by which organizational performance is evaluated; namely, is a particular piece of structure or unit of activity more efficient in the attainment of goals than some other structure or activity? If an organization does not cast its goals in specific, operational language, then goal statements will not direct internal decision-making. This, in turn, seriously limits the extent to which the organization can be viewed as a rational instrument for the pursuit of goals.

A second, related aspect of organizational goals is the amount of consensus that exists among organizational members around the stated goal (assuming that the goal is stated in specific terms). Barnard (1968, p. 65) has drawn attention to the importance of cooperation in organizations in his definition of an organization as a "cooperative system." One factor that affects an individual's willingness to cooperate is the extent to which he or she can identify with the goals of the organization. The degree to which one is able to accept the goals will, in turn, determine the extent to which one will voluntarily submit to the directives of organizational leaders. The voluntary nature of an individual's conformance to organizational directives, moreover, constitutes the heart of Weber's (1964) theory of authority (or "imperative coordination"), which he defines as:

the probability that certain specific commands ... from a given source will be obeyed by a given group of persons. ... A criterion of every true relation of imperative control ... is a certain minimum of voluntary submission; thus an interest (based on ulterior motives or genuine acceptance) is obedience ... It is an induction from experience that no system of authority voluntarily limits itself to the appeal to material or affectual or ideal motives as a basis for guaranteeing its continuance. In addition every such system attempts to establish and to cultivate the belief in its "legitimacy" (pp. 324-325).

However, the degree of consensus about goals in a social agency will, in all likelihood, be fairly low due to the highly normative nature of social welfare activities. That is, social agencies ultimately concern themselves with how people *ought* to behave, and thus must address themselves to some notion of what Donnison (1955, pp. 349-350) has termed the "social health" of its clientele. Moreover, as Donnison goes on to say, "there is no generally understood state of 'social health' toward which all people strive; our disagreements on this question form the subject matter of politics the world over."

From this perspective the goal formation process in a social agency can be seen as essentially a political one in which various interest groups—both within and outside of the organization—attempt to influence or dominate the setting of the agency's major purposes. An example of this is the debates that have taken place over the purposes of day-care programs. One can identify at least three major interests that have opposing conceptions of what functions a day-care center should perform. Feminists see this as a major tool for effecting equality between the sexes since it offers relief from child-care responsibilities and an opportunity for women to pursue other interests. From this perspective the purposes of day care should be just that, to offer care of children during the day to whomever wishes to use it. Another interest group is child-development specialists, who see this as an opportunity to introduce "good" (i.e., middle-class) child-rearing practices to the general population. This group frequently advocates confining daycare services to those people experiencing difficulties in raising their children, and have as their goal the changing of parental attitudes and behavior as well as providing care for children. Finally, the advocates of traditional income maintenance policies see day care as essentially a device for ensuring that income maintenance programs do not undermine work incentives. For them, the major purpose of a day-care program is to reduce the possibility that those receiving public funds will use their parental responsibilities as an "excuse" for not seeking work.

Not only are the goals of social agencies highly controversial, but the people who work in these agencies, that is, social workers and especially professionally trained social workers, are generally sensitive to these controversies and quite likely to have well-developed normative and ideological systems of their own (Scott, 1969; Zald and McCarthy, 1975). To the extent that a consensus about organizational objectives is not present, administrators must pursue a variety of strategies for inducing member participation and cooperation. Cyert and MacCrimmon (1968, pp. 570-72) identify the major strategies used for this purpose as "bargaining" and "side payments," both of which require expenditures of resources beyond what would be required if the member was in agreement with organizational goals. This results in a net loss of efficiency for the organization.

Not only does a lack of consensus affect the nature of member participation, it has an impact on the entire decision-making process within an organization. The rational model assumes that organizational decisions will be made according to the criterion of what is the most effective and efficient way of attaining a given goal. However, when there is no consensus about the purposes of the organization or the means for achieving them (i.e., under conditions of uncertainty), then non-efficiency criteria are used. Pfeffer and his colleagues (1976) found, for instance, that under conditions of uncertainty social influences dominate organizational decision-making, with social relationships and social attraction becoming the bases for decisions. A foster-care agency that is not clear as to what constitutes an "adequate" foster-care family, and has varying points of view about this represented on its staff, is an example of an organization that can be expected to operate on subjective criteria. Families may be selected because they are personally liked by the workers, come from the same ethnic, racial, or religious background, or have similar political and social views. Any decision will be just as good as any other since there is no authoritative statement about what constitutes a "good" family. This procedure is in direct contradiction to Weber's (1958) concept of a bureaucracy (i.e., a rational organization) as an impersonal mechanism:

> Bureaucratization offers above all the optimum possibility for carrying through the principle of specializing administrative functions according to purely objective considerations. . . . The "objective" discharge of business primarily means discharge of business according to *calculable rules* and "without regard for persons" (p. 215, emphasis in original).

Technology in Organizations

A second critical variable in the rational model is the nature of the technologies employed by an organization. Technology in organizations is defined by Perrow (1967) as:

the actions that an individual performs upon an object, with or without the aid of tools or mechanical devices, in order to make some change in that object. The object, or "raw material," may be a living being, human or otherwise, a symbol, or an inanimate object (p. 202).

Thompson (1967) identifies three major types of technologies: long-linked, mediating, and intensive. The first involves serial interdependence, in that act Z can be performed only after the successful completion of act Y, such as the work on an assembly line. Mediating technologies are employed by organizations whose function is to link clients or customers who are or wish to be interdependent, such as commercial banks who link depositors to borrowers. The term intensive is used to refer to technologies in which

a variety of techniques [are] drawn upon to achieve a change in some specific object; but the selection, combination, and order of application are determined by feedback from the object itself. When the object is human this intensive technology is regarded as "therapeutic," but the same technical logic is found also in the construction industry . . . and in research where the objects of concern are non-human (pp. 15-18).

Perrow (1967) develops a typology based on two aspects of technology: the number of exceptional cases encountered in the work, and the nature of the search process undertaken when exceptions occur. The first variable is measured on a scale going from low to high. The second involves two types of search processes:

The first . . . involves a search which can be conducted on a logical, analytical basis. . . . This is exemplified by the mechanical engineering unit of a firm building large machinery. . . . The second . . . occurs

when the problem is so vague and poorly conceptualized as to make it virtually unanalyzable. In this case, no "formal" search is undertaken, but instead one draws upon the residue of unanalyzed experience or intuition, or relies upon chance and guesswork. Examples would be work with exotic metals or nuclear fuels, psychiatric casework, and some kinds of advertising (pp. 195-197).

These and other approaches to classifying organizational technologies (Litwak, 1961; Woodward, 1965) all employ a general analytical framework which looks at the nature of the work done and the nature of the object upon which the work is done. The first factor moves along a continuum that goes from kinds of work in which there is a great deal of knowledge about each component activity that goes into the work, to those kinds of work in which the component activities cannot be separated out and the work is seen as an undifferentiated whole. An example of the former would be a public assistance agency where the major technologies are the determination of eligibility according to predetermined rules; the disbursing of public monies according to established schedules for payment; and accounting for these expenditures. An example of the latter would be a child-guidance clinic in which the diagnosis and treatment of psychological problems in children is the major technology. These activities are usually seen as part of a highly interdependent and interactive process that must be treated as one unitary activity. The degree to which the work of an agency can be disaggregated into finite steps has important implications for the nature of the division of labor in that organization. In the first instance the work can be broken up into its constituent parts and activities assigned to different people. This, in turn, necessitates a large administrative component in the organization so that the various activities can be coordinated. One consequence of this is that the individuals performing the work do not have to be highly trained because they only have to deal with one aspect of the job. In the second case, the child-guidance clinic where the work cannot be disaggregated, the division of labor will be more limited and the individual performing the work will have to do most of the activities entailed in the job. This, in turn, will require more training for the worker and will lessen the need for an elaborate administrative structure, since coordination takes place at the level of the worker. These two ways of organizing work are usually referred to as *bureaucratic* and *professional* organizations, respectively (Litwak, 1961; Scott, 1966).

A salient characteristic of the nature of the object upon which the work is performed is the extent to which the object *reacts* to the worker. This can be measured on a scale that goes from nonreactive objects (e.g., stable metals) to highly reactive objects (e.g., human beings). The amount of reactivity on the part of the object has important implications for the amount of discretion that must be granted to the worker. In the first case the worker will need little discretion because the non-reactive nature of the object means that its characteristics can be predicted over time and the work applied to it routinized. Procedures can be specified in advance and the worker's job will consist, in great part, of applying these predetermined procedures to specific situations. In the case of reactive objects whose characteristics cannot be predicted over time, procedures cannot be specified in advance and the worker will have to have a considerable amount of discretion to take actions based upon the needs of the situation as they arise.

For the most part social agencies deal with situations best characterized as reactive. Within this category, however, the degree of reactivity of the client to the worker will vary, and consequently so will the amount of discretion that has to be given the worker. Two factors affecting the amount of reactivity in a situation are the degree of stress the client is experiencing, and the amount of pathology—physical, psychological, or social—present in the client. Clients experiencing extreme stress, and whose behavior or condition is considered pathological, will tend to be volatile and erratic, and the worker will need considerable leeway in determining the most appropriate course of action. Examples of such situations are the onset of acute illness (physical or mental), sudden death, unexpected loss of a job or living arrangement, and abandonment of a spouse and/or children. These situations tend to be idiosyncratic and unpredictable and agencies find there are few specific guidelines that can be offered to the worker. On the other hand, situations in which clients are not experiencing undue stress, and whose behavior and condition is within normal limits, will be more predictable and thus more amenable to routine, predetermined procedures set by the agency. Examples of this are recreational and leisure-time activities, chronic-care facilities, and long-term counseling.

The reactivity of the client has implications for organizational structure quite similar to those coming out of the nature of the work itself. Organizations dealing with relatively non-reactive situations will lend themselves to a bureaucratic structure more readily, while those dealing with highly reactive situations will be constrained to organize themselves along professional lines because of the need for highly trained workers who will be able to make sound discretionary judgments.

Rationality and Uncertainty

The major dynamic processes within the rational model are the *maximization of rationality* and the *reduction of uncertainty.* Proponents of the rational model argue that the primary force that powers and shapes organizational development is the increase in rational arrangements within the organization. The criterion of efficiency permeates all aspects of organizational behavior with the result that, to paraphrase Gresham's Law, efficiency criteria drive out all other criteria. A major obstacle to the pursuit of rational action is the existence of uncertainty, whether this pertains to confusion or unclarity about organizational goals, the nature of the technologies employed, or unpredictable elements in the environment. In order to increase an organization's capacity for rational action organizational leaders will seek to reduce uncertainty by the extension of administrative controls over both internal and external factors. Uncertainties within the organization will be dealt with by efforts to regularize and routinize as many aspects of organizational behavior as possible. These efforts will persist even when the nature of the activities do not lend themselves to such control. Goffman's (1961) analysis of the nature of "total institutions"

can be seen as one example of an attempt to impose bureaucratic control mechanisms over highly reactive situations (i.e., hospitalized mental patients) as a way of increasing the predictability and tractability of the behavior of the inmates. In that case, concerns of administrative control completely supplanted concerns of therapeutic effectiveness.

When facing uncertainty in the environment, organizations attempt to extend control over critical elements in the environment as a way of reducing this. In economic organizations this is referred to as "vertical integration" whereby a firm extends its control over organizations which supply resources needed for production as well as those organizations responsible for the product's distribution (e.g., oil companies and automobile manufacturers). The social service agency must also deal with an unpredictable environment, although the strategy of directly incorporating other organizations is generally not available to it. One strategy that is often used is that of laying claim to what Levine and White (1961, p. 597) have termed an organization's "domain," which is defined as the "specific goals it wishes to pursue and the functions it undertakes to implement its goals." Warren (1972) extended this concept to include the function domain plays in ensuring to an organization an undisputed claim to necessary resources:

Organizational domain is the organization's locus in the interorganizational network, including its legitimated "right" to operate in specific geographic and functional areas and its channels of access to ... resources. The two important components here are the organization's right to do something, and its access to the resources it needs in order to do it. . . . In its interaction with other organizations, an organization acts to preserve or expand its domain (p. 22).

Establishing a claim to a particular domain, however, is a difficult strategy to employ because claims to legitimacy as a service provider are difficult to advance and sustain in a field where there is so little consensus both about who should offer a particular service and the best way for delivering that service. An example of competition for domain is found in the community mental health field between agencies offering direct services and those offering preventive services (i.e., the "consultation and education" components of community mental health centers). In the area of services to the elderly there has traditionally been competition between social workers and nurses for control of these programs, as there has been in public schools between school social workers and guidance counselors. Lack of "domain consensus" in most service areas means that, in general, the social agency will be less able to control its environment and its efforts at promoting rational internal operations will be hampered to the degree that it must continually deal with uncertainties in terms of funding sources, access to clients, and claims to functional specialization (Kirk and Greenley, 1974).

THE NATURAL-SYSTEM MODEL

In the natural-system approach the organization is seen as a type of social system, and the processes that characterize the functioning of social systems in general are used to explain the operations of complex organizations. A major way in which this approach differs from the rational model is in the number and kinds of goals that an organization is seen as pursuing. In the rational model the organization has only one goal, the efficient production of a service or product. In the natural-system model the generation of products or services is but one of several goals that the organization must attend to. Any social unit that can be viewed as a social system is assumed to have two types of goals. The first is the production of an output, the need for which motivated the founding of the organization (Parsons, 1956). Once the organization has been brought into existence, however, a new set of goals is generated which have to do with the maintenance of the system as a distinct social entity. Moreover, system maintenance goals become as important as the original production goals. Thus, a major concern within the natural-system model is the *relationship between production and maintenance goals* within an organization.

These models also differ in the way an organization member is viewed. In the rational model the individual is seen primarily as a role incumbent. That is, the only part of the individual's total life situation deemed relevant is that part directly pertaining to role performance within the organization. Other factors such as one's emotional or social life are not considered necessary for an understanding of how one behaves in the organization. It is assumed that the organization member will act in a rational manner and thereby complete tasks in the most efficient way possible. The natural-system model, on the other hand, argues that this is an unrealistic and artificial view of human behavior and that the total person must be considered. Attention is therefore directed to the *informal struc-*

ture of an organization, which can be defined as the patterned relationships that evolve between and among organization members based on their total social and emotional needs. This is in contrast to the rational model's emphasis on the *formal structure* of an organization, which is the pattern of interactions between and among members based on the requirements of their official organizational roles.

Subsystem Goals

A social system can be defined as a group of elements (individuals, groups, offices) that exist within some boundary and are related to each other in a patterned way in order to accomplish some goal. The system functions by taking resources (inputs) from its environment, transforming them by means of a production process (throughput), and delivering back into the environment a product made up of the transformed resources (output). Systems are composed of subsystems, each of which performs a function necessary to the system's ongoing operation.

In their analysis of the complex organization as a social system, Katz and Kahn (1966, pp. 39-47) identify the following subsystems within an organization: production or technical, supportive, maintenance, adaptive, and managerial. The production subsystem is concerned with the throughput function of the actual work of the organization. Its goal is the production of a service or product and is thus analogous to the goal of the organization as a whole in the rational model. That is, what the rational model posits as the goal of the entire organization, the natural-system model sees as the goal of the production subsystem only. The

function of the supportive subsystem is to ensure a steady supply of resources and to see that the finished product is distributed, that is, to make sure that there is a consumer for the organization's product. The maintenance subsystem is concerned with what Selznick (1948, p. 29) refers to as the "integrity and continuity of the system itself." Since a social system consists of the patterned interactions of individuals within the system, the goal of the maintenance subsystem is to ensure that organization members function in conformance with organizationally sanctioned procedures. That is, it is concerned with seeing to it that members accept the goals, rules, and general format of operations that have developed in the organization.

The adaptive subsystem is concerned with the capacity of the organization to adjust to changes within its environment. These changes may take the form of shifting values, alterations in the political or economic systems, introduction of new, competitive organizations, and the like. Its goal is to identify changes in the environment pertinent to the operation of the organization and develop ways in which the organization can react to these changes. The managerial subsystem's function is to see that the other subsystems operate in a coordinated fashion. It must ensure the integrated functioning of all parts of the system so that the goals of the system as a whole may be realized.

In a child-welfare agency, for example, the workers dealing directly with clients constitute the production subsystem and their function is to offer the services of the organization (counseling, placement, and adoption). The executive director and the members of the board operate as the supportive subsystem and are concerned with ensuring adequate financing, clients, and facilities. The maintenance subsystem's function of ensuring conformance with agency-prescribed ways of behaving has its formal expression in the written rules and regulations of the organization and in the supervisory structure and procedures. Its equally important but informal expression is found in the ways in which organizational leaders create a "climate" within the organization by espousing and supporting certain ways of acting and thinking and by stigmatizing and opposing ways of behaving that are not considered "appropriate" to the agency (Argyris, 1976). The adaptive function of monitoring and responding to new developments in the organization's environment is performed by those with responsibility for program planning and development. (Interestingly enough, this function is frequently given the least priority in many social agencies because it is seen as diverting resources away from delivering services, yet it probably has the greatest potential for increasing services through the identification of new sources of support.) Finally, the various supervisors and department heads act as the managerial subsystem and function to coordinate the organization's overall activities.

This conceptualization of the organization as composed of subsystems, each performing a different function and pursuing different goals, draws attention to the potential for *goal conflicts within the organization*. The natural-system model assumes that an organization member will be more influenced by the goals of his or her unit than by the overall purposes of the organization. For example, a person involved in the production subsystem will be primarily interested in perfecting the technical capacities of that unit so that it can go about its work in the most efficient and effective way. In the case of the social service agency, the production subsystem will be primarily concerned with improving the technical competence of the members of the unit. Emphasis will be placed on recruiting and hiring individuals with the most and best training possible, reducing staff turnover so that people have sustained experiences in an area of work, and, in general, creating a stable situation in which people will be able to develop their technical skills. In that same agency, however, the program development section (i.e., the adaptive subsystem) will be concerned with increasing the agency's capacity to adapt to a changing and shifting environment. The interests of this unit will probably conflict with those of the service unit since program planners and developers will be concerned with increasing the agency's capacity to respond flexibly to external changes while the service workers will be arguing for stable and routinized operations. As another example, those responsible for fund-raising (the supportive subsystem) may want the service unit to develop new programs in order to attract new monies, an initiative the service people may resist because of their lack of expertise in the proposed program areas. Because of the existence of these potential conflicts between and among subsystems, a major goal for the managerial subsystem is the maintenance of a balance between the units. (This will be discussed at further length below since it constitutes the major dynamic factor within the natural-system model.)

Informal Structure

In addition to the variable of subsystem functions and goals, the natural-system model stresses the importance of the informal (i.e., not organizationally sanctioned) structures in an organization. Gouldner (1959) defines informal structures in the following way:

> Some informal patterns are organizationally unprescribed culture structures—that is, patterns of belief and sentiment; for example, the belief that one should not be a "rate buster." Other informal patterns are organizationally unprescribed social structures, i.e., the cliques that develop among those working near one another (p. 410).

The importance of informal structures in organizations was first noted in the now famous research on worker performance in the Hawthorne Works of the Western Electric Company during the 1920's (Mayo, 1960; Roethlisberger and Dickson, 1939). In that study it was found that the informal relationships that evolve among people who work together are just as important in determining worker behavior as official organizational policies and regulations.

Moreover, the logic of informal structures is based in the social and psychological needs of individuals (i.e., those aspects of one's life not directly connected with performance on the job) and is thus quite different from the logic of the formal structure, which is based in the need to design a structure that will enhance the efficient and effective achievement of organizational goals. One example of the ways in which these two structures conflict has to do with the issue of job security for organization members. Etzioni (1964, p. 3) lists as one of the defining characteristics of an organization "the substitution of personnel, i.e., unsatisfactory persons can be removed and others assigned their tasks." The importance of this is best understood from the rational model perspective, in which the personnel of an organization are viewed, in a sense, as interchangeable parts that can be eliminated, added, or altered depending upon the needs of the organization. From this point of view, job security will be dysfunctional because it may lead to inefficiency if the person is either incompetent or in some other way inappropriate for the position. From an individual perspective, however, job security is of paramount concern; economically, socially, and psychologically, people need steady and rewarding work and adequate income. The need for security serves as the basis for a type of informal structure found in all organizations, namely, some system of mutual protection among people working together. Workers can be expected to "look out" for each other's interests in ways that will run counter to the attempts of organization leaders to develop monitoring and evaluative devices aimed at identifying and weeding out incompetents. These informal arrangements can take the form of a group of workers covering for each other's poor performances, or group resistance to and sabotage of managerial efforts to impose objective and standardized performance-rating devices.

While the informal arrangements within an organization may have negative consequences in terms of undermining efforts to maximize rational procedures, they can have a positive impact on overall organizational functioning because of the role they can play in maintaining a high degree of morale among the workers. Individuals who are able to exert some influence and control over the conditions of their work can be expected to identify more readily with the organization than those who feel powerless in the face of formal organizational requirements (Ouchi and Johnson, 1978). This identification, moreover, serves as the basis of a stronger commitment on the part of the worker to the organization. As an individual's investment in an organization grows because it is a "nice place to work," that is, organization leaders accept and encourage the existence of informal arrangements, then the organization's potential control over the worker is increased since a "nice place to work" is also a hard place to leave, and the worker has a greater stake in remaining with the organization (Tannenbaum, 1968, pp. 3-29). This factor is particularly important in the social welfare agency where, due to the value-laden nature of the work, acceptance of organizational goals and strategies by workers directly increases organizational efficiency since workers will not act in opposition to an organization towards which there are strong commitments.

System Maintenance

The natural-system model posits as a central dynamic process the maintenance of the *character of the system* over time. The word "character" is used advisedly because its reference point in individual personality development provides a useful analogy for looking at organizational development. As an individual grows and matures, a process of character or identity formation occurs. The young person experiments with a variety of ways of doing and being in terms of occupation, interpersonal relationships, and overall conceptions of what kind of person he or she will become. Over time individuals select one or another of these ways, or develop new ones, which then become the dominant ways in which the person conducts his or her life. It is at this point that we say that a person's character or identity has been formed.

In much the same way new organizations experiment with different ways of being. There are many ways to structure an organization. Decision making, for instance, can be centralized so that a few elite members make all major decisions, or it can be decentralized to promote broad participation by many organization members. The strategy for delivering services may emphasize quantity and attach great importance to the number of clients reached; or it may concentrate on quality and direct attention to the technical competence of the staff. Internal relationships may be structured along collegial lines and stress peer interactions, or they may develop along hierarchical lines that emphasize superordinate and subordinate interactions.

As the organization "matures," it selects particular ways of doing things and structuring itself and, like the individual, will be said to have developed a character or, to use Boulding's (1956) term, an "image." The reasons why an organization develops one form and not another are complex and go beyond the scope of the present discussion. Some salient factors in the process, however, are the historical period in which the organization was formed, the nature of the technologies available, dominant values in the larger society, and the values and styles of the founders of the organization (Stinchcombe, 1965).

Once the organization has settled on a purpose, and its internal patterns of relationships have been established, a constant force operates within the organization to maintain this pattern. As the organization becomes an ongoing concern, its members develop commitment to its continued existence; the basis of this commitment is the benefits that organization members derive from the continued existence of the organization in *its present form.* These commitments will vary, therefore, according to benefit received; organizational leaders and those in dominant roles will obviously have a greater investment than others. However, for any organization to continue to function as a system the majority of the members must perceive their situations to be better as a result of their involvement in the organization than would be the case if they were to leave. That is, the organization member must feel that the benefits received are sufficient to warrant her or his continued participation (Barnard, 1968; Simon, 1964).

Commitment to the maintenance of the system, then, is a function of the system's ability to produce benefits for its members. If such benefits are lessened by major changes in the organization's environment, it can be expected that internal commitments to organizational maintenance will also lessen. Changes in the environment usually lead to organizational change, both in overall purposes and internal arrangements; for if the goals pursued by the organization are no longer relevant to its "output set" (Evan, 1966), then it will not be able to recruit the resources necessary for its ongoing operation. In order to survive, the organization will have to alter its goals to conform to new expectations from the environment; this, in turn, will alter the internal structure of the organization as new goals require new patterns of interactions among the organization's subsystems and change the pattern for the distribution of benefits. Once this new pattern is consolidated, however, staff will develop the same strong commitment to its maintenance; this commitment can be expected to continue until the system's function is once again challenged by changes in the environment.

Management of Internal Conflict

Another dynamic process in the organizational system is the need to manage the conflicts that arise from the fact that the system is made up of subsystems which pursue their own goals. Internal conflict is seen as a natural occurrence arising out of the normal operations of the system. That is, the model emphasizes the organization as a cause of intraorganizational conflict rather than the malicious, perverse, or pathological actions of organization members (although they, too, may cause some forms of conflict).

The problem of internal conflict becomes particularly serious when any one of the organizational subsystems emerges as a "leading" subsystem and threatens to dominate or eclipse the other subsystems. While the natural-system model stresses the equal importance of all subsystems for the overall functioning of the organization, one of the subsystems can assume greater importance than others under certain conditions. For example, in the earlier discussion of organizational development it was pointed out that agencies will usually select one or another service strategy as their preferred one, emphasizing either quantity or quality of services. In the former case, where volume is the key, one can expect the supportive and adaptive subsystems to assume key roles because of the constant need for new monies, more clients, and expanded facilities. In a quality strategy, the service or technical subsystem will be predominant, and concerns will be focussed on staff development, inservice training, and similar issues.

A critical function for the manager is the maintenance of equilibrium within the organization. When the functions of one subsystem are stressed by the organization, it would be detrimental to the organization's overall effectiveness to allow that subsystem to dominate others. Such dominance would result in a distortion of the purposes of the organization and a subsequent weakening of the organization's capacities to perform all necessary functions. In the example given above, a social agency in which the technical or service subsystem dominates would have a lessened capacity to recruit new funds and identify critical changes in the environment. If the managerial subsystem is functioning properly (which may not be the case if the agency administrators come from a service background and are biased in that direction), it will develop strategies for reducing the hegemony of the service subsystem and ensure that all functions within the organization are attended to.

THE POWER-POLITICS MODEL

A third theme in the study of organizations is one that views the organization as primarily a political arena in which interest groups compete for the control of organizational resources. While this approach does not have the coherence of the other models, there is a sufficient convergence of the conceptual and analytical emphases of a number of writers that warrant their being grouped as a "power-politics model." Two themes characterize this approach. The first theme is the importance assigned to resources, particularly their source, the amount available, and the means for deciding their distribution within the organization, as determinants of organizational structure and behavior (White, 1974; Zald, 1970). The second is an emphasis on political processes within the organization as the chief mechanism for determining the distribution of resources (Benson, 1977; Burns, 1961; Pettigrew, 1973; Zald, 1970).

All students of organizations recognize the importance of resources since organizations would cease to function if they were unable to secure a regular and sufficient supply of resources. The students of the power-politics approach, however, draw attention to the fact that resources, aside from their importance in the organization's productive work, are also the basis for power, be it on an interpersonal, group, or organizational level. Power has been defined as the ability of person A to control and direct the behavior of person B by means of A's *control over resources* needed by B (Buckley, 1967, pp. 176-185; Dahl, 1957; Emerson, 1962; French and Raven, 1968). By extension, organizational power is generated when a person, or unit, within the organization is able to establish control over resources, thus enabling that person or unit to direct the behavior of other persons or units dependent upon those resources (Tannenbaum, 1968). The power-politics approach, moreover, stresses political processes as the primary way in which individuals or units are able to establish control over resources. Politics is defined by Banfield (1955, p. 304) as "the activity (negotiation, argument, discussion, application of force, persuasion, etc.) by which an issue is agitated or settled." The issue to be settled is how and by whom decisions about resource allocations are to be made, or, in Lasswell's (1958) classic phrase, "who gets what, when, how."

The rational model assumes that resources will be allocated according to rational criteria, that is, they will go where they are most needed for efficient goal attainment. The natural-system model assumes that resources will be allocated along lines that promote system maintenance and enhancement. These assumptions have been criticized as overly simplistic in the first case and overly abstract and unspecified in the second (Benson, 1977; Georgiou, 1973). A political approach to resource allocation proceeds from the assumption that organization members seek to promote their self interests, and their behavior within the organization will be guided by that consideration (Downs, 1967; Tullock, 1965). An individual's organizational interests, moreover, are determined by his or her place within the organization, place being a function of hierarchical position and functional specialty. Political behavior in this context can be viewed as behavior aimed at securing and enhancing one's place in the organization. Pettigrew's (1973) description of organizational politics illuminates this process:

The division of work in an organization creates sub-units. These sub-units develop interests based on specialized functions and responsibilities. Although such sub-units have specialized tasks, they may also be interdependent. This interdependence may be played out within a joint decision-making process. Within such decision-making processes, interest-based demands are made. Given heterogeneity in the demand-generating process and the absence of a clearly set system of priorities between those demands, conflict is likely to ensue. Sub-units with differential interests make claims on scarce organizational resources. . . . The success any claimant has in furthering his interests will be a consequence of his ability to generate support for his demand.

It is the involvement of sub-units in such demand- and support-generating processes within the decision-making processes of the organization that constitute the political dimension. Political behavior is defined as behavior by individuals, or, in collective terms, by sub-units, within an organization that makes a claim against the resource-shaping system of the organization (pp. 17-18).

The major variables in this model are (1) the character of the organization's resources and (2) the nature of its control structure. The central operating dynamic is the impact that shifting patterns of resource availability have on the internal structure of an organization.

Resources

Organizational resources are defined by Yuchtman and Seashore (1967) as more or less "generalized means, or facilities, that are potentially controllable by social organizations and that are potentially usable—however indirectly—in relationships between the organization and its environment" (p. 900). Resources, then, are means for accomplishing organizational purposes that are "imported" by the organization from its environment. In the social welfare organization, for example, the principal resources are money, personnel, clients, and sanctions from the community. Since the present concern is with resources as the bases for power in organizations, the two aspects of this definition that are most critical are the degree to which resources are generalizable and controllable.

The generalizability of a resource has two dimensions: the degree to which one resource can be exchanged for another, or what Yuchtman and Seashore (1967, p. 900) call a resource's "liquidity," and the extent to which one resource can be used for a variety of purposes, which will be referred to here as its "transferability." Money and credit are high in liquidity, while availability of time or ideological commitment to a particular program are low. A psychiatric social worker specializing in the problems of autistic children is an example of a highly nontransferrable resource, while a social worker with a general background is a highly transferrable resource. Organizations with resources high in liquidity and/or transferability can be expected to have a high level of internal political activity due to the efforts of sub-units to gain control of these resources. These kinds of resources, because of their generalizability, can be used by a variety of organizational units, regardless of the unit's functional specialty.

The controllability of a resource refers to the ease with which individuals within the organization are able to establish control over the use of a resource. This, in turn, is a function of the extent to which the resource comes into the organization unencumbered by external constraints on its use. The kinds of external constraints on resources that can be placed on social welfare organizations range from the statutory prescriptions for the use of public monies to the demands of client-advocacy groups that clients be dealt with in ways specified by them (White, 1974, pp. 367-368). The number of external constraints placed on the use of an organizational resource, regardless of the generalizability of the resource itself, will affect the degree of political bargaining that can take place within the organization over the disposition of the resource. That is, resources designated for a particular use by an outside body cannot be bargained for within the organization. An example of a liquid resource that, while highly generalizable, has become less amenable to control by recipient organizations is the federal funds granted to the states in support of social services. In 1963 the federal government spent a little under 200 million dollars in social services grants to the states; by 1972 this figure had risen to over 1.5 billion dollars (Derthick, 1975, table 1 at p. 8). Moreover, as Derthick (1975, pp. 1-14) points out in her thorough and astute analysis of this situation, the funds were "uncontrolled" because the federal government attached few or no conditions to their use. The lack of external constraints on these funds made them highly controllable by the recipient organization, which was free to use them for its own purposes. Since 1972, however, the pendulum has swung in the opposite direction, with the federal government imposing stricter guidelines and accountability procedures on the use of these monies, thus reducing their controllability by recipient organizations (Mogulof, 1973; Newman and Turem, 1974; Smith, 1971). The resource retained its liquidity—it's still money—but lost its controllability (by recipient organizations). Taken together, generalizability and controllability of resources can be viewed as the necessary and sufficient conditions for determining the absolute level of political activity within an organization.

Control Structure

Tannenbaum (1968) defines control in organizations as:

any process in which a person or group of persons or organization of persons determines, that is, intentionally affects, the behavior of another person, group, or organization. . . .The exercise of control may be viewed as an exchange of some valued resource dispensed by one person in return for compliance on the part of another (pp. 5, 15).

Control, then, is synonymous with power, and the control structure of an organization is another way of talking about the distribution of power within the organization. The aspect of the control or power structure most relevant to the present discussion is the extent to which power is concentrated in the hands of a few individuals, or whether it is dispersed among many individuals throughout the organization. The first situation is usually referred to as a *centralized* control structure, while the second is a *decentralized* structure (Meyer, 1968; Scott and Mitchell, 1972, p. 150).

Since power is based on control of resources, the amount of power an individual or unit can exercise is directly related to the amount of resources at their disposal. In organizations where many units have access to resources, and no one unit is in a position to exer-

cise control over the bulk of the resources coming into the organization, we can speak of a highly diffuse power situation in which political activity between units will be high as they compete and negotiate with each other to secure and expand their share of resources. In organizations in which one unit is able to exercise total, or near-total, control over the bulk of the resources, we have a concentrated power situation and can expect internal political activity to decrease. The latter situation will best be analyzed in terms of the rational model since the dominant power group will be able to establish its goals as the overall goals of the organization and will be able to make rational decisions in pursuit of those goals since it has the power to implement decisions.

Politics and rationality can be seen as competing methods for deciding on the distribution of resources within an organization. In a scientifically oriented society such as the American one, rationality is stressed. That is, *ceteris paribus,* rational decisions will be preferred over non-rational ones. However, rationality assumes a clear statement of objectives and the ability to rank preferentially the alternatives for reaching those objectives, with efficiency being the criterion for establishing the rank order. In the absence of either of these conditions another way must be found for deciding how resources are to be distributed. The power-politics approach suggests that the ability to organize and agitate issues (i.e., to engage in political behavior) comes into play when the conditions for rational decision making about resource distribution are not present.

The proponents of the rational model argue that rationality determines the shape of the control structure, that is, those who have the most power in an organization *should* have that power because they are the people or units most suited to direct the operations of the organization, given its goals. The power-politics approach reverses this argument. The goals of an organization are not completely pre-determined, but evolve out of the struggle for control over resources. The goals of an organization at any given time are the goals of the group within the organization that has attained ascendancy in the competition for resources. Those people who are able to gain control over resources are then able to impose their goals on the organization as a whole. Whatever rationality there is in the structure and operations of the organization is a function of the ability of one group, or unit, to "seize the day," to establish its dominance over other groups through their control of resources.

Shifting Patterns of Resource Availability

One of the leading proponents of a political approach to studying organizations argues that a central strength of this orientation is the insights it offers to an understanding of the nature of organizational change: "The political-economy framework is not a substitute for decision-theory, the human-relations approach, or the concept of organizational rationality. For analysis of organizational change, however, it does claim to subsume these others" (Zald, 1970, p. 241). The power-politics approach is explicitly concerned with the processes of organizational change. Flowing from its concern with resources as determinants of organizational behavior, change in organizations is

viewed as primarily a function of the shifting patterns of resource availability. That is, as the kinds and amounts of resources available change, the internal arrangements for their control and distribution (i.e., the structure of the organization) will change in a process of organizational adaptation to its environment.

As a productive system an organization is constantly using up resources in its work. These come from the organization's environment, which allocates resources for those things it "wants done or can be persuaded to support" (Thompson and McEwen, 1958, p. 23). The organization is dependent upon its environment since it must adapt its internal structure and operations to respond to changing environmental requirements. The power-politics model suggests that this process of adaptation can best be understood in terms of the capacities of different units in the organization to establish hegemony over other units by means of their access to and control over new resources.

It has been argued here that the structure of an organization at any given time is best seen as the product of the most recent struggle for power among organizational subunits, with the "winner" (i.e., the unit able to establish control over resources) establishing the agenda for organizational action. The dominant unit is able to elevate its goals and priorities to the level of the goals and priorities for the total organization. The reason why a particular unit is able to establish this control is a function of two factors: the degree to which the unit is organized to take action on its own behalf in negotiating for resources, and the relevance of the unit's functional specialty to the demands placed on the organization by its significant "publics." In a sense, the unit must be able to "sell" itself and have something to "sell." Moreover, of the two factors the second will be the deciding one in a struggle for control. A unit may have great potential for engaging in internal political struggles because of its cohesiveness, high morale, and effective and ambitious leadership, but be lacking in the functional specialization needed by the organization. It is possible that this unit may be able to establish control over resources because of its strength as a cohesive and purposeful social unit. This victory, however, will be short-lived unless the unit is able to acquire or develop the technical capabilities needed by the organization to satisfy the expectations set in its environment.

Developments in the operation of public assistance programs over the past fifteen years offer an illustration of how this process works. Public assistance agencies generally involve three functional specializations: management, eligibility determination, and social services. The period from 1945 to 1962 saw the steady rise in the influence of one of these functional groups, the social services (Gilbert, 1966; Kahn, 1965). Starting with the publication in 1945 of Charlotte Towle's *Common Human Needs* and culminating with the passage of the 1962 Amendments to the Social Security Act (sometimes referred to as the "services amendment"), the influence of the social service (i.e., casework) perspective came to dominate the entire public assistance operation. The functional specialty offered by caseworkers includes a method for individual rehabilitation and change through counseling. The reason why this unit was able to attain the dominance it did within public

assistance was the congruence between its specialized skills and the prevailing mood of the time as regards the nature of financial dependency. Namely, the causes of poverty were to be found in the shortcomings and defects (usually of a psychological nature) of the poor, with the solution being some form of psychological rehabilitation (Mencher, 1963; Lukoff and Mencher, 1962). The goals of social workers became the goals of public assistance, and the 1962 amendments provided for the allocation of monies exclusively for the purposes of expanding the casework capacities of public welfare agencies.

Contrary to all expectations, the 1960's saw the most dramatic rise in the number of people receiving assistance since the inception of the program (Lynch, 1967). As a result, the public agenda shifted from a concern with rehabilitating the poor (assuming that that was once a real concern of the general public and not just of social workers) to ways of dealing with the mounting costs of the public assistance program ("Crisis in Welfare," 1969). Federal and state legislatures began to redeploy public assistance funds from service activities and placed the highest priority on the development of effective management. The influence of the caseworkers waned and the "age of the manager" arrived with consequent changes in the internal structure of the public assistance agency (Gruber, 1974; Turem, 1974).

A NOTE ON THE USE OF THE FRAMEWORK

In order to apply this framework there must be guidelines for its use. The purpose of any conceptual framework is to further understanding through the application of relevant theoretical schemes. Three theoretical models have been presented here and the question now is when and for what purposes are they to be used.

The rational model is most appropriate when there is a clear and concrete specification of objectives and widespread support for these objectives among the members of the organization, and when the means for pursuing these objectives are developed to the point where one alternative can be clearly distinguished from another. (Casework, family therapy, and group therapy, for instance, cannot be neatly separated into three distinct methods because of the considerable overlapping of techniques employed by all three.) The situation conducive to rational analysis must be the *opposite* of what Cohen and his colleagues (1972) refer to as "organized anarchies:"

These are organizations—or decision situations—characterized by three properties. The first is problematic preferences. . . . The organization operates on the basis of a variety of inconsistent and ill-defined preferences. . . .The second property is unclear technology. Although the organization manages to survive and even produce, its own processes are not understood by its members. . . .The third property is fluid participation. Participants vary in the amount of time and effort they devote to different domains, involvement varies from one time to another (p. 1).

Many social welfare organizations do not meet the requirements of the rational model because of dissensus over goals and the diffuse nature of the technologies employed. While this is true for the organization as a whole, it will be less true as one looks at subunits within the organization. As one moves from macro- to micro-levels of analysis,

from the total operation to specific aspects of that operation, the probabilities for rational action increase. This is mainly due to the greater clarity and agreement about goals and means found in small, cohesive groups, compared to large, heterogeneous conglomerates. The rational model, then, will most likely be an appropriate framework for looking at the actions of subunits within organizations. As one goes beyond the operations of a specific unit and looks at overall organizational behavior, the rational approach becomes less useable, except in instances when the total organization is pursuing agreed-upon, specific objectives and has clearly identifiable technological means to choose from.

The natural-system model stresses the importance of coordinating the various subunits of an organization so that the system as a whole can function effectively. This approach assumes a high degree of interdependence among the units of a system in that one unit will not be able to function unless its activities are articulated with all other units. The degree of system interdependence, however, is an empirical question and cannot be assumed. Gouldner (1959) sheds considerable light on the ways in which interdependence can vary in social systems through his concept of the "functional autonomy" of the parts of a system. Functional autonomy is defined as:

the degree to which any one part is dependent on others for the satisfaction of its needs. Systems in which parts have "high" functional autonomy may be regarded as having a "low" degree of system interdependence; conversely, systems in which parts have "low" functional autonomy have a "high" degree of system interdependence. The concept of functional autonomy directs attention to the fact that some parts may survive separation from others, that parts vary in their dependence upon one another, and that their interdependence is not necessarily symmetrical (p. 419).

An organization can be viewed in systemic terms, and analyzed as such, to the extent that the various units comprising it can be shown to *have to rely on each other* in order to get their work done. That is, must I wait until you complete your job before I can start mine? In a child-guidance agency, for example, can the family therapist begin work with a family before the intake worker has completed the initial interviews? Can the intake worker elect to continue seeing a family, thus circumventing the need to involve the family therapist? If either of these situations exist, then these units are operating in a *parallel* rather than interdependent fashion, and it would be inappropriate to view them as part of an integrated system of activities. These are the kinds of empirical questions that must be asked, and answered, about an organization in order to determine the extent of system interdependence and, consequently, the appropriateness of the natural-system model for analysis.

The power-politics approach proceeds from the assumption of the ubiquity of self-interest as a motivating force in all human behavior, including behavior in organizations. Individuals in organizations will act to secure and promote their interests, these being determined by one's location in the structure. Action directed toward the interests of the organization as a whole (whether these interests are defined in terms of maximizing efficient production or securing system integration) will occur only if there is some force operating to constrain self-interest behavior

(Olsen, 1971, pp. 5-52). That is, unless the conditions noted above as necessary for an organization to operate either in the rational pursuit of a goal or to sustain and enhance itself as an integrated social system are clearly present, then it is safe to assume that behavior in the organization will best be explained along the lines suggested in the power-politics model.

REFERENCES

Argyris, Chris. "Single-loop and Double-loop Models in Research in Decision-making." *Administrative Science Quarterly* 21 (1976): 363–375.

Banfield, Edward C. "Note on Conceptual Scheme." In Martin Meyerson and Edward C. Banfield, *Politics, Planning and the Public Interest.* Glencoe, IL: Free Press, 1955.

Barnard, Chester I. *The Functions of the Executive.* 30th ed. Cambridge, MA: Harvard University Press, 1968.

Benson, J. Kenneth. "Organizations: A Dialectical View." *Administrative Science Quarterly* 22, 1 (1977): 1-21.

Boulding, Kenneth. *The Image.* Ann Arbor: University of Michigan Press, 1956.

Buckley, Walter. *Sociology and Modern Systems Theory.* Englewood Cliffs, NJ: Prentice-Hall, 1967.

Burns, Tom. "Micro-politics: Mechanisms of Institutional Change." *Administrative Science Quarterly* 6, 2 (1961): 257-281.

Cohen, Michael D., James G. March, and Johan P. Olsen. "A Garbage Can Model of Organizational Choice." *Administrative Science Quarterly* 17, 1 (1972): 1-25.

"Crisis in Welfare." *The Public Interest,* 16 (Summer 1969), entire issue.

Cyert, Richard M., and Kenneth R. MacCrimmon. "Organizations." In Gardner Lindzey and Elliot Aronson, eds., *The Handbook of Social Psychology,* 1: 568-611. Reading, MA: Addison-Wesley, 1968.

Dahl, Robert A. "The Concept of Power." *Behavioral Science* 2(1957): 201-215.

Derthick, Martha. *Uncontrollable Spending for Social Services Grants.* Washington, DC: Brookings Institution, 1975.

Donnison, David D. "Observations on University Training for Social Workers in Great Britain and North America." *Social Service Review* 29 (1955): 341-350.

Downs, Anthony. *Inside Bureaucracy.* Boston: Little, Brown, 1967.

Emerson, Richard M. "Power-Dependence Relations." *American Sociological Review* 27 (1962): 31-41.

Etzioni, Amitai. *Modern Organizations.* Englewood Cliffs, NJ: Prentice-Hall, 1964.

Evan, William M. "The Organization-set: Toward a Theory of Inter-organizational Relations." In James D. Thompson, ed., *Approaches to Organizational Design.* Pittsburgh: University of Pittsburgh Press, 1966.

French, John R. P., Jr., and Bertram Raven. "The Bases of Social Power." In Dorwin Cartwright and Alvin Zander, eds., *Group Dynamics: Research and Theory.* 3rd ed. New York: Harper & Row, 1968.

Georgiou, Petro. "The Goal Paradigm and Notes towards a Counter Paradigm." *Administrative Science Quarterly* 18 (1973): 291-310.

Gilbert, Charles E. "Policy-making in Public Welfare: The 1962 Amendments." *Political Science Quarterly* 81 (1966): 196-224.

Goffman, Erving. *Asylums: Essays on the Social Situation of Mental Patients and Other Inmates.* Garden City, NY: Anchor, 1961.

Gouldner, Alvin W. "Organizational Analysis." In Robert K. Merton, Leonard Bloom, and L. Edward S. Cottrell, eds., *Sociology Today.* New York: Basic Books, 1959.

Gruber, Murray. "Total Administration." *Social Work* 19 (1974): 625-636.

Gummer, Burton. "A Power-politics Approach to Social Welfare Organizations." *Social Service Review* 52, no. 3 (1978): 349-361.

Kahn, Alfred J. "Social Services in Relation to Income Security." *Social Service Review* 39 (1965): 381-389.

Katz, Daniel and Robert L. Kahn. *The Social Psychology of Organizations.* New York: John Wiley, 1966.

Kirk, Stuart A., and James R. Greenley. "Denying or Delivering Services?" *Social Work* 19 (1974): 439-447.

Lasswell, Harold. *Politics: Who Gets What, When, How.* New York: Meridian Books, World, 1958.

Levine, Sol, and Paul E. White. "Exchange as a Conceptual Framework for the Study of Interorganizational Relationships." *Administrative Science Quarterly* 5 (1961): 583-601.

Litwak, Eugene. "Models of Bureaucracy Which Permit Conflict." *American Journal of Sociology* 67 (1961): 177-184.

Lukoff, Irving F., and Samuel Mencher. "A Critique of the Conceptual Foundation of Community Research Associates." *Social Service Review* 36 (1962): 433-443.

Lynch, John M. "Trends in Number of AFDC Recipients, 1961-1965." *Welfare in Review* 5 (1967): 7-13.

Mayo, Elton. *The Human Problems of an Industrial Civilization.* New York: Compass Books, Viking, 1960.

Mencher, Samuel. "Perspectives on Recent Welfare Legislation, Fore and Aft." *Social Work* 8 (1963): 59-64.

Meyer, Marshall W. "The Two Authority Structures of Bureaucratic Organization." *Administrative Science Quarterly* 13 (1968): 211-228.

Mogulof, Melvin. "Elements of a Special-revenue-sharing Proposal for the Social Services: Goal Setting, Decategorization, Planning, and Evaluation." *Social Service Review* 47 (1973): 593-604.

Newman, Edward, and Jerry Turem. "The Crisis of Accountability." *Social Work* 19 (1974): 5-16.

Olsen, Mancus. *The Logic of Collective Action: Public Goods and the Theory of Groups.* Cambridge, MA: Harvard University Press, 1971.

Ouchi, William G., and Jerry B. Johnson. "Types of Organizational Control and their Relationship to Emotional Well-being." *Administrative Science Quarterly* 23, 2 (1978): 293-317.

Parsons, Talcott. "Suggestions for a Sociological Approach to the Study of Organizations—I." *Administrative Science Quarterly* 1, 1 (1956): 63-75.

Perrow, Charles. "A Framework for the Comparative Analysis of Organizations." *American Sociological Review* 32, 3

(1967): 194-208.

Pettigrew, Andrew M. *The Politics of Organizational Decision-making.* London: Tavistock, 1973.

Pfeffer, Jeffrey, Gerald R. Salancik, and Husespin Leblebici. "The Effect of Uncertainty on the Use of Social Influence in Organizational Decision Making." *Administrative Science Quarterly* 21, no. 2 (1976): 227-245.

Roethlisberger, Fritz J., and William J. Dickson. *Management and the Worker.* Cambridge, MA: Harvard University Press, 1939.

Scott, W. Richard. "Professionals in Bureaucracies—Areas of Conflict." In H. M. Vollmer and D. L. Mills, eds., *Professionalization.* Englewood Cliffs, NJ: Prentice-Hall, 1966.

Scott, W. Richard. "Professional Employees in a Bureaucratic Structure: Social Work." In A. Etzioni, ed., *The Semi-Professions and Their Organization.* New York: Free Press, 1969.

Scott, William G., and T. C. Mitchell. *Organization Theory: A Structural and Behavioral Approach.* Rev. ed. Homewood, IL: Irwin-Dorsey, 1972.

Selznick, Philip. "Foundations of the Theory of Organization." *American Sociological Review* 13 (1948): 25-35.

Selznick, Philip. *Leadership in Administration: A Sociological Interpretation.* New York: Harper & Row, 1957.

Selznick, Philip. *The Organizational Weapon: A Study of Bolshevik Strategy and Tactics.* 2nd ed. New York: Free Press, 1960.

Simon, Herbert A. "On the Concept of Organizational Goal." *Administrative Science Quarterly* 8 (1964): 1-22.

Stinchcombe, Arthur L. "Social Structure and Organization." In James G. March, ed., *The Handbook of Organizations.* Chicago: Rand-McNally, 1965.

Tannenbaum, Arnold S. *Control in Organizations.* New York: McGraw-Hill, 1968.

Thompson, James D., *Organizations in Action.* New York: McGraw-Hill, 1967.

Thompson, James D., and William J. McEwen. "Organizational Goals and Environment: Goal-setting as an Interaction Process." *American Sociological Review,* 23, 1 (1958): 23-31.

Towle, Charlotte. *Common Human Needs.* New York: National Association of Social Workers, 1945.

Tullock, Gordon. *The Politics of Bureaucracy.* Washington, DC: Public Affairs Press, 1965.

Turem, Jerry. "The Call for a Management Stance." *Social Work* 19 (1974): 625-636.

Wamsley, Gary L., and Mayer N. Zald. *The Political Economy of Public Organizations: A Critique and Approach to the Study of Public Administration.* Bloomington, IN: Indiana University Press, 1976.

Warren, Roland L. "The Concerting of Decisions as a Variable in Organizational Interaction." In Matthew Tuite, Roger Chisholm, and Michael Radnoes, eds., *Interorganizational Decision Making.* Chicago: Aldine, 1972.

Weber, Max. "Bureaucracy." In Hans H. Gerth and C. Wright Mills, eds. and trans., *From Max Weber: Essays in Sociology.* New York: Oxford University Press, 1958.

Weber, Max. *The Theory of Social and Economic Organizations,* trans. A. M. Henderson and Talcott Parsons. New York: Free Press Paperbacks, 1964.

White, Paul E. "Resources as Determinants of Organizational Behavior." *Administrative Science Quarterly* 19 (1974): 366-379.

Woodward, John. *Industrial Organization.* London: Oxford University Press, 1965.

Yuchtman, Ephraim, and Stanley E. Seashore. "A System Resource Approach to Organizational Effectiveness." *American Sociological Review* 32 (1967): 891-903.

Zald, Mayer N. *Organizational Change: The Political Economy of the YMCA.* Chicago: University of Chicago Press, 1970.

Zald, Mayer N., and John D. McCarthy. "Organizational Intellectuals and the Criticism of Society." *Social Service Review* 49 (1975): 344-362.

26.

Yeheskel Hasenfeld

PROGRAM DEVELOPMENT

INTRODUCTION

Program development and implementation is a common and crucial task of community organization practitioners, yet it has not received adequate attention in practice theory. There seems to be an implicit assumption that, once the community organization practitioner has successfully mobilized action groups or planning task forces to grapple with important community issues, his function is essentially completed. Yet, the most critical element in any community organization activity is the emergence of some idea and design for a *program,* be it a direct service delivery, a training program, a coordination council, a fund-raising program, or the like.

The implementation of such a program, which in almost all instances requires the development of some organizational framework, is in the last analysis the true test of successful community organization, since the program provides in very concrete terms the outputs or services desired and needed by the community. Thus, the overall thesis of this paper is that the community organization practitioner has the dual role of action mobilizer and planner,

and of organizer and program implementer. In this paper, then, I discuss some of the major tasks and skills that the practitioner needs to know and fulfill in order to successfully implement a community-generated program. The term planner-organizer is used to designate the complexity of such a role.

Most frequently, the planner-organizer is asked to develop a program for direct service delivery. Social action groups often develop service programs in order to serve people ignored by existing services, or as a means of gaining community support, or as a device to stimulate existing service providers to change their own programs. Examples include unions instituting information and referral services and recreation programs for retired workers, and the Black Panthers setting up a breakfast meal service and elementary school education program for neighborhood children. Thus, the discussion that follows will focus on program development for direct services. Nevertheless, the tasks and skills involved are clearly applicable to other types of programs.

Development of a new program is by no means an easy undertaking. It often requires a prolonged process of negotiation and planning. Launching a new service inevitably results in some disruption of the delicate balance that exists among various service providers. Some agency representatives may feel they were excluded from participation. Others may see the new program as a

Source: Adapted from "Guide to Agency Development for Area Planners in Aging," Project T.A.P., funded by the Administration on Aging, Grant SRS-HEW 94-P-76007/5-01 to the Institute of Gerontology, University of Michigan/ Wayne State University and the University of Michigan School of Social Work Continuing Education Program. Reprinted by permission of the author.

challenge to their own domain. While the planner-organizer may find it necessary to disagree with certain groups who oppose the program, he or she must have enough support and sufficient resources to withstand countervailing pressures.

Every new program requires resources—in particular, money and manpower. Without a fair chance of obtaining these, no effort to develop a new program is likely to succeed. The key to the success of a new venture could be the extent to which the planner-organizer is in a position to control at least some of the funds allocable to the relevant social service programs. Yet money without capable or trainable manpower is of little avail. And without facilities, legitimacy, or some other needed resource, both money and manpower may be expended without benefit to consumers. The planner-organizer must be willing to invest a significant proportion of time to mobilize needed resources and to influence this allocation.

THE SYSTEMS PERSPECTIVE

In considering the establishment of a new program or agency, the planner-organizer may find a "systems" perspective to be particularly useful. Each agency can be viewed as an open "system," composed of a set of interrelated units designed to achieve a common objective or complex of objectives. The activities of these units are aimed at (1) recruiting such *inputs* into the agency as money and credit, manpower, and clients; (2) transforming these inputs into actual services such as medical care, counseling, or community planning; (3) producing *output* in such forms as improved social services coordination,

reduction in the incidence of need for protective services, etc.[1]

Service and Maintenance Functions

A second assumption underlying the systems perspective is that the activities of the agency staff are guided by two basic motivations. The first can be termed the goal-seeking motive leading to "service" objectives and the second the self-maintenance motive leading to "survival" objectives. The first motive informs those staff activities designed to achieve the *output* goals of the agency. The self-maintenance motive informs those efforts by staff to maintain the agency through enhancing its access to resources, expanding its services, building a positive climate of public support, etc. Clearly, no agency can achieve its service objectives without consideration of its maintenance needs or survival objectives. Yet if the agency invests all its energies in self-maintenance it will be accused of not accomplishing, indeed of subverting, its service objectives.[2] Both sets of activities are often in tension, causing intraorganizational competition for scarce resources. Improper allocation of these resources reduces the effectiveness of any service provider.

The interplay between the goal-seeking or service function of an agency and its survival needs or maintenance function can be observed in its internal structure. From a systems perspective, five subsystems within an organization

---

[1]See for example, D. Katz and R. Kahn, *The Social Psychology of Organizations* (New York: Wiley, 1966); F. Baker, ed., *Organizational Systems* (Homewood, IL: Richard D. Irwin, 1973).

[2]R. A. Scott, "The Factory as a Social Service Organization," *Social Problems,* 15 (Fall, 1967): 160–75.

are identifiable, each fulfilling an important function without which the agency is likely to experience strain and possible disintegration. Each subsystem is characterized by the function it fulfills in the agency and by a common motivation of those participating in it. The subsystems may be characterized as: (1) the technical, (2) the environmental support, (3) the institutional, (4) the intelligence, and (5) the managerial subsystems.[3]

Subsystems and Their Functions

1. The function of the *technical subsystem* is to provide a service. In a social service agency, it is generally designed to improve or maintain the well-being of a client or client population. The primary motivation of the agency staff providing these services is to achieve proficiency in these assigned tasks. The range of tasks they perform may include assessment of the client's needs; evaluation of the client's resources; counseling or treatment; and referrals to other service providers. The manner in which these tasks are performed is called the agency's service technology.

2. The *environmental support subsystem's* function is to manage or recruit those resources from the environment necessary to the performance of the tasks of the technical subsystems. At least five categories of resources must be brought into the agency: (1) money and credit to cover the costs involved in providing the services and performing other functions; (2) personnel such as administrators, social workers, counselors, clerical staff, and other support staff; (3) clients whose needs or

interests can be served by the agency; (4) knowledge and expertise necessary for the successful implementation of the services; and (5) complementary services of other agencies necessary to ensure that the agency's services are effective.

Procurement and management of these resources requires a variety of transactions or exchanges with those external units in the environment (other systems) that control these resources. This requires that certain agency employees perform what systems theorists call "boundary roles": roles that are necessary to develop and facilitate transactions between the organization and its environment. Boundary relationships are generally managed by agency staff with special responsibility for these tasks. For example, when budget staff negotiates with state and national officials for the allocation of fiscal resources, it manages boundary relationships leading to input of fiscal resources. When personnel workers interview or recruit potential staff, intake workers screen potential clients, and various staff members develop relations with other social service agencies, each also performs a boundary role or assumes a boundary function. In most smaller agencies, many of these boundary relationships are likely to be fulfilled by the same person or persons. These activities enable the agency to achieve some mastery over its environment, leading to procurement of needed resources with some degree of certainty or stability.[4]

3. Staff performing *institutional subsystem* functions seeks to obtain social support and legitimation for the agency from the environment. Without such

---

[3]D. Katz and R. Kahn, op. cit., Chapter 4.

[4]H. Aldrich, "Organizational Boundaries and Inter-organizational Conflict," *Human Relations* 24 (1971): 279–293.

support, the agency cannot hope to obtain the resources necessary for other functions. Sometimes, legitimation is in the form of a legal mandate, such as the Housing Act, Medicare, the Social Security Act, or other legislation.

Without understating the importance of these legislative acts, one should not ignore the importance of obtaining social support in the very community in which the program operates. This includes support from potential clients, various civic organizations, governmental agencies, and other social service agencies. Staff activities involve the development of ties with key community influentials, contribution of resources to important community functions, public exposition of the agency's services, etc. Such activities are oriented toward "institutionalizing" the agency in the community, assuring it will be perceived as integral and indispensable to the community's interests.[5]

4. The ability of the agency to develop effective linkages with its external environment as well as an effective service delivery system is dependent on the operation of the agency's *intelligence and feedback mechanisms*. The functions of the intelligence subsystem are: (1) to gather and interpret vital information about the conditions of the target population for which the service is developed and about other potential client populations, about new service opportunities, about the needs and attributes of the clients served, etc.; and (2) to provide feedback to the staff of the agency on the outcomes of their efforts. This may include information about the results of client referrals to

various services, evaluation of staff activities in the counseling and treatment of clients, or assessment of the "progress" being made by those clients.

Intelligence activities can help the agency to reduce uncertainty about its efforts and can be used to plan on a more rational basis. Without adequate intelligence, any agency is in danger of finding itself off target or out of the mainstream of client needs.

5. Activities of the *managerial subsystem* cut across all the other subsystems in the agency. Management is in charge of making the key decisions regarding what services get delivered, by whom, and how; relations with the environment; and the use of intelligence. The major tasks of management are: (1) to coordinate the activities of the various subsystems in the agency; (2) to resolve conflicts between the various hierarchical levels, and to elicit the compliance of staff to its work requirements; and (3) to effect coordination between the external demands on the agency and its own resources and needs. Management acts to achieve control and stability within the agency and to mediate and achieve a compromise between the various needs and demands of the subsystems of which it is composed.

From this rather brief overview, it should be apparent that each subsystem is dependent on inputs from the others in order to fulfill its function. The quality of the performance of each subsystem profoundly affects the quality of work done in other parts of the agency. A change in one subsystem is likely to affect the performance of the others. For example, increased intelligence activities may result in increased capacity to enlist new services for the target population, which in turn influences the

[5]C. Perrow, *Organizational Analysis* (Belmont, CA: Wadsworth, 1970): 92–132.

ability of those performing the service technology of the agency to help those clients.

Starting a New Service or Program

An understanding of these systemic functions is necessary in any effort to establish a new service or program or to modify and expand an existing one. In choosing whether to work through an existing agency or to establish a new agency, the planner-organizer must consider the costs and advantages of building from what already exists as against building something entirely new.

Developing a new agency to serve certain needs has the clear advantage of freeing the planner from the constraints of existing arrangements. These may include competing objectives of ongoing community agencies as well as tradition, and the custom of following established procedures. Overcoming such obstacles is by no means easy. Consider, for example, the difficulties that might be anticipated in attempting to shift the program focus of a medical clinic serving primarily young mothers and their children, to a medical checkup program for the aging, or of getting a citywide planning agency to develop neighborhood planning "outposts."

Adding a new program to an existing agency may result in serious coordination problems between functional units, may lead to conflict with other agency activities, and may ultimately lead to its "benign neglect."

On the other hand, establishing a new agency is often costlier than expanding the services of an existing organization. An established agency is often well recognized and supported in the community. Its staff has the training and experience to run the agency and knows

how to handle all its administrative details. Moreover, the agency may have all the basic equipment necessary for the new service or program. New agencies often flounder because of the lack of experience and expertise.

PROCEDURES IN ORGANIZING A NEW SERVICE OR PROGRAM

Identifying the Need for Service

No new agency or program should be initiated unless it is propelled by the existence of a concrete and viable need. Self-evident as this may seem, attempts are too often made to develop new services without a clear definition and articulation of the needs to be met. Lack of clarity and specificity of needs is likely to result in two undesirable consequences. First, it makes it far more difficult to mobilize community support for the new program. Second, the actual design of the program may be haphazard, ad hoc, often leading to ineffectiveness and inefficiency. A cardinal principle in program design is that the greater the clarity of the program's objectives, the better its chances for success.

Identifying unmet needs in the community is a complex task that necessitates several steps. The concept of "need" itself often defies adequate definition. What is perceived as a need by one group may not be so considered by another. Nevertheless, there are a number of ways in which planners can get a quick orientation to needs. The following are illustrative strategies:

1. Planners might start by examining available statistical reports such as census data, local Social Security office data, county gov-

ernment surveys, health surveys. While information on the number of potential clients in a given area, their distribution in various neighborhoods, their level of income, housing patterns, health conditions and the like might not indicate what they "need," such information is often suggestive.

2. The planner-organizer might then take a second step: identifying the various agencies in the area that serve the community. This involves finding out whom these agencies serve and what types of services they offer. Statistical reports issued by relevant agencies, the local welfare council and the public social service agencies may be of particular importance. Some communities may have developed information systems for a network of agencies that could provide invaluable data to the planner-organizer.[6]

3. A third step is to explore with the staff of the agencies that are current or potential providers of services to the target population the concerns and problems it has identified regarding gaps or inequities in services.

4. Very early in the process, planners should meet with community groups to discuss their wants, preferences, and interests.

5. A more systematic data-gathering procedure might be developed through a "needs survey" of the neighborhoods in which potential clients are most likely to reside. The facilities of a college or university or a local mental health center, as well volunteers, c· conduct the should be de: mation abou. unmet needs of those interviewed. A social-indicators–type survey is one of the most useful of the new devices to get at such information.[7]

An important concomitant of the planner's information-gathering activities is his or her effort to increase the community's awareness of the needs of the target population. Involvement of community leaders and representatives of agencies in determination of these needs sensitizes them to existing problems and lays the groundwork for mobilizing them into action. Awareness on the part of key groups and agencies in the community is often fundamental to the initiation of new programs.

Mobilizing Support for the Service

It is extremely difficult to develop a new program without the existence and active support of a group in the community that is highly committed to its development. The planner-organizer must often initiate and organize such an action group. The action group then gathers resources and influence, actively representing the new program's objectives, and fights for its support in the community. In short, it assumes an advocate function. Sometimes this group will be the planner's advisory council. At other times it will be a specially organized task force on transpor-

---

[6]See for example, CHILDATA. Council for Community Services in Metropolitan Chicago.

[7]D. Fruin, "Analysis of Need," in M. J. Brown, ed., *Social Issues and the Social Services.* (London: Charles Knight, 1974): 27–56.

n or protective services or some
ner need. Again, it may be a purely ad
hoc coalition of interested parties.

What persons should the planner-organizer mobilize into such a group? Perhaps more than anything else, participants should share a keen interest in and concern for the welfare of the target population. To be truly responsive, it must include representatives of the clients themselves. Potential for influence is another criterion for inclusion. The greater the individual prestige of the members, the greater their potential for collective influence. Influential members may include representatives of civic organizations, financial institutions, church organizations, and the like.

The higher the level of understanding about the problems of the target population among members of this group and the greater their expertise in the delivery of services to them, the more realistic will be the group's efforts and the greater the credibility of its suggestions to the community. Planners often enlist members of professional associations, physicians, social workers, etc., to assure this expertise. Having representatives of community agencies in the group increases the chances that their support for a new program will be forthcoming.

The function of such a group might be: to formulate the overall objectives of the new program; to identify the target population to be served; to identify sources of financial support for the new program; to present the program objectives to important institutions in the community (such as city council, county government, mental health board, United Fund); or all of these.

This group might also examine in detail the information and ideas developed by the planner-organizer.

Although the group itself need not develop a detailed plan for action, consensus regarding the type of program to be developed is helpful. Sometimes, of course, consensus is difficult to reach. Participants must be aware that differences in opinion or in conclusion are possible, and that these experiences can be healthy. An action group should provide the arena where ideas can be exchanged, proposals explored, and creative thinking encouraged. Ultimately, the group should formulate a basic plan for a new program by identifying and agreeing upon its major objectives and the population it should serve.

It is from this action group that a body in charge of defining or reviewing the policies for the new program may ultimately be drawn. This may be formalized as a board of directors, as an advisory council, or as an internal task force within an existing agency. The importance of an action group of this kind cannot be overemphasized. In the founding stages of the new program, the planner-organizer will need to rely heavily on its support, energy, and creativity, and most importantly, on its ability to mobilize necessary resources for the program.[8] The existence of an advocate group is no less crucial when the planner decides to launch the program within an existing agency, than when an entirely new structure is to be developed.

Assigning Responsibilities to a Board or Advisory Council

When the interest group has developed an adequate level of cohesion and

---

[8]M. Zald, "The Power and Function of Boards of Directors: A Theoretical Synthesis," *American Journal of Sociology,* 75 (July, 1969): 97–111.

formulated a basic statement regarding the mandate of the new program, it may be reconstituted as a formal board or council. It might then be given any of the following charges:

1. Development of a specific plan for the implementation of the new program
2. Responsibility for obtaining the basic resources to get the program started
3. Authority to hire or approve the director of the new program
4. Accountability for the activities of the program director and the disbursement of fiscal resources

The board or council must be helped to develop some internal division of labor to ensure that the necessary tasks will be fulfilled. This may involve designating members as president or chairman, secretary, treasurer, program planning subcommittee and the like. In addition, clear procedures for decision making must be formulated. These steps are of particular importance since the board's decisions are bound to have critical impact on the character and direction of the program.

Defining the Mission of the New Agency or Program

Establishment of a new program requires a carefully planned blueprint that specifies both mission and operational objectives. It requires a thoughtful assessment of the feasibility of achieving each objective and identification of the essential means for implementing it. Identified needs coupled with available resources and means must be translated into a series of program objectives aimed at meeting these needs.

The planner-organizer plays a crucial role at this stage. Possessing critical information regarding needs, as well as knowledge about potential resources, he or she must help the board, advisory council, or task force to reach consensus on what the organization's mission will be.

This mission is defined in terms of needs to be met, populations to be served, and services to be given. This mission, however, must be translated into operational terms. This requires first of all, *specification of the needs to be addressed.* These *needs are prioritized* (step no. 1), and *objectives specified* (step no. 2). It is not necessary that the most crucial need be acted on first. Sometimes what is most easily accomplished takes precedence on the planner's timetable. But the ultimate mission must always be kept in mind.

Specifying the Objectives

Specifying the objectives of the program is a process of moving from the general to the specific through careful assessment of alternatives. Assume, for example, that there is a consensus to focus on the needs and problems of aged persons living alone. In the process of identifying the needs of such a population there arises a growing awareness that they are most likely to experience problems in personal management. Such consensus does not lead directly to programs or services. Are these problems expressed in poor household management, in inadequate diet, in poor personal care, in social isolation? Which of these problems are of the greatest urgency? If agreement on the urgency of these problems can be reached, they may be ordered on a chart. In Figure 26.1, four specific problems are identified and ordered in terms of importance.

The next task (step no. 3) is to *specify* the "target" population to determine more exactly what older persons are to be helped by the new or expanded services. A similar process is followed to identify those who manifest the problems most acutely. These may be found in a minority population with low income, residing in a specific neighborhood. Agreements must be reached concerning this target population, as its characteristics will determine the feasibility of various alternatives for responding to the needs.

The choice of the target population should also reflect contingencies regarding the attainment of needed resources. Grants may be earmarked for certain categories of older persons. Certain agencies may be able to provide certain services only to older persons living in their geographical jurisdiction. Also, if it will take two years and $200,000 to develop a service for persons living in neighborhood X, while a similar level of service to persons in neighborhood Y is possible for far less and in only nine months, the choice of initial target population may be clear.

Next comes *exploring alternative program approaches* to dealing with specific problems of the target population (step no. 4). For example, in addressing the problem of nutritional deficiencies the objective may be to provide meals to a given population. Alternatively, the service might be an educational one, in which older persons are taught about proper diet (see Figure 26.2).

Similarly, in response to financial management problems, program objectives may include helping older persons to use their financial resources more efficiently, increasing access and use of banking services, and the like (see Figure 26.3).

Through this process a list of potential agency or program objectives can be developed.

Doing a Feasibility Study

After an inventory of alternative objectives has been formulated, a feasibility study of each (step no. 5) is necessary.

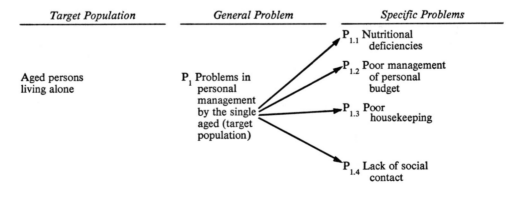

Target Population	General Problem	Specific Problems
Aged persons living alone	P_1 Problems in personal management by the single aged (target population)	$P_{1.1}$ Nutritional deficiencies $P_{1.2}$ Poor management of personal budget $P_{1.3}$ Poor housekeeping $P_{1.4}$ Lack of social contact

FIGURE 26.1

$P_{1.1}$
Nutritional
Deficiencies

O_1 Getting older persons
fed nutritiously

O_2 Increasing knowledge
about diets

FIGURE 26.2

Some of the criteria to be used are as follows:

1. What would be the fiscal cost?
2. What would be the manpower requirements?
3. What facilities and equipment would be needed?
4. How receptive to the objective could the community be expected to be?
5. What would be the anticipated support of the objective by other community agencies?

With such information on each objective, the planning task force must now shift its focus to the other side of the coin, namely *assessing the potential money and credit* the new program could hope to obtain (step no. 6). Some of the elements in such considerations are:

1. The availability of federal and/or state grants

2. Potential contributions by local government
3. Donations and contributions by local private organizations such as United Fund
4. In-kind contributions by social service agencies and social clubs
5. Availability of volunteers to offset or reduce staffing costs

In considering various sources of support, it is often necessary that the new program be affiliated with, or an integral component of, an existing agency. The auspice-giving or sponsoring agency may be able to allocate a certain portion of its budget for the new program, cut the administrative or overhead costs, or provide the organizational auspices required as qualification for grants.

Following the feasibility study, the board, council, or task force must then, on the basis of all the information on options and constraints, determine which services the new program will

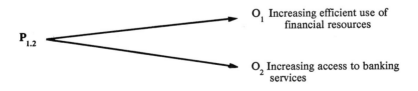

$P_{1.2}$

O_1 Increasing efficient use of
financial resources

O_2 Increasing access to banking
services

FIGURE 26.3

provide. This process culminates in a comprehensive policy statement specifying the consented objectives of the new program, the rationale for their adoption, the kinds of services to be provided, the clients to be served, and the individuals and groups who have assumed responsibility for the program and will be accountable for it to the public. Such a statement may serve as a charter, which may be required if the program is to become incorporated. In any event, it is a claim for domain and a statement of intent.

Obtaining Seed Money for Start-Up

Some planner-organizers assume that no project should commence unless all the resources needed to ensure its success are secured. This view fails to recognize that the most effective way to obtain needed resources may be to start the project and count on its visibility, demonstrated utility, and receptivity by clients to attract new resources. A program once started often generates its own momentum, attracting supporters unknown prior to the project's initiation and quickly developing spokesmen for itself in the community. This, of course, is not always the case. Many programs have foundered on inadequate funding, regardless of the need for the services. Every beginning necessitates some risk taking. The constraint of inadequate financial resources is a limiting factor. but it need not be an inhibiting one.

Nevertheless, basic "seed" or "start-up" money is often necessary. The planner-organizer with his knowledge of federal and state funds and grants, and through his contacts with local agencies, plays a crucial role in locating and obtaining funds. Together with the sponsoring agency or members of the

board, task force, or advisory council, he may initiate or provide technical assistance toward: (1) the submission of grant proposals to federal or state governmental agencies or to private foundations; (2) fund-raising campaigns with the help of local civic associations, fraternal clubs, or churches; (3) solicitation of donations from industrial and commercial organizations; (4) competition for local or revenue-sharing funds; (5) presentations before the United Fund; (6) development of contracts with established community agencies, such as a community mental health board, for the provision of funds for the new program; (7) locating in-kind resources (such as facilities and equipment) through enlistment of the aid of social clubs and the news media; (8) mobilizing volunteers to provide the initial manpower needed to start the program.

The initial resources gathered for the new program must be allocated for two basic purposes: to set up the actual service or program, and to promote the program in the community, attracting additional resources. Often, because of inadequate financing, there is a tendency to ignore the second purpose. Yet if those resources are not allocated to promotion, the program may quickly reach a dead end. While it may be difficult to divert limited dollars from needed services, failure to do so may be shortsighted, ignoring the fact that organizations must survive to be successful. Promotion requires more than money, however. It usually requires the assignment of staff to carry it out.

Specifying the Program Technology

The program objectives formulated in the new program's policy statement do not necessarily define the means to achieve them. The "set of means" by which the objectives are to be accomplished is called the *program technology* of the organization.

As the technology becomes articulated, it provides a series of guidelines for the type of staff and skills needed and the daily tasks to be performed in serving clients.[9]

The components of a program technology can be derived from the program objectives discussed earlier. In the previous example, the problem of nutritional deficiencies led to identification of two objectives—getting older persons fed nutritiously, and increasing their knowledge about diets. In attempting to implement the first of these objectives, the planner-organizer should explore every possible type of service that relates to providing adequate meals for the aging. Schematically, the process can be presented as shown in Figure 26.4.

Thus S_1 may be a meals-on-wheels service, S_2 may represent a cooperative cooking program for small groups of older persons in a given neighborhood, and S_3 might be a hot lunch program at

the neighborhood schools. The choice of the specific service may be based on such criteria as: (1) known success of similar programs elsewhere, (2) availability of expertise to implement it, (3) availability of other necessary resources, (4) receptivity by the aged to be served.

Assuming that the meals-on-wheels program has been adopted, the next series of specifications identifies the major tasks required to provide the service. For example, $S_{1.1}$ stands for organizing volunteers with cars; $S_{1.2}$, preparation of weekly visits by a nutritionist; $S_{1.3}$, preparing the meals at the kitchen of the local church, etc.

In short, this process provides a blueprint of all major tasks necessary to make the program operative.

Implementing the Program Technology

Once the choice of technology is made and its components identified, the new program can proceed to obtain the needed personnel. The program technology itself can be used to provide guidelines for the type of personnel required, and to specify the skills required of staff. It can, in fact, be used as the basis for writing job descriptions—

---

[9]On the concept of human service technology see Y. Hasenfeld and R. English, ed., *Human Service Organizations* (Ann Arbor: University of Michigan Press, 1974): 12–14.

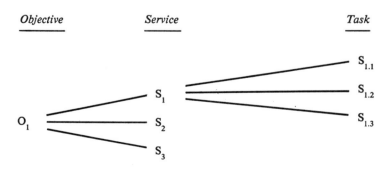

Objective	Service		Task

$$O_1 \quad \begin{cases} S_1 & \begin{cases} S_{1.1} \\ S_{1.2} \\ S_{1.3} \end{cases} \\ S_2 \\ S_3 \end{cases}$$

FIGURE 26.4

although these should not be overly prescriptive or rigid.

Any program, in its initial phase, will require a great deal of flexibility from its staff. Staff may be called upon to switch roles and assume various tasks as the need arises, even though tasks calling for particular skills must be performed by qualified personnel.

The success of the meals-on-wheels-program, for example, may hinge on the skills of a nutritionist needed to plan well-balanced meals. A program in which volunteers cook and deliver meals may only seem to be successful but in fact be missing the objective of getting older people fed nutritiously.

Once personnel are hired they must be given the responsibility to perform those tasks for which they are qualified. A nutritionist, for example, may not be the right person to supervise or organize drivers for the "wheels" part of the meals program. There is often a tendency to assume that a higher level of credentials implies proficiencies in many areas. Yet a nutritionist with an academic degree may know little about counseling or working with volunteers. Often a volunteer is much better qualified.

Developing an Appropriate Delivery Structure

Division of labor, then, is all-important. Effective division of labor requires three critical organizational decisions: Who does what? In what order must various tasks be performed? Who is accountable for what is done? The first decision requires identification of the tasks to be performed and the persons to perform them. The second decision is related to sequence and coordination. Some tasks must be performed before others can be begun.

Those that are performed sequentially may be separated among several work units. Other tasks must be performed together and belong to the same work unit.

In every organization there are certain sets of activities for which a supervisory person may be held accountable. The following principles may prove useful in guiding the development of an appropriate set of structural relationships.[10]

1. Those activities which need to be done simultaneously or in close proximity to each other are generally best grouped together. In the example given, the menu planning and the cooking activities should be in the hands of certain staff, while the handling of the delivery of the meals can be in the hands of another group. A set of activities which must be closely coordinated should be conducted or supervised by a single unit supervisor.

2. Activities that have different time and space schedules and contingencies should generally be grouped separately. For example, the meals-on-wheels program should be separated from a group counseling program.

3. Tasks which can be performed through explicit routines should be separated from tasks that are nonroutine. For example, determination of membership, registration, and fee assessment are routine tasks. They should not be performed by those who provide

---

[10]P. R. Lawrence and J. W. Lorsch, *Organizations and Environment* (Cambridge, MA: Harvard University Press, 1967).

consultation to community groups, a highly nonroutine activity.

4. Activities which require different ways of relating to the clients should be separated. For example, recreational activities for older people should not ordinarily be provided by the staff who give intensive individual counseling. While the same staff could conceivably do both, there ought to be a clear distinction between their two functions.
5. Staff should not be subjected to multiple supervision if at all possible. If it is necessary for more than one supervisor to relate to a particular staff person because of multiple roles that staff person performs, clear distinction must be made regarding the areas of jurisdiction of each supervisor.

The period of initial implementation of program technology is a period of trial and error. It requires a great deal of flexibility and no little tolerance for failure and for ambiguity. Open-mindedness and willingness to explore alternative routes are essential ingredients. During the early stages of program development, lines of communication with staff and clients must be kept as open as possible. Feedback is essential if the program is to adjust to unexpected exigencies. Staff who work directly with the community can provide invaluable information on the operationalization of the technology and its problems, its failures, and its successes.

It is probably desirable to have a "dry run" of the technology to test its organization and to acquaint the staff with its roles and duties. This can be accomplished through simulation techniques prior to putting the program into the field. Another approach is to select clients who are willing to volunteer for the service, even though the "bugs" in it may not have been fully shaken out.

Developing Inter-Agency Relationships

Concurrent with development of the technology of an agency or program is the development of a "support structure." This structure refers to the organization's patterned relationships to those elements in its environment that provide it with the resources necessary to attain its service and maintenance objectives. These elements include:

1. Clients or *consumers* of its service
2. Fiscal, manpower, technical, and other *resources* essential to the goal-oriented performance
3. *Complementary or supportive services* without which an agency's services would be unattainable, inadequate, or ineffective
4. Support or recognition from regulatory and auspice-providing bodies which give the program its *authority or mandate*

Managing the flow of these elements to and from the program requires establishment of a variety of exchange relationships with other organizations in the environment. This environment is described as an agency's "task environment." It is composed of all those groups and organizations whose actions directly affect the agency's goal attainment. Exchange activities leading to receiving elements from the task environment may take the form of: (1) competition, (2) contractual agreements, (3) cooptation, or (4) coalition formation.[11]

Agencies and programs are frequently in *competition* with each other for needed resources. One agency may compete with another for a federal grant by offering to serve more clients per dollar; it may compete to obtain better-trained staff by offering better benefits.

Human services agencies often make *contractual arrangements,* in which one organization agrees to do something for another (often in return for something). Without such arrangements, many services would be poorly performed or left undone. Examples abound. Agencies may exchange staff with complementary competencies on a temporary basis. One agency may do the mailing and publicity for another. A community group may contract with the Welfare Council to assess the service needs of a particular neighborhood. A county department of social services may purchase services from other agencies for its clients, including recreation, mental health, or protective services it does not have the staff to provide directly.

A new program or agency may also attempt to *coopt* key persons from other agencies whose services it seeks. Cooptation is accomplished through involving others in the design of a service or delivery of a service program. Cooptation strategies are employed when involvement and its rewards are likely to give those who might otherwise oppose a program a greater appreciation for why it is needed and what it is intended to accomplish. Their involvement may not only nullify poten-

tial opposition, but may actually increase support.

When agencies pool their resources in a joint venture, they form a coalition. Coalitions differ from contracts in that the latter require explicit agreements about what one party will do for the other. Coalitions, on the other hand, are binding only insofar as working together leads to some mutual goal attainment.

It is not essential for parties in an exchange relationship to benefit equally from the exchange, or to have fully complementary goals. It is only necessary that each part perceive the relationship as being of some benefit to itself.

The choice of each of these strategies depends on numerous conditions, particularly those pertaining to the perceived status and desirability of the new program in the community. The more secure and the greater the importance attached to the agency's services, for example, the more likely it is to employ competitive and contractual strategies.

Enlisting Needed Elements from the Environment

In the discussion that follows, attention will be given to how agencies recruit resources or manage the flow of needed elements from the environment itself.

Clients. Clients can be recruited through referrals by other agencies informed about the new program. Clients may also be informed of a service through the news media. To reach some isolated clients, it is often necessary to launch a door-to-door campaign using volunteers.

---

[11]K. Benson, "The Interorganizational Network as a Political Economy," *Administrative Science Quarterly,* 20 (June, 1975): 229–46.

Inadequate interpretation of an agency's services or intake policy may result in inappropriate referrals. An agency that turns away many ineligible clients causes a serious and unnecessary hardship to those clients and to its staff as well. It does harm to its own image, often damaging its relationships to other agencies. Thus it is critical for the new program to disseminate accurate and specific information about eligibility, both to the public and to other social agencies. Changes in eligibility criteria should be promptly communicated to all referral sources.

Permanent Sources of Funding. Often a new program must expend some of its initial and temporary resources on activities aimed at securing additional, more permanent sources of funding. Examples of such activities include: (1) entering into negotiations with the United Fund or United Way; (2) preparing grant applications to federal and state governmental agencies; (3) organizing a group of community influentials willing to sponsor an annual fund drive; (4) negotiating with local governmental bodies such as community mental health boards or county commissioners to incorporate the program under its sponsorship.

These and other activities require that certain staff members spend considerable time and energy meeting with potential funding sources, exchanging ideas, and presenting the agency's case. It is often desirable to designate a specific staff position for such activities and hire a person with considerable experience in mobilization of resources.

Knowledge and Expertise. No new program can function without adequate access to at least the minimal amount of necessary knowledge and ex-

pertise. In the long run, the success of an agency may hinge on the quality of services it offers, and that quality may be in direct proportion to the knowledge and expertise of its staff. Inadequate and erroneous information could be disastrous.

The planner-organizer can mobilize expertise through: (1) enlisting the services of experts in the field from nearby institutes and universities; (2) consulting with and visiting programs of similar nature in other communities; (3) arranging information exchanges between the staff of the new agency and that of an established one in another area; (4) exploring the available literature on the problems or needs the program attempts to deal with; (5) obtaining consultation and relevant publications from appropriate state and federal agencies; (6) arranging for training and continuing education seminars.

Complementary Services. The effectiveness of any program is dependent in no small measure on the availability of complementary services for its clients. It is not enough to give one's own service well. No matter how highly specialized a service, the organization providing that service must still assume some responsibility for the general welfare of its clients. It cannot shy away from its obligation to make sure that clients receive other needed services.

This is particularly true when the effectiveness of the very services provided by the agency is dependent on the complementary services of other agencies. For example, if an agency develops a child-care program, it cannot in good conscience ignore the health needs of the children, and it may contract for periodic medical examinations with the local "well baby" clinic. A nutrition program for the aged might not be successful unless it also enlisted cooperation from the outreach staff of the Information and Referral Service, the Visiting Nurses Association, or the Mental Health Crisis Center.

A new program must identify the crucial services it will need to enlist from other agencies and programs in order to meet its own objectives. It is within the planner-organizer's responsibility to see to it that such services are or will be made available. Without them, the new program may fail.

These complementary services can be arranged through several means: (1) actual purchase of such services from another agency; (2) contract of exchange of services between the two agencies; (3) a unilateral decision by the other agency to provide the needed services as a gesture of goodwill; (4) a coalition of several agencies with different services all committed to serve the same clients.

Monitoring and Evaluation. Every program is subject to the monitoring and evaluation of some overseeing agencies. These may be state licensing organizations, other governmental units, local administrative boards, professional associations, citizens' groups, or other interested parties. Often these regulatory agencies exert considerable influence. They may impose very specific requirements for the agency to meet.

A state agency, for example, may annually audit the financial transactions of the program, or it may check the extent to which the facilities conform to state regulations. A professional organization may be responsible for accred-

itation without which outside grants cannot be received.

The planner-organizer must see to it that the program has developed the appropriate mechanisms by which it can meet the requirements of these regulatory agencies. This is not a mere bureaucratic formality. Accrediting bodies and standard-setting organizations are often the key sources of legitimation and support of a new program. For example, an agency approved for internship of urban planners will gain considerable prestige and recognition in the professional community and could, therefore, attract good staff. Similarly, an agency that receives a favorable evaluation by a state agency is more likely to obtain future state grants.

Maintaining appropriate relations with the various agencies and organizations necessitates the establishment of "boundary roles" for program staff. Persons in these roles develop and maintain linkages between the new program and relevant organizations in its environment.[12] A staff person may be designated as the liaison with the state social service agency, county government, local hospital, etc. The duties of boundary personnel include: (1) establishment of the necessary relations with outside groups and organizations; (2) resolution of whatever difficulties may arise in the course of a relationship; (3) obtaining relevant up-to-date information about the activities of the partner to the relationship; (4) establishment of contacts with key staff in that organization or group who may be favorable

---

[12]H. Aldrich and D. Herker, "Boundary Spanning Roles and Organization Structure," mimeographed paper (Ithaca, NY: Cornell University, 1974).

toward the agency; (5) alerting the agency to new developments that may alter the relations between the two.

The ability of an agency to seize on new opportunities in the environment, to adapt to new changes, and to be prepared for new constraints depends on the effective job performed by the occupants of these boundary roles. They serve as the ears and eyes of the agency, without which its ability to adapt, grow, and develop would be seriously hampered.

Legitimation and Social Support. Underlying all the inter-agency relations described above is a pervasive need of the program to obtain legitimation and social support. The success of the program in achieving viability is dependent on its ability to become a recognized "institution" in the community. Once the program is perceived by key elements in the community as desirable, indispensable, and an important contributor to the general welfare of the community, it has been "legitimated." Legitimacy implies that the community is willing to accept it as a viable and necessary component of the service structure.[13]

Support and legitimacy do not come easily; neither are they cheap. Concerted efforts to achieve them must be made by program staff. Support generally requires at the very least a satisfied community group or gratified clients. This is the core of an agency's constituent base. This constituency should also include other social service agencies that benefit in some direct way from the services offered by the new program. The constituent base should also include community influentials and professionals who are committed to the well-being of the target population.

Other mechanisms to promote support for the program include: lectures and presentations by staff to various community groups; establishment of an influential board of directors; public visits to the agency's facilities; reports by the news media of the activities of the agency; etc. But necessary as these are, none is sufficient without solid constituent support.

Getting Staff to Perform Adequately

Persons choose to work in organizations and agencies for a variety of reasons. They often join an agency staff with personal expectations and aspirations. The agency, on the other hand, expects them to perform in accordance with its needs, demands, and schedules. There may be many points of incongruity between personal aspirations of staff and organizational expectations. The larger the discrepancies, the greater the strains and the less likelihood that staff will perform adequately.[14]

Planner-organizers can help a new program determine adequate criteria for staff selection and realistic expectations for performance. Individuals who become employees of an agency make a contractual agreement whereby they accept the role requirements assigned to them in exchange for the various inducements provided by the agency (salary, work satisfactions, good working conditions).

A great deal of misunderstanding can be avoided if the agency specifies its re-

---

[13]P. Selznick, *Leadership in Administration* (New York: Harper, 1957).

[14]L. W. Porter, E. E. Lawler and J. R. Hackman, *Behavior in Organizations* (New York: McGraw-Hill, 1975).

quirements at the point of recruitment. Clearly written requirements can guide the agency to hire staff who have the needed skills, aptitudes, and attributes. Recruitment, however, is only a limited mechanism to ensure that staff will perform adequately. Socialization is a critical organizational process through which staff internalizes agency norms and values and learns specific role obligations. Two important socialization mechanisms are training and staff development.

In the final analysis, however, effective and efficient role performance by staff is predicated on the design of a work unit that is congruent with the tasks it has to perform.[15] Tasks can be categorized by two major variables: (1) *Task difficulty,* which refers to the degree of complexity, amount of knowledge needed, and reliance on nonroutine decision making. For example, determination of service eligibility may be a very simple task based on few explicit decision rules, while planning community services necessitates consideration of many factors, reliance on extensive knowledge, and complex decision making. (2) *Task variability,* which refers to the degree of uniformity and predictability of the work to be done. For example, preparation of monthly statistical reports is a relatively uniform and predictable task, while developing ties with various agencies calls for a variety of procedures.

Tasks which are low in complexity and variability call for a work unit structure which is essentially bureaucratic in the classical sense of the word. Tasks which are high in complexity and variability necessitate a work unit structure which is "human relational."

In a bureaucratic structure line staff has very limited discretion; there is a clear hierarchy of authority; and coordination of staff is based on an extensive set of rules and operating procedures. In a human relation structure, the discretion of line staff is high; relations with supervisory staff are collegial; and coordination is based on feedback from the other staff.

When the task has both complex and noncomplex components or variable and nonvariable elements which cannot be separated, a "mixed" structure will be most appropriate.[16] Based on the nature of the "mix" such a structure may provide line staff with high discretion in some specific areas and none in others. For example, the task of intake may be of such type. Workers may have high discretion in defining the problem of the client, but none concerning determination of fees, scheduling, and the like.

It can be readily shown that each structure is most efficient if appropriately matched with the characteristics of the tasks to be performed. This is so because the work unit structure is designed to elicit the behavioral and role prescriptions that each task requires.

When conflict arises between two units or among several staff members because of overlapping jurisdictions, lack of coordination, or lack of mutual understanding, an ad hoc task force to deal with the conflict may prove helpful. In a multi-service center, for example, a conflict could arise between the outreach staff and the counseling staff. The former may feel that they do not get any help in scheduling appoint-

---

[15]C. Perrow, op. cit., Chapter 3.

[16]Eugene Litwak, "Models of Organization Which Permit Conflict," *American Journal of Sociology,* 67 (Sept. 1961), pp. 177–84.

ments and in coping with problems they encounter in the field. The counseling staff, on the other hand, may feel that it is asked to do the work of the outreach staff and that the outreach staff fails to understand what the counselors are trying to accomplish. To resolve the conflict, an ad hoc task force might be established with representatives of both parties to arrive at an acceptable solution, or an integrator position might be created.

The integrator role requires that a third party become the mediator between parties in the dispute. The integrator is generally a person with adequate knowledge of the activities of the units of persons he or she attempts to bring together, and may be in an authority position in relation to both. In the example above, the integrator might be a person who has expertise in both outreach and counseling, so that his directives to both units will be respected. His function is to identify areas where coordination needs to be established and procedures that can be developed to minimize conflict. He also serves as a mediator, interpreting to each unit the issues and problems the other unit needs to solve.[17]

A further word: conflict is not necessarily dysfunctional to an organization. To the contrary. It can help to effectively identify operational problems, philosophical differences, or staff deficiencies. Properly managed, conflict situations assure a changing and responsive pattern of agency operations. Conflict is often a symptom of healthy adaptation to changing needs and expectations.

---

[17]P. R. Lawrence and J. W. Lorsch, op. cit., Chapter 9.

Developing an Intelligence and Feedback System

There is a strong correlation between the extent to which an organization can adapt to changes in its environment and the effectiveness of its "intelligence" system. An effective system enables the organization to evaluate its own activities in relation to changes and developments in its environment. Without such a system, the organization may find that its services and modes of operation are rapidly becoming obsolete. An effective and efficient intelligence system can provide the program with the new information and knowledge required to adjust to changes from both within and without.

In general, an intelligence system fulfills three interrelated functions: monitoring the external task environment of the agency, internal auditing of staff and client activities, and evaluation of the agency's outputs.

The *monitoring of the agency's external environment* is intended to alert the agency to important changes and developments in the various units upon which it is dependent. These include federal and state programs, the programs of local social service agencies, new legislation, etc. Monitoring activities can also be directed at identifying new developments in service techniques. Finally, external monitoring is required to inform the agency of changes in the character of the population it seeks to serve.

The main purpose of *internal auditing* is to inform the agency of the activities of the staff vis-à-vis the clients. Information generated by internal auditing enables staff to assess the progress of the clients and to determine future courses of action, and enables the agency management to evaluate the operation of the service technology. Without such evaluation, the agency has no way of determining whether it is achieving its service goals at some reasonable level.

Evaluation of agency *outputs* occurs after clients have been served by the agency. The emphasis is on what happened to clients and how many were served.

Fulfillment of each of these intelligence functions requires several steps: (1) collection of the necessary data; (2) analysis of those data so that they are useful and used; (3) transmission of relevant information to appropriate decision makers; and (4) interpretation of the information in order to generate additional knowledge. Since the final step of the intelligence process is the generation of knowledge, malfunction in any of the previous steps is likely to adversely affect the capability of the intelligence system to develop that knowledge.

Effective external monitoring systems are dependent on the performance of boundary personnel who maintain close ties with external units and who actively scan the environment for new resources. Staff members assuming boundary roles may develop specialized working relations with a given set of organizations. The contact person gathers essential information about the availability of given resources and the conditions of their use, and transmits this information to staff members who can use it. This is a necessary function if the agency is to remain up-to-date on changes and developments in its environment.

Personnel who perform boundary roles must develop expert knowledge about the characteristics of the resources in their areas of specialization. They must also be able to develop cooperative and informative relationships with the major suppliers of these resources, and must develop analytic skills necessary to assess and evaluate developments and changes in the nature of the environment. Perhaps most important, they must acquire effective and efficient communication channels to decision makers within their own organization.

Internal auditing enables staff to carry out its activities on an informed and rational basis. Internal auditing is directed at (1) the case or client level, and (2) the operational or departmental level. The function of internal auditing at the case or client level is to provide staff with all the necessary information for decision making at every juncture of the client's career in the agency.

This often requires the use of a client "case record." Each client served by the agency should have a record which includes basic information about him, his own perception of his needs, and the service objectives for him. Actions taken by staff and periodic evaluations of the client's performance in the agency should be systematically recorded and the impact of those services noted. A client record could be organized around topics such as background information, health status, income, housing, nutrition needs, and interpersonal problems. Each action or referral should be recorded in the appropriate topic section.

A scheme must also be developed for the uniform classification and codification of the information items to be used; and procedures for information gathering, update, and retrieval must be planned. This process requires that the basic information the agency plans to collect and use be classified and coded in a system of categories that are explicitly defined, unambiguous, and uniformly applied throughout the entire agency. This process can be used to enable staff to develop an orderly and rational sequence of services aimed at assisting the client to achieve his service goals. It can also be used to monitor the actions taken and to signal staff when new or different decisions need to be made.

Auditing procedures at the "operations" level attempt to answer basic managerial questions about the modes of operation of the agency or units thereof. These could include the analysis of all activities done for clients suffering from visual handicaps; the success of various treatment technologies; analysis of the type of referrals used by the agency; or the responses of staff to clients who drop out. The findings of such auditing enable the agency to evaluate its operating procedures and make necessary adjustments or changes.

Findings may specify such information as (1) the type of clients arriving at the agency, the range of problems they present, and the services they request; (2) assessment of the services given to different cohorts of clients, the consequences of those services, or whether adequate follow-up is done by staff; (3) the performance of various staff regarding size of case load; average number of contacts with clients; (4) type of resources or intervention techniques used.

Perhaps the most important function of an intelligence system is to enable the agency to evaluate its service outcomes. In the final analysis, an agency can justify its existence only if it can show competence in attaining its service objectives. To do so, it must develop reliable procedures to evaluate the use of its services. The problems involved in attempts to measure are extremely complex. They stem from the fact that there is no consensus regarding a norm of "success," nor are there valid and reliable methods to measure success.

There is, however, some risk of developing inappropriate *output measures*. This can be observed when the number of clients seen by staff becomes the measure of success. When this criterion is adopted by staff, it may gear its efforts to obtaining a high ratio of clients per worker while reducing the amount of time spent with each. There is also a tendency of organizations to adopt "symbolic" criteria when faced with the difficulties of developing substantive criteria. Symbolic criteria are testimonies by staff or clients, display of the "successful" client, self-evaluation, and other approaches that may be highly misleading and in fact could cover up serious failures by the organization.

Any evaluation of an agency may be painful in that it is likely to expose serious gaps between expectations and accomplishments. Such an exposure may undermine the legitimacy of the agency. Yet an agency cannot improve its services if it lacks adequate outcome measures or fears the consequences of such measures. In the long run, lack of adequate outcome measures may lead toward the deterioration of the organization.

An agency's service goals are often multidimensional, with various subgoals and tasks. The design of valid and reliable outcome measures requires recognition of this fact. In general, outcome measures should relate to the goals of each subsystem in the agency. Outcome measures differentiate between the initial state of the client at the point of entry and the terminal state of that client at point of exit from the agency.

In a complex service program, the new client goes through a series of assessments, which are often updated and corrected with the collection of additional information. These assessments may cover a range of attributes and problems, such as personal care, motivation to participate, health status, financial problems, etc. These include the gamut of areas in which the agency activity plans to intervene in order to improve the status of the client. At point of exit, these same attributes are reassessed and the amount of progress shown by the client through actual performance or his own evaluation is recorded. Because an agency may have succeeded more in some areas than in others, one measure cannot summarize the range of activities undertaken by the agency, nor can it reflect the complexity of attributes and problems presented by the client.

Multiple measures are necessary. Each of these should include concrete and precise descriptions of client attributes and behaviors. These measures must become an integral part of the service technology itself. They may serve as assessment devices for the client's progress in every stage of his association with the agency. In fact, they should logically follow the activities that have been specified in the service technology. They should be embedded in the daily work of the staff and not external measures imposed on the agency without direct reference to what it actually does. Needless to say, such measures must be constantly reexamined, updated and refined.[18]

Successful use of measures for service outcome necessitates a comprehensive and effective *follow-up* system. Without one, the information necessary for evaluation could not be obtained. The basic function of follow-up is to gather the necessary information regarding the consequences for the client of services given. It is the basic mechanism by which the agency can find out what has happened to its clients. Unfortunately, few service agencies have established such sophisticated measures. In a number of cases, in fact, output measures of the type described could be overly costly in relation to the sophistication of the services provided.

CONCLUDING NOTE

The process of establishing a new program is highly complex and requires considerations of many inter- and intra-organizational factors. It is not surprising, therefore, to find that while community workers and action groups may conceive of imaginative and innovative service programs, their ability and success in implementing them are at best modest. As was shown in the above discussion, each step in the process of implementation requires a particular set of skills, expertise, and resources. Inability to enlist them at crucial points in the program development may lead to failure or to detrimental consequences in the ability of the program to fulfill its objectives.

---

[18]C. Weiss, *Evaluation Research* (Englewood Cliffs, NJ: Prentice-Hall, 1972).

Thus, the systems approach used here alerts the planner-organizer to the intricate interrelations among the various building blocks of the program. It identifies the points at which the establishment of certain subsystems must assume priority over other organizing activities. Nevertheless, it should not be concluded that the model presented here is deterministic, in that each of the steps identified must be so followed. It should not be assumed a priori that an organization is a tightly coupled system in which each component must be closely articulated with all others. There is evidence to suggest that many programs may function quite adequately even if some components or subsystems are not fully developed or are not closely inter-linked. The systems approach advocated here enables the planner-organizer to assess at each point in the program development process the need for the establishment of certain organizational components. For example, he may find that a feasibility study is unnecessary since resources have already been earmarked for certain types of programs, or that whatever service technology will be developed, support of key groups in the environment is assured.

Moreover, it has been stressed throughout that agency or program development involves a great deal of trial and error in the face of many unknown parameters. The approach developed here merely attempts to identify the critical parameters the planner-organizer must consider and thus reduce some of the risks that are inherent in any program implementation.

27.

Lynne Clemmons Morris

THE CIRCUIT RIDING ADMINISTRATOR: A NETWORK BASED, MACRO GENERALIST APPROACH TO CAPACITY BUILDING IN SMALL COMMUNITIES

One consequence of the current population redistribution to nonmetropolitan areas and the continued growth of outlying portions of metropolitan areas has been the search by small communities for alternative structures of government and public service delivery. With population growth in small communities has come the need to make decisions concerning appropriate public services in the context of a complex and changing local, regional, state, and federal planning and funding structure. Studies of residents of small communities indicate a preference for retaining the qualities of representativeness and accessibility which characterize government in many small communities (Sokolow, 1981) and a questioning of approaches to development based on centralization, bureau-

Source: Unpublished. Reproduced by permission of the author.

cratization, and regional or county consolidation. The rapid influx of newcomers also has produced some resistance to professionalization of public services, which in many small communities has meant displacement of local leaders, part-time employees, and volunteers by professionals from outside the local community.

Increasingly, small communities are turning to alternative forms of micropolitan development (Tweeten and Brinkman, 1976) characterized by networks and cooperative arrangements for sharing resources among small communities. One such alternative is the circuit riding administrator or planner. The circuit riding approach to service delivery in nonmetropolitan areas is not new, but the use of this approach at the macro level of public service planning and administration is a much more recent development. Circuit riding planning or administration has been implemented in at least twenty states as an alternative to consolidation or technical assistance provided through regional planning structures such as councils of governments. Most of the programs serve nonmetropolitan areas, but they also are developing among groups of small communities within metropolitan areas. The program frequently is initiated in response to requests from a group of small communities. Assistance in formulating an intergovernmental contract for the program usually is provided through an organization such as a state agency, regional council of governments, or state municipal association (Shannon, 1981). Historically, a major source of funding for the program has been the Intergrovernmental Personnel Act. Communities participating in the program must assume increased responsibility for funding over a specified time period.

The title and functions of the position vary and have included descriptions such as circuit riding administrator, circuit riding planner, circuit riding manager, and roving administrator. Most persons occupying or evaluating the position have suggested that such titles accurately describe the intergovernmental or interorganizational character, but not the functions, of the role. A more appropriate description is that of macro generalist (Shannon, 1981), combining planning and administrative functions, who provides advice and consultation and who stimulates coordination and capacity building in a network of small communities. These circuit riding, macro generalist programs provide a unique opportunity to analyse new types of roles combining functions which traditionally are separated in larger bureaucratic organizations, the problems which may arise when these roles are combined, and the potential of these roles for strengthening decision making and the provision of public services at the local community level.

A CASE EXAMPLE

The circuit riding or roving administrator program in South Carolina was begun in 1978. The program first was suggested by the mayors of three small communities. Development of program structure and funding was coordinated through the Upper Savannah Council of Governments. Currently, sixty percent of the program costs are funded through the Council of Governments and forty percent are assumed by the participating local communities.

Currently, the participants in the program include five communities in three adjacent counties. The towns range in size from 500 to 2500 population. Distances between communities range from six to thirty miles. Major sources of employment include agriculture and the textile industry. Much of the land in two of the counties is national forest, a situation which affects community patterns of development in terms of tax base, land availability, and employment opportunities. In all five communities the form of government consists of a part-time mayor and a town council.

The circuit riding or roving administrator provides a needed service which can be developed only through a sharing of resources. Each community could not afford to hire a full-time administrator, although each community felt that current levels of demand for and complexity of public services required administrative assistance beyond that of a part-time mayor. Through participation in the circuit riding administrator program, each community obtained the part-time services of an administrator. The differences between a roving and a full-time administrator are more qualitative than quantitative, however. The result is *not* that each community receives the traditional services of a city administrator one or two days a week. Instead, the roving administrator program has resulted in a unique type of macro practice role which combines more typical administrative tasks such as preparation of budgets and personnel policies with horizontal work roles and relationships involving advice giving, consultation, and network coordination.

Community involvement in the circuit rider network also has produced a number of systemic changes among the participants, both in relationships of the communities to each other and in their relationship to larger structures of decision making such as county government and regional councils of government. An unanticipated consequence of the circuit riding administration program has been its effect on intercommunity coordination of programs and services. This coordination has been achieved indirectly through network participation rather than through creating a superstructure, such as an interagency council, whose primary purpose is coordination. Participation in such an intercommunity network coordinated through the roving administrator also raises a number of questions concerning what factors make successful network functioning possible.

Descriptions of circuit riding administrator programs vary in terms of the degree to which the role is viewed primarily as a way to bring administrative services to small communities which cannot afford a full time administrator (Prince, 1974) or as a purposeful attempt to create alternative forms of public service administration and planning which recognize community diversity and are based on mutual agreement rather than vertical authority (Watts, 1980). These differences may result in part from the varied form which the program has assumed in different community networks. Doherty (1979) has argued that the current state of governmental structure in nonmetropolitan areas is one of innovation, diversity, and natural experimentation with alternative systems and that this situation is preferable to centralized outside efforts to develop more uniform rural public policy. The circuit riding administrator program in South

Carolina provides an opportunity to examine (1) development of a macro practice role which is seen by program participants as having both traditional and innovative components, (2) systemic changes in intercommunity coordination which have resulted from program participation, and (3) factors essential for successful network functioning.

ROLE DEVELOPMENT

Most studies of circuit riding administrator programs describe the role as that of a macro generalist which includes a number of administrative and planning functions. Roles performed by the circuit riding administrator include grant writer, administrative assistant, advisor, consultant, planner, supervisor, staff developer, program developer, coordinator, and provider of technical assistance. In two surveys of circuit riding administrators, the primary roles identified were advisor (Wannamaker and McLeod, 1975) and consultant (Wannamaker and

Stansbury, 1977). Although called a circuit riding administrator or manager, role occupants rarely use the terms administrator or manager in describing their roles. Circuit riders distinguish their position from that of a traditional administrator because of their lack of formal authority to make actual policy decisions or hire and fire staff.

The formal job description for South Carolina's roving administrator program includes eleven functions. Roles indicated by these job activities include administrative assistant, advisor, technical assistant, planner, consultant, and coordinator. The job is described in terms of system support or capacity building activities; the roving administrator "assists," "advises," "prepares," "apprises," "assesses," and "represents." This assistance is provided to mayors, council members, municipal clerks, and employees of public service agencies. Thus the roving administrator works in conjunction with a wide range of small town government officials and public service providers. Examples of the roving administrator's roles and tasks are listed below:*

*Role	*Tasks Performed
Advisor	Makes recommendations on managerial problems
Administrative assistant	Prepares budgets and schedules budget hearings
Coordinator (among communities)	Negotiates intergovernmental service contracts
Technical assistance	Develops options for financial and investment practices. Prepares grant applications.
Mediator	Gets mayors together to discuss problems and develop new ways of working together
Linkage agent (to external agencies)	Represents municipalities in discussions with county, state, and federal agencies
Staff development consultant	Drafts personnel policies. Assists clerks in interpreting policies and municipal ordinances
Evaluator	Assesses efficiency and effectiveness of municipal service delivery systems

The circuit riding administrator has evolved a role in which a wide range of community practice and administrative activities are carried out. Using current community practice terminology, the role could best be described as that of a macro generalist. The role combines many administrative and community practice activities. In the absence of vertical authority usually associated with administrative roles, organizational change and staff development have been promoted through technical assistance, consultation, evaluation, and the creation and maintenance of horizontal working relationships with public agency staff, mayors, and council members. Community practice activities have centered around coordination and capacity building through training and advice giving.

Why has the circuit riding administrator role evolved into that of a macro generalist? What are the advantages and disadvantages of such a practice role in promoting organizational development and building community capacity? Reasons for the combining of administrative and community practice into a macro generalist practice role include:

1. The absence of other professional staff. Carrying out and developing capacity of local government to carry out public service functions requires performance of a variety of macro level tasks. In the absence of other professional staff, these tasks must be assumed by the circuit riding administrator or other staff must be enabled to carry out the tasks.
2. The varying needs of the set of communities employing the circuit rider. Each community requires a somewhat different combination of administrative and planning activities. Adapting to these diverse needs has broadened the practice role of the roving administrator.
3. The need for ongoing administrative activity in the absence of a full time administrator and traditional administrative authority. The roving administrator must use a variety of macro practice roles to mobilize and coordinate the work of others and create a system of shared responsibility for carrying out administrative activity.

The roving administrator's role as an organization generalist evolved over time. Building trust, credibility, and mutual understanding was required before the full range of macro practice roles could be implemented in each community and, over time, the roving administrator became aware of the range of needs of the local governments. Getzels and Thurow (1979) have emphasized the need for role sequencing in establishing the planner's role in small rural communities. They suggest beginning with technical assistance and performing a specific, needed, visible task to establish the planner's credibility and community awareness of the value of planning. Similarly, the circuit riding administrator program began with emphasis on technical aspects of the position: development of personnel procedures, codification of business licensing ordinances, review of changes in state laws affecting municipalities. Over time as trust developed and mayors and council members became more comfortable with the program, the roving administrator's role expanded to include advice regarding financial and investment practices, serving as a sounding board to mayors, responding to requests and complaints of community residents, setting agendas for town councils, and suggesting procedures for decision making in local government. Thus today the role emphasizes advice, planning, and making recommendations regarding financial and political decision-making processes of local government.

From the perspective of the roving administrator, the most important feature of the role is that it allows for periodic advice giving. The roving administrator is present in each community only one or two days a week, although each community can get in touch with the administrator on other days. Since the roving administrator's presence is periodic, continuous administrative activity or supervision of staff is not possible. Rather the administrator must provide good, clear direction and staff training; make recommendations; leave and allow staff, mayors, and council members to carry out an activity themselves; then return, periodically monitor, follow-up, and evaluate performance and progress. The roving administrator views this situation as an ideal environment for capacity building. Local government staff, mayors, and decisionmakers must carry out tasks autonomously rather than relying on a full-time administrator to perform them or supervise performance. In contrast to an outside planner or consultant, the roving administrator does not make recommendations and leave but instead makes recommendations, leaves, gives local staff and decisionmakers time to implement recommendations, and then returns periodically to follow-up and evaluate.

Two major limitations of the role are perceived by the roving administrator.

The first is that the roving administrator does not make decisions concerning staff hiring, firing, or promotion. Instead change in staff composition, roles, and behavior must be negotiated with the staff, mayor, or council members. A second perceived limitation arises from the intermittent presence of the administrator in the organization. The roving administrator cannot always intervene at the appropriate moment. Much intervention occurs after the fact. Actions must be reexamined, undone, and redone. This situation is described by the roving administrator as "the problem of inefficient intervention."

Essential to carrying out this macro generalist role is effective time and task management. The roving administrator's time must be divided up among a variety of tasks and shared by several communities. Initially, time was managed through equal division with the roving administrator spending one day a week in each community. This arrangement was abandoned because the communities' workloads were not equal, blocks of time could not be allocated to undertaking new projects such as preparing grant proposals, and time was needed for work with external organizations such as county government. Currently, a more flexible plan for allocation of time is used. Four days a week are allocated to work in the five communities. One day a week is spent at the regional planning agency or other external organizations. The roving administrator visits each community at least every two weeks. Approximately one to three days are spent in each community depending upon workload. This arrangement allows the circuit riding administrator to modify time spent in each community when special projects are undertaken. Flexibility to respond to immediate needs also has been added. All the communities and the regional planning agency have a copy of the administrator's schedule and can contact the administrator if special assistance is needed. The schedule also is adjusted to coordinate with evening meetings such as council sessions in each community. Although increased flexibility has improved problems of time allocation, some persons interviewed felt that the network of participants was too large. Sharing an administrator among three communities was seen as a preferable network size.

The need to manage travel time is an additional consideration. Participants felt that distance between communities should not be greater than about forty miles. Otherwise, it was felt that too much of the administrator's time would be spent in travel. Communities participating in this program were from six to thirty miles apart; participants felt this was a manageable distance.

SYSTEMIC CHANGES WITHIN COMMUNITIES

The circuit riding administrator's macro generalist practice role has developed and changed over time through a process of negotiation, trust building, and mutual adaptation among program participants. The systemic consequences of this developmental approach to use of professional administrators in small communities appear to have been quite different from situations in which growing small communities have introduced professional administration by replacing part-time local officials with full time administrators. Cortese and Jones (1977) in their study of energy-impacted communities in Colorado, found a 100 percent displacement of local leaders by outside

professional administrators in a three year period. Many displaced oldtimers indicated a sense of loss and estrangement from community life.

In contrast, the circuit riding administrator program has both introduced professional public service administration and retained locally-elected officials. This approach to capacity building in local government is seen in interviews with program participants. Capacity building has resulted from the efforts of both the roving administrator and community leaders to (1) negotiate and renegotiate shared responsibility for public service decision making and administration, and (2) use a systemic perspective in which proposed changes are viewed in terms of their implications for different actors in the structure of local government.

Evidence of continuous working toward shared responsibility is the roving administrator's goal, described as "my number one priority," of helping local communities to look at the way in which they make decisions. The roving administrator observes mayoral and council decision-making processes and has concluded that frequently decisions are made too quickly and with insufficient information. On the basis of this assessment, the roving administrator encourages local governments to examine issues in terms of:

1. What issues raised at council meetings require immediate action?
2. What issues should be received as information to be acted upon at a later date?
3. What issues require additional information and who is responsible for presenting that information to local government officials? This is an activity frequently undertaken

by the roving administrator. Capacity building, however, implies that local government officials can assess and state their information needs with respect to a particular decision. The roving administrator has moved from introducing technical information into local decision-making processes to helping local officials examine information needs.

In the absence of traditional administrative authority, the roving administrator has to negotiate proposed changes with members of local government in each community, including staff of public service agencies, mayors, and council members. Consequently, the roving administrator assesses proposed changes in terms of their systemic impact on local government functioning. An example of this systemic perspective is the activities currently being undertaken by the roving administrator in establishing a computerized information system for local government in one of the communities. Rather than hire outside personnel to operate the computerized system, the roving administrator assessed the career opportunities and problems for local staff which might result from the introduction of the new technology. Having found an assistant town clerk who wanted to take advantage of career opportunities which the introduction of a computerized information system might provide, the roving administrator has become involved in negotiated staff development, community decision making, and fitting the new technology to locally available resources.

Negotiated staff development has involved encouraging the assistant town clerk to take classes in computer literacy at a local technical college, rewriting the assistant town clerk's job description and salary structure to include information processing activities, and building support for this new job description with the mayor and with city council. Other small communities using computers in local government have been identified, and the roving administrator has persuaded a local industrial employer to loan out data processing personnel as consultants in developing the information system. Would that all administrators worked as carefully to adapt technology to local community and organization needs, conditions, and resources!

Participants' sense of capacity building through the gradual development of shared responsibility between the circuit riding administrator and local government officials is reflected in this segment of an interview with a mayor of one of the communities:

MAYOR: "The longer the program is here, the more we learn to do things ourselves and the more we depend on him (the roving administrator)."

INTERVIEWER: "Why do you say that you depend on him more now than you used to?"

MAYOR: "Because he has learned about us, what we need and how we work, and we have learned how he can help us, how we can best use him. The more we learn about each other, the more help we are to each other, and the more we can help ourselves."

This exchange illustrates the introduction of professional administrative activity into an organization through mutual adaptation, so that both the administrative role and the organizational structure itself are strengthened over time. This process results in a sense of both increased interdependence and capacity for independent functioning.

INTERCOMMUNITY COORDINATION THROUGH NETWORK FORMATION

Sharing the services of a circuit riding administrator required the participating communities to engage in joint planning and work out agreements for time sharing and funding of the program. Once the program was established, the participating communities became a network linked together through the shared services of a roving administrator. An unintended consequence of this network formation has been improved cooperation and coordination among the participating communities. Indeed, the program was originally established as an alternative to regional planning and participation in formal coordinating structures. Yet through membership in a decentralized network emphasizing community autonomy, increased cooperation and coordination of public services has occurred among the communities.

Litwak and Rothman (1979) have noted that awareness of interdependence is a key factor influencing levels of interagency coordination. In the formation of a network linked through the sharing of an administrator, a structure was created which facilitated awareness of interdependence. Initially, awareness increased through information sharing. The roving administrator was able to adapt tasks accomplished in one community, such as the development of municipal ordinances, to other communities. Through the roving administrator communities became

aware of the payoffs of sharing information, recognized that they shared some common problems, and began to see each other as problem solving resources.

A second type of coordinating activity was the circuit riding administrator's representing the set of communities in work with county government officials. Communities experienced increased clout when their interests were represented as a group and, when their interests differed, developed trust in the roving administrator's ability to work toward a solution which was fair to all participants. Later efforts at coordination included the roving administrator's taking a mediator role and getting mayors together to work out community disputes. Recently the communities have engaged in joint planning and established a joint fire protection agreement.

Network membership required community officials to meet periodically to evaluate the program, to recognize special community needs for the roving administrator's services which require adjustment of program work schedules, and to maintain an equitable plan for sharing the administrator's services. Network maintenance activities increase awareness of interdependence. Mayors stated that network membership increased the roving administrator's accountability to each community because if an individual community became dissatisfied and pulled out, the entire program could fall apart. Through network maintenance the communities have developed a shared sense that "we are all in this together."

Critical to network development and increased intercommunity coordination has been the central figure linking all the communities together, the roving administrator. Local officials stated that sharing the roving administrator was the key factor which facilitated community coordination. In contrast to efforts at coordination which stress the role of external planning agencies and neutral outside observers who allegedly can help agencies look beyond special interests to see solutions which are for the common good or which are in the public interest, the roving administrator is viewed as essential to intercommunity cooperation because the position requires development of both an insider perspective, representing each individual community's interests, and an outsider perspective, representing common and public interests. In the words of one mayor:

All the communities trust him (the roving administrator) to help us work out fair agreements because he understands each of us and all of us. He is accountable to each of us and all of us.

The circuit riding administrator also has improved linkages between the network of participating local communities and external county, regional, and state level governmental organizations. When dealing with state and county agencies, the roving administrator works first with the set of communities to develop a proposal and then represents the communities in discussions with external agencies. Participants in the program stated that this arrangement was preferable to (1) communities always dealing individually with state and county agencies, (2) removing certain decision-making functions from local governments and consolidating them at the county level—a proposal under consideration in some

states, or (3) dealing with regional liaisons designated by the state agency. The roving administrator emphasized the advantages of being perceived as both an insider and an outsider when acting as a linkage agent between local communities and external agencies.

The circuit riding administrator also acts as a link between the network of local communities and the regional council of governments, which provides the program with an office and secretarial assistance on an ongoing basis. The roving administrator calls upon the council of governments for technical assistance on special projects such as the preparation of grant proposals and has increased the use of this planning expertise by the local communities. By linking local communities with planning resources, the roving administrator has incorporated a greater amount of planning activity into local government. The importance of using the circuit riding administrator in linking local agencies to outside organizations for funding and technical assistance has been particularly stressed by Elam (1978). In terms of macro generalist practice roles, the roving administrator primarily functions not as an individual planner but through assisting local governments in making use of the resources of the regional planning agency. The roving administrator does work in an individual planner role with local communities in the initial phases of planning activity—identification of needs and setting of priorities.

The roving administrator program has resulted in a network of relationships among participating communities. This network has, in turn, through the activities of the roving administrator, developed a set of linkages with external governmental agencies. This pattern of network formation is perceived by the members as increasing (1) coordination among communities, (2) negotiating power of the communities when dealing with external government agencies, and (3) use of external agencies in providing technical planning expertise.

ONGOING ISSUES IN NETWORK DEVELOPMENT

Can this complex network of relationships be maintained over an extended period of time? Participants identified these issues as critical in the future growth and development of the network.

1. Is there an optimum size in terms of network development and, if so, what is that size? Since many other communities wish to participate in the program, how should networks of small communities be organized within a region or state? Several participants stated that three communities constituted the ideal number for a network. Nationally, roving administrator programs range in size from two to five communities.
2. Members stated that a crucial factor in network maintenance is equality of participation and a sense of fair exchange. Ideally, they stated, communities forming a network should be of similar size, be able to contribute equally to the support of the program, and need similar amounts of the roving administrator's time. Since such similarity among communities is unlikely in the real world, the network members must develop a structure for fair and equitable participation acceptable to diverse communities. Members perceive that the greater the diversity of size, need, and resources among communities, the greater the difficulties of network formation. Currently, communities contribute to the program on the basis of population size, and the larger communities receive a somewhat greater share of the administrator's time. Population size was chosen as the basis for funding and allocating the roving administrator's time because, in the words of one participant, it is "the least of the evils." Can such networks be funded on the basis of need while maintaining members' feelings of fairness and equality?
3. What is the future of the program as communities grow and develop? Some planners and political scientists see the circuit riding administrator as an interim program, and that as communities increase in size and complexity of planning problems such as land use, water, sewage, and rapid economic development they will inevitably require the services of a full time administrator. Others assert that the roving administrator program is a new form of public service administration—a decentralized, cooperative, network based approach—representing a search for new forms of governmental arrangements among small communities. Participants themselves acknowledged the possibility of both outcomes, stating that while they could use more of the administrator's time, they expressed reluctance to withdraw from participation in the network

in exchange for a full time administrator.

IMPLICATIONS FOR HUMAN SERVICE ORGANIZATIONS

In summary, the roving or circuit riding administrator program offers an alternative approach to staff, organizational, community, and regional development through the creation and maintenance of networks among small communities. In the absence of a full time position of administrator, and the vertical relationships and authority which accompany such a position, the administrative function is carried out through the negotiated development of a macro generalist practice role emphasizing advice giving, linkage, capacity building, and technical assistance. The experience of small communities with this macro generalist practice role has a number of implications for human service organizations, listed here.

1. Many smaller human service and community organizations might benefit from sharing technical expertise of a macro practice generalist in areas such as proposal writing, development of personnel policies, financial planning, budgeting, and planning information systems. Such a role may be particularly important in an era of declining financial resources.

2. Many of the benefits within each member organization appear to result from the small size of the networks—typically three to five members. Small network size allows the roving administrator to have frequent enough contact with each organization to become accepted as both an insider and an outsider. Interorganizational networks of human service agencies, usually established for purposes of coordination, are typically much larger.

3. The circuit riding administrator, employed by the member organizations, can serve as a linkage agent encouraging network formation and interagency coordination. Within the area of human services, many planned efforts aimed at coordination such as formation of committees and interagency councils result in much time spent in creating awareness of interdependence and actual coordination needs. In the roving administrator program, a network was formed through the circuit riding character of the roving administrator's contacts with member agencies. Through this network of contacts, awareness of interdependence increased and formed the basis for later intercommunity coordination. The program suggests that there may be a variety of preconditions and participative experiences, other than forming a committee, through which groundworks of shared ideas and social relationships necessary for coordination are formed.

4. The roving administrator effectively linked a network of small communities to an external planning organization. Human service planning and coordinating organizations such as United Way or regional offices of public agencies seem logical sources of partial sponsorship or funding for roving administrator programs.

5. The circuit riding administrator program suggests that a number of critical organization activities can, in the absence of a full time administrator, be carried out through processes of negotiation and mutual adaptation. This mode of incorporating administrative activity seems well suited to community organizations because of their member-based decision-making structure and emphasis on member participation. In most human service agencies, the roving administrator would not be an alternative to a traditional, full time administrator. However, the role of circuit riding macro practice generalist might be added to a set of human service organizations. Such a role would expand the organizations' range of macro practice activity, increase interagency communication and coordination, and create a means for not only the introduction but also the monitoring and evaluation of organizational change efforts. Critical to the effectiveness of the role in human service agencies is the issue of accountability. The roving administrator is accountable to a variety of program participants— mayors, council members, staff, the regional planning agency. Perhaps a roving macro practice generalist should be accountable to a similar variety of positions in a network of human service organizations.

6. The roving administrator role provided an effective linkage to external planning organizations. Program participants preferred this arrangement to directly requesting technical assistance from planning agencies. The program's experience suggests ways to link planning into the ongoing operations of human service agencies. Through ongoing agency contacts the roving administrator lays a groundwork for planning by working with communities to identify needs and priorities. Only after this type of discussion took place among communities was the technical expertise of an external agency brought into the planning process.

7. The circuit riding administrator program illustrates the contributions of a generalist macro practice role in human service organizations. The importance of generalist macro practice roles in human services has been emphasized by a number of persons, particularly Yessian and Broskowski (1977). In the roving administrator program, generalist macro practice was not introduced full blown into small communities. Rather the role developed and expanded over time. The program's experience suggests that careful sequencing of activities and roles is critical to introducing generalist macro practice in human service organizations. Second, the generalist macro practice role was developed in conjunction with changes in the roles of other actors in local government; role development was part of a more general process of capacity building. Growing expertise was shared among persons with roles in local government rather than concentrated in the roving administrator. Third, the

generalist macro practice role was effective in linking local communities to specialized expertise in planning organizations, in helping local communities to think about how to use planning, and in initiating with local communities the problem formulation phase of the planning process. This experience suggests that generalist macro practitioners might play an important role in coordinating the appropriate use of specialized technical expertise in human service organizations.

The roving administrator program demonstrates the diverse contributions which can result from the incorporation of a professional macro generalist practice role into local government and public services in small communities. Experience with the program suggests that incorporating such interorganizational roles offers human service agencies one way to carry on essential macro practice activities in an era of declining financial resources. The role also promotes community and intercommunity development by emphasizing those processes which are valued in macro social work practice—participative decision making, coordination, awareness of the systemic impacts of proposed change, ongoing feedback and evaluation, and capacity building at the local community level.

REFERENCES

Cortese, Charles F., and Bernie Jones. "The Sociological Analysis of Boom Towns." *Western Sociological Review,* 8 (1977): 76-90.

Doherty, J. C. "Public and Private Issues in Nonmetropolitan Government." In Glenn V. Fuguitt, Paul Voss, and J. C. Doherty, eds., *Growth and Change in Rural America.* Washington, DC: Urban Land Institute, 1979.

Elam, John. "The Circuit-Riding Manager." *Public Management,* 60 (April 1978): 2-5.

Getzels, Judith, and Charles Thurow. *Rural and Small Town Planning.* Chicago, IL: Planners Press, 1979.

Litwak, Eugene, and Jack Rothman. "The Impact of Organizational Structure and Linkage on Agency Programs and Services." In Fred M. Cox, John L. Erlich, Jack Rothman, and John E. Tropman, eds., *Strategies of Community Organization,* 3rd ed. Itasca, IL: F. E. Peacock Publishers, Inc., 1979.

Prince, Edward L. "Riding the Circuit." *Public Management,* 56 (December 1974): 12-14.

Shannon, Charles P. "The Circuit Rider Program: Lessons from a Short History." *National Civic Review,* 70 (April 1981): 199-203, 210.

Sokolow, Alvin D. "Local Governments: Capacity and Will." In Amos H. Hawley and Sara Mills Mazie, eds., *Nonmetropolitan America in Transition.* Chapel Hill, NC: The University of North Carolina Press, 1981.

Tweeten, Luther, and George L. Brinkman. *Micropolitan Development: Theory and Practice of Greater Rural Economic Development.* Ames, IA: Iowa State University Press, 1976.

Wannamaker, Daniel K., and Alan D. McLeod. "Circuit Riding City Manager." *Public Management,* 57 (August 1975): 22-23.

Wannamaker, Daniel K., and Paul Stansbury. "Riding the Circuit with the Public Administration Specialist." *Public Administration Review,* 37 (May/June 1977): 290-293.

Watts, Ann D. "Planners' Perceptions of Rural/Small Town Issues." *Human Services in the Rural Environment,* 5 (September/October 1980): 15-21.

Yessian, Mark R., and Anthony Broskowski. "Generalists in Human Service Systems: Their Problems and Prospects." *Social Service Review,* 51 (June 1977): 265-288.

Student Study Guide

by Fred. M. Cox

GENERAL INTRODUCTION

Models of Community Organization and Macro Practice Perspectives: Their Mixing and Phasing

Jack Rothman with John E. Tropman

Review Questions

1.   What is the distinction the authors draw between "per-spectives" and "models?"

2.   What led the authors to develop various models of commu-nity organization practice?   What functions does the distinction between models serve?

3.   In general terms, what distinctions do the authors draw between the three models of community organization prac-tice they identify--locality development, social plan-ning and social action?

4.   Name and define the selected practice variables the authors have identified in developing their three mod-els. What are the dimensions along which they vary?

5.   What is the "profile," defined in terms of the practice variables identified by the authors, that distinguishes each of the models from the other?

6.   Name and define the three perspectives on macro social work practice identified by the authors.   How do they differ from one another?

7.   What do the authors mean by "mixing and phasing of approaches?" Illustrate.

Study Questions

1.   Apply the models and perspectives to your own practice. Select a project or activity from your field instruction or employment and analyze it.   Which perspective and/or model does it fit best?   In what respects does it di-verge from that model or perspective?   What revisions, if any, does your analysis suggest for the authors' models or perspectives?

2.   Can you identify, from your field instruction or profes-sional employment, an example of "mixing and phasing" models and/or perspectives?   Are there conflicts or dilemmas for your professional practice inherent in such mixing and phasing? If so, identify them in detail, and indicate how you might minimize them in your practice.

A History of Community Organization Since the Civil War
with Special Reference to Oppressed Communities

Charles D. Garvin and Fred M. Cox

Review Questions

1. How do the authors approach the history of community organizing? How does their approach contrast with Fisher's treatment of the subject? (See Article 22)

2. The authors give emphasis to organizing within certain groups and neglect others. Which groups do they emphasize and why?

3. In the period prior to the first World War, the authors focus on three social conditions and four ideological currents. What were they and how did they affect organizing among each of the identified ethnic minorities, and women, prior to World War I? What organizations were created and what functions did they serve?

4. What were the contributions of the charity organization society and the social settlement to organizing prior to World War I?

5   What social conditions and ideological currents developed in the 1920's? What were their effects upon minorities and women? What was their impact on organizing?

6. What gave rise to community chests and councils of social agencies in the 1920's? What was their significance and what functions did they serve?

7   What factors gave rise to the development of a specialization in community organization in the social work profession during the 1920's?

8. What social conditions and ideological currents developed in the 1930's through the mid-1950's and how did they affect the identified minorities and women? What effects did they have on organizing?

9. What did those writing about the development of professional education for community organization emphasize during this period?

10. What social conditions developed between 1955 and 1968, and how did they affect the development of community organization institutions, including professional education?

11. What social conditions and ideological currents emerged
     after about 1969, and how did they affect the develop-
     ment of community organization institutions, organizing
     among ethnic minorities and women, and developments in
     professional education?

Study Questions

1. What is the history of the organization or agency in
    which you have your field education experience or in
    which you are employed?   How was it affected at various
    points in its history by the social conditions and
    ideological currents identified by the authors?   Are
    there conditions and currents, other than those identi-
    fied by the authors, that had an important part in
    shaping its development? Can you identify how important
    current features of the organization arose from the
    interactions of these conditions and currents?

2. What is the history of organizing activity among an
    ethnic group or among women in the neighborhood, town or
    city you grew up or now live in?   How did the social
    conditions and ideological currents identified by the
    authors affect that history?   Were there important con-
    ditions and currents not identified by the authors that
    affected that history?

PART ONE: COMMON ELEMENTS OF PRACTICE

Need Identification and Program Planning
in the Community Context

Larry M. Siegel, C. Clifford Attkisson and Linda G. Carson

Review Questions

1. What are the three basic assumptions on which Siegel, et
    al., base their discussion of need identification and
    assessment?

2. What is the distinction made between need identification
    and assessment?

3. What are the steps identified in the process of need
    identification and assessment?

4   What does it mean to say "there is a need" for a parti-
    cular program or service?

5. When planning an assessment of human service needs, what
    are the "relevant variables" that should be taken into
    account?

6. What "issues" have the authors identified that should be considered prior to making a needs assessment?

7. What do the authors mean by "convergent" analysis?

8. What purposes are served by need identification and assessment?

9. What are the advantages of a regional needs assessment?

10. What are the eight need identification and assessment approaches noted by the authors?

Study Questions

1. Under what conditions would it be best to avoid need assessment? Under what conditions would need assessment be desirable?

2. In relation to your work or field education setting, and in the light of this article, what are the most appropriate need identification and assessment method(s) that would be suitable for you or your agency's requirements?

The Knowledge Base of Planned Change
in Organizations and Communities

Joseph Katan and Shimon E. Spiro

Review Questions

1. What do the authors mean by "planned change?"

2. Review the contributions from the various social sciences to knowledge of planned change.

3. What types of knowledge have the social sciences contributed to the practice of planned change?

4. What kinds of variables are considered in various hypotheses of planned change?

5. What types of theories or models of planned change have been advanced by social scientists?

6. What methods used by social scientists have been borrowed by those trying to effect planned change?

7. Give one or two examples of strategies or guidelines for practice borrowed from the work of social scientists.

8. What are the criteria to be used by practitioners in selecting knowledge for planned change, as suggested by Thomas?

9.   What is the authors' assessment of the success, to date, in linking relevant knowledge from the social sciences to the practice of planned change? What approaches have been tried and what are the difficulties experienced?

Study Question

1.   Select a problem from your practice or field education experience. Select knowledge relevant to that problem, review several references from the social science literature and generate practice guidelines from that review. If possible, apply them to your practice and assess the outcome.

How To Be an Advocate in Bad Times

Nancy Amidei

Review Question

1.   Describe the five aspects of Amidei's action plan for countering the current decline in support for legislation and appropriations of importance to many Americans.

Study Questions

1.   In relation to your work or field education assignment, which of the six ways to influence politicians do you command? How might you use them in that context?

2.   Would it make sense to organize a voter registration campaign? If so, when and how would you organize it?

3.   Would efforts at coalition building be useful? What groups would you want to include? Around what set of issues would you build a coalition?

Working with Task Groups

Ronald W. Toseland and Robert F. Rivas

Review Questions

1.   What are the tasks a professional worker staffing a task group must attend to (a) between meetings? (b) during meetings? How should these tasks be carried out?

2.   What functions do task groups serve beyond problem solving and decision making? Why are these important?

3. Review the responsibilities of the professional worker staffing a task group with respect to each of these functions.

4. What are the factors that inhibit task groups from generating new ideas and developing creative alternatives for solving problems?

5. Under what conditions do individuals produce better decisions than groups? When do groups do better than individuals?

6. What steps may be taken to help groups avoid "group think" and "risky shifts?"

7. What steps may be taken to reduce conflicts among group members?

8. Describe the six steps in problem solving identified by Toseland.

9. In identifying a problem in need of solution, several things can be done to help a group define the problem in a way that promotes problem solving. What are these, and how can the professional worker help in the process?

10. What are the principles identified by the authors in developing effective goals in group problem solving?

Study Questions

1. Why is it important for community organizers and social administrators to know about working with small groups?

2. Select a problem in your work or field education assignment that requires group effort to solve. Focusing on the step in problem solving you think will be most difficult, specify the measures you would take in facilitating the group in completing that step.

Interpersonal Transactions in Community Organization Practice

Herbert Bisno

Review Questions

1. Give a few examples of the circumstances in which a community practitioner or administrator uses interpersonal skills in practice.

2. Why is little attention given to interpersonal transactions in "macro" social work practice? Why are these reasons invalid, in the author's view?

3. What is the difference between instrumental and subventionary interactions? What is the meaning of these terms?

4. The author cites four ways in which goals and interests may differ such that they affect interpersonal transactions. What are these differences, and give examples to illustrate.

5. How do the obligations and accountability of the practitioner differ between instrumental and subventionary interactions? Give some examples to make your points clear.

6. How do authority, dependency and exchange relations differ between instrumental and subventionary interactions?

7. How do the motivations for engaging in interactions differ between instrumental and subventionary relationships?

8. How does the focus on task achievement and maintaining relationships, sometimes referred to as "process," differ between instrumental and subventionary interactions?

9. What are the principal methods and techniques engaged in by the practitioner when carrying out instrumental interactions? How do these differ from one another?

Study Question

1. With one or more classmates, invent situations that call for the application of the four methods identified by the author: adversative, developmental, rule-making and rule-implementation. Assign roles to one another, and role play each situation. Ask other members of the class to critique each of your role playing situations. If time permits, do some reading in the relevant literature that will help guide your interactions during the role playing situations.

Community Problem Solving: A Guide to Practice with Comments

Fred M. Cox

Review Questions

1. What are the conflicts, tensions or strains that may be found in various kinds of agencies sponsoring social action, locality development and social planning?

2. Describe the two perspectives discussed by the author for understanding the practitioner's behavior in carrying out community organization practice.

3. Describe the various ways of viewing the problems addressed by community organization practitioners, and their implications for practice.

4. How is the client of a community organization practitioner defined? What difference does the degree of homogeneity of the client group make in practice? What difference does the consistency between the sponsoring organization's primary beneficiary and the practitioner's definition of client make for practice?

5. Describe and discuss the factors that need to be taken into account in selecting goals in community organization practice.

Study Questions

1. What impact may internal strains within agencies sponsoring community organization practice have on the ability of the agency to sponsor that practice?

2. Apply one of the two analyses of the practitioner to your own work or field education experience as it applies to one specific job or learning assignment.

3. How do you perceive any important assignment in your job or field education setting? Does your perception differ from the way others view it? What impact does this have on your practice?

4. Analyze the extent of consistency between the primary beneficiary of your employer or your field education agency and the client of your major assignment, and describe the impact of such consistency or lack of consistency.

5. Develop at least two possible and plausible strategies for dealing with the problem that is a major focus of your job or field education assignment and indicate why you believe one is superior to the other.

Program Evaluation and Administrative Control

Steven Maynard-Moody

Review Questions

1. Describe the content out of which an emphasis on program evaluation has grown.

2. Describe three program evaluation strategies, and how they are related to Thompson's work.

3. What does Perrow mean when he raises the question of "effectiveness for whom" in organizational functioning?

4. What are the three major ways of examining organizational effectiveness that reflect the heterogeneity of the concept?

5. What are the results of the author's two studies? How do they conform to the norm of rationality, and conflict with what Thompson's model predicts?

6. Do the study results support or contradict the view that high level management controls evaluation studies? Describe how.

7. What are the consequences of emphasizing goal attainment in program evaluation?

Study Question

1. If the project or program to which you have been assigned in your job or field education were subjected to an evaluation that was based entirely on goal attainment, what do you think would be the consequences for you, your agency and your client?

PART TWO: ARENAS

Introduction

Fred M. Cox

Review Questions

1. What does the author mean by "arenas" of community practice? What are the objections to viewing arenas as contexts of practice? How does the author answer those objections?

2. Define the arenas identified by the author.

3. What is the relation between the author's perspective on arenas and community organization practice? How may such practice be defined in terms of relations among arenas?

4. What are the functions of all social systems? Why are some regarded as instrumental and others as consummatory? Why are they regarded as universals? How may some systems be regarded as primarily serving one or another function? How may the primary functions served

by systems vary for different groups of participants? How may the primary functions served differ for various systems external to the system in question?

5. What are the organizational variables the author has identified as important to the community organization practitioner? Describe them and illustrate how organizations may differ in these respects.

6. Litwak and Meyer point out that all formal organizations and parts of many do not conform to the traditional bureaucratic features identified in the literature. What are those traditional features, and how do some "human relations" organizations differ from them? How do the capabilities of traditional bureaucracies and human relations organizations differ?

7. Thompson and Tuden identify characteristics of four types of organizations, and relate those characteristics to their capabilities. What are the characteristics of each type and to what capabilities do those features give rise?

8. How do Thompson and Tuden's and Litwak and Meyer's analyses correspond and differ with one another?

9. Rein and Morris provide still another analysis of the relation between certain organizational features and their capabilities. What are those features and to what capabilities are they related?

10. How are Rein and Morris' and Thompson and Tuden's conclusions related? What relation do the latter authors' conclusions have for those of Blau and Scott?

11. When a single organization must exercise a variety of capabilities which are not congenial to its major features, how may it adapt to this problem?

12. Connor discusses a number of organizational capabilities. What are they?

13. Connor identifies four sets of structural characteristics of organizations which are related to various types of capability. What are these structural characteristics and their sub-dimensions?

14. Review the relation between organizational structure and the ability to (1) pursue various types of goals, (2) cope with differing characteristics of the organization's environment, (3) create and maintain various kinds of organizational climate, and (4) operate effectively.

15. Galbraith identifies two essential and required charac-
    teristics of every organization of any size and com-
    plexity: differentiation of activities and their coor-
    dination. He identifies various principles used in
    organizational differentiation, mechanisms for coordina-
    tion and problems that arise in coordination. He sug-
    gests mechanisms for mitigating these problems, and the
    conditions under which various mechanisms are satisfac-
    tory and unsatisfactory. Review his analysis.

16. Translating Galbraith's analysis into the author's
    terms, the two types of organizational structure identi-
    fied by Galbraith--service and functional--work well
    under certain conditions. What are these conditions?
    Galbraith introduces the concept of a matrix organiza-
    tional structure. What is this, and under what condi-
    tions does it work best? Illustrate.

17. Under what conditions must one depend upon what Connor
    calls "clan control?" In what ways does this discussion
    parallel what Thompson and Tuden or others said earlier?
    Hint: How is clan control similar to collegial struc-
    ture and human relations organizational structure? What
    are the conditions necessary for clan control to operate
    properly?

18. Litwak and Meyer discuss the importance of linking for-
    mal organizations, including schools and social agen-
    cies, with primary groups, such as neighborhoods and
    families. What are the four barriers to communication
    (linkages) they identify? What are the guidelines they
    offer for overcoming these barriers? How can these
    guidelines aid the practitioner in selecting appropriate
    means of communicating under the different conditions
    identified by these authors?

19. As identified by Thompson and McEwen, what are the
    various ways organizations interact, depending on their
    relative positions of power in relation to one another?

20. When organizations are approximately equal in power, and
    interact through various forms of exchange, what are the
    factors, identified by Levine, White and Paul, that
    affect those exchanges?

21. What are the factors, identified by Morris, affecting
    cooperation between agencies ?

22. What are the two types of cooptation, identified by
    Selznick, and why are their differences important?

23. Litwak and Hylton studied the formation of alliances
    between agencies in the form of coordinating agencies.
    Under what conditions did such agencies arise? What
    different levels of interdependence led to what differ-

ent types of coordination? What different levels of standardization led to what different types of coordination? What differences in the number of units requiring coordination led to what different types of coordination?

24. Halpert identifies interpretive and contextual factors leading to coordination among organizations. Review these factors, and give examples from your practice experience.

25. Halpert also identifies interpretive and contextual factors that tend to inhibit coordination. Review these factors, and give examples from your practice experience.

26. What additional barriers to coordination did Halpert identify when coordination is mandated? Review these factors, and give examples from your practice experience.

27. Coleman has identified a number of factors influencing the way individuals, groups and organizations relate to one another. He states the results in terms of interests and residues of sentiment that develop as a result. What are the various sets of conditions he identifies that characterize interaction and what results arise from them?

28. When people engage in dissimilar but interdependent activities which produce unequal costs and benefits for those interacting, and interests which are at least partially opposed to one another, the results may be conflict, unilateral action or inaction. What factors determine which of these three outcomes is likely to occur? How do they produce these different results?

Study Questions

1. Identify a practice problem from your field education or employment experience which requires the practitioner to mobilize certain organizational capabilities to achieve a measure of success. Apply what you learned in this Introduction to that problem, and develop a prescription to guide the practitioner in mobilizing those organizational capabilities.

2. Identify a practice problem from your field education or employment experience which requires the practitioner to affect the relationships between organizations, promoting communication, coordination, conflict or some other form of relationship. Apply what you learned in this Introduction to that problem, and develop a prescription to guide the practitioner in achieving the appropriate forms of relationship.

Society: American Values as a Context for Community
Organization and Macro Practice

John E. Tropman and Fred M. Cox

Review Questions

1. What is the relationship between social values and social policy?

2. How do political factors affect the relationship between
values and policy?

3. In what three ways do values conflict, according to the
authors?

4. What is the meaning of "close effects?" Theory and
practice? How do they affect social policy?

5. How is it that an understanding of the complexity of
values may illuminate without resolving the value conflicts found in community practice?

6. One of the authors provides an example of the complexities involved in applying values to policy decisions.
Describe that example and indicate the several points
that it illustrates.

7. Review and describe each of the conflicts of values
identified by the authors, and provide an illustration
to make clear your understanding.

8. What is expected of the individual in American society?

9. Americans honor achievement. How do they respond to
failure? What distinctions are made in our responses to
those who fail? Between those who succeed fairly and
unfairly?

10. What economic conditions do Americans want for themselves?

11. What do Americans mean when they say they believe in
equality?

12. What is the meaning of freedom and liberty to Americans?
What are their limits?

13. When freedom must be constrained by group action, Americans turn to democratic values. What does democracy
mean in the American context?

14. What is the distinction between democratic and republican forms of government? Why do Americans prefer one or
the other?

15. What is the distinction between political and social democracy?

16. How do Americans value families? In what forms?

17. What do the concepts of humanitarianism and human rights mean to Americans?

Study Questions

1. The authors have stressed the complexity and dilemmas involved in applying values to social policy. Identify a policy issue current in your state legislature or local government that interests you. Working with a group of your classmates, develop at least two sides to the issue. Dividing your group in two or more teams, debate the issue in class.

2. Over the course of a few weeks or a semester, collect newspaper clippings on a current social policy issue in your state or locality, and write a short paper showing how the debate reflected in those clippings illustrates the complexities and conflicts in some of the values discussed in this paper.

3. Identify an issue of social policy that is being played out in the agency in which you are engaged in field instruction or are employed. Interview the principal participants in the issue, such as the agency executive, your supervisor, board members and clients, and define the issue as clearly as possible. Develop an argument for how the issue should be resolved, taking into account and answering the objections to your solution that you have heard or would anticipate. Be sure to include conditions, other than values, in your considerations (e.g., limitations in funding, lack of trained staff, etc.) but highlight the value considerations, both those that reinforce your position and those that tend to undermine it.

Community: Alternative Conceptions of Community:
Implications for Community Organization Practice

Fred M. Cox

Review Questions

1. Define and describe the three major types of concepts of community, identified by the author.

2. Describe the seven conceptions of community, organized under the three major categories noted above, and indicate what the implications of each may be for community organization practice.

Study Question

1. Each of the seven conceptions of community were grouped
    under three major types of conceptions, based on judg-
    ments about the relevance of each conception. Discuss
    one of the conceptions categorized as a "context" and
    show its relevance as a "vehicle" or "problem" for the
    community organization practitioner.

Organizations: Organizations as Polities:
An Analysis of Community Organization Agencies

Mayer N. Zald

Review Questions

1. What does Zald mean by organizational analysis? Why is
    this approach useful in analyzing community organization
    practice?

2. What is the constitution of an organization? What sig-
    nificance does it have for community organization prac-
    tice?

3. What are the factors affecting an organization's autono-
    my in making basic decisions?

4. What difference does the social class of the constituen-
    cy make in a community organization agency?

5. What difference does it make in community organization
    practice whether the agency constituency consists of
    organizations or individuals?

6. Under what conditions is it best to employ "specialists"
    vs. "generalists" to do community work? When it is
    important to employ generalists, what should be their
    qualifications?

7. When Zald advises the practitioner to make "the most
    precise diagnosis of the chain of influence and mecha-
    nisms of decision making for each specific decision,"
    what does he mean? What are the implications for "the
    democratic process?"

Study Questions

1. Identify the location of the organization that employs
    you or to which you are assigned for field instruction,
    among the various cells of Zald's figure describing goal
    dimensions for community organization agencies. Now

suppose you thought you should undertake a goal of another type. Describe the goal and identify the cell into which it falls. What problems would you face with the organization's constituency?

2. Is an organization that is dependent upon a few large benefactors who make decisions at periodic intervals on refunding the organization likely to be more or less autonomous in making basic decisions about program than an organization that depends on the United Way for funding or one that depends on one or a series of endowments administered by a bank's trust department? Why?

3. If an organization's goals are accomplished mainly by member volunteers, is it likely to be more or less autonomous in making basic decisions than one that uses paid professionals? Why?

4. If it is necessary to promote coordination among agencies to achieve an objective, what conditions would you look for or try to create to foster such coordination?

PART THREE: STRATEGIES

Introduction

John L. Erlich and John E. Tropman

Review Questions

1. How is strategy, as a form of activity, different from other activities if viewed from the perspective of game theory?

2. How is strategy defined or conceptualized in this book?

3. What is the relation between conflict and consensus in working out a strategy?

4. What are "task" and "process" goals, and how are they related to one another?

5. What is the relation between means and ends in developing strategy? Why should they be public and measurable rather than private and vague?

6. What is the relation of resources and strategy? How do the conditions of resources--scarcity and availability, amount and type of resources available to the practitioner--affect the type of strategy selected?

7. How do resistance to goals and goal complexity affect selection of strategy?

8. How do social class and related status factors affect the selection and success of a strategy?

9. How do factors such as the legitimacy of the change agent or target of change and their organizational strength affect selection of strategy?

10. What are the three basic forms of influence or social power that may be marshalled by a change agent in developing strategy?

11. What additional properties do these three forms of influence have that are of importance to the community practitioner?

12. How are these forms of influence related to the five models cited by Rothman in the first article in this book?

Study Questions

1. Get several of your fellow students together and discuss the application of Figure I to case situations known to you through your field education or employment experiences. First, can you agree, in a given example, that "the problem" exists or is maintained primarily by one of the three means of influence identified by the authors? Second, does the sequence of actions suggested by the authors for mitigating the problem fit your experience? What problems do you see? Does Figure I require modification, based on your experience?

2. Repeat the above exercise in relation to the particular type of intervention to which you or the agency sponsoring your field education or employment experience are committed. Is the sequence of actions suggested by the authors for those with each "mode of intervention" commitment consistent with your experience? What inconsistencies do you see? Does Figure I require modification, based on your experience?

Social Planning, Social Policy and Political Change

Eugen Pusic

Review Questions

1. Pusic links his analysis of social planning and social policy to an evolutionary view of social thought, particularly social science, and to ideas about societal and political change or development. What are his views on these matters and how are they linked to social policy and social planning?

2. What does Pusic mean by social policy? Social planning?

3. What is the role of power and knowledge in social planning?

4. What is the role of social planning, in Pusic's view?

Study Questions

1. Pusic's views may be expected to be influenced by the social and political conditions of his homeland, Yugoslavia. In what ways are Pusic's views on social policy similar to and different from common views held in the United States and Western Europe? Is social policy "oriented toward the neutralization of some of the effects of social stratification and the domination of privileged interest groups over the majority?"

2. In what ways are Pusic's views on social planning similar to and different from Western views? Is planning in the West best characterized as going "from the periphery to the center in order to return again to the periphery for implementation?" Is "our information about resources . . . sufficient to achieve the coordinating and regulating effect of the plan?" Is power "an unnecessary addition" to planning?

3. Is Pusic's vision of the increasing importance of social planning, coupled with a decreasing role of government in such planning, likely to occur? "Can there be a whole society . . . that is self-regulated on the principle of maximizing chances of interest satisfaction and minimizing possibilities of interest domination?"

Theories of Choice and Making Decisions

James G. March

Review Questions

1. What are the elements of the model of rational choice which March asserts are common to "standard theories of choice?"

2. What elements of this model are called into question by empirical studies of choice and decision making and why are they placed in doubt by the research? What are the elements of a revised model coming out of such studies?

3. How is conflict treated in "standard choice theory" and how are models of choice modified by empirical studies of decision making? How do "tradeoffs" among conflicting objectives figure into such theories?

4. How does "understanding a political process that allows decisions to be made without necessarily resolving conflict among parties" help our understanding of the process of decision making?

5. What is the role of information? How is it used? Alliances? Mobilization, involvement and attention as a scarce resource? Agents and their reliability? Power? Trustworthiness? Log-Rolling?

6. How are rules or "standard operating procedures" treated in understanding decision making? How may they serve, in part, as a substitute for rational choice? How do rules develop and what may be learned from an understanding of those processes? What are the implications for understanding how decisions are made?

7. How does the prevalence of disorder affect decision making? What kind of order does March find and how does it affect decision making? What is the effect of multiple and shifting demand on the individual's time and attention? What are the implications for institutional leaders?

8. In what ways is the process of decision making symbolic, related to the reinforcement of values and meaning in our lives?

9. How does the theory of the need for and use of information in decision making differ from the observed practice?

Study Questions

1. What does March's discussion of choice and decision making have to do with the shaping of social policy?

2. How do March's views relate to Pusic's, as expressed in the previous article?

3. Suppose you and your agency wish to get a piece of legislation passed or rules changed by a large bureaucracy. How would you apply what you have learned from March to that problem?

Homelessness as a Public Concern:
How to Develop a Community Approach to Solving the Problem

Milan J. Dluhy

Review Questions

1.   How is the current problem of homelessness different
     today than it was in the Great Depression of the 1930's?

2.   What are the trends in the U.S. during the 1980's that
     have contributed to the increase in homelessness?

3.   What are the troubling and unanswered questions concern-
     ing the problem of homelessness which face us?

4.   In the author's opinion, where are the major initiatives
     in dealing with the problem likely to come from and why?

5.   What are the most critical assumptions in dealing with
     the problem?

6.   What are the different types of homelessness and why are
     these distinctions important?

7.   What do research findings show, consistently and
     throughout the United States (ignoring important local
     variations for the moment), about the problem?

8.   What are the key issues a community needs to resolve in
     dealing with the problem?

Study Questions

1.   Apply the author's approach to the study and implementa-
     tion of a plan for dealing with homelessness in your
     community.

2.   With respect to another problem of local concern, devel-
     op an approach which follows the general outline of the
     author's method adapted to the change in problem focus.
     If there is time, apply the adapted method to the prob-
     lem you have identified in your community.

Social Planners and Social Planning in the United States

Armand Lauffer

Review Questions

1.   Lauffer observes that planning is based on the assump-
     tion that free market forces do not adequately distri-
     bute resources or opportunities; opponents respond that
     the results of planning are no more beneficial than

those resulting from the unplanned interplay of forces, and may pose dangers to democratic values, i.e., freedom and choice vs. constraints. How does Lauffer answer this criticism?

2. Lauffer describes American social planning as <u>ad hoc</u> (non-comprehensive) and localized (non-centralized). What does he mean by this? What are the arguments he cites against central planning? What are the implications for social planning?

3. Lauffer indicates that planners are seldom free agents, and answer to "input" and "output" constituencies. Which type of constituency exercises the greatest control? Why?

4. How does Lauffer describe the ways that social planning has been defined? He begins with five somewhat conflicting definitions, drawn from the literature, and then discusses Hudson's list of five types of social planning. Review each of these and describe how they differ.

5. Lauffer prefers an approach which tries to describe what planners do, distinguishing between analytic and interactive activities. Review his efforts in this regard. Are the steps he describes necessarily ordered? If not, why not? What influences the relative emphasis placed on one step or another in the planning process? To what extent is the process rational? If not fully rational, why is it not so?

6. Describe what Lauffer means by "planning as a corrective in the service-delivery system." What are the five kinds of problems that may be the focus of attention and the three elements that may be missing (and therefore constitute problems) in such planning.

7. Describe sectoral and inter-sectoral planning. What is involved in each?

8. What are the different ways Lauffer describes planning from the perspective of the planner? Describe them and indicate why they may be important.

9. What does Lauffer foresee for the future of social planning?

Study Questions

1. Lauffer provides five definitions of social planning, drawn from his review of the literature. How do you assess the strengths and weaknesses of each definition?

2. Lauffer characterizes social planning in modest terms, focusing on corrections to the service delivery system rather than solutions to social problems, recognizing the limits to rationality and the significant part played by competing and conflicting interests. Is Lauffer's "modesty" justified? If so, why? If not, why not?

3. Lauffer describes several important differences in planners' perspectives. Indicate how they fit or conflict with your own perspectives and indicate what you would do if you had a planning task that required a perspective different from your own.

4. What does the future hold for social planning? What is the evidence for your views? Compare and contrast them with Lauffer's speculations about planning of the future.

Political Strategy for Social Planning

Barry Checkoway

Review Questions

1. Checkoway makes a detailed argument in favor of the development of political strategy for social planning. Summarize that argument. What does he mean by "political strategy?" Why do social planners neglect political strategy?

2. The bulk of Checkoway's paper discusses a number of skills that may be used as tools in political strategy. Describe them and how they may be used to serve the purposes of what Lauffer calls "output constituencies."

3. Checkoway discusses obstacles to developing and using political strategy among planners, and suggests some ways around such obstacles. What are the obstacles and, without exaggerating the ease of surmounting them, what are some approaches to overcoming them?

Study Questions

1. Does political strategy have a place in social planning? If so, what is that place? If not, why not?

2. From your own practice or field instruction experience, describe one effort to apply political strategy in a social planning task. Analyze the reasons for its success, failure or mixed results.

3. How is the use of political strategy in social planning related to what Rothman refers to as "mixing and phasing" models?

Citizen Input and Professional Responsibility

Carl V. Patton

Review Questions

1. What are the problems in using citizen input in social planning, identified by Patton?

2. In the case studies reported, what were the differences between the majority opinions of the groups (a) at the two public hearings, (b) between the public hearings and the sample surveys, (c) between residents and neighbors of the affected areas and (d) between renters and owners?

Study Question

1. What are the implications of Patton's findings in these cases for planning theory and practice? What do the cases tell us about (a) motives of citizens in expressing opinions through public hearings and surveys, (b) the limitations in information gained through public hearings, (c) technical superiority of plans and political priorities bearing upon them? In each instance, what does the analysis suggest for planning practice?

Community Development: Potentials and Limitations

Shanti K. Khinduka

Review Questions

1. How does Khinduka define and describe community development?

2. What is Khinduka's view of community development's potential as a strategy for social change?

3. What is the basis for Khinduka's view that community development theory and practice (a) give unwarranted precedence to process rather than task achievement, (b) place excessive emphasis on change in values and attitudes as precursors to social and economic change, (c) mistakenly oppose rapid change, (d) erroneously favor consensus as the only satisfactory basis for major community decisions, (e) overemphasizes citizen involvement, (f) erroneously emphasize the importance of identification with and loyalty to the local community, (g) in their emphasis on local autonomy present a dilemma for practitioners, (h) are limited by the emphasis on psychological rather than a socioeconomic approach to social problems?

4.   What are the appropriate uses of community development practice, in Khinduka's view?

Study Questions

1.   If changes in attitude are not a necessary precondition for social change, as Khinduka argues, how might one go about producing "development" in a community or locality in need of it without attempting first to change attitudes? Apply this, if possible, to a practice situation with which you are familiar.

2.   Given Khinduka's critical analysis of community development theory and practice, under what conditions should it be applied? Discuss this, if possible, in relation to a practice situation with which you are familiar.

Needs Assessment and Community Development:
An Ideological Perspective

Sylvia Martí-Costa and Irma Serrano-García

Review Questions

1.   The authors regard needs assessment as "an integral part of community development, the process of consciousness raising" which "implies a political commitment. . . to the exploited, underprivileged and powerless groups in society." Describe their argument and how they arrived at this conclusion.

2.   Review the "control system maintenance" and "social change" purposes served by needs assessment.

3.   If needs assessment is to serve basic social change on behalf of the oppressed, what must the techniques selected accomplish, in the authors' view? Which techniques tend to achieve those objectives and which tend not to achieve them?

4.   What are the criteria used for judging the adequacy of needs assessment techniques?

5.   Describe the model of "intervention within Research" discussed by the authors, including its four phases and purposes.

Study Questions

1.   How do the authors' analysis of community development respond (or fail to respond) to Khinduka's critique in the previous article?

2. What is your critique of the authors' efforts to link needs assessment to community development and to a professional commitment to oppressed groups in society? Do you agree or disagree with various parts of their argument, and if so, why?

3. The authors believe that certain techniques provide more contact with the agency or community and, hence, serve the purpose of consciousness raising and social change better than other approaches. Based on a more detailed knowledge of these techniques derived from your reading of article #3 by Siegel and his colleagues, how would you judge this assertion?

4. Given the authors' purposes in using needs assessment for community development, what, if anything, have they overlooked?

Community Involvement in Desegregation: The Milwaukee Experience

Ian Harris

Review Questions

1. Review the origins, organizational sponsorship and support, and composition of "The Committee of 100" and "The Coalition for Peaceful Schools."

2. Describe the "seven stage continuum to evaluate the functions of citizen participation," which the author discusses.

3. How does the author view the stage(s) at which the Committee operated? Why does he believe that the Committee had more influence on policy than it might have had in the absence of intervention by the Court?

4. Answer question number 3 in relation to the "Coalition."

5. How does the author view the impact of (a) the middle-class membership of the Committee and (b) the shift in membership to a more "grass-roots" base toward the end of the Coalition's existence?

6. What are the major contributions of the Committee and the Coalition in the author's view?

7. Review the author's views on the factors which determine the success of such voluntary action as exemplified by the Committee and the Coalition.

Study Questions

1. Can you identify functions performed by the Committee and the Coalition for various groups in Milwaukee (citizens, school board, students, etc.) beyond those the author cited? Give particular attention to what sociologists call "latent (or not immediately visible) functions" and "unintended consequences."

2. What are the various meanings of the term "representation," and how do you assess the "representativeness" of the Committee and the Coalition in terms of these various meanings?

3. In our system of representative democracy, is it appropriate for an elected school board to adopt a policy for decision making that corresponds to Koneya's sixth stage of citizen participation? If so, why? If not, why not?

4. How do you view the major contribution(s) of the Committee and the Coalition? Do these coincide with or diverge from the author's views? How and why?

Community Organizing in Historical Perspective: A Typology

Robert Fisher

Review Questions

1. What are some of the indications of a resurgent interest in neighborhood organizing?

2. What is the major motivation for this resurgence?

3. What are the three approaches to community organization identified by the author? How do they differ?

4. Describe and illustrate the three approaches with historical and contemporary examples.

5. Describe the ways in which the approaches have overlapped in their applications at various periods during the 20th century.

Study Question

1. Compare and contrast Fisher's three approaches to community organization with Rothman's three models of community organization practice. How are they similar to and different from one another, conceptually and empirically?

Can't Ya Hear Me Knocking?: An Organizing Model

Lee Staples

Review Questions

1. What are the characteristics of community organizations
    that Staples' organizing model is designed to build?
    Touch on questions of constituency, issues and tactics,
    membership, leadership, structure, finances and staff.

2. Describe briefly the four phases of the organizing pro-
    cess identified by Staples.

3. What are the basic questions the organizer tries to
    answer during the groundwork phase of organizing?

Study Question

1. Think about the neighborhoods served by the agency in
    which you are engaged in field instruction or are em-
    ployed. Would any of those neighborhoods be appropriate
    for organizing along the lines Staples describes? If
    so, why? If not, why not?

The Tactics of Organization Building

Warren Haggstrom

Review Questions

1. What is the significance of "collectively held meanings"
    to the people of a low income area in beginning to work
    with them on building an organization? How does this
    apply to the situation in the neighborhood, including
    the presence of the organizer and what does it imply for
    the way the organizer works with the people?

2. How is the organizer like and unlike a salesman in
    beginning to work with a neighborhood? What is the point
    of meetings and of organization in beginning to work in
    a neighborhood?

3. In the example of the meeting with the district sanita-
    tion inspector, how did he insult the neighborhood and
    how was this used by the organizer and neighborhood to
    their advantage?

4. How does the enabler differ from the organizer? How is
    it possible to "disagree aggressively with people while"
    remaining "clearly on their side?" What does the author
    mean by "the necessary self-discipline" of the organi-
    zer?

5. What are the structural requirements of an effective
    organization, in the author's view? What are the common
    mistakes of an inexperienced organizer in building an
    organization?

6. The author views the conflict situation as a "morality
    drama." From the point of view of the organizer and the
    neighborhood organization, what is the purpose of the
    "plan" and what should be its outcome as the conflict
    subsides and the "audience" departs?

7. What must be done to turn "symbolic concessions" into
    real ones?

8. What are the needs of the opposition and "opposition
    tactics" and how can they be turned to the advantage of
    the neighborhood organization?

9. What are the functions of "unpredictability" on the part
    of the neighborhood organization?

10. What are the functions of campaign (a) actions and (b)
    activities and of (c) services in neighborhood organi-
    zing? How do they differ? Which take precedence? Why?

11. The author identifies six approaches that "will not
    work." What are they and why are they important?

12. What are the functions of making people in the neighbor-
    hood aware of changes and particularly of changes
    brought about by local people through their own organi-
    zation?

13. Why is it important that members of the neighborhood
    organization make their own decisions about actions to
    be taken and believe that the results attained are due
    to their own efforts rather than those of the organizer
    or the neighborhood's opponents? How can the organizer
    facilitate this process?

14. What kind of relationship should organizers strive to
    develop between themselves and members of the neighbor-
    hood organization? Why?

Study Questions

1. The author contends that "When an organizer helps people
    to begin to act on central problems. . . the organizer
    deliberately creates conflict [which requires no] arti-
    ficial confrontations." How does your own experience
    support or question that contention? Is conflict inevi-
    table? If so, why? If not, why not?

2. Community organizers do not always operate from a base of a neighborhood community organization. (If they do, it is often from the point of view of cooperating with the established local powers to obtain some mutually agreeable ends.) So the practitioner may be "on the other side" of strategies and tactics such as those described here. Imagine a scenario in which you, perhaps in connection with your work or field education, were faced with "actions" such as those discussed by the author. How would you deal with them in a "constructive" way, i.e., with a view to protecting the interests that you (and your employer) represent but without destroying the neighborhood organization that opposes you and that, from a broader professional point of view, you recognize has a right to exist and have its views taken into account in decisions affecting the neighborhood?

3. Now suppose you were the neighborhood organizer confronted with the "progressive" or "liberal" professional planner characterized in study question 2, above. How would you deal with the planner and his actions in a way most consistent with the author's point of view?

Organization Theory for Social Administration

Burton Gummer

Review Questions

1. What are the three models of organizational behavior discussed by Gummer? What are the principal variables in each model and along what dimensions do they vary?

2. What is the significance of variations in the degree to which goals may be specified and the degree of consensus on goals?

3. The author points out that organizational technologies may be classified according to (a) the nature of the work done (from well understood and analyzed to poorly understood and undifferentiated) and (b) the nature of the objects on which the work is done (reactive or nonreactive). Give an illustration of each from the human services and indicate what the consequences are for the organization.

4. What methods are used by organizations to reduce uncertainty? Why is such reduction important for organizations?

5. In addition to the efficient production of goods and/or services, the natural system model of organization takes account of of what other type of goals? In addition to viewing the organizational member as a role player within the formal structure, how does the natural systems model view the participant?

6. What are the four subsystems of the natural systems model, and what functions do they perform? Illustrate the four subsystems by reference to a human service organization with which you are familiar. How might the existence of four subsystems lead to goal conflicts within the organization? Illustrate from your experience.

7. What is "informal structure," and how can it produce conflict within organizations? How can it also have a positive impact?

8. What is the likely impact of changes in an organization's environment on organizational character? How does this impact occur and with what results?

9. What are the responsibilities of organizational leaders for managing internal conflict? Why is this important?

10. What is the significance of control over the resources needed by an organization for the organization? What difference does it make who controls resources? What is the difference between "liquidity" and "transferability" of resources?

11. What is the relevant dimension of control structures discussed by the author? How is power and control viewed from the perspective of the rational model of organization? How does that view differ in the power politics model?

12. If organizational change can best be understood from the perspective of the power politics model, as the author suggests, what explains which faction or unit gains power within an organization?

13. Under what conditions is it appropriate to apply each of the three models of organization discussed by the author?

Study Questions

1. Describe the organizational character of the organization that employs you or in which you have your field instruction. What difference does its character make in the way it operates?

2. Suppose you wanted to promote some change you regard as
    desirable in the organizational character of the agency
    that employs you or in which you do your field practice.
    What alternatives are open to you, based on the natural
    systems model? First, describe the change you think is
    necessary and then describe the theoretical approaches
    to bringing it about, illustrating with specific actions
    that might be taken or encouraged.

3. Apply the explanation of organizational change from the
    perspective of the power politics model to an agency
    with which you are familiar. Can you explain a recent
    significant change in that organization using this per-
    spective? If yes, how? If not, why not? What is a
    better explanation?

Program Development

Yeheskel Hasenfeld

<u>Review Questions</u>

1. Compare and contrast the social systems model developed
    by Hasenfeld and the natural systems model discussed by
    Gummer in the previous chapter. Give particular atten-
    tion to both authors' analyses of subsystems-systems and
    their function.

2. Review the procedures or steps in organizing a new
    service program.

3. What kinds of persons should be brought together to
    support a new program? Why?

4. What is involved in defining the mission of a new pro-
    gram, specifying objectives and doing a feasibility
    study?

5. Review the potential sources of seed money for getting a
    new program started.

6. How is a decision made about appropriate program tech-
    nology?

7. What principles should be used in dividing up specific
    program responsibilities?

8. What forms may relationships among organizations take in
    implementing a new program?

9. How is "effective and efficient role performance" relat-
    ed to "the design of a work unit congruent with the
    tasks it has to perform?" Compare this discussion with
    the related information provided in the Introduction to
    "Arenas."

Study Questions

1. Identify a need in the agency that employs you or in
    which you are engaged in field instruction that requires
    the development of a new program or substantial modifi-
    cation of an existing one. Identify the steps that
    would be necessary in program development or reorganiza-
    tion and why it would be unnecessary to engage in the
    remaining steps listed by the author.

2. Select and develop one or more steps in the development
    of a program, the need for which is identified above,
    and indicate in detail how you would carry them out.

3. With the cooperation of your employer or field instruc-
    tor, take the steps necessary to develop a new program
    or substantially revise an existing one (or some part of
    one), and report your findings and conclusions, using
    the guidance provided by the author. Take only those
    steps found necessary in this instance, and assess any
    changes in your plans that you find necessary or desir-
    able as you move through the process.

The Circuit Riding Administrator: A Network Based, Macro-
Generalist Approach to Capacity Building in Small Communities

Lynne Clemmons Morris

Review Questions

1. What is a "circuit riding administrator--macro general-
    ist?" What conditions have prompted its development?

2. What does the author mean by the statement that "the
    difference between a roving and a full-time administra-
    tor is more qualitative than quantitative?

3. In studies of circuit riding administrators, how are the
    roles described? Why do they generally avoid the term
    "administrator?" What are the major roles and tasks
    performed in South Carolina's program?

4. How has the circuit riding administrator's role grown
    and changed over time? Why has this happened?

5. What are the two major limitations of the role of roving
    administrator?

6. What are the problems in the allocation of time to several communities? How have these problems been managed?

7. What does the author mean by the importance of a "systematic perspective" on the role of the roving administrator and the emphasis on "capacity building?"

8. How has the development of the role of roving administrator led inadvertently to "improved cooperation and coordination among the participating communities" when the position was created originally as "an alternative to regional planning and participation in formal coordinating structures?" In what specific ways did coordination take place?

9. What are the "ongoing issues" that face those interested in developing programs of roving administration?

10. What are the implications of the circuit riding administrator role for human service organizations?

Study Questions

1. Apply the circuit riding administrator model to the problems of three to five functionally related human service organizations with which you are familiar in your work or field education experience. Does the model have promise for these organizations? If so, why? If not, why not? If possible, explore the idea with representatives of the organizations involved.

2. If you are located in a rural or small-town area, do the same exercise for three to five small towns.

3. Does the model hold promise for application to the human service responsibilities of village, township and county governments in rural areas? Assuming that each of three to four adjacent counties have full-time county administrators, but lack full-time administrators for a number of human service activities within the responsibility of county government (e.g., nutrition and subsidized housing for the aged, subsidized transportation for the disabled, certain child welfare services such as foster care or adoption of hard-to-place children), assess the possibilities and problems of applying this model. If you are working in or assigned for your field education in such a locality, explore the possibilities with those responsible and report your findings.

Bibliography of Selected Readings

I. General Introduction

A. Conceptions

Gilbert, Neil and Specht, Harry. "Social Planning and Community Organization: Approaches." In Turner, John B. (ed.), *Encyclopedia of Social Work.* Washington, DC: Nat. Assn. Soc. Wkrs., 1977, pp. 1412-1424.

Harper, Ernest B. and Dunham, Arthur. "What Is Community Organization? Selected Definitions." In Harper, Ernest B. and Dunham, Arthur (eds.), *Community Organization in Action.* New York: Association Press, 1959, pp. 54-59.

Kramer, Ralph M. and Specht, Harry. "Introduction." In Kramer, Ralph M. and Specht, Harry (eds.), *Readings in Community Organization Practice.* 3rd ed. Englewood Cliffs, NJ: Prentice-Hall, 1983, pp. 1-23.

Perlman, Robert. "Social Planning and Community Organization." In Turner, John B. (ed.), *Encyclopedia of Social Work.* Washington, DC: Nat. Assn. Soc. Wkrs., 1977, pp. 1404-1412.

Ross, Murray G. with Lappin, B. W. *Community Organization: Theory, Principles and Practice.* 2nd ed. New York: Harper, 1967. pp. 3-99.

Staples, Lee. "An Organizing Model." In *Roots of Power.* New York: Praeger, 1984.

B. History

Addams, Jane. *Forty Years at Hull House.* New York: Macmillan, 1935.

Arnold, Joseph. "The Neighborhood and City Hall: The Origins of Neighborhood Associations in Baltimore, 1880-1911." *Journal of Urban History* 6: 3-30 (November 1979).

Austin, Michael J. and Betten, Neil. "Intellectual Origins of Community Organizing, 1920-1939." *Social Service Review,* 51:1:155-170 (March, 1977).

Axinn, June and Levin, Herman. *Social Welfare: A History of the American Response to Need.* New York: Dodd, Mead, 1975.

Breines, Wini. *Community and Organization in the New Left, 1962-1968: The Great Refusal.* New York: Praeger, 1982.

Carson, Clayborne, Jr. *In Struggle: SNCC and the Black Awakening of the 1960's.* Cambridge, MA: Harvard Univ. Press, 1982.

Chafe, William. *Civilities and Civil Rights: Greensboro, North Carolina and the Black Struggle for Freedom.* New York: Oxford Univ. Press, 1980.

Chambers, Clark A. *Seedtime of Reform: American Social Service and Social Action, 1918-1933.* Minneapolis: Univ. of Minn. Press, 1963.

Coit, Stanton. *Neighborhood Guilds: An Instrument of Social Reform.* London: Sonnenshein, 1891.

Connolly, Michael P. "An Historical Study of Changes in Saul D. Alinsky's Community Organization Practice and Theory, 1939-1972." Ph.D. dissertation, Univ. of Minnesota, School of Social Work, 1976.

Davis, Allen F. *Spearheads for Reform: The Social Settlements and the Progressive Movement, 1890-1914.* New York: Oxford Univ. Press, 1967.

Dunham, Arthur. "Historical Perspectives." In Dunham, Arthur, *The New Community Organization.* New York: Crowell, 1970. pp. 35-55.

Evans, Sara. *Personal Politics: The Roots of Women's Liberation in the Civil Rights Movement and the New Left.* New York: Random House, 1979.

Fisher, Robert and Romanovsky, Peter (eds.). *Community Organization for Urban Social Change: A Historical Perspective.* Westport, CT: Greenwood, 1981.

Gilbert, Neil and Specht, Harry. *The Emergence of Social Welfare and Social Work.* Itasca, IL: F.E. Peacock Publishers, 1976.

Goodwyn, Lawrence. *The Populist Movement: A Short History of Agrarian Revolt in America.* New York: Oxford Univ. Press, 1978.

Leiby, James. *A History of Social Welfare and Social Work in the United States: 1815-1972.* New York: Columbia Univ. Press, 1978.

Lewis, Verl S. "Charity Organization Society." In Turner, John B. (ed.), *Encyclopedia of Social Work.* Washington, DC: Nat. Assn. Soc. Wkrs., pp. 96-100.

Lubove, Roy. *The Professional Altruists: The Emergence of Social Work as a Cause, 1880-1930.* Cambridge, MA: Harvard Univ. Press, 1965.

Philpott, Thomas Lee. *The Slum and the Ghetto: Neighborhood Deterioration and Middle-Class Reform in Chicago, 1880-1930.* New York: Oxford Univ. Press, 1978.

Rosenzweig, Roy. "Organizing the Unemployed: The Early Years of the Great Depression, 1929-1933." *Radical America.* 10:37-60 (July-August 1976).

Schaffer, Anatole. "The Cincinnati Social Unit Experiment, 1917-1919." *Social Service Review.* 45:159-172 (June 1971).

Teodori, Massimo. *The New Left: A Documentary History.* New York: Bobbs Merrill, 1969.

Trattner, Walter I. *From Poor Law to Welfare State.* 2nd ed. New York: Free Press, 1979.

Wald, Lillian. *The House on Henry Street.* New York: Holt, 1915.

II. Common Elements

A. Need Identification

League of California Cities. *Handbook: Assessing Human Need.* Sacramento: League of Calif. Cities, 1975.

Mager, Robert F. *Goal Analysis.* Belmont, CA: Fearon, 1972.

Neuber, Keith A., et al. *Need Assessment: A Model for Community Planning.* Beverly Hills, CA: Sage, 1980.

Rothman, Jack. *Social R & D: Research and Development in the Human Services.* Englewood Cliffs, NJ: Prentice-Hall, 1980.

Siegel, L. M., et al. *Mental Health Needs Assessment: Strategies and Techniques.* Washington, DC: Nat. Institute for Mental Health, 1974.

Smith, Frank J. and Hester, Randolph T., Jr. *Community Goal Setting.* New York: Van Nostrand Reinhold, 1982.

Twain, David. *Creating Change in Social Settings: Planned Program Development.* New York: Praeger, 1983.

B. Advocacy

Berry, Jeffrey. *Lobbying for the People.* Princeton, NJ: Princeton Univ. Press, 1977.

Dear, Ronald B. and Patti, Rino J. "Legislative Advocacy: Seven Effective Tactics." *Social Work.* 26:4:289-296 (July 1981).

Dluhy, Milan J. *Changing the System: Political Advocacy for Disadvantaged Groups.* Beverly Hills, CA: Sage, 1981.

Patti, Rino J. and Dear, Ronald B. "Legislative Advocacy: One Path to Social Change." *Social Work.* 20:2:108-114 (March 1975).

C. Working with Groups

Bertcher, Harvey J. *Group Participation: Techniques for Leaders and Members.* Beverly Hills, CA: Sage, 1979.

Corey, Gerald and Corey, Marianne. *Groups: Process and Practice.* Monterey, CA: Brooks/Cole, 1977.

Maguire, Lambert. *Understanding Networks: Intervention Strategies.* Beverly Hills, CA: Sage, 1983.

Swap, Walter C., et al. *Group Decision-Making.* Beverly Hills, CA: Sage, 1984.

Toseland, Ronald W. and Rivas, Robert F. *An Introduction to Group Work Practice.* New York: Macmillan, 1984.

Tropman, John E., et al. *Essentials of Committee Management.* Chicago: Nelson-Hall, 1979.

Tropman, John E. *Effective Meetings: Improving Group Decision-Making.* Beverly Hills, CA: Sage, 1980.

Zander, Alvin. *Making Groups Effective.* San Francisco: Jossey-Bass, 1982.

D. Program Evaluation

Anderson, Scarvia and Ball, Samuel. *The Profession and Practice of Program Evaluation.* San Francisco: Jossey-Bass, 1978.

Austin, Michael J., et al. *Evaluating Your Agency's Programs.* Beverly Hills, CA: Sage, 1982.

Besag, Frank P. and Besag, Peter L. *Statistics for the Helping Professions.* Beverly Hills, CA: Sage, 1984.

Carter, Reginald K. *The Accountable Agency.* Beverly Hills, CA: Sage, 1983.

Lauffer, Armand. *Assessment Tools: For Practitioners, Managers and Trainers.* Beverly Hills, CA: Sage, 1982.

Rutman, Leonard and Mowbray, George. *Understanding Program Evaluation.* Beverly Hills, CA: Sage, 1983.

Sichel, Joyce L. *Program Evaluation Guidelines: A Research Handbook for Agency Personnel.* New York: Human Sciences Press, 1982.

Weiss, Carol (ed.). *Evaluating Action Programs.* Boston: Allyn & Bacon, 1972.

III. Arenas

A. Society

Crozier, Michael. *The Trouble with America.* Trans. by Peter Heinegg. Los Angeles: Univ. of California Press, 1984.

Drucker, Peter. *The Age of Discontinuity: Guidelines to Our Changing Society.* New York: Harper & Row, 1969.

Etzioni, Amitai. *The Active Society: A Theory of Societal and Political Processes.* New York: Free Press, 1968.

Greer, Germain. *Sex and Destiny.* New York: Harper & Row, 1984.

Janowitz, Morris. *The Last Half Century: Societal Change and Politics in America.* Chicago: Univ. of Chicago Press, 1978.

Lipset, Seymour M. and Schneider, William. *The Confidence Gap.* New York: Free Press, 1983.

Mayhew, Leon H. "Society." In Sills, David L. (ed.), *International Encyclopedia of the Social Sciences.* New York: Macmillan, 1968. Volume 14, p. 583ff.

Perry, Ralph B. *Characteristically American.* New York: Knopf, 1949.

Tropman, John E. "Societal Values and Social Policy." In Tropman, John E., et al., *Strategic Perspectives on Social Policy.* Elmsford, NY: Pergamon, 1976.

Williams, Robin M., Jr. *American Society.* New York, Knopf, 1958.

Yankelovitch, Daniel. *New Rules.* New York: Random House, 1981.

B. Community

Banfield, Edward C. and Wilson, James Q. *City Politics.* New York: Vintage Books, 1963.

Bourne, Larry S. and Simmons, J. W. (eds.). *Systems of Cities.* New York: Oxford Univ. Press, 1978.

Coleman, James S. *Community Conflict.* Glencoe, IL: Free Press, 1957.

Dahl, Robert A. *Who Governs? Democracy and Power in an American City.* New Haven: Yale Univ. Press, 1961.

Drake, St. Clair and Cayton, Horace R. *Black Metropolis.* New York: Harper, 1962.

Gans, Herbert J. *The Urban Villagers.* New York: Free Press, 1962.

Gitlin, Todd and Hollander, Nanci. *Uptown: Poor Whites in Chicago.* New York: Harper and Row, 1970.

Goodman, Paul and Goodman, Percival. *Communitas.* 2nd ed. New York: Vintage, 1980.

Gottschalk, Simon. *Communities and Alternatives.* Cambridge, MA: Schenkman, 1975.

Greeley, Andrew. *Neighborhood.* New York: Seabury, 1977.

Hunter, Floyd G. *Community Power Structure.* Chapel Hill: Univ. of North Carolina Press, 1953.

Kanter, Rosabeth M. *Community and Commitment.* Cambridge, MA: Harvard Univ. Press, 1972.

Presthus, Robert. *Men at the Top: A Study in Community Power.* New York: Oxford Univ. Press, 1964.

Stein, Maurice R. *The Eclipse of Community: An Interpretation of American Studies.* Princeton, NJ: Princeton Univ. Press, 1960.

Sussman, Marvin (ed.), *Community Structure and Analysis.* Westport, CT: Greenwood, 1978.

Swanson, Bert and Swanson, Edith. *Discovering the Community.* New York: Irvington, 1977.

Warren, Donald I. "Neighborhoods in Urban Areas." In Turner, John B. (ed.), *Encyclopedia of Social Work*. Washington, DC: Nat. Assn. Soc. Wkrs., 1977, pp. 993-1005.

Warren, Roland L. *The Community in America*. 3rd ed. Chicago: Rand McNally, 1978.

Warren, Roland L. (ed.). *New Perspectives on the American Community*. 3rd ed. Chicago: Rand McNally, 1977.

C. Organizations

Blau, Peter M. and Scott, W. Richard. *Formal Organizations*. San Francisco: Chandler, 1962.

Camerons, Kim and Whetten, David A. *Organizational Effectiveness: A Comparison of Multiple Models*. New York: Academic Press, 1983.

Connor, Patrick E. *Organizations: Theory and Design*. Chicago: Science Research Associates, 1980.

Etzioni, Amitai. *A Comparative Analysis of Complex Organizations*. New York: Free Press, 1975.

Evan, William M. "Organization Theory and Organizational Effectiveness: An Exploratory Analysis." *Organization and Administrative Science*. 7:15-28 (Spring/Summer, 1976).

Galbraith, Jay R. *Organizational Design*. Reading, MA: Addison-Wesley, 1977.

Grusk, Oscar and Miller, George. *The Sociology of Organizations*. New York: Free Press, 1981.

Hall, Richard. *Organizations: Structure and Process*. 3rd ed. Englewood Cliffs, NJ: Prentice-Hall, 1982.

Hasenfeld, Yeheskel. *Human Service Organizations*. Englewood Cliffs, NJ: Prentice-Hall, 1983.

Hasenfeld, Yeheskel and English, Richard A. (eds.). *Human Service Organizations*. Ann Arbor, MI: Univ. of Michigan Press, 1974.

Katz, Daniel and Kahn, Robert L. *The Social Psychology of Organizations*. New York: Wiley, 1966.

Lauffer, Armand. *Understanding Your Social Agency*. 2nd ed. Beverly Hills, CA: Sage, 1984.

Levine, Sol, et al. "Community Interorganizational Problems in Providing Medical Care and Social Services." *American Journal of Public Health*, 53:3:1183-1195 (August 1963).

Lipsky, Michael. *Street Level Bureaucracy*. New York: Harper and Row, 1980.

Litwak, Eugene. "Models of Bureaucracy Which Permit Conflict." *American Journal of Sociology*. 62:2:177-184 (September 1961).

Maniha, John and Perrow, Charles. "The Reluctant Organization and the Aggressive Environment." *Administrative Science Quarterly*, 10:2:238-257 (September 1965).

March, James G. and Simon, Herbert. *Organizations*. New York: Wiley, 1967.

Messinger, Sheldon. "Organizational Transformation: A Case Study of a Declining Social Movement." *American Sociological Review*, 20:3-10 (February 1955).

Nystrom, Paul C. and Starbuck, William H. *Handbook of Organizational Design*. New York: Oxford Univ. Press, 1981.

Perrow, Charles. *Organizational Analysis: A Sociological View*. Monterey, CA: Brooks/Cole, 1970.

Pfeffer, Jeffrey. *Organizational Design*. Arlington Hgts, IL: AHM Publishing, 1978.

Pinner, Frank, et al. *Old Age and Political Behavior*. Berkeley, CA: Univ. of California Press, 1959.

Rein, Martin and Morris, Robert. "Goals, Structures and Strategies for Community Changes." In *Social Work Practice 1962*. New York: Columbia Univ. Press, 1962. pp. 127-145.

Seely, John R., et al. *Community Chest: A Case Study in Philanthropy.* Toronto: Univ. of Toronto Press, 1957.

Selznick, Philip. *TVA and the Grass Roots.* Berkeley, CA: Univ. of California Press, 1949.

Sills, David L. *The Volunteers: Means and Ends in a National Organization.* Glencoe, IL: Free Press, 1957.

Thompson, James D. *Organizations in Action.* New York: McGraw-Hill, 1967.

Thompson, James D. and Tuden, Arthur. "Strategies, Structures and Processes of Organizational Decision." In Thompson, James D., et al. (eds.), *Comparative Studies in Administration.* Pittsburgh: Univ. of Pittsburgh Press, 1959.

Zald, Mayer N. and Ash, Roberta. "Social Movement Organizations: Growth, Decay and Change." *Social Forces.* 44:327-341 (1966).

D. Linkages

Evan, William M. "The Organizational Set: Toward a Theory of Interorganizational Relations." In Thompson, James D. (ed.), *Approaches to Organizational Design.* Pittsburgh, PA: Univ. of Pittsburgh Press, 1966.

Gilbert, Neil and Specht, Harry. *Coordinating Social Services: An Analysis of Community, Organizational and Staff Characteristics.* New York: Praeger, 1977.

Litwak, Eugene and Hylton, Lydia F. "Interorganizational Analysis." *Administrative Science Quarterly.* 6:4:395-420 (March 1962).

Litwak, Eugene and Meyer, Henry J. "The School and the Family: Linking Organizations and External Primary Groups." In Lazarsfeld, Paul F., et al. (eds.), *The Uses of Sociology.* New York: Basic Books, 1967, pp. 522-543.

Litwak, Eugene and Rothman, Jack. "Toward the Theory and Practice of Coordination between Formal Organizations." In Rosengren, William R. and Lefton, Mark (eds.), *Organizations and Clients.* Columbus, OH: Merrill, 1970.

Miller, Walter B. "Inter-Institutional Conflict as a Major Impediment to Delinquency Prevention." *Human Organization,* 17:3:20-23 (Fall 1968).

Morris, Robert and Randall, Ollie A. "Planning and Organization of Community Services for the Elderly." *Social Work,* 10:1:96-102 (January 1965).

Reid, William J. "Interagency Coordination in Delinquency Prevention and Control." *Social Service Review,* 38:4:418-423 (December 1964).

Rogers, David L., et al. *Interorganizational Coordination.* Ames: Iowa State Univ. Press, 1982.

Simpson, Richard L. and Gulley, William H. "Environmental Pressures and Organizational Characteristics." *American Sociological Review.* 27:3:344-351 (June 1962).

IV. Strategies

A. Social Policy

Anderson, James. *Policy Making.* New York: Praeger, 1975.

Coplin, Merry. *Library Research for Public Policy Issues.* New York: Learning Research Institute Studies, 1975.

DeNitto, Diane M. and Dye, Thomas R. *Social Welfare Politics and Public Policy.* Englewood Cliffs, NJ: Prentice-Hall, 1983.

Dunn, William N. (ed.) *Values, Ethics and the Practice of Policy Analysis.* Lexington, MA: D. C. Heath, 1982.

Flynn, John P. *Social Agency Policy.* Chicago: Nelson Hall, 1985.

Galper, Jeffrey H. *The Politics of Social Services.* Englewood Cliffs, NJ: Prentice-Hall, 1975.

Gil, David G. *Unraveling Social Policy.* 2nd ed. Cambridge, MA: Schenkman, 1976.
Gilbert, Neil and Specht, Harry. *Dimensions of Social Welfare Policy.* Englewood Cliffs, NJ: Prentice-Hall, 1974.
Jansson, Bruce S. *Theory and Practice of Social Welfare Policy.* Englewood Cliffs, NJ: Prentice-Hall, 1983.
Majchrzak, Ann. *Methods for Policy Research.* Beverly Hills, CA: Sage, 1984.
Morris, Robert. *Social Policy of the American Welfare State: An Introduction to Policy Analysis.* New York: Harper and Row, 1979.
Pierce, Dean. *Policy for the Social Work Practitioner.* New York: Longman, 1984.
Rein, Martin. *Social Policy: Issues of Choice and Change.* New York: Random House, 1970.
Tropman, John. *Policy Management in the Human Services.* New York: Columbia Univ. Press, 1984.
Tropman, John E., et al. *New Strategic Perspectives on Social Policy.* New York: Pergamon, 1981.
Wildavsky, Aaron. *Speaking the Truth to Power: The Art and Craft of Policy Analysis.* Boston: Little, Brown & Co., 1979.

B. Social Planning

Banfield, Edward C. *Political Influence.* New York: Free Press, 1961.
Checkoway, Barry (ed.) *Citizens and Health Care: Participation and Planning for Social Change.* New York: Pergamon, 1981.
Fisher, Jack C. and Henderson, Henry P. "Regional Planning and Development." In Turner, John B. (ed.), *Encyclopedia of Social Work.* Washington, DC: Nat. Assn. Soc. Wkrs., 1977, pp. 1175-1183.
Gans, Herbert J. *People and Plans: Essays on Urban Problems and Solutions.* New York: Basic Books, 1968.
Gilbert, Neil and Specht, Harry. *Dynamics of Community Planning.* Cambridge, MA: Ballinger, 1977.
Gilbert, Neil and Specht, Harry. *Planning for Social Welfare: Issues, Models and Tasks.* Englewood Cliffs, NJ: Prentice-Hall, 1977.
Green, Robert. *The Urban Challenge: Poverty and Race.* Chicago: Follett, 1977.
Hanson, John E. "Social Planning, Governmental: Federal and State." In Turner, John B. (ed.), *Encyclopedia of Social Work.* Washington, DC: Nat. Assn. Soc. Wkrs., 1977, pp. 1443-1448.
Kahn, Alfred J. *Theory and Practice of Social Planning.* New York: Russell Sage, 1969.
Kettner, P., et al. *Initiating Change in Organizations and Communities.* Monterey, CA: Brooks/Cole, 1985.
Lauffer, Armand. *Social Planning at the Community Level.* Englewood Cliffs, NJ: Prentice-Hall, 1978.
Mahaffey, Maryann and Hanks, John W. *Practical Politics: Social Work and Political Responsibility.* Silver Springs, MD: Nat. Assn. Soc. Wkrs., 1982.
Marris, Peter and Rein, Martin. *Dilemmas of Social Reform.* New York: Atherton Press, 1967.
Mayer, Robert R., et al. *Centrally Planned Change.* Urbana, IL: Univ. of Illinois Press, 1974.
Meltzer, Jack. "Environment: Urban Planning and Development." In Turner, John B. (ed.), *Encyclopedia of Social Work.* Washington, DC: Nat. Assn. Soc. Wkrs., 1977, pp. 341-349.
Moroney, Robert M. "Social Planning: Tools for Planning." In Turner, John B. (ed.), *Encyclopedia of Social Work.* Washington, DC: Nat. Assn. Soc. Wkrs., 1977, pp. 1448-1452.

Morris, Robert, et al. *Feasible Planning for Social Change*. New York: Columbia Univ. Press, 1966.

Palmiere, Darwin. "Health Services: Health and Hospital Planning." In Turner, John B. (ed.), *Encyclopedia of Social Work*. Washington, DC: Nat. Assn. Soc. Wkrs., 1977, pp. 595-602.

Rein, Martin. "Social Planning: Welfare Planning." In *International Encyclopedia of the Social Sciences*. New York: Macmillan, 1968, pp. 142-154.

Zaltman, Gerald and Duncan, Robert. *Strategies for Planned Change*. New York: Wiley, 1977.

C. Locality Development

Cary, Lee J. (ed.) *Community Development as a Process*. Columbia, MO: Univ. of Missouri Press, 1983.

Chekki, Dan A. (ed.) *Participatory Democracy in Action: International Profiles of Community Development*. New York: Advent Books, 1980.

Chekki, Dan A. (ed.) *Community Development: Theory and Methods of Planned Change*. New York: Advent Books, 1980.

Clay, Philip L. *Neighborhood Renewal: Middle Class Resettlement and Incumbent Upgrading in American Neighborhoods*. Lexington, MA: Lexington Books, 1979.

Clinard, Marshall B. *Slums and Community Development: Experiments in Self-Help*. New York: Free Press, 1966.

Davis, Frank G. *The Economics of Black Community Development: An Analysis and Program for Autonomous Growth and Development*. Lanham, MD: Univ. Press of America, 1976.

Fessler, Donald R. *Facilitating Community Change: A Basic Guide*. San Diego: University Associates, 1976.

Fitzsimmons, Stephen J. and Freeman, Abby J. *Community Development: A Program, Policy and Research Model*. Lanham, MD: Univ. Press of America, 1984.

Goodenough, Ward H. *Cooperation in Change: An Anthropological Approach to Community Development*. New York: Russell Sage, 1963.

Hardiman, Margaret and Medgley, James. *The Social Dimensions of Development: Social Policy and Planning in the Third World*. New York: Wiley, 1982.

Henderson, Paul and Thomas, David N. *Skills in Neighborhood Work*. Winchester, MA: Allen & Unwin, 1981.

Henig, Jeffrey R. *Neighborhood Mobilization: Redevelopment and Response*. New Brunswick, NJ: Rutgers, 1982.

Long, Norman. *An Introduction to the Sociology of Rural Development*. Boulder, CO: Westview, 1982.

Mayer, N. *Neighborhood Organizations and Community Development*. Washington, DC: Urban Institute, 1984.

Mayer, N. *Keys to the Growth of Neighborhood Development*. Washington, DC: Urban Institute, 1981.

Mulford, Charles. *Interorganizational Relations: Implications for Community Development*. New York: Human Sciences Press, 1983.

Nesman, Edgar G. *Peasant Mobilization and Rural Development*. Cambridge, MA: Schenkman, 1980.

O'Brien, David J. *Neighborhood Organization and Interest-Group Process*. Princeton, NJ: Princeton Univ. Press, 1975.

Perry, David G. and Bussey, Kay. *Social Development*. Englewood Cliffs, NJ: Prentice-Hall, 1984.

Sanders, Daniel S. (ed.) *The Developmental Perspective in Social Work*. Honolulu: Univ. of Hawaii Press, 1982.

Sorrentino, Anthony. *Organizing Against Crime: Redeveloping the Neighborhood*. New York: Human Sciences Press, 1977.

Specht, Harry. *The Community Development Project: National and Local Strategies for Improving the Delivery of Services.* New York: State Mutual, 1976.

Spergel, Irving A. "Social Planning and Community Organization: Community Development." In Turner, John B. (ed.), *Encyclopedia of Social Work.* Washington, DC: Nat. Assn. Soc. Wkrs., 1977, pp. 1425-1433.

Spiegel, Hans B. C. (ed.). *Citizen Participation in Urban Development.* Vol. 1, *Concepts and Issues.* Washington, DC: NTL Inst. for Applied Behavioral Science, 1968.

Spiegel, Hans B. C. (ed.) *Citizen Participation in Urban Development.* Vol. 2, *Cases and Programs.* Washington, DC: NTL Inst. for Applied Behavioral Science, 1969.

Stern, Gloria. *How to Start Your Own Food Co-op.* New York: Walker, 1974.

Thomas, David. *Skills in Neighborhood Work.* New York: State Mutual, 1980.

Toch, Hans and Grant, J. Douglas. *Reforming Human Services: Change Through Participation.* Beverly Hills, CA: Sage, 1982.

Warren, Rachelle and Warren, Donald L. *The Neighborhood Organizer's Handbook.* Notre Dame, IN: Univ. of Notre Dame Press, 1977.

Weissman, Harold H. *Community Councils and Community Control: The Workings of Democratic Mythology.* Pittsburgh, PA: Univ. of Pittsburgh Press, 1970.

Wireman, Peggy. "Citizen Participation." In Turner, John B. (ed.), *Encyclopedia of Social Work.* Washington, DC: Nat. Assn. Soc. Wkrs., 1977, pp. 175-179.

D. Social Action

Alinsky, Saul D. *Reveille for Radicals.* Chicago: Univ. of Chicago Press, 1946.

Alinsky, Saul D. *Rules for Radicals.* New York: Random House, 1971.

Bailey, Robert, Jr. *Radicals in Urban Politics: The Alinsky Approach.* Chicago: Univ. of Chicago Press, 1974.

Berkowitz, William R. *Community Impact: Creating Grass Roots Change.* Cambridge, MA.: Schenkman, 1982.

Berube, Maurice and Gittell, Marilyn (eds.) *Confrontation at Ocean-Hill Brownsville.* New York: Praeger, 1969.

Boyte, Harry C. *The Backyard Revolution: Understanding the New Citizen Movement.* Philadelphia: Temple Univ. Press, 1980.

Burghardt, Steve. *The Other Side of Organizing: Personal Dilemmas and Political Demands.* Cambridge, MA: Schenkman, 1982.

Burghardt, Steve. *Organizing for Community Action.* Beverly Hills, CA: Sage, 1982.

Case, John and Taylor, Rosemary (eds.) *Co-ops, Communes and Collectives: Experiments in Social Change in the 1960's and 1970's.* New York: Pantheon, 1979.

Cassidy, Robert. *Livable Cities: A Grass-Roots Guide to Rebuilding Urban America.* New York: Holt, Rinehart & Winston, 1980.

Fish, John Hall. *Black Power/White Control: The Struggle of the Woodlawn Organization in Chicago.* Princeton, NJ: Princeton Univ. Press, 1973.

Fisher, Robert. *Let the People Decide: Neighborhood Organizing in America.* Boston: G. K. Hall, 1984.

Gamson, William. *The Strategy of Social Protest.* Homewood, IL: Dorsey, 1975.

Kahn, Si. *Organizing: A Guide for Grass Roots Leaders.* New York: McGraw-Hill. 1982.

Lancourt, Joan E. *Confront or Concede: The Alinsky Citizen-Action Organizations.* Lexington, MA: Lexington Books, 1979.

Morris, David and Hess, Karl. *Neighborhood Power: The New Localism.* Boston: Beacon Press, 1975.

Piven, Frances F. and Cloward, Richard. *Poor People's Movements: Why They Succeed, How They Fail.* New York: Pantheon, 1977.

Sanders, Marion K. *The Professional Radical: Conversations with Saul Alinsky.* Evanston, IL: Harper & Row, 1965.

Shockley, John S. *Chicano Revolt in a Texas Town.* Notre Dame, IN: Univ. of Notre Dame Press, 1974.

Staples, Lee. *Roots to Power: A Manual for Grassroots Organizing.* New York: Praeger, 1984.

Thurz, Daniel. "Social Action." In Turner, John B. (ed.), *Encyclopedia of Social Work.* Washington, DC: Nat. Assn. Soc. Wkrs., 1977, pp. 1274-1280.

Trapp, Shel. *Dynamics of Organizing.* Chicago: Nat. Training and Info. Center, 1976.

Wellstone, Paul. *How the Rural Poor Got Power: Narrative of a Grass-Roots Organizer.* Amherst: Univ. of Mass. Press, 1978.

E. Administration and Management

Ables, P. and Murphy, M. *Administration in the Human Services: A Normative Systems Approach.* Englewood Cliffs, NJ: Prentice-Hall, 1981.

Aldridge, Martha. *Beyond Management.* Iowa City: Univ. of Iowa Press, 1982.

Austin, Michael. *Supervisory Management for Human Services.* Englewood Cliffs, NJ: Prentice-Hall, 1981.

Azarnoff, R. and Seliger, J. *Delivering Human Services.* Englewood Cliffs, NJ: Prentice-Hall, 1982.

Bamford, Terry. *Managing Social Work.* New York: Methuen, 1983.

Brager, George and Holloway, Stephen. *Changing Human Service Organizations.* New York: Free Press, 1978.

Brawley, Edward A. *Mass Media and Human Services: Getting the Message Across.* Beverly Hills, CA: Sage, 1983.

Burke, W. Warner (ed.) *Current Issues and Strategies in Organization Development.* New York: Human Sciences Press, 1977.

Cherniss, Cary. *Staff Burnout: Job Stress in the Human Services.* Beverly Hills, CA: Sage, 1980.

Christian, Walter and Hannah, Gerald T. *Effective Management in Human Services.* Englewood Cliffs, NJ: Prentice-Hall, 1983.

Edelwich, Jerry with Brodsky, Archie. *Burn-Out: Stages of Disillusionment in the Helping Professions.* New York: Human Sciences Press, 1980.

Farmer, Richard E., et al. *Stress Management for Human Services.* Beverly Hills, CA: Sage, 1984.

Fischer, Constance T. and Brodsky, Stanley L. (eds.) *Client Participation in Human Services: The Prometheus Principle.* New Brunswick, NJ: Transaction Books, 1978.

Gambrill, Eileen and Stein, Theodore J. *Supervision: A Decision-Making Approach.* Beverly Hills, CA: Sage, 1983.

Gates, B. *Social Program Administration: The Implementation of Social Policy.* Englewood Cliffs, NJ: Prentice-Hall, 1980.

Knighton, Art and Heidelman, Nancy. *Administration of the Human Services: A Practical Workbook for Managers.* Ann Arbor, MI: Univ. of Michigan Press, 1983.

Lauffer, Armand. *Getting the Resources You Need.* Beverly Hills, CA: Sage, 1982.

Lauffer, Armand. *Strategic Marketing for Not-for-Profit Organizations.* New York: Free Press, 1984.

Lauffer, Armand. *Grantsmanship and Fundraising.* Beverly Hills, CA: Sage, 1984.

Levin, Henry M. *Cost Effectiveness.* Beverly Hills, CA: Sage, 1983.

Levy, Charles. *A Guide to Ethical Decisions and Actions for Social Service Administrators: A Handbook for Managerial Personnel.* New York: Haworth, 1982.

Lohmann, Roger A. *Breaking Even: Financial Management in Human Service Organizations.* Philadelphia: Temple Univ. Press, 1980.

Lurie, Abraham and Rosenberg, Gary (eds.) *Social Work Administration in Health Care.* New York: Haworth, 1984.

Martin, Shan. *Managing Without Managers: Alternative Work Arrangements in Public Organizations.* Beverly Hills, CA: Sage, 1983.

Middleman, Ruth R. and Rhodes, Gary B. *Competent Supervision: Making Imaginative Judgments.* Englewood Cliffs, NJ: Prentice-Hall, 1985.

Mintzberg, Henry. *The Nature of Managerial Work.* New York: Harper & Row, 1973.

Nadler, David A., et al. *Managing Organizational Behavior.* Boston: Little, Brown & Co., 1979.

Paine, Whiton S. (ed.) *Job Stress and Burnout: Research, Theory and Intervention Perspectives.* Beverly Hills, CA: Sage, 1982.

Patti, Rino J. *Social Welfare Administration: Managing Social Programs in a Development Context.* Englewood Cliffs, NJ: Prentice-Hall, 1983.

Perlmutter, Felice D. and Slavin, Simon (eds.) *Leadership in Social Administration.* Philadelphia: Temple Univ. Press, 1980.

Pressman, Jeffrey and Wildavsky, Aaron. *Implementation.* Berkeley, CA: Univ. of California Press, 1974.

Rothman, Jack, et al. *Marketing Human Service Innovations.* Beverly Hills, CA: Sage, 1983.

Sarri, Rosemary C. and Hasenfeld, Yeheskel (eds.) *The Management of Human Services.* New York: Columbia Univ. Press, 1978.

Seashore, Stanley S., et al. (eds.) *Assessing Organizational Change: A Guide to Methods, Measures and Practices.* New York: Wiley, 1983.

Skidmore, Rex. *Social Work Administration: Dynamic Management and Human Relationships.* Englewood Cliffs, NJ: Prentice-Hall, 1983.

Slavin, Simon (ed.) *Applying Computers in Social Services and Mental Health Agencies: A Guide to Selecting Equipment, Procedures and Strategies.* New York: Haworth, 1982.

Slavin, Simon (ed.) *Social Administration: The Management of the Social Services.* New York: Haworth, 1978.

Smith, Craig and Skjei, Eric. *Getting Grants.* New York: Harper and Row, 1981.

Taylor, James B. *Using Microcomputers in Social Agencies.* Beverly Hills, CA: Sage, 1981.

Toch, Hans and Grant, J. Douglas. *Reforming Human Services: Change Through Participation.* Beverly Hills, CA: Sage, 1982.

Weiner, Myron E. *Human Services Management: Analysis and Applications.* Homewood, IL: Dorsey, 1982.

Indexes

NAME

Aberle, David F., 190
Addams, Jane, 28, 36, 391
Adler, Felix, 34
Aiken, M., 101
Alford, R., 101
Alinsky, Saul D., 7, 9, 12, 16, 17, 54, 165, 188, 210, 236, 241, 385, 393, 396, 399, 400
Alvarez, Salvador, 37
Amidei, Nancy, 69
Anthony, Susan B., 37
Argyris, C., 173, 181
Aristotle, 217
Arnold, Joseph, 394
Attkisson, C.C., 80, 86, 87

Bacon, Francis, 278
Baker, F., 75
Baker, Flory, 336
Bakke, E. Wright, 245n
Banfield, Edward C., 441
Barbee, Lloyd, 374
Barnard, Chester I., 429
Barnett, Samuel, 34
Batalla, Guillermo Bonfil, 357
Baumheier, Edward C., 19
Bedics, B. C., 6

Bell, Budd L., 336
Bell, R. A., 74
Bell, Wendell, 234
Bell, William G., 336
Bengston, Vern L., 213-214
Benne, K. D., 102
Bennis, W. G., 102
Bergman, Edward M., 337
Berry, Jeffrey M., 335
Biddle, Loureide J., 5, 6, 13, 16, 359
Biddle, William W., 5, 6, 13, 16, 359-360
Biegel, A., 76
Binstock, Robert H., 6, 7, 8, 14, 15, 16
Bisno, Herbert, 69
Blakely, Edward J., 6, 9, 12, 14
Blau, Peter M., 162, 189, 196-197
Bloom, B. L., 74
Blum, H. L., 71, 72, 75
Bohlen, Janet, 335
Bokemeir, Janet, 335
Booth, Heather, 330
Boulding, Kenneth, 438
Boyte, Harry C., 243, 397
Bradley, John, 333
Brager, George, 102
Brandwein, Ruth, 323

Brawley, Edward A., 334
Braybooke, David, 315
Brecht, Bertolt, 384
Brill, N., 115, 119
Broskowski, Anthony, 75, 485
Bryson, John M., 329
Burke, R., 126

Campbell, D. T., 73
Carter, Jimmy, 57, 321, 387
Chapin, E. H., 76
Chavez, Cesar, 53
Checkoway, Barry, 309
Chin, R., 102
Christensen, Terry, 335
Clark, Peter, 247
Cloward, Richard, 101, 241
Cohen, Michael D., 279, 447
Cohen, Wilbur J., 272
Cohn, A. H., 93
Coit, Stanton, 34
Coleman, James S., 160, 168, 169, 210
Collier, John, 49
Commons, John R., 272
Connor, Patrick E., 197-202
Coolidge, Calvin, 41
Corey, K., 102
Cortes, Ernie, 393
Cortese, Charles F., 479
Cox, Fred M., 70, 87
Creighton, James L., 333
Cremer, Nancy Sheldon, 337
Crowell, L., 136
Cullen, Countee, 39
Cummings, L., 172
Cyert, Richard M., 430

Dahrendorf, Ralf, 219
Dale, Duane, 333
Davidoff, Paul, 325
Dear, Ronald B., 335
DeBono, E., 137
Delbecq, A. L., 88-89
Derthick, Martha, 442
Deutscher, I., 173
Dewey, John, 31
Dluhy, Milan, 272, 335, 336
Doelker, R., 6
Doherty, J. C., 475
Donnison, David D., 429

Dornbusch, S., 179
Douglass, Frederick, 36
Downing, George T., 36
DuBois, W. E. B., 36
Dunham, Arthur, 5, 14, 351

Edson, J., 115
Eisenhower, Dwight D., 54
Eisenstadt, S. N., 251
Elam, John, 482
Eliot, T. S., 41, 294
Epstein, T. Scarlett, 355
Etzioni, Amitai, 172, 315, 437

Feldman, Martha, 279
Feldstein, Paul J., 331
Ferraro, Geraldine, 61
Festinger, Leon, 355
Filley, A., 126
Fishel, Leslie H., Jr., 28
Fisher, Robert, 26, 27, 385
Fiske, D. W., 73
Fitzgerald, F. Scott, 41
Follett, Mary, 46, 396
Fraga, Felix, 393
Franklin, John Hope, 45
Frazier, W. D., 102
Freeman, Edward, 329
Freud, Sigmund, 41
Friedmann, John, 315, 316

Galbraith, Jay R., 201
Gamson, William, 260
Gans, Herbert J., 235
Garvey, Marcus, 45
George, Henry, 31
Gershenfeld, M., 115, 127
Getzels, Judith, 477
Gibb, J., 136
Glenn, Karen, 334
Goffman, Erving, 433
Gordon, Robbie, 334
Gouldner, Alvin W., 427-428, 437, 446
Gronouski, John, 373
Gross, Edward, 199
Grosser, Charles, 13
Guetzkow, H., 126
Gummer, Burton, 329, 425
Gurin, Arnold, 24, 150
Gyr, J., 126

Haggstrom, Warren, 385, 398
Halpert, Burton P., 207
Hanks, John W., 329
Harbach, Franklin, 392
Hare, A., 124
Harris, Ian, 352
Hart, Joseph K., 46
Hart, P., 171
Hasenfeld, Yeheskel, 329, 426
Havelock, R. G., 102
Haynes, George Edmund, 36
Heilbroner, Robert L., 357
Hemmens, George C., 337
Henderson, Paul, 5
Hoffer, Eric, 260
Hollingshead, August B., 239
Holloway, S., 102
Homans, George C., 189
Howard, John R., 36-37
Huber, G., 120, 122
Hudson, Barclay, 315
Hughes, Langston, 39
Hunter, E. H., 76
Hunter, Floyd, 238, 239, 240, 252
Hylton, Lydia F., 206-207

Irizarry, I., 369

Jackson, Jesse, 61
James, William, 31
Jansson, Bruce S., 19, 270
Johnson, K. W., 102
Johnson, Lyndon B., 55, 113, 168, 321
Jones, Bernie, 479
Joslyn-Scherer, M. S., 334
Jung, C., 220

Kahn, S., 9, 11, 12, 15, 17
Kahn, Robert L., 435
Kaplan, Abraham, 323
Katan, Joseph, 68
Katz, Daniel, 215, 435
Katz, Elihu, 251
Kaufman, Harold J., 237
Kelly, Florence, 36
Kennedy, John F., 55, 168
Khinduka, S. K., 351
King, Martin Luther, Jr., 52, 211, 257
Kirchoff, B., 172
Kitano, Harry H. L., 49

Klosterman, Richard E., 318
Koneya, Mele, 377
Kramer, Ralph M., 4, 232, 242
Krumholz, Norman, 330

Lancourt, Joan, 330
Lasswell, Harold, 441
Lauffer, Armand, 6, 309, 334
Leinberger, Paul, 333
Lerner, Max, 30, 31, 39
Levine, Sol, 205, 433
Lewis, Sinclair, 41
Lindblom, Charles, 315
Lindeman, Eduard C., 47
Lippitt, Ronald, 150, 156, 164
Litwak, Eugene, 194, 195, 203, 206-207, 481
Long, Norton E., 190
Lopez y Rivas, Gilberto, 45
Lovejoy, Mary C., 214
Lowery, M. J., 76
Lowi, T., 169
Loye, David, 324
Lubove, Roy, 42, 44, 47
Lynd, Helen Merrell, 238
Lynd, Robert S., 238

MacCrimmon, Kenneth R., 430
Machiavelli, 238
Machlowitz, Marilyn, 219
Mahaffey, Maryann, 329, 336
Maier, N., 120, 126, 133
March, James G., 271
Martí-Costa, Sylvia, 352
Marx, Karl, 238
Masi, Dale, 323-324
Max, Steve, 333
Mayer, N., 5
Mayhew, Leon H., 190
Maynard-Moody, Steven, 70
McCabe, Irene, 53
McCabe, T. R., 76
McCarthy, Eugene, 55
McCarthy, Joseph, 47
McEwen, William J., 204
McGowan, E., 179
Mead, George Herbert, 31
Mead, Margaret, 357
Meier, R., 84, 85
Merton, Robert K., 158, 220
Messinger, Ruth W., 336

Meyer, Henry J., 194, 195, 203
Mills, C. Wright, 252
Moe, Edward O., 190, 236
Moore, Joan, 40
Moroney, Robert M., 337
Morris, Robert, 6, 7, 8, 14, 15, 16, 155, 196, 205
Morris, Lynne Clemmons, 426
Moynihan, Daniel P., 55
Murphy, Campbell G., 32

Naisbitt, John, 57, 58, 59
Napier, H., 115, 124, 127
Nelkin, D., 170
Neven, David, 333
Nixon, Richard M., 57, 227, 321

Ohlin, Lloyd E., 101
Olsen, Johan, 279
Osterman, Paul, 337

Pareto, 220, 238
Parsons, Talcott, 22, 191-192, 237
Patti, R., 169, 329, 335
Patton, Carl, 310
Paul, Benjamin D., 205
Peirce, Charles S., 31
Perlman, Janice E., 60
Perlman, Robert, 150
Perrow, Charles, 171, 172, 430-431
Perry, Charles, 337
Perry, Ralph Barton, 230
Pettigrew, Andrew M., 441
Pfeffer, Jeffrey, 430
Picasso, Pablo, 294
Pierce, Dean, 19, 270
Pierce, Franklin, 168
Pines, Burton Yale, 331
Piven, Frances Fox, 241
Poplin, Dennis E., 243
Pusic, Eugen, 271

Quarles, Benjamin, 28

Randolph, A. Phillip, 48
Reagan, Ronald, 57, 58, 59, 169, 321
Rein, Martin, 6, 14, 155, 196
Reynolds, Judge John, 377
Riddick, M. F., 102
Roberts, Robert W., 4

Robeson, Paul, 39
Robin, S. A., 81-82
Roche, Joseph L., 330, 335
Roering, William D., 329
Rogers, E. E., 102
Rokeach, Milton, 214
Romelaer, Pierre, 291
Roosevelt, Franklin D., 48, 49
Rose, Arnold, 158-159
Ross, Murray G., 8, 9-10, 13, 150, 188
Rossi, Peter, 173
Rothman, Jack, 6, 102, 103, 162, 163, 325, 481
Ruskin, John, 34

Sacco, Nicola, 41
Salcito, Ramon, 336
Scheidel, T., 136
Schlitz, Michael, 214-215
Schone, Donald A., 325, 337
Schorr, Alvin L., 19
Schwab, J. J., 74
Scott, W. Richard, 162, 171, 179, 189, 196-197
Seashore, Stanley E., 441-442
Selznick, Philip, 206, 427, 428, 435
Serrano-García, Irma, 352, 369
Sevon, Guje, 279
Shapira, Zur, 279
Shevky, Eshref, 234
Shoemaker, F., 102
Siegel, Larry M., 68
Simon, Herbert, 163, 281, 318
Sinclair, Upton, 393
Smith, Adam, 277
Smith, R., 101
Specht, Harry, 4, 13, 232, 242
Spiro, Shimon E., 68
Staples, Lee, 385
Steers, R., 177
Steiner, I., 120
Steiner, Jesse, 392
Stoner, J., 125
Suchman, E., 180

Taft, Jesse, 41
Tait, John L., 335
Tamerin, J. S., 76
Tannenbaum, Arnold S., 443
Taylor, Samuel H., 4

Thomas, David N., 5
Thomas, Edwin, 100, 102
Thompson, James D., 170, 171, 178, 195, 196, 204, 431
Thrasymachus, 238
Thurow, Charles, 477
Toseland, Ronald W., 69
Towle, Charlotte, 445
Trecker, H., 115
Tropman, John E., 19, 116, 117, 133, 270
Trounstine, Philip J., 335
Truman, Harry S, 48
Tsanoff, Corinne, 392
Tuden, Arthur, 195, 196
Turk, H., 101
Tyler, William B., 198

Van de Ven, A. H., 89
Van Gogh, Vincent, 296
Vanzetti, Bartolomeo, 41
Vickers, Geoffrey, 316

Wald, Lillian, 36, 391
Wallace, George, 53

Warheit, George J., 74, 85
Warner, W. Lloyd, 238
Warren, Roland L., 11, 12, 150, 189, 232, 235, 236, 238, 242, 322, 433
Washington, Booker T., 36
Watson, Frank D., 33
Weber, Max, 172, 198, 233, 239, 259, 355, 428, 429, 430
Weeks, John, 46
Weick, K., 171, 180
Whitaker, D., 127
Whitaker, William H., 336
White, Paul E., 205, 433
Whitman, Alberry, 29
Williams, Robin M., Jr., 216
Wilson, Woodrow, 38
Woods, Robert, 391

Yessian, Mark R., 485
Yuchtman, Ephraim, 441-442

Zald, Mayer N., 6, 155, 425
Zander, A., 120
Ziller, R., 125

SUBJECT

Aberrant behavior: description of, 158
Abortion, 110, 145
Accountability: efforts at, 379, 485; in instrumental activities, 146; purpose of, 180
Action: basis for, 288-289, 399, 404; and decision rules, 289-290; differentiated from community action, 237; examples of, 289, 414-415; implementation suggestions for, 153; nature of, 415, 416; objective of, 407; requirements for, 235-236
Action group, 455, 456
Action guidelines, 102
Action system, 163, 165, 166
Action-reaction-action pattern: description of, 165
Activism, 26
Actors: in conflict situation, 412; organizing search for, 403-404
Adaptation: functions, 191; in organizations, 444

Adaptive subsystem: aspects of, 435-436
Administration: definition of, 21; focus of, 18, 423-425; macro generalist role in, 484; organizations as setting for, 20; phases in, 269; skills of, 24; value agreement in, 266
Administration in Social Work, 20
Administrative practice, 22-23
Administrator: roles and functions of, 21-22, 423, 424, 477; and value orientation, 25
Adult foster care: description of, 306
Adversity: conditions of, 282
Advice: nature of, 295-296
Advice giving: role of circuit rider, 478
Advocacy: definition of, 335; elements of, 69, 106, 114, 335-336
Advocacy planners: views of, 316
Advocate: definition of, 13; role of social worker, 389
Affective conflict, 126

Africa, 45
Afro-American League, 36
Agencies: characteristics of, 151; future forms of, 324; need assessment in, 76; and practice settings, 154-155; types of, 21
Agency staff: and goal conflict, 145
Agency structure, 151
Agenda: development of; 121, elements of, 116, 133; pacing, 117-118
Agents: roles and functions of, 286
Agreements: between agencies, 207-208; and sanctions, 413
Aid to Families with Dependent Children (AFDC): media hostility about, 108
Alameda, California, 329
Alcatraz Island, 53
Alien Land Bill, 30
Alliance: aspects of, 285, 286
Alliance for Vounteerism, 60
Alternatives: decisions based on, 280-281
Ambiguity and Choice in Organizations, 291
Ambulatory: definition of, 306
American Association of University Women, 46
American Equal Rights Association, 38
American Hospital Association, 326
American Medical Association, 326-327
American Woman Suffrage Association, 38
Annual meeting: evaluation reports at, 166
Anomic collectivity, 195
Anonymity: issues regarding, 344-345
Anthropology: and studies of change, 99
Antiabortion movement, 110
Antihunger movement: history of, 113
Appalachia: strip mining in, 113
Area Agencies on Aging, 321
Arenas: description of, 187-188
Aristocracy: meanings of, 223
Assessment: nature of, 74, 75, 166. *See also* Needs Assessment
Assignment: meanings of worker, 151, 154
Association of Community Organizations for Reform Now (ACORN), 9, 60, 384, 393
Association of Training Schools for Professional Social Work, 38
Associations: development of, 276
Attacks: on low income organizations, 410, 414; on organizer, 420
Attention: claims on, 292
Auditing: case or client record, 470; operations

level, 471; purpose of, 469
Authority: imbalance in, 147; relations in social programs, 179
Authority theory: defined, 429
Autonomy: loss of community, 242

Back of the Yards: Chicago, 393
Backyard revolution: description of, 385; in Houston, 388
Baltimore, 394; characteristics of homeless in, 301
Barriers: in service systems, 74
Behavior: as output measure, 202
Behavioral management theory, 173
Behavioral sciences: concepts of change in, 100
Beliefs: ideas about, 220
Beneficiaries: organizations and, 162
Benefits: elements of community development, 348; issues around, 228-229
Bill of Rights, 227
Black power: growth of, 9, 53
Blacks: and community issues, 61; conditions of, 28; conflicts between, 53; and New Deal programs, 48; opportunities for, 48; organizations of, 36, 44-45, 51, 53; repression of, 39
Block grants: examples of, 322
Board of directors: tasks of, 457
Boston, 394
Boundaries: community, 233, 236; for organizing neighborhood, 403; for problem solving in task groups, 130-131
Boundary roles: in transactions, 452; staff, 466; working relations in, 470
Brandeis University, 7
Brazil, 58
Brotherhood of Sleeping Car Porters, 48
Budget: and voter campaigns, 111
Bums: description of, 223
Bureaucracies: planner role in, 324
Bureaucracy: characteristics of, 194, 195, 197, 415, 430; structure of, 432-433, 468
Buy out: organization's power to, 204-205
Bylaws: requirements of, 400

California: gold rush, 30
Campaigns: activities of, 416
Career expectations, 222-223
Case conference: establishment of, 32
Case management, 320
Case record: elements of, 470

Casework, 46, 445: role, 359
Categorical programs, 321
Causal knowledge, 170
Census: types of data, 234
Central planning: arguments against, 312-313
Centralization: organizational, 198
Change: agent, 263; basis of decisions for, 188; orientation, 246; strategy, 12; target, 251, 263
Character: organizational, 438
Charity: notions of, 297
Charity endorsement bureau, 42-43
Charity Organization Society, 32-33, 34: in Denver, 42
Chicago, 39: characteristics of homeless in, 301
Chicago Commons, 396
Chicago school of human ecologists: study of community dynamics, 233-234
Chicanos: history of protest, 29; immigration, 39-40, 48; organizations of, 51; organizing efforts of, 53
Child guidance clinic: technology of, 431
Child labor laws: attack on, 46
Child welfare agency: subsystems of, 435-436
Children: status of, 229
China, 58
Chinese: immigration curbs on, 40; immigration to California, 30; organizations of, 37
Chinese Exclusion Act, 30
Chinese-Americans: changes for, 51; status of, 49
Choice: elements of, 318, 226; ideas about, 279-280; model of, 280; orchestrations of, 293
Choice process: symbolic nature of, 293
Circuit riding administrator: development of, 474; as linking agent, 482; roles of, 475, 476, 477-478
Circuit riding administrator program: characteristics of participants in, 475; organizational activities, 485
Citizen demands: unfulfilled, 379
Citizen input, 343
Citizen opinion: comparative study of, 344-347; elements of, 343
Citizen participation: benefits of, 332, 381; in community forums, 86-88; evaluation guidelines for, 377; forms of, 357; and planning, 322, 331; problems with, 358; various aspects of, 332-333

Citizens' Councils, 394
City: defined, 233
Civic clubs: purposes of, 395
Civil disobedience, 221
Civil liberties: in 1920s, 39
Civil Rights Act of 1875, 28
Civil War: social issues after, 27
Clan control: in professional organizations, 202
Class: as variable in strategy, 262
Classroom exercise: value conflict in, 217-219
Cleveland Chamber of Commerce, 43
Client system: defined, 14-15
Clients: characteristics of, 152, 162; definitions of, 161; measuring attributes of, 472; recruiting of, 464-465; stress of, 432; roles of, 16-17
Close effects: meaning of, 215
Closed loop, 180
Coalition: meanings of, 286, 287, 288; stage of planning, 316; of truth squads, 112
Coalition for Peaceful Schools: activities, 376; advocacy role, 378; benefits, 382; membership, 375, 376, 379-380; purpose, 375-376; reasons for decline, 380-381
Coalition model: characteristics of, 399-400
Coalitions: definition of, 335; elements of, 464; forming, 206; ways of building, 335
Coding: in effectiveness study, 174-175
Cognitive dissonance, 355
Cognitive style: of planners, 322-323
Cold War: in 1950s, 50
Collaboration: agency, 320
Collective action: nature of, 210
Collectivities: decisions in, 227
Collegial body: problem solving in, 195
Colorado: study of, 479
Colored Farmers Alliance and Cooperative Union, 36
Combat: conflict and, 285
Commissioner of Indian Affairs, 40
Committee of 100: activities, 375; difficulties, 377; and hostile School Board, 382; membership, 375, 379-380; purpose of, 374; successes, 378
Committee on Community Organization: of NASW, 56
Committee on Fair Employment Practices, 48
Common Human Needs, 445
Communication: channels for, 94; facilitating good, 136; steps in task groups, 119-20
Communications: barriers to group and organi-

zational, 203, 204

Communist Party, 48; organizing efforts, 394, 395

Community: characteristics of, 11; conceptions of, 233; as context and vehicle, 242; definition of, 189-190, 232; elements of simple, 274; factors in breakdown of, 242; functions of, 190; shortcomings of, 9; social system aspects of, 236; as target of change efforts, 242; views of, 14-15. *See also* Client system

Community action agencies: objectives and programs of, 321

Community action process, 237

Community Action Programs, 55, 228

Community attitudes: and assessment efforts, 72

Community awareness: and homeless issues, 300; mobilizing, 455

Community capacity building, 477-479

Community Chest: evolution of, 41, 42-43; formation of, 206; membership of, 43; primary function of, 192; relation to council of social agencies, 44

Community development: components of, 353-354; definition of, 5; ideological bias of, 354; process of, 362; strategic weakness in, 356, 360; strengths of, 360. *See also* Locality development

Community Development Block Corporation: description of, 322

Community development program: case study of, 344-347

Community forums: aspects of, 79, 87-88, 94

Community group survey, 86, 96

Community impressions, 80, 93-94

Community integration, 188, 196

Community interviews, 85

Community meetings, 371

Community mental health boards, 321

Community mental health field: competition, 434

Community organization: changing practice modes of, 104; curriculum in social work schools, 56; origins of training for, 46; political activist tradition in, 389-390

Community organization agencies: characteristics of, 244

Community organization practice: conceptualization of, 4; critical issues for, 55, 68, 150; definition of, 191; differing perspectives on, 56, 67, 238; objectives of, 52; organizational relations to, 244; roles in, 22

Community organizing: withdrawal of funding from, 59-60

Community power structure: studies of, 238-241

Community practice: alternative roles in, 477

Community structure: studies of change and, 101

Community support: agency mobilization of, 320

Community welfare council: structure of, 44

Competence, 296

Competition: factors in, 205; within communities, 234

Competitive market, 164

Complementary services, 465-466

Complexity: communicating, 203-204; factors in organizational, 198

Compromise, 127, 214

Concessions: nature of, 413

Confederácion de Uniones Obreras Mexicanos, 51

Conflict: analysis of, 171, 210-211, 406; causes of organizational, 439; generated by public meetings, 345, 346; in task groups, 126, 132; managing, 148-149, 231, 285, 412, 439, 468-469; relations, 209-210; strategy dimension of, 259, 264; tactics, 12-13; value, 214, 216

Conflict theory, 159

Conformity: issue in evaluation, 180

Congress of Industrial Organization (CIO), 47, 393

Congress of Racial Equality (CORE), 52

Consciousness raising, 352, 363

Consensus: aspects of, 107, 316; difficulties with, 227; limits of, 357; meanings of, 264-265; on organizational goals, 429; tactics, 12; uses of, 127, 259, 322

Consequences: decisions based on, 280-281

Consolidation: alternative approaches to, 474

Constituency: based on class, 249, 262; characteristics of, 151; definition of, 245, 330; in social action, 15; powerless, 398; relation to organizational constitution, 248; support for program, 467; of welfare councils, 44

Constitution: kinds of, 151, 244-245, 249

Consumer, 16, 23

Consummatory activities, 192

Contagion: in decision making, 290

Contest strategy: in planning, 322
Context, 208-209
Continuing education: for social work practitioners, 103
Contra Costa County, California: mental health survey in, 84-85
Contracts: meanings of, 165, 285, 464
Control: defined, 443
Control systems, 287
Controllability as resource, 442
Convergent analysis, 76, 88, 94, 95-96, 367: definition of, 73; uses of, 73
Cooperation: aspects of, 205, 361, 429, 481
Cooptation, 265, 464: Nature and types of, 206
Coordination: barriers to, 209; conditions of, 71, 206-207, 253-54; elements in, 484; forms of, 475; among small communities, 481; among social agencies, 41
Core group: roles, 369-371, 402
Corporate organizations, 196
Costs and benefits, 347
Council of Agencies: in Cincinnati, 42
Council of governments, 474, 482
Council of social agencies, 43-44, 192
Council of Social Work Education (CSWE), 56, 150
Counseling: macro practice neglect of, 143
County government, 481
County infirmary, 306
Criteria: in decision making, 125, 138-139
Cross pressures: organizational, 211
Cultural structure, 203, 214
Culture, 213
Curriculum reform: in Milwaukee public schools, 381
Curriculum study: for community organization practice, 56-57

Dallas, Texas, 329
Data: collection and compilation, 78, 79, 136, 366; planners' reliance on, 323
Dawes Act of 1887, 29-30, 40
Day care, 429-430
Decentralization, 58, 169
Decision group, 22
Decision makers, 179
Decision making: analysis of, 125, 150-153, 164, 252, 279-280, 292, 479; forms of, 288, 295, 306, 438; methods of, 124, 126-127, 239, 287; paradox of, 178; participation in, 122, 283-284, 293, 294, 343, 350; problems in, 286-287, 290
Decision process, 284, 291-293
Decision rule, 280
Deed restrictions, 395
Delinquency: theories about, 160
Delphi technique, 79-80, 90-92
Democracy, 35, 227-228
Democratic structure: organizational, 411
Demographic data: uses of, 234-235, 403
Density: organizational, 211
Department of Health and Human Services (DHSS): program decline in, 57
Department of Housing and Urban Development (HUD), 60, 299
Dependency: breaking, 421
Depression of 1929, 47, 50
Desegregation, 378
Deviant behavior, 157-158
Differentiation: organizational, 201
Direct membership model, 399-400
Direct service agencies, 320
Disaggregation, 431-432
Discrimination, 225, 226
Discussion: procedures, 120, 132
Disjunctive theory, 159
Distribution: organizational, 211
Distributive justice, 229
Divide and conquer technique, 414
Division of labor, 432, 457, 462-463
Domain, 433-434
Domination, 241
Double standard, 224
Dropouts, 56
Dues, 401
Dysfunction, 161

Ecological relations: in community context, 233-235
Economic development: views of, 277, 354-355
Economic interests, 224, 239
Economic Opportunity Act of 1964, 206
Economic system: in the 1920s, 39
Education: in democracy, 227; and planning efforts, 333-334; in social settlements, 35-36
Effectiveness: nature of, 172, 174
Efficiency: aspects of, 92, 177, 433; strategies, 170, 174-176
Elderly: relative power of, 109
Elites: roles of, 17, 228, 249

Embarrassment: tactic, 109-110
Enabler: role, 13, 25, 389, 408
Ends and means, 192, 260, 291
Environment: social and organizational issues in, 172, 274, 435, 452
Environmentalists: coalition with poor, 112-113
Equal Rights Amendment, 46, 53
Equality, 225
Equity, 218-219, 229
Ethnic institutions, 53, 60-61
Evaluation, 153: and consequences, 222; methods, 166, 174-175; need for, 70, 471; in planning, 317; research, 171-172, 179, 180; and values, 216-217
Evaluation Studies Review Annual, 173, 174
Evaluators: study of, 175-177
Exchange relationships, 147, 205, 285
Executive roles, 248
Expediter, 306
Expertise: program and evaluation, 170, 465
External relations: organizational, 245

Factional interests, 196
Fair Budget Action Campaign, 112
Fair hearing, 132
Fairness: measure of, 223, 224
Family: aspects of, 59, 229-230
Family Assistance Plan, 227
Feasibility, 131, 459
Federal agencies: influence on evaluation, 177
Federal Emergency Management Assistance, 306
Federal Emergency Relief Administration, 50
Federal government: programs in 1960s and 1970s, 54, 60; roles, 54-55, 57, 168
Federal Program Evaluations, 174
Federal revenue sharing, 321
Federal Security Agency, 50
Federated finance, 42
Federated organizations, 47, 196
Federation for Charity and Philanthropy: in Cleveland, 43
Feedback: agency linkages for, 453; Delphi technique for, 91-92; uses of, 123, 128, 140, 317, 361
Feminization of poverty, 61
Field survey, 74
Findings, 471
Fluoridation, conflict over, 211

Follow-up, 472
Food stamp program, 108
Force: issues regarding, 264, 265, 268
Formal organizations, 189
Formalization, 198
Forum: use of, 304-305. *See also* Community forums
Functional autonomy, 446-447
Functional structure, 201
Fund raising, 248
Funding: sources, 154-155, 400-401, 459, 460

Game theory, 257
Garbage can decision process, 292
Gender: roles in planning field, 323
General assistance: defined, 306
Generalist, 251
Generational conflict, 220
Goal achievement: factors in, 177, 180, 191
Goal conflicts, 436
Goal displacement: defined, 162-163
Goal distortion, 314
Goal idealization, 260
Goal model, 172, 173, 177, 179-180
Goal setting, 135, 162-163, 329-330
Goal specification, 138, 428
Goals: classification of organizational, 245, 246; definition of, 329; definition of organizational, 428; development of, 134-135, 162, 286; kinds of, 14, 21, 145, 152, 163, 258; measuring, 176, 282; multiple, 434; threats to, 247
God, 230
Goods, 264
Government: roles and problems of, 155, 224-225, 274, 277
Government programs: growth of, 47
Grade tax: example of, 217-218
Grassroots movement, 60
Grassroots organizations, 60
Great Society, 312, 321
Greater Milwaukee Conference on Religious and Urban Affairs, 375-376
Gresham's Law, 433
Grey Panther groups, 53
Group decision making, 90
Group pressure: in task groups, 124
Group work, 360
Groups: elements in, 189, 197, 344
Groupthink, 125

Guesswork: in choice theory, 281

Handicapped: concerns of, 53
Hawthorne Works: of Western Electric Company, 437
Headmistress: advice for making choices by, 279, 281, 282, 284, 290, 292, 294, 297
Henry Street Settlement, 396
Hierarchy: organizational, 291
Homeless: assumptions about the, 297, 300; definition of, 306; population characteristics, 300; typology of, 302-303; welfare for, 304
Homelessness: in United States, 297, 298-299
Homosexuals: organizing efforts of, 53
House Subcommittee on Housing and Community Development: hearings of, 299
Housing Counseling Assistance Program, 306
Housing voucher, 306
Houston, Texas, 387, 395
Hull House: Chicago, 396
Human behavior: choice theories of, 279
Human relation structure: tasks in, 468
Human relations model, 173
Human relations organizations, 194
Human resource commission: role of, 321
Human rights, 231
Human service needs: assessing, 72, 82, 87, 88, 89, 93
Human services: assessment and planning, 75, 80-81, 91, 484
Humanistic pragmatism, 222
Humanitarianism, 230, 231
Hypocrisy, 284

Idea generation: examples of, 89-90, 136
Identification: lack of community, 242
Ideology: in research and policy making, 169-170
Illinois: AMA activity in, 327
Image: organizational, 438
Immigrant Protective League, 35
Immigration: to United States, 28, 30, 39-40, 48-49
Implementation: factors in, 139, 140, 317; problems in, 169, 327; task of, 450
Incrementalism, 315
India: untouchable issue in, 358
Indian Reorganization Act of 1934, 49
Individuals: roles of, 89-90, 91, 93, 222, 250, 363

Inducement: meanings of, 264, 268
Industrial Areas Foundation, 9, 17
Industrial Revolution, 52
Industrialization, 9, 27, 230
Influence: analysis of, 175, 191, 238-241, 265. See also Power
Influentials, 335, 456
Informal structure: defined, 434-435, 437
Information; 296, 318: for assessing needs, 72; basis for goal selection, 163; collection and development, 78, 79-80; convergent analysis of, 96; displaying, 137; gathering of, 73, 76-80, 282; integration, 78-79; power of, 275; role in rule persistence, 289; sharing, 119, 120, 122-123; sources of, 75, 101, 455; techniques for ordering and clarifying, 137; uses of, 73, 94, 285-286, 295
Information and referral, 84
Information society, 57
Information system: design of, 294-296
Input constituency, 314
Inputs, 451
Institutional relationships, 241, 246
Institutional subsystem, 452-453
Institutions: locating, 235-236, 403
Instrumental activities, 147-148, 149, 192: description of, 144
Instrumental strategies: examples of, 171; use of, 174, 176
Integration: concepts of community, 274; in human service programs, 71; function of social system, 191
Integrator role, 469
Intelligence: function, 453, 470
Intensive technology: defined, 431
Interaction: community, 233-234, 236; maintaining organizational, 435; patterns of power leaders, 239; techniques of needs assessments, 366-367; understanding process of, 237
Interagency relationships, 83-84
Interagency task groups, 119
Interdependence: features of, 412-413, 446-447, 481
Interest groups: analysis of, 86, 177, 179, 240, 429
Interests: nature of, 144-145, 161-162, 210-211, 214-215
Intergovernmental contract, 474
Intergovernmental Personnel Act, 474
Interlocking: organizational, 211

International Ladies' Garment Workers' Union, 38

Interorganizational coordination: factors in, 207-209

Interpersonal activities, 143-144

Interpersonal skills, 69

Intersectoral planning, 321, 324

Intervention: problems, 478

Intervention within research: a model, 369-371

Intuition, 431

Iowa: AMA activity in, 327

Irrational beliefs: in task groups, 132

Issues: definition of, 330; uses of, 324, 399, 404, 479-480

J. P. Stevens strike, 241

Japan, 58

Japanese: immigration of, 30, 40; organizations of, 37

Japanese Americans, 37, 49-50, 51

Job security, 437

Justice, 229

Key informant: interviews: 93, 94-95

Knights of Labor, 37

Knowledge: analysis of, 102, 104, 149, 153-154; sources of, 99-100, 103, 249

Ku Klux Klan, 39, 45

La Raza Unida, 53

Labor and management, 211-212

Landlords: conflict with, 145

Lateral thinking, 137

Law: as function of change, 99

Lazy poor, 223-224

Leadership: elements in, 240, 333, 399-400

League of Latin American Citizens, 45

League of Women Voters, 46, 52

Learning: ideas about, 289

Legitimacy: aspects of, 407-408, 467; building, 263

Leverage, 139

Liberalism, 31

Liberty, 226

Ligatures, 219

Limited rationality, 281-282

Line workers, 251

Linkage: elements of, 102-104, 203-204, 319, 484

Liquidity, 442

Living situations: for homeless, 304

Local autonomy, 358-359

Local government, 313, 477

Locale, 405

Locality: analysis of, 358

Locality development: characteristics of, 25, 155, 266, 351-352; definition of, 5, 351, 352; examples of, 5; guidelines for using, 23; phases in, 269; and practice variables, 17; problem description for, 157; and process goals, 8; view of problems, 158, 159, 160

Log-roll, 288

Los Angeles: characteristics of homeless in, 301; railway strike in, 40

Louisville Convention of Colored Men, 36

Love: meanings of, 230

Lynching, 29

Macro generalist, 474, 477

Macro practice: common elements of, 68; contexts of, 3, 62, 67; evolution of, 61; motivations in relationships in, 147-148; student training for, 62; role elements of, 475

Mail surveys, 84

Maintenance: organizational, 246-247, 439

Maintenance functions, 192

Maintenance goals, 434, 451

Maintenance sybsystem, 435-436

Majority rule, 127, 227

Management: functions, 445, 453; information system, 296; roles, 179, 424; subsystem, 436, 440

Mandate: views of, 128, 155, 252

Map: in key informant interview, 93-94

Marginal profits, 254

Marijuana, 159

Market, 317

Mass communication, 203

Mass societies: characteristics of, 242

Massachusetts Fair Share, 384, 398

Material balances, 276

Matrix organization, 202

Maximum feasible participation, 55, 59, 228

Means tested programs, 226

Means-ends: aspects of, 258, 260, 261, 268, 269, 317

Media, 108, 334

Meetings: characteristics of, 115, 117, 407, 411

Membership organization: forms of, 399

Mental health, 74, 84-85, 360

Merger, 206-207
Meriam Report of 1928, 45
Message distortion, 203
Meta-analysis, 103
Mexican-Americans, 29, 36-37, 45, 49
Mexico, 40
Michigan, 53, 113
Micropolitan development: described, 474
Middle class criminals, 224
Middletown study, 238
Migrant farm labor, 48
Milwaukee Plan, 374
Milwaukee School Board: desegregation efforts, 373, 374, 379
Minneapolis: characteristics of homeless in, 301
Minority interests, 227, 228
Minutes: elements of, 116, 117
Misinformation, 108, 109
Mistrust, 251
Mitigating circumstances, 218-219
Mitigating disastrous results, 218-219
Mixing approaches, 7-8
Mobilization: fostering, 367, 368-369; problems of, 286
Mobilization for Youth, 101
Model: definition of, 3-4
Model Cities, 55, 227, 228, 321
Monitoring: activities in, 128, 295, 317, 466, 469
Montgomery, Alabama bus boycott, 52, 211
Moral communities, 242
Morale, 437-438
Morphological revolution, 358
Motivation: aspects of, 139, 347-348
Mutual adaptation, 480
Mutual benefit, 37
Mutual support, 232
Myth of neutrality, 363
Myths: about welfare programs, 108

Narrow-mindedness, 181
NASA: need for urban, 313-314
National American Woman Suffrage Association, 38
National Association for the Advancement of Colored People, 36, 39, 51, 374
National Association of Colored Women, 36
National Association of Social Workers (NASW), 56, 194

National Coalition for the Homeless, 299
National Commission on Neighborhoods, 60
National Farm Workers' Union, 51
National Federation of Business and Professional Women's Clubs, 46
National Federation of Settlements and Neighborhood Centers, 393
National Institute of Drug Abuse, 92-93
National Labor Relations Act of 1935, 47-48
National Neighborhood Policy Act, 387
National Urban League, 36
National Welfare Rights Organization, 398
National Women Suffrage Association, 38
National Women's Party, 46
Native Americans: changes for, 49; and federal actions, 45; organizing efforts of, 53; problems for, 29-30, 37, 40; tribal growth of, 51
Natural sciences, 273
Natural systems model: described, 434; use of, 425, 439, 441, 446
Need: defined, 72
Needs assessment: approaches, 76-78, 79-80, 352, 362; definition of, 71; differentiated from program evaluation, 75; political process of, 364; steps in, 71-72; strategies of, 71; techniques, 95, 367-368.
Need identification: aspects of, 78-79, 81, 454-455; definition of, 71, 95; problems with, 84
Needs survey, 455
Negotiation: uses of, 205, 480
Neighborhood maintenance: approaches, 26, 391, 395, 396-397
Neighborhood organization: aspects of, 387, 388-389, 400, 420
Networks: elements of, 59, 475, 481, 482-483, 484
Neutrality: definition of, 363, problems with, 364, 415
New Deal, 168
New Federalism, 313
New Politics, 55
New York, 111, 299
New York City, 60: characteristics of homeless in, 301
New York Charity Organization Society, 38
New York Consumer's League, 38
Niagara Movement, 36
Nineteenth Amendment, 38
Nisei, 40
Nominal group technique: advantages and dis-

advantages of, 90, 367; description of, 79, 88-89; methods of, 89-90; research findings about, 89; uses of, 88
Nonconformist, 158
Nonuniform events, 195
North Boston, 235
North Division High School (Milwaukee), 378-379
Nuclear family, 230
Numerical equality, 217

Objectivity: definition of, 363; elements of, 136, 276, 364
Obligations: in instrumental activities, 145
Observation, 188
Office of Community War Services, 50
Office of Economic Opportunity, 57
Ohio, 113
Oil industry, 109
Opposites: logic of, 273
Opposition: knowing the, 165, 414
Optimization, 318
Options, 304-305, 347
Order of Sons of America, 45
Oregon, 113
Organization building, 407, 410
Organization theory, 427
Organizational analysis: aspects of, 100-101, 155, 171, 252-253, 444
Organizational climate, 200, 436
Organizational development, 477
Organizational effectiveness, 170, 173-176, 177, 200
Organizational goals, 199, 248
Organizational strength, 263
Organizational structure: capabilities, 197-200, 202; definition of, 197; democratic nature of, 409; elements of, 332; in relation to problem solving, 195
Organizational variables, 193
Organizations: as constituent base, 250; as context for practice, 21, 314; differing functions of, 21, 172, 193; goals within, 244; impacts on, 423-424; and surrounding environment, 204-205
Organized anarchies, 446
Organizer: characteristics and roles of, 406, 408-409, 417, 419-422
Outcomes: measuring, 166, 170, 294, 471, 472

Outputs: goals of, 199, 451; measuring, 202
Outsiders, 94

Participant interests, 193-194
Participation: elements of, 35, 55-56, 59, 71, 120, 155, 483
Participatory corporation, 59
Participatory democracy, 360
Patriotism, 221
Peace Corps, 54
Pearson Product Moment Correlation, 174
Penitente Order, 37
People's organizations, 188, 236
Perceptions, 131-132
Personal worth, 217
Personality theory, 427
Personnel, 179, 461-462
Phasing: of Strategies, 25
Philadelphia: characteristics of homeless in, 301
Phoenix: characteristics of homeless in, 301
Physical sciences, 314
Pilot program: use of, 138
Pittsburgh Survey, 33
Pittsburgh: characteristics of homeless in, 301
Placement: for homeless people, 300
Planned change: defined, 98; elements of, 99-100, 102; theories of, 101
Planner: approaches of, 349, 456; program development function of, 450; relationship to employer, 14; roles of, 266, 316, 327-328, 330, 336, 337, 465; and value orientation, 25; view of community, 11
Planning: activities of, 74, 319, 334; constituencies of, 330-331; definition of, 266, 311-312; dilemmas of, 312; image problems of, 308-309; linkages to small organizations, 485, local, 312, 482; modifications toward, 284; policy as precursor to, 309; sequences of approaches to, 317; trends in, 324, 325; typology of, 315; use of inducement in, 266; variety of views of, 309
Planning issues: difference by gender, 323-324
Playfulness: in decision making, 284-285
Police cooperation, 254
Policy: concepts of, 18, 20, 270-271; definition of, 213; documents, 271; draft, 22; statement, 460; steps in, 19, 24. *See also* Social policy
Policy for the Social Work Practitioner, 270

Policy Management in the Human Services, 270

Policy manager, 19, 25

Policy practice: aspects of, 19-20, 22, 23

Political activist, 389-391, 394

Political analysis, 107, 273, 349, 418

Political science, 99

Political strategy, 329, 336-337

Political tactics, 318, 331

Politicians, 110, 331

Politics, 214, 441

Polity: elements of, 244, 264, 425

Poor: participation of, 111, 382; programs for, 112, 223

Populist Movement, 28

Portland, Oregon: characteristics of homeless in, 301

Postpower society, 275

Poverty, 159, 355, 359

Power: analysis of, 241, 262, 443; defined, 239, 440; elements of, 275, 287; and planning, 276; political activist view of, 393; process of building, 417; ways to wield, 109; within community organizations, 244

Power leaders: study of, 239

Power politics model, 440, 444, 447

Power structure: elements of, 11, 239, 240; uses of, 13-14, 23, 252

Practitioner: characteristics, 24, 151, 160, 325; identity issue, 235; knowledge base for, 101-102, 103, 150, 236, 237; mixing and phasing of roles, 24-25; needs of, 68; perspectives on activities of, 156; roles of, 13, 22, 52, 98, 191, 203-204, 258, 300; settings for planning, 327; skills, 61, 164-165; and values, 216

Pragmatism, 31, 323

Preferences: aspects of, 280-284, 287, 318

President's Committee on Equality of Treatment in the Armed Services, 48

Prevention, 363

Primary groups, 194

Private interests, 336, 337

Private sector, 334

Problem definition, 130, 134, 138, 161, 260, 316

Problem field, 245

Problem identification, 129-130, 132, 137, 302

Problem situation, 133

Problem solving: aspects of, 70, 129, 136, 138, 139

Problem specification, 457-458

Problem-solving guide: purpose of, 154

Problematization, 369

Problems: analysis of, 151, 152, 180-181, 263; causes and objectives of, 195; describing, 157, 406

Process goals: 166, 354; definition of, 8; described, 8-9, 259; example of, 163; limits on, 252

Production goals, 434

Production subsystem, 435-436

Program alternatives, 458

Program development, 72, 250, 450-451, 454, 461, 463

Program evaluation research, 168, 169

Proportionate equality, 217

Psychoanalysis, 41

Psychology, 99, 359

Public assistance: agencies, 431, 445; aspects of, 225-226, 445

Public hearings, 343, 348

Public interest, 147, 228, 313

Public meetings: nature and purposes of, 344, 349-350. *See also* Meetings

Public opinion, 345, 346-347

Public poor law, 33

Public schools: community values toward, 235

Public service administration, 483

Public services, 473-474

PUSH, 61

Questionnaires: kinds of, 85; uses of, 81, 90-92

Raleigh, North Carolina, 329-330

Rank orders, 127-128

Rational analysis: described, 169-170

Rational model: aspects of, 327-328, 430, 435; definition of, 428; personnel issues in, 437; resource allocation in, 441; uses of, 443, 446

Rationality: assumptions about, 443-444; in choice theory, 280-281; evaluators' strategies regarding, 176; limits of, 425; normative pressure for, 171; and planning, 71, 318; in relation to reality, 178-179

Reactivity, 432

Recession: and cutbacks, 328

Recruitment, 399, 402

Referendum: uses of, 252

Referral systems: used by homeless, 302

Reframing technique, 134
Regional City: study of, 239
Regional planning, 73, 75
Regulation: economic aspects of, 277
Rehabilitation: strategy for homeless, 304
Relationships: organizer and neighborhood, 421
Removal Act of 1830, 29
Reports: presentation of, 117; recipients' use of, 175, 176
Representatives: roles of, 195, 228, 375
Republic (Plato's), 238
Republican Party, 387
Research: history of, 168; use of, 102, 103-104, 181, 301-302
Residues of organization: explained, 160
Resistance: elements of, 262, 264
Resource distribution: conflict theory about, 159
Resources: allocation of, 451; defined, 441-442; needs for, 72, 140; power to control, 440; strategies for scarce, 261; ways to secure, 149, 465
Restore our Alienated Rights (ROAR), 394
Revelatory strategies, 171, 174-175, 176
Rewards, 223
Rhode Island: AMA activity in, 327
Risk taking: by planners, 323
Risky shift, 125
Rituals: in decision making, 293
Robert's Rules of Order, 121, 382
Rochester, New York, 43
Role theory, 156
Roles: circuit rider, 477-478, 485; description of, 13, 19, 156, 189, in instrumental relations, 148; organizational, 411
Round robin: uses of, 89-90, 120
Rule development: theories of, 289-291
Rule implementation, 149
Rules: definition of, 288; organizational, 411; purposes of, 149
Ruling class: theory of, 238
Rusk Settlement: in Houston, 391

Salesman: organizer as, 406
Salience, 330
San Antonio, 45
Sanctions, use of, 123
Sanitation services: action for, 407-408
School desegregation, 373

School of Public Health, University of California, 93
School of Social Service Administration, University of Chicago, 156
Schools of social work: aspects of, 7, 38, 56, 103
Scope: in communications, 203-204
Scopes trial, 41
Seattle, Washington, 37, 382
Sectarian federations: roles of, 321
Section 8: described, 306
Sectoral planning, 320, 324
Selective listening, 203, 204
Self-determination, 359
Self-esteem: issues around, 9, 219, 418-419
Self-help, 58-59
Self-interest, 145, 286, 447
Self-reliance, 222
Self-responsibility, 420
Services: delivering, 201-202; planning for, 303-304
Shared decision making, 122
Shared goals, 145
Shared responsibility, 479, 480
Shared services, 481, 484
Shelters: for homeless, 304
Size: of networks, 483
Slack: theories of, 281-282
Small towns: and circuit riders, 474, 476
Snyder Act of 1921, 45
Social action: agency auspices for, 154-155; and coercive approach, 15-16, 266; and community development goals, 361-362; and conflict, 159, 259; description of, 6-7; elements in, 9, 158, 385, 418; guidelines for using, 23; phases in, 269; practice variables, 17-18; problem basis for, 157, 160; value orientation, 25
Social action model, 398-401
Social and Health Indicator Analysis, 78, 80, 96
Social area survey, 78-79, 80, 82-83, 96
Social areas: identification of, 234-235
Social change, 61, 354, 365
Social conditions: interpretations of, 72
Social control: defined, 232
Social Darwinism, 30-31, 33
Social disorganization, 158, 392
Social functions: described, 232

Social organization, 213
Social planners, 311
Social planning, definition of, 275, 312, 315; description of, 6, 15; functions of, 278; guidelines for using, 23; impetus from federal government, 50; phases in, 269; problem definition in, 157-158; process, 327; setting for, 273; and task goals, 9; view of problems, 160; strategies in, 158, 164; and sponsoring organizations, 155
Social policy: definition of, 20, 275; description of, 18; government influence on, 277; historical stages of, 275, 276; instrumental use of, 276-277; misunderstanding of, 108; phases in, 269; relationship to force, 266; values debate in, 213
Social power: defined, 238
Social problems, 156-159, 163
Social psychology, 99
Social reform: in social settlement movement, 35
Social research, 277
Social research and development (R&D), 325
Social sciences, 68, 99-100, 103-104, 273
Social scientist: and research, 169
Social security: elements of, 107, 164, 219, 225, 226
Social Security Act: principles of, 168, 217-218, 445; Title II, 218
Social service: role for community development, 360
Social service agencies: clientele vs. beneficiaries, 162
Social service indexes, 32
Social service systems, 277, 278
Social services: development of, 392-393; financing in low income area, 416-417; implications for future, 180; problem areas in, 319; grants, 422
Social settlements: history and programs of, 34-36, 46, 391-392
Social structure, 161, 214
Social survey: early example of, 33
Social system: defined, 435; elements of, 214, 236, 237; functions of, 191-193
Social ties, 203
Social unit plan, 44
Social welfare: aspects of, 224, 226-227, 230, 231, 418
Social work: approaches, 26, 99, 389; and change, 46-47, 62, 98; student orientations toward, 56
Socialist Labor Party, 31
Socialist Party, 31
Socialization, 232, 265, 288
Society: aspects of, 9, 190, 213, 273
Socioeconomic issues: for community development, 359
Sociology of community organization, 99, 243, 254
Solidarity: in communities, 274
South Carolina: circuit riding program in, 474-475, 476
South Korea, 58
Southern Christian Leadership Conference, 52
Southwest Civic Club: Houston, 395
Spain, 58
Special issue groups: coalitions of, 113
Special master: court overseer of desegregation, 373-374
Specialist role, 251
Specialization: in organizations, 198
Sponsorship: organizational, 411
Staff: aspects of, 401, 462, 467-468
Standardized operating procedures, 288
State: nature of the, 274
Status: meaning of, 265; in task groups, 122-123, 124
Steering committee: roles of, 375
Storefront office, 417-418
Strategies: for dealing with homelessness, 300-301; planner analysis of, 319; variables in, 266-268
Strategy: analysis of, 152-153; defined, 257, 258, 261, 328; guide to selecting, 164; problems for planners, 328-329; and roles people play, 241
Student Non-violent Coordinating Committee (SNCC), 52
Students for a Democratic Society, 54
Sub-units: aspects of, 444-445, 446; description of, 441
Subgoals, 135
Subsidy programs, 229
Substantive conflict, 126
Subsystem: nature of, 236-237, 435-436
Subventionary activities, 144
Summary: of meeting, 118
Supplemental Security Income (SSI), 218
Support: goals, 199; structure, 463

Supreme Court: decision on school desegregation, 52

Survey: of homeless population, 302

Survey sample: case example of, 344, 345-347

Surveys: advantages and disadvantages of, 85-86; design characteristics of, 85; elements of, 82, 367; issues in using, 348; purposes of, 349-350

Symbiosis: between agencies, 253-254

Symbols: nature of, 293

Synoptic models: process of planning, 315

Syracuse University, 7

System maintenance: activities of, 364-365

Systems perspective, 451

Systems-resource model, 172

Tactics: analysis of, 153; use of, 172, 331; targets of, 164-165

Target: defined, 232

Target group: defining characteristics of, 458; definition of, 248n; effective relations with, 251-252; involvement of, 456; mobilizing, 252; of organizations, 245, 246

Target system, 268

Task environment: for agency, 463

Task functions, 148, 191

Task goals, 8-9, 135, 163, 166, 259

Task groups: elements of, 69, 114, 115, 371; functions of, 118-129

Task management, 478

Taxation: issues in, 226, 229, 247

Technical assistance: steps in, 452, 477

Technology: development of new, 58; introduction of, 480; organizational, 430-431; planner role in, 313, 324; and social change, 318; typology of, 431

Telephone survey: uses of, 85

Texas, 39: AMA activity in, 327

The Metropolitan Organization (TMO): Houston, 393

"The New Negro": meanings of, 39, 45

The Rape of Florida, 29

Theory and Practice of Social Welfare Policy, 270

Third world: issues of, 356-357, 361

Time management, 478

Timing: in social change efforts, 357

Title VII of Elementary and Secondary Assistance Act, 376, 382

Toynbee Hall, 34

Training: aspect of action plan, 165

Transactive approach: in planning, 316

Transferability: of resources, 442

Travel time: circuit rider, 479

Treatment groups, 118

Treaty of Guadalupe Hidalgo, 29

Tribal government, 49

Trust: elements of, 287, 406, 477

Trustworthiness: political nature of, 287-288

Truth squads: uses of, 108-109

Turf: meaning of, 398

Tuskegee Institute, 28

U.S. Chamber of Commerce, 328

U.S. Commission on Civil Rights: report on desegregation, 381

U.S. Office of Education, 376

U.S. Supreme Court, 373

Uncertainty: elements of, 170-171, 178-179, 180, 430, 433

Unionism: after the Depression, 47

United Fund. *See* Community Chest

United Jewish Appeal, 42

United States Air Force: use of Delphi technique, 91

Universal Negro Improvement Association, 45

University of Missouri, 7

University Settlement, 34

Unmet needs: assessing, 93-94

Unpredictability: in low income organization, 416

Upper Savannah Council of Governments, 474

Urban League, 51

Urban poor: community development focus on, 361-362

Urbanization: outcomes of, 9, 27-28, 41

Utility theory, 138

Values: as criteria for evaluation, 171, 217; definition of, 214; description of, 213, 318; juxtaposition of, 220; nature of, 26, 216, 219, 264-265, 356; social science, 364; in social work profession, 25; understanding differences in, 235

Vehicle: meaning of, 232

Vertical integration: described, 433

Vertical thinking: described, 137

Vested interests, 313

Veterans: benefits, 226

Vietnam War, 54, 113

VISTA, 54
Voters: issues for, 110-111, 264-265

War on Poverty: elements of, 55, 164, 168, 169, 206
Washington: economy of, 113
Welfare: issues, 55; strategy for homeless, 304
Welfare agencies: functions of, 192
Welfare council. *See* Community welfare council
Well-being, 146-147
Willful choice, 279-280
Winnetka, Illinois, 329

Women's movement: issues in, 37-38, 52, 53, 61
Women's suffrage movement, 38, 46
Work: issues about, 58, 219, 229
Working-class: difficulties involving, 249
Workshops: uses of, 371
World economy: and United States, 58
World War I, 39, 43, 45
World War II, 48, 50
Worthy poor: described, 33, 223

Yankee City study, 238-239

Civil litigation

SECOND EDITION

Laurence Olivo and Mary Ann Kelly

2009
EMOND MONTGOMERY PUBLICATIONS LIMITED
TORONTO, CANADA

Emond Montgomery Publications Limited
60 Shaftesbury Avenue
Toronto ON M4T 1A3
http://www.emp.ca/college

Printed in Canada.

We acknowledge the financial support of the Government of Canada through the Book Publishing Industry Development Program (BPIDP) for our publishing activities.

The events and characters depicted in this book are fictitious. Any similarity to actual persons, living or dead, is purely coincidental.

Acquisitions and developmental editor: Peggy Buchan
Marketing manager: Christine Davidson
Sales manager, higher education: David Stokaluk
Production and copy editor: Cindy Fujimoto, WordsWorth Communications
Proofreader: Debbie Gervais, WordsWorth Communications
Indexer: Paula Pike, WordsWorth Communications
Cover designer: John Vegter

Library and Archives Canada Cataloguing in Publication

Olivo, Laurence M., 1946-
    Civil litigation / Laurence Olivo and Mary Ann Kelly. — 2nd ed.

Includes bibliographical references and index.
ISBN 978-1-55239-318-5

    1. Civil procedure — Ontario — Textbooks.   2. Actions and defenses —
Ontario — Textbooks.   3. Civil procedure — Ontario — Forms.   4. Actions
and defenses — Ontario — Forms.   I. Kelly, Mary Ann, 1948-   II. Title.

KEO1119.O45 2009   347.713'05   C2009-900294-9